THE PROGRAMMING
PROCESS WITH PASCAL

THE PROGRAMMING PROCESS WITH PASCAL

JUDITH L. GERSTING

Indiana University/Purdue University

WEST PUBLISHING COMPANY
St. Paul   New York   Los Angeles   San Francisco

PRODUCTION CREDITS

Copyeditor Barbara Bergstrom
Compositor Carlisle Communications, Ltd.

COPYRIGHT ©1989   By WEST PUBLISHING COMPANY
50 W. Kellogg Boulevard
P.O. Box 64526
St. Paul, MN 55164–1003

Printed in the United States of America

96 95 94 93 92 91 90 89   8 7 6 5 4 3 2 1 0

Library of Congress Cataloging-in-Publication Data

Gersting, Judith L.
   The programming process with Pascal.

   Includes index.
   1. Pascal (Computer program language)   I. Title.
QA76.73.P2G47   1989   005.13′3   88–20847
ISBN 0–314–44532–3

To our children –
  life's ultimate programming challenge!

PREFACE

Philosophy of the book...

This book is intended for use in a first course in computer science or programming that uses Pascal as the programming language. It provides the necessary material to teach the Association for Computing Machinery CS1 course, or a course oriented toward the Educational Testing Service Advanced Placement examination. No programming background on the part of the student is assumed.

Like most modern textbooks in this area, the emphasis is on problem-solving using the computer rather than on syntax details. More than this, however, the book is intended to prepare future computer professionals for the workplace. From the first, the book stresses the importance of the entire programming process, from problem specification through maintenance. It has been argued that this "professional" approach is not meaningful to students who lack experience with large-scale programming projects. However, it is the very lack of experience that allows us as instructors the best opportunity to implant and cultivate those thought processes and habits that will be desirable later on!

Outline of the chapters...

The Prologue introduces terminology about the computing environment. Depending on the background of the students, this material can be skipped.

Chapter 1 gives a brief introduction to the various steps of the programming process, which will be examined in more detail in later chapters. Chapter 2 presents all of the information necessary to write a simple program, including standard data types, input, and output. It also examines issues involved in problem specification.

Chapter 3 begins with a discussion of algorithm development, with a particular emphasis on top-down design. This leads naturally into the topics of procedures and parameters. Chapter 4 presents more technical issues on parameters, including the different mechanisms of parameter passing associated with variable and value parameters, scope of identifiers, and side effects. The important skill that students learn from these two chapters is modularization of the problem solution through the use of procedures; at this stage the procedures themselves are simple, or are handled by stubs. There is, however, a brief optional section in Chapter 3 on **if-then-else** and **for** loops that can be covered to allow for more complex procedures to be written at this time. (Asterisks denote those optional end-of-chapter questions in Chapters 3-7 that make use of this material.)

Chapter 5 discusses further details of arithmetic computations, as well as internal program documentation. Chapter 6 covers user-defined and standard functions, plus material on program debugging.

Control structures are covered in Chapters 7 and 8. Chapter 7 presents boolean expressions and decision structures (**if-then-else** and **case.**) User-defined data types are also introduced, and program testing is discussed. Chapter 8 covers loop structures (**while, repeat,** and **for**), as well as program maintenance and external program documentation. An introduction to text files also appears here.

Chapters 9 and 10 cover arrays and records, as well as the **set** data type. Text files and binary files are presented in Chapter 11. Chapter 12 deals with recursion, and Chapter 13 covers pointer variables, linked lists, and additional searching and sorting algorithms.

The order of topics in the table of contents should not be viewed as the only possible sequence. For example, files can be covered earlier, as can recursion. Functions can be postponed until after control structures. Omitting or including the optional early section on simple control structures, as well as optional sections on functions and procedures as parameters, variant records, and forward declarations, increases the instructor's flexibility in tailoring the course to specific needs.

The text adheres to Level 0 ISO Pascal, equivalent to ANSI/IEEE standard Pascal. Footnotes throughout point out some system deviations from standard. An appendix presents a brief look at Turbo Pascal. Throughout the book, a different typeface distinguishes program code from text, and reserved words are shown in boldface.

Special features...

As befits the emphasis on the programming process, each chapter contains a complete example of a software development project, from problem statement through problem specification, algorithm development, discussion of procedures and procedure interfaces, a structure chart, often a data flow diagram, the complete program, and a sample program execution. Many other complete programs, with sample program executions, are presented. The book also contains two running case studies, one completely worked out and the other left for the student; these case studies first appear in Chapter 1 and evolve in complexity as new topics are introduced; by Chapter 13, they are fairly significant examples, and students have seen program modification in action.

CHECKUPS are short-answer questions sprinkled throughout the chapters and are meant to be done when they are encountered. At the end of the chapter, Exercises provide paper-and-pencil questions, and Skill Builders are short programming projects. Software Development Projects are also given at the end of each chapter; it is intended that students model their work for these on the chapter examples, complete with problem specification, details of algorithm development, data flow diagrams, documentation, etc. A Testing and Maintenance Department asks students to test and/or modify the example software development program from the chapter (the example program is available on disk). Finally, a Debugging Clinic provides programs (again on disk) for students to correct. Errors in these programs (after the first one) are much more subtle than mere syntax errors.

Programming "tips" appear as summaries and reminders in the margins throughout the chapters.

Answers to CHECKUPS, as well as answers to about half the Exercises and one Skill Builder per chapter (marked in the text by the symbol #), are in the back of the book. A Glossary and various Appendices are also included. The Instructor's Manual contains answers to the remaining Exercises, another Skill Builder, a Software Development Project, and the Debugging Clinic for each chapter.

Acknowledgments...

A published book is never the work of the author alone, although he or she takes full responsibility for its faults. Thanks go to Rich Jones and Jerry Westby at West Publishing Company for their patience with my ideas and my diversions while the manuscript was being written. Conscientious reviewers provided many comments that were extremely helpful:

Stephen Allan
Utah State University

Mark A. Bernard
Marquette University

Andrew Bernat
University of Texas at El Paso

Doug Bickerstaff
Eastern Washington University

Sue Chavin
University of California—Santa Barbara

Robert Christiansen
University of Iowa

Cecilia Daly
University of Nebraska—Lincoln

Richard Easton
Indiana State University

Henry A. Etlinger
Rochester Institute of Technology

Mark Foehse
Kansas State University

John Goda
Georgia Institute of Technology

Cynthia M. Hanchey
Oklahoma Baptist University

Robert M. Holloway
University of Wisconsin—Madison

Lawrence J. Kotman
Grand Valley State College

Richard Larson
University of Illinois at Chicago

Thomas T. Lin
Slippery Rock University

James L. Lyle
California State University—Dominguez Hills

Andrea Martin
Louisiana State University

Dan Matthews
Tri State University

Wanda Meyer
University of North Dakota—Williston

William Nico
California State University—Hayward

Gary A. Phillips
Oakton Community College

Robert Riser
East Tennessee State University

Lawrence L. Rose
University of Pittsburgh

Ron Sandstrom
Fort Hays State University

John Townsend
Bowling Green University

Sister Martina Van Ryzin
Silver Lake College

Stewart Venit
California State University—Fullerton

Melanie Wolf-Greenberg
California State University—Fullerton

Henderson Yeung
California State University—Fresno

Last but far from least, my family gave me continual support throughout this project, never complaining when I typed till all hours on my micro, and welcoming me warmly whenever I emerged to attend soccer matches!

Judith L. Gersting

CONTENTS

CHAPTER THREE

ALGORITHM DEVELOPMENT; PROCEDURES; SIMPLE CONTROL STRUCTURES

55

CHAPTER FOUR

MORE ON PROCEDURES AND PARAMETERS   91

CHAPTER SEVEN

DECISIONS; NEW DATA TYPES; 171
PROGRAM TESTING

CHAPTER EIGHT

REPETITIONS; PROGRAM 217
MAINTENANCE; EXTERNAL
DOCUMENTATION

CHAPTER NINE

ARRAYS   265

CHAPTER TEN

RECORDS AND SETS   313

CHAPTER ELEVEN

FILES 365

CHAPTER TWELVE

RECURSION 435

CHAPTER THIRTEEN

DYNAMIC VARIABLES;   483
ABSTRACT DATA TYPES;
SORTING AND SEARCHING

GLOSSARY   567

APPENDICES   583

INDEX   675

THE PROGRAMMING
PROCESS WITH PASCAL

THE COMPUTING ENVIRONMENT

This section gives a brief introduction to computer systems in general and some of the terminology associated with them The details of how to access and use a particular computer system can vary considerably from one installation to another. Local authorities such as your instructor, user manuals, computer center documentation, and other students will be valuable sources for this nitty-gritty (and important) information.

Computer Classifications

Computers are roughly classified according to their physical size, the amount of information they can store, and the speed with which they can process that information. These factors determine the uses to which various machines are put. **Microcomputers** are desk-top (or even lap-size) machines that serve one user at a time. **Minicomputers** are the size of a small cabinet and may satisfy the computing needs of a small or medium-sized business, often serving more than one user at a time. **Mainframe** machines are larger, usually requiring a separate room with special air-conditioning facilities and power requirements; they service a number of users at once, and are found in large businesses, universities, etc. **Supercomputers** represent the ultimate in computing power and are found in government or research installations where there is a massive amount of computation to be done, often of a scientific or engineering nature. The boundaries between these classifications are fuzzy because advances in electronic technology mean that today's microcomputer can store as much information and process it as quickly as the mainframes of a few years ago.

Components of a Computing System

Any computing system has the same components. These are:

- input and output devices
- memory
- central processing unit

Input devices and *output devices* are part of a computing system, but, unlike memory and the central processing unit, are not part of the computer itself; they are called *peripheral devices*.

Input and Output Devices

Input and output devices translate information from a form that we humans can use into a form that the computer can use (input device) and vice versa (output device). We represent information in alphanumeric form (using words and numbers), while a computer represents information in *binary form* (using only the numbers 0 and 1). Letters of the alphabet and numbers are translated or coded by an input device into sequences of 0s and 1s. The output device decodes sequences of 0s and 1s into numbers and letters, or sometimes into sounds or graphic images.

A microcomputer keyboard is an input device and the screen and the printer are output devices. (Printed output is called *hard copy* output.) A *terminal* connected to a mainframe computer also has a keyboard for input and either a screen or printer for output. A mainframe computer may be able to service several hundred terminals, some directly wired to it, others temporarily connected to it by a telephone line connection. Specialized input and output devices exist, for example, a *graphics tablet* is an input device that accepts information traced on its surface.

A computer can also store information on storage media such as magnetic *disks* or *tapes* Once information has been recorded on disk or tape, it can be read back into the computer at a later date by means of a *disk drive* or a *tape drive*. Therefore disk and tape drives are also input devices (and output devices) in the sense that they load and unload information to and from the computer; however, the information stored on disk or tape is in "machine readable," not "human readable," form.

Memory

The input information that we have been talking about consists of both a program and data that the program uses. Each program instruction and each item of data is stored in binary form in a specific location in the computer's memory. The computer keeps track of where everything is stored. New results that are generated during program execution are also stored in memor in binary form. An output device retrieves data, including the new results, from the computer's memory, converts it from binary to ordinary representation, and displays or prints it for human use.

In addition to the memory resident within the computer itself, called *main memory,* disks or tapes serve as *secondary storage* or *auxiliary memory* for the computer. Many microcomputers have built-in hard disks that store large quantities of information. Related items of information in auxiliary memory are stored in *files*. A single computer program, for example, would be contained in one file. A file might be created to hold the input data for that program, and still another file could be used to hold the output data so that it would be available for later inspection. The user chooses names for these files as they are created.

Central Processing Unit

The computer's *central processing unit* (CPU) consists of two components, the arithmetic-logic unit (ALU) and the control unit. The *arithmetic-logic unit* actually carries out operations such as basic arithmetic and comparisons between two values. Each program instruction that the user types into the computer gets broken down into sequences of very simple instructions, so the ALU may have to perform a number of operations to achieve the effect of a single program instruction.

The *control unit* directs the activities within the computer. This includes: getting from memory the next instruction to be executed, together with any data the instruction needs to operate upon; giving this information to the ALU; moving the results back into memory; and generally timing and sequencing events in an orderly fashion.

Software

The components of a computing system that we have discussed are the physical components of the system, the *hardware.* The system also needs *software,* computer programs, in order to run. Of course the user will supply a program to do a particular job, but there must also be programs resident within the computer itself. These programs are the *system software* for the particular computing system.

One essential piece of system software is the *operating system*. It is responsible for overall management of the computer's resources, including peripheral devices. The operating system, for example, supervises the entry of input data from the input device into memory. It accepts computer user commands telling the computer to do various tasks such as run a particular program, or display the contents of a file. Another essential piece of system software called an *editor* allows the user to create files and edit (make changes in) existing files. The details of the commands the operating system and editor accept vary from system to system—this is some of the information you need to know in order to use your local system. Microcomputer word processing software can also be used to create and edit files.

Figure P-1 represents the various components of a computing system.

Languages

Recall that the computer only deals with information in binary form (as sequences of 0s and 1s). The computer is designed to recognize and can carry out certain binary-form instructions. A program using such instructions is said to be written in *machine language.* Early programming was

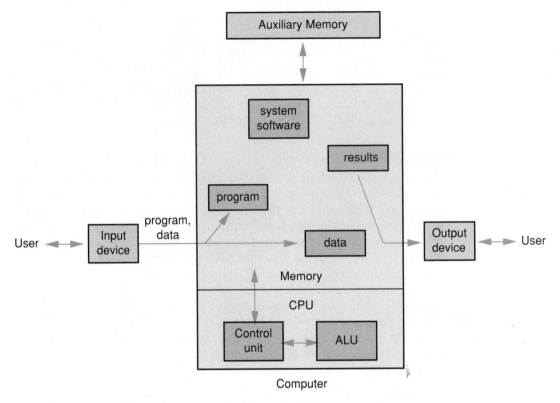

FIGURE   P-1   A computing system.

all done using machine language. Machine language programming is tedious, and the details of the language depend upon the design of the computer. A later improvement allowed the use of English abbreviations such as ADD R1,R2,R3 meaning "add the numbers stored in memory locations R1 and R2 and store the result in memory location R3." This is *assembly language* programming. While its instructions seem more natural than machine language, assembly language still has the disadvantages of being machine-dependent, and of requiring the programmer to keep track of various memory locations and what they contain. A program written in assembly language must be translated into machine language, because the computer still understands only machine language. A piece of system software called an *assembler* does this translation.

An improvement over assembly language came in the form of *higher level languages,* also called *programming languages*. Such languages allow more powerful instructions that more closely follow the steps we want the program to carry out to solve a particular problem; thus it is easier to design such programs, or to understand a program someone else has written. The programmer need not keep track of the memory locations where items are stored but can simply refer to each item by some meaningful name. As another advantage, programming languages are standardized, not dependent upon a particular machine.

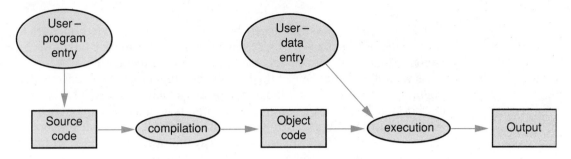

FIGURE P-2 Program compilation and execution.

However, programs written in higher level languages must also be translated into machine language form for the particular computer being used. A piece of system software called a **compiler** does this translation job from a program in a high level language (the **source code**) into a corresponding machine language program (the **object code**). Once a program has been entered, it must go through a compilation phase before the execution phase that actually produces answers (see Fig. P-2). If the computer saves the object code and no changes are made in the program from one run to the next, the program can be executed directly from the object code, and the compilation phase can be skipped. Some programming languages are **interpreted** rather than compiled, meaning that program instructions are translated and executed one at a time, and no object code is saved; the language interpreter that does this task must be invoked each time the program is executed.

Pascal, the programming language we will use in this book, is only one of many higher level languages. Some of the other common ones are:

- **BASIC:** an easy-to-learn, all-purpose language universally available on microcomputers.
- **FORTRAN:** a language especially suited to scientific and engineering applications.
- **COBOL:** a language used primarily for business data processing.
- **PROLOG:** a language that simulates deductive reasoning, useful for applications in artificial intelligence.
- **LISP:** the original, and still widely used, language for artificial intelligence work.
- **Modula-2:** a language designed to extend Pascal's capabilities.
- **Ada:** a language developed for the Department of Defense as a standardized language for military and defense use.
- **C:** originally a systems programming language, now supported on many machines and used in a variety of applications.

As indicated, some languages were designed for specific purposes and are more suited than other languages to carry out certain kinds of tasks. Pascal, named after the seventeenth-century mathematician and philosopher Blaise Pascal, was developed by Professor Niklaus Wirth of Zurich, Switzerland, in the early 1970s. It was intended to be an easy but powerful language that would encourage good programming techniques.

As we noted earlier, one of the benefits of a higher level language is that programs written in such a language are not machine-dependent, so they are "portable" from one computer to another as long as the computer has a compiler for that language. However, there may still be several versions of a language, some allowing extensions, or capabilities, not provided for in the standard core of the language. Such extensions can be very useful if a program will only be run on a system supporting these extensions. However, to ensure that programs really are portable, only the standard features of a language should be used. Only ISO (International Standards Organization) standard Pascal is used in this book.

Computing Modes

If a number of users are connected by terminals to a mainframe computer, the computer system is operating in a ***timesharing*** mode. This means that the computer is servicing all the users by doing a little bit for each user at a time in a round-robin fashion. For example, while one person is typing in a line of input, the computer can be running a piece of someone else's program. Unless the system is being heavily used and the ***response time*** (the time it takes the computer to carry out some work for a particular user) slows down, the user will not even notice that the system is operating in timesharing mode, rather than the ***stand-alone*** mode that services the single user of a microcomputer. As a consequence, whether the computer system is operating in timesharing or stand-alone mode won't generally have much effect on program execution.

Two other computing modes can affect program execution. If the computer system is operating in an ***interactive*** mode, the user can "interact" with the computer while it is running a program. For example, the program might contain an instruction that causes the computer to print a message on the screen asking for some item of data. Execution of the program stops until the user supplies the data. What the program does next could be determined by the value of the data supplied. The user and the computer can have a sort of conversation, with each one reacting to what the other is "saying." In a ***batch processing*** mode, on the other hand, the user gives the computer a program and a complete file of data, and the computer processes the program using this data, finally returning the results to the user. During program execution, the user has no interaction with the computer. This text assumes that an interactive computing mode is available.

CHAPTER ONE

INTRODUCTION TO THE PROGRAMMING PROCESS

1.1 Problem Solving—An Example

Imagine you are a home builder who, like many residential builders, also designs the homes. A customer asks you to design and construct a house that will meet certain requirements, such as provide a given amount of space and stay within a certain budget. How can this problem be solved?

Consider the following scenario: you listen to the client at the initial meeting, nod in agreement, go out to the empty lot, and, without plans or blueprints, begin to lay down a few bricks. Wherever it seems there ought to be a door or window, you leave space. When the walls don't quite fit together at the corners, you squeeze in a few extra bricks near the top. When part of the wiring is forgotten, you tear out a section of wallboard, add the wiring, and cover it up again. This all costs extra time and money, which you pass on to the client. The final result is a poorly constructed house (Fig. 1.1) that is also late and over budget.

Of course this is a farfetched scenario. No builder, no matter how experienced, would consider beginning a house without a detailed set of plans. First, however, comes extensive consultation with the client so that the finished product will satisfy all of the client's requirements, even those the client hadn't thought about initially. Understanding the problem, that is, specifying the complete set of requirements to be met, is an important part of the problem-solving process.

The builder then develops the house plans. Major decisions—the number of bedrooms, two story vs. ranch style, etc.—are made first, referring to the problem specifications (or the client) for guidance. After this initial pass at the design, the builder fills in more details, perhaps sketching out room layout, dimensions, and location of doors and windows. Results are checked against the problem requirements, then still more detailed decisions are made. This process may be repeated many times until final

FIGURE 1.1 The house that "no plans" built.

decisions (e.g., doorknob styles or carpet colors) are made. Planning the solution is another part of the problem-solving process.

At each pass through the building design, decisions too detailed to be considered at the moment are left until later. The builder may never even consider the details of some tasks but will entrust these lower-level decisions to qualified subcontractors after giving them the specifications needed for their part of the job.

The builder and subcontractors then carry out the solution plan, that is, they actually construct the house. This is done in stages or "modules." Payment of many construction loans is tied to signing off at the completion of each stage of a project. Each stage is checked against the problem specifications, i.e., the house plans. In this way any errors are caught early, while they are easier and less expensive to correct. After the building is complete and accepted, the building plans are available to the owner in case subsequent changes (adding an extra room, for example) are ever made. The building plans serve as "documentation," explaining the details of the construction to anyone who needs to know.

The steps the builder uses to solve the problem of constructing a house can be summarized as follows:

- Understand the problem
- Plan the solution, making major decisions first
- Carry out the solution in careful stages
- Check each stage as it is completed
- Leave documentation of the solution for future use

By now, you may have concluded that you are in the wrong class; don't worry, this is not a textbook for Housebuilding 101! The problem-solving steps outlined here are applicable to any type of problem to be solved, including writing a computer program.

Programming, like home building, is not a natural talent one is born with, but a skill to be mastered with practice. The programs that result, like the completed home, can be monuments to the individual style of the "designer" and the technical skills of the "builder."

1.2 The Programming Process

1. Problem
   specification
2. Algorithm
   development
3. Coding
4. Debugging
5. Testing
6. Documenting
7. Maintenance

The process of writing a computer program can be broken down into seven steps that closely parallel those of the home-builder example. These steps are:

1. Problem specification
2. Algorithm development
3. Coding
4. Debugging
5. Testing
6. Documenting
7. Maintenance

(The drawing and list shown here in the margin will serve as a reminder whenever the programming process is being discussed later in the book.)

Although the steps of the programming process are numbered sequentially, their boundaries are not that distinct. Part of problem specification is done concurrently with algorithm development, and documenting occurs continually throughout all of the other phases.

1.2.1 *Problem Specification*

In order to write a computer program to solve a particular problem, we must understand the problem completely. This means knowing what information is available to help solve the problem, and what the outcome of solving the problem should be. In terms of a computer program, what is the data on which the program will act (the program *input*), and what is to be the result of executing the program (the program *output*)?

Suppose we are asked to write a program to balance a checkbook. The input consists of the balance at the beginning of the month, and a list of deposits made and checks written during the month. The output is to be the new balance at the end of the month. This seems pretty clear—start with the old balance, subtract the checks, add the deposits, and the result will be the new balance. But think about what the client said was wanted for output. Just the new balance? Surely the client also wants to see to whom the checks were written, and the amount of each check. Perhaps even a running balance for the month should be given, with entries for each day checks are written or deposits made. Is this an interest-bearing checking account? How is the interest computed? Are there bank service charges on this account? How are they computed? The details of this problem have not been completely specified. There are certain situations, likely to occur, for which we haven't been told what to do. What if someone makes an error in giving us the input data for this program? How should the program handle checks for negative amounts, for example, or for amounts over $1,000,000? There are certain situations, unlikely but possible, for which we haven't been told what to do.

Gaps in the original problem specification occur because the person who poses the problem does not give complete information. He or she may leave out information that seems obvious and may fail to cover all the likely scenarios or the unlikely, but possible, scenarios.

Many of these gaps will become apparent while planning the problem solution. Consultation with the client is often necessary in order to complete the problem specification. Final problem specification is thus accomplished in an iterative fashion along with the development of the problem solution, step 2 in the programming process.

1.2.2 Algorithm Development

An **algorithm** is a procedure to do a certain task, presented as a series of actions that can be carried out mechanistically, without any special insight, additional knowledge, or subjective judgment required. The task we want to do is solve a problem, obtaining the desired output from the given input. The algorithm is our plan of attack to accomplish this. Developing this plan is the most creative part of the programming process. Here we may be somewhat imaginative, while at the same time producing a solution that conforms to the problem specifications.

It can be overwhelming to be faced with how to solve an entire problem all at once. To make the job more manageable, we first break the problem into a few major tasks that, if indeed they could be carried out, would solve the problem. At this first pass we are only concerned with identifying the tasks, not with detailing how they will be done. At the next pass we examine each of these major tasks and identify subtasks of which it is composed. Again, we do not consider the details of how to do the subtasks. This decomposition process continues until the subtasks are so small and represent such simple jobs that it is easy to see how to do them. The plan for the solution is then complete. A simple problem will require few passes, a complex problem more.

This process is known as **top-down design.** It is also called **stepwise refinement** because at each pass the design gets "refined" with the addition of further details. A **structure chart** (Fig. 1.2) can be used to represent the various subtasks and the relationships among subtasks.

1.2.3 Coding

So far we have not even mentioned a computer. Only after the algorithm design is complete is it time to actually write program instructions,

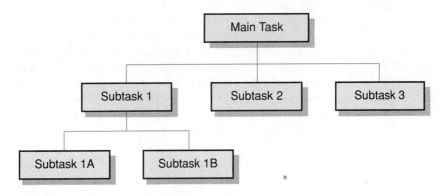

FIGURE 1.2 A structure chart.

statements in the programming language being used that tell the computer how to do the various subtasks of the design and get them to work together correctly. Statements written in a programming language constitute ***computer code.*** Translation into computer code is easily accomplished if we have described the subtasks in ***pseudocode*** form, using language that is a cross between purely prose English and computer code. There are no formal "rules" for writing pseudocode, and there will be many examples as we go along.

Because we have refined the algorithm into very simple subtasks and have described these subtasks in pseudocode, it is almost routine to generate the corresponding sections of computer code. Furthermore, the structure chart graphically illustrates how the subtasks work together, so we can integrate the sections of code properly.

Unfortunately, a widely held misconception equates programming with coding and identifies typing at a keyboard to enter the program into the computer as the only activity involved. Coding is but one step in the programming process (and the least interesting step at that).

1.2.4 *Debugging*

Once the program has been coded and entered, it is time to execute it on some data and compare the output with the problem specification. Alas, the initial attempt at program execution often doesn't produce any output at all! The program may not get as far as execution because it does not successfully complete the compilation phase, when translation from the programming language to the computer's machine language takes place.

Three types of errors can occur in a program: ***syntax errors,*** the potential for ***run-time errors,*** and ***logic errors***. Locating and correcting errors (***bugs***) in a program is called ***debugging.***

Syntax errors are illegal combinations of symbols that do not obey the rules of the programming language, and therefore cannot be translated by the compiler. Syntax errors show up during the compilation phase, before the program is executed. If a syntax error exists, the compiler will send a message to help locate the problem (e.g., "semicolon expected here").

Messages may be more obscure than this, depending on the type of error and the "user-friendliness" of the compiler.†

Once the program is executing on some data, the possibility for run-time errors exists. These errors reflect illegal operations attempted due to the particular data values being used. For example, an instruction that would result in division by zero for a particular set of data will produce a run-time error when the program is executed on that data set. A message ("division by zero attempted") will indicate each run-time error. The compiler was unable to spot these problems during compilation because it did not see the data.

Even when the program successfully executes and produces answers, the results may not be correct. Two types of errors are possible here. An error may have been made in translating the algorithm into code. More likely, however, the program accurately reflects the algorithm, but the algorithm does not really solve the problem it was intended to solve. In this case the algorithm, and the resulting program, has a logic error. Logic errors are more difficult to find and correct than syntax or run-time errors because they are errors in the thought process of designing the problem solution, and no messages pinpoint them. Logic errors require a retreat to step 2 (algorithm development) in the programming process. Fortunately, there are some guidelines to use in debugging logic errors; we'll say more about this in Chapter 6.

1.2.5 *Testing*

What more can we ask for than a debugged program that gives correct results? Aha!—do we know that the program always gives correct results, or does it only work for the particular data values we've tried? Have all logic errors been corrected, or do some lurk in unexpected sections of the program, waiting for new data values to cause them to appear?

Unless the program is extremely simple, the answers to these questions are unknown. It is not sufficient to stop with one or two correct runs and feel that the programming process is complete. The programmer must now become the devil's advocate and actively search for circumstances under which errors are likely to occur. The larger and more complex the problem, and the more critical the application, the more important testing becomes. A 20-line program written for your first programming assignment does not warrant much testing, but you should be aware of program testing and increase the effort spent on testing as your programs become more complex.

1.2.6 *Documenting*

Documentation refers to all material that makes a program easy to understand and use, both for the person who wrote it and for anyone else. It begins with the problem specification phase. The original problem descrip-

---

†Some Pascal systems for microcomputers feature syntax checks as each statement is entered, so errors are easily located and corrected on the spot. By the time the program has been completely entered, it has been compiled and is free of syntax errors. This check-as-you-go system also avoids ***cascading errors,*** where 20 or 30 error messages referring to various statements throughout the program occur, all because of a single error that caused many subsequent statements to appear wrong.

tion, plus additional decisions or assumptions made as the specification was developed, contribute to an understanding of *what* the program does. Notes on the algorithm development are critical in explaining *how* the program does what it does. The structure chart gives an overview of the logic of the program. The pseudocode descriptions for each subtask provide detailed information on how the subtasks work. Notes on debugged logic errors, program changes, and data sets used for program testing also help describe the program. All of this material is in addition to the program itself and is called ***external documentation. Internal documentation*** consists of elements incorporated within the program itself to help explain how it works.

Documentation goes on concurrently with the rest of the programming process. Waiting until the end to go back and recreate material for documentation causes too much loss of detail and too much misinformation. After you work for days on a program, the meaning of every line may seem unforgettable, but a month later you will have trouble understanding the program. Imagine how difficult it would be for someone else. That's why documentation is important, and why it should not be left until last.

1.2.7 *Maintenance*

Large and complex pieces of software can be used for years, long after the original programmers are no longer associated with the project. Maintaining an existing piece of software involves three concerns. First, new uses of the program or new data values can expose previously undetected logic errors that must be fixed. Second, the program may need to be modified in order to allow it to perform new tasks, or to do old tasks in a different way. Finally, new hardware or system software may require changes in existing code so that established programs will run on new machines. If the program was written using only standard features of the language, such changes should be minimal.

The maintenance programmer relies heavily on the program's documentation. He or she will also contribute to that documentation, noting any errors found and program changes made.

> Each phase of the programming process provides its own psychic rewards. Design is programming in the large; coding is programming in the small. . . . The pleasures of programming are the pleasures of shape and form, of the broad stroke, of the thought made flesh. The pleasures of coding are the pleasures of refinement, of the perfection of detail.
>
> The pleasures of debugging are the pleasures of the sleuth; of drawing key inferences from the tiniest and most ephemeral aspects of the behavior of a malfunctioning program. . . Patience is rewarded by the joy of sudden enlightenment and conquest, reinforced by the sight of a sick program springing to life.
>
> Few programs of any consequence are written, turned loose on the world, and then abandoned. . . As the lapidary polishes a gem to elicit its brilliance and clarity, so does the programmer refine and improve a program to enlarge its functionality, enhance its hospitality, boost its performance, and simplify its structure. The pleasures of refinement are the pleasures of acquired wisdom and its fruits.
>
> From the "President's Letter" by Paul Abrahams, *Communications of the ACM*, vol. 30, No. 12, December 1987

We'll look at the phases of the programming process in more detail as we proceed through this book. Also throughout this book, we will follow two case studies of program development, one in which the work is completely done, and one in which you must do some of the work. We'll introduce the case study problems now.

CASE STUDY ONE   View #1

The Lodestone County Water Pollution Department of the Board of Health checks bacteria levels in various bodies of water around the county on a regular basis. In particular, bodies of water used for recreational swimming are tested for fecal coliform bacteria, which would indicate the presence of raw sewage. Five samples per month are taken from each site, and bacteria levels that are sufficiently high are flagged for investigation.

The department asks Sterling Software Systems to develop a program that will automate its record keeping, take the data from a sample, and indicate whether the site should be flagged.

CASE STUDY TWO   View #1

The Lodestone County Hospital Hypertension Clinic monitors a number of outpatients with hypertension (high blood pressure) and does public health testing for potential high blood pressure patients. On each visit to the clinic, a patient's blood pressure is taken three times over a half-hour period. Each reading gives a systolic and diastolic figure. For example, with a blood pressure of 120/80, the systolic pressure (when the heart is pumping) is 120 and the diastolic pressure (when the heart is relaxed between beats) is 80. The clinic averages the three readings and classifies the patient as normal, mild hypertensive, moderate hypertensive, or severe hypertensive.

The clinic wants Sterling Software Systems to develop a program that will automate its record keeping, take the data on a patient, and classify that patient.

EXERCISES   *1.* Consider the following problem: Given the names and ages of two people (this is the input), find (this is the output) twice the age of the person whose name comes first alphabetically.

    # a) Write a more complete problem specification.
    b) Describe the major subtasks.
    c) Give data sets to test a program that is supposed to solve this problem.

\# For problems marked by #, answers are given in Appendix K.

2. Locate a source of information (a manual, a computer center consultant, your instructor, a friend) for the computer system you will be using. Learn how to log on to the system if it is a mainframe or multi-user system, or how to bring up the system if it is a stand-alone microcomputer. Use the editor to create a file called NAME or something similar (different systems have different rules for allowable file names—be sure to check the details for your system), and type your name and address into the file. Be sure to make some typographical errors while doing this, so you can learn how to correct them. Save your file. Now use the operating system commands to

    a) Display your directory (a list of your files—NAME will be the only file, unless your system has already included others).

    b) Copy your file to a second file with a different name.

    c) Delete the original file.

    d) Type the contents of the new file on the screen.

    e) Print the contents of the new file on a printer.

CHAPTER TWO

SIMPLE PROGRAMS; PROBLEM SPECIFICATION

2.1 A Pascal Program Template

Every Pascal program follows a certain basic form, so we begin by looking at this pattern or "template" for any program. The template looks like this:

program heading
declarations
begin
   statements
end.

   The program heading indicates the program name, where the input will be found, and where the output should be sent. The declarations section sets aside memory locations for the data the program will use and the results it will generate, and establishes the kind of information to be stored there so that it can be properly interpreted. The "body" of the program consists of the statements between **begin** and **end.** These are the actual program instructions, and program execution begins with the first such statement.

2.1.1 A Sample Program

Figure 2.1 shows a complete Pascal program, followed by a sample program execution that shows exactly what you would see on the screen if you ran the program. First there is a message: "What is the average number of miles per week you usually drive? (to the nearest mile)." You enter 235 (in the sample execution shown), followed by a RETURN. The program responds with "That's about 378.115 kilometers." This response leads us to suspect that the program is converting a distance in miles to the equivalent value in kilometers. Turning to the actual code, this suspicion is confirmed by the second line, which is a comment enclosed within curly braces { and }. Although we have given no information about Pascal statements yet, you probably can get the drift of how the program works just by reading it, especially if we mention that an * stands for multiplication. By the time we are done with this chapter, we'll have examined the entire program in detail.

```pascal
program Mileage(input, output);
{converts distance in miles to distance in kilometers}

const
    MilesToKmsConversion = 1.609;    {conversion factor}

var
    Miles : integer;            {input distance in miles}
    Kms : real;                 {corresponding distance in kms}

begin
    writeln('What is the average number of miles per week ');
    writeln('you usually drive?    (to the nearest mile)');
    writeln;
    readln(Miles);
    Kms := (MilesToKmsConversion)*Miles;
    writeln;
    writeln('That' 's about ', Kms:7:3, ' kilometers.');
end.
```

RUNNING THE PROGRAM...

What is the average number of miles per week
you usually drive?   (to the nearest mile)

235

That's about 378.115 kilometers.

FIGURE 2.1 A complete Pascal program and a sample program execution.

2.2 The Program Heading

The program heading in our sample program is

```pascal
program Mileage(input, output);
```

The first word is **program,** which is a Pascal *reserved word,* meaning that it can only be used for a special purpose. The purpose of **program** is to indicate the beginning of the code for a Pascal program. Other reserved words in our program are **const, var, begin,** and **end.** There aren't many reserved words, and a complete list appears in Appendix A.

2.2.1 *Identifiers*

The word *Mileage* in the program heading is the name we chose for the program itself. We will name lots of things in our programs—the program itself, various data items and results, subtasks carried out within the program. Names are called **identifiers.** An identifier can be any string of letters and digits starting with a letter, except it can't be a reserved word. This restriction is not much of a problem—it's hard to see why anyone would be tempted to name a program **end,** for example. Other identifiers in our sample program are *Miles, Kms,* and *MilesToKmsConversion.*

Identifiers are not "case-sensitive." *MILES, Miles,* or *miles* are all treated as the same identifier. An identifier can be of any length, so it can be long enough to help make its purpose clear.†

This brings up an important point. The computer understands code as long as the rules are followed. Things can be named X, Y, and Z, for example, because these are legal identifiers. However, programs are also read by those who have to use them and maintain them. Choices of names meaningful in the context of the program greatly aid in explaining the program to others. In our sample program the line

```
Kms := (MilesToKmsConversion)*Miles;
```

is practically self-explanatory (i.e., kilometers are computed by multiplying miles by the proper conversion factor) while

Use descriptive identifiers, and rely on only the first eight characters to distinguish them.

```
Z := X*Y;
```

or

```
Sleepy := Doc*Grumpy;
```

might do the same task, but their identifiers do not enlighten. The compiler will enforce the correct **syntax rules** (rules for how symbols may be combined in the language), but the programmer is responsible for the readability of a program over and above the syntax rules.

Syntax rules in Pascal can be represented by **syntax charts** or **syntax diagrams.** The syntax diagram for an identifier is

---

†On some systems, a distinction is made between upper- and lower-case letters, and *MILES, Miles,* and *miles* would be treated as three different identifiers. It is best not to make use of such distinctions, whether the computer does it or not, because keeping track of them is confusing for the humans who must read the program and makes the program less portable. Some systems only look at the first eight characters of an identifier. In this case, *CorporateTax* and *CorporateRate* would be indistinguishable. To be safe, rely on only the first eight characters to distinguish the identifier. Some versions of Pascal allow an underscore as part of an identifier, as in *Miles_to_kilometers_conversion,* but this is not standard.

The arrows show that the initial character is a letter, followed by any number of letters or digits in any order. Syntax diagrams for all Pascal constructions can be found in Appendix E.

CHECKUP 2.1   Which of the following are not legal Pascal identifiers?
ARobin A_Robin Robin2 2Robin Robin.x

2.2.2 *Files*

The computer's system software allows the user to create and edit files, select names for these files, and view a directory of the files on the user's disk (single-user system) or in the user's area (multi-user system). A file must be created to contain a program. The name of the file is a system file name rather than a Pascal identifier. For example, we might use a file called SAMPLE.PAS to hold our sample program *Mileage*.

Files to hold the program input and output are also needed. The files the program will use are written in parentheses behind the program name in the program heading, as in

program Mileage(input, output);

In an interactive computer environment, the file name *input* refers to the keyboard, so that the input "file" contains whatever data the user enters. The file name *output* refers to the screen, so the output "file" contains whatever the computer writes on the screen. In batch processing, the input file is created by the user ahead of time and stored on a disk, and the output file is created and stored by the computer as the program executes. These stored files for input and output usually must have other names within the program because *input* and *output* refer to communication with the user through the keyboard and screen.

A program may use more than just one file for input and one file for output. For example, even an interactive program may use a large amount of data that is kept stored in a file so that it does not have to be re-entered each time the program is run, and also use additional data entered from the keyboard as the program executes. We'll see how to deal with files other than *input* and *output* in Chapter 11.

If a program does not need an input file, the program heading could omit the file name *input* and just be written

program NoInputRequired(output);

2.3 Comments

Several items throughout the sample program are written within curly braces { and }. These are treated as program ***comments.*** A comment is entirely ignored by the compiler and has no effect on the computer's actions while executing the program, so in some sense it is not part of the program code. Its sole purpose is to provide information for the humans who read the code. Like the use of reasonable and helpful identifiers, program comments help make the program easier to understand. Because our sample program is such a short and simple one, we've used only minimal commenting. A comment at the beginning gives a general description of the program, and comments describe the purpose of each of the quantities used in the program. From the start, make it a habit to include comments in programs. At first, as in our sample program, only minimal comments will be necessary, but your use of comments should increase as programs get longer and more complex.

Comments may also be enclosed within the symbol pairs (* and *). A single comment may extend over several lines, but braces are needed only at the beginning and end of the entire comment. Anything enclosed within a pair of braces becomes a comment, except that comments cannot be nested within comments. Comments can also go on the same line as other program statements, as in the sample program, where "in-line" comments are useful to describe the individual quantities.

Use comments to give at least a general description of the program and to explain the purpose of each quantity used in the program.

Anything enclosed within { and } is treated as a comment.

2.4 Declarations

In the declarations section of the program, memory is allocated to store quantities with which the program deals. The number of miles and the equivalent number of kilometers are two such quantities in the sample program; these quantities are **variables** in that their specific value is not known until the program is executed. However, the sample program also uses another quantity whose value is the same for every program execution, namely, the conversion factor between miles and kilometers. The declarations section also stores this **constant** quantity in memory. We'll look at how to declare constants and how to declare variables in turn.

2.4.1 *Constants*

A constant quantity has a fixed value that cannot be affected by program execution. A constant can be named using any legal identifier. Constants in a program are declared by the reserved word **const,** followed by a list of statements of the form

identifier = constant value;

In our sample program, the single constant is declared by

```
const
    MilesToKmsConversion = 1.609;     {conversion factor}
```

This sets aside a location in memory that contains the value 1.609, and that can be referred to by the identifier *MilesToKmsConversion*. Anywhere this identifier appears in the program, it will be replaced with the value 1.609 when the program is executed (or even when it is compiled).

Our sample program could be written in two different ways without using a constant. The conversion factor could be a variable whose value is entered as part of the input data every time the program is run. The disadvantage is that the user must supply this value (and then, presumably, doesn't need this program at all). Even if the user knows the conversion factor, asking for it every time the program runs is extra trouble for the user and introduces another potential source for mistakes due to typographical errors.

Another way would be to simply use the numerical value 1.609 in the program statement where it is needed:

```
Kms := (1.609)*Miles;
```

However, it isn't very clear what this line of code accomplishes, unless one recognizes the conversion factor from miles to kilometers. The constant identifier gives a more explanatory statement:

```
Kms := (MilesToKmsConversion)*Miles;
```

Another advantage to the use of constants is illustrated by the following scenario. A program to compute interest rates based on the prime rate uses the constant value 0.085 (the prime rate when the program is written) throughout the program. A change in the prime rate requires changing every statement that uses this value. If *PrimeRate* had been declared as a constant, however, only this single line of code would need to be changed.

In summary, constant declarations help make a program more readable and easier to modify.

Constants do not have to have numerical values; they can be declared as strings of characters, given by enclosing the string in single quote marks. The following is a valid set of constant declarations:

```
const
    Pi = 3.1416;            {geometric constant pi}
    PrimeRate = 0.085;      {current prime rate}
    Base = 5000;            {sample population in the experiment}
    Prompt = 'Enter next set of durations.';    {instruction to
                                                    user}
```

Note the use of comments that clarify what the constant values represent. *Prompt* can be used to save typing a fixed output message many different places in a program.

One predefined constant that does not have to be declared is *maxint*; *maxint* gives the value of the largest integer that can be stored in a single memory location. This is determined by the number of **bits** (binary digits) that make up a memory location, which is a function of the architecture of the particular computer being used. Running the following program will determine the value of *maxint* for your system.

```
program LargestInteger(output);
{Finds the largest allowable integer for this system.}
```

begin
  writeln('Largest allowable integer for this system is ', maxint);
end.

Computations that result in an integer value larger than *maxint* will cause an error message such as ***integer overflow.*** The lower boundary on negative integer size will be close to $-maxint$.

Declarations of constants, if present, precede variable declarations.

Not every program requires constant declarations, but if they appear, they must be placed before the variable declarations. Any subsequent attempt by the program to modify the value of a declared constant will result in an error.

2.4.2 *Variables*

Variables are quantities whose values are unknown ahead of program execution, or whose values can change during execution. The quantities *Miles* and *Kms* are variables in the sample program.

Variables can be named by any legal identifier. The declaration of a variable sets aside a location in memory that can be referred to by this identifier. Whenever a program statement containing this identifier is executed, the current value in the corresponding memory location is used for the identifier. Figure 2.2 illustrates the contents of the three memory locations set aside by the declarations section of the sample program at different points in the sample program execution.

A program might use several kinds of data. For example, the sample program asks for input data "to the nearest mile," so it expects to store an integer value for the variable *Miles*. After multiplying this value by 1.609, the program expects to store a real number (a number with a decimal point) for the variable *Kms*. The translation rules that convert data into binary

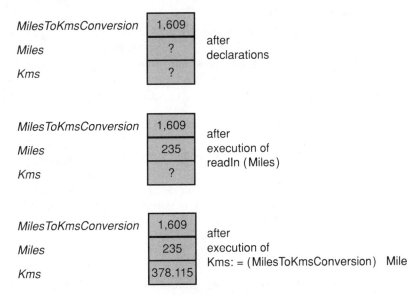

FIGURE 2.2 Memory locations during the sample program execution.

form to be stored in memory are different for each type of data. A given pattern of 0s and 1s could be the coded form of an integer, or it could be the coded form of some real number with a value nowhere near the value of the integer, or it could even represent an alphabetic character. In order to properly code and decode the binary information it stores and retrieves from a given memory location, the computer must know the type of data being stored there. This information is provided as part of the variable declaration; once a certain location is assigned a data type, no other type of data can be stored there.

Declare all variables.

The form for variable declarations is the reserved word **var** followed by a list of statements of the form

list of identifiers : data type;

The variable declarations in the sample program are

```
var
    Miles : integer;        {input distance in miles}
    Kms : real;             {corresponding distance in kms}
```

More than one variable of a given type can be declared in the same statement, but not all the variables of a given type need appear in the same statement. The following is a valid declaration:

```
var
    Wins : integer;
    Average : real;
    Losses, Ties : integer;
```

2.4.3 *Data Types*

Standard data types are integer, real, char, and boolean.

Pascal defines a number of interesting data types and even allows us to invent our own, but for now, we'll use the four *standard data types*—integer, real, character, and boolean.

A variable of type *integer* can take on a value of zero, or positive or negative counting-number values. Examples of integers are

0   17   −2357   84561

No sign is included for a positive number, and no commas are written within large integers. Integers must fall within the range −*maxint* to *maxint* (although the lower limit is somewhat approximate).

A variable of type *real* can take on decimal number values. Examples of real values are

3.461   −27.4   635.0476   17.0   0.9

Such numbers must contain a decimal point, and at least one digit before and after the decimal point. No commas are used. The internal computer representation of the real number 17.0 is quite different from that of the integer 17, even though these are the same quantity mathematically.

Real numbers can also be expressed in "E format," essentially, scientific notation. The "E" stands for exponent, a power of 10. A number written in E format always gives the digits of the number first. These digits might not contain a decimal point, but if a decimal point is included, there must be at least one digit on either side. Next comes an E, followed by a positive or negative integer that is the power of 10. For example, the number 3.47E+03 has digits 3.47 and an exponent, or power of 10, of 3. This says that the number 3.47 is to be multiplied by 10 to the power 3. Therefore

$$3.47E+03 = 3.47 \times 10^3 = 3470.0$$

Other examples of E format numbers and their values are

$$-135E+02 = -13500.0$$
$$4.78E-03 = 0.00478$$
$$0.4E+05 = 40000.0$$

Many electronic calculators display values in E format.

CHECKUP 2.2   Write the following numbers in decimal form:
  a. 234E−02
  b. 3.89E+04
  c. −24E−05

CHECKUP 2.3   Which of the following are not valid *real* values?
  3.28   .60   42.   2.46E+02   3434E−01   2.59 E+01   4.67E+1.0

Real numbers are also called **floating-point numbers** because of the way the decimal point can get moved about in E format. The E format is convenient for representing very large or very small real numbers. Any real number is stored in the computer's memory essentially in E format. However, only a certain number of bits of the memory location are devoted to storing the exponent. Therefore numbers that are too big in absolute value (have a positive exponent too large to store) will result in a **floating-point overflow;** the consequences here depend upon the system. Those numbers that are too close to zero (have a negative exponent too large to store) will result in a **floating-point underflow;** when this occurs, most systems use 0 for the number.

The remaining bits of the memory location store the representation of the digits of the real number. Therefore there is a limit to the number of significant digits for any real number, which may lead to unexpected

There is a system-dependent limitation on the size of integer values, and on the size and number of significant digits for real values.

inaccuracies in real number computations. As a simple example, suppose we are limited to 5 significant digits for any real number. In decimal form, we then express 1/3 as 0.33333, and 3*(1/3) results in 0.99999. This does not agree with 1.0, the exact answer. Of course, 1/3 is not a terminating fraction in ordinary decimal arithmetic, but even some terminating fractions, when translated into binary representation, become nonterminating. We should avoid exact comparisons of real number values and instead look for values that are very close. Quantities that are integers within the allowable range of integers should be declared type *integer* rather than type *real*, because integral values have exact internal representations.

Use integer data where possible, avoiding exact comparisons of real values.

A variable of type *char* can take on values consisting of any single character on the keyboard. Thus a variable declared by the declaration

var
    Initial : char;

A variable of type char holds only a single character; a blank is a valid character.

could at various times have the values 'J', 'm', or even '7', ';', or '$'. A character variable holds only one character, not a string of characters. To represent the word "dingbat" using character variables would require seven such variables, one for each letter. The character '7' that might be assigned to a variable of type *char* is not the same as the numerical value 7 that might be assigned to a variable of type *integer*. Also, single quote marks must be used within a program to distinguish the character 'J' from *J*, which could be an identifier.

A variable of type *boolean* can only take on one of two values, *true* or *false*. Boolean variables are used for decision making—if a variable has the value *true*, do something, if it has the value *false*, do something else. Boolean variables have one peculiarity—they cannot be read in as data, although they can be written as output.

A final example of a valid variable declaration section is

var
    FirstInitial, LastInitial : char;   {subject's initials}
    Age : integer;   {subject's age}
    Resident : boolean;   {state residency status}
    GPA : real;   {grade average}

Later we will see other constructions that belong in the declarations section of a program.

2.4.4 *Strong Typing*

Pascal is a **strongly typed language** in that every variable in the program must be declared and its data type fixed once and for all. Some languages are not strongly typed, and a new variable name can be used any time. The data type of the variable is the data type of the variable's current value. This seems appealingly simple, especially after struggling to figure out ahead of time what all the variables will be called, and what kind of data they will hold.

However, there are advantages to all of this work required ahead of time for Pascal variable declarations. First, it forces the programmer to plan a solution carefully, determining exactly what quantities the program deals with. (Something overlooked can always be added to the declaration section.) Second, the Pascal compiler helps correct typographical errors; if an incorrect identifier is typed in, an error message notes that it is illegal because it hasn't been declared. The use-a-new-variable-whenever-you-want-to school of thought will never catch these. Third, the compiler performs **type checking** to make sure that only the right kind of data is in each variable and that ill-advised activities with data, such as subtracting a character value from a real number, are not attempted.

2.5 **Punctuation and Formatting**

Program statements must be separated by semicolons.

In Pascal programs the semicolon separates one statement from another. Semicolons are one of the Pascal details that can drive the beginning programmer crazy. A missing semicolon forces the compiler to treat what was intended to be two statements as one; this one so-called statement will probably not be syntactically acceptable as a single statement, and an error message results. After this happens a half-dozen times, you'll begin to remember the necessary semicolons!

Statements can also be combined into compound statements bounded by the reserved words **begin** and **end.** The general form for a compound statement is

begin $s_1; s_2; \ldots s_k$ **end**

where $s_1, s_2, \ldots, s_k$ are statements. No semicolon is needed after statement s_k, because the reserved word **end** is not another statement; separators are necessary only between statements. Similarly, no semicolon is needed after **begin.** Pascal is tolerant of a semicolon used after **begin** or before **end.** In order to have this conform to the general form for a compound statement given above, Pascal inserts a **null statement** that has absolutely no effect. The compiler treats

begin; $s_1; s_2; \ldots s_k;$ **end**

as

begin   null statement; $s_1; s_2; \ldots s_k;$ null statement   **end**

It is actually advantageous to use a semicolon after s_k so that if another statement later gets added after s_k, the necessary separating semicolon is already in place.

The term "statement" always includes the possibility of a compound statement. As a consequence, any of the statements in a compound statement can also be compound statements. Compound statements can be nested within compound statements that are nested within compound statements, and so forth. This ability to combine statements in rather complex ways is what allows us to do powerful things with computer programs.

Pascal is a ***free format*** language, meaning that where things are placed on a line does not matter; only the separating semicolons are required for the compiler to make sense of the statements in the code. We could write

```
Mileage      program        (input ,
          output) ;
```

or

```
var Miles:integer;{inputdistanceinmiles}Kms:real;{corresponding
distanceinkms}begin
```

and the compiler could cope. (We humans, however, would have a hard time reading this code.) There must be blanks between words, such as between **program** and *Mileage*. Also, blanks cannot be inserted in the middle of a word (**pro gram** would not be recognizable). Other than these restrictions, blanks inserted in a line of code are ignored by the compiler, unless they are included as part of a string constant declared in a **const** declaration, or as part of a string constant to be written as output, as in

```
writeln('What is the average number of miles per week ');
```

Since the compiler doesn't care, we will write our programs in a way that makes them as readable as possible for humans. This means that we won't put more than one statement per line.

The final **end** in a program must be followed by a period. This signals to the compiler that this is indeed the end of the entire program, rather than the end of some compound statement contained within the program.

2.6 Input, Output, and Assignment

In the body of our sample program,

```
begin
  writeln('What is the average number of miles per week ');
  writeln('you usually drive? (to the nearest mile)');
  writeln;
  readln(Miles);
  Kms := (MilesToKmsConversion)*Miles;
  writeln;
  writeln('That' 's about ', Kms:7:3, ' kilometers.');
end.
```

we write a message to the user, collect an input value, do a computation, and write output to the user. We'll look first at how to handle input.

2.6.1 *Reading Input*

Most programs require some input data, so there will be values to collect from the input file and store in memory locations referred to by some of the variable identifiers. This process is handled by a *read* or *readln* statement. The sample program uses

readln(Miles);

to obtain the value for *Miles* from the input file (keyboard) and store it in the memory location designated by *Miles*. The general form of the *read* or *readln* statement for input from the keyboard is

$read(\text{variable}_1, \text{ variable}_2, \ ..., \text{ variable}_k);$

or

$readln(\text{variable}_1, \text{ variable}_2, \ ..., \text{ variable}_k);$

Both *read* and *readln* statements assign the first value from the input file to variable$_1$, the second value to variable$_2$, and so forth. We can think of a "pointer" going along the input file and hunting for values. The difference between the two statements is that after reading the value for variable$_k$, the pointer remains on the same line for the *read* statement, and moves to the beginning of the next line (throwing away anything remaining on the current line) for the *readln* statement.

Suppose, for example, we have made the following declaration:

var
　　　number1, number2, number3, number4 : integer;

Using the statement

read(number1, number2, number3);

starts the pointer looking for integer values. These values will be read and assigned, in order, to *number1*, *number2*, and *number3*. Intervening blanks will be skipped, and the pointer will move to subsequent lines, if necessary, to find three values. If the input consists of

```
    44      − 53
  155              6
    12
```

then after execution of the above *read* statement, the three variables have values of *number1:* 44   *number2:* −53   *number3:* 155

and the pointer is positioned after the 155. Execution of a subsequent statement

read(number4);

causes the value 6 to be assigned to *number4.*

Now consider the same input and execute the statement

readln(number1, number2, number3);

This again causes these three variables to take on values of

number1: 44   *number2:* −53   *number3:* 155

but after execution of this statement, the pointer goes to the beginning of the next line. It is now impossible to *read* the value 6, and a subsequent statement

read(number4);

assigns the value 12 to *number4.*

The *read* and *readln* statements behave the same way when the input values are real numbers instead of integers. Real number input can be expressed in either decimal form or E format. All numerical values must be separated by one or more blanks and, again, no commas are used within numbers.

Values found in the input must be of the data type expected. If the next variable to receive a value in a *read* or *readln* statement has been declared to be of data type *XXX*, then the next value must be of data type *XXX*, or a **type clash** will occur, generating an error. The only exception to this rule is that an integer value can be read for a variable of data type *real,* and the integer will be converted to its corresponding real representation. For example, if *Time* has been declared to be a *real* variable, a value of 6 can be read in, and the value will be converted to 6.0. However, if *Number* has been declared to be type *integer,* an attempt to read the value 3.7 results in an error. An attempt to read the value 8.0 also results in an error—this will **not** be converted to the corresponding integer value of 8.

Variables of different types can receive values in the same *read* or *readln* statement. A program with the declaration

var
    TaxRate : real;
    UnitsSold: integer;

could contain the statement

readln(UnitsSold, TaxRate);

and input values of

122   0.05

could be given. Note, however, that input values of

0.05   122

would result in an error.

CHECKUP 2.4   With the declarations
var
    X, Y : integer;
    Z : real;

and input data of
2   7   1.4
3.5
2.1

what will be the value of X, Y, and Z in each of the following three cases?
    a. read(X);
          read(Y);
          readln(Z);
    b. read(X);
          readln(Y);
          readln(Z);
    c. readln(X);
          readln(Y);
          readln(Z);

If a *read* or *readln* statement has three variables in its list, the pointer will search for three values. It does not matter if there are more than three values, but if there are fewer than three values available, difficulties occur. If the program is operating in batch mode, reading from a data file, some nasty message such as "Tried to read past end of file" will result and the program will "crash." In an interactive mode, the program "hangs" waiting for further input from the keyboard. No message will be forthcoming, as no "error" has been committed. If an interactive program seems to stop during execution with nothing happening, check to see that enough input values have been supplied.

Interactive programs must prompt the user for input.

This brings up another important point about interactive programs. Because the computer gives no message when it is waiting for data, the programmer must put a message in the program (a **prompt**) telling the user when to enter data and giving information on the kind of data expected. Note the prompt in our sample program:

```
writeln('What is the average number of miles per week ');
writeln('you usually drive? (to the nearest mile)');
```

The prompt tells the user to enter data about mileage and (indirectly) tells the user that the value should be an integer.

Read or *readln* statements assign values to variables in a "destructive" way. If a value is read in for a variable, that value gets placed in the memory location referred to by the variable and the previous value in that memory location is destroyed.

Reading character data is slightly more confusing than dealing with numerical data because any symbol on the keyboard can be thought of as an item of character data type. In particular, a blank is a character. If the next variable to be assigned a value is of type *char*, then the next symbol read, blank or not, will be given to that variable. Suppose a program has the declarations

```
var
    Initial : char;
    number1, number2 : integer;
```

and contains the statement

```
readln(Initial, number1, number2);
```

Input data of

J   12   55

result in the assignment of the following values:

Initial: J   *number1:*   12   *number2:*   55

However the statement

```
readln(number1, Initial, number2);
```

with input data of

12   J   55

Blanks in input are ignored when reading numeric data but are significant when reading character data.

gives the following result. The first variable, *number1*, is given the value 12. After reading this value, the pointer is positioned directly after the 12, ready to begin searching for a value for the second variable listed in the *readln* statement. Because this is a variable of type *char*, the blank following the 12 is the value given to *initial*. The pointer is now positioned immediately after this blank, and next looks for an integer value to assign to *number2*. The pointer passes over intervening blanks because it's looking for a number, but when the J is encountered, a type clash occurs—a noninteger value was found next.

Input data of

12J55

or

12J   55

would work here, but these are a bit ugly and unnatural. Putting the data on separate lines and using separate *readln* statements will solve this problem. We could use

```
readln(number1);
readln(Initial);
readln(number2):
```

with input data

12
J
55

Provide enough data values to satisfy the input statement; values are assigned to variables in order, and must be of the correct data type.

The summary rule about reading input data is that the data values must match the list of variables in the *read* or *readln* statement in

- number (there can be too many values, but there can't be too few)
- order (values are assigned to variables in the order that the variables appear in the list)
- type (values must agree with the data type of the variable to which they are assigned)

2.6.2 *Writing Output*

A *write* or *writeln* statement is used to output string constants or values currently stored in memory locations named by identifiers within the program. The prompt in our sample program,

```
writeln('What is the average number of miles per week ');
writeln('you usually drive? (to the nearest mile)');
```

writes out two string constants. String constants are bounded by single quote marks. We used two *writeln* statements here because a single string constant can't be split across two lines.

The current value of the variable *Kms* in the sample program is written out in the middle of two string constants by the statement

```
writeln('That' 's about ', Kms:7:3, ' kilometers.')
```

To print a single quote mark—an apostrophe—as part of a string constant, as in the word

That's

requires a special device, because using a single quote would denote the end of a string constant. The trick is to use two single quotes (not a double quote, which would be printed as what it is, a regular quotation mark "). A blank space at the end of the string constant

```
'That' 's about '
```

and at the beginning of the string constant

```
' kilometers.'
```

ensures space between the text and the numerical value when the output is printed.

For output to the screen, the *write* or *writeln* statement has the form

write(list of string constants and identifiers);

or

writeln(list of string constants and identifiers);

Values are written out corresponding to the order in the list.

When a *write* statement is used, the "pointer" for writing remains at the end of the last value written. Subsequent *write* or *writeln* statements add additional output to the same line. With a *writeln* statement, the pointer positions itself at the beginning of the next line, and subsequent output appears there. Thus the statements

```
write('Rainy day in ');
writeln('Georgia');
```

produce

```
Rainy day in Georgia
```

while

```
writeln('Rainy day in ');
writeln('Georgia');
```

produce

Rainy day in
Georgia†

A *writeln* statement without a list of identifiers or string constants introduces a blank line in the output. This is very useful for "vertical formatting," making the output easier to read. We used two such statements in the sample program, one to put a blank line after the prompt message and before the input value, and one to put another blank line between the input and the output (see the sample session).

Write and *writeln* statements also control horizontal formatting. With no further instructions, horizontal formatting—the number of spaces used to print output—follows certain default conventions. String constants are written using as much space as they require. Character variables are written using one space. Numerical values are allotted some system-dependent amount of space and right justified within this space. To override the default spacing and impose our own horizontal formatting, we can use a colon and a positive integer after any identifier listed in the *write* or *writeln* statement. This number specifies the **field width,** or number of spaces, to be used to print the value of that identifier. Integer values are right justified within this space. If *number* and *size* are *integer* variables with values of 22 and 55, then

writeln(number:4, size:5);

results in

__22__55

Character values and string constants are also right justified within the field width. If we choose too small a field-width specification for a numerical value, this will be overridden and enough space used to print the entire numerical value. A string constant, however, will be truncated to fit a too-small field width, and the right-hand characters will be lost. A field-width specification of 1 forces the value of a boolean variable to be written as T or F, rather than the default True or False.

Real values without field-width specification are written in E format. If *Average* has been declared type *real,* the result of

---

†Some systems collect output in a storage area (a **buffer**) until it is "dumped" to the output device by a *writeln* statement. On such systems, the code

write('Enter the next input value');
read(Value);
writeln('Thanks');

does not write out the prompt, so the user does not know to enter input data, and the program hangs. *Writeln* statements avoid this difficulty. Also, systems implementing early versions of Pascal require an input value to be present at the beginning of program execution. This is not a problem with batch processing, where the data file already exists, but does cause a peculiarity in interactive processing. The solution is to type a carriage return, which sends a type of input character, in order to get the program started.

writeln(Average);

could be

5.6728000000E + 01

The exact number of spaces used and the number of digits allocated to the exponent are system-dependent. The many 0s before the E are no doubt there to fill up the default field width and are not significant digits; we should do something to suppress them. Using a field-width specification defines the number of spaces for E format output. Thus

writeln(Average:10);

results in

5.6728E + 01

(a total of 10 spaces used to write the output). This eliminates the nonsignificant digits. If the specified field width is too small, enough space will be used to print the value anyway.

To force the output into decimal form, a second specification is used that indicates the number of digits behind the decimal point to print (the number is rounded to fit). The statement

writeln(Average:6:2);

results in the decimal output

_56.73

(a total of 6 spaces for the output with 2 digits behind the decimal point). This type of formatting is particularly useful for writing out dollar-and-cent values.

CHECKUP 2.5   What does the output look like after executing

```
writeln(X:5);
write(Y:7);
writeln(Z:6:2);
```

if X, Y, and Z have the values 46, 231, and 2.432, respectively?

CHECKUP 2.6   Use a single *writeln* statement to produce the output

    Size = 15.98   Cost = $299.31

if *Size* has the value 15.98 and *Cost* has the value 299.3054.

Horizontal formatting can be tricky. Try to get the correct output first, then experiment with horizontal formatting to get the output lined up and looking pretty.

Words like *read, readln, write,* and *writeln* have very specific meanings, yet they are not Pascal reserved words. They are **standard identifiers.** This means that one could declare a variable *readln*, which would then be treated everywhere in the program as an ordinary variable, rather than with its standard meaning as part of an input statement. The resulting program would be confusing to read; use of standard identifiers as variable names should be avoided. (Appendix B has a list of standard identifiers; like reserved words, they are unlikely candidates for variable names anyway.)

2.6.3 *The Assignment Statement*

One way to assign values to variables is by the input process, using *read* or *readln* statements. Another way is to use the **assignment statement.** The sample program uses the statement

Constant declarations use an = sign, variable declarations use the : symbol, and assignment statements use the := symbol.

    Kms := (MilesToKmsConversion)*Miles;

to assign a new value to the variable *Kms.* The general form of the assignment statement is

    variable identifier := new value;

where the new value can be given by another variable or by an arithmetic expression involving constants or variables.

The assignment statement can be thought of as being carried out in two steps. First, the right side of the assignment statement is used to compute the new value, using the current values of any variables. Then the single variable that appears on the left side of the assignment statement receives the new value; its previous value is destroyed. This means that if X is an *integer* variable, the assignment statement

    X := X + 1;

is legal. It says to compute a new value by adding 1 to the current value of X, then to give this new value to X.

The value assigned to the variable must be of the same data type as the variable itself, otherwise a type clash will occur, just as when reading input values. For example, with the declaration

var
    number1, number2, B : integer;
    letter : char;

the assignments

number2 := 2 + number1;
letter := 'B';

are legal, while

letter := 3*number1;

would cause a type mismatch. The assignment

letter := '3';

is legal because the 3 is here being treated as a character (because of the quote marks). Also, the assignment

number2 := B;

is legal; it says to replace the integer value of variable *number2* with the integer value of variable *B*.

The one exception to the rule of matching data types in an assignment statement is the same one as for input—an integer value can be assigned to a variable of type *real*.

CHECKUP 2.7   If *X* is an *integer* variable, what is its value after the following sequence of statements has been executed?

    X := 3;
    X := X + 2;
    X := X - 1;

---

1. Problem
   specification
2. Algorithm
   development
3. Coding
4. Debugging
5. Testing
6. Documenting
7. Maintenance

We have beaten our original sample program to death. Sample Software Development Project Catalog Order at the end of this chapter gives another complete Pascal program. The programs in the Sample Software Development Project in each chapter will be developed from problem statements using the steps of the programming process outlined in Chapter 1, so before we turn to Catalog Order, let's look again at the first step—problem specification.

2.7 Problem Specification

The written problem specification serves as the basis for understanding between the client and the software developer, almost like a legal contract.

It should not be dashed off quickly in order to get on to the more "interesting" work of solving the problem.

While the original problem statement gives information about the program input and output, it may still leave many questions unaddressed. The software developer must discover such questions and interact with the client to find the answers. This work may be done by the programmer, or it may be the job of an analyst, software engineer, or technical manager. In a classroom setting, the instructor typically supplies beginning students with a completely specified problem. Nonetheless, this idyllic situation won't continue throughout one's professional career, so consider what is involved in being responsible for the problem specification.

2.7.1 *Format for Input and Output*

Even when the program input and output are stated, questions such as the following may arise:

What is the form the input will take? Does a large body of data already exist in a file to be used without retyping? If so, how is the data arranged in the file; for example, are there five data values on a line, or does each value have a separate line? If the data will be read from a file but we can design the file, how should the data be arranged? If the data will be entered from the keyboard, how should the program ask the user for input, i.e., what should the user expect to see? Is all of the input necessary to solve the problem available?

What is the desired form for the output? Should it be displayed graphically, as a table, as a paragraph? Must the output meet certain reporting needs of the client that would dictate particular display formats, headings, margins, etc.? Must the output be consistent with the input requirements of some other piece of software?

2.7.2 *Special Cases of Legal Data*

The problem statement may describe only the typical instance of the problem to be solved and neglect to mention legitimate special cases. In a program to automate an instructor's gradebook, for instance, a student may be able to earn enough extra credit to have an average over 100 percent. This is legitimate data that the program should be able to handle successfully. Consultation with the client is essential to help reveal special cases and determine how they are to be treated. A program designed to deal only with the typical majority of cases may make assumptions about input data that will prevent it from handling the unusual exception.

2.7.3 *Illegal Data Handling*

It may be possible to catalog all the legitimate special cases of data. It is not possible to catalog all the illegal data that can arise due to typographical errors, misreading data, fatigue, carelessness, etc. Such input should always be anticipated, however, and some blanket mechanism defined for dealing with it. The best approach is to test, if possible, whether the input falls within some expected range or has some expected characteristic. If not, the program writes an error message and either goes on to the next case or stops in some organized fashion. Such a program is *robust,* able to deal with any input. A program not designed for robustness may, in the face of illegal input, "crash" (stop running) with little or no indication of the reason. Even worse, it may give erroneous results without warning the user that anything is amiss.

2.7.4 *Special Requirements*

Aside from input and output, other areas to address with the client concern any special requirements that will influence program development. Perhaps the program must run on a particular computing system with some limitations that may affect the program. The client may require a particular method or formula to be used in computing results. If the amount of data expected is huge, this can influence the program design. The client's priorities should be determined in terms of certain trade-offs that might arise—is processing speed all-important, or can some speed be sacrificed for a slightly slower method that will make the program easier to understand? In a *real-time* system (a process control system in a factory or laboratory, an air-traffic control system, etc.) time constraints are very important. What are the program's reliability requirements; must it be guaranteed to operate correctly at least 98 percent of the time? (A video game can tolerate a lower level of reliability than an automated-bank-teller program.) If this is an interactive program, what assumptions can be made about the typical user? A program to interact with the general public will require a different level of *user interface* than, for example, a program a professional geologist uses to monitor earthquake activity.

2.7.5 *Generalizations*

While it is important to understand the client's present needs, it is also important to anticipate his or her future needs. Additional output that can be obtained either from the input data already planned or from additional available data should be suggested. Perhaps the client originally requested a special case of a more general solution that can be provided. In anticipation of the client's future needs, additional capabilities should be built into the program, or the program should at least be designed so that additional capabilities can be added easily.

2.7.6 *Functional Requirements and Data Flow*

At this point in the problem specification the *functional requirements* of the program as a whole, that is, what the overall program is to do, have been established. We know that problem specification blends in with step 2 of the programming process, algorithm development. Applying the top-down design technique, the overall task is broken down into major subtasks, these are refined into sub-subtasks, etc. This work can be used to advantage in the more detailed aspects of problem specification. We determine the functional requirements of the program modules that correspond to the various subtasks—what data each will receive and what information each will produce. This helps define the logical components of the program.

To see how those components interact, a ***data flow diagram*** is useful. This is intended to illustrate the flow of information in the program (somewhat like a fluoroscope of the body shows the workings of the circulatory system). Figure 2.3 illustrates a data flow diagram for a simple program that asks the user for a number, doubles the number, and writes out the result. Three main subtasks have been identified—getting the input, doing the calculation, and writing the output. The "Main Program" here simply facilitates the data flow, receiving values from some modules and giving them to others. How the individual subtasks are accomplished is not shown and indeed will not even have been decided when a data flow diagram is drawn.

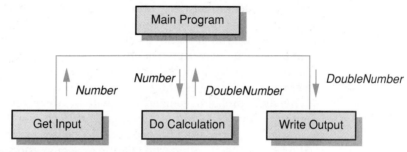

FIGURE 2.3 Data flow diagram.

Figure 2.4 summarizes issues in problem specification. These are shown chronologically as they would probably be addressed, but some reordering is possible.

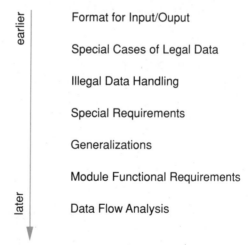

FIGURE 2.4 Problem specification.

2.7.7 *Formal Specification Languages*

The original problem statement was no doubt expressed in English (or some other human language), which has many shades and nuances of meaning. Because the whole point of problem specification is to clarify the problem, formal specification languages have been developed. Statements in these languages have a precise meaning and help avoid ambiguities. However, these statements generally apply at the level of the functional requirements and data flow for each module, already a long way from the original English language problem statement.

2.7.8 *The Specification Document*

The answers to all the questions we have raised—the form of input and output data, treatment of special cases, etc.—become part of the problem specification document. They represent agreements reached with the client. Any assumptions made in the absence of specific guidelines must also be included in this document; as the client reviews the document, these assumptions can be accepted or challenged. Once the problem specification document is finally accepted, the assumptions included in it also represent agreements with the client.

The final problem specification will be the overall reference as the program is developed, and the ultimate test for accepting the software and signing off. If there are ambiguous terms or unanswered questions in the final problem specification, the client can accuse the software developer of not delivering what was agreed upon. If, however, the problem specification is stated in terms of well-defined and testable events (the input looks exactly like this, the initial screen display for the user has this form, the response time is thus and so), everyone knows exactly what the rules are. The program can be tested against these specifications and the developer can demonstrate that the product has met them.

2.7.9 *Prototype Software*

Once the functional requirements and data flow have been tentatively agreed upon, a **prototype** software system can illustrate the form for the user interface and the form for final output. To go back to the construction analogy in Chapter 1, the builder can do a mock-up, a small model house that will show how the real house will look. Changes in the model can easily be made before a lot of time has been invested in actual construction. The same is true of prototype software. The client can see the parts of the program that most interest him before the algorithms that carry out the processing have been developed. Changes are much easier to implement at this stage.

We can see that even after the problem specification is agreed to by both parties, it may still be necessary to make mutually acceptable changes. Much of the problem specification document will become part of the documentation for the program itself, so the documentation phase of the programming process is already underway.

In the beginning, we will be writing rather simple programs, and our problem specifications will not be as formal or extensive as we have described here.

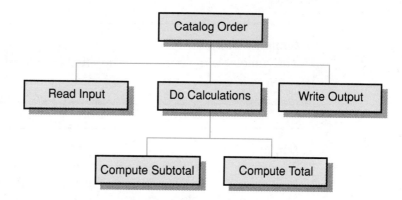

FIGURE   2.5   Structure chart for program *CatalogOrder.*

2.8 Sample Software Development Project—Catalog Order

Problem Statement

Automate the process of catalog shopping. Given the quantity of a certain item ordered and the unit price, compute the subtotal, the sales tax (at 5 percent), and the total price.

Problem Specification

Items are identified by a 3-character catalog "number," such as 4AC or B5M. The catalog number of the item, the quantity, and unit price, comprise the customer order. All of this input data should appear as part of the program output in order to confirm the customer's order. The output should also contain the subtotal, the tax amount, and the total price. The tax rate will be a constant. We will use output formatting that assumes "reasonable" values for the unit price and the totals; if the field width we select is too small, the necessary space to print the value will be used anyway.

Input: 3-character catalog number, quantity, unit price
Output: catalog number, quantity, unit price, subtotal, tax amount, total price

Algorithm Development

This task breaks down into three major subtasks: read the input, do the calculations, write the output. "Do the calculations" breaks down into two smaller tasks: compute the subtotal and compute the total. This gives us the structure chart of Figure 2.5.

> **Read Input**
> We must prompt the user for the catalog number of the item to be ordered; we will store this as three variables of type *char*. We should also ask for the quantity to be ordered (an integer), and the unit price (a real number). Three separate *writeln* and *readln* pairs seems the simplest approach.

Compute Subtotal
The subtotal is the product of the number ordered times the unit price.

Compute Total
To compute the total cost, we first find the amount of tax. This is the product of the tax rate times the subtotal. Then we add the tax amount to the subtotal, giving the total.

Write Output
As part of the output, we repeat the catalog number, quantity, and unit price for the item ordered. Then we write the subtotal, tax amount, and total price. Several *writeln* statements will be needed. We will format the output representing money as decimal numbers with two digits behind the decimal point, so that it looks like dollars and cents. We also will experiment with the output horizontal spacing so that the dollar values line up (our efforts here may go somewhat awry if the values exceed the field-width specification).

The complete program is:

```
program CatalogOrder(input, output);
{Computes total price for order of some quantity of an item}

const
    TaxRate = 0.05;              {sales tax rate}

var
    ID1, ID2, ID3 : char;       {3-character catalog "number"
                                  for item}
    Quantity : integer;         {quantity of item ordered}
    UnitPrice : real;           {unit price of item ordered}
    Subtotal, Total : real;     {subtotal & total (with tax) for
                                  order}
    TaxAmount : real;           {amount of sales tax on subtotal}

begin

    {input section}
    writeln('Please give catalog number of the item you wish');
    writeln('to order.    Catalog number must be 3 characters.');
```

```
      readln(ID1, ID2, ID3);
      writeln('What quantity of this item do you wish to order?');
      readln(Quantity);
      writeln('What is the unit price of this item?');
      readln(UnitPrice);

      {calculations section}
      Subtotal  := Quantity*UnitPrice;
      TaxAmount := TaxRate*Subtotal;
      Total  := Subtotal + TaxAmount;

      {output section}
      writeln;
      write('You ordered ', Quantity:2, ' of catalog item ');
      writeln(ID1, ID2, ID3, ' at $', UnitPrice:5:2, ' each.');
      writeln('This comes to        $', Subtotal:8:2);
      writeln('plus sales tax of     $', TaxAmount:8:2);
      writeln('for a total cost of $', Total:8:2);
end.
```

RUNNING THE PROGRAM...

```
      Please give catalog number of the item you wish
      to order.    Catalog number must be 3 characters.
      n28
      What quantity of this item do you wish to order?
      8
      What is the unit price of this item?
      13.95

      You ordered    8 of catalog item n28 at $13.95 each.
      This comes to        $   111.60
      plus sales tax of    $     5.58
      for a total cost of  $   117.18†
```

CASE STUDY ONE

View #2

As a project manager at Sterling Software Systems, you are responsible for developing the problem specification for the water pollution program (see CASE STUDY ONE in Chapter 1). You formulate the following list of questions to pose to the Lodestone County Water Pollution Department.

■ How are sites identified?

---

†Field-width specifications for numerical output can always be chosen to make sample data look exactly right, but other legitimate data values may not use the same amount of space. We've used "reasonable" field widths throughout.

- How is the date of a reading recorded?
- What is the form of the data from the sample?
- What is the cutoff point at which a site should be flagged?
- What is the form of the "flag" or message if a site has too high a level?
- Should this program operate in interactive or batch mode?

Consultation with the client yields the following information. The program should be interactive because the department wants to use it in the lab to enter data and obtain results whenever a test is completed. Each site is identified by a unique integer number. The department has no standard format for dates, so any reasonable form can be selected. The data from a sample consists of the amount of water in the sample (given in ml—an integer value) and the count of the bacteria found in that sample (also an integer value). A site should be flagged if the bacteria level exceeds 200 per 100 ml of water, and the flag should just be some appropriate message identifying the site and the date of the violation.

You note that in a future interview the client should provide some range of reasonable sample sizes and bacteria counts and a range of reasonable site ID numbers so that some error checking can be done on the input data. You determine that an appropriate form for the date on which the sample was taken is month/date/year, as in 03/28/89 (March 28, 1989). The cutoff ratio will be a constant in the program so that it can be easily modified in the future if that becomes necessary or desirable. You decide that the output should include the input data as well as the computed values as a further check on the correctness of the input data. The program's input and output values have now been determined.

Input: site ID, date, water volume, bacteria count
Output: site ID, date, water volume, bacteria count, bacteria level, violation message if appropriate

You now feel you have enough information to begin the algorithm development.

(Note: The manager of the Lodestone County Water Pollution Department should expect to work with Sterling Software Systems on further details of the problem specification after the initial problem statement. The problem specification really determines what SSS contracts to do for the department. It is the department manager's responsibility to budget time to spend with the software developer over questions that arise, and to present the details of the problem as completely and accurately as possible.)

CASE STUDY TWO	View #2

As project manager at Sterling for the hypertension patient program, formulate a list of questions to pose to the Lodestone County Hospital Hypertension Clinic. (Try to guess the answers, too.)

EXERCISES

#1. With the declarations

var
M, N, P, Q : integer;

and input data of

```
74      51
62     −14
26      18
```

find the value of M, N, P, and Q after execution of the statements

```
readln(M);
readln(Q, N, P);
```

2. With the declarations

var
X, Y : integer;
A : char;

and input data of

```
12   6
8
```

find the value of X, Y, and A after execution of the statements

```
read(Y, A);
readln;
readln(X);
```

3. What does the output look like after executing

```
write('This is the value of X', X:3, 'and of Y');
writeln(Y:5);
writeln('Done.');
```

if X and Y have values of 483 and 32, respectively?

#4. What does the output look like after executing

```
writeln(X:4);
```

#For problems marked by #, answers are given in Appendix K.

```
write(Y:6:2, Z:3);
```

if X, Y, and Z have values of −35, 46.786, and 2, respectively?

#5. What is the output from the following program?

```
program Guess(output);

var
    One, Two : integer;

begin
  One := 2;
  Two := 1;
  One := One + Two;
  Two := One + Two;
  writeln(One, Two);
end.
```

6. Given the input data

3 − 6

what is the output from the following program?

```
program Switch (input, output);

var
    value1, value2 : integer;

begin
  readln(value1, value2);
  value1 := value2;
  value2 := value1;
  writeln(value1, value2);
end.
```

#7. The following statements are from a Pascal program to read in a three-letter abbreviation for a month and write it out again. Arrange the statements in the correct order.

```
read(name1);
begin
name1 : char;
program Month(input, output);
```

```
writeln(name1, name2, name3);
var
writeln('What month is this?');
name2 : char;
read(name2);
name3 : char;
end.
write('The month is now ');
readln(name3);
```

8. Arrange the following statements to form a Pascal program that converts a person's height in feet and inches into height in inches.

```
begin
writeln('How tall are you?');
InchesPerFoot = 12;
writeln('____ in');
program height(input, output);
var
readln(Feet);
writeln('____ ft');
const
write(Inches);
writeln(' inches.');
Feet, Inches : integer;
Inches := (InchesPerFoot*Feet) + Inches;
end.
write('Your height is ');
readln(Inches);
```

#9. What are the errors in the following program (lines are numbered for reference only)?

```
1.    program (input, output);

2.    var
3.        capitol, state = integers;

4.    begin
5.        readln(capitol, state);
6.        print('capital of ', state:7:2, ' is');
7.        writeln(capital);
8.    end.
```

10. What is the error in the following program (lines are numbered for reference only)?

```
1.    program NoNo(input, output);

2.    const
3.        Fix = 4.7;

4.    var
5.        over, under : integer;

6.    begin
7.      writeln('Enter data');
8.      read(Fix);
9.      readln(over);
10.     under := over + 2*Fix;
11.     writeln('Now under is ', under);
12.    end.
```

For each of Exercises 11-14 list four questions that should be addressed in the problem specification.

11. A bank maintains a number of different loan options. When a monetary amount is entered, along with a fixed interest rate and a period of years representing the time period of the loan, the output should be the total monthly payment.

12. Customers at a pharmacy fill out information on known allergies. When a new prescription is issued, the patient's name is entered along with the new prescription drug, and the output should be a warning if the new drug may trigger allergic effects.

#13. Student grades are entered into a program that computes the semester average and letter grade.

14. A parts inventory system should keep a record of the number of each part on hand. Inputs will be either

- A query giving the part name and asking for the number on hand
- The number of units of a particular part sold; outputs here would be the new total on hand

When the number of units of a particular part gets low, the output should be a message to order more of that part.

SKILL BUILDERS   Skill Builders are short programming problems that emphasize a specific idea learned in the chapter.

1. Write a program that prints the message

HELLO

2. Write a program to print the table

Week's Schedule

	MON	TUE	WED	THUR	FRI
AM					
PM					

3. Write a program to print the following design:

```
            *
          *   *
        *       *
      *           *
      *   *   *   *   *
          *   *
```

#4. Write a program that assigns an integer value of your choice to X and an integer value to Y and prints

X = (your value for X)

Y = (your value for Y)

5. Write a program that reads the user's initials (don't forget a prompt) and prints the message

Hello, J. G.

(using the appropriate initials).

SOFTWARE DEVELOPMENT PROJECTS

Software Development Projects present only the problem statement. Write up the problem specification, identifying any assumptions, and develop the algorithm, identifying and describing the subtasks and drawing a structure chart. Then write the program, including appropriate comments, and produce at least one sample program execution. In other words, follow the format of Sample Software Development Project Catalog Order in this chapter.

1. Develop software that asks the user for an integer value between 10 and 20 and prints

Your value was --.

Twice this value is --.

(Note the single space between the text and the number.)

2. Develop software that asks the user for two integer values and computes their sum and product.

3. Develop software to read the width and length of a rectangular lot in feet, along with the price per square foot; the program computes the total price of the lot.

4. Develop software that reads in the user's lifetime average pulse rate (in beats per minute) and age (in years); the program finds the total number of heartbeats in the person's life up to the most recent birthday.

5. Develop software that computes the circumference and area of a circle after reading in the radius.

6. A worker gets a certain base rate of pay, and then is paid time-and-a-half for overtime over forty hours per week. Develop software that reads in the total hours worked for the week and the base pay rate, and then computes the total wages for the week. Assume the worker works at least forty hours.

TESTING AND MAINTENANCE DEPARTMENT

1. Run program *CatalogOrder* with several different input values. In particular, see what happens if:

- the catalog number consists of all numerical digits
- the unit price, subtotal, and total are such as to exceed their field-width specifications
- the number of items ordered is 0

2. Modify program *CatalogOrder* to change the tax rate to 7 percent.

3. Modify program *CatalogOrder* to require the user to enter a $ along with the unit price.

4. Modify program *CatalogOrder* to add 6 percent of the subtotal for postage and handling, and to include this amount in the output information.

5. Modify program *CatalogOrder* to read in data for a second item ordered, and to output the subtotal, tax, and total for the two items combined.

DEBUGGING CLINIC

Run and debug the following program:

```
program TripLength(input, output);
{program to compute the roundtrip distance from your home to
 the  grocery store}
```

```
var
    two : integer;          {multiplication factor}
    distance : real;        {distance to store - input
    roundtrip : real;       {roundtrip distance}

begin
    writeln('How far is it from your home to the grocery store');
    writeln('(to the nearest tenth of a mile)?');
    readln(distance)
    two := 2.0;
    roundtrip := two*distance;
    writeln('The roundtrip distance is ', roundtrip:5:1, ' miles.');
end.
```

CHAPTER THREE

ALGORITHM DEVELOPMENT; PROCEDURES; SIMPLE CONTROL STRUCTURES

3.1 Algorithm Development

1. Problem specification
2. Algorithm development
3. Coding
4. Debugging
5. Testing
6. Documenting
7. Maintenance

Algorithm development is step 2 of the programming process. The goal of this phase is to devise the actual method for solving the problem, the "blueprint" from which the program will be constructed. Algorithm development is a key step; programs with errors can be written from correct algorithms, but correct programs cannot be written from incorrect algorithms!

Even after the problem has been completely specified, thinking up the solution method is one of the hardest parts of the programming process. There is no "formula" for doing this because every problem is different. However, some general clues will provide a starting point for algorithm development.

3.1.1 *Stay Calm*

The first clue is just a bit of advice. Many students faced with a programming problem read the problem once and panic when an idea does not immediately present itself. Remember that the problem is very likely to be solvable, particularly if it is a class assignment. Mull over the problem statement for a day or two, think about it in your odd moments, and try some of the other clues suggested below. Don't give up!

3.1.2 *Break Down the Problem*

The original problem may be complex enough to overwhelm us if we try to figure out all at once how to do the entire job. Instead, we break down the problem into major tasks, break each task into subtasks, etc. This makes the "size" of the problem manageable. During this process, we do not try to figure out how to do the subtasks, we only look at the overall structure of the

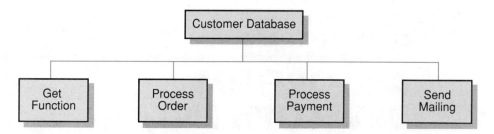

FIGURE 3.1 First pass at structure chart for customer database.

solution as built from a number of smaller parts. When the parts get sufficiently small, then we can see how to do them.

The Catalog Order problem in Chapter 2 was initially broken down into three parts: read the input, do the calculations, write the output. This is a little simplistic, but it is often a good idea to view input gathering and writing output as separate tasks. This still leaves the great middle ground of "do the calculations."

Suppose we want to write a program to manage the customer database for a company that sells whackbonks to the general public. Even without a problem specification, we can identify likely subtasks that the program should handle. Let's assume a datafile of records for existing customers already exists, and that the clerical staff will use the program interactively to manage this file. The input subtask here could give the user a menu of choices from which to select the function to be carried out. Probable functions would be to process an order, process a payment, and send out a mailing. Our first pass at a structure chart looks like Figure 3.1. Not every subtask will be performed every time the program is executed. Get Function will be carried out and, depending on the results from Get Function, one of the other subtasks will then be selected.

Get Function may be further broken down into the two subtasks of displaying the menu of choices for the user and collecting the choice made by the user. Processing an order has three possible subtasks. First, if the customer is new, data needs to be added to the customer database. Second, order information has to be sent to the shipping department. Third, the customer has to be billed. Now that we've thought of adding a new customer, there are probably occasions when a customer's record should be deleted from the database. We'll add this subtask as one of the function choices at a higher level of the structure chart. Figure 3.2 shows the second pass at the structure chart.

We could continue this process, refining the subtasks in even more detail. Add New Customer, for example, might be broken down further into subtasks of entering the customer name, address, and other information.

Get in the habit of breaking the problem to be solved into smaller components.

Any given problem may be "decomposable" into subtasks in more than one way. No matter how the decomposition is done, it is easier to see how to solve many small problems than it is to see how to solve the entire problem at once. Furthermore, we know how the subtasks should be reassembled to accomplish the original overall task. We earlier called this process top-down design, but it is also known as a ***divide-and-conquer*** strategy—divide the problem into small, individually manageable parts, and then "conquer" them one by one.

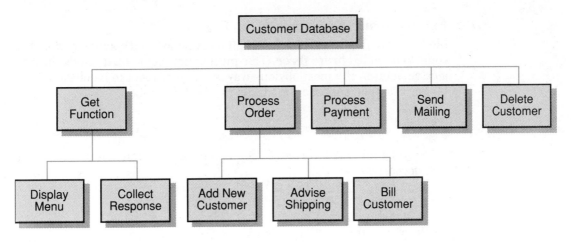

FIGURE **3.2** Refinement of the structure chart for customer database.

3.1.3 *Emulate a Solution by Hand*

Begin by thinking of how to solve the problem by hand.

The divide-and-conquer strategy still tells us nothing about how to actually solve a problem, it merely helps us reduce the scale of the problem to be solved. Suppose that the time has come to actually figure out how to do a subtask. Thinking about how we would solve the same task if we were going to do it by hand, without benefit of a computer, is often helpful. We may be able to translate our by-hand solution method rather directly into code.

For example, suppose we want to find the smallest value in a long list of numbers. Imagine how we might do this by hand if someone gave us a pack of index cards with a number on each one. We would write down the first number (or try to remember it), put the first card aside and look at the second card. If the number there is smaller than the one currently on our sheet of paper, we cross out the number on the sheet of paper and write down the new, smaller number. If the number on the second card is not smaller, we don't change the number written down. Setting the second card aside, we deal with the third card the same way, and proceed in this fashion until we are out of cards. At that point, the number on the sheet of paper is the smallest value we saw in the entire pack of cards, so it is the minimum.

We could write a program using this same algorithm. A pseudocode version follows; we will be able to translate this pseudocode into a Pascal program when we learn more Pascal.

```
read the first number
set Min equal to first number
while there are more numbers in the list
   begin
      read the next number
      if this number is smaller than Min,
         set Min equal to this number
   end
write Min
```

3.1.4 *Employ Brute Force as a First Try*

Methods that duplicate what we might do by hand often operate by what has come to be called **brute force.** This means that the method grinds through a calculation in the most obvious way, with no attempt to be elegant.

For example, suppose the task is to add the numbers

$$2 + 4 + 6 + 8 + ... + 100$$

A straightforward (brute force) approach is given by the following pseudocode:

```
set Sum equal to 0
set x equal to 2
while x ≤ 100
   begin
      add x to Sum
      add 2 to x
   end
write Sum
```

To see that this works, notice that x has the value 2 when we first test whether $x \leq 100$. Because 2 is ≤ 100, we add 2 to *Sum*, which now has the value $0 + 2 = 2$, and add 2 to x, which now has the value $2 + 2 = 4$. The value of x is still ≤ 100, so we add 4 to *Sum*, which now has the value $2 + 4$, and we add 2 to x, which becomes $4 + 2 = 6$. The successive values of *Sum* are

```
0
2
2 + 4
2 + 4 + 6
.
.
.
```

When x finally has the value 100, we add it to *Sum*, change x to $100 + 2 = 102$, and, because x is no longer ≤ 100, proceed to the "write *Sum*" statement. The value of *Sum* at that point is

$$2 + 4 + 6 + ... + 100 = 2550$$

This approach produces the correct answer and proceeds in a very direct way. There is, however, a more elegant approach. The task at hand is to compute the sum of an arithmetic series, where each term differs from the preceding one by a constant amount (2 in this case). The formula for the sum of an arithmetic series says that the sum is the average of the first term and the last term, multiplied by the number of terms in the series. In this case there are 50 terms in the series (half of the 100 integers from 1 to 100). The average of the first and last term is

$$\frac{2 + 100}{2}$$

Therefore we could compute *Sum* in one step, namely,

```
Sum := 50*(1/2)*(2 + 100);
```

Which is the better approach? Certainly the second approach is more elegant. In addition, the second approach is more efficient. It requires only one computation—and would require only one computation even if we changed the 100 in the problem to 1000. The brute force method requires doing a sequence of steps repetitively, and the number of repetitions increases if we change 100 to 1000.

But there are drawbacks to the elegant approach. For one thing, we have to know the formula. Also, even if *we* understand this single line of code, it might not be clear to someone else reading the program. We may have traded clarity for elegance and efficiency, which is not always a good idea. The brute force approach has some advantages, not the least of which is it may be the solution method that first comes to mind when no other ideas present themselves.

3.1.5 *Look for Well-Known Algorithms*

Some tasks, such as putting a list of items into numerical or alphabetical order (**sorting**), or looking for a particular item in a list of items (**searching**), are done so frequently on large data sets that finding efficient algorithms for these tasks has been a high priority. We'll look at some algorithms for sorting and searching later in this book. The point here is that classic algorithms have been developed to carry out certain classic tasks. If we have to do one of these tasks, we should look for an existing algorithm rather than attempting to find one of our own. (We must be sure, of course, that we understand the algorithm and know that it really does what we want.)

3.1.6 *Exploit Similarity*

When faced with a problem to solve, a quick mental review of other problems whose solutions we have seen can be helpful. Suppose that our problem is somewhat similar to another problem for which we already have an algorithm. Can the previous algorithm be modified to solve the new problem? Is there some piece of the previous algorithm, or some approach that it uses, that we can adapt to this new situation? (Studying more problem solutions, and more algorithm techniques, increases your store of programming experience so that similarities become easier to find. It is also a good idea to keep your already-written programs organized for future reference.)

Think about similar problems already solved.

For example, suppose that we want to keep adding together the integers in a list as long as those integers are less than or equal to some fixed value denoted by the identifier *Top*. This is similar to our earlier problem of computing

$$2 + 4 + 6 + 8 + \ldots + 100$$

In that problem, we added as long as the integers were less than or equal to 100; however, the items to be added followed a pattern and could be computed. In our new problem the integers will have to be read in as data items. If we "similar out" the brute force approach to the earlier problem, we get the following pseudocode:

```
set Sum equal to 0
read a value for x
while x ≤ Top
  begin
    add x to Sum
    read a value for x
  end
write Sum
```

3.1.7 Check the Problem Specification

One of the features of the problem specification may be special requirements imposed on the solution method. For example, it may be specified that a system of linear equations must be solved by Gaussian elimination. A requirement like this determines the formula, equation, or steps to be used in the solution process.

3.1.8 Take Advantage of the Data Structures

The basic idea of **data structures** (covered later in this book) is that data items are not treated as individual items but are organized and connected by means of logical relationships. One organization of data may lend itself to a particular solution approach, whereas another organization of that same data may suggest a different approach.

As a simple example, names, addresses, and phone numbers in a telephone directory are never treated as individual items but are always structured in a name-address-number relationship. Furthermore, the name-address-number units are arranged alphabetically. This organization of data greatly influences our "algorithm" for looking up an individual's telephone number.

The programmer determines the data structure. Therefore, the choice of how to structure the data should be made somewhat concurrently with algorithm development because the data structure will affect the algorithm, and conversely, what is to be done with the data should affect the choice of data structure. Since we're now getting way ahead of ourselves, save this last clue on algorithm development for future reference.

3.2 Top-Down Design

We have emphasized top-down design as an important strategy in algorithm development. Breaking down a problem into tasks and subtasks allows us to control its complexity because we do not have to think about all of the details of the entire problem at once. How the problem is broken down into separate subtasks or **modules** may vary from one person to another. That's why the structure chart is an important piece of documentation: it shows how the programmer thought about the problem, what he or she identified as the program modules, and how those modules are related.

Often a beginning programmer can't understand why there is so much fuss about top-down design, modularity, etc. Indeed, if the task to be done is a simple one, it is not hard to "see" the entire program at once. Only when the size of the problem grows beyond what we can keep in mind at any one time does the value of this approach become evident. The point at which this occurs varies with the intellectual capacity of the individual, but it happens to everyone sooner or later! Programs that involve half a million lines of code, for example, simply cannot be dealt with as a unit. We are trying to learn approaches that will serve us well when we cross the threshold of our own particular mental limitations. Bear with us, then, as we point out the advantages of the top-down, modular approach.

3.2.1 *Easier to Design*

Breaking down a problem gives us a handle on the design process, a way to proceed that does not let the size or complexity of the problem overwhelm us and that postpones the worries about how to actually do the specific tasks. We've emphasized this as the chief value of the top-down approach, but there are other benefits as well.

3.2.2 *Easier to Understand*

When a program is designed in a top-down, modular fashion, these modules and their relationships become a skeleton of the program design, clearly indicating the overall approach to anyone who wants to understand the program. This information will still be valuable after the program itself has been written.

3.2.3 *Easier to Implement*

One question that arises in the top-down approach is how far should one break down the problem? A reasonable answer is that one should break down the problem until the subtasks are easy to implement, but what is "easy" for one person may be difficult for another. A general rule-of-thumb might be that no module in the program should end up much larger than one written page of code, or two screens on a video display.

3.2.4 *Easier to Debug and Test*

The debugging and testing phases of the programming process can also be done in a modular fashion if we have designed and written the program this way. Each individual module can be tested separately by providing a minimal framework in which it can be compiled and executed. (We'll say more about how to do this in Chapter 4.) This process allows many errors to be detected in a "local" environment, where the cause of the problem can be more easily pinpointed. If the program has not been designed and implemented in a modular fashion, then the entire program is suspect when an error occurs. Worse yet, an error that becomes apparent in one section of the program may actually have its source in another section because the erroneous data have propagated and interacted with various parts of the program code. Using separate modules and carefully controlling the data that can pass from one module to another has been called **building firewalls** within the program. This terminology emphasizes the idea of trying to control the spread of erroneous data throughout the rest of the program.

3.2.5 *Easier to Modify*

After a program has been designed, written, debugged, and tested, subsequent modifications become easier if the program has been organized in a modular fashion. Changes that need to be made tend to be more localized because all the code pertaining to a particular subtask has been kept together as a module. A new module can replace an old module without changing the rest of the program.

3.2.6 *Multiple Uses*

A module of code designed to do a particular subtask may be used at several different points in a program. Each time the particular subtask needs to be performed, the appropriate program module can be invoked; the code for the subtask is written once and called upon as needed. In addition, the module may represent a generic task that would be useful in many applications. The code for the module, once developed and tested, can be copied and included as part of other programs.

Figure 3.3 summarizes these advantages to the top-down design process.

3.3 Information Hiding

Carefully controlling the data that can pass between modules is part of a larger concept called **information hiding.** To understand this idea, let's suppose that the program designer and the person who implements a program module (the "builder" and the "subcontractor" of our opening analogy) are two different people. (A programmer might play both of these roles, but at different times.) While the concept of "hiding" information seems like the exact opposite of what is desired in communication between two people, there are advantages to both the designer and the programmer.

The designer identifies *what* is to be done but does not care *how* it is done. Such an arrangement frees the designer from lower-level details and greatly simplifies the design task. The designer must tell the programmer in what form the rest of the program will supply data to the subtask, and what the rest of the program expects to see as output from the subtask. This defines the "interface" between the module and the rest of the program.

The programmer is free to use any implementation he or she wishes, providing the specifications of the interface are met. In addition, the details of the implementation can be modified at any time, as long as the interface agreements are upheld. Such changes are said to be **transparent** to the rest

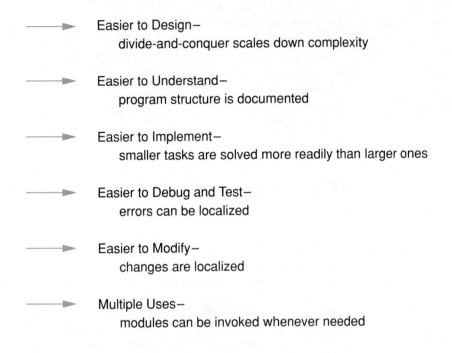

Easier to Design—
divide-and-conquer scales down complexity

Easier to Understand—
program structure is documented

Easier to Implement—
smaller tasks are solved more readily than larger ones

Easier to Debug and Test—
errors can be localized

Easier to Modify—
changes are localized

Multiple Uses—
modules can be invoked whenever needed

FIGURE 3.3 Advantages to the top-down design approach.

of the program (or to the program user) because from all outward appearances (i.e., the interface), nothing has been changed.

Clearly, the interface between the program module and the rest of the program must be carefully specified. The functional requirements of each module should indicate not only what the module does, but also what data it will receive from, and what data it will return to, the rest of the program. We'll spend the rest of this chapter and the next discussing how to create and use program modules, and how to control the flow of data through the interfaces between these modules and the rest of the program.

3.4 Procedures

Two types of modules are available in Pascal programs, **procedures** and **functions.** Functions will be considered in Chapter 6.

A procedure is a module of code to carry out a specific subtask identified in the program design. In order to use a procedure in a program we must know (a) how to write the code for the procedure itself, (b) how to invoke the procedure from another part of the program when the subtask is to be done, and (c) how to exchange the data back and forth across the module interface.

3.4.1 *The Procedure Itself*

The overall format for a procedure is

procedure heading
declarations
  begin
    statements
  end;

This is very similar to the overall format for an entire Pascal program, but there are three differences:

1. Instead of the reserved word **program** in the heading, the reserved word **procedure** is used.

A procedure heading needs a formal parameter list if it is to exchange any data with the rest of the program.

2. Instead of a list of file names appearing in the heading behind the program name, a list of variable names, called ***formal parameters,*** appears in the heading behind the procedure name. These control the flow of data into and out of the procedure. The data types of the formal parameters must be indicated as part of this list even though, as will be seen later, formal parameters are not program variables in the usual sense.

3. Instead of a period after the final **end,** there is a semicolon.

As a simple case, suppose there is some fixed message to be output every so often. A procedure could be used to write the message. The procedure would need no data from the rest of the program, nor would the rest of the program need any results from the procedure. Because no data values are to be passed into or out of the procedure, item 2 above does not apply. Procedure *Chorus* below does such a task (any legitimate Pascal identifier can be used for a procedure name).

procedure Chorus;
{writes a Happy Birthday message}

  begin
    writeln('Happy Birthday to You!');
  end;

Outside of the three changes mentioned above, procedures look just like programs. In particular, procedures can declare their own constants and variables (called ***local*** constants and variables). Thus another version of procedure *Chorus* could be written using local string constants to hold the message.

procedure Chorus;
{writes a Happy Birthday message}

const
    message1 = 'Happy Birthday ';
    message2 = 'to You!';

```
    begin
        write(message1);
        writeln(message2);
    end;
```

The code for a procedure must be inserted within the code for the rest of the program. It goes into the declarations section of the main program, after any constant or variable declarations.

3.4.2 *Invoking a Procedure*

Whenever the particular subtask represented by a procedure is to be done, we insert the procedure name at the appropriate point or points in the program code. The procedure name is followed by a list of variables, called **actual parameters,** used to pass data between the rest of the program and the procedure. In program *Birthday* below, no data is being passed, so procedure *Chorus* is invoked by simply giving its name.

```
program Birthday(input, output);
{traditional birthday song}

{if the program needed any constant or variable declarations,
 they would go here}

procedure Chorus;
{writes a Happy Birthday message}

const
    message1 = 'Happy Birthday ';
    message2 = 'to You!';

    begin    {procedure Chorus}
        write(message1);
        writeln(message2);
    end;      {procedure Chorus}

begin {main program}
    writeln('Here''s a message from all your friends:');
    writeln;
    Chorus;
    Chorus;
    writeln('Happy Birthday, Happy Birthday');
    Chorus;
end.   {main program}
```

Comments at the **begin** and **end** marking the body of the procedure, as well as at the **begin** and **end** of the main program, help distinguish code for the procedure from code for the main program. As programs grow more complex, there will be many **begin-end** pairs. It is a good idea to denote by a comment what is beginning and ending in each case.

Even though code for a procedure appears first in the program listing, program execution always begins with the first statement in the body of the main program. At the point in the program where execution reaches the procedure name, control is transferred to the procedure. After the procedure module has been executed (when the procedure **end** statement is reached), control returns to the next line of code after the procedure invocation.

CHECKUP 3.1   What is the output when program *Birthday* above is executed?

Procedures are declared in the declarations section of a program, but execution begins in the main program.

In the birthday example, the procedure is invoked from the main program. However, it is possible to invoke a procedure from within a procedure. One can think of the *invoking* program segment (which could be the main program or a procedure) being temporarily suspended while the *invoked* procedure module is executed.

If procedure B is invoked by procedure A, which is itself invoked by the main program, then the sequence of activities described below is possible. In each part of Figure 3.4, execution is currently taking place in the top module; lower level modules are temporarily suspended.

■ The main program is executing (Fig. 3.4a).
■ At some point the main program invokes procedure A; control transfers to execution of A (Fig. 3.4b).
■ At some point, procedure A invokes procedure B; control transfers to execution of B (Fig. 3.4c).
■ At the end of executing procedure B, control returns to procedure A (Fig. 3.4d).
■ At the end of executing procedure A, control returns to the main program (Fig. 3.4e).

The boxes shown in Figure 3.4 are arranged in a stack, a word that actually has a technical meaning. A **stack** is an arrangement of items that always grows or shrinks from the top, that is, a new item can only be added to the top of the stack, and only the item currently on top of the stack can be removed. The changes in the stack in Figure 3.4 represent the order of execution of the program modules. However, the boxes in the stack also represent the memory requirements for each new invocation. Box A, for example, represents stor-

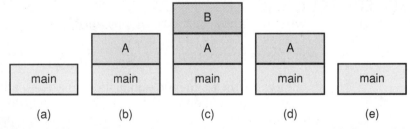

(a)   (b)   (c)   (d)   (e)

FIGURE   3.4 Activation records for procedure invocations—the top module is currently being executed.

age locations for data used by procedure *A*, such as *A*'s local variables. This storage (box *A*) is called an ***activation record*** for the invocation of *A*.

The following version of program *Birthday* has exactly the same output as the first version, but it uses two procedures. The main program invokes *Chorus1*, which in turn invokes *Chorus2*. *Chorus2* is declared before *Chorus1* so that when the identifier *Chorus2* appears in a program statement inside *Chorus1*, the compiler will recognize it as a procedure name.

```
program Birthday2(input, output);
{traditional birthday song}

{if the program needed any constant or variable declarations,
 they would go here}

procedure Chorus2;
{Writes second part of Happy Birthday message}

    begin    {procedure Chorus2}
      writeln('to You!');
    end;      {procedure Chorus2}

procedure Chorus1;
{writes first part of Happy Birthday message}

    begin    {procedure Chorus1}
      write('Happy Birthday ');
      Chorus2;
    end;      {procedure Chorus1}

begin {main program}
  writeln('Here' 's a message from all your friends:');
  writeln;
  Chorus1;
  Chorus1;
  writeln('Happy Birthday, Happy Birthday');
  Chorus1;
end.    {main program}
```

CHECKUP 3.2   Draw a figure similar to Figure 3.4 to describe the execution of program *Birthday*2 above.

3.5 Parameters

When a procedure and the rest of the program must exchange information, formal parameters in the procedure heading and actual parameters in the statement that invokes the procedure control this flow of information. To get a better idea of how this works, let's consider parameters in a different setting.

3.5.1 *An Analogy*

Imagine that you are the invoking program in the guise of a customer at the drive-through window of a fast-food restaurant. To pass certain "data values" to the clerk working inside, you invoke a procedure *FastFood* by executing the statement

FastFood(food1, food2, amount);

When this statement is executed, the variables *food1* and *food2* could have the values hamburger-order and fries-order, respectively, while the variable *amount* could have the value $5.00. These variables are actual parameters; their values are the specific ones involved in this particular transaction with the restaurant.

You expect the clerk to take these values and carry out a task with them, namely, convert each item ordered into the genuine article, compute the change, then return the genuine articles and change to you. After execution of procedure *FastFood, food1,* and *food2* should have the values hamburger and fries, respectively (i.e., the real things), and *amount* could have the value $2.39 (depending on local prices). The procedure's task changed the values of the actual parameters. Figure 3.5 illustrates your view of this interaction with procedure *FastFood.* What goes on behind the window can't be seen.

Now imagine you are the procedure in the guise of the fast-food drive-through-window employee. The company training manual for filling an order might consist of the following pseudocode procedure:

procedure FastFood(**var** item1, item2: MenuItem;
                                    var money: Cash);
{services drive-through customer's order for two items}

    begin
        assign to *item1* the genuine article named in *item1;*
        assign to *item2* the genuine article named in *item2;*
        assign to *money* the correct change;
    end;

As this procedure is written in the training manual, *item1, item2,* and *money* have no values associated with them. They are formal parameters—"dummy variables" with no values. They take on values when the procedure is invoked by an executing program (i.e., by a customer at the drive-through window). The data type declarations "MenuItem" and "Cash" (not standard Pascal data types!) in the procedure heading imply that the actions described make sense for the kinds of values the formal parameters will have. Figure 3.6 illustrates your view of the task, which may be repeated many times for different customers. Each time, the formal

FIGURE 3.5A

FIGURE 3.5B Customer view of procedure *FastFood*.

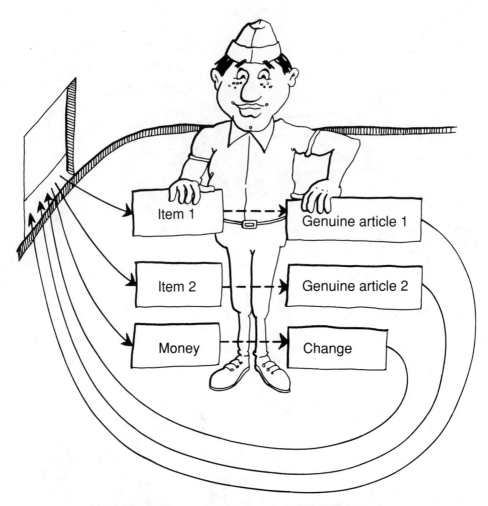

FIGURE 3.6 Employee view of procedure *FastFood*.

Correspondence between actual and formal parameters is done entirely by position in the respective parameters lists, not by name.

The actual and formal parameter lists must match in number, order, and type.

parameters will take on the values passed to them by the particular customer.

A correspondence exists between the actual parameters when the procedure is invoked and the formal parameters in the procedure heading. The value of the first actual parameter is taken on by the first formal parameter, the value of the second actual parameter is taken on by the second formal parameter, and so forth. The respective identifiers used for actual and formal parameters do not matter, only their relative positions in the actual parameter list and the formal parameter list. Figure 3.7 shows this correspondence for the *FastFood* example. Because of this correspondence, *the actual parameter list and the formal parameter list must match in number, order, and type.*

Before leaving the drive-through-window analogy, note that the window serves as the interface between the invoking program (customer) and the procedure (employee). Consistent with the concept of information hiding, communication through the interface is controlled and limited to necessary information.

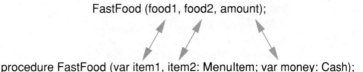

FIGURE **3.7** Correspondence between actual parameters in procedure invocation and formal parameters in procedure heading.

3.5.2 *Variable and Value Parameters*

A procedure may need to know data values from the invoking program segment in order to carry out its task, and the invoking program segment may need data values back from the procedure after the procedure has carried out its task. The same item of data can fall into both categories: a value for the item is passed to the procedure by the invoking program segment, but the procedure changes this value. When execution transfers back to the invoking program segment, it needs to know the new value for this data item.

Whenever the procedure needs to return a data value to the invoking program segment, a ***variable formal parameter*** is used. Variable formal parameters are preceded by the reserved word **var** in the formal parameter list of the procedure heading. To illustrate, let's personalize the birthday song program by finding out the user's current age. We'll use a procedure *AskAge* to obtain this information and return it to the main program by means of a variable parameter. When control returns to the main program after execution of *AskAge*, *AgeNow* has the value passed to it by the variable parameter *CurrentAge*.

```pascal
program Birthday3(input, output);
{traditional birthday song, personalized with user's age}

var
    AgeNow : integer;          {user's age now}

procedure Chorus;
{writes a Happy Birthday message}

const
    message1 = 'Happy Birthday ';
    message2 = 'to You!';

  begin   {procedure Chorus}
    write(message1);
    writeln(message2);
  end;     {procedure Chorus}

procedure AskAge(var CurrentAge: integer);
{gets the user's current age and returns it to the main program}

  begin    {procedure AskAge}
    writeln('Today is your birthday - how old are you?');
    readln(CurrentAge);
  end;     {procedure AskAge}
```

```
begin {main program}
  AskAge(AgeNow);

  writeln('Here' 's a message from all your friends:');
  writeln;
  Chorus;
  Chorus;
  writeln('Happy Birthday, Happy Birthday');
  Chorus;

  writeln;
  writeln(AgeNow:3, ' years old - congratulations!');
end.  {main program}
```

RUNNING THE PROGRAM...

```
Today is your birthday - how old are you?
24
Here's a message from all your friends:

Happy Birthday to You!
Happy Birthday to You!
Happy Birthday, Happy Birthday
Happy Birthday to You!

  24 years old - congratulations!
```

If a procedure needs a data value from the invoking program segment but does not need to return a new value, a **value formal parameter** can be used. A value parameter is denoted by the absence of the word **var** preceding it in the formal parameter list. In the following birthday program, *CurrentAge* is a value parameter of procedure *CenturyAge*; it is used by the procedure but its value is not changed, and a new value is not returned to the main program. (Note that just as in program *Birthday3*, procedure *AskAge* has a variable parameter with the identifier *CurrentAge*. The two formal parameters named *CurrentAge* will not be confused, even though they have the same identifier, because they are in separate procedures.) *FutureAge* is a variable parameter in procedure *CenturyAge*; its value is computed within the procedure and returned for use by the main program. *Year* is a local variable within procedure *CenturyAge*.

```
program Birthday4(input, output);
{traditional birthday song, personalized with user's age and a
 projected age in the year 2000}

var
    AgeNow : integer       {user's age now}
    FutureAge : integer    {age in year 2000}

procedure Chorus;
{writes a Happy Birthday message}
```

```
const
    message1  =  'Happy  Birthday ';
    message2  =  'to You!';

  begin     {procedure Chorus}
    write(message1);
    writeln(message2);
  end;     {procedure Chorus}

procedure AskAge(var CurrentAge: integer);
{gets the user's current age and returns it to the main program}

  begin {procedure AskAge}
    writeln('Today is your birthday - how old are you?');
    readln(CurrentAge);
  end;   {procedure AskAge}


procedure CenturyAge(CurrentAge: integer;
                         var FutureAge : integer);
{determines age in year 2000}

var
    Year : integer;                {present year}

  begin     {procedure CenturyAge}
    write('What year is this? ');
    readln(Year);
    FutureAge := (2000 − Year) + CurrentAge;
  end;      {procedure CenturyAge}

begin {main program}
  AskAge(AgeNow);

  writeln('Here' 's a message from all your friends:');
  writeln;
  Chorus;
  Chorus;
  writeln('Happy Birthday, Happy Birthday');
  Chorus;

  writeln;
  writeln(AgeNow:3, ' years old - congratulations!');

  writeln;
  CenturyAge(AgeNow, FutureAge);
  write('In the year 2000, you will be ', FutureAge:3);
  writeln(' years old.');
end.   {main program}
```

RUNNING THE PROGRAM...

Today is your birthday - how old are you?
24
Here's a message from all your friends:

Happy Birthday to You!
Happy Birthday to You!
Happy Birthday, Happy Birthday
Happy Birthday to You!

24 years old - congratulations!

What year is this? 1989
In the year 2000, you will be   35 years old.

The formal parameter list for a procedure must specify the data types of all parameters and identify those that are variable parameters with the reserved word var.

As the previous program shows, the formal parameter list of a procedure can contain both variable and value parameters. Variable parameters of the same data type can be grouped together, but each group must be preceded by the word **var** and separated by semicolons. Value parameters can also be grouped by data type. In procedure *XRay* below, *Number* and *Day* are variable parameters of type *integer*, *Initial* is a value parameter of type *char*, and *Level* is a variable parameter of type *real*. In procedure *Never* below, *A* and *B* are value parameters of type *integer*, *When* is a variable parameter of type *real*, and *Next* is a value parameter of type *real*.

Variable formal parameters in a procedure heading carry data out of or both into and out of a procedure; value parameters only carry data into a procedure.

```
procedure XRay(var Number, Day: integer; Initial:  char;
               var Level: real);
```

```
procedure Never(A, B: integer; var When: real; Next: real);
```

Again, a variable parameter is required whenever a procedure must return a new data value to the invoking program segment. A value parameter can be used if a data item is only coming into the procedure and a new value need not be passed back to the invoking program segment. The technical differences between variable and value parameters that justify this distinction will be discussed in the next chapter.

CHECKUP 3.3   For the procedure heading

```
procedure MixUp(var A, B: integer; C: real; var D: real;
                var E: integer; F, G: integer);
```

which are value parameters?

CHECKUP 3.4   The heading for procedure *Funny* is

procedure Funny(X, Y: integer);

and the procedure is invoked by the program statement

Funny(A, B);

where the current value of *A* is 7 and the current value of *B* is 19. What values are associated with the formal parameters *X* and *Y*, respectively, when this statement is executed?
If procedure *Funny* is invoked by the program statement

Funny(Y, X);

and the current value of *Y* is 12 and the current value of *X* is -3, what values are associated with the formal parameters *X* and *Y*, respectively, when this statement is executed?

After this discussion about parameters, it's well to remind ourselves that decomposing the problem into logical subtasks (program modules) should come first. Only then is it appropriate to assess what the information flow across the module interfaces should be.

3.6 Simple Control Structures (Optional)

Pascal provides program statements (called ***control structures***) that allow a choice of actions depending on some condition, and that allow repetition of an action. We will investigate these possibilities in detail in Chapters 7 and 8, but we'll introduce two simple control structures here.
     What happens when the following program statement is executed?

```
if Number < 3 then
   writeln('Less than 3')
else
   writeln('Not less than 3');
```

One of two messages is written, depending upon the current value of *Number*. We can compare two quantities of the same data type by using relations such as

= (equal)
<> (not equal)
< (less than)
<= (less than or equal to)
> (greater than)
>= (greater than or equal to)

Then we can use a statement of the form

if comparison **then**
   statement1
else
   statement2;

If the result of the comparison is true, statement1 is executed and statement2 is ignored. If the result of the comparison is false, statement1 is ignored and statement2 is executed. This **if** statement is itself a single statement, and it is illegal to put a semicolon before the **else.**
   A variation is to omit **else** and statement2, leaving

if comparison **then**
   statement1

In this case, if the result of the comparison is true, statement1 is executed, but if it is false, nothing happens and the program proceeds to the next statement.

CHECKUP 3.5   If the current value of X is 7 and the current value of Y is 12, what is the value of A after the following statement is executed?

```
if Y <= X then
   A := X − 1
else
   A := X + 1;
```

One way to repeat an action in a program is to put that action within a counting loop, called a **for** loop. In the following statement, a variable *Count* takes on the values 1, 2, and 3. For each value of *Count*, the statements (in this case, only one statement) within **begin..end** are executed.

```
for Count := 1 to 3 do
   begin
      writeln('This is line number ',Count:1);
   end;
```

The output from execution of this counting loop would be:

```
This is line number 1
This is line number 2
This is line number 3
```

The following program illustrates both the **if** statement and the **for** loop. The program counts the number of students in each of 10 school districts and finds the total number of students who go to school in districts with fewer than 500 students. The main program consists of a **for** loop to process each of the 10 districts. Within the body of the loop, a procedure is invoked to read the input data, and an **if** statement is used to direct different courses of action for small and large districts.

```
program School(input, output);
{computes total number of students in small (fewer than 500
 students)  school districts out of 10 districts reporting}

var
     Number : integer;        {counting variable for the 10 school
                               districts}
     Students : integer;      {number of students in a district}
     Total : integer;         {total number of students in districts
                               with < 500 students}

procedure GetData(Number: integer; var Kids: integer);
{collects number of students, Kids, in school district Number}

  begin    {procedure GetData}
     write('Enter the number of students in School ');
     writeln('District ', Number:1);
     readln(Kids);
  end;      {procedure GetData}

begin    {main program}
   Total := 0;
   for Number := 1 to 10 do
     begin
       GetData(Number, Students);
       if Students < 500 then
         Total := Total + Students;
     end;
   writeln;
   writeln('The total number of students in school districts');
   writeln('with under 500 students is ', Total:4);
end.    {main program}
```

RUNNING THE PROGRAM...

```
Enter the number of students in School District 1
450
Enter the number of students in School District 2
900
Enter the number of students in School District 3
1300
Enter the number of students in School District 4
1560
Enter the number of students in School District 5
820
Enter the number of students in School District 6
900
```

Enter the number of students in School District 7
520
Enter the number of students in School District 8
380
Enter the number of students in School District 9
430
Enter the number of students in School District 10
1100

The total number of students in school districts
with under 500 students is 1260

CHECKUP 3.6   Recall our discussion earlier in this chapter on exploiting similarity. Change program *School* to a program that reads 10 quiz grades for a course and writes out the number of such grades that are below 70.

3.7 Sample Software Development Project—Carpet Sales

Problem Statement

Compute the cost to carpet a room, given the size of the room, the cost of the carpet, and the installation charge.

Problem Specification

We'll assume that the room is rectangular in shape. Carpet costs are given in dollars per square yard, so we must find the area of the room in square yards. Room dimensions are usually given in feet, however, so we will read in the room length and width in feet, change these dimensions to yards, and then compute the area. Installation charge is a function of the area only, independent of the carpet price; it will be given in dollars per square yard also but is a program constant. Sales tax is not included in the cost. Output should be the total cost (carpet plus installation).

Input: room length, room width (in feet)
      carpet cost (in dollars/sq. yd.)
Output: total cost (carpet + installation)

Algorithm Development

There is a logical flow of subtasks to solve this problem, illustrated in the structure chart of Figure 3.8:

- Find the area
- Compute the carpet cost
- Compute the installation cost
- Find the total cost
- Write output

Although we could combine some of these subtasks, we'll use a procedure for each one. The main program will only invoke these procedures in the proper order and hold values to pass back and forth between procedures as needed.

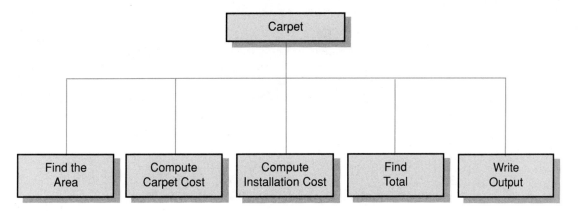

FIGURE 3.8 Structure chart for program *Carpet.*

Find Area
This procedure needs to collect the input data of length and width (in feet), convert these measurements to yards, and compute the area. Only the area needs to be returned to the rest of the program for other procedures to use, so *Area* should be a variable formal parameter. *Length* and *Width* can be local variables. The form of the procedure is

```
procedure FindArea(var Area: real);
{reads room dimensions in feet, converts to yards, computes
 Area and returns it to main program}

var
     Length, Width : real;     {room dimensions in feet}

begin     {procedure FindArea}

   read Length and Width
   change to yards
   multiply to find Area

end;     {procedure FindArea}
```

Notice that we've used a pseudocode mixture of actual computer code and English. We've given the heading, with the formal parameter list, and some variable declarations exactly as they will appear in the final code because we've already made decisions on these details. We haven't yet written the exact code for the body of the procedure, but our pseudocode tells us what will be happening. We may need additional local variables when we implement the pseudocode, but we can always add them later—they will not affect the procedure's interface with the rest of the program.

Compute Carpet Cost

This procedure needs to know the value of *Area* from the main program and should read in the price of the carpet in dollars per square yard. It should compute the cost of the carpet and return this to the main program. Thus, *CarpetCost* should be a variable formal parameter, while *Area* can be a value parameter because this procedure does not change *Area*. *CarpetPrice* can be a local variable.

```
procedure ComputeCarpetCost(Area: real;
                            var CarpetCost: real);
{computes CarpetCost for a room of size Area}

var
    CarpetPrice : real     {price of carpet in dollars/sq. yd}

begin     {procedure ComputeCarpetCost}
    read in CarpetPrice
    multiply CarpetPrice by Area to find CarpetCost
end;      {procedure ComputeCarpetCost}
```

Compute Installation Cost

This procedure needs to know the value of *Area* from the main program and will use the local constant *ChargeToInstall* to compute *InstallationCost,* which it passes to the main program.

```
procedure ComputeInstallationCost(Area: real;
                                  var InstallationCost: real);
{computes InstallationCost for a given Area using local
 constant ChargeToInstall}
```

Find Total

This procedure simply receives two numbers, adds them, and returns the result. To emphasize the general nature of this computation, we can use *Number1* and *Number2* as value formal parameters. The corresponding actual parameters will be numbers representing carpet cost and installation cost when this procedure is invoked. Remember that the correspondence between actual and formal parameters is done by position in the respective lists, and not by the identifiers used.

```
procedure FindTotal(Number1, Number2: real;
                    var Sum: real);
{adds Number1 and Number2 to give Sum}
```

Write Output

This procedure receives the total cost from the main program and writes it out. *Total* can be a value formal parameter, as the procedure does not have to return a new value for *Total*. Again, when writing this procedure we don't have to worry about what identifier the main program (which someone else might be writing if this were a large project) will use for the corresponding actual parameter. We only need to agree that there will be one value of data type real passed to this procedure as a value parameter.

procedure WriteOutput(Total: real);
{writes the total carpet cost along with a sales pitch}

Once procedure interfaces and program variable identifiers have been decided, data flow information can be added to the structure chart, resulting in Figure 3.9. Such a data flow diagram summarizes at a glance how procedures are invoked. It also indicates which actual parameters only carry data into a procedure ("in arrows"), which carry data into a procedure but receive new values from the procedure ("in/out arrows"—there are none of these in Figure 3.9), and which receive values that are read in or initialized within the procedure ("out arrows").

Now finishing each of the pieces and assembling them into the complete program is quite easy. Notice that the main program below is short, consisting simply of invocations of the various procedures, for which we chose rather informative names. The main program expresses the flow of the program logic, and the data flow diagram, very clearly. Anyone who wants to understand the general idea of how the program works can just read the main program. Details can then be found in the code for the various procedures. The variables declared in the main program are used by more than one procedure; these variables receive values from some procedures and pass them to others.

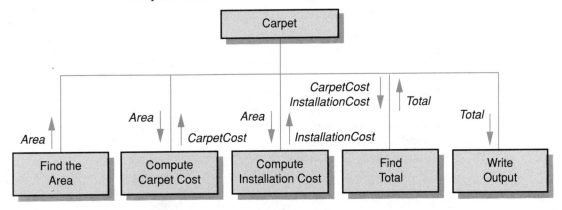

FIGURE 3.9 Data flow diagram for program *Carpet*.

```
program Carpet(input, output);
{computes the cost of carpeting a rectangular room, given the
 dimensions and the carpet price; installation charge is a
 constant function of area}

var
    Area : real;                    {room area in square yards}
    CarpetCost : real;              {cost for carpet only}
    InstallationCost : real;        {cost for installation, based on
                                     area and fixed rate}
    Total : real;                   {total carpet costs,
                                     carpet + installation}

procedure FindArea(var Area: real);
{reads room dimensions in feet, converts to yards, computes Area
 and returns it to main program}

var
    Length, Width : real;    {room dimensions in feet}
    LengthInYards,
    WidthInYards : real;     {room dimensions in yards}

  begin     {procedure FindArea}
    write('Please give the room dimensions, ');
    writeln('to the nearest foot');
    write('Length: ');
    readln(Length);
    write('Width: ');
    readln(Width);
    LengthInYards := Length/3;
    WidthInYards := Width/3;
    Area := LengthInYards*WidthInYards;
  end;       {procedure FindArea}

procedure ComputeCarpetCost(Area: real; var CarpetCost: real);
{computes CarpetCost for a room of size Area}

var
    CarpetPrice : real;        {price of carpet in dollars/sq. yd}

  begin     {procedure ComputeCarpetCost}
    write('What is the price per sq. yd of the carpet');
    writeln(' you have selected?');
    readln(CarpetPrice);
    CarpetCost := CarpetPrice*Area;
  end;       {procedure ComputeCarpetCost}

procedure ComputeInstallationCost(Area: real;
                                  var InstallationCost: real);
{computes InstallationCost for a given Area using local constant
 ChargeToInstall}
```

```
const
    ChargeToInstall = 2.33; {installation charge per sq. yard}

    begin    {procedure ComputeInstallationCost}
    InstallationCost := ChargeToInstall*Area;
    end;    {procedure ComputeInstallationCost}

procedure FindTotal(Number1, Number2: real; var Sum: real);
{adds Number1 and Number2 to give Sum}

    begin    {procedure FindTotal}
    Sum := Number1 + Number2;
    end;    {procedure FindTotal}

procedure WriteOutput(Total: real);
{writes the total carpet cost along with a sales pitch}

    begin    {procedure WriteOutput}
    writeln;
    writeln('Now for a total of only $ ', Total:7:2);
    write('you can have this fine carpet installed');
    writeln(' in your home.');
    writeln('Why wait? Act now!');
    end;    {procedure WriteOutput}

begin    {main program}
    FindArea(Area);
    ComputeCarpetCost(Area, CarpetCost);
    ComputeInstallationCost(Area, InstallationCost);
    FindTotal(CarpetCost, InstallationCost, Total);
    WriteOutput(Total);
end.    {main program}
```

RUNNING THE PROGRAM...

```
Please give the room dimensions, to the nearest foot
Length: 17
Width: 14
What is the price per sq. yd of the carpet you have selected?
14.99

Now for a total of only $   458.02
you can have this fine carpet installed in your home.
Why wait? Act now!
```

CASE STUDY ONE	View #3

As project manager at Sterling Software Systems, you are engaged in the algorithm development process for the water pollution problem. You have identified four subtasks the program must carry out in order to solve this problem. The program needs to collect the input data for a site reading (site

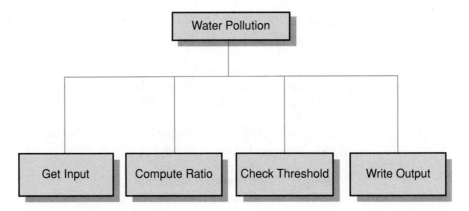

FIGURE 3.10 Structure chart for program *WaterPollution*.

ID, date, amount of water, and bacteria count), compute the ratio of bacteria to water, determine whether the ratio exceeds the safe threshold value, and write the output. This results in the structure chart shown in Figure 3.10.

CASE STUDY TWO   **View #3**

Sterling Software Systems and the Hypertension Clinic have worked out the problem specification for the hypertension data processing.

Patients are identified by an integer ID number, and the date of their visit is recorded in month/date/year fashion. Each patient has three pairs of readings, each consisting of a systolic and a diastolic pressure. These three pairs of readings are to be averaged, and patient classification is based on the average diastolic pressure according to the following scale:

- below 90 normal
- 90-104   mild hypertensive
- 105-114   moderate hypertensive
- over 115 severe hypertensive

The program should operate in an interactive mode and display the following typical output:

Patient ID	Date	Average Pressure	Classification
137	02/20/87	128/95	mild hypertensive

As project manager for this project, identify subtasks and draw a structure chart for the program to solve this problem.

---

*(Items marked with * make use of optional material on Simple Control Structures.)*

EXERCISES   **#1.** A factory manufactures, on the average, *A* widgets and *B* gadgets per month. Each widget costs *C* dollars to manufacture and sells for *D* dollars.

Each gadget costs E dollars to manufacture and sells for F dollars. A program is to be written to find the factory's profit for the month. Identify major subtasks that such a program must carry out; break some of these down into lower levels of detail; draw a structure chart for the resulting program design.

2. Write the procedure heading for a procedure *Chemistry* that uses integer variable parameters *Sodium* and *Calcium*, a real value parameter *Iron*, and an integer value parameter *Manganese*.

#3. Procedure *P1* has the heading

```
procedure P1(A, B: integer; var C: real);
```

and is invoked in the following section of the main program:

```
X := 15;
Y := 12;
Z := 8.9;
X := X + 2*Y;
P1(Y, X, Z);
```

What values are associated with the formal parameters A, B, and C at this point?

4. Procedure *P1* from Exercise 3 is invoked in the following section of the main program:

```
C := 3;
A := 7;
C := C + A;
B := 2.0;
P1(C, A, B);
```

What values are associated with the formal parameters A, B, and C at this point?

#5. A procedure to compute the volume of a rectangular solid has the parameters *Length, Width, Height,* and *Volume* in its formal parameter list. Which of these must be variable parameters and which can be value parameters?

6. Write pseudocode for a procedure to find the maximum of two integers *Number1* and *Number2*; the procedure should not read or write any data values. Use English to describe the body of the procedure and computer code for the rest, including the procedure heading.

*7. Consider the following section of code:

```
readln(A);
if A < 7 then
  writeln (2*A)
else
  writeln(3*A);
```

What is the output when *A* has the value 5? 10? 7?

#*8. Consider the following section of code:

```
readln(A);
if A >= 15 then
  A := A + 1;
writeln(A);
```

What is the output when *A* has the value 20? 10?

*9. Write a single **if** statement to carry out the body of the procedure in Exercise 6.

*10. What is the output when the following statement is executed?

```
for Index := 2 to 5 do
  begin
    write('Index = ');
    writeln(Index:1);
  end;
```

SKILL BUILDERS

1. Write a program that invokes a procedure to print your name and address.

2. Write a program that twice invokes a procedure with a single value parameter; the output of the program should be:

```
The next value is 3
The next value is 5
```

#3. Write a program that reads in an integer, doubles it, and writes the result; use a procedure to do the doubling.

4. Modify the program from #3 to do the reading, doubling, and writing process for two numbers.

5. Modify the program from #4 to use three procedures, one to read, one to double, and one to write.

*6. Write a program that reads in an integer and writes out one of the following two messages, as appropriate:

```
Twice your number, —, was less than 50.
Twice your number, —, was not less than 50.
```

*7. Modify the program from #5 to process 10 numbers; use a counting loop.

SOFTWARE DEVELOPMENT PROJECTS

For the following projects, follow the format of Sample Software Development Project Carpet Sales, including problem specification, algorithm development, structure chart, discussion of and pseudocode for program modules, data flow diagram, the program itself—with appropriate comments—and at least one sample program execution.

1. Develop software that prompts the user for appropriate input and then generates the following report:

**Quarterly Report of the
United Truffles and Escargot Society**

Sales	Expenses	Profits
$ _ _ _ _ . _ _	$ _ _ _ _ . _ _	$ _ _ _ _ . _ _

2. A shipping company ships three cargoes per month. Develop software to collect the weight of each cargo and to output the average shipping weight per cargo for the month. (The symbol / is used for division, so *A/B* means *A* divided by *B*.)

3. A wildlife management project has to estimate the number of a particular species in a nature preserve. This is done by counting the number found in a small area and assuming that the number-to-area ratio is a constant. Develop software that reads in the acreage of the sample area, the acreage of the total preserve, and the number of the species counted in the sample, performs the necessary calculation, and writes the output. (The symbol / is used for division, so *A/B* means *A* divided by *B*.)

4. At Dapper Dan's Dealership, a new car is sold with a 10 percent discount off the sticker price. Sales tax is 5 percent of the amount paid, and license plate fees are one-half of 1 percent of the amount paid. Develop software to read the sticker price of a new car and determine the total price a buyer must pay.

5. A lawn service charges for mowing and spraying based on the square footage of the (rectangular) lawn. Develop software to find the monthly cost to a customer based on multiple mowings and one spraying per month. The program should obtain as input not only the lawn dimensions, but also the (rectangular) house dimensions, as the house does not get sprayed or mowed!

***6.** Develop software to read the user's total income and compute the user's tax bill if the tax rate is 15 percent of total income for the first $20,000 or less, plus 28 percent of total income above $20,000.

***7.** Redo Software Development Project #2 above to handle 25 cargoes per month; use a counting loop.

**TESTING
AND
MAINTENANCE
DEPARTMENT**

1. Run program *Carpet* with various input values. What happens if the room dimensions are given as real numbers instead of integers?

2. Modify program *Carpet* to change the installation cost per square yard to $3.50.

3. Modify program *Carpet* to make the installation charge 10 percent of the carpet cost.

4. Modify program *Carpet* to handle two different rooms.

*5. Modify program *Carpet* to eliminate the installation charge if the price for the carpet exceeds $25.00 per square yard.

DEBUGGING CLINIC

Find and correct the errors in the following program.

```
program Washer(input, output);
{program to compute the area of one face of a flat circular
 washer given the outer and inner radii}

var
    BigRadius : real;        {outer radius of washer in cm}
    SmallRadius : real;      {inner radius of washer in cm}
    Area : real;             {area of one face of washer}

procedure GetInput(var OuterRadius, InnerRadius: real);
{collects outer and inner radius in cm}

  begin    {procedure GetInput}
    writeln('Enter the outer radius of the washer, in cm');
    readln(BigRadius);
    writeln('Enter the inner radius of the washer, in cm');
    readln(SmallRadius);
  end;      {procedure GetInput}

procedure FindArea(BigRadius, SmallRadius: real);
{computes area by subtracting inner circle area from outer circle
 area}

const
    pi = 3.14157;

var
    BigArea : real;          {area of outer circle}
    SmallArea : real;        {area of inner circle}
    Area : real;             {area of one face of washer}

  begin    {procedure FindArea}
    BigArea := pi*(BigRadius)*(BigRadius);
    SmallArea := pi*(SmallRadius)*(SmallRadius);
    Area := BigArea — SmallArea;
  end;      {procedure FindArea}
```

```
procedure WriteOutput(Area: real);
{writes out the area}

    begin    {procedure WriteOutput}
      writeln ('The area of the washer is ', Area:7:2, ' sq. cm');
    end;    {procedure WriteOutput}

begin    {main program}
  GetInput(BigRadius, SmallRadius);
  FindArea(BigRadius, SmallRadius);
  WriteOutput(Area);
end.    {main program}
```

CHAPTER FOUR

MORE ON PROCEDURES AND PARAMETERS

The main use of procedures, as we discussed in Chapter 3, is to help us structure our programming problem into a series of manageable subtasks. Some of the technical details of parameter passing among these subtasks and how multiple procedures in a program can be related to one another deserve further explanation. We'll also look at some subtle sources of error and how to avoid them.

4.1 Parameters Again

4.1.1 How Variable Parameters Work

Recall that a variable formal parameter, indicated by **var** in the procedure heading, returns values to the invoking program segment by means of the corresponding actual parameter. A program variable used as an actual parameter has already been allocated memory space before the procedure is invoked. When the actual parameter corresponds to a variable formal parameter, the procedure invocation serves to temporarily add the name of the formal parameter as another label for that memory space. If the procedure changes the value stored in this memory space, the new value persists when control is returned to the invoking program segment and the temporary label is removed.

For example, program *CashRegister* below computes a total price for two purchases. The main program first initializes the variable *Total* to $0.00. It then reads in a purchase price. Invoking procedure *ComputeTotal* labels as *Sum* the memory location known to the main program as *Total*. The procedure modifies the value stored there by adding the price for the current item. Because *Sum* is a variable parameter, the change made in this value is retained after the procedure is exited and the memory space is once again labeled only by *Total*. The main program then reads in a second purchase price and invokes procedure *ComputeTotal* again. Finally the main program writes the output.

```
program CashRegister(input, output);
{computes total price for two items purchased}

var
    Total : real;              {running total for items purchased}
    Price1, Price2 : real;     {prices of purchased items}

procedure ComputeTotal (var Sum, SalePrice: real);
{adds SalePrice to Sum -
 both Sum and SalePrice are variable parameters}

  begin {procedure ComputeTotal}
    Sum := Sum + SalePrice;
  end;   {procedure ComputeTotal}

begin {main program}
  Total := 0.0;

  writeln('What is the price of the first item?');
  readln(Price1);
  ComputeTotal(Total, Price1);

  writeln('What is the price of the second item?');
  readln(Price2);
  ComputeTotal(Total, Price2);

  writeln;
  write('The prices for the two items are $', Price1:7:2);
  writeln(' and $', Price2:7:2);
  writeln('The total price for the two items is $', Total:7:2);

end.    {main program}
```

RUNNING THE PROGRAM...

```
What is the price of the first item?
42.95
What is the price of the second item?
16.49

The prices for the two items are $    42.95 and $    16.49
The total price for the two items is $    59.44
```

Figure 4.1 shows what happens to the memory location allocated to the variable *Total* during the sample program execution.

In this program the actual parameter *Total* and the formal parameter *Sum* correspond by virtue of their positions in their respective parameter

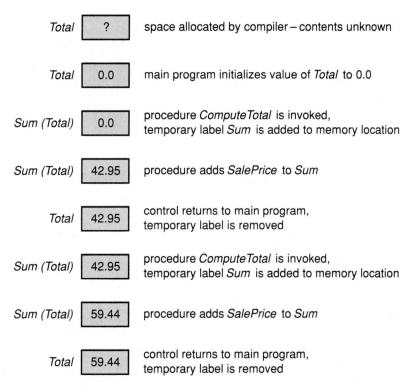

FIGURE 4.1 Memory location *Total* during execution of program *CashRegister.*

lists. The identifiers used do not matter; the formal parameter could also have the identifier *Total.* Additional labeling of the memory space would still occur, but the new temporary label would be the same as the permanent label.

Procedure *ComputeTotal* needs to know the value of *Total* from the main program, and the main program needs to know the new value of *Total* after procedure *ComputeTotal* is done. Therefore *Sum,* the formal parameter corresponding to the actual parameter *Total,* is both an "input parameter" and an "output parameter" to the procedure, which is why it is a variable formal parameter. However, *SalePrice* is a different story. The procedure needs to know a value for *SalePrice,* but it does nothing to modify this value. *SalePrice* is only an "input parameter" and consequently could be a value parameter.

4.1.2 *How Value Parameters Work*

When an actual parameter corresponds to a value formal parameter, the procedure invocation serves to create a new temporary memory location, labeled by the formal parameter. The value passed to the formal parameter is stored there. That memory location is completely "local" to the procedure; it is part of the activation record for that invocation of the procedure. While the procedure can access and even change that value, the new value is in no way associated with the actual parameter. Once the procedure is exited and control is returned to the invoking program segment, the content of that temporary memory location is no longer available. The actual parameter still has whatever its value was before the procedure was invoked. In the next version of the cash register program, *SalePrice* is a value parameter. An extra

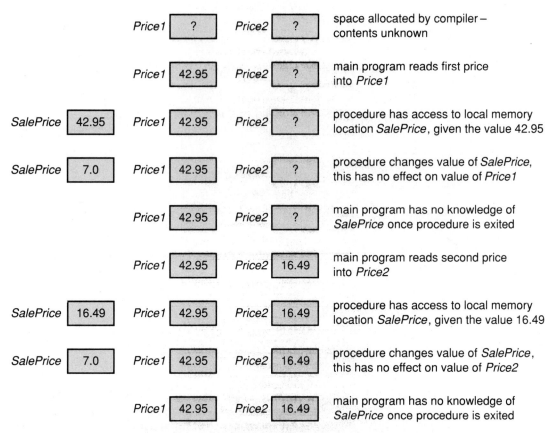

FIGURE 4.2 Selected memory locations during execution of program
NewCashRegister.

line (completely extraneous and unnecessary) has been inserted in the
procedure to illustrate the effect of changing the value of *SalePrice.* Figure
4.2 shows what happens to various memory locations during the sample
program execution.

program NewCashRegister(input, output);
{computes total price for two items purchased}

var
    Total : real;   {running total for items purchased}
    Price1, Price2 : real;   {prices of purchased items}

procedure ComputeTotal (**var** Sum: real; SalePrice: real};
{adds SalePrice to Sum - Sum is a variable parameter, SalePrice
is a value parameter}

    begin {procedure ComputeTotal}
    Sum := Sum + SalePrice;
    SalePrice := 7.0;   {this statement has no effect outside
                          of procedure ComputeTotal because
                          SalePrice is a value parameter}
    end;   {procedure ComputeTotal}

```
begin {main program}
   Total := 0.0;

   writeln('What is the price of the first item?');
   readln(Price1);
   ComputeTotal(Total, Price1);

   writeln('What is the price of the second item?');
   readln(Price2);
   ComputeTotal(Total, Price2);

   writeln;
   write('The prices for the two items are $', Price1:7:2);
   writeln(' and $', Price2:7:2);
   writeln('The total price for the two items is $', Total:7:2);

end.   {main program}
```

RUNNING THE PROGRAM...

```
What is the price of the first item?
42.95
What is the price of the second item?
16.49

The prices for the two items are $    42.95 and $    16.49
The total price for the two items is $    59.44
```

CHECKUP 4.1   What is the output from the following program?

```
program Numbers(input, output);

var
   X, Y : integer;

procedure Changes(var P: integer; Q: integer);
   begin
     P := P + 1;
     Q := 2*Q;
   end;

begin
  X := 3;
  Y := 7;
  Changes (X, Y);
  writeln(X, Y);
end.
```

4.1.3 *Comparing Variable and Value Parameters*

Value parameters may receive values from expressions as well as from variables; variable parameters may only receive values from variables.

Because a value formal parameter only receives a copy of a value and does not temporarily take over memory space previously allocated to an actual parameter, it is possible to pass to a value parameter anything that has a value of the correct data type. Thus expressions, as well as variables, can be used as actual parameters that correspond to value formal parameters, while actual parameters that correspond to variable formal parameters must be variables. Again, assume that procedures *XRay* and *Never* have the headings

```
procedure XRay(var Number, Day: integer; Initial: char;
                var Level: real);

procedure Never(A, B: integer; var When: real; Next: real);
```

Then the following procedure calls are legitimate, assuming that *N, D, I,* and *J* are integers and that *Level, Time,* and *Soon* are type *real:*

```
XRay(N, D, 'p', Level);

Never(3*I + J, 17, Time, Soon);
```

Regardless of whether a formal parameter is a variable parameter or a value parameter, no memory space is allocated and labeled with a formal parameter identifier when a program is compiled. This is why we said in the previous chapter that formal parameters are not program variables in the usual sense.

How can one decide whether to use a value parameter or a variable parameter? The overriding rule is: If the invoking program segment needs to know the new value of a quantity changed within a procedure, that quantity must be represented by a variable parameter. In other words, "output parameters" or "input/output parameters" must be variable parameters. "Input parameters"—those that bring information to the procedure but need not return information to the invoking program segment—can be value parameters. However, there is an exception. Later, we will see data types that consist of multiple memory locations. Using value parameters for these data types would cause large amounts of storage to be allocated to the temporary memory locations. Because of memory limitations, then, variable parameters are often used (and sometimes required) even if the procedure will make no changes in the data values.

An alternative is to make all parameters variable parameters, but this is not a good idea for three reasons. First, having to decide whether a formal parameter should be a value parameter or a variable parameter forces the programmer to think about the role of that parameter. This process clarifies the program/procedure interface in the programmer's mind. Second, using both types of parameters documents this interface—the procedure heading describes what will be available to the invoking program segment and what will not. Finally, the program/procedure interface should be as tightly controlled as possible to reduce the possibility of undesirable "side effects."

A **side effect** occurs when a procedure modifies a variable to achieve some result within the procedure, but the modification persists outside of the procedure to adversely affect the rest of the program. We'll see an example of this in the next section.

The formal and actual parameter lists constitute the interface between the procedure and the rest of the program. Interface specifications, part of the functional requirements of a module, are agreements about these parameter lists in regard to number, order, and type, which identifiers in the lists represent what items of data, and which should be variable parameters rather than value parameters.

4.2 Scope of Identifiers

Value formal parameters for a procedure, like the identifier *SalePrice* in program *NewCashRegister*, are treated as identifiers completely local to the procedure. The **scope** of an identifier is the range of the program in which that identifier has meaning.

4.2.1 Scope of Variable Identifiers

Program blocks, established by where procedures are declared, determine the scope of identifiers.

Procedures are declared within the main program and can also be declared within (contained or **nested** within) other procedures. The main program and each procedure may be viewed as a block, as in Figure 4.3. Here the main program contains two procedure blocks, X and Y, indicating that procedures X and Y are part of the declaration section of the main program. Procedures V and W are part of the declaration section of procedure Y. Figure 4.4 illustrates how the declaration sections might look; the main program and any procedures can declare their own constants and variables. Let's determine the scope of each of the variables declared in Figure 4.4.

A variable declared within a block has as its scope that block and any blocks contained within that block, but nothing outside that block. Here *time* and *money*, declared in the main program, are **global variables** available to the entire program. The variable *sum*, declared within procedure X, is local to procedure X and has no meaning in the main program or in procedure Y. A separate memory location for *sum* is established when X is invoked and abandoned when X is exited. If X is invoked again at a later time, another memory location for *sum* is established, therefore *sum* cannot be assumed to have the value it had when execution last left X. The variables *name, I,* and *J* are local to procedure Y and have meaning only within block Y, including within procedures V and W. From the point of view of procedures V and W, these variables are global.

The variable *time*, declared in procedure Y, represents a potential conflict because this declaration defines *time* as a local variable within procedure Y, yet an identifier *time* is also available to Y as a global variable. In such cases, a locally declared variable takes precedence over a global variable. Here the identifier *time* used within procedure Y will mean a variable local to Y. This local variable uses a completely separate memory location from the space set aside for the global identifier *time*, and changes made to *time* within procedure Y will have no effect on the value of the global *time*. The same is

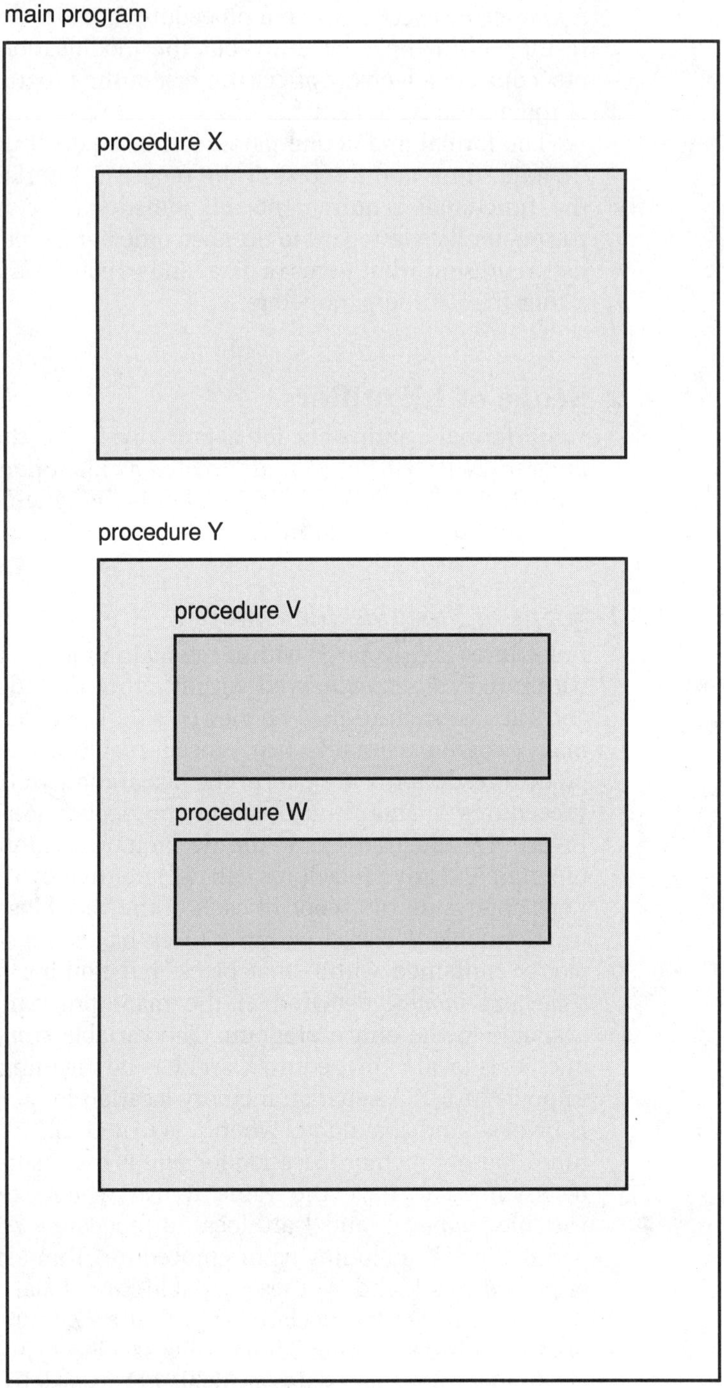

main program

procedure X

procedure Y

procedure V

procedure W

FIGURE 4.3 Example of blocking structure.

```
program - - -
const
        pi = 3.14;
var

        time: integer;
        money: real;

        ┌──────────────────────────────────────────────┐
        │   procedure X;                               │
        │   var                                        │
        │           sum: integer;                      │
        │   begin {procedure X}                        │
        │   .                                          │
        │   .                                          │
        │   end; {procedure X}                         │
        └──────────────────────────────────────────────┘

        ┌──────────────────────────────────────────────┐
        │   procedure Y;                               │
        │   var                                        │
        │           name: char;                        │
        │           I, J:  integer;                    │
        │           time:  real;                       │
        │                                              │
        │    ┌──────────────────────────────────────┐  │
        │    │    procedure V;                      │  │
        │    │    var                               │  │
        │    │            I:  integer;              │  │
        │    │            done:  boolean;           │  │
        │    │    begin {procedure V}               │  │
        │    │    .                                 │  │
        │    │    .                                 │  │
        │    │    end; {procedureV}                 │  │
        │    └──────────────────────────────────────┘  │
        │    ┌──────────────────────────────────────┐  │
        │    │    procedure W;                      │  │
        │    │    var                               │  │
        │    │            last:  char;              │  │
        │    │    begin {procedure W}               │  │
        │    │    .                                 │  │
        │    │    .                                 │  │
        │    │    end; {procedure W}                │  │
        │    └──────────────────────────────────────┘  │
        │                                              │
        │   begin {procedureY}                         │
        │   .                                          │
        │   .                                          │
        │   end; {procedure Y}                         │
        └──────────────────────────────────────────────┘

begin {main program}
.
.
end.  {main program}
```

FIGURE   4.4   Possible declarations for the program of Figure 4.3.

true for the variable *I* declared in procedure *V*. Within procedure *V*, the identifier *I* refers to a variable local to *V*, while outside of *V* (but within *Y*), the identifier *I* refers to the variable declared within *Y*. Identifiers *done* and *last* are local to *V* and *W*, respectively.

While use of a local variable with the same name as a global variable is legal, a human reading the program may find it confusing to remember whether a particular reference to *time* means "local time" or "global time." Such a situation should be avoided, if possible. On the other hand, procedures may be developed independently of other parts of the program, even by different people if the program is a large project. A procedure writer is only required to meet the interface requirements; the identifiers chosen for local variables are no one else's business. If one person uses identifier *Rate* as a local variable because it seems the most descriptive identifier, and another person who writes the invoking program segment also uses *Rate* for the same reasons, no changes are necessary to incorporate the two sections of code into a single program. (Similarly, while it may be clearer to have formal parameter identifiers that are the same as their corresponding actual parameter identifiers, differences cause no problem.)

Value parameters in a formal parameter list for a procedure act like variables local to the procedure. Variable parameters act as alternate names for variables global to the procedure.

Local variables take precedence over global variables, so a local variable can use the same identifier as a global variable if this seems appropriate.

CHECKUP 4.2   What is the output from the following program?

```
program Scope(input, output);

var
    A, B : integer;

procedure NotMuch;
var
    A : integer;
  begin
    A := 7;
    B := 10;
    writeln(A, B);
  end;

begin
    A := 5;
    B := 15;
    writeln(A, B);
    NotMuch;
    writeln(A, B);
end.
```

4.2.2 *Scope of Procedure Identifiers*

Rules of scope also apply to procedure names. A procedure name is meaningful, that is, the procedure can be invoked, within the block in which it is declared. In Figure 4.3, the main program can invoke procedures X or Y. The main program cannot invoke procedures V or W because these are local to procedure Y. Procedure Y can invoke V or W. Procedures V or W could invoke procedures X or Y, which are "global" from the point of view of V or W. This brings up the possibility of procedure Y invoking procedure V that in turn invokes procedure Y, etc.; this is legal. It is even legal for a procedure to invoke itself directly, a process known as **recursion.** Recursion is a powerful intellectual idea, and we'll save it for Chapter 12.

Finally, procedure Y can invoke procedure X because X is declared in the main program, the block that contains Y, and the declaration for X is made before the declaration for Y. Some thought must be given to the order in which procedures are declared so that those to be invoked by other procedures are declared first. (The section on Forward Declarations in Chapter 12 provides a way around this restriction.)

Figure 4.5 summarizes what identifier can be used where for the structures shown in Figures 4.3 and 4.4. Note that scope is entirely determined by where procedures and variables are declared, not from the sequence of invocations that may occur as the program executes. This is known as **static scoping;** scope is determined once and for all when the program is compiled.

Much confusion over scope would be eliminated if there were no nested procedures. Procedures need not be nested; the situation in Figure 4.3 could, with some changes in variables, be organized into four separate procedures X, Y, V, and W within the main program. Use of nested procedures may more accurately reflect the structure chart, with subtasks of subtasks. If a procedure will be called by more than one other procedure, it should not be nested. Otherwise there are no hard-and-fast rules as to nested vs. sequential procedure declarations.

We have now raised several questions that have no "right" answers. Should local and global variables ever have the same names? Should corresponding formal and actual parameters always have the same names? Should procedures be nested or sequential? In some programs, one way may be preferable to the other, but most allow judgment calls that exercise personal preferences (part of something called **programming style.**)

4.2.3 *Side Effects*

Confusion over scope would also be reduced if only global variables were used. Then every procedure would know about everything and we wouldn't even need parameters! In the long run this would cause more problems than it solves. Use of global variables within procedures violates the principle of information hiding. It lets procedures know more than they need to know and allows them to unwittingly modify a variable that will later cause an error somewhere else in the program. As can be imagined, tracking down errors caused by these side effects can be difficult. In most cases, a procedure should use only the variables in its formal parameter list

Within   **Can Use**

main program

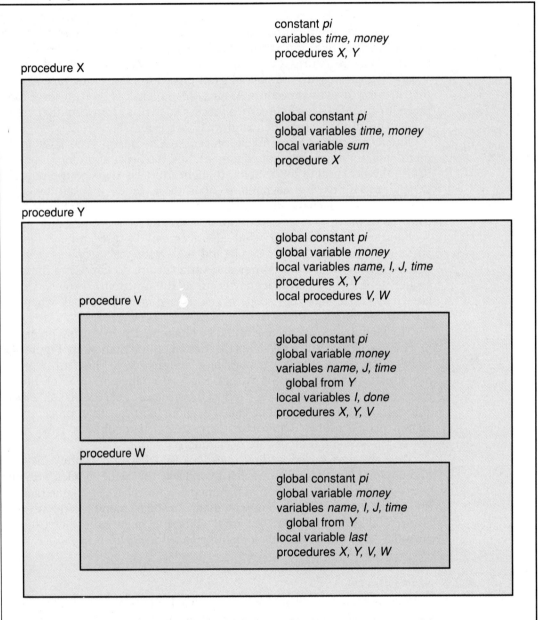

FIGURE 4.5 Scope of identifiers for the program of Figure 4.4.

and its local variables. Then the procedure heading and declarations section document what the procedure can access. Global constants can be used because their values can't be changed during program execution. Data items used by most of the procedures in a program may be justifiable as global variables to avoid long and cumbersome parameter lists but should be treated with great care.

Limit a procedure's ability to generate side effects by avoiding the use of global variables within a procedure, and using value parameters instead of variable parameters where possible.

In the following program, four students have three grades each. Procedure *Student* computes the average for a student by reading in the grades, adding them up, and dividing by 3. The main program invokes this procedure four times, once for each student, and computes the class average by adding up the four averages and dividing by 4.[†] Looking at the output, it is clear that the program contains an error. The error is caused by a side effect. Can you find the difficulty?

```pascal
program BadAverage(input, output);
{is supposed to compute the class average for four students, each
 with three grades}


var
    Sum : real;          {running sum of student averages}
    Average : real;      {an individual student average}
    ClassAverage : real; {average for the class}


procedure Student(var Average: real);
{computes average grade, Average, for an individual student with
 three grades}

var
    Gr1, Gr2, Gr3 : integer;     {3 grades for the student}

  begin     {procedure Student}
    writeln('Give the three grades for the student:');
    readln(Gr1, Gr2, Gr3);
    Sum := Gr1 + Gr2 + Gr3;
    Average := Sum/3;
  end;       {procedure Student}

begin {main program}
  Sum := 0.0;
  Student(Average);
  Sum := Sum + Average;
  Student(Average);
  Sum := Sum + Average;
  Student(Average);
  Sum := Sum + Average;
  Student(Average);
  Sum := Sum + Average;

  ClassAverage := Sum/4;
  writeln;
  writeln('The class average is ', ClassAverage:6:2);
end.    {main program}
```

[†]A counting loop could have been used here—see the section on Simple Control Structures in Chapter 3.

RUNNING THE PROGRAM...

```
Give the three grades for the student:
89 91 93
Give the three grades for the student:
92 95 90
Give the three grades for the student:
93 88 94
Give the three grades for the student:
20 20 30

The class average is   23.33
```

Both the main program and the procedure need a variable that represents the sum of the quantities to be averaged, but in the main program these quantities are the student averages, while in the procedure, these quantities are the individual grades. Because *Sum* is a global variable, every time the statement

```
Sum := Gr1 + Gr2 + Gr3;
```

is executed in procedure *Student,* it changes the value of *Sum* in the main program. Hence the next statement in the main program,

```
Sum := Sum + Average;
```

is actually adding the total of the student's three grades to the average of those three grades. *Sum* is a reasonable identifier for both the procedure and the main program, but there are two different "sums"! Making *Sum* a local variable in procedure *Student* will solve the problem. A corrected version of the program appears below. *Average* is a variable parameter because the main program needs the result of the procedure's computation of *Average.* The first time *Student* is called, the value for *Average* is unknown, but *Student* merely assigns a value <u>to</u> *Average,* it does not need a value <u>from</u> *Average.* In other words, *Average* is an "output only" parameter.

```
program GoodAverage(input, output);
{computes the class average for four students, each with three
 grades}

var
    Sum : real;            {running sum of student averages}
    Average : real;        {an individual student average}
    ClassAverage : real;   {average for the class}

procedure Student(var Average: real);
{computes average grade, Average, for an individual student with
 three grades}
```

```
var
    Gr1, Gr2, Gr3 : integer;       {3 grades for the student}
    Sum : integer;                 {sum of student grades}

    begin      {procedure Student}
    writeln('Give the three grades for the student:');
    readln(Gr1, Gr2, Gr3);
    Sum := Gr1 + Gr2 + Gr3;
    Average := Sum/3;
    end;        {procedure Student}

begin      {main program}
    Sum := 0.0;

    Student(Average);
    Sum := Sum + Average;
    Student(Average);
    Sum := Sum + Average;
    Student(Average);
    Sum := Sum + Average;
    Student(Average);
    Sum := Sum + Average;

    ClassAverage := Sum/4;
    writeln;
    writeln('The class average is ', ClassAverage:6:2);
end.        {main program}
```

RUNNING THE PROGRAM...

```
Give the three grades for the student:
89 91 93
Give the three grades for the student:
92 95 90
Give the three grades for the student:
93 88 94
Give the three grades for the student:
20 20 30

The class average is    74.58
```

4.3 Procedures and Testing

Designing a program in a modular fashion, using procedures, makes it easier to test. Suppose that the procedures and the functional requirements of each procedure, what it is to do and what its formal parameter list will be, have been decided upon. Then the structure of the program and the module interfaces can be tested before the details of a single procedure have been written. This is done by using **stubs** where the procedure code will eventually go. A stub for a procedure carries the appropriate procedure heading but does not actually do anything. It should write out a message such as "now executing procedure ABC," and it may contain assignment statements that set formal parameters equal to artificial values so that parameter passing can be tested. Running the main program with these stubs for all the procedures that will eventually be added is like tuning up an orchestra—a peep or a toot is requested from and sent to the conductor from each section as a signal that the section is ready to perform, but the actual performance comes later.

Once the code for a procedure has been written, it can also be tested as a stand-alone unit without plugging it into the entire program. To do this, a **driver** program that provides a minimum shell in which to run the procedure is written. The driver simply initializes any values the procedure needs passed to it as parameters and receives any values passed back from the procedure. These can be artificial values; the purpose here is to test whether the procedure is properly performing its computations.

The stub-and-driver system involves writing extra, if simple, code. This may not seem worth the effort—why not just put the whole program together and give it a whirl? This will work for small programs. The value of the stub-and-driver system occurs in larger programs where it becomes easier to debug a section at a time rather than face an entire, complex program with an error "somewhere." Once again, writing stubs and drivers to test procedures and program structure on small programs is a good habit to acquire so that you'll have these tools mastered when you need them for testing larger programs.

Write stubs for procedures to test overall program structure and procedure interfaces; write driver programs to test procedures.

4.4 Sample Software Development Project—Postage

Problem Statement

Compute the postal charge for mailing an item.

Problem Specification

Postal rates depend upon the category of item being mailed (for example, letter, book, or package), the destination (domestic or foreign), as well as the weight. For simplicity, we'll allow the category to be identified by the letters *L, B,* or *P,* and the destination by the letters *D* or *F.* Input will consist of these two items, together with the weight. Postal rates for domestic mail are based on weight by the ounce, for foreign mail on weight by the half-ounce. We'll require that the input be given in ounces, and we'll convert it to half-ounces if necessary. Output should consist of a printed receipt in the following form:

```
U.S. Postal Service
*********
Category:      (L, B, or P)
Destination:    (D or F)
```

```
Weight in ounces: __
*********
Charge:   $___ . __
```

Input: category, destination, weight
Output: receipt in proper form

Algorithm Development

We can break the task into three major subtasks: getting the input, computing the charge, and printing the receipt. Figure 4.6 shows the structure chart. We'll make each of these subtasks a procedure.

Get Input

A series of three prompt-read pairs should serve to collect the three values of *Category*, *Destination*, and *Weight*. Each of these values is needed by other procedures in the program, so each should be a variable formal parameter.

procedure GetInput(**var** Category, Destination: char;
                         var Weight: real);
{collects the Category, Destination, and Weight of the item to be mailed}

begin {procedure GetInput}

   prompt for and read *Category*, *Destination*, *Weight*

end;   {procedure GetInput}

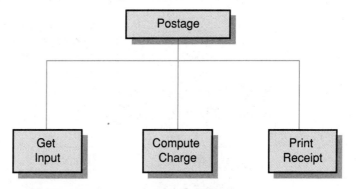

FIGURE 4.6 Structure chart for program *Postage*.

Compute Charge

This procedure needs to know the category and destination of the mail, as well as the weight. The postal rate scale varies with the category of mail and whether it is domestic or foreign. We won't write the code for this procedure now. First, we don't have the postal rates available, but even if we did, one among many courses of action must be taken based on the values of *Category* and *Destination*. We'll be able to handle this easily after Chapter 7. For the moment, then, we'll write a stub for this procedure. We'll print a message that says the program got here, and we'll assign some phony value to *Charge*. We do know what the procedure interface should look like.

```
procedure ComputeCharge(Category, Destination: char;
                         Weight: real;
                         var Charge: real);
{computes the Charge to mail to Destination an item of type
 Category weighing Weight}
   begin    {stub for procedure ComputeCharge}
     writeln('Execution has reached procedure ComputeCharge');
     Charge := 5.00;    {phony value assigned to Charge}
   end;     {procedure ComputeCharge}
```

Print Receipt

Procedure *PrintReceipt* needs all of the data values, and can accomplish its task with several *writeln* statements.

```
procedure PrintReceipt (Category, Destination: char;
                         Weight, Charge: real);
{procedure to print the postal receipt as a table}
```

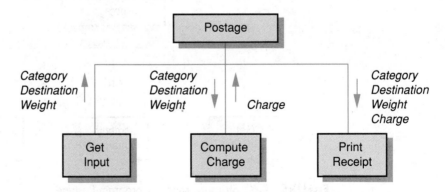

FIGURE 4.7 Data flow diagram for program *Postage*.

Adding data flow information to the structure chart gives us Figure 4.7. The complete program (as complete as we can make it at this time) is shown below. Again, the main program displays the structure of the program logic and shuffles values between the procedures. The sample session indicates that the input and output procedures are working, and that we did get to the *ComputeCharge* procedure. We have some confidence that the total program would work properly if *ComputeCharge* were correctly completed.

```pascal
program Postage(input, output);
{computes postal charges for mailing an item
 given the category, destination, and weight}
var
      Category : char;      {designates letter, book, or package}
      Destination : char;   {designates domestic or foreign destination}
      Weight : real;        {weight of item in ounces}
      Charge : real;        {standard postal charge to mail this item}


procedure GetInput(var Category, Destination: char;
                   var Weight: real);
{collects the Category, Destination, and Weight of the item to be
 mailed}

   begin     {procedure GetInput}
     writeln('Enter category of item: Letter, Book, or Package: ');
     write('(L, B, or P) ');
     readln(Category);

     writeln('Enter destination of item: Domestic or Foreign: ');
     write('(D or F) ');
     readln(Destination);

     writeln('Enter weight of item (in ounces):');
     readln(Weight);
   end;      {procedure GetInput}

procedure ComputeCharge(Category, Destination: char;
                        Weight: real;
                        var Charge: real);
{computes the Charge to mail to Destination an item of type
 Category weighing Weight}

   begin     {stub for procedure ComputeCharge}
     writeln('Execution has reached procedure ComputeCharge');
     Charge := 5.00;     {phony value assigned to Charge}
   end;      {procedure Computecharge}

procedure PrintReceipt(Category, Destination: char;
                       Weight, Charge: real);
{procedure to print the postal receipt as a table}
```

```
const
   blanks = '                    ';  {to space over the output}
   stars = '*********';            {part of output}

   begin      {procedure PrintReceipt}
     writeln;
     writeln(blanks, 'U.S. Postal Service');
     writeln(blanks, stars);
     writeln(blanks, 'Category:    ', Category);
     writeln(blanks, 'Destination: ', Destination);
     writeln(blanks, 'Weight in ounces: ', Weight:4:1);
     writeln(blanks, stars);
     writeln(blanks, 'Charge: $', Charge:6:2);
   end;      {procedure PrintReceipt}

begin      {main program}
  GetInput(Category, Destination, Weight);
  ComputeCharge(Category, Destination, Weight, Charge);
  PrintReceipt(Category, Destination, Weight, Charge);
end.      {main program}
```

RUNNING THE PROGRAM...

```
Enter category of item: Letter, Book, or Package:
(L, B, or P) B
Enter destination of item: Domestic or Foreign:
(D or F) D
Enter weight of item (in ounces):
6.8
Execution has reached procedure ComputeCharge

            U.S. Postal Service
            *********
            Category:    B
            Destination: D
            Weight in ounces:   6.8
            *********
            Charge: $    5.00
```

CASE STUDY ONE   View #4

In the water pollution problem, you have identified the major subtasks. Now you review the problem specification. Your notes indicate that the program is to read in an integer site ID number, a date in the form month/date/year, an integer volume of water measured in ml, and an integer value for the bacteria count found in that sample. The program is to write some appropriate message if the bacteria-to-water ratio exceeds the specified ratio of 200 per 100 ml. (Because it has now been several days since you last looked at this problem, you are grateful for the careful documentation you made of the problem specification. It allows you to refresh your memory quickly, without having to call your client to repeat a question because you forgot the answer!) Working from the problem specification and the structure chart, you can now do the functional requirements for your procedures. Your main program will simply call the various procedures and pass values among them.

Get Input

This procedure needs to collect values for the site ID number, the amount of water in the sample, and the bacteria count in the sample. These are all integer quantities. The procedure also needs to collect the date; this is harder because the date is in the form 03/28/89, so it can't be read as an integer value (which probably wouldn't make much sense anyway). You decide to read a series of *char* data types, reading in but ignoring the separating slashes. (In the case of dates such as 03/28/89, the leading zero is one of the characters read and must be present as part of the data.) All of this data is needed by the rest of the program, so it is passed to the main program through variable parameters.

```
procedure GetInput(var ID, Water, Bacteria: integer;
                   var Mon1, Mon2, Day1, Day2,
                       Yr1, Yr2: char);
{procedure to collect input for water pollution data; amount
 Water of water and count Bacteria of bacteria were
 obtained from site  ID on date Mon1Mon2/Day1Day2/Yr1Yr2}
```

Compute Ratio

This procedure needs the bacteria count and the amount of water as input and returns the ratio of the two quantities.

```
procedure ComputeRatio(Bacteria, Water: integer;
                       var Ratio: real);
{computes the Ratio of Bacteria to Water}
```

Check Threshold

Procedure *CheckThreshold* takes the ratio computed by *ComputeRatio* and tests to see whether it exceeds the threshold value *Threshold*, which is a global constant. It sets a boolean value *Over* to true if the threshold is exceeded.

```
procedure CheckThreshold(Ratio: real;
                         var Over: boolean);
{compares Ratio to the global constant Threshold and sets
 Over to true if that limit is exceeded}
```

Write Output

This procedure echoes the input data and writes a violation message if the pollution level is too high. The procedure needs all of the input data and the boolean value that determines whether a warning message should be written.

```
procedure WriteOutput(ID, Water, Bacteria: integer;
                      Mon1, Mon2, Day1, Day2,
                      Yr1, Yr2: char;
                      Ratio: real;
                      Warning: boolean);
{echoes site input data and writes warning message if
 warranted}
```

Main program

The main program needs to call the respective procedures and store values passed between procedures. The structure of the main program is the following:

```
program WaterPollution(input, output);
{tests water sample from a site against a pollution threshold,
 issues a warning if the bacteria level is too high}

const
    Threshold: = 2.0     {200 bacteria per 100 ml water}

var
    ID : integer;              {site ID number}
    Water : integer;           {amount of water sampled, in ml}
    Bacteria : integer;        {bacteria count in sample}
    Mon1, Mon2 : char;         {two-digit month notation}
    Day1, Day2 : char;         {two-digit date notation}
    Yr1, Yr2 : char;           {two-digit year notation}
    Warning : boolean;         {flag for warning message if
                                pollution level too high}
    Level : real;              {pollution level for this
                                sample}

{procedure declarations}

begin    {main program}
    GetInput(ID, Water, Bacteria,
            Mon1, Mon2, Day1, Day2, Yr1, Yr2);
    ComputeRatio(Bacteria, Water, Level);
    CheckThreshold(Level, Warning);
```

Continued

```
WriteOutput(ID, Water, Bacteria,
            Mon1, Mon2, Day1, Day2, Yr1, Yr2,
            Level, Warning);
end.    {main program}
```

(Note: The contract for this project should have required that the program development be reviewed with the manager of the Lodestone County Water Pollution Department. At this point the manager should expect to see something like a structure chart, together with a description of each program module. While it is not the manager's job to worry about details such as parameter passing, it is his or her job to check that the modules, if correctly implemented as described, would solve the problem. This is the final chance to clear up any misunderstandings between the department and the software developer about the problem that is to be solved.)

CASE STUDY TWO

View #4

For the hypertension clinic program, give a description of and the procedure heading for each of your procedures (i.e., do the functional requirements). Identify the global variables in your program, and give the outline of the main program, with procedure calls and actual parameters specified.

(Items marked with * make use of optional material on Simple Control Structures from Chapter 3.)

EXERCISES

#1. Is the formal parameter *Sum* in program *NewCashRegister* an "output parameter" or an "input/output parameter"? Explain.

#2. Procedure *Q* has the heading

procedure Q(**var** A: char; B: integer; **var** C: integer);

and is invoked in the following section of the main program:

```
A := 'B';
B := 7;
C := 12;
Q(A, C*B — 5, B);
```

What values are associated with the formal parameters *A*, *B*, and *C* at this point?

3. Procedure *W* is given by

procedure W(M: integer; **var** N: integer);

```
begin
  M := N + 7;
  N := 2*M;
end;
```

What is the output from the following section of code?

```
X := 6;
Y := 2;
W(X, Y);
writeln(X, Y);
```

#4. Procedure *Multiply* is given by

procedure Multiply(Factor1, Factor2, Product: integer);

```
begin
  Product := Factor1*Factor2;
  writeln(Product);
end;
```

What is the output from the following section of code?

```
Product := 0;
N1 := 3;
N2 := 4;
Multiply(N1, N2, Product);
writeln(Product);
```

5. What is the output from the following program?

program Zebra(output);
var
    X, Y : integer;

procedure P2(**var** X: integer);
var
    Y : integer;

```
  begin {procedure P2}
    Y := 5;
    writeln(X, Y);
    X := X + Y;
    writeln(X, Y);
  end;   {procedure P2}

begin {main program}
  X := 2;
  Y := 3;
```

```
    writeln(X, Y);
    P2(Y);
    writeln(X, Y);
end.  {main program}
```

#6. What is the output from the following program?

```
program Kangaroo(output);
var
    X : integer;

procedure Kanga(var X: integer);

  procedure Roo(var Y: integer);

    begin {Roo}
      Y := 3;
      X := 7;
      writeln(X, Y);
    end;    {Roo}

  begin {Kanga}
    writeln(X);
    Roo(X);
    writeln(X);
  end; {Kanga}

procedure Roo2(var X: integer);

  begin {Roo2}
    writeln(X);
    X := 2;
    Kanga(X);
    X := 5;
  end; {Roo2}

begin {main program}
  X := 19;
  Roo2(X);
  writeln(X);
end. {main program}
```

7. What is the output from the following program? (Be careful—think about how variable parameters deal with memory spaces.)

```
program Gnu(output);
var
    A, B : integer;
```

```
procedure P3(var A, B: integer);

   begin {procedure P3}
     A := 2*A;
     writeln(A, B);
     B := A + B;
     writeln(A, B);
   end;  {procedure P3}

begin {main program}
  A := 5;
  B := 6;
  writeln(A, B);
  P3(B, B);
  writeln(A, B);
end.  {main program}
```

*8. What is the output from the following program?

```
program Doubler(output);
var
    Number, I : integer;

procedure DoThis(var A: integer);
  begin
    A := 2*A;
  end;

begin
  Number := 2;
  for I := 1 to 5 do
    begin
      DoThis(Number);
      writeln(Number);
    end;
end.
```

*9. What is the output from the following program if *Value* has the value 3.2?

```
program Choice(input, output);
var
    Value : real;

procedure Compute(Number: real);
  begin
    if Number > 4.5 then
      writeln(4*Number:3:1)
    else
```

```
        writeln(2*Number:3:1);
      end;


  begin
    readln(Value);
    Compute(Value);
    writeln(Value:3:1);
  end.
```

SKILL BUILDERS

1. Write a program to read in the base and height of a triangle and compute the area. Let the main program handle input and output but use a procedure to compute the area.

2. Modify your program from #1 to have the main program handle input while the procedure computes the area and writes the output.

3. Modify your program from #2 to use three procedures, one for input, one for computing the area, and one for output.

#4. Write a procedure that receives a parameter value for the radius of a sphere and returns the surface area $(A = 4(\text{pi})(\text{radius})^2)$.

5. Write a procedure that receives a parameter value for a distance in miles and returns the number of seconds and the number of minutes it takes for light to travel that distance (speed of light = 186,000 miles per second).

*6. Write a procedure that receives a parameter value for x and returns the value of the function $f(x) = 3x + 7$ if x is less than 5.0 and returns the value of the function $g(x) = 2x - 4$ otherwise.

SOFTWARE DEVELOPMENT PROJECTS

For the following projects, follow the standard Sample Software Development Project format, including problem specification, algorithm development, structure chart, discussion of program modules—including establishing the appropriate parameter lists, but using stubs where necessary—data flow diagram, the program itself, and at least one sample execution.

1. Develop software that reads in the present population of a country and that country's annual percentage rate of growth. The output is a table showing the population at the end of each of the next five years.

2. The volume V of a gas is given in terms of the temperature T and pressure P by the equation $V = kT/P$, where k is a constant. Develop software that reads one set of data for V, T, and P to determine the constant k and then computes the volume given any T and P values.

3. A bank customer will be paid simple interest based on a scale according to the amount of principal deposited. Develop software to read in the principal and a number of years and to write out the interest accumulated at the end of that number of years. (For simple interest, interest = (principal)*(rate)*(time).) Use a stub for a procedure to determine the interest rate.

4. A rectangular plaque can be manufactured in gold, silver, or bronze finish. The price of the plaque depends on the choice of material, the current market price of the material, and the dimensions. Develop software to read in the choice of material (use character data—G, S, or B), the market price per ounce of that material, and the dimensions of the plaque; the output consists of the total price for the plaque. Use a stub for a procedure to determine the cost per square inch based on the material and its current market price.

5. A nursery grows several different types of plants. Each type has a different water and nutrient requirement. Develop software to read in the plant type (use an integer), the number of square feet devoted to that plant type, and the cost per unit volume for water and nutrients. The program should output the total water and nutrient cost to the nursery for that plant type. Use stubs for two procedures that determine the volume of water per square foot for a plant type, and the volume of nutrients per square foot for a plant type, respectively.

*6. Use a counting loop to modify Sample Software Development Project #1 to print out the population at the end of each of the next twenty years.

TESTING AND MAINTENANCE DEPARTMENT

1. Test program *Postage* for all combinations of category and destination. How many possibilities are there?

2. Modify program *Postage* to print duplicate receipts, one for the post office and one for the customer.

3. Modify program *Postage* to read the current date and print it on the receipt.

4. Rewrite program *CatalogOrder* on page 44 to use three procedures, one for input, one for calculations, and one for output.

DEBUGGING CLINIC

Run and debug the following programs.

1. **program** Paint1(input, output);
{collects dimensions of rectangular area and cost of paint/gallon, computes cost to paint based on constant coverage of 500 sq. ft. per gallon}

const
    Coverage = 500;   {500 sq. ft. per gallon of paint}

```
var
    Length, Width : integer;    {dimensions of area to paint, in ft}
    Area : integer;             {area to paint}
    Gallons : real;             {gallons needed to cover Area}
    Cost : real;                {cost per gallon of paint}

procedure PaintNeeded(Length, Width: integer;
                        var Area: integer; var Gallons: real);
{computes Area from Length and Width, finds gallons needed
 to cover Area}

    procedure FindGallons(Area: integer; var Gallons: real);
    {computes Gallons needed to cover Area}

        begin    {procedure FindGallons}
        Gallons := Area/Coverage;
        end;     {procedure FindGallons}

    begin    {procedure PaintNeeded}
    Area := Length*Width;
    end;     {procedure PaintNeeded}

procedure ComputeCost(Gallons: real; var Cost: real);
{computes Cost for amount of paint Gallons}

var
    Price : real;                        {price per gallon}

    begin    {procedure ComputeCost}
    writeln('What is the price per gallon for paint? ');
    readln(Price);
    Cost := Price*Gallons;
    end;     {procedure ComputeCost}

begin    {main program}
  writeln('Give length and width of area to be painted.');
  writeln('Length (in feet): ');
  readln(Length);
  writeln('Width (in feet): ');
  readln(Width);
  PaintNeeded(Length, Width, Area, Gallons);
  FindGallons(Area, Gallons);
  ComputeCost(Gallons, Cost);
  writeln('The cost to paint this area is $', Cost:6:2);
end.    {main program}
```

2. **program** Paint2(input, output);
{collects dimensions of rectangular area and cost of paint/gallon,
 computes cost to paint based on constant coverage of 500 sq. ft.
 per gallon}

```pascal
const
    Coverage = 500;      {500 sq. ft. per gallon of paint}

var
    Area : integer;              {area to paint}
    Gallons : real;              {gallons needed to cover Area}
    Cost : real;                 {cost per gallon of paint}

procedure FindArea(var Area: integer);
{reads Length and Width, computes Area}

var
    Length, Width : integer;   {dimensions of area to paint, in ft}

  begin    {procedure FindArea}
  writeln('Give length and width of area to be painted.');
  writeln('Length (in feet): ');
  readln(Length);
  writeln('Width (in feet): ');
  readln(Width);
  Area := Length*Width;
  end;      {procedure FindArea}

procedure FindGallons(Area: integer; Gallons: real);
{computes Gallons needed to cover Area}

  begin    {procedure FindGallons}
  Gallons := Area/Coverage;
  end;      {procedure FindGallons}

procedure ComputeCost(Gallons: real; var Cost: real);
{computes Cost tor amount of paint Gallons}

var
    Price : real;                    {price per gallon}

  begin    {procedure ComputeCost}
  writeln('What is the price per gallon for paint? ');
  readln(Price);
  Cost := Price*Gallons;
  end;      {procedure ComputeCost}

begin    {main program}
  FindArea(Area);
  FindGallons(Area, Gallons);
  ComputeCost(Gallons, Cost);
  writeln('The cost to paint this area is $', Cost:6:2);
  end.      {main program}
```

3. **program** Paint3(input, output);
{collects dimensions of two rectangular areas and cost of paint/gallon, computes cost to paint based on constant coverage of 500 sq. ft. per gallon}

const
    Coverage = 500;   {500 sq. ft. per gallon of paint}

var
    Area1, Area2 : integer;   {areas of 2 rectangles}
    Area : integer;   {total area to paint}
    Gallons : real;   {gallons needed to cover Area}
    Cost : real;   {cost per gallon of paint}

procedure FindArea(**var** Area: integer);
{reads Length and Width, computes Area}

var
    Length, Width : integer;   {dimensions of area to paint, in ft.}
    begin   {procedure FindArea}
    writeln('Give length and width of area to be painted.');
    writeln('Length (in feet): ');
    readln(Length);
    writeln('Width (in feet): ');
    readln(Width);
    Area1 := Length*Width;
    Area2 := Length*Width;
    end;   {procedure FindArea}

procedure FindGallons(Area: integer; **var** Gallons: real);
{computes Gallons needed to cover Area}

    begin   {procedure FindGallons}
    Gallons := Area/Coverage;
    end;   {procedure FindGallons}

procedure ComputeCost(Gallons: real; **var** Cost: real);
{computes Cost for amount of paint Gallons}

var
    Price : real;   {price per gallon}

    begin   {procedure ComputeCost}
    writeln('What is the price per gallon for paint? ');
    readln(Price);
    Cost := Price*Gallons;
    end;   {procedure ComputeCost}

```
begin    {main program}
  FindArea(Area1);
  FindArea(Area2);
  Area := Area1 + Area2;
  FindGallons(Area, Gallons);
  ComputeCost(Gallons, Cost);
  writeln('The cost to paint this area is $', Cost:6:2);
end.    {main program}
```

CHAPTER FIVE

MORE ARITHMETIC; INTERNAL DOCUMENTATION

5.1 Arithmetic Expressions

The standard arithmetic operations of addition, subtraction, multiplication, and division are represented by the arithmetic operator symbols $+$, $-$, $*$, and $/$, respectively. We have already used *arithmetic expressions,* which consist of combinations of numeric constants, numeric variables, and arithmetic operators. For example,

A + 2*B and 3.4 − Value

are arithmetic expressions, where *A, B,* and *Value* are numeric variables. There are some details about expressions that haven't been mentioned, however.

The division operator / works exactly as one would expect. For example, 13/4 gives the real value 3.25. This division problem can also be expressed by saying that 13 divided by 4 gives a quotient of 3 with a remainder of 1. The Pascal reserved words **div** and **mod** represent the operations of finding the integer quotient and the integer remainder, respectively, that result from dividing two integers. These words are used like the other arithmetic operator symbols. From the above example,

$$13 \textbf{ div } 4 \ = 3 \text{ (quotient)}$$
$$13 \textbf{ mod } 4 = 1 \text{ (remainder)}$$

As another example,

$$-18 \textbf{ div } 6 \ = -3$$
$$-18 \textbf{ mod } 6 = \ 0$$

Operands		Operator					
		+	−	*	/	div	mod
integer	integer	integer	integer	integer	real	integer	integer
integer	real	real	real	real	real	illegal	illegal
real	integer	real	real	real	real	illegal	illegal
real	real	real	real	real	real	illegal	illegal

FIGURE 5.1   Data type of the result when a binary operation is performed.

The second value in the **mod** operation must be positive, so the above expression could not be written as 18 **mod** −6.

Because the variables and constants in an arithmetic expression are numeric, a data type is associated with each one. The result of evaluating an expression will also be numeric and must have an associated data type. How is that data type determined?

The operators div and mod can only be used with integer operands and produce integer values.

The **div** and **mod** operators can use only type *integer* values for the numbers upon which they operate (their **operands**), and the resulting value will be an integer. The other four operators (+, −, *, /) can use any combination of type *integer* and type *real* operands. The result will always be type *real* for /. For the other three operators, the result will be type *integer* if both operands are type *integer*, otherwise it will be type *real*. This information is summarized in Figure 5.1.

As an example, the result of evaluating

$3*2.4$

*The arithmetic operators +, −, *, and / will always produce a real value if either of the operands is real.*

is the real value 7.2. Because integers and real numbers are represented differently in memory, the process for arithmetic on the binary representation of two integers differs from that for arithmetic on the binary representation of two real numbers. There's no way to handle a mixture. The expression 3*2.4 is evaluated as follows: The representation in memory of the integer value 3 is changed to the representation of the real number 3.0, and the operation is then carried out using real number arithmetic. The result is a real number representation.

The operations of Figure 5.1 are **binary operations** because they manipulate two operands to produce a third value as a result. The operation of taking the negative of a number is a **unary operation.** Pascal uses the standard minus sign as the operator symbol for this operation. Just as in ordinary algebra, two operators cannot appear together. To multiply 5.1 by −6.4, for example, we have to write

$5.1*(-6.4)$

One operation available in many programming languages is, unfortunately, not included in Pascal: the operation of **exponentiation,** raising to a power. No nice symbol, say, @, exists that will allow us to write $X @Y$ and mean

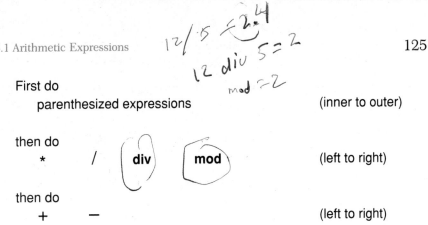

First do

    parenthesized expressions   (inner to outer)

then do

    *   /   div   mod   (left to right)

then do

    +   —   (left to right)

FIGURE 5.2 Rules of operator precedence.

$$X^Y$$

If the power to which we want to raise X is a positive integer, we can do repeated multiplications, as in

$$X^3 = X*X*X$$

For a more general way to do exponentiation, we'll wait until the next chapter. The lack of an exponentiation operation is a minor irritation when dealing with scientific or engineering applications where formulas often involve exponents.

5.1.1 *Operator Precedence*

In complex expressions, there must be a way of deciding which operations will be performed first. Just as in ordinary algebra, parentheses help make clear the order of evaluation, as quantities in parentheses are evaluated first. In case of nested parentheses, the evaluation is done from the innermost set of parentheses outward. Some parentheses can be omitted because of precedence rules, conventions about which operators take **precedence** (are performed first) over others. Multiplications and divisions (including **div** and **mod**) are done before additions and subtractions. If there is a "tie," that is, the operators are of equal precedence, then the operations are done from left to right (see Fig. 5.2).

According to these rules of operator precedence,

    1 + 3/4

is interpreted as 1 + (3/4) because / has a higher precedence than +. If we want to indicate that the addition is to be done first, then we must write (1 + 3)/4.

The expression

    2 + 6 **div** 2 − 4/2 + 5

is evaluated as follows:

$$2 + 6 \textbf{ div } 2 - 4/2 + 5 = 2 + (6 \textbf{ div } 2) - (4/2) + 5 \text{ (divisions}$$
$$\text{have higher}$$
$$\text{precedence)}$$
$$= 2 + 3 - 2.0 + 5$$
$$= 5 - 2.0 + 5 \text{ (left to right)}$$
$$= 3.0 + 5 \text{ (left to right–note real result after}$$
$$\text{subtraction of a real value from}$$
$$\text{an integer value)}$$
$$= 8.0$$

CHECKUP 5.1   What is the value of each of the following expressions? Assume that X has the value 4.2, Y has the value 6.0, and Z has the integer value 3.

a. $Z/Y + Z \textbf{ div } 3*8$
b. $(X - Y)/Z + 2$
c. $3*Z \textbf{ mod } 7 + (X - Y)*2$
d. $Z*(2 + 3*(4 - Z*(2 - 5 \textbf{ mod } 3)))$
e. $2*Z \textbf{ div } (Z - 3)/(Y - 7)*X$

Use parentheses to override the default rules of operator precedence or to clarify the order of operations in an expression.

Although rules of operator precedence allow elimination of some parentheses, the object is to write an expression in the clearest possible manner. Even though

$$A/B*C \text{ and } (A/B)*C$$

give the same value, the second expression is clearer. Parentheses should always be used when there might be the slightest possibility of confusion for the human reader.

Clarity in writing expressions is often a judgment call. Is it clearer to write the expression

```
(Temp2 - Temp1)/(time2 - time1)
```

or to assign

```
TemperatureDifference := Temp2 - Temp1;
TimeDifference := time2 - time1;
```

and then write

```
TemperatureDifference/TimeDifference
```

Although a particular application may make one approach preferable, the choice is probably a matter of programming style. Above all, the decision should be based on achieving maximum clarity, not on the fact that one approach requires three statements and the other only one. Typing time is cheaper than confusion time!

5.1.2 *New Uses for Expressions*

Expressions can be used in place of single variables or constants in two instances we haven't yet mentioned. One is in a *write* or *writeln* statement. The following is a legitimate statement:

writeln(Distance, 3*Speed/10);

Expressions can be used in write statements; integer expressions can be used as field width specifications.

Second, an integer expression (one that evaluates to an integer value) can be used as a field-width specification. For example,

write(X:Tab + 1);

writes the value of X in a field of width (*Tab* + 1) spaces. This idea is useful if the spacing of the program output depends in some way on the program data.

5.1.3 *Surprising Arithmetic with Real Numbers*

Because the number of significant digits of a real number that can be stored in computer memory is limited, inaccuracies can be introduced into real number computations even when the original data has been stored accurately. As a decimal number illustration, if our computer can store only five significant decimal digits, then it can represent the values 324.15 and 4.2 accurately. When these numbers are multiplied, their product is 1361.43. Because memory has a five significant-digit limit, this product is stored as 1361.4, a value 0.03 off from the correct answer. If this answer is then used in another computation, and that result used in still another computation, etc., the cumulative effect of such **round-off errors** can be significant.

Real number arithmetic can cause a seeming violation of the rules of algebra. Algebraically, the two quantities

$$(A - B) + C \text{ and } (A + C) - B$$

produce identical results for any real values A, B, and C. But, if the values A and C differ greatly in size, the computed results may not be identical. Try the following two statements on your computer system:

writeln((2.0E16 − 2.0E16) + 1.0);
writeln((2.0E16 + 1.0) − 2.0E16);

The correct result is 1.0 in either case. The first statement probably gives the correct result; the second statement may give 0.0 as an answer. (If not, raise the exponent to a larger value.) What has happened here?

The grade-school algorithm to add decimal values is to line up the decimal points and add the digits. The computer works with its binary representation in much the same way. If the two numbers being added are of vastly different sizes, as is the case with 2.0E16 + 1.0 above, then after "lining up the decimal points," the total spread of digits may exceed the number of significant digits that can be stored. The least significant digits (the number 1 in this case) are lost. Exactly when this becomes a problem depends on the architecture of the particular computer; that's why the second statement above may or may not give the correct answer on your system.

5.1.5 Assignment Statements Again

Integer values can be assigned to variables of type real, but real values cannot be assigned to variables of type integer

The assignment statement allows the current value of an expression to be assigned to a variable. For a numerical expression, we use our knowledge of how expressions are evaluated to avoid type clashes. Either real or integer values can be assigned to a real variable, but an integer value will get changed to the corresponding real value. Only integer values can be assigned to integer variables.

For example, if *I* is an integer variable, the assignment

```
I := I + 12/4;
```

would result in a type clash, although at first glance it seems that only integers are involved. However, 12/4 always produces a value of type *real*—the result is not 3, but 3.0. Then *I* + 12/4 also becomes a real value and cannot be assigned to an integer variable.

Any variables used in an expression must have already received a value, either by a *read* or *readln* statement, or by an assignment statement. If we want a running total, for example, we can use a statement like

```
Total := Total + NewTerm;
```

a number of times. We can give *Total* an initial value (perhaps 0.0) by an assignment statement preceding the first instance of the above statement. Often the first few statements in the body of a program are for **initialization of variables.** (We cannot assume that uninitialized variables have a value of zero, or any other particular value.)

CHECKUP 5.2   Which of the following assignments are not legal? Assume that *I* and *J* are type *integer*, *X* is type *real*.

```
a. X := 2*J;
b. I := 3.0 + J;
c. J := 4*J/I;
d. I := 6*J mod 5;
e. J := X div J;
```

---

6. Documenting

5.2 Internal Documentation

We have stressed that program documentation is an ongoing part of the programming process. It helps the program developer keep in mind all the details of the program. It helps others who may be part of the same programming team to understand how this code will fit in with the rest of the program. It helps the program user, and it helps those who must maintain the code in the future. In this section we'll discuss ***internal documentation,*** documentation that is part of the program code itself.

5.2.1 *Comments*

The prologue comment for a program should give a problem statement and perhaps a "history" of the program and overview of the solution method.

Comments are an important part of internal documentation. The program should contain an opening comment or ***prologue comment*** that appears right after the program heading and explains the overall nature of the problem to be solved. The prologue comment might also include a general description of the approach used to solve the problem, and any special restrictions or assumptions about the problem that have been incorporated into the program. It may list the procedures invoked by the main program and briefly describe the purpose of each as part of the overall algorithm. Information on the program's author and the completion date of the initial program version can be included. Over the life of the program, brief descriptions of program modifications, their dates, and their authors should be added to this opening comment.

The prologue comment for a procedure should include a statement of what the procedure does, explanations of the formal parameters, and, perhaps, what procedures invoke this one, and what procedures it invokes.

Each procedure should also contain an opening comment describing the particular subtask that the procedure carries out and perhaps an indication of the method used. The opening comment is also a good place to describe the purpose of each formal parameter in the heading. It might also include a list of the procedures that invoke this procedure, and a list of the procedures invoked by this procedure. This information should be consistent with the data flow diagram, if one was done as part of the program design.

Opening comments for both the main program and for procedures should be sufficiently descriptive that a quick reading of these comments provides an overview of the entire program. Most of the content for opening comments should not require a special effort to obtain. The problem statement, with any restrictions or assumptions, is part of the problem specification. The breakdown into modules, with the establishment of the module interfaces, was part of the algorithm development process. Early pseudocode descriptions of what a procedure does and how it does it can be incorporated as part of the procedure opening comment. If you use a word processor to outline your initial thinking about the problem, this information will even be electronically stored, ready to incorporate into a program file as comments.

Comments in the declarations section of the main program and of the procedures explain the meaning and purpose of constants and variables. Unlike some languages, Pascal allows comments to be "in line," part of a line of code that contains another program statement. The comment for a particular constant or variable can be written right on the same line in which that item is declared. In large programs, it is helpful to group the variables in the declarations section, either alphabetically or by their function in the program. This makes it easier to look back and find a particular variable when you read the program and want a reminder of what that variable stands for.

The various **begin-end** pairs that occur throughout the program should be commented to denote what is being bounded. This helps point out the structure of the program logic.

Our programs so far have been quite simple. As programs get more complex, it is helpful to indicate by a comment what a particular section of code accomplishes. A series of comments like

Use comments to describe variables, explain sections of code, and identify begin-end pairs.

```
X := X + 1;              {adding 1 to X}
```

provides little illumination about the nature of the algorithm; indeed, it just distracts. Too many trivial comments, then, are not helpful. On the other hand, several hundred lines of code without a comment is not a good idea either. Use comments roughly in the manner paragraphs are used in English—when a major new idea comes along, describe what's happening. Comments should make the program easier to understand, so the comments themselves should be easy to understand. "Computerese"—technical comments that are rather meaningless to the uninitiated, or that describe low-level details of the code—should be avoided. Comments are supposed to provide the big picture.

Comments can help in program development. They outline the program structure and should therefore, in some sense, be done first, with the rest of the code filled in later. Students who display programs without comments often say, when asked where the comments are, "I haven't put them in yet." These folks have missed the point and have also bypassed a valuable programming tool.

Keep comments up-to-date as the program changes.

As with all parts of program documentation, it is important to keep comments up-to-date. A comment that no longer describes the current code is worse than none at all. As changes in the program are made, comments must be changed accordingly. Documentation, as we stated earlier, is an ongoing part of the programming process.

5.2.2 Self-Documenting Code

A program is **self-documenting** when elements of the program itself help document the program, i.e., explain how it works. (Although "self-documenting program" or "self-documenting code" is standard terminology, it should not be taken to mean that no other form of documentation is necessary.)

Meaningful identifiers for both variables and modules are part of self-documenting code. "Cute" identifiers should be avoided. The point is to be enlightening about the nature of the item being named, not to be witty or clever.†

Identifiers for procedures should be especially meaningful. It should be possible to read the main program, consisting of a number of procedure invocations, and tell by the names of the procedures the general idea of what

---

†As we noted earlier, an underscore in an identifier, used to separate words, is not allowed in standard Pascal. In our sample programs we have used capitalization to help distinguish words, as in RateOfPay.

Use meaningful identifiers for variables and procedures.

the program does. (The very fact that the program is written as a series of modules, instead of as one huge piece of code, is also part of the internal documentation of the program because it makes the program easier to understand.)

Another aspect of self-documenting code is the use of **white space,** that part of a printed page that is blank. Margins, blank lines, and indentations are white space. We earlier agreed to put only one program statement (or a statement plus a comment) on a line. We have used blank lines to separate various parts of the program declaration section, and to set off groups of related statements in a program, much as paragraphs are used in English. We have indented to help distinguish one procedure from

Use white space to clarify the code.

another, and to help distinguish procedures from the main program. As our programs use more complex structures, we will make further use of indentation to identify a compound statement. None of this spacing is required by Pascal, so it is up to us to impose these additional aids to program readability.

The format to be followed for indenting is a matter of choice–programming style again. The important thing is to settle on a system of indentation that seems clear and to be consistent in its use. We have used a consistent indentation system in our sample programs, and you may choose to use that as a model. Some Pascal systems for microcomputers have a built-in indentation system as part of the program entering process; the cursor on the screen is automatically placed at what the system considers the appropriate column for the start of each program statement. Many mainframes have a **pretty printer** program that takes a Pascal program as input and returns as output that same program in a consistently indented style. These aids to indentation are nice as long as the system-imposed indentation format is acceptable. A company may, for consistency or compliance with government documentation standards, enforce its own indentation conventions on all of its programs.

5.3 Sample Software Development Project—Shipping

Problem Statement

You work in the shipping department of the Byte-Right Dog Food Company. Retail stores send orders for shipments of dog food. The dog food comes in 100-lb., 10-lb., and 1-lb. bags. You want to ship the order using the fewest number of bags.

Problem Specification

An order is an integer value giving the amount in pounds to be shipped. In order to use the fewest number of bags, you want to send as many 100-lb. bags as possible, then as many 10-lb. bags as possible, and then 1-lb. bags to finish the order. Output should be the original order and the number of bags of each size required to fill the order.

Input: order size (in pounds)

Output: order size
> number of 100-lb. bags to send
> number of 10-lb. bags to send
> number of 1-lb. bags to send

Algorithm Development

As a sample calculation, if the order is for 437 lb. of Byte-Right dog food, you want to ship this order using four 100-lb. bags, three 10-lb. bags, and seven 1-lb. bags. You need to determine the number of 100s, the number of 10s, and the number of 1s in the order. This can be accomplished by using the **div** and **mod** operations. Computing 437 **div** 100 will give the value 4, the number of 100-lb. bags to ship, and 437 **mod** 100 will give the remainder 37. We repeat the process with the value 37 and the divisor 10. Computing 37 **div** 10 will give the value 3, the number of 10-lb. bags to ship, and 37 **mod** 10 will give the value 7, which is the number of 1-lb. bags to ship. We'll put all these calculations in a procedure, with separate procedures to read the size of the order and to write the output. The structure chart appears in Figure 5.3.

Read Order

This procedure collects the order and returns it to the main program. The procedure thus has only one parameter, the variable parameter *Order*.

```
procedure ReadOrder(var Order: integer);
{gets the order amount, Order, and returns it to the main
 program}

begin   {procedure ReadOrder}

  prompt for and read order size

end;    {procedure ReadOrder}
```

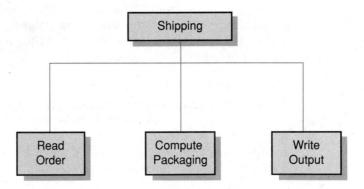

FIGURE 5.3 Structure chart for program *Shipping*.

Compute Packaging

This procedure needs to know the value of *Order* from the main program and returns the number of each size bag to ship to fill the order. As discussed above, we'll use the **div** and **mod** operations.

```
procedure ComputePackaging(Order: integer;
                        var Hundreds, Tens, Ones: integer);
{finds the number of Hundreds, Tens, and Ones in the
 integer Order}

var
    RestOfOrder : integer;   {order after removing the 100s}

begin   {procedure ComputePackaging}

    find Order div 100    (number of 100-lb. bags)
    find Order mod 100    (RestOfOrder)
    find RestOfOrder div 10 (number of 10-lb.  bags)
    find RestOfOrder mod 10 (number of 1-lb.  bags)

end;   {procedure ComputePackaging}
```

Write Output

This procedure needs to know the results from *ComputePackaging* in order to write them out; it will also write out the original order.

```
procedure WriteOutput(Order, Hundreds, Tens, Ones: integer);
{writes the number of each size bag to ship}
```

As usual, the main program will simply call the three procedures in the appropriate order. We'll leave the data flow diagram for an exercise. The complete program appears below.

```
program Shipping(input, output);
{given an order for Byte-Right Dog Food, decides on number
of 100-lb. bags, 10-lb. bags, and 1-lb. bags needed to fill order
with  fewest  number  of  bags}

var
    Order : integer;        {size of order in lbs.}
    Hundreds : integer;     {number of 100-lb. bags to fill order}
    Tens : integer;         {number of 10-lb. bags to fill order}
    Ones : integer;         {number of 1-lb. bags to fill order}
```

```
procedure ReadOrder(var Order: integer);
{gets the order amount, Order, and returns it to the main
 program}

  begin      {procedure ReadOrder}
    write('Give the order size in lb. : ');
    readln(Order);
  end;      {procedure ReadOrder}

procedure ComputePackaging(Order: integer;
                              var Hundreds, Tens, Ones: integer);
{finds the number of Hundreds, Tens, and Ones in the
 integer Order}

var
    RestOfOrder : integer;    {order after removing the 100s}

  begin      {procedure ComputePackaging}
    Hundreds := Order div 100;    {number of 100s in Order}
    RestOfOrder := Order mod 100;
    Tens := RestOfOrder div 10;    {number of 10s in Order}
    Ones := RestOfOrder mod 10;    {number of 1s in Order}
  end;      {procedure ComputePackaging}

procedure WriteOutput(Order, Hundreds, Tens, Ones: integer);
{writes the number of each size bag to ship}

  begin      {procedure WriteOutput}
    writeln;
    writeln('Fill order of ', Order:5, ' lb. as follows:');
    writeln;
    writeln('      100-lb. bags: ', Hundreds:3);
    writeln('       10-lb. bags: ', Tens:3);
    writeln('        1-lb. bags: ', Ones:3);
  end;      {procedure WriteOutput}

begin      {main program}
  ReadOrder(Order);
  ComputePackaging(Order, Hundreds, Tens, Ones);
  WriteOutput(Order, Hundreds, Tens, Ones);
end.      {main program}
```

RUNNING THE PROGRAM...

Give the order size in lb. : 437

Fill order of   437 lb. as follows:

        100-lb. bags: 4

10-lb. bags:	3
1-lb. bags:	7

View #5

The water pollution project at Sterling is coming along nicely. You have now identified the modules for your program and the functional requirements for each. At this point you can write the input procedure, since it consists only of a series of prompts and reads, and the procedure to compute the bacteria-to-water ratio, since it consists of a simple real number division. You can also determine the form for the output. You decide to write stubs for the procedure that checks whether the threshold has been exceeded and for the output procedure. In this way you can get a running program.

The output must include the site ID number, the date of the sample, the amount of water, the bacteria count, the resulting bacteria-to-water ratio, and possibly a warning message. You decide that a table of the following form would make the information easy to understand at a glance.

Site ID	Date	Water	Bacteria	Level	Warning
235	04/17/87	1200 ml	3600	3.00	***

Nothing would appear under the column "Warning" if the level is not exceeded.

The following version of the program builds upon the outline developed in Chapter 4. There the main program had already been completed, along with the procedure headings, including the formal parameter lists, for each of the four procedures. In the following version, the procedures *GetInput* and *ComputeRatio* have been completed. A stub has been written for *CheckThreshold*. *WriteOutput* has been partially completed, dealing with everything except the flag for the warning, which needs information from *CheckThreshold*. A sample program execution shows that the logic of the program is working as far as it has been implemented.

```
program WaterPollution(input, output);
{tests water sample from a site against a pollution threshold,
 issues a warning if the bacteria level is too high}

const
    Threshold = 2.0;        {200 bacteria per 100 ml water}

var
    ID : integer;           {site ID number}
    Water : integer;        {amount of water sampled, in ml}
    Bacteria : integer;     {bacteria count in sample}
    Mon1, Mon2 : char;      {two-digit month notation}
    Day1, Day2 : char;      {two-digit date notation}
    Yr1, Yr2 : char;        {two-digit year notation}
```

```
Warning : boolean;      {flag for warning message if
                         pollution level too high}
Level : real;           {pollution level for this
                         sample}

procedure GetInput(var ID, Water, Bacteria: integer;
               var Mon1, Mon2, Day1, Day2,
               Yr1, Yr2: char);
{procedure to collect input for water pollution data; amount
 Water of water and count Bacteria of bacteria were obtained
 from site  ID on date Mon1Mon2/Day1Day2/Yr1Yr2}

var
    Slash : char;       {separating / in date format}

  begin      {procedure GetInput}
    write('Enter the site ID number: ');
    readln(ID);
    writeln;

    writeln('Enter the date of this sample.');
    write('Use month/date/year format: ');
    readln(Mon1, Mon2, Slash, Day1, Day2, Slash, Yr1, Yr2);
    writeln;

    write('Enter the amount of water in sample (in ml): ');
    readln(Water);
    writeln;

    write('Enter the bacteria count found in this sample: ');
    readln(Bacteria);
  end;        {procedure GetInput}

procedure ComputeRatio(Bacteria, Water: integer;
                      var Ratio: real);
{computes the Ratio of Bacteria to Water}

  begin      {procedure ComputeRatio}
    Ratio := Bacteria/Water;
  end;       {procedure ComputeRatio}

procedure CheckThreshold(Ratio: real;
                       var Over: boolean);
{compares Ratio to the global constant Threshold and sets
 Over to true if that limit is exceeded}

  begin      {stub for procedure Check Threshold}
    writeln;
    writeln('execution has reached procedure CheckThreshold');
  end;        {procedure CheckThreshold}
```

```
procedure WriteOutput(ID, Water, Bacteria: integer;
                      Mon1, Mon2, Day1, Day2,
                      Yr1, Yr2: char;
                      Ratio: real;
                      Warning: boolean);
{echoes site input data and writes warning message if warranted}

    begin    {procedure WriteOutput}
      writeln;
      writeln;
      write('Site ID', 'Date':8, 'Water':12, 'Bacteria':13);
      writeln('Level':9, 'Warning':10);
      write('_____' );
      writeln('_____' );
      writeln;
      write(ID:5, Mon1:6, Mon2, '/', Day1, Day2, '/', Yr1, Yr2);
      write(Water:8, ' ml', Bacteria:9, Ratio:11:2);
      writeln;
    end;     {procedure WriteOutput}

  begin    {main program}

    GetInput(ID, Water, Bacteria,
             Mon1, Mon2, Day1, Day2, Yr1, Yr2);

    ComputeRatio(Bacteria, Water, Level);

    CheckThreshold(Level, Warning);

    WriteOutput(ID, Water, Bacteria,
                Mon1, Mon2, Day1, Day2, Yr1, Yr2,
                Level, Warning);
  end.       {main program}
```

RUNNING THE PROGRAM...

Enter the site ID number: 235

Enter the date of this sample.
Use month/date/year format: 04/17/87

Enter the amount of water in sample (in ml): 1200

Enter the bacteria count found in this sample: 3600

execution has reached procedure CheckThreshold

Site ID	Date	Water	Bacteria	Level	Warning
235	04/17/87	1200 ml	3600	3.00	

In program *WaterPollution*, blank lines have been inserted in procedure *GetInput* and in the main program to add to readability. In procedure *WriteOutput* fieldwidth specifications are used to space the columns in the table. Lining up the column headings and the data, and getting the underline the right length, took a couple of tries.

(Note: Sterling Software Systems should show the manager of the Lodestone County Water Pollution Department output from this prototype software, and explain how the "Warning" column will be handled. If the manager wishes to make changes in the user interface, i.e., how the input is entered or what the output should look like, now is the time. Having agreed to the prototype, the manager cannot change his or her mind after Sterling has invested a lot of development time without expecting to pay them for the extra trouble. However, if the final product does not perform according to this prototype, the manager has the right to refuse to sign off on the contract.)

CASE STUDY TWO

View #5

Sterling's project for the hypertension clinic is also making progress. Building on your work in Chapter 4, write the modules of the program that collect the input and that compute the average pressure for the patient. Write stubs for any remaining modules but partially complete the output module so that it prints the table headings as designed in Chapter 3 and also the patient ID number, date, and average pressure. The column under "Classification" will be blank for now. Run the program for several different sets of input.

*(Items marked with * make use of optional material on Simple Control Structures from Chapter 3.)*

EXERCISES

1. Is the following equation true?
   18.0 **div** 6.0 = 3.0

#2. Is the following equation true?
   24 **mod** 7 = 3

3. What is the result of evaluating 4 **div** 8?

#4. What is the data type of the result of evaluating the expression
   4 **div** 2 + 7 + 6/2

#5. Evaluate the expression
   $8*A + B/C + D$
where $A = 3, B = 10, C = 5, D = 2$.

6. Evaluate the expression
   $4*A - (B*A + 5/(A - 6 \text{ mod } B))$
where $A = 2$ and $B = 3$.

7. What output is produced by

```
        writeln(2*A  +  2:  2*A  −  2);
```
if *A* has the value 3?

#8. Add data flow information to the structure chart of Figure 5.3.

*9. Write a single statement that prints a 1-digit positive integer *M* in column *T* if $M \geq 5$ and prints it in column $T + 4$ if $M < 5$; *T* is a positive integer less than 60.

SKILL BUILDERS

1. Write a program that reads a real number and prints its square.

2. Write a program that reads an integral value for *x* and evaluates the polynomial $4x^2 + 3x - 6$.

#3. Write a program that reads a real value for *x* and evaluates the expression

$$\frac{2x - 1}{4x - 2}$$

4. Write a program that reads a real value for *x* and evaluates the expression

$$\frac{2x - 1}{4x} - 2$$

5. Write a program that reads a temperature in degrees Fahrenheit and converts it to degrees Celsius, using the formula

$$F = \frac{9}{5} C + 32$$

*6. Write a program that evaluates the polynomial of Skill Builder #2 above for all integral values of *x* between 1 and 10, inclusive; use a counting loop.

SOFTWARE DEVELOPMENT PROJECTS

Remember that Software Development Projects are to follow the format of the Sample Software Development Projects and include problem specification, algorithm development, structure chart, discussion of and pseudocode for program modules, the program itself—with good internal documentation—and at least one sample program execution.

1. The height *S* (in feet) of a thrown or dropped object at time *T* (seconds) is given by the equation

$$S = -16T^2 + V_0 T + S_0$$

where V_0 is the initial velocity (positive if object is thrown up, negative if object is thrown down) and S_0 is the initial height. Develop software to read in V_0 and S_0 and compute *S* for any time *T.*

2. The electrical resistance R of a wire is given in terms of the length L and the diameter D by the equation $R = kL/(D)^2$, where k is a constant that depends on the material in the wire. Develop software that reads one set of data for R, L, and D to determine the constant k, and then computes the resistance given any L and D values.

3. A full page of text contains 60 lines; an average word contains 7 characters. Develop software to help the Petunia Printing Press estimate the number of characters in a book, given the number of full pages and the average number of words per line; figure an additional half page for every 20 full pages.

4. The current I in an electrical circuit is given in terms of the resistance R by the equation $I = k/R$. Develop software that computes the change in I for a given change in R.

5. As a security measure, the Hotel Swank codes the room number on its guest room keys. The code on the key is a three-digit integer that is the reverse of the actual room number; if the integer 321 appears on the key, for example, the room number is 123. Develop software to read in the coded number (as a single integer) and output the room number.

*6. Develop software to add an even parity bit to a 5-bit binary word, that is, a string of 5 0s and 1s is read in and a sixth bit is added to the end so as to make the total number of 1s an even number. The program should write out the 6-bit result. Parity bits provide a simple form of error detection when transmitting binary messages.

TESTING AND MAINTENANCE DEPARTMENT

1. Run program *Shipping* for order values that are over 1000 lbs. Run it for order values that are less than 100 lbs. What happens with an order value of 0 lbs?

2. Byte-Right Dog Food is no longer packaging dog food in 100-lb. bags; the largest bag is now 50 lb. Modify program *Shipping* accordingly.

DEBUGGING CLINIC

1. What's wrong with the following program?

```
program cookie(input, output);
{divides an even number N of cookies into 2 piles of N/2 cookies
 each}

var
     N : integer;      {original number of cookies, an even number}

begin
   writeln('Enter number of cookies, an even number: ');
```

```
      readln(N);
      writeln;
      write('Dividing these cookies into 2 piles, each pile');
      writeln(' contains ', N/2:5:2, ' cookies.');
   end.
```

2. Improve the internal documentation of the following "correct" program.

```
program Poor(input, output);
var    R,S,X,Y,Z,W : real;
procedure A(var P,Q,R:real);
begin
R := P*Q;
end;
begin
write('Enter price per pound for meat: ');readln(X);
write('Enter price per gallon for drink: ');readln(Y);
write('Enter amount of meat in pounds: ');readln(Z);
write('Enter amount of drink in gallons: ');readln(W);
A(X,Z,R);writeln('$',R:7:2);
A(Y,W,S);writeln('$',S:7:2);
end.
```

CHAPTER SIX

FUNCTIONS; DEBUGGING

6.1 Functions

Functions, like procedures, are modules of code to carry out a specific subtask identified in the program design. The overall format for a function declaration is

function heading
declarations
  begin
    statements
  end;

A function may be thought of as a procedure with limited capabilities in that a function computes only a single value, based upon any number of input values, and returns that single value to the invoking program.

6.1.1 A Function Example

As an example, suppose we want to read three real values and compute their average. We can use the main program to read the values and write the output, and a function to compute the average. The program below does the job.

```
program Average1(input, output);
{reads and averages three real values; values assumed to be under
 100,000 with no more than three decimal places}

var
     Value1, Value2, Value3 : real;    {the values}
```

143

```
function Average(x, y, z: real): real;
{finds the average of three real values}

    begin    {function Average}
      Average := (x + y + z)/3.0;
    end;     {function Average}

begin    {main program}

  {input section}
  writeln('Give the three values to be averaged.');
  write('First value: ');
  readln(Value1);
  write('Second value: ');
  readln(Value2);
  write('Third value: ');
  readln(Value3);

  {output section}
  writeln;
  write('The average of ', Value1:9:3, ', ', Value2:9:3, ', and ');
  writeln(Value3:9:3, ' is:');
  writeln;
  writeln(Average(Value1, Value2, Value3):25:3);
end.     {main program}
```

RUNNING THE PROGRAM...

```
Give the three values to be averaged.
First value: 2576.04
Second value: 347.897
Third value: 87005.67

The average of    2576.040,    347.897, and 87005.670 is:

        29976.536
```

In program *Average1*, the module of code that declares the function consists of

```
function Average(x, y, z: real): real;
{finds the average of three real values}

    begin    {function Average}
      Average := (x + y + z)/3.0;
    end;     {function Average}
```

This code is similar to a procedure declaration. In the heading, the reserved word **function** is used, rather than **procedure,** followed by the function name. This can be any Pascal identifier but, unlike a procedure name, it not only references a module of code but also refers to a memory location where the single value computed by the function will be stored. This location, that is, this function value, must be assigned a data type; this assignment occurs at the very end of the function heading. Between the function name and the function value data type in the heading appears the list of formal parameters the function will use, together with their data types. The body of the function computes the average of the three formal parameter values and assigns the result to the function name. A function declaration appears in the declarations section of the main program after any constant or variable declarations and among any procedure declarations.

Within the statement

```
writeln(Average(Value1, Value2, Value3):25:3);
```

in the main program, the "function designator"

```
Average(Value1, Value2, Value3)
```

appears. A **function designator** consists of the function name and a list of actual parameters. The function designator causes the function to be invoked, with values passed to the function's formal parameters by means of the actual parameter list. After the function module has been executed, the computed function value then replaces the function designator in the program statement. In this example, the program statement that contains the function designator is a *writeln* statement, so the program writes out the function value.

Unlike a procedure invocation, a separate program statement is not used to invoke a function. The function designator is simply placed within another program statement wherever the function value is desired. The function designator could be part of an expression on the right side of an assignment statement; it could even be part of an actual parameter list, passing the computed function value to a value formal parameter in another function or procedure. Of course, attention must be paid to the data type of the function value in order to avoid type clashes.

Because of the nature of a function, parameter passing is simpler than for procedures. A function computes a single value; this "output" value replaces the function designator, so there is no "output" formal parameter in the function heading. The formal parameters simply receive input values (**arguments**) to the function, so they should be value parameters. This also means that the actual parameters used in a function designator can be expressions as well as variables. Actual and formal parameters, as for procedures, correspond by their relative positions in their respective parameter lists.

Rules of scope, local and global variables, and the possibility of side effects all hold for function modules just as for procedure modules. Function side effects are controlled by using value parameters for all formal parameters and using no global variables within the function declaration. A function module can declare its own local constants and variables, as well as its own local procedures and functions.

The body of the function declaration must assign a value to the function name.

Note that somewhere in the body of the function an assignment must be made to the function name. Otherwise when the function is invoked, the value of the function designator cannot be determined; this will generate an error message. It is also important to note that the function name itself can only receive the computed function value; it cannot subsequently be used as an ordinary variable. Consider the following two statements to replace the body of function *Average:*

```
Average := x + y + z;
Average := Average/3.0;
```

Aside from the fact that this is a confusing use of the identifier *Average,* the appearance of *Average* on the right side of the second assignment statement is illegal. A function designator could appear here (functions as well as procedures can be recursive and invoke themselves, as we will see in Chapter 12), but in the above statement no actual parameter list is given, and an error message to this effect will be generated.

CHECKUP 6.1   Can the following replace the last two lines of program *Average1?* Why or why not?

```
        Average(Value1, Value2, Value3);
        writeln(Average:25:3);
end.      {main program}
```

6.1.2 *Alternatives to Functions*

Functions are a convenience, not a necessity. If a function value can be computed by a single expression, as in the above example, that expression could be used wherever the function is invoked. The next program is a version of the previous program that takes this approach to eliminate the function module.

```
program Average2(input, output);
{reads and averages three real values; values assumed to be under
 100,000 with no more than three decimal places}

var
     Value1, Value2, Value3 : real;    {the values}

begin    {main program}

  {input section}
  writeln('Give the three values to be averaged.');
  write('First value: ');
```

```
readln(Value1);
write('Second value: ');
readln(Value2);
write('Third value: ');
readln(Value3);

{output section}
writeln;
write('The average of ', Value1:9:3, ', ', Value2:9:3, ', and ');
writeln(Value3:9:3, ' is:');
writeln;
writeln((Value1 + Value2 + Value3)/3.0:25:3);
end.  {main program}
```

Use of a function is preferable in that it shields the main program from the computation details. A function is also more convenient than rewriting the expression if the same computation must be done at several different places in the program.

A procedure can always be used in place of a function. The procedure would have exactly one variable parameter, which would return the function value. The next version of the example program uses a procedure rather than a function.

```
program Average3(input, output);
{reads and averages three real values; values assumed to be under
 100,000 with no more than three decimal places}


var
    Value1, Value2, Value3 : real;      {the values}
    Ave : real;                         {average of the 3 values}

procedure Average(x, y, z: real; var Ave: real);
{finds the average of three real values}

  begin    {procedure Average}
    Ave := (x + y + z)/3.0;
  end;      {procedure Average}

begin    {main program}

  {input section}
  writeln('Give the three values to be averaged.');
  write('First value: ');
  readln(Value1);
  write('Second value: ');
  readln(Value2);
  write('Third value: ');
  readln(Value3);
```

```
{output section}
writeln;
write('The average of ', Value1:9:3, ', ', Value2:9:3, ',  and ');
writeln(Value3:9:3, ' is:');
writeln;
Average(Value1, Value2, Value3, Ave);
writeln(Ave:25:3);
end.     {main program}
```

Any function can be replaced by a procedure; always use a procedure if more than one value is to be returned to the invoking program.

A function handles the compute-one-value task a bit more efficiently than a procedure. Because the function name takes on the value, we don't have to think up both a module name and a variable name, as we did in program *Average3*. Also, the ability to use the function designator directly in an expression, rather than having to invoke a procedure and then use the resulting value, may be more convenient. (Note the two statements required in program *Average3* to mimic one statement in *Average1*). Whether you prefer functions or procedures to compute single values is yet another facet of programming style; remember that if you have to compute more than one value, a procedure is the appropriate choice.

6.1.3 *Functions and Procedures as Parameters (Optional)*

Functions can be passed as actual parameters to procedures (or other functions). Because of this, we can use procedures to perform tasks involving functions just as we have used procedures to perform tasks involving data values. Formal parameters in such procedures represent generic functions that will be specified by actual parameters when the procedure is invoked.

Functions may be passed as actual parameters to procedures, but the function arguments must be passed separately.

In the formal parameter list of such a procedure, the entire function heading is used, that is, the word **function,** the function identifier, the function's formal parameter list, and the data type of the function value are all given as a single formal parameter. When the procedure is invoked, the corresponding actual parameter gives only a specific function name, and none of its arguments. The function arguments are passed as additional actual parameters in the procedure call. In the following example, procedure *WriteValue* writes the integer value of a function *f* evaluated at a single integer argument value *a*. The main program uses this procedure to write values for a doubling function and a squaring function; these functions are also declared in the program.

```
program FunctionCompute(input, output);
{compares values of 2*a and a*a for integer values of a}

var
    a : integer;     {input value—argument for the two functions}

function Double(x: integer): integer;
{computes the function 2*x}
```

```
begin    {function Double}
  Double := 2*x;
end;     {function Double}
```

function Square(x: integer): integer;
{computes the function x*x}

```
begin    {function Square}
  Square := x*x;
end;     {function Square}
```

procedure WriteValue(function f(x: integer): integer; a: integer);
{writes the value of f(a)}

```
begin    {procedure WriteValue}
  writeln(f(a));
end;     {procedure WriteValue}
```

begin   {main program}

```
  {input section}
  write('Enter an integer value: ');
  readln(a);

  {output section}
  writeln;
  write('The value ', a, ' when doubled is ');
  WriteValue(Double, a);

  writeln;
  write('The value ', a, ' when squared is ');
  WriteValue(Square, a);
end.      {main program}
```

RUNNING THE PROGRAM...

```
Enter an integer value: 4
The value    4 when doubled is    8
The value    4 when squared is    16
```

The first formal parameter in the heading for procedure *WriteValue* above specifies an integer-valued function with a single integer argument. Only functions matching this description can be passed as actual parameters to the procedure. The body of the procedure makes no use of the *x* given in the first parameter; it actually evaluates a function using the second formal parameter, *a*. (To be more accurate, the procedure itself does not evaluate a function—it invokes a function module, passing the parameter *a* as an actual parameter, and then writes out the function value returned by that module.)

The variable *a* plays a number of different roles in the above example. It is a global variable declared in the main program. It is passed by the main program as an actual parameter to the procedure. Within the procedure heading, *a* is also the name of the corresponding formal parameter. When a function is invoked by the procedure, *a* becomes an actual parameter that corresponds to the formal parameter *x* in the function heading. Got all that?

Procedures can also be passed as actual parameters. As in the case of function parameters, the corresponding formal parameter consists of the entire procedure heading, with additional parameters to receive the actual parameters for this procedure.

6.1.4 *Standard Functions*

The function modules discussed so far are also called **user-defined functions.** In addition, Pascal provides a number of built-in or **standard functions.** To use a standard function, we need not write the module for the function but only invoke the function using the proper name and actual parameter list. Just as for user-defined functions, the function value has a data type. Figure 6.1 shows the standard functions that must be present in any legitimate Pascal system; a particular implementation may well support additional built-in functions. The functions of Figure 6.1 are all one-argument functions. The data type of the single argument and of the function value are shown.

The majority of the standard functions are mathematical in nature. The first three functions of Figure 6.1 are trigonometric. Note that the argument value for the sine and cosine functions is in radians. (The remaining trigonometric functions can be computed by using trigonometric identities, such as tan x = sin x/cos x.) The functions *exp* and *ln* compute the exponential and logarithm functions to the base *e*, where *e* has the approximate value 2.71828. The remaining mathematical functions are self-explanatory from Figure 6.1. Standard functions are convenient. Writing code to evaluate the sine function, for example, would involve a series expansion, something we would just as soon not have to do.

The next three functions have type *boolean* values. *Odd* just provides a way to test whether an integer value is an odd number. The functions *eoln* and *eof* give important information about the data file. (If no argument is given, the data file is assumed to be *input*.) Roughly, *eoln* is true when no more data appears on the current line, and *eof* is true when no more data appears in the current file. This allows us to process data until we get to the end of the line or the end of the file. We'll look at *eoln* and *eof* again in Chapters 8 and 11.

The ordinal functions have to do with ordering. Many data types, called **ordinal** types, involve data items that can be enumerated in some standard way. For integers, the standard enumeration is

$$\dots -4, \ -3, \ -2, \ -1, \ 0, \ 1, \ 2, \ 3, \ 4,\dots$$

The standard enumeration for boolean data is

false, true

There are several (machine-dependent) enumerations for character data, differing in the relative placement of uppercase vs. lowercase letters, where

FIGURE 6.1 Standard functions in Pascal.

Function name	Purpose	Argument type	Value type
Mathematical functions			
$sin(x)$	computes the sine of x (x in radians)	real or integer	real
$cos(x)$	computes the cosine of x (x in radians)	real or integer	real
$arctan(x)$	computes the arctangent of x, result in radians	real or integer	real
$exp(x)$	computes e^x	real or integer	real
$ln(x)$	computes the natural logarithm of x ($x > 0$)	real or integer	real
$abs(x)$	computes the absolute value of x	real or integer	same as x
$sqr(x)$	computes x^2	real or integer	same as x
$sqrt(x)$	computes $\sqrt{x}$ ($x \geq 0$)	real or integer	real
$round(x)$	rounds x to nearest integer	real	integer
$trunc(x)$	truncates (drops the decimal part of) x	real	integer
Boolean functions			
$odd(x)$	true if x is odd	integer	boolean
$eoln(x)$	true if no more data on current line of file x	file	boolean
$eof(x)$	true if no more data in file x	file	boolean
Ordinal functions			
$succ(x)$	gives value after x in standard enumeration of x's data type	ordinal type	same as x
$pred(x)$	gives value before x in standard enumeration of x's data type	ordinal type	same as x
$ord(x)$	gives position of x in standard enumeration of x's data type	ordinal type	integer
$chr(x)$	gives char data item with ordinal number x	integer	char

digits and punctuation symbols are included, etc. In any of these arrangements, or **collating sequences,** one can count on the fact that "a" will precede "b," which will precede "c," that "3" will precede "4," and so forth.

Appendix G gives the most commonly used collating sequences for character sets.

Thus *integer, boolean,* and *char,* as well as some other data types we'll see later, are ordinal. The data type *real* is not an ordinal type, however, because there is no clear sequence of values. The next value after 1.5 might be 1.6, or 1.55, or 1.50001—there's no way to specify an enumeration.

A data item x with an ordinal data type has a position in the data type's enumeration. The functions *succ(x)* and *pred(x)* give the data item after x (the successor of x) and before x (the predecessor of x), respectively, in the standard enumeration. As examples, *succ*(4) = 5, *succ*('b') = 'c', and *pred*(true) = false. Asking for the predecessor of the first item in the enumeration, or for the successor of the last item, will result in an error.

The function *ord* gives the integer value (the **ordinal number**) representing the position of the argument in the enumeration. Enumerations are numbered beginning with 0 except for integers, where the enumeration begins with the minimum integer value. This means that an integer's position in the enumeration of all integers is the value of the integer itself. For example, *ord*(0) = 0, *ord*(−235) = −235, *ord*(7) = 7. The value of *ord*(false) is 0 because false is first in the enumeration of type *boolean* data items. The result of applying function *ord* to character data is unpredictable because of the variations in collating sequences; such things as *ord*('A') < *ord*('B') will always be true, however.

Finally, the *chr* function takes an integer value and returns the character whose ordinal value is that integer, if such a character exists. Thus *chr(ord*('j')) = 'j'.

User-defined functions take precedence over standard functions with the same name.

User-defined function names take precedence over standard function names. Consequently, we can declare a function named *odd* (if that seems appropriate). If a program statement containing the function name *odd* is executed, this user-defined function will be invoked rather than the standard function.

Because built-in functions are so convenient, why not have built-in procedures for often-done tasks? In fact, we have already been using such procedures—*read* and *readln, write* and *writeln* are standard procedures for handling input and output. The variables listed in the *read* statement can be thought of as the actual parameters for the *read* procedure.

The standard functions *exp* and *ln* allow us to implement an exponentiation operation. In order to compute

$$x^y$$

we use the expression

exp(y*ln(x))

which represents the mathematical expression

$$e^{y(ln\ x)}$$

The equation *ln x* = *p* says $e^p = x$, which can then be written as $e^{\ ln\ x} = x$. Using this fact along with the laws of exponents, we can see that

Exponentiation can be implemented using the standard functions exp and ln.

$$e^{y(\ln x)} = (e^{\ln x})^y = x^y$$

This approach has one drawback because the function *ln* is not defined for other than positive values of its argument. Therefore we cannot use this expression to compute $(-8)^{1/3}$, even though this is mathematically reasonable.

CHECKUP 6.2   What is the value of each of the following?

> ***a)*** *abs*(-5)
> ***b)*** *sqr*(7)
> ***c)*** *sqr*(7.0)
> ***d)*** *trunc*(4.9)
> ***e)*** *succ*('m')
> ***f)*** *pred*(-5)

CHECKUP 6.3   Write a Pascal expression for the mathematical expression
$$2^x + b^2 + 4\,\sin x$$

---

1. Problem specification
2. Algorithm development
3. Coding
4. Debugging
5. Testing
6. Documenting
7. Maintenance

6.2 Debugging

No doubt by now you have already had some experience with debugging programs. Unlike some of the other steps in the programming process, it's impossible to bypass the debugging phase, even if you are willing to abandon the guidelines of good programming practice.

As mentioned earlier, syntax errors and run-time errors produce system messages that help pinpoint the source of the difficulty. Sometimes these errors still take a little time to find, often because we read what we want to see in a program statement, not what is actually there. Spotting a typographical error, like *BloodTypeO2* for *BloodType02*, requires careful proofreading, even when the compiler sends an error message about trying to use an undeclared identifier. Also, an early syntax error can cause a number of spurious error messages later in the program (the cascading error effect); once the legitimate error is corrected, these error messages go away. Despite such difficulties, we'll assume that you can now find and correct syntax and run-time errors.

Far more serious debugging problems arise in tracking down logic errors. The computer does not announce a logic error. The program runs, it terminates normally, output is produced. Recognizing when the output is wrong is a big part of the debugging process. Erroneous output can often be detected by doing the same calculation by hand for a few test cases, running the program for those cases, and comparing results. (We'll talk more about selecting test data in the next chapter.) Even if you don't do an entire calculation by hand, you may be able to estimate the range of values appropriate for the answer and detect when the program output does not fall within this range. Other cases of incorrect output may be more obvious. It is easy, for example, to check the output of a program to print a list of names in alphabetical order. At any rate, let's assume that you have detected the presence of a logic error; what steps can be taken to locate the source?

There are four general types of debugging actions you can take. First, the output may be incorrect because the input is not what you think it is. Maybe the program is really working correctly *on the input that it is seeing.* Have your program **echo the input**—list the input values right after they have been read in, before there is a chance for the program to change the values in any way. This list is for debugging purposes only; it is not "pretty" and not intended to be part of the final program output. (It is, however, often appropriate to incorporate input values as part of the final output, as we did in program *CatalogOrder* in Chapter 2.)

Input echo helps to detect program errors in reading input.

A series of *writeln* statements can accomplish the input echo; after the program has been debugged, the *writeln* statements can be deleted. A better way to "disable" these *writeln* statements is to enclose them in braces { } after the program is debugged so that they are treated as comments and ignored. Then the *writeln* statements can be easily recovered by removing the braces if program maintenance requires a further debugging session. An even easier way to "disable" and "enable" debug *writeln* statements will be discussed in the next chapter.

It may seem unlikely that errors could be made in reading input. (Remember that we are not talking here about run-time errors like type clashes. We are talking about values that get read and assigned to variables without generating run-time errors but are not the values we thought we were assigning to those variables.) Keep in mind that so far our programs (and input statements) have been fairly simple. We also have not yet done much with character data. Character data are especially prone to errors creeping into the input process because blanks are treated as characters.

Desk checking a program for simple cases may pinpoint logic errors.

The second debugging action is to **desk check** the program. Use a pencil and paper and follow the instructions in the program by hand. Write down the value of each variable as the program proceeds, crossing out (instead of erasing) old values as they are replaced by new values. You may be able to spot the point at which the program deviates from the correct algorithm. Here again, a lot of concentration is required to carry out the program instructions as they are actually written in the program, not as you intended to write them.

Use writeln statements to check the value of variables at specified points in the program; use some mechanism to enable and disable these diagnostic statements.

The third and fourth debugging actions are automated forms of desk checking and are useful for larger programs. The third action is to introduce *writeln* statements at various points in your program to give the current values of the program variables. These are called **diagnostic statements,** as they help "diagnose" a "sick" program. Every time some action is taken that changes the value of a variable, the new value should be written out. This gives an ongoing picture of the program variables and helps isolate the first time one of them takes on an incorrect value. Again, comment braces can be used for now to disable diagnostic *writeln* statements.

The fourth debugging step involves using your computer system's debugging facilities. These generally allow you to get a "snapshot" of the program variables at any points you set in the program execution and save you the trouble of putting in your own diagnostic *writeln* statements. The ultimate snapshot effect is ***single-stepping*** your program, halting program execution after each instruction to display the contents of the program's variables. A ***trace program*** may also tell you what procedure you are currently in, what procedure invoked that procedure, etc. This tells you how deep you are in nested procedures.

One of the most important debugging steps occurs in the initial design phase of the program, and that is the decision to design and develop the program in a top-down, modular fashion. Although we've talked about debugging a "program," the same techniques can be used to debug individual modules as they are implemented, using appropriate drivers. The scope of the debugging task is thereby reduced. Then when the entire program is finally assembled, much of the debugging has already been done and, in addition, the modular structure makes it easier to localize the probable sources of any remaining errors. For example, diagnostic *writeln* statements can be interspersed between procedure invocations in the main program to determine which module seems to be at fault. Once the faulty module has been pinpointed, then debugging efforts can be applied at a finer level of detail in that section of the program. Even within a module, debugging efforts should focus on localizing the suspect region of code, narrowing it down to successively smaller sections.

As a final thought about debugging logic errors, beware of the ***used-car syndrome,*** which goes like this: You have already poured a lot of time into "repairs" on your current program, but it isn't running right. You continue to work on it, in hopes that this will be the last "repair" needed, instead of the (expensive) alternative of throwing out the old program and starting all over again. It is natural to try to salvage an investment; it is also sometimes false economy. If you seem to be finding one logic error after another, fixing one only to have something else go wrong, or if you reach a point where you can't even figure out what the problem is, be brave enough to scrap it all and start fresh. This is only a last resort, not an excuse to avoid working hard trying to debug your current program. If you do start over, try to bring a fresh perspective and a different approach to the problem so you don't fall into the same traps as before. (Finally, you might check with your instructor before you take this radical step—and be sure to save the previous version of the program.)

Become familiar with the local computer system's Pascal debugging tools.

Don't fall victim to the "used-car syndrome" by hanging on to the original code at all costs.

6.3 Sample Software Development Project—Bacteria

Problem Statement

A certain colony of bacteria grows at a rate proportional to the number present—the more there is, the faster the total number grows. The number of bacteria in the colony after t hours is given by the function

$$y = y_0 e^{0.2t} \tag{1}$$

where y_0 is the number of bacteria present at the start of the experiment.

Graph the growth of the colony for the first five hours of the experiment, given the initial number of bacteria.

Problem Specification

To see the sort of values we have to graph, let's try some different values for y_0 and use equation (1) (and a calculator) to compute the approximate number present at different times.

y_0	t = 0	t = 1	t = 2	t = 3	t = 4	t = 5
1000	1000	1221	1492	1822	2226	2718
2000	2000	2443	2984	3644	4451	5437
3000	3000	3664	4476	5466	6677	8155

The values can get quite large. In order to be able to fit the graph on the screen or page, we have two choices. One possibility is to compute the range of values for the given input and then do a scaling operation so that the largest value will fit. The second possibility is to limit the input size so that we know ahead of time what the maximum value can be and set up the program accordingly. The first approach is certainly more general, but we'll take the second approach for now. We will limit the maximum initial number of bacteria to 3000; then the maximum value we must be able to plot is approximately 8155.

Most graphs present the values of the argument along the horizontal axis, and the function values along the vertical axis. This presents some complications for us with our current programming capabilities, so we'll present the argument values (the values of t) along the vertical axis, and the function values (the values of y) horizontally. (Such a graph is sometimes called a **histogram.**) We'll evaluate the function at half-hour intervals from $t = 0$ to $t = 5$.

Input: initial number of bacteria present
Output: graph of number of bacteria present at half hour intervals from $t = 0$ to $t = 5$.

Algorithm Development

We need to read the program input and then do a series of computations to plot the points of the graph. Each such point will require that we evaluate the function (which we'll do by using a function subprogram) and then actually plot the point. The structure chart (Fig. 6.2) shows the procedures we will need: one procedure to read the initial value, and one procedure to plot a point, within which will be nested the function subprogram. The main program will invoke the plotting procedure once for each half-hour interval, i.e., once for each point to be plotted.

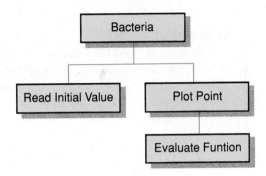

FIGURE 6.2 Structure chart for program *Bacteria*.

Read Initial Value

This procedure gets the initial number of bacteria present (an integer no greater than 3000) and returns it to the main program.

procedure ReadInitialValue(**var** InitialNumber: integer);
{gets the initial number of bacteria and returns it to the main program}

begin {procedure ReadInitialValue}

prompt for and read initial number of bacteria present

end; {procedure ReadInitial Value}

Plot Point

This procedure needs to know the value of y_0, the initial number of bacteria, and the current value of t in hours in order to pass these along to the function that is computing the value of y. In addition, the current value of t will be used to mark the vertical axis.

We still have to do a scaling operation because the range of values we must be able to plot goes from 1 (for $y_0 = 1$ and $t = 0$) to about 8155 (for $y_0 = 3000$ and $t = 5$). If we scale the values by dividing by 150 (somewhat of an arbitrary choice) and then adding 1, i.e., if we compute

$$round((\text{function value})/150) + 1 \qquad (2)$$

then the resulting values range from 1 (when the function value is 1) to 55 (when the function value is 8155). This gives us a comfortable range of values to plot horizontally. We'll make the scaling factor a constant local to *PlotPoint;* then it will be easy to

Continued

Plot Point—Continued

modify if we should later change the restrictions on the input values
or decide to stretch or shrink the graph. Each value that we
compute using equation (2) determines the distance along the
horizontal axis at which the point being plotted should be placed.
We can use the "*" character for the point and use the integral
value determined by (2) for the horizontal field width within which
to print this character. Since a character is written right-justified in
its field width, this technique places the "*" the desired number of
spaces to the right along the horizontal axis.

procedure PlotPoint(yzero: integer; t: real);
{plots an * for the number of bacteria present at time t,
 given the initial number of bacteria yzero}

const
     ScaleFactor = 150;   {scales the range of values to a
                                    manageable range to plot}
var
     Horizontal : integer;   {space to move horizontally to
                                    plot the point}

declaration for function to compute $y_0 e^{0.2t}$

begin   {procedure PlotPoint}

     mark the vertical axis with the current value of t
     plot the * for the function value at distance *Horizontal*
     label the point with the function value

end   {procedure PlotPoint}

Evaluate Function

The function we must evaluate is given by equation (1). It is
straightforward to translate this equation into a function declaration.

function y(yzero: integer; t: real): real;
{computes the number y of bacteria present at time t given
 an initial number yzero}

begin   {function y}
  y := yzero*exp(0.2*t);
end;   {function y}

The main program will first get the input, then plot each of the points for
the values of t at half-hour intervals from $t = 0$ to $t = 5$. Finally, it will write

out the horizontal axis on the bottom of the graph. The complete program is shown below.

```pascal
program Bacteria(input, output);
{graphs the growth of a certain colony of bacteria for the first
5 hours of an experiment, given the initial number of bacteria
(no more than 3000).}

var
     InitialNumber : integer;      {original number of bacteria
                                    present}

procedure ReadInitialValue(var InitialNumber: integer);
{gets the initial number of bacteria and returns it to the main
 program }

  begin    {procedure ReadInitialValue}
    write('What is the initial number of bacteria present');
    writeln(' at the start of the');
    write('experiment?    (value limited to 3000): ');
    readln(InitialNumber);
  end;     {procedure ReadInitialValue}

procedure PlotPoint(yzero: integer; t: real);
{plots an * for the number of bacteria present at time t, given
 the initial number of bacteria yzero}

const
     ScaleFactor = 150;       {scales the range of values to a
                               manageable range to plot}

var
     Horizontal : integer;    {space to move horizontally to
                               plot the point}

function y(yzero: integer; t: real): real;
{computes the number y of bacteria present at time t given an
 initial number yzero}

  begin    {function y}
    y := yzero*exp(0.2*t);
  end;     {function y}

  begin    {procedure PlotPoint}
    {label the vertical axis}
    write('t = ', t:3:1, ' | ');

    {plot the point}
    Horizontal := round((y(yzero, t))/ScaleFactor) + 1;
    write('*':Horizontal);
```

```
        {label the point}
        writeln(y(yzero, t):6:1);
        writeln(' | ':8);
    end;      {procedure PlotPoint}


begin      {main program}
    ReadInitialValue(InitialNumber);

    {plot points}
    writeln;
    writeln;
    PlotPoint(InitialNumber, 0.0);
    PlotPoint(InitialNumber, 0.5);
    PlotPoint(InitialNumber, 1.0);
    PlotPoint(InitialNumber, 1.5);
    PlotPoint(InitialNumber, 2.0);
    PlotPoint(InitialNumber, 2.5);
    PlotPoint(InitialNumber, 3.0);
    PlotPoint(InitialNumber, 3.5);
    PlotPoint(InitialNumber, 4.0);
    PlotPoint(InitialNumber, 4.5);
    PlotPoint(InitialNumber, 5.0);

    {now draw horizontal axis}
    write('_____');
    writeln('_____');
    write('        0  1000  2000  3000  4000  5000  6000  7000');
    writeln('   8000');
end.        {main program}
```

RUNNING THE PROGRAM 1...

What is the initial number of bacteria present at the start of the experiment?   (value limited to 3000): 1000

```
t = 0.0  |       *1000.0

t = 0.5  |       *1105.2

t = 1.0  |        *1221.4

t = 1.5  |         *1349.9

t = 2.0  |          *1491.8

t = 2.5  |           *1648.7

t = 3.0  |            *1822.1

t = 3.5  |             *2013.8
```

```
t  =  4.0 |                    *2225.5

t  =  4.5 |                       *2459.6

t  =  5.0 |                          *2718.3
          |
          |
          |_____
          0   1000   2000   3000   4000   5000   6000   7000   8000
```

RUNNING THE PROGRAM 2...

What is the initial number of bacteria present at the start of the experiment? (value limited to 3000): 3000

```
t  =  0.0 |                 *3000.0

t  =  0.5 |                   *3315.5

t  =  1.0 |                     *3664.2

t  =  1.5 |                       *4049.6

t  =  2.0 |                         *4475.5

t  =  2.5 |                           *4946.2

t  =  3.0 |                             *5466.4

t  =  3.5 |                               *6041.3

t  =  4.0 |                                 *6676.6

t  =  4.5 |                                   *7378.8

t  =  5.0 |                                     *8154.8
          |
          |
          |_____
          0   1000   2000   3000   4000   5000   6000   7000   8000
```

Because we have scaled the values along the horizontal axis by a factor of 150, if program *Bacteria* were to run with an input value of, say, 100, its output would not display the growth rate very effectively because the range of values would be small. This is the major reason to do a scaling operation as a function of the input value.

Finally, note that the series of procedure invocations in the main program is extremely repetitious. We had to type eleven of these; what if one hundred such invocations were required? We need a better way to handle repetitious actions, and we'll learn how to do this in Chapter 8. (If you learned about simple control structures in Chapter 3, you'll recognize that a counting loop would be appropriate here.)

<table>
<tr><td>CASE
STUDY
ONE</td><td>View #6</td></tr>
</table>

Sterling's water pollution program uses procedure *ComputeRatio* to compute the ratio of bacteria to water in a given sample. Because this procedure returns only one value, it could be implemented as a function. Procedure *Check-Threshold* makes use of this ratio, and so does procedure *WriteOutput*. The function could be declared in the main program and be invoked by each of these two procedures; then there would be no need of a global variable *Level* to be passed between procedures, as each procedure would simply invoke the function when it needed this value. On the other hand, input values for the function would have to be passed to the invoking procedures. A more efficient approach, and one closer to the original design, is to retain the global variable *Level* and simply use the function (once) to compute its value.

You decide to modify the program from Chapter 5 using a function to compute the ratio of bacteria to water. At the same time, you must also modify the documentation to reflect this change in the program design. The following program shows the new version. Of course you test the new version to be sure that the modification has not introduced errors and caused the program to lose some of its previous functionality.

```
program WaterPollution(input, output);
{tests water sample from a site against a pollution threshold,
 issues a warning if the bacteria level is too high}

const
    Threshold = 2.0;           {200 bacteria per 100 ml water}

var
    ID : integer;              {site ID number}
    Water : integer;           {amount of water sampled, in ml}
    Bacteria : integer;        {bacteria count in sample}
    Mon1, Mon2 : char;         {two-digit month notation}
    Day1, Day2 : char;         {two-digit date notation}
    Yr1, Yr2 : char;           {two-digit year notation}
    Warning : boolean;         {flag for warning message if
                                pollution level too high}
    Level : real;              {pollution level for this
                                sample}

procedure GetInput(var ID, Water, Bacteria: integer;
                   var Mon1, Mon2, Day1, Day2,
                   Yr1, Yr2: char);
{procedure to collect input for water pollution data; amount
 Water of water and count Bacteria of bacteria were obtained
 from  site ID on date Mon1Mon2/Day1Day2/Yr1Yr2}
```

```
var
     Slash : char;      {separating / in date format}

  begin     {procedure GetInput}
     write('Enter the site ID number: ');
     readln(ID);
     writeln;

     writeln('Enter the date of this sample.');
     write('Use month/date/year format: ');
     readln(Mon1, Mon2, Slash, Day1, Day2, Slash, Yr1, Yr2);
     writeln;

     write('Enter the amount of water in sample (in ml): ');
     readln(Water);
     writeln;

     write('Enter the bacteria count found in this sample:  ');
     readln(Bacteria);
  end;      {procedure GetInput}

function Ratio(Bacteria, Water: integer): real;
{computes the Ratio of Bacteria to Water}

  begin     {function Ratio}
     Ratio := Bacteria/Water;
  end;      {function Ratio}

procedure CheckThreshold(Ratio: real;
                         var Over:  boolean);
{compares Ratio to the global constant Threshold and sets
 Over to true if that limit is exceeded}

  begin     {stub for procedure CheckThreshold}
     writeln;
     writeln('execution has reached procedure  CheckThreshold');
  end;      {procedure CheckThreshold}

procedure WriteOutput(ID, Water, Bacteria: integer;
                      Mon1, Mon2, Day1, Day2,
                      Yr1, Yr2: char;
                      Ratio: real;
                      Warning: boolean);
{echoes site input data and writes warning message if  warranted}

  begin     {procedure WriteOutput}
     writeln;
     writeln;
     write('Site ID', 'Date':8, 'Water':12, 'Bacteria':13);
     writeln('Level':9, 'Warning':10);
```

```
        write('_____');
        writeln('_____');
        writeln;
        write(ID:5, Mon1:6, Mon2, '/', Day1, Day2, '/', Yr1,  Yr2);
        write(Water:8, ' ml', Bacteria:9, Ratio:11:2);
        writeln;
    end;     {procedure WriteOutput}


begin     {main program}

    GetInput(ID, Water, Bacteria,
             Mon1, Mon2, Day1, Day2, Yr1,  Yr2);

    Level := Ratio(Bacteria, Water);

    CheckThreshold(Level, Warning);

    WriteOutput(ID, Water, Bacteria,
                Mon1, Mon2, Day1, Day2,  Yr1, Yr2,
                Level, Warning);
end.     {main program}
```

| CASE STUDY TWO | View #6 |

Modify Sterling's current program for the hypertension clinic so that the average patient blood pressure is computed by a function that is invoked once for the systolic pressure and once for the diastolic pressure. Rewrite the program documentation to reflect this modification, and test the program for several input cases.

(Items marked with ∗ make use of optional material on Simple Control Structures from Chapter 3.)

EXERCISES

 1. What is the value of *succ*('B')?

 #2. What is the value of *pred*(2.0)?

 #3. What is the value of *sqrt*(*sqr*(−2))?

 4. Write an expression to compute 2^4 (other than by repeated multiplication).

 #5. What is the output from the following program?

```
program positive(input, output);

function funny(x, y: integer): integer;
  begin
    funny := abs(x*y);
  end;
```

```
begin
  writeln(funny(-4, funny(3,-2)));
end.
```

6. Given the input data

    2 3 4

what is the output from the following program?

```
program stir(input, output);

var
    first, last,
    next, big :      integer;

function mult(OneNumber, AnotherNumber: integer): integer;
  begin
    mult := OneNumber * AnotherNumber;
  end;

begin
  readln(first, last, next);
  big := mult(first, last);
  next := mult(last, next);
  last := mult(big, next);
  writeln(big, last, next, first);
end.
```

#*7. Given the function declaration

```
function Compute(Number: real): real;

var
    Count : integer;          {loop index}

begin
  for Count := 1 to 3 do
    begin
      Number := sqr(Number);
    end;
  Compute := Number;
end;
```

write a single expression that could replace a function designator for this function if *Number* is always positive.

*8. What value is computed by the following function if *x* receives the value 4?

```
function Loopy(x: integer): integer;
```

```
var
     Index : integer;              {loop index}

begin
  for Index := 1 to 3 do
    begin
      Loopy := x*Index;
    end;
end;
```

**SKILL
BUILDERS**

1. Write a program that reads two integers and uses a function to compute the square of their difference.

#2. Write a program that reads a character between 'a' and 's' and writes out the next alphabetical character.

3. Redo Skill Builder #5 from Chapter 5, this time using a function.

4. Write a program that asks for the radius of each of two spheres and computes the volume of each sphere (use a function).

5. Write a program that asks for an angle in degrees and writes out the sine of that angle.

*6. Write a function that computes the minimum of two integer values that are passed as parameters.

**SOFTWARE
DEVELOPMENT
PROJECTS**

Remember the total design effort that these projects entail.

1. In 12-meter yacht racing, such as for the America's Cup, a complex formula is used to determine if a boat's rating R qualifies it as a 12-meter craft ($R = 12$). An approximation to this formula is given by

$$R = \frac{L + 2*D + \sqrt{S} - F}{2.37}$$

where L is the "rated length" of the boat (close to the length along the water line), D is the difference between the "skin girth" and the "chain girth"—see Figure 6.3—S is the sail area, and F is the average freeboard (height of the deck above water). L, D, and F are measured in meters, S in square meters. Develop software that collects the necessary data and computes R.

2. Interest on an annuity is compounded quarterly. At the end of T years, the amount A in the account is given by the equation

$$A = P(1 + 0.25r)^{4T}$$

where P is the amount of principal and r is the annual interest rate. Develop

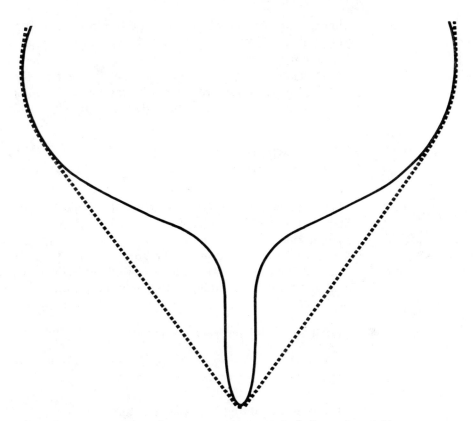

FIGURE 6.3 "Skin girth" is measured against the hull—on the solid line. "Chain girth" is measured on the dotted line.

software to read in P, r, and T and compute the amount A in the account.

3. The number of mosquito larvae L in pond water as a function of surface area A (in m^2) is modeled by the equation

$$L = 0.002A^4 + A^3 - 8A^2 + 16A + 20$$

Superbugs, Inc., estimates that one gallon of spray per 200,000 larvae is needed to kill off the mosquito population. Develop software to read in the dimensions of a rectangular pond, in feet, and determine the number of gallons of spray required.

4. Develop software to read in two digits between 0 and 9 (as characters) and write out the sum of their corresponding integer values.

5. An object floating in water is pushed down a distance x_0 feet from its equilibrium position and then released. Ignoring friction, it will bob up and down with a displacement of x feet about its equilibrium position as a function of time T in seconds given by the equation

$$x = x_0 \cos(T \sqrt{(1996.8A/W)})$$

where A is the cross-sectional area of the object in square feet, and W is the weight of the object in pounds. Develop software to graph the displacement as a function of time.

*6. Develop software to write out an amortization table for a mortgage. The mortgage is written for a period of Y years, with an annual interest rate R and payments to be made at the end of each month. The monthly payment P is given by the formula

$$P = \frac{A*MR(1 + MR)^N}{(1 + MR)^N - 1}$$

where A is the amount borrowed, MR is the monthly interest rate, and N is the total number of months of the loan. For each payment, the interest due for that month is taken out and the remainder of the payment is credited toward the amount borrowed. The program should display summary information about the terms of the loan, as well as the total amount paid and the total interest paid. In addition, it should print a table of the form

Month #	Interest Paid	Principal Paid	Remaining Balance
―――	―――	―――	―――
―――	―――	―――	―――

(Hint: Use a counting loop that runs from 1 to N.)

TESTING AND MAINTENANCE DEPARTMENT

1. Run program *Bacteria* with several different input values. In particular, try 0, 100, and 4000.

2. Run program *Bacteria* with some different values for *ScaleFactor*. How does this affect the program output?

3. Modify program *Bacteria* so that procedure *PlotPoint* invokes function y only once instead of twice.

4. Modify program *Bacteria* to remove the restriction on the initial amount of bacteria present; the program should scale the graph in some reasonable way based on the initial value that is input.

*5. Modify program *Bacteria* to invoke *PlotPoint* within a counting loop.

DEBUGGING CLINIC

1. Run and debug the following program:

```
program FunFunction(input, output);
{what is wrong with this program to compute the square of an
integer?}
```

```
var
    little : integer;

function square(number: integer): integer;

  begin
    square := number;
    square := square * square;
  end;

begin
  writeln('Enter an integer: ');
  readln(little);
  writeln('The square of your integer is ', square(little));
end.
```

2. Insert diagnostic *writeln* statements to help debug the following program.

```
program Pythagoras(input, output);
{computes the length of the hypotenuse of a right triangle,
 given  the lengths of the sides}

var
    a, b : real;      {lengths of sides of right triangle}
    c    : real;      {length of hypotenuse}

function Hypotenuse(a, b: real): real;
{uses Pythagorean theorem c² = a² + b²}

  begin
    c := sqr(a*a + b*b);
  end;

begin
  writeln('Enter the lengths of two sides of a ');
  write('right triangle: ');
  readln(a, b);

  writeln;
  writeln('The length of the hypotenuse is ', c);
end.
```

CHAPTER SEVEN

DECISIONS; NEW DATA TYPES; PROGRAM TESTING

When a program is executing, we may think of the program statement currently being executed as the "active point" in the program. This active point traces a path through the program that is called the *flow of control.* The default flow of control, which is followed in the absence of instructions to the contrary, is *sequential.* In sequential flow of control, program statements are executed in the order in which they occur in the code. Sequential flow of control can be temporarily sidetracked by procedure or function invocations that transfer control to a program module. When execution of the program module is complete, however, control returns to the invoking program segment and picks up where it left off. Our programs so far have proceeded sequentially (with the single exception of program *School* in the optional section on "Simple Control Structures" in Chapter 3).

Control structures are the statements available in a programming language to redirect the flow of control out of the sequential mode. Pascal provides control structures for *conditional flow of control* and *looping.* Conditional flow of control allows one section of code to be executed while other sections are omitted, the choice to be determined by some condition that is evaluated during program execution. Looping allows repetition of a section of code without writing the same instructions over and over. In this chapter we will learn how to implement conditional flow of control; looping is covered in the next chapter.

Conditional flow of control requires a new kind of expression, called a boolean expression.

7.1 Boolean Expressions

An arithmetic expression, such as $3*4 - 7$, has an associated numeric value (5, in this case). A *boolean expression* has an associated *truth value,* either true or false.

7.1.1 *Simple Boolean Expressions*

There are four simple kinds of boolean expressions. First, there are the built-in boolean constants *true* and *false,* whose truth values are self-evident. Second, additional boolean constants can be declared in the declarations section of the program, as in

```
const
    Always  =  true;
    Never  =  false;
```

Third, boolean variables can be declared in the declarations section of the program, as in

```
var
    top, finished : boolean;
```

A boolean variable, like any other variable, takes on a value by a read statement or an assignment statement.

The fourth kind of simple boolean expression arises when we compare two items using **relational operators.** For example, if *A* is an integer variable, the expression $A = 4$ asserts that the current value of variable *A* equals 4. This statement is either true or false, so $A = 4$ has a value of true or false—it is a boolean expression. Figure 7.1 shows the relational operators in both their standard mathematical form and the Pascal equivalent. Although we've used mathematical symbols, relational operators can be applied to nonnumeric items. For example, "less than" applied to character data means "precedes, according to the collating sequence being used." (See Appendix G for common collating sequences.)

Relational operators apply to expressions as well as to single items, but the expressions must represent quantities of the same data type. Comparing character data to integer data, for example, is senseless (and illegal). The

Rational operators are used to compare expressions of the same data type; integer vs. real comparisons are also legal.

FIGURE 7.1   Relational operators

Mathematical Form	Pascal Equivalent	Meaning
=	=	The two quantities are equal.
≠	<>	The two quantities are unequal.
<	<	The first quantity is less than the second.
≤	<=	The first quantity is less than or equal to the second.
>	>	The first quantity is greater than the second.
≥	>=	The first quantity is greater than or equal to the second.

only exception to the same-data-type rule is that an integer quantity can be compared to a real quantity: the integer is converted to its real equivalent.

Real values should not be compared with the equality operator; rather the values should be tested for a very small difference.

Because the computer representation of a real number may only approximate the exact value, it is unwise to use the relational operator = to compare two real quantities. This operator does a bit-by-bit comparison of the memory locations of the two quantities; a disagreement in a single bit will make the result of the comparison false. To test whether the real variables *Sum* and *Limit* are equal, for example, a boolean expression such as

abs(Sum − Limit) < Tolerance

can be used, where *Tolerance* is some appropriate small constant value such as 0.0001.

CHECKUP 7.1

What is the value of each of the following boolean expressions if the current values of *Time, Class,* and *Key* are 3.4, 'X', and 6, respectively?

a. Key = 10 − 4
b. Time <= 4.0
c. Time + 1.0 >= Key − 1
d. Class <> Time + Key
e. Class = X
f. Class < 'Z'

7.1.2 *Boolean Operators*

Boolean expressions can be combined with boolean operators to produce more complex boolean expressions. There are three **boolean operators,** symbolized by the words "and," "or," and "not."

If X and Y are boolean expressions, the expression

X **and** Y

will have the value true only if both X and Y have the value true. The expression

X **or** Y

will have the value true if X is true or if Y is true or if both X and Y are true. The expression

not X

will have the truth value opposite to that of X.

The effect of the boolean operators is summarized in the **truth tables** of Figure 7.2.

FIGURE 7.2 Truth tables for boolean operators

X	Y	X and Y		X	Y	X or Y		X	not X
T	T	T		T	T	T		T	F
T	F	F		T	F	T		F	T
F	T	F		F	T	T			
F	F	F		F	F	F			

As an example of a more complex boolean expression, consider

(Total < 100) or (Price <= 3.99)

If the current value of *Total* is 120 and the current value of *Price* is 2.49, then one of the two subexpressions is true and the entire **or** expression is also true.

A boolean expression can be used on the right side of an assignment statement. If *SmallLot* has been declared as a boolean variable, then the statement

SmallLot := not(Order > 10);

assigns the value true to *SmallLot* if the current value of *Order* is 7.

Relational operators cannot be "chained" together in a boolean expression.

Pascal relational operators differ from their mathematical equivalent in that they cannot be chained together. While $1.0 < X < 2.0$ is perfectly acceptable in mathematics, it is not allowed in Pascal. The desired effect can be obtained by writing

(1.0 < X) and (X < 2.0)

Boolean operators have an order of precedence. The operator **not** is applied first, then **and,** and then **or**. This means that

In the absence of parentheses, the boolean operator not is applied first, then and, and then or.

A and B or not C

is evaluated as

(A and B) or (not C)

Parentheses can be used to overrule the natural order of precedence or to make the order of evaluation clearer to the human who is reading the program.

When relational operators are involved, parentheses are required, not optional. This is because boolean operators take precedence over relational operators. In the expression

A < B and C < D

the operator **and** is applied first, giving

```
A < (B and C) < D
```

Boolean operators take precedence over relational operators, so use parentheses.

which results in chained inequalities (illegal) and the attempt to use what is probably numeric or character data with a boolean operator (illegal). The correct syntax for the expression is

```
(A < B) and (C < D)
```

The moral is: USE PARENTHESES WITH BOOLEAN OPERATORS. Figure 7.3 summarizes the rules of operator precedence.

CHECKUP 7.2 What is the value of each of the following boolean expressions if the current values of *Time, Class, Key,* and *Over* are 3.4, 'X', 6, and *false*, respectively?

a. `(1.0 <= Time) or (Class = 'Y')`
b. `(not Over and (Time < 5.0)) or (Key <> 6)`
c. `(5 < Key) and (Key < 10) and not(odd(Key))`

CHECKUP 7.3 Assuming the same current values as in CHECKUP 7.2, what is the value of the boolean variable *Flag* after execution of each of the following?

a. `Flag := Time > Key;`
b. `Flag := ('M' < Class) and Over;`
c. `Flag := Over or (Time + 4.2 > 6.0);`

First do
    parenthesized expressions (inner to outer)

then do
    not

then do
    * / **div** **mod** **and** (left to right)

then do
    + − **or** (left to right)

then do
    = <> < <= > >=

FIGURE 7.3 Rules of operator precedence for arithmetic, boolean, and relational operators.

7.2 **The If Statement**

Now we are ready to see how to implement conditional flow of control, where a section of code is executed or omitted based upon some condition. The condition is whether a particular boolean expression has the value true or false. If the expression is true, one segment of program code is executed, if the expression is false, a different segment of code is executed.

For example, the program below executes one write statement if the user enters an odd value, and a different write statement if the user enters an even value.

```
program EvenOdd(input, output);
{asks for an integer value and tells whether the value is even or
  odd}

var
    Number : integer;          {Number the user enters}

begin
  writeln('Enter an integer value');
  readln(Number);
  writeln;
  if odd(Number) then
    writeln('Your number, ', Number, ', was odd.')
  else
    writeln('Your number, ', Number, ', was even.');
  writeln('Wasn' 't that interesting?');
end.
```

RUNNING THE PROGRAM...

```
Enter an integer value
17

Your number,    17, was odd.
Wasn't that interesting?
```

In an if statement, the then clause is executed if the current value of the boolean expression is true, the else clause is executed if it is false.

The general form of the Pascal **if** statement is

```
if boolean expression then
    statement1
else
    statement2;
```

If the boolean expression is true, statement1 is executed and statement2 is not; if the expression is false, statement1 is not executed but statement2 is. Control then proceeds to the next program statement following this **if** statement. The **if** statement is a single statement; a semicolon inserted at the end of statement1 will act as a statement separator, but because

```
else
    statement2
```

*Do not use a ";"
between the end
of the then
clause and the
word else in an
if statement.*

is not a legitimate statement, a compiler error will result. Always make sure there is no semicolon directly before the **else** in an **if** statement.

An **if** statement involving a complex boolean expression may be simplified by using a boolean variable having the truth value of this expression, rather than the expression itself. For example,

```
if ((Rate < 0.08) and (DOW > 1600.0)) or not(Stable) then
   writeln('Sell this stock')
else
   writeln('Keep this stock');
```

could be handled with a declaration

```
var
   SellCondition : boolean;
```

the assignment statement

```
SellCondition := ((Rate < 0.08) and (DOW > 1600.0))
                     or not(Stable);
```

and the **if** statement

```
if SellCondition then
   writeln('Sell this stock')
else
   writeln('Keep this stock');
```

Program readability and clarity should govern such decisions.

7.2.1 *Compound* **Then** *or* **Else** *Clauses*

Remember from Chapter 2 that statements can be compound statements, framed by **begin** and **end.** Consequently, the general form of the **if** statement above really represents

*If more than one
statement is to
be executed in a
then clause or
an else clause, a
begin-end is
required in order
to define the
clause.*

```
if boolean expression then
   begin
      statement;
      statement;
         ⋮
      statement;
   end
else
   begin
      statement;
      statement;
         ⋮
      statement;
   end;
```

That's why we said earlier that *sections* of code are executed or omitted based upon some condition. Notice how we've used indenting to help highlight the **then** and **else** clauses of the **if** statement.

Program *Commission* illustrates the **if** statement with compound statements for both the **then** clause and the **else** clause.

```
program Commission(input, output);
{computes real estate commission plus bonus for an individual
real estate agent based on total sale amount and number of
high-priced sales}

var
    TotalSales : real;          {dollar value of total monthly sales}
    HighNumber : integer;   {number of sales for month over
                                 $200,000}

procedure GetInput(var TotalSales: real;
                        var HighNumber: integer);
{collects information on total monthly sales and number of
high-priced sales}

  begin    {procedure GetInput}
    writeln('Enter the total dollar amount in sales for');
    write('this month (no commas, please): $ ');
    readln(TotalSales);

    writeln('Enter the number of sales made');
    write('this month that exceeded $200,000: ');
    readln(HighNumber);
  end;     {procedure GetInput}

procedure WriteOutput(TotalSales: real; HighNumber: integer);
{writes message and amount of compensation for this individual}

const
    BonusRate = 800;            {reward for high-priced sales}
    CutOff = 3;                 {number to make high-priced
                                 seller}
    HighCommissionRate = 0.03;  {base commission rate for
                                 high-priced seller}
    LowCommissionRate = 0.02;   {base commission rate for
                                 regular seller}

var
    Commission : real;          {amount of commission}
    Bonus : real;               {amount of bonus for high-priced
                                 seller}

begin {procedure WriteOutput}
```

```
        if HighNumber < CutOff then
          begin {then}
            Commission := TotalSales*LowCommissionRate;

            writeln;
            writeln('At Cockroach Realty, your ability to');
            writeln('earn is bounded only by your own');
            writeln('abilities.    Get out there and sell!');
            writeln;
            write('Your commission for this month is $ ');
            writeln(Commission:10:2);
          end     {then}

        else
          begin {here's a high-priced seller}
            Commission := TotalSales*HighCommissionRate;
            Bonus := HighNumber*BonusRate;

            writeln;
            write('You have sold ', HighNumber, ' houses this');
            writeln(' month for over $200,000.    That' 's the');
            writeln('kind of thing we like to see from our');
            writeln('agents here at Cockroach Realty.');
            writeln('Congratulations; keep up the good work!');
            writeln;
            write('Your commission for this month is $ ');
            writeln(Commission:10:2, ' plus your bonus for');
            write(HighNumber, ' high-priced sales of $ ');
            writeln(Bonus:10:2, ' giving a total for the month of');
            writeln;
            writeln('***** $ ':25, Commission + Bonus:10:2, ' *****');
          end; {high-priced seller}
      end; {procedure WriteOutput}

  begin {main program}
    GetInput(TotalSales, HighNumber);
    WriteOutput(TotalSales, HighNumber);
  end.   {main program}
```

RUNNING THE PROGRAM...

```
Enter the total dollar amount in sales for
this month (no commas, please): $ 275000
Enter the number of sales made
this month that exceeded $200,000: 0

At Cockroach Realty, your ability to
earn is bounded only by your own
abilities.    Get out there and sell!

Your commission for this month is $      5500.00
```

RUNNING THE PROGRAM...

> Enter the total dollar amount in sales for
> this month (no commas, please): $ 832000
> Enter the number of sales made
> this month that exceeded $200,000: 3
>
> You have sold 3 houses this month for over $200,000. That's the
> kind of thing we like to see from our
> agents here at Cockroach Realty.
> Congratulations; keep up the good work!
>
> Your commission for this month is $ 24960.00 plus your bonus for
> 3 high-priced sales of $ 2400.00 giving a total for the month of
>
> ***** $ 27360.00 *****

In program *Commission,* procedure *WriteOutput* consisted of one single **if** statement. Had there been some common computation involved in both clauses of the **if** statement, that common work could have been done outside the **if** statement. For example, if the commission rate is the same for both classes of sellers and the bonus is the only distinction, we could write procedure *WriteOutput* as follows:

```
procedure WriteOutput(TotalSales: real;  HighNumber: integer);
{writes message and amount of compensation for this individual}

const
    BonusRate = 800;        {reward for high-priced sales}
    CutOff = 3;             {number to make high-priced seller}
    Rate = 0.02;            {base commission rate}

var
    Commission : real;      {amount of commission}
    Bonus : real;           {amount of bonus for high-priced
                             seller}

  begin {procedure WriteOutput}
  Commission := TotalSales*Rate;

  if HighNumber < CutOff then
    begin    {then}
      writeln;
      writeln('At Cockroach Realty, your ability to');
      writeln('earn is bounded only by your own');
      writeln('abilities.   Get out there and sell!');
      writeln;
      write('Your commission for this month is $ ');
      writeln(Commission:10:2);
    end      {then}
```

```
    else
      begin {here's a high-priced seller}
        Bonus := HighNumber*BonusRate;

        writeln;
        write('You have sold ', HighNumber, ' houses this');
        writeln(' month for over $200,000.   That''s the');
        writeln('kind of thing we like to see from our');
        writeln('agents here at Cockroach Realty.');
        writeln('Congratulations; keep up the good work!');
        writeln;
        write('Your commission for this month is $ ');
        writeln(Commission:10:2, ' plus your bonus for');
        write(HighNumber, ' high-priced sales of $ ');
        writeln(Bonus:10:2, ' giving a total for the month of');
        writeln;
        writeln('***** $ ':25, Commission + Bonus:10:2, ' *****');
      end;      {high-priced seller}
  end;    {procedure WriteOutput}
```

7.2.2 *The Empty* Else *Clause*

One variation in the **if** statement allows for an empty **else** clause. To have some action taken when a condition is true and to have control simply proceed to the statement following the **if** statement when the condition is false, the **else** part of the statement is omitted. The statement

```
  if Count > 10 then
    writeln('Too many');
```

will write the message "Too many" when the value of *Count* exceeds 10, and will do nothing for other values of *Count*.

7.2.3 *Nested* If *Statements*

Some statements in a compound statement could be **if** statements themselves, leading to ***nested* if *statements.*** This allows multiple courses of action to be taken. Program *Grade* below is a classic example of the use of nested **if** statements. Note how comments indicate what condition holds true at each level of nesting.

```
program Grade(input, output);
{assigns student letter grade based on percent}

var
    Average : integer; {average percent grade for student}

begin
  write('Enter the student''s grade average: ');
  readln(Average);
  writeln;
```

```
  if Average >= 90 then
    {Average >= 90}
    writeln('Grade for this student is an A')

  else
    if Average >= 80 then
      {80 <= Average < 90}
      writeln('Grade for this student is a B')

    else
      if Average >= 70 then
        {70 <= Average < 80}
        writeln('Grade for this student is a C')

      else
        if Average >= 60 then
          {60 <= Average < 70}
          writeln('Grade for this student is a D')

        else
          {Average < 60}
          writeln('Grade for this student is an F');
end.
```

RUNNING THE PROGRAM...

```
Enter the student's grade average: 74
Grade for this student is a C
```

The possible paths of action these nested **if** statements allow can be represented as branches in a "decision tree," as in Figure 7.4a. In "Running the Program..." above, *Average* is 74. Because *Average* is not greater than or equal to 90, the **then** clause in the main **if** statement is not executed, and control passes to the **else** clause. The **else** clause isitself an **if** statement; because *Average* is not greater than or equal to 80, control passes to the **else** clause. This **else** clause is also an **if** statement; this time, the boolean condition to execute the **then** clause is true, and the appropriate message is written out. Control then transfers to the statement after the major **if** statement, which is the end of the program. Figure 7.4b shows the path through the decision tree for this case.

The empty **else** clause, together with the ability to use nested **if** statements, leads to a potential ambiguity known as the ***dangling else*** problem. A statement of the following form

```
  if boolean expression 1 then
    if boolean expression 2 then
      statement1
    else
      statement2
```

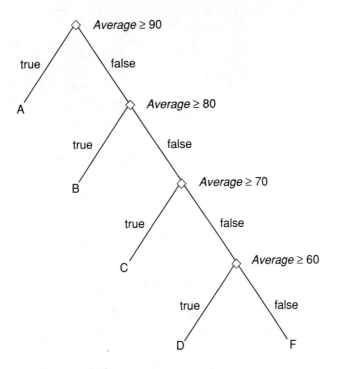

FIGURE   7.4A   "Decision tree" for nested **if** statements in program *Grade*.

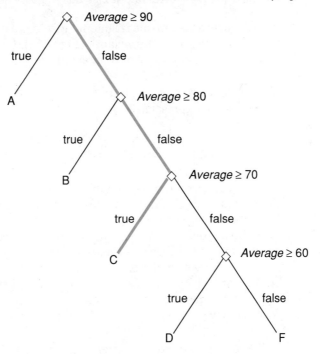

FIGURE   7.4B   Path through decision tree for sample program execution.

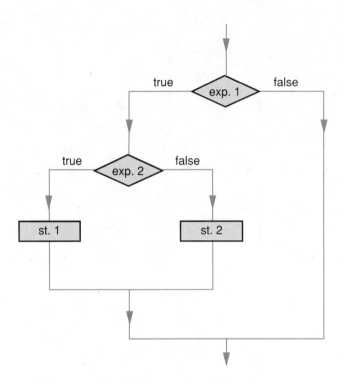

FIGURE 7.5A Pascal resolves the dangling else ambiguity as above.

appears to be a case of one **if** statement, with an empty **else** clause, and with an if-then-else for its **then** clause (Fig. 7.5a). But indenting is meaningless to the compiler, so the above statement is syntactically equivalent to

if boolean expression 1 **then**
   if boolean expression 2 **then**
      statement1
else
      statement2;

Use begin-end pairs to clarify then-else relationships in nested if statements; do not require that the program reader recall the dangling else convention.

This appears to be a case of one if-then-else statement, with a **then** clause that is an **if** statement with an empty **else** clause (Fig. 7.5b). Which interpretation is correct?

Pascal associates an **else** with the nearest preceding **then** statement not already associated with an **else.** Based on this, the first interpretation above is correct. Use of **begin-end** can clarify matters. In the version below, the **begin-end** forces the **else** to be part of the major **if** statement's **then** clause. This has exactly the same effect as using no **begin-end,** but one does not have to remember the dangling **else** convention.

  if boolean expression 1 **then**
    begin {then}
      if boolean expression 2 **then**

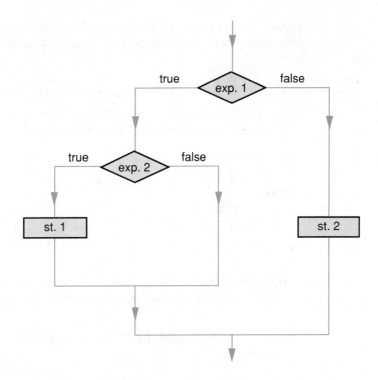

FIGURE   7.5B   The dangling else convention does <u>not</u> give this interpretation.

```
        statement1
     else
        statement2;
   end;   {then}
```

The intent of the second interpretation can also be accomplished by using **begin-end** to override the default treatment of the dangling **else**. In the following version, the **begin-end** forces the **else** to be associated with the first **then.**

```
if boolean expression 1 then
   begin {then}
     if boolean expression 2 then
        statement1;
   end    {then}
else
   statement2;
```

It is a good idea to use **begin-end** pairs even when only a single statement is included within the pair. That way if additional statements are added later, the framework for a compound statement already exists (see the next CHECKUP problem, which probably does not do what its author intended). Comments with **begin** and **end** provide clarification, especially important where nested statements result in complex constructions.

CHECKUP 7.4   What is the output from the following section of code if *A* has the value 7? If *A* has the value 4? If *A* has the value 12?

```
if A < 5 then
  writeln('small A')
else
  writeln('big A');
  writeln('Next time make A smaller.');
```

Because of the way most Pascal systems evaluate boolean expressions, an unpleasant surprise may occur. Consider the statement

```
if (Next < 100) and (Quantity/(GroupSize − Next) > 1.0) then
  statement1;
```

and suppose that *Next* and *GroupSize* are integer variables each with a current value of 100. An attempt to evaluate the boolean expression

```
Quantity/(GroupSize − Next) > 1.0
```

will provoke a run-time error (attempt to divide by zero). However, the boolean expression

```
Next < 100
```

Both components in a boolean expression using and are evaluated, even if the first component evaluates to false. If there is a possibility of a problem, use nested if statements.

is false. The result of the boolean operator **and** when one of the operands is false will be false, regardless of the truth value of the other operand. One might think that the entire expression is assigned the value *false* as soon as the first operand is evaluated, that the second operand is never evaluated, and that trouble is avoided. This is not a good assumption because generally both operands are evaluated in any case. Nested **if** statements can be used to avoid such a problem. Thus

```
if Next < 100 then
  if Quantity/(GroupSize − Next) > 1.0 then
    statement1;
```

has the desired effect of allowing statement1 to be executed only when both boolean expressions are true, and if *Next* has the value 100, the second expression is not evaluated.

7.2.4 *Enabling/Disabling Diagnostic Writes*

If statements can be used with diagnostic *writeln* statements in order to quickly and easily enable or disable these debugging aids. A boolean constant called *debug* is declared, and each diagnostic *writeln* statement is written in the form

if debug **then** writeln(...);

These *writeln* statements are activated if the constant value for *debug* is set to *true* and ignored if the constant value for *debug* is set to *false*. Enabling/disabling diagnostic statements becomes a matter of changing the value of one program constant.

7.3 **The** Case **Statement**

The **if** statement allows us to direct the program into one of two actions. The **case** statement allows choices among multiple actions. In the **case** statement, the choice of action depends on the value of an ordinal expression, that is, an expression that takes on values from an ordinal data type. (Recall that *real* is not an ordinal data type, so a real-valued expression cannot be used to determine the choice of action.)

In the following sample **case** statement, a *char* expression, in fact, a single *char* variable with the identifier *transaction*, is evaluated. Based upon the value, exactly one of three procedures is invoked.

```
case transaction of
   'D' : DepositProcess;
   'W' : WithdrawalProcess;
   'B' : BalanceProcess;
end {case statement}
```

A value for *transaction* of 'W', for example, causes the *WithdrawalProcess* procedure to be invoked; after *WithdrawalProcess* has been executed, control goes to the statement following the **case** statement. Note that the **case** statement requires an **end** that has no corresponding **begin,** and that semicolons are used to separate the action statements.

Multiple values can produce the same action. The following statement is similar to the one above but takes lower-case letters into account.

```
case transaction of
   'D','d' : DepositProcess;
   'W','w': WithdrawalProcess;
   'B','b' : BalanceProcess;
end {case statement}
```

Each course of action in a **case** statement must be preceded by a list, called a ***case label*** list, of the values that will initiate that action. Values in the list are separated by commas, and a colon separates the list from the action statement. Each value in each case label list must be a particular constant value (not an expression) of the same data type as the expression being evaluated. In particular, a string constant such as 'Deposit' would not be a legal entry in a label list. A particular constant value cannot appear in more than one label list because then it would not be clear which action should be taken for that value.

The course of action associated with a case label list must be a single Pascal statement. However, this statement can be a compound statement or a procedure invocation, thus allowing an entire section of code to be executed. The compound statement could contain **if** statements, or other **case** statements, leading to nested **case** statements. The statement following a label list can also be the null statement, so that some values of the case expression result in no action being taken. Comments describing each different course of action may be helpful.

CHECKUP 7.5   What will be the output if the following section of code is executed when X has the value 4?

```
case 2*X + 1 of
   2,4,6,8,10 : writeln('EVEN');
   1,3,5,7,9  : writeln('ODD');
end;
```

CHECKUP 7.6   What will be the output if the following section of code is executed when Y has the value 'C'?

```
case Y of
   'A','B',1,2 : writeln('early');
   'C','D',3,4 : writeln('middle');
   'E','F',5,6 : writeln('late');
end;
```

If the expression in a **case** statement evaluates to a value not found in any of the case label lists, standard Pascal gives an error message and terminates the program. This makes it important to consider all possible values of the expression. Some implementations allow an "else" or "otherwise" clause to take care of values not appearing in any case label list; the action associated with the "else" could be to write a message that the value is not legitimate. This is a handy feature, because errors in data entry may lead to unexpected values for the expression, and it is better to deal with them gracefully by providing an appropriate message than to have the program crash. Something similar can be accomplished in standard Pascal by using a new relational operator **in,** together with set notation.

Mathematically, sets are collections of elements represented by listing the elements within curly braces, as in {1,2,3}. Since curly braces denote comments in Pascal, sets are denoted by square brackets, as in [1,2,3]. A given set can contain elements from only one ordinal type. A short-cut form to denote consecutive values is to write [1..5] instead of [1,2,3,4,5].

The relational operator **in** returns *true* if a value is an element of a set and *false* if it is not. To allow for bank-machine-customer mistakes in data entry in the example above, we could write

```
if transaction in ['D','d','W','w','B','b'] then
   case transaction of
      'D','d' : DepositProcess;
      'W','w': WithdrawalProcess;
      'B','b' : BalanceProcess;
   end {case statement}
else
   writeln('Request not valid, try again.');
```

A **case** statement can always be replaced by nested if statements, but the **case** statement is usually more readable.

CHECKUP 7.7   Replace the statement

```
if transaction  in  ['D','d','W','w','B','b'] then
   case transaction of
      'D','d'  : DepositProcess;
      'W','w' : WithdrawalProcess;
      'B','b'  : BalanceProcess;
   end {case statement}
else
   writeln('Request not valid, try again.');
```

with nested **if** statements.

Replacing nested **if** statements with a single **case** statement is not always possible, although the following program reworks the earlier student grade assignment program using a **case** statement. The **in** operator is used to check on the validity of the data, and a procedure replaces multiple *writeln* statements.

```
program Grade(input, output);
{assigns student letter grade based on percent}

var
      Average : integer; {average percent grade for student}
```

```pascal
procedure WriteOutput(Lettergrade: char);
{writes student letter grade message}

  begin {procedure WriteOutput}
    write('Grade for this student is ');
    if (Lettergrade = 'A') or (Lettergrade = 'F') then
      writeln('an ', Lettergrade)
    else
      writeln('a ', Lettergrade);
  end;  {procedure WriteOutput}

begin   {main program}
  write('Enter the student' 's grade average: ');
  readln(Average);
  writeln;

  {Average div 10 gives the 10s digit of the average - this
   determines the letter grade}

  if Average div 10 in [0..10] then
    case Average div 10 of
      9,10  : WriteOutput('A');
      8     : WriteOutput('B');
      7     : WriteOutput('C');
      6     : WriteOutput('D');
      5,4,3,2,1,0: WriteOutput('F');
    end
  else
    writeln('Grade average not between 0-100, enter  again.');
end.    {main program}
```

7.4 New Data Types

Type declarations by themselves do not create any variables of that type.

Pascal provides four standard simple data types—*integer, real, char,* and *boolean.* Legitimate values of these data types are automatically recognized. Pascal also allows us to define our own data types. The first step in this process is to do a type declaration that describes the form of legitimate values of the new data type. The type declaration by itself does not create any variables of this data type. That must be done by a variable declaration, the same as for any other data type. A type declaration in a program or module appears in the declarations section, after any constant declarations and before any variable declarations. Rules of scope apply to type declarations; once a type has been declared, it is recognized within that program block and any internal blocks.

7.4.1 *Enumerated Types*

An *enumerated data type,* also called a *user-defined data type,* has as its legitimate values those elements that we list in a finite list. An enumerated type, as the name suggests, is an ordinal data type, so the order in which we list these elements is the ordering that will be used by the ordinal functions of *succ* and *pred*, for example.

To declare an enumerated type, we use the reserved word **type** followed by an identifier for the type, an equal sign, and the list of elements enclosed in parentheses. The elements must be identifiers, not numbers or characters. The statement

type
    Direction = (North, South, East, West);

declares a new data type called *Direction*. The legitimate values of this data type are the four listed elements. Given the variable declaration

var
    Compass, Wind : Direction;

then the assignment

  Compass := South;

is legal, just as assigning a value of 3 to an *integer* variable is legal because 3 is one of the allowable integer values. The assignment

  Compass := 5;

is illegal in the same way that assigning a value of 'B' to an *integer* variable is illegal. Although the type declaration uses an identifier to name the type, remember that it does not itself create any variables. The type declaration only sets up the collection of legal values that variables of that type can take on. Variable declarations, as for *Compass* above, are required to create variables of that type.

A given identifier can appear in only one enumerated-type declaration list. The following would be illegal:

Identifiers cannot appear in more than one enumerated type declaration list.

type
    Direction = (North, South, East, West);
    Region = (Midwest, South, Atlantic);

Because we need separate identifiers for a type and a variable of that type, it may seem difficult to come up with enough meaningful identifiers. If we have a meaningful identifier for a particular variable in mind, and that variable will be the only one of its type, we can "borrow" the identifier name for use as the type identifier as well by a trick such as

type
    HouseType = (Ranch, Trilevel, TwoStory, TownHouse);

var
    House : HouseType;

As we have seen, variables of an enumerated type can receive values in assignment statements. Given the earlier declarations we made, the statement

```
Compass := Wind;
```

assigns the current value of *Wind* (which must be one of the four allowable values) to *Compass*. Relational operators can be used. For example, the expression

```
Wind < East
```

is true if the current value of *Wind* is *North* because *North* precedes *East* in the type declaration for *Direction*. Of course only variables or values of the same enumerated type can be compared, otherwise a type clash results. Variables of enumerated types can be used as procedure or function parameters, and function values can be declared as enumerated types. The standard ordinal functions certainly apply; for example *succ(North)* is *South,* and *ord(North)* is 0.

In summary, it appears we can do the same things with enumerated-type variables that we can with any other kind of variable; however, there is one major drawback. We cannot read or write values for enumerated-type variables. We cannot, for instance, use a statement like

```
readln(Wind);
```

with input data of *East* in order to assign a value of *East* to *Wind.* Enumerated-type variables are strictly internal variables. This restriction makes enumerated data types a less nifty idea than if such variables could communicate directly with the outside world. Nevertheless, they still aid internal program documentation because they can provide a more meaningful description of the program's intent. The following **case** statement

```
case Compass of
   North : writeln('Turn left');
   South : writeln('Turn right');
   East  : writeln('Go forward');
   West  : writeln('Go backward');
end;
```

conveys more information (to the human reader) than the one below, which could be used if *CompassChar* had been declared a *char* variable:

```
case CompassChar of
   'N' : writeln('Turn left');
   'S' : writeln('Turn right');
   'E' : writeln('Go forward');
   'W': writeln('Go backward');
end;
```

Enumerated-type
variables cannot
be read in or
written out; a
"translation
table" must be
used to simulate
this capability.

Although we can't directly read values for *Compass*, we can fake the process by using an intermediate *char* variable, such as *CompassChar*, to read the data and then building a "translation table" using another **case** statement:

```
case CompassChar of
  'N' : Compass := North;
  'S' : Compass := South;
  'E' : Compass := East;
  'W' : Compass := West;
end;
```

A similar "translation table" can be used to fake the process of writing out enumerated type values.[†]

CHECKUP 7.8   Given the declarations

```
type
    Meal = (Appetizer, Soup, Salad, Entree, Dessert);
    Wine = (White, Red, Rose);
var
    Course : Meal;
    Drink, Beverage : Wine;
```

a c d – legal

which of the following are legal statements? For any that are not, why not?

Drink

✓ *a.* Course := Soup;
✗ *b.* Wine := White;
   c. **if** Drink < Beverage **then** Course := Entree;
   d. **if** Course >= Soup **then** Drink := Red;
✓ *e.* **if** Drink = Red **then** writeln(Red);   *cannot writ out enumerated type*
   f. **if** Meal = Soup **then** Beverage := White;

7.4.2 *Subrange Types*

Subrange types
can only be
defined for
ordinal data
types.

Another way to create a new data type is to select a "subrange" of values from an existing ordinal type. The subrange is described by giving the first and last values to be included. The ordering of elements in the original ordinal type is preserved in the subrange. The declaration

```
type
    PositiveInteger = 1..maxint;
```

[†]Some Pascal versions do allow variables of enumerated type to be written out directly.

selects all integers between 1 and *maxint*, inclusive, as values for the type *PositiveInteger*. Note that no parentheses are needed in the declaration statement. The declarations

type
```
    Negatives   =  −100.. −1;
    FirstGroup  =  'A'..'H';
    Direction   =  (North, South, East, West);
    NonWest     =  North..East;
```

select the negative integers from −100 through −1 as elements of *Negatives*, characters from 'A' through 'H' as elements of *FirstGroup*, and the values *North*, *South*, and *East* as elements of *NonWest*. The declaration for *NonWest* must follow the declaration for *Direction*, otherwise the elements for the subrange of values are not recognized. (Note that *North* is not being used in two different enumerated-type declarations, which would be illegal.)

Suppose that along with the above type declarations we also have the following variable declarations:

var
```
    Total    :  PositiveInteger;
    Missing  :  Negatives;
    Initial  :  FirstGroup;
    Tide     :  Direction;
    Heading  :  NonWest;
```

Then an assignment statement such as

```
    Heading := West;
```

will usually produce a (fatal) run-time error, because *West* is a value outside the range of allowable values for *Heading*.

However, the assignment statement

```
    Tide  := Heading;
```

is legal, even though *Tide* and *Heading* are not the same data type. This is because the two data types *Direction* and *NonWest* are **compatible,** that is, the underlying set from which their values are taken is the same. Assignments can be made between type-compatible variables. In this case, because the possible values for *Heading* are a subrange of those for *Tide*, the current value of *Heading* will always be one that can legally be assigned to *Tide*. The assignment statement

```
    Heading := Tide;
```

will produce no compilation error, since the two types are compatible, but a run-time error will probably occur if the current value of *Tide* is *West*. Similarly,

Assignment statements and relational operators can be used between type-compatible variables.

    Missing : = Total;

is syntactically correct, because the underlying values for each data type are integers, but an error is almost sure to occur.

Comparisons using relational operators can also be made between type-compatible variables. Also, the actual parameter corresponding to a value formal parameter need only be type-compatible with the formal parameter, although a run-time error will usually occur if the value of the actual parameter at execution is out of the range of values for the formal parameter. However, the actual parameter corresponding to a variable formal parameter must be of the exact same type as the formal parameter, not just type-compatible.

Subrange data types serve two purposes. First, they give the reader of the program additional information about variables. Declaring *Initial* to be of type *FirstGroup* provides more information about *Initial* than if it had simply been declared as a type *char* variable. Second, subrange data types provide us with a defense mechanism against some programming errors. As a simple example, still using the above type declarations, suppose that a program contains *integer* quantities *Sum1* and *Sum2,* and the intended assignment statement

    Total : = Sum1 + Sum2;

is mistakenly entered as

    Total : = Sum1 − Sum2;

No compilation error results, but if *Sum1 − Sum2* evaluates to a negative value, a run-time error usually occurs because of the attempt to assign a negative (out-of-range) value to *Total*. (Nothing would have been detected if *Total* had been declared only as type *integer*.) This usually causes the program to crash—not a desirable situation, but one preferable to carrying out a computation with an erroneous value without a clue that anything is wrong.

Out-of-range assignments within a program to variables of a subrange data type should cause an error, but out-of-range input data may not.

While subrange checks generally guard against erroneous values being assigned to a subrange variable by an assignment statement, they often do not guard against out-of-range values being assigned through a *read* statement. The statement

    readln(Total);

may not produce an error message if the value 0 is provided as input. **Data validation** for input data should be handled by the program itself, using **if** statements, for example. In this way, not only can out-of-range input values be detected, but at the same time the user can also be given the opportunity to enter correct data and the program can continue to execute. We'll see some examples shortly.

7.5 Program Testing

Program testing occurs after the initial debugging of a program or program module, when there appears to be a correct version.

7.5.1 Black-Box and White-Box Testing

1. Problem
   specification
2. Algorithm
   development
3. Coding
4. Debugging
5. Testing
6. Documenting
7. Maintenance

There are two approaches to program testing. One approach assumes no knowledge of the internal structure of the program but does assume that a very detailed problem specification exists. The program is tested against the specifications by selecting sets of test data that will demonstrate all the different conditions the program is supposed to handle. The difficulty is that the number of possibilities is usually very large, so that dealing with all possible combinations of legitimate input data, to say nothing of testing how the program handles erroneous data, is a monumental task. Except for very simple programs, it will not be feasible to test all cases. Testing may proceed from the most likely or most important classes of input down to the point where time or money dictates that testing be concluded. Therefore, errors may still lurk in the program, to appear months or years later under some unusual combination of input values.

Here again we see the importance of a careful problem specification against which to test the final product. Because no internal knowledge of the program is assumed, this testing approach is known as **black-box testing**— the program is treated as a "black box" (an engineering term) that accepts input and produces corresponding output for inspection.

The second approach uses knowledge about the internal structure of the program, leading this approach to be called **white-box testing.** In all but the simplest of programs, the path that the program logic takes during execution depends on the data values. Most programs will have many different paths; now that we know how to do decision statements such as **if** and **case,** we see how it is possible to execute one section of code at one time and another section of code at another.

The goal of white-box testing is to exercise the program as thoroughly as possible, choosing various sets of data values that force the program to execute as many different paths as possible. Although this sounds like a simple task, in large programs there are at least four difficulties. First, it may be hard to actually identify all the possible paths. Second, the number of such paths may be very large. Suppose, for example, that a program has four points at which one of two courses of action is possible (four **if-then-else** statements, for instance); even this simple situation provides $2^4 = 16$ different paths of execution through the program. Third, it may be hard to identify a data set for each particular path–what data characteristics force program execution to follow this particular path, as opposed to some other one? Fourth, even if a particular branch executes correctly for one set of data, it may still contain an error that might surface under another set of data.

In either testing approach, the absolute "answer" for a given set of input values may not be known. The program is judged to "pass" a particular trial if its behavior seems normal and the output falls within an expected range of values and is consistent (e.g., if X items went in, then Y items should come out). Thus, for a number of reasons, neither testing approach can guarantee that a large program is error-free. Black-box and white-box testing should both be used as complementary approaches to detecting as many errors as possible.

7.5.2 Test-Set Generation

Test programs on both typical and special cases of data.

Test-set generation–the task of constructing sets of data for either black-box or white-box testing–is a big job. It is important to test typical cases, because these will constitute the largest volume of input over the life of the program. Special cases, however, usually reveal more errors. Of particular interest are "boundary values." If something is supposed to work for a range of values, the upper and lower limits should be tested, along with beginning and ending conditions.

In a large programming project, there may be a group of people whose sole job is generating test sets. Often an independent group, not the one that did the program development, is contracted to do program testing. The theory is that outsiders have no special interests to protect, since they have invested nothing in the program development. They may be more zealous in their attempts to flush out errors, as well as bringing a fresh viewpoint to observing program behavior. Independent testing provides a sort of checks-and-balances system. Research is being done on automatic test-set generation, so that test-set candidates are constructed as part of program development itself.

7.5.3 Defensive Programming

Because data to a program can't always be guaranteed to be error-free, programs must be tested for their behavior on illegal, as well as legal, data. While the program is being written, the programmer should adopt an attitude of **defensive programming,** assuming that errors in input data will occur and trying to minimize their damage. The objective is to make the program as **robust** as possible: in the presence of unexpected data values, while it may not be possible for the program to provide correct answers, it still must proceed in a controlled manner. As a simple example of defensive programming, suppose the *real* value *Distance* is to be divided by the *real* value *Time* and the result assigned to the *real* variable *Rate*. The beginning programmer will write

```
readln(Time);
Rate  := Distance/Time;
```

The defensive programmer will take steps to validate the input data and write

```
readln(Time);
if Time <> 0 then
   Rate  := Distance/Time
else
```

```
begin
  writeln('Time cannot have value 0;');
  writeln('please enter value for Time again: ');
  readln(Time);
  Rate  := Distance/Time;
end;
```

This gives the user a second chance to enter valid data. In the next chapter, we'll be able to give the user multiple retries.

Defensive programming techniques like the above **if** statement guard against wrong but reasonable data. Total garbage entered in response to the *readln* statement (input such as g$3#, for example) will still cause the program to crash because of a type clash. The ultimate in data validation is to read everything in as character data, one character at a time. Then, no matter what keys on the keyboard are struck, there is no possibility of a type clash on input. The character data then has to be searched to pick out meaningful characters. Characters that represent numeric values can be used to internally construct a numeric value and assign it to a numeric-type variable. Whether these extreme measures are justified depends on the task at hand and how critical it is that failure be avoided.

Use defensive programming techniques to validate input data.

Extremely critical situations exist where human life is at stake and time is essential, such as in the flight-control software that actually controls the plane in military fighter aircraft. In this split-second environment, a software failure could result in the loss of crew and plane. Defensive programming and program testing should be carried to the ultimate in such a situation. Yet it has come to be recognized that despite adherence to the philosophy of top-down design and careful attention to the steps of the programming process, despite employing defensive programming techniques and extensive testing, bugs may remain in large software systems. Research is being done on **fault-tolerant software,** software that is able to continue functioning even when deeply hidden bugs appear. Approaches to achieving fault tolerance rely on multiple versions of software on the theory that a bug in one piece of software is not likely to appear in quite the same way in a different, independently developed version of that software.

Extensive testing still does not guarantee detecting all errors; the level of testing depends on the application.

7.5.4 Bottom-up and Top-down Testing

Testing should not be done only on the entire, completed program. Both black-box and white-box testing can be carried out incrementally on the program modules as they are developed. We discussed the use of stubs and drivers for testing program modules in Chapter 4.

In **bottom-up testing,** individual modules are tested using driver code. After individual modules have been developed and tested, they are combined and the resulting program tested in an **integration testing** phase. Numerous integration phases may occur as more of the program is completed. Finally, the entire piece of software is tested as part of the computing environment in, which it will be used—interacting with other applications software, using a particular operating system, compiler, and input/output devices, perhaps telecommunications hardware and software, etc. After successfully completing all these levels of testing, the software is issued in a "limited release" version. The software is released first to an **alpha test site,** consisting of in-house users other than the program developers. After successful alpha testing, the software is released to **beta test sites,** consisting of external users. Alpha and beta test sites get use of the program with forewarning that some errors may remain; these users help further exercise the code. Finally, the program passes final acceptance tests and is signed off by the client or marketed for general use.

One drawback of bottom-up testing is that problems that are easiest to solve—bugs in individual modules—are discovered first. Problems of interfacing modules and interfacing the software with the rest of the computing system are more difficult to solve and will typically involve more design-level changes. Allowing discovery of such problems to occur only at the end of the programming process, when it is more costly and time-consuming to fix them, is poor planning. The entire programming effort may be halted until such problems can be solved.

Top-down testing, like top-down design, considers the program in large pieces first, then successfully refines the level of testing. Major modules and their interfaces are tested first, using stubs for modules. As the program design is refined, stubs for submodules are used and lower-level interfaces tested. The advantage to this approach is that it can be carried on concurrently with program development, and it finds major errors early, when there is less involved in making changes.

Do not postpone program testing until the end; use both bottom-up and top-down testing.

In practice, a combination of top-down and bottom-up testing is employed. The overall approach is one of top-down testing, but individual modules are inserted as they are tested. Once again, the budget for testing—time and money to be allocated to this activity—will depend on the application.

7.6 Sample Software Development Project—Diving

Problem Statement

Write a program to automate the process of computing the score for an individual dive in a diving competition.

Problem Specification

According to the rules of the United States Diving Association, there are seven judges in a diving meet. Each judge may award a score for a dive as any whole or half value between 0 and 10, for example, 8.5 is a valid score. The high and low scores from the seven scores are eliminated. The remaining five scores are added together. Then three-fifths of this total score is multiplied by the degree of difficulty of the dive. The result is the final score for that individual dive. The degree of difficulty of a dive is determined by the particular dive attempted and can run from 1.0 to 4.0 to the nearest tenth, for example, 3.2 is a valid degree of difficulty.

Input: degree of difficulty, seven scores
Output: input echo
        final score for dive

Algorithm Development

Since the algorithm is already contained in the problem specification, we simply need to break it down into manageable subtasks. As usual, we'll isolate the process of getting the input to a single procedure. Then we have to find the high and low judging score—we'll use a separate module for each of these two tasks. We'll do the rest of the calculations in another module and, finally, write the output. Figure 7.6 shows the structure chart.

Because we have some ranges of values on both the possible scores and the degree of difficulty, it would be a good idea to validate the input data.

Get Input

This procedure must request and collect the degree of difficulty for the dive and the seven judges' scores. All of these values are returned for use by the rest of the program, so all will be variable parameters of type *real*.

```
procedure GetInput(var Degree, S1, S2, S3, S4, S5, S6,
                       S7: real);
{gets the degree of difficulty of the dive, and the seven
 individual judges' scores for the dive, and returns these to
 the main program.}


begin    {procedure GetInput}

    prompt for and read degree of difficulty and seven scores
    check for valid range of data

end;     {procedure GetInput}
```

For data validation, we'll use boolean-valued functions to check that a real value is given to the nearest tenth, and that the degree of difficulty falls within the proper range. We'll also use a boolean-valued function to validate each score; bad input for an individual judge's score will be handled by a procedure. Each erroneous entry will result in a second chance to enter valid data. This refinement leads to the structure chart of Figure 7.7. Because the new subprograms are fairly simple, we won't do separate algorithm developments for them.

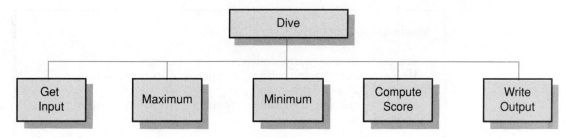

FIGURE 7.6 Structure chart for program *Dive*.

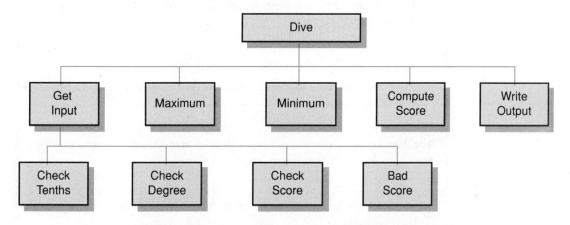

FIGURE 7.7 Refinement of structure chart for program *Dive*.

Maximum

This module receives seven values and must find the largest value. This is a very common task, and we have pulled it out into a separate module partly for this reason. In fact, because only the single maximum value must be returned, we'll use a function. The idea behind the algorithm for this function is to scan the list of input values and set the current maximum value equal to the largest value found so far. Initially, the current maximum value is set to the first value. When each new value is examined, it is tested against the current maximum; if it is larger, it is made the new current maximum value. When all values have been examined, the current maximum is the overall maximum. The pseudocode version below calls for successive **if** statements with empty **else** clauses.

function Maximum(S1, S2, S3, S4, S5, S6, S7: real): real;
{this function computes the maximum value from among
 seven input values}

begin   {function Maximum}

Continued

Maximum—Continued

set current maximum to S1
if S2 > current maximum, change current maximum to S2, otherwise leave it alone
if S3 > current maximum, change current maximum to S3, otherwise leave it alone

.
.
.

if S7 > current maximum, change current maximum to S7, otherwise leave it alone
set *Maximum* to current maximum

end;   {function Maximum}

Minimum
We'll make this a function also; it works just like *Maximum*, except that it looks for successively smaller values.

function Minimum(S1, S2, S3, S4, S5, S6, S7: real): real;
{this function computes the minimum value from among seven input values}

Compute Score
This procedure needs to know the seven scores and the degree of difficulty. It invokes the *Maximum* and *Minimum* functions to find the high and low scores and throw them away. It then carries out the rest of the arithmetic and returns the final score to the main program.

procedure ComputeScore(Score1, Score2, Score3, Score4,
                          Score5, Score6, Score7,
                          DegreeOfDifficulty: real;
                          var FinalScore: real);
{uses U.S. Diving Association rules for championship diving meets: eliminate high and low score, take 3/5 of the remaining total, multiply by degree of difficulty of the dive}

begin   {procedure ComputeScore}

add the scores, subtract the maximum and minimum value
multiply the total by 3/5 and the degree of difficulty

end   {procedure ComputeScore}

> **Write Output**
>
> This procedure needs to know the input data and the final score.
>
> **procedure** WriteOutput(Degree, S1, S2, S3, S4, S5,
>   S6, S7, Score: real);
> {writes the degree of difficulty of the dive, the seven
> original judges' scores, and the final score for the dive}

The complete program appears below.

program Dive(input, output);
{computes the score for an individual dive using U.S. Diving
Association rules}

var

    DegreeOfDifficulty : real;   {the degree of difficulty of
                                     the dive attempted}
    Score1,Score2,Score3,Score4,   {the individual judges'}
    Score5,Score6,Score7 : real;   {scores for this dive}
    FinalScore : real;   {final score for this dive}

procedure GetInput(**var** Degree, S1, S2, S3, S4, S5, S6, S7: real);
{gets the degree of difficulty of the dive, and the seven
 individual judges' scores for the dive, and returns these to the
 main program}

var
    Number : integer;   {individual judge's number}

function TenthsOnly(Value: real): boolean;
{checks that a real value is given only to the nearest tenth.}

    begin   {function TenthsOnly}
      if (abs(round(10*Value) − 10*Value) < 1.0E−10) **then**
        TenthsOnly := true
      else
        TenthsOnly := false;
    end;   {function TenthsOnly}

function DegreeCheck(Degree: real): boolean;
{performs a check on the degree of difficulty value; should be
 between 1.0 and 4.0}

    begin   {function DegreeCheck}
      if ((1.0 <= Degree) **and** (Degree <= 4.0)) **then**
        DegreeCheck := true

```
    else
       DegreeCheck := false;
  end; {function DegreeCheck}


function ScoreCheck(Score: real): boolean;
{performs a check on the individual judge's score for the dive;
should be between 0.0 and 10.0, in increments of 0.5; note
that if Score is given to the nearest tenth, then
round(10*Score) should be an integer ending in 0 or 5}

  begin    {function ScoreCheck}
    if ((0.0 <= Score) and (Score <= 10.0) and
       (round(10*Score) mod 5 = 0)) then

       ScoreCheck := true
    else
       ScoreCheck := false;
  end;     {function ScoreCheck}


procedure BadScore(Number: integer);
{invalid score entered for judge # "Number," another try
permitted}

  begin {procedure BadScore}
    writeln('This score is not valid.');
    write('The individual judge' 's score must be ');
    writeln('between 0.0 and 10.0,');
    writeln('to the nearest half.');
    write('Try again.    ');
    write('Enter score for judge # ', Number:1,': ');
  end; {procedure BadScore}

  begin    {procedure GetInput}
    writeln('What is the degree of difficulty of this dive?');
    write('(enter value between 1.0 and 4.0,');
    writeln(' to the nearest tenth):');
    readln(Degree);
    if not DegreeCheck(Degree) or not TenthsOnly(Degree) then
       begin    {not valid data}
         writeln('This degree of difficulty is not valid.');
         write('The degree of difficulty must be ');
         writeln('between 1.0 and 4.0,');
         writeln('to the nearest tenth.');
         write('Try again.    ');
         write('Enter degree of difficulty: ');
         readln(Degree);
       end;    {not valid data}
    writeln;
```

```
{now for the rest of the input, the seven scores}
writeln('Give the seven judges'' scores.');
write('(enter values between 0.0 and 10.0,');
writeln(' to the nearest half):');

Number := 1;
write('Judge #', Number:1, ': ');
readln(S1);
if not ScoreCheck(S1) or not TenthsOnly(S1) then
  begin
    BadScore(Number);
    readln(S1);
  end;

Number := 2;
write('Judge #', Number:1, ': ');
readln(S2);
if not ScoreCheck(S2) or not TenthsOnly(S2) then
  begin
    BadScore(Number);
    readln(S2);
  end;

Number := 3;
write('Judge #', Number:1, ': ');
readln(S3);
if not ScoreCheck(S3) or not TenthsOnly(S3) then
  begin
    BadScore(Number);
    readln(S3);
  end;

Number := 4;
write('Judge #', Number:1, ': ');
readln(S4);
if not ScoreCheck(S4) or not TenthsOnly(S4) then
  begin
    BadScore(Number);
    readln(S4);
  end;

Number := 5;
write('Judge #', Number:1, ': ');
readln(S5);
if not ScoreCheck(S5) or not TenthsOnly(S5) then
  begin
    BadScore(Number);
    readln(S5);
  end;
```

```
        Number := 6;
        write('Judge #', Number:1, ': ');
        readln(S6);
        if not ScoreCheck(S6) or not TenthsOnly(S6) then
          begin
            BadScore(Number);
            readln(S6);
          end;

        Number := 7;
        write('Judge #', Number:1, ': ');
        readln(S7);
        if not ScoreCheck(S7) or not TenthsOnly(S7) then
          begin
            BadScore(Number);
            readln(S7);
          end;
    end;      {procedure GetInput}


function Maximum(S1, S2, S3, S4, S5, S6, S7: real): real;
{this function computes the maximum value from among seven
 input values}

var
    CurrentMax : real;         {current maximum value}

  begin      {function Maximum}
    CurrentMax := S1;
    if S2 > CurrentMax then CurrentMax := S2;
    if S3 > CurrentMax then CurrentMax := S3;
    if S4 > CurrentMax then CurrentMax := S4;
    if S5 > CurrentMax then CurrentMax := S5;
    if S6 > CurrentMax then CurrentMax := S6;
    if S7 > CurrentMax then CurrentMax := S7;
    Maximum := CurrentMax;
  end;       {function Maximum}


function Minimum(S1, S2, S3, S4, S5, S6, S7: real): real;
{this function computes the minimum value from among seven
 input values}

var
    CurrentMin : real;         {current minimum value}

  begin    {function Minimum}
    CurrentMin := S1;
    if S2 < CurrentMin then CurrentMin := S2;
    if S3 < CurrentMin then CurrentMin := S3;
    if S4 < CurrentMin then CurrentMin := S4;
```

```
        if S5 < CurrentMin then CurrentMin :=  S5;
        if S6 < CurrentMin then CurrentMin :=  S6;
        if S7 < CurrentMin then CurrentMin :=  S7;
        Minimum := CurrentMin;
     end;   {function Minimum}

procedure ComputeScore(Score1, Score2, Score3, Score4, Score5,
                        Score6, Score7, DegreeOfDifficulty: real;
                        var FinalScore:  real);
{uses U.S. Diving Association rules for championship diving
 meets: eliminate high and low score, take 3/5 of the remaining
 total, multiply by degree of difficulty of the dive}

var
    Total : real;        {total of scores without max and min}

  begin    {procedure ComputeScore}
    {add all the scores and subtract the max and min}
    Total := Score1 + Score2 + Score3 + Score4 + Score5
           + Score6 + Score7
           - Maximum(Score1, Score2, Score3, Score4,
                     Score5, Score6, Score7)
           - Minimum(Score1, Score2, Score3, Score4,
                     Score5, Score6, Score7);
    FinalScore := Total*(3/5)*(DegreeOfDifficulty);
    end;    {procedure ComputeScore}

procedure WriteOutput(Degree, S1, S2, S3, S4, S5, S6, S7,
                      Score: real);
{writes the degree of difficulty of the dive, the seven original
 judges' scores, and the final score for the dive}

  begin    {procedure WriteOutput}
    writeln;
    writeln;
    write('This dive has a degree of difficulty of ');
    writeln(Degree:3:1);
    writeln('The seven original judges' ' scores are:');
    writeln(S1:8:1, S2:8:1, S3:8:1, S4:8:1, S5:8:1, S6:8:1,  S7:8:1);
    writeln;
    writeln('The final score for this dive is ', Score:6:2);
    end;    {procedure WriteOutput}

begin {main program}

  GetInput(DegreeOfDifficulty, Score1, Score2, Score3, Score4,
           Score5, Score6, Score7);

  ComputeScore(Score1, Score2, Score3, Score4, Score5, Score6,
               Score7, DegreeOfDifficulty, FinalScore);
```

WriteOutput(DegreeOfDifficulty, Score1, Score2, Score3,
        Score4, Score5, Score6, Score7, FinalScore);

end.   {main program}

RUNNING THE PROGRAM...

What is the degree of difficulty of this dive?
(enter value between 1.0 and 4.0, to the nearest tenth):
3.4

Give the seven judges' scores.
(enter values between 0.0 and 10.0, to the nearest half):
Judge #1: 8.0
Judge #2: 7.5
Judge #3: 7.5
Judge #4: 8.5
Judge #5: 9.0
Judge #6: 9.0
Judge #7: 8.0

This dive has a degree of difficulty of 3.4
The seven original judges' scores are:
  8.0   7.5   7.5   8.5   9.0   9.0   8.0

The final score for this dive is   83.64

RUNNING THE PROGRAM...

What is the degree of difficulty of this dive?
(enter value between 1.0 and 4.0, to the nearest tenth):
2.88
This degree of difficulty is not valid.
The degree of difficulty must be between 1.0 and 4.0,
to the nearest tenth.
Try again.   Enter degree of difficulty: 2.8

Give the seven judges' scores.
(enter values between 0.0 and 10.0, to the nearest half):
Judge #1: 8.1
This score is not valid.
The individual judge's score must be between 0.0 and 10.0,
to the nearest half.
Try again.   Enter score for judge #1: 8.0
Judge #2: 7.5
Judge #3: 7.0
Judge #4: 17.5
This score is not valid.
The individual judge's score must be between 0.0 and 10.0,

to the nearest half.
Try again.   Enter score for judge #4: 7.5
Judge #5: 8.5
Judge #6: 8.6
This score is not valid.
The individual judge's score must be between 0.0 and 10.0,
to the nearest half.
Try again.   Enter score for judge #6: 8.5
Judge #7: 8.0

This dive has a degree of difficulty of 2.8
The seven original judges' scores are:
  8.0   7.5   7.0   7.5   8.5   8.5   8.0

The final score for this dive is   66.36

Notice how much of this program is devoted to input validation. Although the *GetInput* procedure can be shortened by employing techniques for looping and arrangements of data that we will learn later, it is still the case that data validation is costly in terms of the amount of code required. This is not surprising, because the purpose of data validation is to guard against incorrect values. This means it must deal with all sorts of "weird" cases, instead of the expected values that the program was designed to handle in a straightforward manner. However, skipping data validation efforts in a program may ultimately be even more costly.

CASE STUDY ONE   **View #7**

The water pollution project at Sterling Software Systems has two unfinished modules: the *CheckThreshold* procedure that decides whether the ratio of bacteria to water for a particular sample exceeds the threshold value, and the *WriteOutput* procedure that still has to handle the warning message based on the results of *CheckThreshold*. Because of the modular design of the program, the careful delineation of module interfaces, and the attention paid to documentation—including the use of descriptive identifiers and the opening comment in the stub for *CheckThreshold*—you can turn the task of writing this procedure over to someone else, who can complete the procedure without any knowledge of the rest of the program. Meanwhile, you can modify procedure *WriteOutput* to handle the warning message.

You also obtain from the Lodestone County Water Pollution Department ranges of values for the site ID numbers. You decide to incorporate some input data validation. The complete program appears below.

```
program WaterPollution(input, output);
{tests water sample from a site against a pollution threshold,
 issues a warning if the bacteria level is too high}
```

```
const
    Threshold = 2.0;            {200 bacteria per 100 ml water}

var
    ID : integer;               {site ID number}
    Water : integer;            {amount of water sampled, in ml}
    Bacteria : integer;         {bacteria count in sample}
    Mon1, Mon2 : char;          {two-digit month notation}
    Day1, Day2 : char;          {two-digit date notation}
    Yr1, Yr2 : char;            {two-digit year notation}
    Warning : boolean;          {flag for warning message if
                                  pollution level too high}
    Level : real;               {pollution level for this sample}

procedure GetInput(var ID, Water, Bacteria: integer;
                   var Mon1, Mon2, Day1, Day2,
                       Yr1, Yr2: char);
{procedure to collect input for water pollution data; amount
 Water of water and count Bacteria of bacteria were obtained
 from site ID on date Mon1Mon2/Day1Day2/Yr1Yr2}

var
    Slash : char;       {separating / in date format}

  begin     {procedure GetInput}
    write('Enter the site ID number: ');
    readln(ID);
    if not((1 <= ID) and (ID <= 1000)) then
      begin {ID out of range}
        write('Check the site ID number and enter again: ');
        readln(ID);
      end;  {ID out of range}
    writeln;

    writeln('Enter the date of this sample.');
    write('Use month/date/year format: ');
    readln(Mon1, Mon2, Slash, Day1, Day2, Slash, Yr1, Yr2);
    writeln;

    write('Enter the amount of water in sample (in ml): ');
    readln(Water);
    if not (Water > 0) then
      begin   {error in amount of water}
        write('Check the amount of water & enter again: ');
        readln(Water);
      end;    {error in amount of water}
    writeln;

    write('Enter the bacteria count found in this sample:  ');
    readln(Bacteria);
```

```
    if not (Bacteria >= 0) then
      begin   {error in amount of bacteria}
        write('Check the amount of bacteria & enter again: ');
        readln(Bacteria);
      end;    {error in amount of bacteria}
  end;     {procedure GetInput}


function Ratio(Bacteria, Water: integer): real;
{computes the Ratio of Bacteria to Water}


  begin     {function Ratio}
    Ratio := Bacteria/Water;
  end;      {function Ratio}


procedure CheckThreshold(Ratio: real;
                         var Over: boolean);
{compares Ratio to the global constant Threshold and sets
 Over to true if that limit is exceeded}

  begin     {procedure CheckThreshold}
    Over := false;    {initialize Over}
    if Ratio > Threshold then
      Over := true;
  end;       {procedure CheckThreshold


procedure WriteOutput(ID, Water, Bacteria: integer;
                      Mon1, Mon2, Day1, Day2,
                      Yr1, Yr2: char;
                      Ratio: real;
                      Warning: boolean);
{echoes site input data and writes warning message if warranted}


  begin      {procedure WriteOutput}
    writeln;
    writeln;
    write('Site ID', 'Date':8, 'Water':12, 'Bacteria':13);
    writeln('Level':9, 'Warning':10);
    write('_____');
    writeln('_____');
    writeln;
    write(ID:5, Mon1:6, Mon2, '/', Day1, Day2, '/', Yr1, Yr2);
    write(Water:8, ' ml', Bacteria:9, Ratio:11:2);


    if Warning then
      write('     ** HIGH **');
    writeln;
  end;      {procedure WriteOutput}
```

begin   {main program}

GetInput(ID, Water, Bacteria,
            Mon1, Mon2, Day1, Day2, Yr1, Yr2);

Level := Ratio(Bacteria, Water);

CheckThreshold(Level, Warning);

WriteOutput(ID, Water, Bacteria,
            Mon1, Mon2, Day1, Day2, Yr1, Yr2,
            Level, Warning);

end.   {main program}

RUNNING THE PROGRAM...

Enter the site ID number: 115

Enter the date of this sample.
Use month/date/year format: 08/22/79

Enter the amount of water in sample (in ml): 420

Enter the bacteria count found in this sample: 1230

Site ID	Date	Water	Bacteria	Level	Warning
115	08/22/79	420 ml	1230	2.93	** HIGH **

You have also developed sets of test dat to exercise the program, and you run the program on these test sets, making sure that it behaves according to the specifications in each case.

(Note: The little extra time spent by the manager of the Lodestone County Water Pollution Department providing SSS with information on reasonable input values will pay dividends in a more robust program, one able to stand up even at the hands of Kevin Klutz, the department's worst lab technician.)

CASE STUDY TWO   # View #7

The deadline for the hypertension clinic project is drawing near. Complete the program as originally designed, then modify the program to include some data validation. Devise sets of test data that will exercise the program as thoroughly as possible, and make sure that it performs according to the specifications for all test cases.

(Items marked with ∗ make use of optional material on counting loops from Chapter 3.)

EXERCISES

#1. If *N* has the current value 5 and *M* has the current value 7, what is the truth value of each of the expressions below?

    not (N >= 5) **and** (M < 7)
    not ((N >= 5) **and** (M < 7))

#2. Write a statement that prints the message "too hot" only if *Temp* is greater than 98.

#3. Write a statement that prints the message "too hot" if *Temp* is greater than 98, but otherwise prints the message "just right."

4. Write a statement that, if *Y* >= *X*, subtracts *X* from *Y* and reads a new value for *X*, and, if *Y* < *X*, subtracts *Y* from *X* and reads a new value for *Y*.

5. For *M* and *N* with values of 3 and 5, respectively, what is the output from the following statement?

```
if N < M then
  if 2*N < M then
    writeln('yes')
else
  writeln('no');
```

6. Use a **case** statement to write "positive" if *I* has the value 1, "zero" if *I* has the value 0, and "negative" if *I* has the value −1.

#7. Write a type declaration for an enumerated type whose values are the days of the week. Write a subrange type declaration for weekdays. Declare a variable of the subrange type.

8. What is wrong with the following type declaration?

type interval = 0.0..1.0;

∗9. What is the output when the following statement is executed?

```
for Index := 5 to 10 do
  if odd(Index) then
    writeln(2*Index)
  else
    writeln(Index + 1);
```

SKILL BUILDERS

#1. Write a program to prompt for and read two *char* values, then write an appropriate message noting that the characters are the same or different.

2. Write a program to ask for five *integer* values and write out the number of odd values that were entered.

3. Write a program to solve the quadratic equation $ax^2 + bx + c = 0$, given the real number coefficients a, b, and c.

4. Write a program that asks the user to make an inquiry about one of three candidates for mayor; based on the choice, the appropriate short campaign message is displayed. (Use a **case** statement.)

5. Write a program to read in three different integers and write them out in increasing size.

*6. Rewrite Skill Builder #2 above to process 25 integer values.

SOFTWARE DEVELOPMENT PROJECTS

1. Complete program *Postage* on page 109. Use the following rates (which are simplifications of the actual rate scales): for domestic mail, letters are 25 cents for the first ounce and 20 cents for each additional ounce; book rate is 25 cents for the first ounce, 20 cents for each additional ounce up to 4 ounces, 10 cents for each additional 2 ounces over that up to 1 pound, when it becomes package rate. Package rate is $2.35 for the first two pounds and an additional 48 cents for each additional pound. For foreign mail, letter rate is 44 cents for each half-ounce; book rate is 96 cents for the first pound and 61 cents for each additional pound; package rate is $3.90 for the first 2 pounds and $1.30 for each additional pound.

2. Develop software that asks the user for the length of a word (1 to 5 characters), then the word itself, and reports whether that word is a palindrome. (***Palindromes*** are words or phrases that read the same forward and backward, like "madam" or "pop.")

3. The sign of the zodiac is determined by date of birth according to the following table:

Aries	March 21-April 19
Taurus	April 20-May 20
Gemini	May 21-June 21
Cancer	June 22-July 22
Leo	July 23-August 22
Virgo	August 23-September 22
Libra	September 23-October 23
Scorpio	October 24-November 21
Sagittarius	November 21-December 21
Capricorn	December 22-January 19
Aquarius	January 20-February 18
Pisces	February19-March 20

Develop software to read the user's date of birth and write the user's horoscope. There should be a fixed message for each sign. The message should also include a reference to a related sign occurring two months later, for example, the related sign for Virgo is Scorpio, and that for Capricorn is Pisces. For instance, the output message for a Virgo could be: "As a Virgo, you will face difficulties in your work. Look for a Scorpio to help you." Use an enumerated data type for the signs of the zodiac.

4. Develop software that asks the user for the current date (in month/date/year format) and computes how many days remain in the year. Be sure to account for leap year: years evenly divisible by four, like 1988, are leap years, except for the century years. The only century years that are leap years are those divisible by 400, such as 1600, 2000, etc.

5. Develop software for ticket-pricing information on round-trip airline tickets from Wilbursville to Orvillesburg and back. The base round-trip rate is $140.00, but reservations made more than 30 days ahead get a 20% reduction. In addition, flights on Tuesday or Wednesday get a $15.00 discount, and flights on Saturday or Sunday cost an additional $20.00. A stay of longer than 7 days earns a $30.00 rebate. After the ticket price is computed, first-class passengers pay a surcharge of 15% on all tickets, economy passengers get a 10% reduction on all tickets. The program should ask for the current date, the date and day of the flight, the date and day of the return, and the passenger class. The program should compute the ticket price.

***6.** Job applicants at a major company are interviewed in five different rooms, according to the following table:

Initial of last name	Room #
A-E	123
F-K	124
L-P	125
Q-S	126
T-Z	127

Develop software that asks the user for his or her last name and then directs the user to the correct room. The program should process 20 applicants.

TESTING AND MAINTENANCE DEPARTMENT

1. Modify program *Dive* so that the output indicates the maximum score and minimum score that get discarded.

2. Modify the program for Software Development Project #6 in Chapter 2; this time, allow for the possibility that the worker works fewer than 40 hours in a week.

3. Modify program *WaterPollution* so that when the date for the sample is entered, the input validation checks that the limit for the number of days in the month has not been exceeded. For example, 09/31/68 is invalid because September has only 30 days. Ignore leap years.

4. Repeat modification #3 above, but do not ignore leap years (see Software Development Project #4 above for a discussion on how to compute leap years).

5. Design test sets for program *Dive*. Be sure to test boundary values of legal input data, as well as the input validation features of the program. Try to test as many logic branches of the program as possible.

DEBUGGING CLINIC   Test the following program and see if it conforms to the "specifications" given in the initial comment. If not, write a correct version.

```pascal
program bookie(input, output);
{judges the price of a book based on the following scale:
    under $3.00 - inexpensive
    $3.00-$15.00 - moderate
    over $15.00 - expensive}

var
    bookprice : integer;

begin
    writeln('What is the selling price of the book ');
    write('to the nearest dollar (no decimal point, please):  ');
    readln(bookprice);
    if bookprice < 3 then
      writeln('inexpensive');
    if bookprice <= 15 then
      writeln('moderate')
    else
      writeln('expensive');
end.
```

CHAPTER EIGHT

REPETITIONS; PROGRAM MAINTENANCE; EXTERNAL DOCUMENTATION

Pascal provides three control structures for looping, wherein sections of code are automatically repeated.

8.1 Conditional Loops

8.1.1 The While Statement

We may want an action to be performed as long as (while) some condition is true; when that condition becomes false, the action should no longer be performed. The **while** statement accomplishes this. We formulate a boolean expression and define the action to be taken as a (possibly compound) statement S. When

> **while** boolean expression **do**
>   statement S;

is encountered in a program, the expression is evaluated. If its value is true, statement S is executed. Then the expression is evaluated again; if it is still true, statement S is executed again. Then the expression is evaluated again, etc. If the expression ever evaluates to false, control transfers to the next program statement following this **while** statement. Statement S is called the **body** of the loop—it is the action that may be executed many times.

As a simple example, suppose we want to add the total cash register receipts for the day. This involves maintaining a *Sum* variable by successively reading an amount and adding it to *Sum.* Therefore it seems that "read and add" constitute the body of the loop, the action to be cycled through as many times as necessary. We must initialize *Sum* so that we start with a clean slate (or more properly speaking, a clean memory location). Our thinking to this point goes something like

A while statement tests a boolean expression at the beginning of a loop; the loop body will be executed as long as this expression evaluates to true.

217

```
Sum  :=  0.0;
while another  amount  remains  to  process  do
  begin
    read(Amount);
    Sum  :=  Sum  +  Amount;
  end;
readln;
writeln('The  total  receipts  for  the  day  add  to  $',  Sum:8:2);
```

The boolean expression "another amount remains to process" has not been specified. How do we know whether another amount remains to be processed, i.e., how do we know when to terminate the loop? There are several possible loop termination mechanisms when reading data. In this case we will use a **sentinel value** (a **trailer value**). A sentinel value is a recognizable signal for the end of the data because it is not itself a legitimate data value. In our example, we expect that all of the receipts will be positive real numbers, so zero or a negative value would serve as a sentinel value. We modify our first pass to read

A sentinel value must be a recognizable value that will not be confused with legitimate data.

```
program ReceiptTotal1(input, output);
{is supposed to add up the day's receipts}

var
    Sum, Amount : real;

begin
    writeln('Enter  the  day' 's  receipts  -  do  not  separate  ');
    writeln('values  with  commas;  use  0  as  the  last  value.');
    writeln;
    Sum  :=  0.0;
    while Amount  >  0.0 do
      begin
        read(Amount);
        Sum  :=  Sum  +  Amount;
      end;
    readln;
    writeln;
    writeln('The  total  receipts  for  the  day  add  to  $',  Sum:8:2);
end.
```

CHECKUP 8.1   Desk check the above program for the input values
35.29   7.35   16.98   0

CHECKUP 8.1 was a bit of a dirty trick. If you actually traced the program execution—not what you thought the program was supposed to do—you did not get very far. When a value for *Amount* hasn't yet been read in, then the current value of *Amount* is undefined. We can't test whether it is greater than zero. To fix this, we'll do one *read* statement before the loop and change the body of the loop itself to process an amount, then read the next value. This corrected version appears below.

```
program ReceiptTotal2(input, output);
{adds up the day's receipts - uses while loop}

var
    Sum, Amount : real;

begin
  writeln('Enter the day' 's receipts - do not separate ');
  writeln('values with commas; use 0 as the last value.');
  writeln;
  Sum := 0.0;
  read(Amount);
  while Amount > 0.0 do
    begin
      Sum := Sum + Amount;
      read(Amount);
    end;
  readln;
  writeln;
  writeln('The total receipts for the day add to $', Sum:8:2);
end
```

RUNNING THE PROGRAM...

```
Enter the day's receipts - do not separate
values with commas; use 0 as the last value.

14.95  16.70  13.82  0

The total receipts for the day add to $      45.47
```

In program *ReceiptTotal2*, the repetitive sequence of events is still read-and-add, read-and-add . . .; the first read is done outside of the loop and then the repetition begins, so that it looks like read, add-and-read, add-and-read. . . . The final *read* statement before the loop is exited reads the sentinel value, which should not be processed.

If the boolean expression in a **while** statement evaluates to false the very first time, the body of the loop is never executed at all. This occurs in our example program if the first data value read is not positive.

The body of a while loop will not be executed at all if the boolean condition evaluates to false on the first pass.

If nothing within the body of the loop affects the boolean expression, then that expression, once true, will always remain true. In this case, the loop will continue forever. Everyone sooner or later gets to debug an ***infinite loop!*** On a mainframe, there is usually a system-imposed time limit for job execution and a program in an infinite loop will get kicked out when it exceeds this limit. On a microcomputer, a program in an infinite loop is usually detected by the absence of output for a long period of time, and the programmer must then force an execution interrupt.

8.1.2 *The* Repeat *Statement*

Although the **while** statement is sufficient to carry out any sort of loop activity, Pascal provides two other looping control structures. In the program to total receipts, we described the loop as "while there are more values, process." This could also be described as "process until there are no more values." The **repeat** statement takes this point of view—repeat an action until some condition becomes true. The general form of the repeat statement is

A repeat..until statement tests a boolean expression at the end of a loop; the loop body is always executed at least once and will be executed again as long as the expression evaluates to false.

```
repeat
    body of loop
until boolean expression;
```

The loop body is executed once, and the boolean expression is then evaluated. If its value is not true, the body of the loop is repeated. Then the expression is evaluated again, etc. Once the expression becomes true, control passes to the next program statement after the **repeat** statement. A version of the receipts program using a **repeat** loop follows.

```
program ReceiptTotal3(input, output);
{adds up the day's receipts - uses repeat loop}

var
    Sum, Amount : real;

begin
    writeln('Enter the day' 's receipts - do not separate ');
    writeln('values with commas; use 0 as the last value.');
    writeln;
    Sum := 0.0;
    read(Amount);
    repeat
      Sum := Sum + Amount;
      read(Amount);
    until Amount <= 0.0;
    readln;
    writeln;
    writeln('The total receipts for the day add to $', Sum:8:2);
end.
```

RUNNING THE PROGRAM...

```
Enter the day's receipts - do not separate
values with commas; use 0 as the last value.

14.95
16.70
13.82
0
```

The total receipts for the day add to $ 45.47

If the first value read is a sentinel value (there is no legitimate data), the program above is in error. For one thing, the sentinel value gets added to *Sum*, even though the sentinel value is not legitimate data. In addition, the program will then try to read a value beyond the sentinel value. The body of the loop gets executed once before any test about repeating the loop occurs. A **repeat** statement should not be used if there is the possibility that the loop body should not be executed at all.

No begin..end is needed for a repeat loop but is required in a while loop whenever the body of the loop contains more than one statement.

Notice that the body of the loop is not a compound statement framed by **begin-end.** The reserved words **repeat-until** frame the body of the loop, so **begin-end** is not required. **Begin-end** is required for the body of a **while** loop (unless the loop body can be expressed by a single, noncompound statement), because no framing word separates the end of the loop body from the next program statement. Finally, note that the condition for terminating the **repeat** loop is the negation of the condition for continuing the **while** loop: **while** A **do**.. is the same as **repeat..until** not A.

CHECKUP 8.2   Recall that to get a correct version of the receipts program using a **while** loop, an initial *read* had to be done outside the loop body. Because the test to continue a **repeat** loop occurs at the end of the loop, we might try to avoid this initial *read*. What's wrong with the following version of the receipts program, even if the first value is not a sentinel value? Hint: Use a negative number as the sentinel value.

```
program ReceiptTotal4(input, output);
{is supposed to add up the day's receipts}

var
    Sum, Amount : real;

begin
    writeln('Enter the day' 's receipts - do not separate ');
    writeln('values with commas; use a negative number ');
    writeln('as the last value.');
    writeln;
    Sum := 0.0;
    repeat
      read(Amount);
      Sum := Sum + Amount;
    until Amount <= 0.0;
    readln;
    writeln;
    writeln('The total receipts for the day add to $', Sum:8:2);
end.
```

CHECKUP 8.2 illustrates one of many ways loops can go wrong! We'll say more later about loop errors and testing loops.

In either a while loop or a repeat loop, something within the loop body must affect the boolean condition controlling the continuation of the loop, or an infinite loop will result.

To summarize, both the **while** loop and the **repeat** loop evaluate a boolean expression to decide whether to continue (**while** loop) or exit (**repeat** loop) the loop. A **while** loop makes this decision at the beginning of the loop body and a **repeat** loop at the end. In neither case is the decision made in the middle of the loop body, even if the boolean expression has assumed the proper value at that point; loops are not exited from the middle. For both kinds of loops, the loop body must affect the boolean expression in order to avoid an infinite loop. The major difference between a **while** loop and a **repeat** loop is that the loop body will always be executed at least once in a **repeat** loop. The **while** statement won't allow the loop body to execute when it shouldn't, so it may be the preferred control structure. However, in a situation where the loop body should be executed at least once, either statement form can be used.

8.1.3 *Multiple Conditions for Loop Exit*

When a conditional loop has a compound exit condition, check after exiting the loop to determine which condition holds.

The boolean expression in a **while** loop or a **repeat** loop can be a compound expression. If so, we may exit a loop without specifically knowing why. As an example, the following program searches a list of *integer* values for a specific *integer* value called *TicketNumber*. The repetitive action (loop body) consists of reading a list value and incrementing a counter for the number of values read so far. If *TicketNumber* appears, we can stop reading the list (the counter will tell us where we were in the list when *TicketNumber* appeared). If *TicketNumber* is not in the list, however, we have to enter the entire list before we can come to this conclusion. The boolean expression that controls the **while** loop uses two expressions joined by **and.** Whenever either becomes false—that is, we have just found *TicketNumber* or just read the last value—the entire boolean expression becomes false and the loop is exited. Then we test which of the two conditions caused us to exit and act accordingly.

```
program SearchList(input, output);
{searches a list of n integers for a specific value}

var
     n : integer;              {number of elements in the list}
     value : integer;          {current value read from the  list}
     TicketNumber : integer;   {number being searched for}
     counter : integer;        {keeps track of current position in
                                the list}

begin
   writeln('How many integers are in the list?');
   readln(n);
   writeln('What is the value of TicketNumber?');
   readln(TicketNumber);
   writeln('Enter the list of integers, one per line:');
```

```
{begin to search the list for TicketNumber}
readln(value);
counter := 1;
while (value <> TicketNumber) and (counter < n) do
  begin
    readln(value);
    counter := counter + 1;
  end;

{loop has been exited - either TicketNumber has been found
 or list was exhausted - let's see which}

if value = TicketNumber then
  begin
    writeln('TicketNumber is item ', counter:3, ' in the list.');
    writeln('You do not need to enter the rest of the list.');
  end
else
  begin
    writeln('TicketNumber did not appear in the list.');
  end;
end.
```

RUNNING THE PROGRAM...

```
How many integers are in the list?
17
What is the value of TicketNumber?
34
Enter the list of integers, one per line:
16
82
47
34
TicketNumber is item    4 in the list.
You do not to need to enter the rest of the list.
```

In program *SearchList*, if we were to test for the exit condition in the other order, i.e., test first for the end of the list, we still would not have complete information. The very last item in the list could have been *TicketNumber*, and both subexpressions in the **and** expression would have become false simultaneously.

Another implementation of the loop part of program *SearchList* sets a flag when the desired value is found, and this causes a loop exit. This section of code would be written as follows (*found* has been declared as a boolean variable); no initial *read* is required, but the counter must be initialized differently:

```
found := false;
counter := 0;
```

```
while (counter < n) and (not found) do
  begin
    readln(value);
    counter := counter + 1;
    if value = TicketNumber then
      found := true;
  end;
```

Searching a large list makes more sense when the list already exists in some data file. Then we enter at the terminal just the value we are seeking and read the list values from the file. Chapter 11 discusses files, and we'll refer to program *SearchList* again there (see Skill Builder 11.5).

8.2 Counting Loops

Events that take place during loop execution govern the number of times a conditional loop executes. A third kind of loop statement can be used to execute a loop some fixed number of times that can be determined before the loop begins. Such a loop is called a **counting loop** or **definite loop,** as opposed to a conditional loop, and is handled by the **for** statement.

For example, the following statement writes the integers from 1 to 5 (*Number* is an *integer* variable):

```
for Number := 1 to 5 do
  writeln(Number);
```

Number gets set to 1 and the loop body is executed; *Number* then gets incremented to 2, and the loop body is executed again. *Number* continues to be incremented (and the loop body executed) through the value 5.

The general **for** statement follows this same pattern. It looks like

In a for loop, the variable that controls the loop execution must be of the same ordinal type as the expressions that give the initial and final values to that variable.

```
for loop-control-variable := initial-exp. to final-exp. do
  statement S;
```

where, as usual, statement S can be a compound statement. The loop control variable can be of any ordinal type; the initial and final expressions must also be of this ordinal type. The loop control variable is set equal to the initial value (determined by evaluating the initial expression) and then incremented to the final value (determined by evaluating the final expression) by whatever enumeration scheme is used in that ordinal type. For each value of the loop control variable, the loop body is executed. The enumeration scheme in *char* variables is alphabetic so

```
for Letter := 'j' to 'q' do
  write(Letter);
```

would produce

jklmnopq

In a **for** loop, a program statement to explicitly increment the loop control variable, such as

Number := Number + 1;

is not required. In fact, it is illegal to to anything within the loop body to change the value of this variable. (This would mess up the counting scheme.) In the same spirit, the initial and final expressions are evaluated and the number of times the loop will execute is determined before the loop body is entered. Any changes within the loop that affect the current value of either the initial or final expression are ignored as far as the loop-counting mechanism is concerned.

The loop control variable is a "dummy variable" intended merely as a loop counter. This view is reinforced by the requirement that the loop control variable be locally declared if the **for** statement appears within a procedure or function. Furthermore, the loop control variable has an undefined value once the **for** statement is exited; it does not, for example, retain the final value of the loop. However, the loop control variable can later be reinitialized and used again.

If the initial and final values are the same, the body of a **for** loop is executed exactly once; if the initial value is greater than the final value, the loop body is not executed at all, and control passes directly to the next statement in the program. It is possible, however, to have loops that count down instead of up by using the syntax

for loop-control-variable := initial-exp. **downto** final-exp. **do**
    statement S;

where the initial value is at least as large as the final value (if not, the loop body is not executed at all).

CHECKUP 8.3   What is the output from the statement

```
for I := 12 downto 7 do
   write(I:3);
```

CHECKUP 8.4   What is the output from the following section of code?

```
for Index := 0 to 2 do
   write(2*Index + 1:3);
   write(' ** ');
```

The loop control variable is incremented by one ordinal value on each pass through the loop body, but clever use can be made of this variable within the loop body. The following section of code writes a table of values of the $ln(x)$ function between $x = 1$ and $x = 2$, where *NumberOfPoints* controls the step size in x from 1 to 2. Here the final expression for the **for** loop is a program variable rather than a constant.

```
writeln('    x            ln(x)');
writeln;
for Point := 0 to NumberOfPoints do
  begin
    x := 1 + Point/NumberOfPoints;
    writeln(x:5:3, ln(x):12:5);
  end;
```

If *NumberOfPoints* has the value 10 when this section of code is executed, then the output is

x	ln(x)
1.000	0.00000
1.100	0.09531
1.200	0.18232
1.300	0.26236
1.400	0.33647
1.500	0.40547
1.600	0.47000
1.700	0.53063
1.800	0.58779
1.900	0.64185
2.000	0.69315

Using enumerated-type variables as loop control variables can make **for** loop statements self-documenting. With declarations of

```
type
    Workday = (Monday, Tuesday, Wednesday, Thursday,  Friday);
var
    Day : Workday;
```

the purpose of the statement

```
for Day := Monday to Friday  do
    ComputeProductionTotal(Day);
```

is easily understood.

For loops are somewhat simpler to read and understand than **while** or **repeat** loops and should be used whenever the situation allows it, i.e., whenever the loop is to be executed a fixed number of times.

CHECKUP 8.5   What is the output from the following section of code? Rewrite this as a **for** loop:

```
even := 2;
while even <= 10 do
  begin
    write(even:3);
    even := even + 2;
  end;
```

8.3 Nested Loops

The body of a loop contains other program statements. One of these may be a loop statement, leading to **nested loops.** Nested **for** loops are particularly handy, as in the short and neat program below that writes out the multiplication tables from 1 to 5. For each pass through the outer **for** loop that is, for each value of *I*, the inner **for** loop is executed, i.e., *J* takes on the values 1 through 5.

```
program MultTable(input, output);
{writes out the multiplication tables from 1 to 5}

var
     I, J : integer;     {loop counters}

begin
   writeln('Multiplication table from 1 to 5');
   writeln;
   writeln('  |     1     2     3     4     5');
   writeln('_____');

   for I := 1 to 5 do
     begin
       write(I:1,' |');
       for J := 1 to 5 do
         write(I*J:5);
       writeln;
     end;
end.
```

The output from this program is

Multiplication table from 1 to 5

	1	2	3	4	5
1	1	2	3	4	5
2	2	4	6	8	10
3	3	6	9	12	15
4	4	8	12	16	20
5	5	10	15	20	25

As another example of nested loops, the following program modifies the cash register receipts problem to read a subtotal of receipts from each of a number of cash registers and then output a grand total.

```
program ReceiptTotal5(input, output);
{adds up the day's receipts from a number of cash registers; uses
 a while loop nested within a for loop}

var
    NumberRegisters : integer;      {number of cash registers}
    Sum : real;                     {subtotal for one register}
    Amount : real;                  {current value read in}
    Total : real;                   {grand total for all registers}
    Index : integer;                {loop index}

begin
  write('Enter the number of cash registers: ');
  readln(NumberRegisters);
 ,writeln;

  Total := 0;

  for Index := 1 to NumberRegisters do
    begin    {for loop}
      write('Enter the day' 's receipts for register ');
      writeln(Index:2);
      write('Do not separate values with commas; ');
      writeln('use 0 as the last value.');
      writeln;

      Sum := 0.0;
      read(Amount);
      while Amount > 0.0 do
        begin
          Sum := Sum + Amount;
          read(Amount);
        end;    {while Amount  > 0.0}
      readln;
      writeln;
      write('The receipts for register ', Index:2);
      writeln(' for the day add to $', Sum:8:2);
      writeln;

      Total := Total + Sum;
    end;    {for loop}

  writeln;
  writeln('The grand total from all registers is $', Total:10:2);
end.
```

RUNNING THE PROGRAM...

Enter the number of cash registers: 4

Enter the day's receipts for register   1
Do not separate values with commas; use 0 as the last value.

44.52 6.78 9.10 0

The receipts for register   1 for the day add to $ 60.40

Enter the day's receipts for register   2
Do not separate values with commas; use 0 as the last value.

150.85
62.89
0

The receipts for register   2 for the day add to $ 213.74

Enter the day's receipts for register   3
Do not separate values with commas; use 0 as the last value.

0

The receipts for register   3 for the day add to $ 0.00

Enter the day's receipts for register   4
Do not separate values with commas; use 0 as the last value.

23.49 88.17
0

The receipts for register   4 for the day add to $ 111.66

The grand total from all registers is $ 385.80

8.4 Loop Termination Mechanisms

We have looked at two ways to terminate a loop that is reading input data—use of a sentinel value with a **while** loop or a **repeat** loop, and use of a counting loop with its built-in termination mechanism.

8.4.1 *User-Controlled Termination*

Another possibility lets the user in an interactive system control loop termination. For example, a game might have the following control structure, where *Response* is a type *char* variable.

```
repeat

        .
        .
     game
        .
        .

   writeln('Do you want to play again? Answer Y or  N');
   readln(Response);
until (Response = 'N') or (Response = 'n');
```

User-controlled termination is especially useful in input validation. In the last chapter, **if** statements gave the user a second chance at entering data. A **repeat** loop will not allow the program to proceed until valid data has been entered, as in

Use loops to validate input data.

```
repeat
   write('Enter your choice of A, B, C, D, or E: ');
   readln(Response);
until Response in ['A'..'E'];
```

8.4.2 *Text Files*—eoln *and* eof

Another termination mechanism depends upon the structure of the input data file. This is most easily understood if we think about batch processing, where a data file has been created ahead of time and is available when the program begins to execute. Such a file must usually have some name other than *input,* to avoid confusion with input values read from the keyboard, but let's pretend that the file is still called *input* (see Chapter 11 for details on files). When the user creates this file using the system editor, each line is typed on the keyboard, followed by a carriage return. The carriage return enters a special character, called an end-of-line character, into the file. This character can be read as a single item of type *char,* but if it is then written out, it is represented by a blank.

The fact that the end-of-line character can be read as *char* data can cause problems when reading type *char* input. Suppose we are doing a **text-processing** task, where we want to treat the file entirely as lines of characters. If we go along the first line reading, one symbol at a time, data of type *char,* we are very likely to read the end-of-line character and move on to the second line of text without even noticing. In text processing, we probably want to handle each line of text separately, or at least we want to know when we've finished one line and begun another. Here is where the standard boolean function *eoln(x)* comes in. This function is true if the read "pointer" is positioned so that the next character in file *x* is the end-of-line character; if the filename *x* is omitted, it is assumed to be file *input.*

The end-of-line character in a text file can be read as character data; use the eoln function to detect it.

A procedure very similar to the following one can be used to read and write one line of text from file *input.* Due to the details of naming batch files that we mentioned earlier, this exact procedure may not work on a given system.

```
procedure ReadWriteLine;
{general idea to read one line of text from file input, write it
 to file output; may not work as is due to system-dependent
 details of naming files}

var
    NextCharacter : char;     {next character in file}

begin     {procedure ReadWriteLine}
  while not eoln do
    begin {while not eoln}
      read(NextCharacter);
      write(NextCharacter);
    end;  {while not eoln}

  {now deal with end-of-line character}
  readln;   {read end-of-line and go to next line}
  writeln;  {advance to next line for more output}
end;        {procedure ReadWriteLine}
```

In procedure *ReadWriteLine,* we used a **while** loop instead of a **repeat** loop, just in case the line has nothing in it but the end-of-line character. The final *readln* and *writeln* move the "pointers" for the input and output files to the beginning of the next line in their respective files.

Use the eof function to detect the end-of-file marker since trying to read it will cause an error.

A batch file also has a marker for the end of the file. The standard function *eof(x)* is true when the "pointer" is positioned just before the end of file *x*; if the filename *x* is omitted, it is assumed to be file *input.* While the end-of-file marker can be recognized, trying to read it will cause an error. Reading until *eof* is true (i.e., stopping just before the end-of-file marker) is another technique for loop termination. This technique has two advantages: there is no ahead-of-time knowledge required about how many data items are in the file (in which case a counting loop could be used), and the data does not have to end with a special sentinel value.

Something like the following program, with its nested loops, can be used to read and write an entire text file line by line. Figure 8.1a illustrates how we can think of the input file, with the read "pointer" positioned just before the end-of-file marker; this terminates the outside loop and ends the program below. (Although we can visualize a file this way, it is actually stored in a string of contiguous memory cells, as in Figure 8.1b.)

```
program ReadWriteText(input,output);
{general idea to copy the text file input into output; may not
 work as is due to system-dependent details of naming files}

var
    NextCharacter : char;     {next character in file}

begin
  while not eof do
```

```
begin    {while not eof}
  while not eoln do
    begin {while not eoln}
      read(NextCharacter);
      write(NextCharacter);
    end;    {while not eoln}

  {now deal with end-of-line character}
  readln;    {read end-of-line and go to next line}
  writeln;   {advance to next line for more output}
  end;       {while not eof}
end.
```

In the program above, a test such as

while (not eof) **and** **(not** eoln) **do**

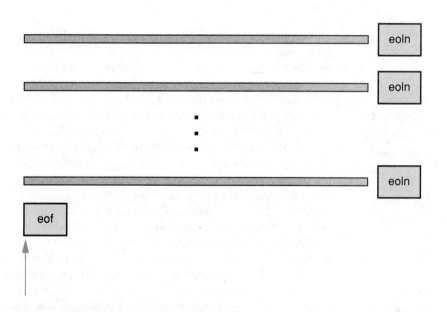

FIGURE 8.1A Mental model of a text file.

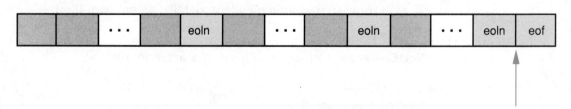

FIGURE 8.1B A text file as stored in auxiliary memory.

will not work. When *eof* is true, *eoln* and hence **not** *eoln* are undefined. Even though **not** *eof* is false at this point, most systems will evaluate both parts of the boolean expression anyway; this will generate an error message or unexpected results.

The *eoln* function is also meaningful in interactive programming where the input file really is the characters entered at the keyboard. In the following program, the details of batch files are not a problem.

```pascal
program Poetry(input, output);
{echoes user's poetry}

var
    Stop : char;   {condition to terminate}

procedure ReadWriteLine;
{reads one line of text from file input, writes it to file output}

var
    NextCharacter : char; {next character in file}

  begin   {procedure ReadWriteLine}
    while not eoln do
      begin {while not eoln}
        read(NextCharacter);
        write(NextCharacter);
      end;   {while not eoln}

    {now deal with end-of-line character}
    readln; {read end-of-line and go to next line}
    writeln; {advance to next line for more output}
  end;    {procedure ReadWriteLine}

begin {main program}
  repeat
    writeln('Enter the next line of of your poem.¹);
    ReadWriteLine;
    writeln;
    writeln('Do you want to stop now? If so, answer Yes.');
    readln(Stop);
  until (Stop = 'Y') or (Stop = 'y');
end.   {main proram}
```

RUNNING THE PROGRAM...

```
Enter the next line of your poem.
FOR loops are a real treat
FOR loops are a real treat
```

Do you want to stop now? If so, answer Yes.
no
Enter the next line of your poem.
and WHILE loops just can't be beat.
and WHILE loops just can't be beat.

Do you want to stop now? If so, answer Yes.
Yes

For each line of the poem, the first copy on the screen is the input echo and the second copy is the output. One might expect that a sequence of *read* and *write* statements would cause a copy of each letter to be output on the screen immediately after it is typed, as in

FFOORR llooooppss, etc.

However on most systems, the entire line of input, terminated by the carriage return, is stored in an input buffer from which the successive *read* statements then pick out one character at a time. Of course, it would make more sense to capture the poem in some permanent output file, not just reproduce it on the screen.

What constitutes the end-of-file marker in an interactive environment? The last carriage return just marks the end of the last line of data. The end-of-file marker is system dependent; it might be control-Z, for example, or a special function key. Because of this variation, we won't use *eof* in an interactive environment. (By the way, once an *eof* marker is entered in an interactive environment, the program cannot later request and read further data from the user—this would cause an attempt to read past end-of-file.)

To summarize, the various mechanisms to force loop termination when reading data are: sentinel values, use of counting loops, user-controlled termination, *eoln,* and *eof.*

8.5 Testing Loops

Test loops carefully for off-by-one values—wrong starting or ending values.

The last chapter talked about the importance of program testing. Loops seem particularly prone to engendering logic errors. Perhaps we initialize a counter variable to 1 when it should be initialized to 0, or vice versa. Perhaps we exit the loop one pass too soon—or one pass too late—by using a "less than" condition when we should use "less than or equal to" or vice versa. As a result, some value after the loop exit is not quite large enough or a bit too large. These errors fall into the **off-by-one** category. A conditional loop controlled by a compound boolean expression that uses **and** instead of **or,** or vice versa, will behave improperly on some sets of data. Often there is more than one way to implement a loop, and bits and pieces of each correct implementation—good ideas in the right context—are gathered together into incorrect code. Using *real* values in an exact comparison as the loop condition will frequently cause the loop to execute the wrong number of times due to the inexact representation of real numbers. Nested loop structures compound the difficulties.

Our earlier programs *ReceiptTotal1* and *ReceiptTotal4* illustrated some common loop errors. For simpler examples, the following six **while** loops are attempts to add the integers from 1 to 5 (assume that appropriate variable declarations have been made).

a.
```
Sum := 0;
I := 1;
while I < = 5 do
  begin
    Sum := Sum + I;
    I := I + 1;
  end;
```

b.
```
Sum := 0;
I := 1;
while I < = 5 do
  begin
    I := I + 1;
    Sum := Sum + I;
  end;
```

c.
```
Sum := 0;
I := 0;
while I < 5 do
  begin
    I := I + 1;
    Sum := Sum + I;
  end;
```

d.
```
Sum := 0;
I := 0;
while I < = 5 do
  begin
    I := I + 1;
    Sum := Sum + I;
  end;
```

e.
```
Sum := 0;
I := 1;
while I < 5 do
  begin
    Sum := Sum + I;
    I := I + 1;
  end;
```

f.
```
Sum := 0;
I := 1;
while not (I > = 5) do
  begin
    Sum := Sum + I;
    I := I + 1;
  end;
```

CHECKUP 8.6   Which of the above sections of code are correct and which contain errors? For those with errors, explain the problem.

CHECKUP 8.7   Use a **for** loop to solve the problem of adding the integers from 1 to 5.

In this simple problem the errors are fairly easy to find, but these are just the kinds of errors that creep into more complex examples. Diagnostic *writeln* statements, including *writeln* statements just before the loop is entered and just after it is exited, help trace values during loop execution and may help pinpoint difficulties.

CHECKUP 8.8   Insert diagnostic *writeln* statements in program *ReceiptTotal4*.

8.6 Program Verification

Because of the near impossibility of guaranteeing program correctness by testing, computer scientists have borrowed tools of mathematical logic to attempt to *prove* that programs are correct. Originally, it was hoped that **proof of correctness** or **program verification** could itself be done by computer, but the task has proved to be quite difficult.

"Correctness" has a rather narrow meaning here. Proving a program correct does not mean that the program correctly solves the problem it was intended to solve. It means that the program obeys certain characteristics of its specification, which may or may not reflect a correct solution to the original problem. In particular, it is shown that if the input values to the program satisfy certain relationships, then the output values satisfy certain (other) relationships. For example, if the program finds the hypotenuse of a right triangle given the lengths of the legs, then we have two input values a and b that satisfy the relationships

$$a > 0 \text{ and } b > 0$$

and an output value c that should satisfy the relationship

$$c^2 = a^2 + b^2$$

Instead of having just an initial relationship and a final relationship, the program is broken down into smaller sections, even individual statements. Then relationships about program variables that should hold in between statements are formulated. These relationships are called **assertions** because they assert what is supposed to be true about the program variables at that point. If A_i stands for the ith assertion and S_i stands for the ith program statement, then there is a sequence of assertions and statements of the form

A_0
S_1
A_1
S_2
.

.

.

S_k
A_k

The idea is that if assertion A_{i-1} is true before statement S_i is executed, then assertion A_i will be true after statement S_i is executed. The intermediate assertions are usually obtained by working backwards from the desired final assertion.

As an example, suppose that statement S_i is

```
X := X - 1;
```

and that after this statement is executed the assertion A_i is $X > 0$. Then assertion A_{i-1} is the relationship $X - 1 > 0$. If $X - 1 > 0$, that is, $X > 1$, before the statement is executed, then after the value of X is reduced by 1, it will be true that $X > 0$.

8.6.1 Loop Invariants

For a loop structure, we specify an assertion that holds before the loop is entered and continues to hold after each loop iteration. Such an assertion is called a **loop invariant** because it is a relationship that remains constant as the loop progresses. The values of the variables involved in the loop assertion will no doubt be changed by an iteration of the loop, but the relationship among these values will not change.

Consider the following section of code to compute the product of two nonnegative integers X and Y; the algorithm repeatedly adds Ys until there are X terms in the sum:

$$X*Y = \underbrace{Y + Y + \ldots + Y}_{X \text{ terms}}$$

Count keeps track of the number of terms accumulated so far, so the current value of *Product* should always be *Count*Y.*

```
Count := 0;
Product := 0;
```

```
while Count <> X do
  begin
    Product := Product + Y;
    Count := Count + 1;
  end;
writeln(Product);
```

The loop invariant, *Product* = *Count*Y*, is true before the loop begins because both *Product* and *Count* have the value 0. At each pass through the loop, the value of *Product* is increased by *Y* and the value of *Count* is increased by 1, so if

$$(\text{old})Product = (\text{old})Count*Y$$

then

$$(\text{old})Product + Y = (\text{old})Count*Y + Y = ((\text{old})Count + 1)*Y$$

or

$$(\text{new})Product = (\text{new})Count*Y$$

and the loop invariant is still true.

The loop terminates when *Count* has the value *X*. At that time the invariant *Product* = *Count*Y* becomes *Product* = *X *Y*, exactly what want. This "proof of correctness" increases our confidence that the loop behaves as we wish.

We proved that the loop behaves correctly provided that it terminates, but we need some assurance that it does terminate. Some quantity must change in such a way as to eventually satisfy the exit condition for the loop. In this case, an appropriate **variant assertion** is to note that *Count* is initially less than or equal to *X* and increases on each pass through the loop. Including the assertions as comments in the code, we get

Loop invariants and variant assertions can help prove that a loop behaves as intended.

```
Count := 0;
Product := 0;

{loop invariant: Product = Count*Y}
while Count <> X do
  {variant assertion: Count ≤ X and increasing until exit
   condition Count = X is reached}

  begin
    Product := Product + Y;
    Count := Count + 1;
  {loop invariant: Product = Count*Y}
  end;

{assertion Product = X*Y}
writeln(Product);
```

This seems like overkill for such a simple program. (Indeed, the product could be found by using the single statement **Product** := **X∗Y**.) This illustrates the level of detail involved in program verification. It is extremely difficult to apply these techniques to large, already existing programs. Program verification is easier, but still time-consuming, when done along with program development. The list of program assertions describes the intended program behavior and, therefore, has a place in the program design process. In addition, these assertions, left as program comments, provide valuable documentation.

8.7 Program Maintenance

1. Problem specification
2. Algorithm development
3. Coding
4. Debugging
5. Testing
6. Documenting
7. Maintenance

Software does not wear out in the same way a piece of machinery does, so one might wonder why it needs to be maintained. As we mentioned in Chapter 1, maintenance activities are necessary for three reasons:

1. Previously undetected errors may come to light, even in "mature" software that has been thoroughly tested, released, and used for some time.
2. The functional requirements of the program may change. New laws, changes in company policy, larger quantities of data, marketplace competition, etc., may dictate that a task the program already performs must be done in a different way or that new, related tasks must be performed.
3. Hardware or system software upgrades (i.e., changes in the program's environment) may necessitate changes in an existing program.

The fact that a lot of maintenance activity is required for a certain program does not necessarily indicate that the original program development was faulty. Quite the opposite may be true—it may be that the program is exceedingly dependable, useful, and important, and that is exactly why it gets used enough to discover new errors, why people want to add to its capabilities, or why they want to prolong its usefulness by adapting it to new environments.

Nevertheless, many people view maintenance programming as a demeaning activity without the "glamour" and importance of new program development—rather akin to mending as opposed to fashion design. This is an unfortunate attitude; maintenance activities occupy a large part of the software budget, in both time and money. Studies done on software costs reveal that:

■ Over a ten-year period in the "life cycle" of a major software system, i.e., starting with development through release and subsequent use, between 60-75 percent of the overall costs will be spent on maintenance. (Note that this means that program development costs do not exceed 25-40 percent of the overall costs.)
■ Over a ten-year period, more than half of a programmer's time will have been devoted to maintenance programming.
■ As hardware costs decline and labor costs rise, maintenance programming occupies about half of the total computing budget.

■ The cost per programming instruction (line of code) in maintenance programming of a large software system can be fifty times more expensive than the cost per instruction of development programming.

Clearly maintenance is an expensive activity. In an effort to hold down costs, planning for maintenance should be incorporated as part of program development. Fortunately, this does not require any additional measures beyond those we have already stressed. A careful statement of the problem specification, a modular design of the program, clearly written and well-commented code, and thorough testing will all contribute to ease of program maintenance. Most important of all is program documentation, the written record of these activities.

Plan for program maintenance by careful program development and good documentation.

Documentation is important because even the programmer who wrote the original program will not be able to remember the details of how it works for very long. A large program is seldom developed by a single individual, and over a period of time, perhaps none of the individuals involved in the original development of the program is still around. Documentation is the only reliable form of communication that the maintenance programmer can have with the thinking of a program's original developers. Of course, it is also important for the maintenance programmer to thoroughly document any of his/her own changes.

Conversely, lack of good documentation, poor program design, use of nonstandard language features, "cute" or "tricky" code, less-than-thorough testing, all present problems to the maintenance programmer. The older the software, the more these problems may exist—the ideas of good programming practice have developed over the years. The maintenance programmer may face further problems because of the nature of maintenance tasks. If an error in a working system has surfaced, chances are that the user will want it corrected yesterday, at the latest. Also, changes to a working system require caution and thorough testing; they can have a ripple effect that introduces unexpected errors in other parts of the program. (Perhaps you yourself have made one final cosmetic change to a program just before you handed it in only to watch the entire program seem to unravel before your very eyes and completely stop working.)

If involved with program maintenance, learn about the program before having to solve some problem under pressure.

There are lessons here for all concerned. Those working on program development need to think ahead and provide the necessary tools for the maintenance programmers (after all, they may eventually *be* the maintenance programmers). Maintenance programmers should view their task as a challenging activity without which the program would not continue to be useful. Project managers must budget time and money to allow for thorough and professional program development and maintenance. This includes time for maintenance programmers to spend becoming familiar (*before* a crisis develops) with programs for which they are responsible.

8.8 External Documentation

Internal documentation—the bits of information or aids to readability that are incorporated in the program listing itself—does not give the entire story

1. Problem
   specification
2. Algorithm
   development
3. Coding
4. Debugging
5. Testing
6. Documenting
7. Maintenance

about the program. For more extensive information *external documentation,* written material about the program apart from the program listing, should be provided. Some internal documentation, such as prologue comments, may be condensations from the external documentation.

External documentation should contain a written record of all useful information about the program. This includes the original problem statement and problem specification, modifications or additions made to the problem specification as the project progresses, and names, dates, and references to any legal documents. It includes the structure chart for the program, a description of the algorithms used, the functional requirements of each module—what it does, its interface with the rest of the program, perhaps a data flow diagram—and a pseudocode description of the module. We've tried to provide most of this information in the Sample Software Development Projects. The documentation should also provide information on the testing done for the program, what testing approach was used, the data sets used, the results at each step, a description of any errors that were found and how they were corrected.

Any subsequent modifications to the program must be incorporated into the documentation. Documentation that does not reflect the current status of the program is misleading and causes more confusion than no documentation at all. Efforts are underway to design programming environments that automatically update on-line documentation files according to changes made to the program code, thereby forcing documentation to remain current.

All of the above documentation is rather technical in nature and is needed by someone who must understand the details of how the program works, either to use it in a very sophisticated way or to modify it. The ordinary user of the program needs other information that includes:

- how to run the program;
- how to set up the data;
- what the restrictions on the data may be;
- what form to expect for the output;
- an interpretation of what the output values stand for;
- the hardware and software requirements needed to run the program;
- what input will be expected from the user or what commands the user can issue if it is an interactive program;
- what facilities are included for data validation;
- anything else that needs to be known in order to use the program effectively.

The amount of such information needed depends on the complexity of the program and its intended use. Children learn to run video games without any such instructions! Also, documentation for a commercial product may differ somewhat from that for an in-house product.

The two kinds of external documentation therefore are a *technical reference manual* and a *user's manual.* Both are communication vehicles for understanding the program, and it is important that they be written as clearly as possible. The user's manual especially must avoid computerese

Keep notes for a technical reference manual and a user's manual as the program is developed.

jargon and must include the minor (to the initiated) but crucial details on how to run the program and how to recover from errors that the user makes while running the program.

To produce documentation of the highest quality possible, many companies hire technical writers. Ideally, the technical writer is a part of the development team and involved with the project from the beginning. As we've said before, documentation that is tacked on at the end is seldom satisfactory. In addition, early versions of the user's manual can help the project manager interface with the client to be sure that the project is progressing in a mutually desirable fashion.

8.9 Sample Software Development Project— A Bank Statement

Problem Statement

Write a program to issue the bank statement for one month's set of transactions on a checking account at Scrooge Federal.

Problem Specification

The account must be identified; a valid ID for a checking account at Scrooge Federal consists of a four-character string, two letters followed by two digits. The initial balance in the account must be known. Two types of transactions can be done: a check can be written against the account, or a deposit can be made to the account. Data about each transaction must supply the following information: the date of the transaction (in the form 02/04/89), a transaction code (C for check, D for deposit), a check number if the transaction processes a check, and the amount of the check or deposit. A running balance must be maintained, and the final statement for the month should be a nicely formatted report giving the account ID, the month and year being reported (in the form "February, 1989"), the initial balance, the total number and amount of deposits, the total number and amount of checks, and the closing balance.

The following assumptions are made: there are no input errors (Scrooge employs only the highest-caliber workers), the user always has data to enter when the program is run (but note that there may be no transactions on an account for the month), the account never gets overdrawn, and the balance never reaches six figures (i.e., \$99,999.99 is the maximum balance).

Input: account ID, initial balance, and a series of transactions, each consisting of a date, a transaction code, a check number if the transaction involves a check, and an amount
Output: bank statement

Algorithm Development

The algorithm to process transactions just involves adding the amount of a deposit to the running balance or subtracting the amount of a check from

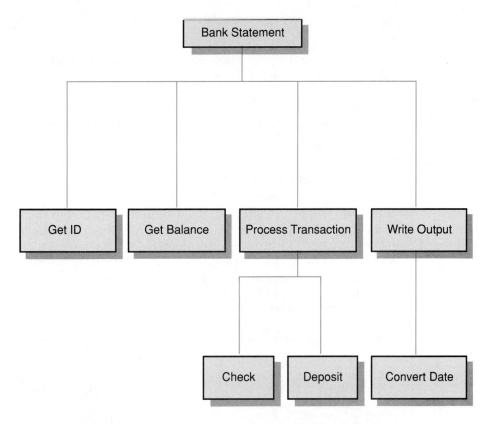

FIGURE 8.2 Structure chart for program *BankStatement*.

the running balance, and incrementing a counter and a running total for the type of transaction. The problem breaks down easily into subtasks as shown in Figure 8.2. The Process Transaction task will be carried out as long as there are more transactions for the month, so this will be contained in a conditional loop. Because of the possibility of no transactions on the account for the month, a **while** loop will be used instead of a **repeat** loop. Note the extra bit of work involved in converting to the month and year format required for the output. We'll also need to be careful in how we prompt the user for data entry (even the folks at Scrooge need guidance).

Get ID

This procedure prompts for and reads the account ID as four items of character data, passing the result to global variables for use by the output procedure.

```
procedure GetID(var ID1, ID2, ID3, ID4: char);
{gets the four characters of the account ID and returns these
 to the main program}
```

Get Balance

This procedure prompts for and reads the value of the initial balance in the account, a real variable.

procedure GetBalance(**var** InitialBalance: real);
{gets the initial balance for the month for this account}

Process Transaction

This procedure first reads the date. The month and year characters of the date will be used to write the date in the output, but the rest of the date information can be discarded. The check number can also be discarded. (If we were creating a file to keep a permanent record of the input data, we would keep all of this information.) Then the transaction code is read and, depending on the code, either the Check procedure or the Deposit procedure is invoked to finish processing the transaction.

procedure ProcessTransaction(**var** Month1, Month2,
                                   Year1, Year2: char;
                                   var Balance: real;
                                   var CheckCount, DepositCount:
                                   integer;
                                   var CheckTotal, DepositTotal:
                                   real);
{reads a date for an individual transaction, the transaction code for either a deposit or a check, and adjusts balance and totals accordingly; invokes procedure CheckProcess or DepositProcess}

var
    dummy : char;   {dummy variable to read input
                      characters that won't be used
                      - part of the date}
    TransactionCode : char; {C or D for check or deposit}

begin {procedure ProcessTransaction}

    prompt for and read the date
    prompt for and read the transaction code
    if transaction code is C or c, invoke *CheckProcess*, passing
        Balance, *CheckCount*, and *CheckTotal*, and receiving
        updated values for them
    if transaction code is D or d, invoke *DepositProcess*, passing
        Balance, *DepositCount*, and *DepositTotal*, and receiving
        updated values for them
end {procedure ProcessTransaction}

```
procedure CheckProcess(var CheckCount: integer;
                       var Balance, CheckTotal: real);
{carries out the details of a check transaction; invoked by
 ProcessTransaction}

var
    Amount : real;    {amount of check}
    dummy : integer; {to read and discard check number}

begin {procedure CheckProcess}

  prompt for, read, and discard check number
  prompt for and read Amount
  add Amount to Balance to get new Balance
  add Amount to CheckTotal
  add 1 to CheckCount

end;  {procedure CheckProcess}
```

```
procedure DepositProcess(var DepositCount: integer;
                         var Balance, DepositTotal : real);
{carries out the details of a deposit transaction; invoked by
 ProcessTransaction}

var
    Amount : real;    {amount of deposit}

begin    {procedure Deposit Process}

  prompt for and read Amount
  subtract Amount from Balance to get new Balance
  add Amount to DepositTotal
  add 1 to DepositCount

end;    {procedure DepositProcess}
```

Write Output
This procedure receives values for the date, the old and new balance, and the number and amount of checks and deposits. Then it writes the output. It invokes a *DateFormat* procedure to change the date into the format required for the output by the problem specification.

Continued

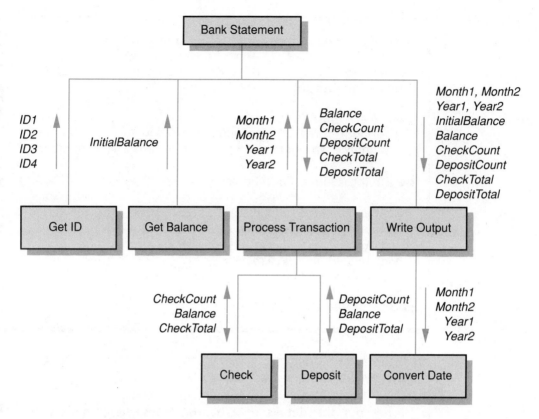

FIGURE 8.3 Data flow diagram for program *BankStatement*.

Write Output—Continued

procedure WriteOutput(Month1, Month2,
                         Year1, Year2: char;
                         InitialBalance, Balance : real;
                         CheckCount, DepositCount: integer;
                         CheckTotal, DepositTotal: real);
{writes the final bank statement; invokes procedure
 DateFormat}

procedure DateFormat(Month1, Month2, Year1, Year2: char);
{converts the date to the proper form and writes it out;
 invoked   by procedure WriteOutput}

Figure 8.3 illustrates the data flow diagram.

In the complete program below, notice that the local variable *dummy* in *CheckProcess* takes precedence over the local variable of the same name in the procedure *ProcessTransaction* in which *CheckProcess* is declared. (Since none of these values are used anyway, this doesn't matter, but if these were meaningful variables, the use of *dummy* in *CheckProcess* would not affect the value of *dummy* in *ProcessTransaction*.)

```
program BankStatement(input, output);
{processes the deposit and check transactions for a given month
 on a particular account and writes out a summary statement}

var
    ID1, ID2, ID3, ID4 : char;    {the account ID}
    key : char;                   {symbol for more transactions}
    Month1, Month2 : char;        {the month part of the date for
                                   each transaction}
    Year1, Year2 : char;          {the year part of the date for
                                   each transaction}
    InitialBalance : real;        {starting balance for the month}
    Balance : real;               {current balance in the account}
    CheckCount : integer;         {total number of checks written
                                   on this account for the month}
    DepositCount : integer;       {total number of deposits made
                                   to this account for the month}
    CheckTotal : real;            {total amount for checks written
                                   on this account for the month}
    DepositTotal : real;          {total amount for deposits made
                                   to this account for the month}

procedure GetID(var ID1, ID2, ID3, ID4: char);
{gets the four characters of the account ID and returns these to
 the main program}

    begin    {procedure GetID}
    writeln('Please give the account ID - two letters');
    write(' followed by two digits: ');
    read(ID1);
    read(ID2);
    read(ID3);
    readln(ID4);
    writeln;
    end;     {procedure GetID}

procedure GetBalance(var InitialBalance: real);
{gets the initial balance for the month for this account}

    begin    {procedure GetBalance}
    writeln('Enter the starting balance for this account - ');
    write(' no $ sign, please: ');
    readln(InitialBalance);
    writeln;
    end;     {procedure GetBalance}
```

```pascal
function Continue: boolean;
{determines if there are more transactions to process}

var
    key : char;    {symbol to check for continuation}

  begin {function Continue}
    writeln;
    write('More transactions? (Y or N): ');
    readln(key);
    if (key = 'N') or (key = 'n') then
      Continue := false
    else
      Continue := true;
  end;   {function Continue}

procedure ProcessTransaction(var Month1, Month2,
                             Year1, Year2: char;
                             var Balance: real;
                             var CheckCount, DepositCount:
                             integer;
                             var CheckTotal, DepositTotal: real);
{reads a date for an individual transaction, the transaction code
 for either a deposit or a check, and adjusts balance and totals
 accordingly; invokes procedure CheckProcess or  DepositProcess}

var
    dummy : char; {dummy variable to read input characters
                   that won't be used - part of the date}
    i : integer;      {loop index}
    TransactionCode : char; {C or D for check or deposit}

procedure CheckProcess(var CheckCount: integer;
                       var Balance, CheckTotal : real);
{carries out the details of a check transaction; invoked by
 ProcessTransaction}

var
    Amount : real;    {amount of check}
    dummy : integer; {to read and discard check number}

  begin {procedure CheckProcess}
    writeln;
    write('Check number: ');
    readln(dummy);
    write('Amount of check: ');
    readln(Amount);
    Balance := Balance - Amount;
    CheckTotal := CheckTotal + Amount;
    CheckCount := CheckCount + 1;
  end;   {procedure CheckProcess}
```

```
procedure DepositProcess(var DepositCount: integer;
                         var Balance, DepositTotal : real);
```
{carries out the details of a deposit transaction; invoked by ProcessTransaction}

```
var
    Amount : real;     {amount of deposit}

  begin {procedure DepositProcess}
    writeln;
    write('Amount of deposit: ');
    readln(Amount);
    Balance := Balance + Amount;
    DepositTotal := DepositTotal + Amount;
    DepositCount := DepositCount + 1;
  end;    {procedure DepositProcess}

  begin {procedure ProcessTransaction}
    writeln;
    writeln;
    writeln('Enter the following data for this transaction:');
    writeln;

    write('Date (month/date/year): ');
    read(Month1);
    read(Month2);
    for i := 1 to 4 do
      read(dummy);
    read(Year1);
    readln(Year2);
    writeln;

    write('Transaction code (C for check, D for deposit): ');
    readln(TransactionCode);
    if (TransactionCode = 'C') or (TransactionCode = 'c') then
      CheckProcess(CheckCount, Balance, CheckTotal)
    else
      DepositProcess(DepositCount, Balance, DepositTotal);
  end;    {procedure ProcessTransaction}

procedure WriteOutput(Month1, Month2, Year1, Year2: char;
                      InitialBalance, Balance : real;
                      CheckCount, DepositCount: integer;
                      CheckTotal, DepositTotal: real);
```
{writes the final bank statement; invokes procedure DateFormat}

```
procedure DateFormat(Month1, Month2, Year1, Year2: char);
```
{converts the date to the proper form and writes it out; invoked by procedure WriteOutput}

```
begin    {procedure DateFormat}
  {write the month part of the date}
  case Month2 of
    '3' : write('March');
    '4' : write('April');
    '5' : write('May');
    '6' : write('June');
    '7' : write('July');
    '8' : write('August');
    '9' : write('September');
    '0' : write('October');
    '1' : if Month1 = '0' then
            write('January')
          else
            write('November');
    '2' : if Month1 = '0' then
            write('February')
          else
            write('December');
  end;    {case statement}

  {now write the year part of the date}
  writeln(', 19', Year1, Year2);
end;    {procedure DateFormat}


begin {procedure WriteOutput}
  writeln;
  writeln('              ------Scrooge Federal--------');
  writeln;
  write('           Summary Statement for Account ');
  writeln(ID1, ID2, ID3, ID4);
  writeln;
  write('           Month of ');
  DateFormat(Month1, Month2, Year1, Year2);
  writeln;

  write('Initial Balance:                    $');
  writeln(InitialBalance:8:2);
  writeln;
  write('     ', DepositCount:3, ' deposits, totaling        $');
  writeln(DepositTotal:8:2);
  write('     ', CheckCount:3, ' checks, totaling         $');
  writeln(CheckTotal:8:2);
  writeln;
  writeln('Final Balance:                    $', Balance:8:2);
end;    {procedure WriteOutput}


begin    {main program}
```

```
          {initialize variables}
          CheckTotal  := 0.0;
          DepositTotal := 0.0;
          CheckCount := 0;
          DepositCount := 0;

          GetID(ID1, ID2, ID3, ID4);
          GetBalance(InitialBalance);
          Balance := InitialBalance;

          writeln('Transactions for this account for one month:');
          writeln;
          while Continue do
            ProcessTransaction(Month1, Month2, Year1, Year2, Balance,
                            CheckCount, DepositCount,
                            CheckTotal, DepositTotal);

          WriteOutput(Month1, Month2, Year1, Year2,
                    InitialBalance, Balance,
                    CheckCount, DepositCount,
                    CheckTotal, DepositTotal);
       end.    {main program}
```

RUNNING THE PROGRAM...

```
          Please give the account ID - two letters
           followed by two digits: jg22

          Enter the starting balance for this account -
           no $ sign, please: 800.00

          Transactions for this account for one month:


          More transactions? (Y or N): y


          Enter the following data for this transaction:

          Date (month/date/year): 12/05/88

          Transaction code (C for check, D for deposit): d

          Amount of deposit: 19.50

          More transactions? (Y or N): y


          Enter the following data for this transaction:

          Date (month/date/year): 12/07/88
```

Transaction code (C for check, D for deposit): c

Check number: 341
Amount of check: 45.60

More transactions? (Y or N): y

Enter the following data for this transaction:

Date (month/date/year): 12/17/88

Transaction code (C for check, D for deposit): d

Amount of deposit: 60.00

More transactions? (Y or N): n

------Scrooge Federal--------

Summary Statement for Account jg22

Month of December, 1988

Initial Balance:		$ 800.00
2 deposits, totaling	$ 79.50
1 checks, totaling	$ 45.60
Final Balance:		$ 833.90

**CASE
STUDY
ONE**   View #8

Sterling Software System's program for the Lodestone County Water
Pollution Department has been tested and meets all specifications, so it
could be delivered now. However, the program design makes it an easy
modification to allow multiple sites to be processed in one run without
restarting the program. The input validation features can also be strengthened to allow multiple chances for valid data entry. You propose these
changes to the department manager, who agrees to a contract extension to
allow the program modifications to be made. You turn this job over to one of
your maintenance programmers.

The resulting program appears below. The previous **if** statements that
provided one re-entry in the case of invalid *ID, Water,* or *Bacteria* data have
been changed to **while** loops. A **while** loop is also used to validate the date
information entered; this loop uses as its boolean expression a function
designator that involves boolean function *ValidDate. ValidDate,* in turn,
invokes function *Value* that converts character data to numerical equiva-

lents. Finally, the previous main program body has been embedded in a **repeat** loop so that multiple data sets can be accommodated.

(Note: The manager of the Lodestone County Water Pollution Department may wish that these requirements had been incorporated into the original program specification. Nevertheless, the manager appreciates the suggestions SSS has made that will allow this tool to be used more effectively. The manager requests that a test version of the program without the modifications be delivered so that the department lab can begin to use it, and agrees to a new deadline date and a fee to cover the modifications.)

```pascal
program WaterPollution(input, output);
{tests water sample from a site against a pollution threshold,
 issues a warning if the bacteria level is too high}

const
    Threshold = 2.0;            {200 bacteria per 100 ml water}

var
    ID : integer;                {site ID number}
    Water : integer;             {amount of water sampled, in ml}
    Bacteria : integer;          {bacteria count in sample}
    Mon1, Mon2 : char;           {two-digit month notation}
    Day1, Day2 : char;           {two-digit date notation}
    Yr1, Yr2 : char;             {two-digit year notation}
    Warning : boolean;           {flag for warning message if
                                   pollution level too high}
    Level : real;                {pollution level for this sample}
    Continue : char;             {signal to terminate execution}

procedure GetInput(var ID, Water, Bacteria: integer;
                   var Mon1, Mon2, Day1, Day2,
                   Yr1, Yr2: char);
{procedure to collect input for water pollution data; amount
 Water of water and count Bacteria of bacteria were obtained
 from  site ID on date Mon1Mon2/Day1Day2/Yr1Yr2}

var
    Slash : char;       {separating / in date format}

function Value(FirstChar, SecondChar: char): integer;
{function to convert two characters to a two-digit integer}

var
    FirstDigit : integer;        {the integer equivalents}
    SecondDigit : integer;       {of numerical characters}

    begin    {function Value}
    FirstDigit := ord(FirstChar) − ord('0');
    SecondDigit := ord(SecondChar) − ord('0');
    Value := 10*FirstDigit + SecondDigit;
    end;     {function Value}
```

```
function ValidDate(Mon1, Mon2, Day1, Day2: char): boolean;
{function to do some validation on date entered}

var
    MonthValue : integer;       {numerical value for month}
    DayValue : integer;         {numerical value for day}
    ValidMonth : boolean;       {MonthValue in range 1-12}
    ValidDay : boolean;         {DayValue in range 1-31}

  begin       {function ValidDate}
    MonthValue := Value(Mon1, Mon2);
    DayValue := Value(Day1, Day2);

    ValidMonth := (0 < MonthValue) and (MonthValue < 13);
    ValidDay := (0 < DayValue) and (DayValue < 32);

    ValidDate := ValidMonth and ValidDay;
  end;        {function ValidDate}


  begin       {procedure GetInput}
    writeln;
    write('Enter the site ID number: ');
    readln(ID);
    while not((1 <= ID) and (ID <= 1000)) do
      begin {ID out of range}
        write('Check the site ID number and enter again: ');
        readln(ID);
      end;    {ID out of range}
    writeln;

    writeln('Enter the date of this sample.');
    write('Use month/date/year format: ');
    readln(Mon1, Mon2, Slash, Day1, Day2, Slash, Yr1, Yr2);
    while not ValidDate(Mon1, Mon2, Day1, Day2) do
      begin {error in date input}
        write('Please enter the date again: ');
        readln(Mon1, Mon2, Slash, Day1, Day2, Slash, Yr1, Yr2);
      end;    {error in date input}
    writeln;

    write('Enter the amount of water in sample (in ml): ');
    readln(Water);
    while not (Water > 0) do
      begin {error in amount of water}
        write('Check the amount of water & enter again: ');
        readln(Water);
      end;    {error in amount of water}
    writeln;
```

```
      write('Enter the bacteria count found in this sample:  ');
      readln(Bacteria);
      while not (Bacteria >= 0) do
        begin   {error in bacteria count}
          write('Check the bacteria count & enter again: ');
          readln(Bacteria);
        end       {error in bacteria count}
    end;   {procedure GetInput}


function Ratio(Bacteria, Water: integer): real;
{computes the Ratio of Bacteria to Water}

  begin {function Ratio}
    Ratio := Bacteria/Water;
  end;   {function Ratio}


procedure CheckThreshold(Ratio: real;
                         var Over: boolean);
{compares Ratio to the global constant Threshold and sets
 Over to true if that limit is exceeded}

  begin     {procedure CheckThreshold}
    Over := false;   {initialize Over}
    if Ratio > Threshold then
      Over := true;
  end;       {procedure CheckThreshold}


procedure WriteOutput(ID, Water, Bacteria: integer;
                      Mon1, Mon2, Day1, Day2,
                      Yr1, Yr2: char;
                      Ratio: real;
                      Warning: boolean);
{echoes site input data and writes warning message if  warranted}

  begin     {procedure WriteOutput}
    writeln;
    writeln;
    write('Site ID', 'Date':8, 'Water':12, 'Bacteria':13);
    writeln('Level':9, 'Warning':10);
    write('_____');
    writeln('_____');
    writeln;
    write(ID:5, Mon1:6, Mon2, '/', Day1, Day2, '/', Yr1,  Yr2);
    write(Water:8, ' ml', Bacteria:9, Ratio:11:2);

    if Warning then
      write('      ** HIGH **');
    writeln;
  end;       {procedure WriteOutput}
```

```
begin        {main program}

  repeat

    GetInput(ID, Water, Bacteria,
             Mon1, Mon2, Day1, Day2, Yr1, Yr2);

    Level := Ratio(Bacteria, Water);

    CheckThreshold(Level, Warning);

    WriteOutput(ID, Water, Bacteria,
                Mon1, Mon2, Day1, Day2, Yr1, Yr2,
                Level, Warning);
    writeln;
    writeln;

    writeln('Do you have more sites to process?');
    writeln('(Answer Y or N): ');
    readln(Continue);

  until (Continue = 'N') or (Continue = 'n');
end.        {main program}
```

RUNNING THE PROGRAM...

```
Enter the site ID number: 3240
Check the site ID number and enter again: 320

Enter the date of this sample.
Use month/date/year format: 22/13/87
Please enter the date again: 12/13/87

Enter the amount of water in sample (in ml): 700

Enter the bacteria count found in this sample: 1100
```

Site ID	Date	Water	Bacteria	Level	Warning
320	12/13/87	700 ml	1100	1.57	

```
Do you have more sites to process?
(Answer Y or N):
y

Enter the site ID number: 556

Enter the date of this sample.
Use month/date/year format: 07/36/89
Please enter the date again: 07/26/89
```

Enter the amount of water in sample (in ml): 520

Enter the bacteria count found in this sample: 1340

Site ID	Date	Water	Bacteria	Level	Warning
556	07/26/89	520 ml	1340	2.58	** HIGH **

Do you have more sites to process?
(Answer Y or N):
n

CASE STUDY TWO   **View #8**

As project manager for the hypertension clinic program, you realize that this' program would be more useful if it were modified to handle more than one patient without having to exit and restart the program. Also, the data validation mechanisms could be strengthened by using loop structures. Carry out these program modifications. Be sure to test the new program thoroughly.

EXERCISES

#1. What is wrong with the following section of code to add integers from 1 to 10? (Assume that all variables have been properly declared.)

```
value := 0;
top := 10;
score := 1;
while score < top do
  begin
    value := value + score;
  end;
```

2. Write a section of code that reads odd integers until an even integer is encountered and then writes the number of odd integers read.

#3. Write a section of code using a **while** loop to read and add together positive integer values until the total exceeds 100; write the total at that point.

4. Redo Exercise 3 using a **repeat** loop.

#5. Write a section of code to read and add together positive integers as long as the total is less than 100; write the final total (note that the final total should be less than 100).

#6. What would be a reasonable next statement after a loop that has the form

repeat
  . . .
until (A <= B) **or** (C > D);

7. What is the output from the following section of code?

```
n := 7;
for row := 18 to 3*n  do
   writeln(2*row);
```

8. Write a section of code to read and write *n* characters, where the value of *n* is a positive integer; use a **for** loop.

#9. If program statement S_i is

```
X := X + 2;
```

and the assertion A_i to be true after this statement is executed is $X > Y$, what is assertion A_{i-1}?

10. In the following section of code to compute the sum of two nonnegative integers X and Y, show that the assertion $Sum = X + I$ is a loop invariant and that when the loop terminates, $Sum = X + Y$.

```
I := 0;
Sum := X;
while I <> Y do
   begin
      Sum := Sum + 1;
      I := I + 1;
   end;
writeln(Sum);
```

SKILL BUILDERS

1. Write a program that reads and writes a string of character values until an 'a' is encountered; use a **repeat** loop (you may assume that an 'a' appears somewhere in the first line read).

2. Rewrite the program for Skill Builder #1 above using a **while** loop.

3. Write a program that prints out all the capital letters on one line with all the lowercase letters on the next line.

#4. Write a program that prints out the multiples of 10 from 0 to 100.

5. Write a program to prompt for, read, and average a series of positive integers. Use a sentinel value.

SOFTWARE DEVELOPMENT PROJECTS

1. Develop software that asks the user for two positive integers *n* and *m* and computes their **greatest common divisor,** i.e., the largest integer that divides both *n* and *m*.

2. A motorist fills the tank and notes the mileage on the odometer at the beginning of a trip. Thereafter, the mileage and the number of gallons of gas purchased at each stop, as well as at the final destination, are recorded. Develop software to prompt for and read the data and output the gasoline mileage obtained for the trip.

3. The most frequently occurring letter in the English alphabet is considered to be "e," followed by "t." Develop software to read a text file (entered at the keyboard) until a terminating symbol of * is read as the first character in a line and then output a frequency count of e's and t's.

4. Suppose a polynomial p(x) is evaluated at $x = a$ and then at $x = b$. If p(a) > 0 and p(b) < 0, or conversely, we may assume that the polynomial has a root at some point c between a and b. Assuming that the polynomial looks like a straight line between a and b allows us to approximate the value of c by a process called linear interpolation. For example, Figure 8.4 shows a polynomial p(x) where p(0) = 4 and p(1) = −2. We have assumed a straight line between (0,4) and (1, −2). Because of the similarity of the two right triangles, the ratio

$$\frac{x}{4} = \frac{1}{6}$$

holds and can be solved for x: $x = 0.66$. We then compute p(0.66); if this is within some tolerance of 0, we use 0.66 as the root. If not, we repeat this process with 0 and 0.66 if p(0.66) is negative, or we repeat this process with 0.66 and 1 if p(0.66) is positive (as will be the case shown in Figure 8.4).

Develop software to read in a polynomial of degree 3 with integer coefficients that has a root between 0 and 1. Find that root to a tolerance of 0.01. Some sample test cases are:

$$x^3 - 3x^2 + 1$$
$$x^3 + x - 1$$
$$x^3 - 5x^2 + 7x - 2$$

5. Consider a positive integer n. If n is even, compute $n/2$; if n is odd, compute $3n + 1$. Then repeat this process on the result, and continue to do this. The original number n is called a ***wondrous number*** if the number 1 is ever generated by this process. (See ***Gödel, Escher, Bach: An Eternal Golden Braid*** by Douglas R. Hofstadter, Basic Books, Inc., 1979, for an amusing dialogue on wondrous numbers.) Develop software that asks for a positive integer as input and writes out one of two messages: "Your number, —, is a wondrous number" or "After 20 calculations, I was not able to decide whether your number, —, is wondrous."

TESTING AND MAINTENANCE DEPARTMENT

1. Modify program *Bacteria* on page 159 to replace the repetitious series of calls to procedure *PlotPoint* by a loop construction.

2. Modify program *BankStatement* by adding each of the following features in turn, being sure to test the program thoroughly as modifications are added:

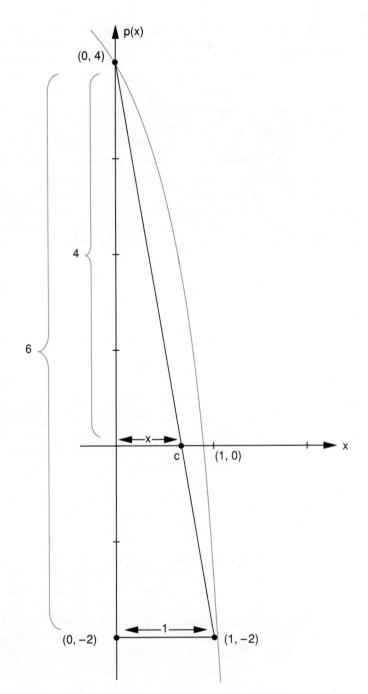

FIGURE 8.4 Linear interpolation to find a polynomial root.

a. Incorporate some validity checking on the input data, as described
by the following list. Allow multiple tries (with appropriate
prompts) for invalid input.
valid ID (right number of letters & digits)

$0 \leq$ initial balance $\leq \$99,999.99$
$1 \leq$ month ≤ 12
month the same as for previous transaction
$1 \leq$ day $\leq$ right number of days for month (ignore leap years)
transaction code $=$ 'C', 'c', 'D', or 'd' only
$0 <$ check number
$0 \leq$ transaction amount $\leq \$50,000.00$

b. Be able to process multiple sets of data, i.e., multiple accounts for a given month, or multiple months for the same account.

c. Be able to deal with overdrafts by printing an appropriate message containing at least the check number and the amount and assessing a \$10.00 fine (or as much of the \$10.00 as can be assessed before a negative balance results); do not process the check.

d. If the account balance ever reaches six figures, set the balance at \$99,999.99 and continue processing, writing an appropriate message.

e. These are interest-bearing accounts, so compute an average daily balance (assume all transactions take effect at the end of the day) for the month. If the average $\geq \$1500$, then at the end of the month, add interest at the rate of 5.25% annual rate on the average daily balance. If the average $< \$1500$, assess a service charge at the end of the month as follows:

$\$1000 \leq$ average daily balance $< \$1500$ $\quad \$3.00$
$\$500 \leq$ average daily balance $< \$1000$ $\quad \$5.00$
$\$0 \leq$ average daily balance $< \$500$ $\quad \$8.00$

3. Write both a technical reference manual and a user's manual for program *BankStatement* modified as outlined in #2 above.

DEBUGGING CLINIC

Run and debug the following programs.

1.

```pascal
program Addition(input, output);
{program to add up integers until a negative value occurs;
 assumes first integer is not the terminator}

var
    Number, Sum : integer;

begin
  Sum := 0;
  writeln('Please enter next integer;');
  writeln('a negative number terminates.');
  readln(Number);
  repeat
    Sum := Sum + Number;
    writeln('Please enter next integer;');
```

```
        writeln('a negative number terminates.');
        readln(Number);
      until Number > 0;
      writeln (Sum);
end.
```

2.
```
program Echo1(input, output);
{program to read and write five characters}

var
      Next : char;
      Count : integer;

begin
  Count := 1;
  while Count <= 5 do
    writeln('Type a single character.');
    readln(Next);
    writeln(Next);
    Count := Count + 1;
end.
```

3.
```
program Echo2(input, output);
{program to read and write five characters}

var
      Next : char;
      Count : integer;

begin
  for Count := 1 to 5 do;
    begin
      writeln('Type a single character.');
      readln(Next);
      writeln(Next);
    end
end.
```

4.
```
program Factorial(input, output);
{program to compute n! where n! = n(n − 1)(n − 2)...(3)(2)(1) and
0! = 1}

var
      n, nFactorial, value : integer;
```

```
begin
  writeln('Give a value for n');
  readln(n);
  nFactorial := 1;
  if (n = 0) or (n = 1) then
    writeln(nFactorial)
  else
    begin       {n > 1}
      value := 2;
      repeat
        nFactorial := nFactorial * value;
        value := value + 1;
      until value = n;
      writeln(nFactorial);
    end;
end.
```

CHAPTER NINE

ARRAYS

Up to this point, each item of data needed by a program has been stored in a separate memory location with its own individual variable name. There was no relationship between any of the variables, although choices of variable identifiers such as *ID1, ID2*, etc., indicated that we probably had a mental model of relationships among these variables.

We will work more and more from now on with mental models of relationships among variables. A **data structure** is the name given to a mental model of a collection of variables that, instead of being totally individual items, are related or "structured" in some way. We will also consider the kinds of manipulations or operations we would like to perform on the models. A given model and its associated operations are purely "pencil and paper" stuff, so together they form an **abstract data type.** We can talk about abstract data types without knowing anything at all about a programming language. Ultimately, however, we have to use the capabilities of our programming language in order to implement these abstract ideas in our programs. Pascal provides us with additional data types, beyond those we have already seen, in order to help with this task.

9.1 The Array **Data Type**

The **array** data type is provided in Pascal and in most other programming languages. The name suggests an orderly arrangement or display of values. Such an arrangement could consist of a one-dimensional display, as in Figure 9.1a, or a two-dimensional table, as in Figure 9.1b, or a three-dimensional arrangement like Figure 9.1c, or arrangements of even higher dimensions that we can't draw.

9.1.1 An Example

To see why an array is useful, let's deal with a simple one-dimensional case. Suppose our data consist of the national average price per gallon of gasoline

265

1	3	7	−4	19

(a)

25	−6	31	0	8
−1	2	5	26	−12
15	47	−9	52	26

(b)

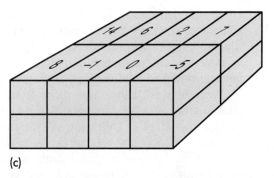

(c)

FIGURE 9.1 One-dimensional, two-dimensional, and three-dimensional arrays.

for each month of the year. If we only want to compute the average of these twelve values, we need only one variable, say, *NextPrice,* to hold the current value. We loop through a *read* statement twelve times, adding the current value of *NextPrice* to a *Sum* variable each time. Finally we divide by twelve. Because we have no further use for a value in *NextPrice* once it is added to *Sum,* one variable whose content keeps getting destroyed by the next *read* does the job.

Suppose, however, that our output is to be a report that displays the data in some nice form, indicates the maximum value from the twelve values, and tells what percentage of the maximum price each month's price represents. In order to be able to write out all twelve values and also to be able to compare each with the maximum value, we need to keep all twelve values. Rather than work with twelve individual variables such as *Price1, Price2,* etc., let's use a one-dimensional array called *Price* and then reference the individual elements by their position in the array, *Price[1], Price[2],* etc. (see Fig. 9.2). The position of a value in the array is called the array **index** of the value; in Pascal, the index is always enclosed in square brackets. The

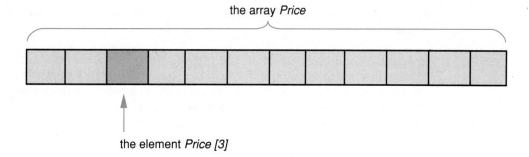

the array *Price*

the element *Price [3]*

FIGURE 9.2 A one-dimensional array *Price* with twelve elements.

advantage to this approach is not apparent until we learn that an array index can be an expression instead of just a number; then we can imagine constructions such as

```
for i := 1 to 12 do
    read(Price[i]);
```

to read in all of the array values. This is certainly handier than previous alternatives, which were to use twelve individual *read* statements, one for each of the twelve variables, or to list all twelve variable names in a single *read* statement.

The variable *Price* refers to an array, so it has an array data type. This data type needs a type declaration. Recall that type declarations come between constant and variable declarations. To declare an array type, we must name the type, indicate that it is an array, describe the dimensions of the array, and indicate the data type of the array elements. This points up an important restriction about arrays: All of the elements of an array must be of the same data type. An appropriate type declaration for the twelve-element array we want to use is

All the elements of an array must have the same data type.

```
type
    PriceArray = array [1..12] of real;
```

This declaration defines a data type whose legitimate values are one-dimensional arrays of twelve real values. We can now declare variables to be of this type, as in

```
var
    Price : PriceArray;
```

It is this variable declaration that actually sets aside the twelve memory locations collectively referred to as *Price*.

Before we go into more detail about array declarations, let's write the entire program *GasolinePrice*. We've borrowed the idea for the function that finds the maximum value in the array from program *Dive* (Sample Software Development Project, Chapter 7). Notice how we pass the entire array *Price* as a parameter to function *Maximum*, as well as to the two procedures used.

```pascal
program GasolinePrice(input, output);
{Given the national average price per gallon of gasoline for each
 month of the year, finds the maximum price and what percentage of
 the maximum price each month's price represents}

type
    PriceArray = array [1..12] of real;

var
    Price : PriceArray;        {array to hold the 12 monthly
                                 average prices}
    MaxPrice : real;           {maximum of the 12 prices}

function Maximum(Price: PriceArray): real;
{finds the maximum value among the elements of array Price}

var
    CurrentMax : real;         {current maximum value}
    i : integer;               {array index}

  begin    {function Maximum}
    CurrentMax := Price[1];
    for i := 2 to 12 do
      begin
        if Price[i] > CurrentMax then
          CurrentMax := Price[i];
      end;
    Maximum := CurrentMax;
  end;      {function Maximum}

procedure GetInput(var Price: PriceArray);
{reads the 12 monthly price averages into array Price}

var
    i : integer;      {array index}

  begin    {procedure GetInput}
    write('Enter the national average price ');
    writeln('per gallon of gasoline');
    write('for each month of the year');
    writeln(' - no dollar signs, please:');
    writeln;
    for i := 1 to 12 do
      read(Price[i]);
    readln;
  end;      {procedure GetInput}
```

```
function Percent(x, y: real): integer;
{finds x as a percentage of y}


   begin    {function Percent}
     if y <> 0.0 then
       begin
         Percent := round((x/y)*100);
       end
     else
       begin
         writeln('attempt to divide by zero, check data');
         Percent := -500;
       end;
   end;    {function Percent}


procedure WriteOutput(Price: PriceArray; Max: real);
{writes out the array values (the 12 price averages), the maximum
value, and the percentage of maximum of each of the 12
values}

var
     i : integer;       {array index}

   begin    {procedure WriteOutput}
     writeln;
     writeln;
     write('Monthly national average price ');
     writeln('per gallon of gasoline');
     writeln;
     write('JAN    FEB    MAR    APR    MAY    JUN   ');
     writeln('JUL    AUG    SEP    OCT    NOV    DEC');
     for i := 1 to 12 do
       write(Price[i]:4:2, '    ');

     writeln;
     writeln;
     writeln('The maximum price is $   ', Max:4:2);
     writeln;
     writeln;

     write('Here' 's the percentage of the ');
     writeln('maximum for each month:');
     writeln;
     write('JAN    FEB    MAR    APR    MAY    JUN   ');
     writeln('JUL    AUG    SEP    OCT    NOV    DEC');
     for i := 1 to 12 do
       write(Percent(Price[i], Max):3, '       ');
   end;    {procedure WriteOutput}
```

```
begin    {main program}
  GetInput(Price);

  MaxPrice  : =  Maximum(Price);

  WriteOutput(Price, MaxPrice);
end.      {main program}
```

RUNNING THE PROGRAM...

Enter the national average price per gallon of gasoline
for each month of the year - no dollar signs, please:

1.02 1.01 0.98 0.97 0.98 0.94 0.95 0.89 0.87 0.91 0.99 1.04

Monthly national average price per gallon of gasoline

JAN	FEB	MAR	APR	MAY	JUN	JUL	AUG	SEP	OCT	NOV	DEC
1.02	1.01	0.98	0.97	0.98	0.94	0.95	0.89	0.87	0.91	0.99	1.04

The maximum price is $ 1.04

Here's the percentage of the maximum for each month:

JAN	FEB	MAR	APR	MAY	JUN	JUL	AUG	SEP	OCT	NOV	DEC
98	97	94	93	94	90	91	86	84	88	95	100

All the previous data types we have encountered, whether user-defined types or the standard types of *integer, real, char,* or *boolean,* are **simple data types.** This means that a variable of that data type is one indivisible item of data—an integer or a character, for example. An array is a **structured data type,** meaning that a variable of that type can be thought of as either a single variable (*Price*) or as a collection of component variables (*Price[1], Price[2],...*). Program *GasolinePrice* illustrates both of these points of view. Individual elements of the array *Price* are referenced for the purpose of reading in and writing out values and for other operations done within the program modules, but the entire array is passed as an actual parameter to function *Maximum* and the procedures.

9.1.2 *The Array Type Declaration*

The type declaration for an array must give the array dimensions and the data type of the elements.

Let's consider the type declaration for an array in more detail. It must include the name of the type, the reserved word **array,** and the type of the array elements. Array elements can be of any type, but remember that all elements of a single array must be of the same type.

The array declaration must also include the dimensions of the array and the size of each dimension. The size of a dimension is generally given as a subrange of values from an ordinal type. A multi-dimensional array (two-dimensional, three-dimensional, etc.) will have a list of such subranges, which gives the dimensions and the size of each dimension at the same time. The arrays in Figures 9.1a and 9.1b consist of integer elements, so

type
    OneD = **array** [1..5] **of** integer;
    TwoD = **array** [1..3,1..5] **of** integer;

would be appropriate type declarations. Arrays of type *TwoD* have three rows, numbered 1, 2, and 3, and five columns, numbered 1, 2, 3, 4, and 5.

Even for multi-dimensional arrays, the actual memory space allocated consists of the proper number of contiguous memory cells, like one long one-dimensional array. Specifying the size of each dimension tells the system not only what that proper number is, but also how to locate each array element. For example, an array *A* with two rows and three columns (Fig. 9.3a) may be stored as

A[1,1] *A[1,2]* *A[1,3]* *A[2,1]* *A[2,2]* *A[2,3]*

and *A[2,2]* is the fifth element after the beginning of the array storage; but if *A* has three rows and two columns (Fig. 9.3b), it may be stored as

A[1,1] *A[1,2]* *A[2,1]* *A[2,2]* *A[3,1]* *A[3,2]*

In this case, *A[2,2]* is the fourth element. Fortunately, this is all handled automatically from information in the type declaration, and we may continue to use our mental model of two-dimensional tables and three-dimensional cubes.

Consider the following declarations:

A[1,1]	A[1,2]	A[1,3]
A[2,1]	A[2,2]	A[2,3]

(a)
Array with Two Rows, Three Columns

A[1,1]	A[1,2]
A[2,1]	A[2,2]
A[3,1]	A[3,2]

(b)
Array with Three Rows, Two Columns

FIGURE 9.3 Two different arrangements of six elements in two-dimensional arrays.

type
        Stock = **array** [−5..5] **of** integer;
        Fruit = (apple, berry, peach, lemon, lime);
        Pie = **array** [berry..lemon] **of** integer;
        JuiceOrder = **array** [1..8] **of** Fruit;
        TableArray = **array** ['A'..'C',1..7] **of** char;
        Spock = **array** [1..5,1..8,'M'..'T',0..3] **of** real;

Stock declares a one-dimensional array type for a display of eleven integer values and *Pie* declares a one-dimensional array type for a display of three integer values. *JuiceOrder* declares a one-dimensional array type for a display of eight elements of type *Fruit*. *TableArray* declares a two-dimensional character array type arranged in three rows ('A', 'B', and 'C'—the first subrange) and seven columns (1 through 7—the second subrange). *Spock* declares a four-dimensional array type of real values. Variables could now be declared to be of any of these types.

CHECKUP 9.1   How many memory locations would be reserved for a variable declared as one of the following types?
a. **type** NameArray = **array** [0..5] **of** char;
b. **type** BoxArray = **array** [1..3,1..5] **of** integer;
c. **type** SpaceArray = **array** ['A'..'Z',1..4,−7..−4] **of** real;

CHECKUP 9.2   *a.* Write a type declaration for arrays that look like the one in Figure 9.3a; assume character array elements.
     b. Write a type declaration for arrays that look like the one in Figure 9.3b; assume integer array elements.

Constants can also be used to describe the subrange for an array dimension. The declarations

const
        top = 10;

type
        DaysToWork = **array** [1..top] **of** char;

indicate that arrays of type *DaysToWork* will have ten elements. As usual, the use of a constant makes subsequent program modifications easier. It is not possible to use a variable to describe the subrange for an array dimension (**type** Wrong = **array** [1..n], for example) because the amount of memory to set aside for an array-type variable must be known when the program is compiled.

An alternative to using a subrange for the size of a dimension is simply to use the name of an ordinal or subrange type, as long as this does not allow too many values. The declaration

type
    Directory = **array** [char] **of** real;

indicates that arrays of type *Directory* will have as many (real) elements as there are in the character set of the computer. Although *integer* is an ordinal type name, it cannot be used in this way because it would allow an array dimension to be too big.

9.1.3 *Referencing Array Elements*

As with any other type declaration, the array type declaration describes the form that variables of that type will have. Suppose we have made the following variable declarations, after making the type declarations shown earlier:

var
    Inventory : Stock;
    Table : TableArray;

Then we can imagine *Inventory*, once values have been associated with its elements, to be arranged as a display of eleven integers, as in Figure 9.4a. To refer to a specific element of *Inventory*, we must include the index of that element, as determined by the type declaration. According to the declaration for array type *Stock*, the pattern for *Inventory*, the indices are integers from -5 to 5. Thus:

- *Inventory[− 3]* has the value 14.
- *Inventory[4]* has the value 0.
- *Inventory[− 5]* has the same value as *Inventory[3]*.

Note that the value of the array index is not to be confused with the value of the array element stored at that index. Also, even though *Inventory* contains eleven integer values, there is no such thing as *Inventory[11]* because, according to the type declaration, 11 is not a legal index value.

| 3 | −1 | 14 | 20 | 7 | 4 | −5 | 2 | 3 | 0 | 12 |

FIGURE 9.4A Array *Inventory*

FIGURE 9.4B Array *Table*

The array *Table* might contain the values shown in Figure 9.4b. A reference to an element of *Table* needs two indices; the first index is always the row value and the second index is the column value. Here

- *Table['B',3]* has the value 'e'.
- *Table['A',1]* has the value 'b'.
- *Table['A',6]* has the same value as *Table['C',2]*.

An array index expression must evaluate to the correct data type for the index.

An expression can serve as an array index provided that (a) the expression evaluates to a value of the index type, and (b) the expression evaluates to a value within the index range. A violation of the first condition can be detected when the program is compiled, but a violation of the second condition will (we hope) be a run-time error producing a message such as "index out of range."[†]

Defensive programming suggests using input validation, **if** statements or other means of condition testing, subrange data types, etc., to attempt to prevent array indices taking on out-of-range values.

Guard against out-of-bounds array indices—they can cause trouble.

Multi-dimensional arrays must have an index expression for each dimension. These index expressions are matched in order against those of the type declaration. For example, in a reference to an element of *Table* such as *Table[exp1,exp2]*, *exp1* would have to evaluate to a *char* value of 'A', 'B', or 'C', and *exp2* would have to evaluate to an *integer* value between 1 and 7.

As a final reminder, individual array elements are accessed by giving the array name followed by the index value or values in square brackets. Such individual array elements can be treated like any simple variable and used in read or write statements, assignment statements, expressions, actual parameter lists, etc.

[†]If such an error message is not generated, the system may simply pick up and use a value from an adjacent memory location. For example, suppose you want to use *Inventory[i]* and through some error, *i* is allowed to take on the value 6, which is outside of the range of index values for *Inventory*. If the memory location adjacent to *Inventory[5]* contains 3400, this totally unrelated value may be used instead. This is an obscure error to find! Some compilers have a range-checking switch that can be deactivated, but this should certainly not be done during program development.

CHECKUP 9.3   Suppose that variables *Name* and *Box* have been declared to be of type *NameArray* and *BoxArray*, respectively (see CHECKUP 9.1), and that these arrays contain the values shown below. What is the

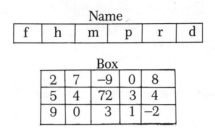

Name

f	h	m	p	r	d

Box

2	7	−9	0	8
5	4	72	3	4
9	0	3	1	−2

effect of each of the following?

a. writeln(Name[4]);
b. writeln(Box[1,4]);
c. writeln(Box[4,1]);
d. Box[1,3] := 2*abs(Box[1,3]);
e. Sum := 0;
   for i := 1 **to** 3 **do**
     begin
       Sum := Sum + Box[i,i];
     end;
   writeln(Sum);

CHECKUP 9.4   What will be the output from the following section of code, using *Inventory* and *Table* from Figure 9.4?

```
n := 7;
letter := 'D';
writeln(Inventory[n mod 3]:3);
writeln(Table[pred(pred(letter)),trunc(sqrt(n))]);
```

9.2 Array Traversal and For Loops

In most situations where we are dealing with arrays, we need to reference the individual array elements. For example, in loading input data into an array, we cannot simply say *read(Table)* and expect all of the values to be picked up at once and dropped into their appropriate locations; we have to read each array element one at a time, as we did in program *GasolinePrice*. The same holds true for writing out the values in an array. A **for** loop provides a natural mechanism to systematically traverse array elements.

For loops are an organized way to traverse all the array elements, with nested loops for multi-dimensional arrays.

Traversing multi-dimensional arrays calls for nested **for** loops. The following (rather pointless) program reads values into the two-dimensional array *Box* and writes them out again.

```
program BoxReadWrite1(input, output);
{reads in and writes out values for Box, a two-dimensional
 integer array}

type
    BoxArray = array [1..3,1..5] of integer;

var
    Box : BoxArray; {two-dimensional integer array}
    i, j : integer;    {array indices}

begin
  write('Box is a 3 x 5 integer array - ');
  writeln('please enter 15 values for Box');
  writeln;
  for i := 1 to 3 do
    begin    {outer read loop - rows}
      for j := 1 to 5 do
        begin    {inner read loop - columns}
          read(Box[i,j]);
        end;    {inner read loop - columns}
    end;    {outer read loop - rows}
  readln;
  writeln;

  writeln('Box looks like this:');
  writeln;
  for i := 1 to 3 do
    begin    {outer write loop - rows}
      for j := 1 to 5 do
        begin    {inner write loop - columns}
          write(Box[i,j]:2);
        end;    {inner write loop - columns}
      writeln;
    end;    {outer write loop - rows}
end.
```

RUNNING THE PROGRAM...

Box is a 3 x 5 integer array - please enter 15 values for Box

1 2 3 4 5 6 7 8 9 0 2 4 6 8 0

Box looks like this:

```
1 2 3 4 5
6 7 8 9 0
2 4 6 8 0
```

The prompt for program *BoxReadWrite1* was unsatisfactory because it did not tell the user whether to supply the values for *Box* by row or by column. The program itself, by the way the **for** loops are organized, loads *Box* by rows. For each of the three values of *i* (the row index, established by the outer **for** loop), *j* (the column index—inner loop) runs through the columns from 1 to 5. In the following version, the prompt has been improved, and the **for** loops rewritten, this time to load *Box* by columns.

```pascal
program BoxReadWrite2(input, output);
{reads in and writes out values for Box, a two-dimensional
 integer array}

type
    BoxArray  =  array [1..3,1..5] of integer;

var
    Box : BoxArray; {two-dimensional integer array}
    i, j : integer;    {array indices}

begin
  write('Box is a 3 x 5 integer array - ');
  writeln('please enter 15 values for Box');
  write('Give the values by column - column 1, ');
  writeln('then column 2, etc.');
  writeln;
  for j := 1 to 5 do
    begin    {outer read loop - columns}
      for i := 1 to 3 do
        begin    {inner read loop - rows}
          read(Box[i,j]);
        end;    {inner read loop - rows}
    end;      {outer read loop - columns}
  readln;
  writeln;

  writeln('Box looks like this:');
  writeln;
  for i := 1 to 3 do
    begin    {outer write loop - rows}
      for j := 1 to 5 do
        begin    {inner write loop - columns}
          write(Box[i,j]:2);
        end;       {inner write loop - columns}
      writeln;
    end;    {outer write loop - rows}
end.
```

RUNNING THE PROGRAM...

Box is a 3 x 5 integer array - please enter 15 values for Box
Give the values by column - column 1, then column 2, etc.

0 1 2 3 4 5 6 7 8 2 4 6 3 5 7

Box looks like this:

0 3 6 2 3
1 4 7 4 5
2 5 8 6 7

Any single array element can be accessed directly by giving its index or indices in the array.

Instead of doing some uniform process with all of the array elements, we may want to access a single array element from somewhere in the array (perhaps to write out its value in response to a query from the user). This is easily done provided we know the index value or values. We can access any array element without having to traverse the array to get there; this **random-access** property is one of the most attractive features of arrays.

CHECKUP 9.5   Give a single program statement that will write out the value of the fourth element in the second row of *Box* from program *BoxReadWrite2*.

9.3 Allocated Storage vs. Used Storage

One of the less-attractive features of arrays has to do with storage requirements. When a variable is declared to be an array type, the amount of memory storage set aside is determined from the type declaration. This is a fixed amount of storage, and cannot be changed except by changing the type declaration (or a constant used in the type declaration). If we are not sure how many elements we will need in an array, our only choice is to set the type declaration to the maximum size we think we might ever want. If the array is not entirely filled, the unused memory space is wasted. Furthermore, since we do not want to process unused memory cells, we need some variable or variables in the program to keep track of just how much of the array is filled. These variables will then serve as upper limits on any **for** loops that process the array elements.

If an array is not filled, variable(s) can be used to keep track of how much of the array is filled.

The following program allows a user to enter a string of characters, up to a maximum of sixty. The output is the same string of characters reversed. The input is stored in a one-dimensional array *Message* that can hold at most sixty characters, but this array may only be partially filled. The variable *n* keeps track of the actual number of characters read in, and it is only the first *n* elements of *Message* that we want to manipulate. Notice that a warning is issued if the user's string of characters exceeds the maximum value of sixty (of course this value, since it is a program constant, can easily be changed).

In order to reverse the n characters, we could create a second array *Copy* and move *Message[n]* into *Copy[1]*, *Message[n − 1]* into *Copy[2]*, etc. This would involve a construction like

```
for i := 1 to n do
    Copy[i] := Message[n − i + 1];
```

However, we don't actually have to store the array elements in reverse order, we only need to write them out that way. A **for..downto** loop will work.

```
program MirrorWriting(input, output);
{reads in a line of characters - current limit 60 - and writes it
 out in reverse order}

const
    Max = 60;
    Blank = ' ';
    Terminator = '#';

type
    Index = 1..Max;
    LineOfText = array [Index] of char;
    CountValue = 0..Max;

var
    Message : LineOfText;    {array to hold the line of
                              characters}
    n : CountValue;          {number of characters actually
                              read}

procedure FillBlank(var X: LineOfText);
{initializes array X to blanks - not necessary, but tidy}

var
    i : Index;        {array index}

    begin     {procedure FillBlank}
      for i := 1 to Max do
        X[i] := Blank;
    end;      {procedure FillBlank}

procedure Load(var X: LineOfText; var n: CountValue);
{reads n values into array X}

var
    symbol : char;    {current character}
```

```
    begin    {procedure Load}
      n := 0;
      write('Write the line of characters ');
      writeln('-maximum ', Max:2, ' please-');
      writeln('that you want MirrorWriting to reverse.');
      writeln('Use # to denote the end of the message.');
      writeln;

      read(symbol);
      while (symbol <> Terminator) and (n < Max) do
        begin
          n := n + 1;
          X[n] := symbol;
          read(symbol);
        end;

      if (symbol <> Terminator) then
        begin    {more than Max valid characters were  entered}
          writeln('You entered more than ', Max:2, ' characters.');
          writeln('Only the first ', Max:2, ' will be reversed');
        end;
      readln;
    end;    {procedure Load}

procedure WriteReverse(X: LineOfText; n:  CountValue);
{writes out the reversed array}

var
    i : Index;           {array index}

  begin    {procedure WriteReverse}
    writeln;
    writeln('The reverse of your message is:');
    writeln;
    for i := n downto 1 do
      write(X[i]);
  end;    {procedure WriteReverse}

begin    {main program}
  FillBlank(Message);
  Load(Message, n);
  WriteReverse(Message, n);
end.    {main program}
```

Write the line of characters -maximum 60 please-
that you want MirrorWriting to reverse.
Use # to denote the end of the message.

Have a good day!#

The reverse of your message is:

!yad doog a evaH

CHECKUP 9.6   In program *MirrorWriting* above, what happens if the first character entered is the terminator character?

9.4 Arrays as Single Variables

There are a few occasions when we can treat an array variable as a single variable.

9.4.1 *Array Assignment*

One such occasion is in an assignment statement. If *Array1* and *Array2* are array variables of the same type, then the statement

```
Array2 := Array1;
```

has the effect of making *Array2* an exact copy of *Array1*. This wholesale assignment will work only if the two arrays are of the same type, and this means that they have the same type identifiers. Consider the following declarations:

```
const
    Max = 10;
type
    TypeOne = array[1..10] of integer;
    TypeTwo = array[1..Max] of integer;
var
    A : TypeOne;
    B : TypeTwo;
```

Under these circumstances, the assignment statement

```
A := B;
```

is illegal because of a type mismatch—the two types are not the same, even though they describe arrays of identical characteristics.

Even if two arrays are of the same type, arithmetic operations such as addition are not defined on variables of array type, so a statement such as

```
Array3 := Array1 + Array2;
```

is not legal. To add two arrays, element-by-element addition must be done, as in the following statement that assumes that *Array1* and *Array2* are one-dimensional arrays:

```
for i := 1 to n do
  Array3[i] := Array1[i] + Array2[i];
```

The details of this activity can be relegated to a procedure (we'll talk about arrays as parameters next), so that to the invoking program segment, it appears as if adding arrays is a one-step operation.

9.4.2 *Arrays as Parameters*

An array can be passed as a single actual parameter. The corresponding formal parameter must indicate the correct array data type. In program *GasolinePrice*, for example, function *Maximum* was invoked by the statement

An array name can be treated as a single variable in an assignment statement or in a parameter list.

```
MaxPrice := Maximum(Price);
```

and the function heading was

```
function Maximum(Price: PriceArray): real;
```

No indices appeared in either the actual or formal parameter. If we wanted to pass an array element as a parameter, an index would appear as part of the actual parameter and the data type of the array element (not the array) would be given in the formal parameter list. An example might be

```
ABC(Price[i]);
```

to invoke procedure *ABC* and pass the element of the *Price* array indexed by the current value of *i*. The procedure heading for *ABC* would have the form

```
procedure ABC(Amount: real);
```

indicating that a single real value is expected. A formal parameter cannot contain an indexed variable, so something like

```
procedure ABC(X[i]: real);
```

is illegal.

If an array being passed as a parameter to a procedure or function may be only partially filled, then a variable or variables indicating how much of the array has been used should be passed as well, as in program *Mirror-Writing*. If an array is passed as a value parameter, then, like any other value parameter, a local copy of the array is made available for the procedure to use. This means that, temporarily at least, twice the memory space required for the original array must be allocated. A program using large arrays and many procedures runs the risk of exceeding memory space. This can be solved by passing all arrays as variable parameters even when these arrays serve as "input only" parameters. However, using a variable parameter removes the protection against side effects that use of a value parameter provides.

While an array can be passed as a single parameter to a function, a function cannot be defined to return an array as the function value. Functions are intended to return only single values, and a function value cannot be a structured data type. A procedure could return an array through a variable parameter.

9.5 Packed Arrays

Handling strings of character data has so far been rather awkward. Each character requires an individual memory location, so in order to read or write a string of characters a loop must deal with each memory location individually. Using a one-dimensional array of type *char* makes the loop easier to write by allowing us simply to increment the array index, but each array element still requires individual attention.

Some improvement on this situation can be obtained by using a **packed** array of type *char*. Declaring an array to be "packed" instructs the compiler to economize on the storage requirements. For example, the binary-coded form of character data is rather short. It may be possible to store the code for more than one character in a single memory location provided that this storage is done in some organized way that allows for retrieving the individual character codes when required. The extra work to retrieve a single character means that the saving in storage space obtained by using packed arrays may be offset by slower execution time. The potential slowdown in execution or savings in memory would be of real concern only in large programs. We are interested in packed arrays because they allow us to manipulate strings of characters in a more natural fashion.

To describe a string of characters, we declare a packed one-dimensional array data type with elements of type *char*, as in

```
type
    String = packed array [1..10] of char;

var
    Line1, Line2 : String;
```

Line1 and *Line2* can now each hold a ten-character string. By declaring them to be packed arrays, rather than just arrays, we gain three nice features:

1. Packed arrays can be written out "in a hunk" with a single write statement, instead of one element at a time. The statement

```
writeln(Line1);
```

causes *Line1*'s ten characters to be written out. Unfortunately, this provision does not apply to read statements.[†] The ten characters have to be read into *Line1* by the usual looping process

```
for i := 1 to 10 do
    read(Line1[i]);
```

If the character string to be read will ever be less than ten characters, a conditional loop rather than a **for** loop should be used, just as in program *MirrorWriting*. In order to maintain control over the entire content of *Line1*, it should either be initialized to all blanks before reading or filled ("padded") with blanks in any remaining space to the right of the actual input. Also, as with any partially filled array, a variable such as *Length* can be kept to denote the actual string length. Then a cute trick like

```
write(Line1: Length);
```

will write the character string *Line1* in a field width of length *Length*, which will truncate the blanks on the right and only allow the actual characters to be written out.

2. A single assignment statement can be used to place a string constant of the appropriate size into a packed array. The assignment statement

```
Linel := 'Tinkerbell';
```

has the same effect as

```
Line1[1] := 'T';
Line1[2] := 'i';
etc.
```

The string constant must be exactly the length of the packed array. To insert fewer characters, the string constant must be padded with blanks to make it the right length, as in

```
Line1 := 'Peter Pan ';
```

3. Comparisons can be made between packed arrays or between packed arrays and string constants of the appropriate length by using relational operators. Thus

```
Line1 < Line2
```

is a legitimate boolean expression. Its value is true if *Line1* "alphabetically" precedes *Line2*, but this is subject to the collating sequence of characters in

---

[†]Some extensions to standard Pascal define a built-in "string" data type, in which case **string** becomes a reserved word. These systems usually allow string-type variables to be read with a single *read* statement.

the computer. If *Line1* contains the string 'Peter Pan ' and *Line2* contains the string 'Wendy   ', then

> Line1 < Line2

A string (packed array of char) can be treated like a single variable in write statements, assignment statements, or boolean expressions, but not in read statements.

is true because 'P' always precedes 'W'. If *Line2* contains the string 'nevernever', then

> Line1 < Line2

is still true if uppercase letters precede lowercase letters in the collating sequence of the character set, otherwise it is false. Also,

> Line1 < '   Wendy'

may or may not be true, depending on where blanks fall in the collating sequence.

CHECKUP 9.7   Given the declarations

> **type**
>   String = **packed array** [1..7] **of** char;
>
> **var**
>   name : String;

which of the following are legitimate statements?
a. name := 'Bob';
b. writeln(name);
c. read(name);
d. **if** name <> 'Betsy   ' **then** writeln('Not Betsy');

9.5.1 Arrays of Arrays

Because the elements of an array can belong to any single data type, it is possible to have an array whose elements are themselves arrays. For example, a block of text can be thought of as a (vertical) one-dimensional array whose elements are strings (packed arrays of characters). Each index in the array determines one line of text. Given the declarations

type
    String = **packed array** [1..80] **of** char;
    PageType = **array** [1..55] **of** String;

var
    Page : PageType;

then *Page* looks like

Page
[1] -
[2] -
.
.
[55] -

Page can hold up to fifty-five lines of text, each with up to eighty characters. In the type declarations, *String* is used in the declaration for *PageType*, so of course *String* has to be declared first.

A page of text can also be represented as a two-dimensional array of *char* elements. Either representation allows us to access single characters in the text. Under the above type declarations, the third character in line 5, for example, is referenced by *Page[5][3]*. *Page[5]* picks out the fifth element in the array *Page*, which is a string; the index 3 picks out the third element in this string array. This is somewhat awkward, but the form *Page[5,3]* is also allowed. This latter form would also be the one to use if *Page* had been declared as a two-dimensional array.

We now have a choice of data structures—mental models about the elements of data and their relationships—for representing a block of text. Should our model be that of a two-dimensional array of characters, or of a one-dimensional array of strings of characters? In this particular case, it makes little difference, unless what we want to do involves lines of text, like moving a line or deleting a line. Then the array-of-strings model seems preferable. This sort of decision will come up more and more later—the application influences the choice of an appropriate data structure.

9.5.2 *Faking Enumerated-Type Read/Write*

An array of character strings is also helpful in overcoming the inability to read in or write out enumerated-type variables. We found one way around this difficulty in Chapter 7, namely, to use a **case** statement to link *char* variables, which can be read and written, to internal enumerated-type variables. This same linking can be accomplished by an array indexed by the enumerated-type variables with the corresponding character strings as the array entries. For example, with the declarations

type
    Direction = (North, South, East, West);
    String = **packed array** [1..5] **of** char;
    TableType = **array** [Direction] **of** String;

var
    Table : TableType;
    Compass : Direction;
    Buffer : String;

we would initialize the contents of array *Table* as follows:

```
Table[North]  : =  'North';
Table[South]  : =  'South';
Table[East]   : =  'East ';
Table[West]   : =  'West ';
```

Then to simulate writing out the enumerated-type variable *Compass,* we do **write(Table[Compass]).** If the current value of *Compass* is North, then the string 'North' gets written out.

Reading values is a bit more complicated. To simulate reading a value for *Compass,* the string of characters must be read, one element at a time, into a temporary variable such as *Buffer. Buffer* then gets compared with the elements of *Table* until a match is found. Because we are comparing two packed arrays, this comparison can be done by using the relational operator "=" and a character-by-character match is not required. When a match is found, the corresponding index is the enumerated-type variable we want. The code, given appropriate declarations for *i* and *Index,* looks like

```
for i := 1 to 5 do
   read(Buffer[i]);
for Index := North to West do
   begin
      if Buffer = Table[Index] then
         Compass := Index;
   end;
```

This code has some problems. What happens if *Buffer* does not match any of the elements of *Table?* Also, if a match is found at the first index, why waste time searching the rest of the array? A problem at the end of this chapter (Skill Builder #4) asks you to improve upon the array search technique given by the above code.

9.6 Sorting

Searching through the elements of an array to find a particular value (as we searched *Table* above for the value of *Buffer*) is a task that occurs frequently, so it is important to develop correct and efficient ways to do it. Sorting the elements of an array into numerical or alphabetical order is also an important task. A number of algorithms have been devised for sorting. The technique we will describe is not the most efficient, but it is easy to understand how it works.

As an example, let's consider the array *A* of integers shown in Figure 9.5a and see how we could sort it in increasing order. Working backwards, once the array is sorted the maximum array value, 9, should be stored in *A[4].* This maximum value occurs at index 2. If we simply give *A[4]* the value 9, then this value is now in the right place, but we have to keep the original value of *A[4]* somewhere. Why not keep it at index 2? In other words, we can simply exchange the values of *A[4]* and *A[2].* This results in the array of Figure 9.5b. In abbreviated form, what we have done is

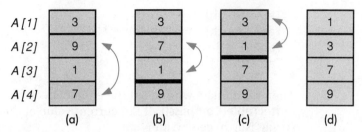

FIGURE 9.5

> consider indices 1..4
> find *MaxIndex* {the index where the maximum value is stored}
> exchange *A[4]* and *A[MaxIndex]*

Now we can repeat this process, but only consider the range of indices from 1 to 3 (*A[4]* is now correct and should not be changed).

> consider indices 1..3
> find *MaxIndex* {index where the maximum value occurs}
> exchange *A[3]* and *A[MaxIndex]*

The result is shown in Figure 9.5c. Then

> consider indices 1..2
> find *MaxIndex*
> exchange *A[2]* and *A[MaxIndex]*

This gives us the array of Figure 9.5d. A final pass considering indices 1..1 is not necessary because *A[1]* must be correct.

We are clearly repeating a process where we consider indices from 1 to *i*. The variable *i* is initially the last index of the array, and decreases by 1 until it has the value 2 on the last pass. This can be handled by a **for** loop:

```
for i := last downto 2 do
begin
    find MaxIndex for the range of indices from 1 to i
    exchange A[i] and A[MaxIndex]
end;
```

The sorting method we have described is called a ***selection sort;*** at each pass the maximum value is selected and moved into place. We used a function in program *GasolinePrice* that returned the maximum value from an array; we can modify that function to return the index in the array where the maximum value is found. This function will need to know the range of indices to consider, so the value of *i* should be passed as a parameter.

CHECKUP 9.8   Fill in the missing parts in the following procedure that implements a selection sort on an array indexed by integers.

```
procedure SelectionSort(var A: ArrayType; n: integer);
{sorts first n elements in array A}

var
    i : integer;                        {index in array A}

function MaxIndex(A: ArrayType; i: integer): integer;
{finds the index of the maximum value from 1 to i in
 array A}
var
    CurrentMaxIndex : integer;      {index of current max.
                                     value}
    j : integer;                    {array index}

    begin    {function MaxIndex}
    CurrentMaxIndex := ----;
    for j := 2 to ---- do
      begin
        if A[----] > A[CurrentMaxIndex]  then
            ---- := j;
      end;
    ---- := CurrentMaxIndex;
    end;     {function MaxIndex}

procedure Exchange(var X, Y: ArrayElementType);
{exchanges elements X and Y}

var
    Temporary : ArrayElementType;

    begin    {procedure Exchange}
    Temporary := X;
    ---- := ----;
    Y := Temporary;
    end;      {procedure Exchange}

    begin    {procedure SelectionSort}
    for i := ---- ---- ---- do
      begin  {for loop}
        Exchange(----, A[MaxIndex(----,----)]);
      end;   {for loop}
    end;      {procedure SelectionSort}
```

9.7 Sample Software Development Project—Players

Problem Statement

The coach at Touchdown Tech must keep information on his student athletes, in particular, their grade-point average, which determines their eligibility. He wants a program that will enable him to enter names (for simplicity, last names only) and grade-point averages (GPAs) for his players, and then print out two tables showing

    a. the players and their GPAs in alphabetical order;

    b. the players and their GPAs in order of GPA.

Problem Specification

The program must handle two types of data, players' names and players' grade-point averages. Names will be strings of characters and GPAs will be real numbers. Players' names form a collection of related data items, as do players' GPAs, so it is reasonable to think of storing them in array form. However, an array can store elements of only one data type, so we'll use two separate arrays, a one-dimensional array of strings for the names, and a one-dimensional array of real numbers for the GPAs. The two items of data about a given player will be related by the array indices—a player's name and that player's GPA have the same index in each array. If items in two separate arrays are related by means of the array indices, the arrays are called *parallel arrays.*

We must estimate the maximum array dimensions and write the array type declarations accordingly. For this problem, the following assumptions are made: the maximum number of characters in a player's name is 10, and the maximum number of players is 50. However, the program should accommodate attempts by the user to enter more than 10 characters in a name or more than 50 names. The user should be allowed to use a sentinel value to end the input rather than have to supply a count of the number of players. The program should be able to handle an empty input list.

Some input validation should be done to ensure that the GPA falls within a reasonable range of values; the assumption is made that Touchdown Tech is on a 4.00 grade point system. Also, the list of "players and their GPAs in order of GPA" is assumed to mean increasing numerical order. Grade-point averages will be displayed to two decimal places.

Input: players' names, players' GPAs
Output: a list of players and their GPAs sorted in alphabetical order
        a list of players and their GPAs sorted in increasing order of GPA

Algorithm Development

A breakdown into subtasks yields something like Figure 9.6. We want to sort the array of names to get them in alphabetical order, and we also want to sort the array of GPAs. Because we already have a procedure to do selection sort on an array (see CHECKUP 9.8), it would seem that we are home free—just use this procedure twice, passing the array of names as a

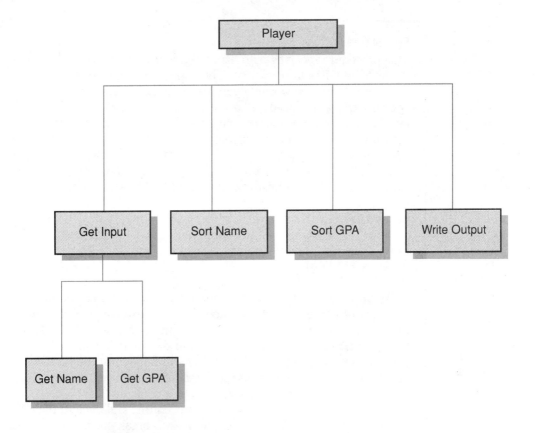

FIGURE 9.6 Structure chart for program *Player*.

parameter the first time, and the array of grade-point averages as a parameter the second time.

This approach has two problems. First, the sort procedure must declare the array type in its formal parameter list. The two arrays that we want to sort will be of two different types because their respective elements are of two different types. A solution is to use two distinct sort procedures, even though they do virtually the same thing. What we would really like to have is a generic "sort an array" procedure that would carry out the right operations no matter what data type the elements are, but Pascal does not provide us with this capability. (The programming language Ada does provide the ability to write "generic" procedures.)

The second problem arises because the names array and the GPAs array are parallel arrays. We must be sure that each player's GPA stays related to that player's name. Therefore when we sort and rearrange the array of names, we must rearrange the parallel GPA array in exactly the same way. Similarly, when we sort the GPA array, we must make corresponding moves in the names array. This means that the selection sort procedure we have developed will have to be modified.

Sort Name

This procedure receives both arrays—the array of names to sort and the array of GPAs to rearrange. The corresponding formal parameters must be variable parameters because the results of applying the sort procedure to these two arrays are to be made known to the main program. The sort procedure also needs to know the number of actual array elements used; this can be passed to the value parameter *Length,* declared to be type *integer.* Because the two arrays will be indexed by integers, *Length* is also an array index value. The procedure heading can have the following form:

```
procedure SortName(var Name: NameArray; var GPA:
                    GradeAveArray; Length: integer);
{sort array of players' names - move items in GPA
 array accordingly}
```

Within the sort procedure, when elements in two positions in the array of names have been exchanged, an exchange of elements in the same two positions must be done in the array of GPAs. Thus the *SortName* procedure needs access to the *Exchange* procedure for elements of type *real.* The same thing will happen in the *SortGPA* procedure—it will need access to the *Exchange* procedure for elements of type *String.* We will therefore break out the *Exchange* procedure from each of the two sort procedures and declare them within the main program. We might as well break out the corresponding *MaxIndex* functions as well. At this point, we are looking at three pairs of modules in the main program—two *MaxIndex* functions, two *Exchange* procedures, and two *Sort* procedures.

After removing the *MaxIndex* function and the *Exchange* procedure from the sort procedure, all that is left is a counted loop of exchanges. Each exchange of the form

```
ExchangeName(Name[i], Name[MaxIndex]);
```

must be followed by an exchange of the form

```
ExchangeGPA(GPA[i],   GPA[MaxIndex]);
```

Sort GPA

This is exactly analogous to procedure *SortName.*

Get Input

This procedure loads the name array and the GPA array and keeps track of the number of array elements entered.

procedure GetInput(**var** Name: NameArray; **var** GPA:
                    GradeAveArray; **var** Length: integer);
{collects input of players' names and GPAs}

begin   {procedure GetInput}

  prompt the user to enter data

  as long as the sentinel value has not yet been seen and the array length has not been exceeded, invoke *GetName* and *GetGPA*, loading the results into the name array and the GPA array; increment the number of array elements entered

  if the user attempts to exceed the array bounds by entering too many names, write a message

end;   {procedure GetInput}

Get Name

This procedure collects, one at a time, the characters for one player's name and loads them into an array *NextName*, which is a string (packed array of characters). *NextName* is returned to *GetInput* to be loaded into the names array. *GetName* is only invoked when a valid name, not the sentinel value, has been entered. In order to tell the difference, the first character must have already been read (by *GetInput*); if it is not the sentinel value, it is passed to *GetName* to be loaded into *NextName*.

procedure GetName(symbol: char; **var** NextName: String);
{collects a valid player name}

begin   {procedure GetName}

  make *symbol* the first character of *NextName*

  as long as there are more characters (the *eoln* has not been reached) and as long as the string length is not exceeded, read the next character and load it into *NextName*; increment the number of characters in *NextName*

Continued

Get Name—Continued

if the user has entered a name that is too long, write a warning message and use only the maximum number of characters allowed

end;   {procedure GetName}

Get GPA

procedure GetGPA(**var** NextGPA: real);
{reads current player's GPA}

begin   {procedure GetGPA}

read GPA until valid input

end;   {procedure GetGPA}

(We'll actually do a minor modification on the parameter list for this procedure based on the error message we decide to use for invalid input—see the program code below.)

We'll let the main program take care of writing the output. This means that the WriteOutput subtask shown on the structure chart for this program is not a separate module, and the data flow diagram, Figure 9.7, shows no parameter-passing information for this subtask. The complete program appears below.

```
program Player(input, output);
{sorts athletes by name and by GPA; uses selection sort on
 parallel arrays}

const
    MaxArraySize = 50;        {at most 50 players}
    NameLength = 10;          {maximum 10 characters per name}
    GPAMax = 4.00;            {maximum GPA value}

type
    String = packed array [1..NameLength] of char;
    Index = 1..MaxArraySize;
    NameArray = array [Index] of String;
    GradeAveArray = array [Index] of real;
```

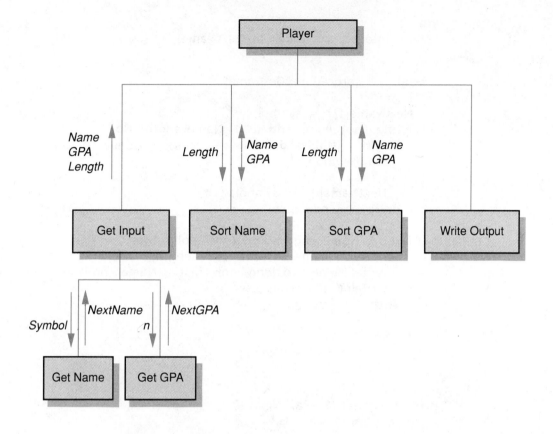

FIGURE 9.7 Data flow diagram for program *Player.*

```
var
    Name : NameArray;          {array to hold players' names}
    GPA : GradeAveArray;       {array to hold players' GPAs}
    Length : integer;          {number of array entries}
    i : Index;                 {array index}

procedure GetInput(var Name: NameArray;
                   var GPA: GradeAveArray;
                   var Length: integer);
{collects input of players' names and GPAs}

var
    NextName : String;         {next name to read}
    NextGPA : real;            {next GPA to read}
    symbol : char;             {first character in player's name}
    n : integer;               {index in Name array}

procedure GetName(symbol: char; var NextName: String);
{collects a valid player name}
```

```
var
    i : integer;      {index in NextName}


  begin    {procedure GetName}
    i := 1;
    NextName[1] := symbol;
    while (not eoln) and (i < NameLength) do
      begin    {still valid Name characters, continue to  collect}
        read(symbol);
        i := i + 1;
        NextName[i] := symbol;
      end;     {end while}

    if (i = NameLength) and (not eoln) then
      begin     {name exceeds NameLength}
        write('Name too long, only first ', NameLength:2);
        writeln(' characters used.');
      end;       {end if}

    readln ;
  end;    {procedure  GetName}



procedure GetGPA(var NextGPA: real; n: integer);
{reads current player's GPA}

  begin    {procedure GetGPA}
    readln(NextGPA);
    while not ((0 <= NextGPA) and
               (NextGPA <= GPAMax)) do
      begin {GPA not valid, try again}
        writeln;
        writeln('GPA must be between 0.00 and ', GPAMax:4:2);
        write('Enter again.    Player', n:3, ' GPA: ');
        readln(NextGPA);
      end;  {end while - now valid GPA}
  end;      {procedure  GetGPA}


begin     {procedure GetInput}
  writeln;
  write('Enter each player' 's last name - maximum ');
  writeln(NameLength:2, ' characters - ');
  write('and press the RETURN key.   ');
  writeln('Then enter that player' 's GPA ');
  write('and press RETURN.    Number of players limited to  ');
  writeln(MaxArraySize:3, '.');
  writeln('Use * to denote end of input.');
  writeln;
```

```
n := 1;
NextName := '                    ';        {initialize NextName}
write('Player', n:3, ' name: ');
read(symbol);
while (symbol <> '*') and (n <=  MaxArraySize) do
  begin    {more input, collect it}
    GetName(symbol, NextName);
    Name[n] := NextName;
    writeln;
    write('Player', n:3, ' GPA: ');
    GetGPA(NextGPA, n);
    GPA[n] := NextGPA;
    writeln;

    {nth element now entered for each array}
    n := n + 1;
    NextName := '                  ';
    if n > MaxArraySize  then
      begin    {can't process more names}
        writeln('Maximum number of names entered');
      end
    else
      begin    {can accept more input, prompt for it}
        write('Player', n:3, ' name: ');
        read(symbol);
      end;
  end; {while loop for more input}

Length := n - 1;    {number of elements entered in
                        each  array}
end;    {procedure GetInput}


function MaxIndexName(Name: NameArray; i: Index):  Index;
{finds the index of the maximum value from 1 to i in
 array Name}


var
    CurrentMaxIndex : Index;      {index of current max. value}
    j : Index;                    {array index}

  begin    {function MaxIndexName}
    CurrentMaxIndex := 1;
    for j := 2 to i do
      begin
        if Name[j] > Name[CurrentMaxIndex]  then
          CurrentMaxIndex := j;
      end;
    MaxIndexName := CurrentMaxIndex;
  end;    {function MaxIndexName}
```

```
function MaxIndexGPA(GPA: GradeAveArray; i: Index):  Index;
{finds the index of the maximum value from 1 to i in
 array  GPA}

var
    CurrentMaxIndex : Index;        {index of current max.  value}
    j : Index;                      {array index}

  begin    {function MaxIndexGPA}
    CurrentMaxIndex := 1;
    for j := 2 to i do
      begin
        if GPA[j] > GPA[CurrentMaxIndex]  then
          CurrentMaxIndex := j;
      end;
    MaxIndexGPA := CurrentMaxIndex;
  end;      {function  MaxIndexGPA}

procedure ExchangeName(var X, Y: String);
{exchanges string elements X and Y in array Names}

var
    Temporary : String;

  begin    {procedure ExchangeName}
    Temporary := X;
    X := Y;
    Y := Temporary;
  end;      {procedure ExchangeName}

procedure ExchangeGPA(var X, Y: real);
{exchanges real elements X and Y in array GPA}

var
    Temporary : real;

  begin    {procedure ExchangeGPA}
    Temporary := X;
    X := Y;
    Y := Temporary;
  end;      {procedure ExchangeGPA}

procedure SortName(var Name: NameArray;
                       var GPA: GradeAveArray; Length: integer);
{sort array of players' names - move items in GPA array
 accordingly}

var
    i : Index;                {index in Name array}
    MaxIndex : Index;         {index of current maximum in
                               Name  array}
```

```
begin    {procedure SortName}
  for i := Length downto 2 do
    begin
      MaxIndex := MaxIndexName(Name, i);
      ExchangeName(Name[i], Name[MaxIndex]);

      {exchange done in Name array, now exchange same
       elements in GPA array}

      ExchangeGPA(GPA[i], GPA[MaxIndex]);
    end;    {for loop}
end;      {procedure SortName}

procedure SortGPA(var Name: NameArray;
                  var GPA:  GradeAveArray; Length: integer);
{sort array of players' GPAs - move items in Name array
 accordingly}

var
  i : Index;                    {index in GPA array}
  MaxIndex : Index;             {index of current maximum in
                                 GPA  array}

  begin    {procedure SortGPA}
    for i := Length downto 2 do
      begin
        MaxIndex := MaxIndexGPA(GPA, i);
        ExchangeGPA(GPA[i], GPA[MaxIndex]);

        {exchange done in GPA array, now exchange same
         elements in  Name array}

        ExchangeName(Name[i], Name[MaxIndex]);
      end;    {for loop}
  end;      {procedure SortGPA}

begin    {main program}

  GetInput(Name, GPA, Length);

  if Length > 0 then
    begin    {arrays are not empty, write output}

      SortName(Name, GPA, Length);
      writeln;

      writeln('Players sorted alphabetically by name are: ');
      writeln;
```

```
            writeln('         Name                    GPA');
            writeln;
            for i := 1 to Length do
              writeln('         ', Name[i], GPA[i]:14:2);

            SortGPA(Name, GPA, Length);
            writeln;

            writeln('Players sorted according to GPA:');
            writeln;
            for i := 1 to Length do
              writeln('         ', Name[i], GPA[i]:14:2);
          end;   {if statement}
      end.    {main program}
```

RUNNING THE PROGRAM...

Enter each player's last name - maximum 10 characters -
and press the RETURN key.   Then enter that player's GPA
and press RETURN.   Number of players limited to   50.
Use * to denote end of input.

Player   1 name: Jones

Player   1 GPA: 2.74

Player   2 name: TerribleTurk
Name too long, only first 10 characters used.

Player   2 GPA: 1.78

Player   3 name: Boomer

Player   3 GPA: 3.24

Player   4 name: Strongarm

Player   4 GPA: 4.21

GPA must be between 0.00 and 4.00
Enter again.   Player   4 GPA: 3.21

Player   5 name: Hawk

Player   5 GPA: 2.91

Player   6 name: *

Players sorted alphabetically by name are:

Name	GPA
Boomer	3.24
Hawk	2.91
Jones	2.74
Strongarm	3.21
TerribleTu	1.78

Players sorted according to GPA:

TerribleTu	1.78
Jones	2.74
Hawk	2.91
Strongarm	3.21
Boomer	3.24

CASE
STUDY   **View #9**
ONE

The Lodestone County Water Pollution Department will soon be required to file semiannual reports with the State Board of Environmental Affairs. An output format from the water pollution program that displays a table of all the test results at once, after all of the input has been obtained, would be consistent with the required report format. You are asked to make this program modification, which can easily be done if the data is structured in parallel arrays.

Separate arrays could be used to store site ID, date, water amount, bacteria count, and level. However, the site ID, water amount, and bacteria count are all integers, so another choice is to use a two-dimensional integer array with three columns for these items. The completed program below uses this latter approach. Also, the date could be stored in one array whose elements are character strings. However, in order to make the code for the input validation that is done on the date data easier to understand, you decide to use separate arrays for month, day, and year.

Although your mental model for the data items this program uses has now expanded to include a data structure (parallel arrays), you do not want to change the *user interface*—how the user interacts with the program. After all, this program has now been successfully in use for several months. Your internal changes should be *transparent* to the user, meaning that the user does not see them in his or her interaction with the program. The only difference will be the appearance of the output.

The real value of the modular design of this program becomes apparent in this (fairly major) modification. Most of the program modules can be used intact in the new version. *WriteOutput* will be split into two modules, one to write the table heading, and one to write the table entries.

(Note: The manager of the Lodestone County Water Pollution Department should require in the specification for the modification that upgrading to the new version of the program impact the current program users as little as possible.)

program WaterPollution(input, output);
{tests water sample from a site against a pollution threshold, issues a warning if the bacteria level is too high; processes multiple sites and readings in this way and prints results in tabular form}

const
    Threshold = 2.0;   {200 bacteria per 100 ml water}
    MaxNoOfReadings = 30;   {maximum number of readings
                                       program can handle}

type
    SampleVariables = (ID, Water, Bacteria);
    Index = 1..MaxNoOfReadings;
    SiteDataArray = **array** [Index,SampleVariables] **of** integer;
    MonthArray = **array** [Index,1..2] **of** char;
    DayArray = **array** [Index,1..2] **of** char;
    YearArray = **array** [Index,1..2] **of** char;
    LevelArray = **array** [Index] **of** real;

var
    SiteData : SiteDataArray;   {array to hold site ID,
                               amount of water sampled,
                               in ml, bacteria count
                               in sample}

    Month : MonthArray;   {array to hold month - two
                               characters - of sample date}

    Day : DayArray;   {array to hold day - two
                               characters - of sample date}

    Year : YearArray;   {array to hold year - two
                               characters - of sample date}

    Level : LevelArray;   {array to hold pollution level
                               of sample data}

    Warning : boolean;   {flag for warning message if
                               pollution level too high}

    Continue : char;   {signal to terminate execution}

    n : integer;   {number of readings to process}
    i : integer;   {array index}

procedure GetInput(**var** ID, Water, Bacteria: integer;
                        var Mon1, Mon2, Day1, Day2,
                    Yr1, Yr2: char);

```
{procedure to collect input for water pollution data; amount
Water of water and count Bacteria of bacteria were obtained
from site ID on date Mon1Mon2/Day1Day2/Yr1Yr2}

var
    Slash : char;      {separating / in date format}

function Value(FirstChar, SecondChar: char): integer;
{function to convert two characters to a two-digit integer}

var
    FirstDigit   : integer;      {the integer equivalents}
    SecondDigit : integer;      {of numerical characters}

  begin   {function Value}
    FirstDigit := ord(FirstChar) − ord('0');
    SecondDigit := ord(SecondChar) − ord('0');
    Value := 10*FirstDigit + SecondDigit;
  end;     {function Value}

function ValidDate(Mon1, Mon2, Day1, Day2: char): boolean;
{function to do some validation on date entered}

var
    MonthValue : integer;      {numerical value for month}
    DayValue : integer;        {numerical value for day}
    ValidMonth : boolean;      {MonthValue in range 1-12}
    ValidDay : boolean;        {DayValue in range 1-31}

  begin   {function ValidDate}
    MonthValue := Value(Mon1, Mon2);
    DayValue := Value(Day1, Day2);

    ValidMonth := (0 < MonthValue) and (MonthValue < 13);
    ValidDay := (0 < DayValue) and (DayValue < 32);

    ValidDate := ValidMonth and ValidDay;
  end;     {function ValidDate}

  begin     {procedure GetInput}
    writeln;
    write('Enter the site ID number: ');
    readln(ID);
    while not((1 <= ID) and (ID <= 1000)) do
      begin {ID out of range}
        write('Check the site ID number and enter again: ');
        readln(ID);
      end; {ID out of range}
    writeln;
```

```
        writeln('Enter the date of this sample.');
        write('Use month/date/year format: ');
        readln(Mon1, Mon2, Slash, Day1, Day2, Slash, Yr1, Yr2);
        while not ValidDate(Mon1, Mon2, Day1, Day2) do
          begin {error in date input}
            write('Please enter the date again: ');
            readln(Mon1, Mon2, Slash, Day1, Day2, Slash, Yr1, Yr2);
          end;    {error in date input}
        writeln;

        write('Enter the amount of water in sample (in ml): ');
        readln(Water);
        while not (Water > 0) do
          begin   {error in amount of water}
            write('Check the amount of water & enter again: ');
            readln(Water);
          end;    {error in amount of water}
        writeln;

        write('Enter the bacteria count found in this sample:  ');
        readln(Bacteria);
        while not (Bacteria >= 0) do
          begin   {error in bacteria count}
            write('Check the bacteria count & enter again: ');
            readln(Bacteria);
          end;    {error in bacteria count}
    end;    {procedure GetInput}


function Ratio(Bacteria, Water: integer): real;
{computes the Ratio of Bacteria to Water}

    begin      {function Ratio}
      Ratio := Bacteria/Water;
    end;       {function Ratio}


procedure CheckThreshold(Ratio: real;
                            var Over: boolean);
{compares Ratio to the global constant Threshold and sets
 Over to  true if that limit is exceeded}

    begin     {procedure CheckThreshold}
      Over := false;    {initialize Over}
      if Ratio > Threshold then
        Over := true;
    end;       {procedure CheckThreshold}


procedure WriteHeader;
{writes output table heading}
```

```
  begin     {procedure WriteHeader}
    writeln;
    writeln;
    write('Site ID', 'Date':8, 'Water':12, 'Bacteria':13);
    writeln('Level':9, 'Warning':10);
    write('_____');
    writeln('_____');
    writeln;
  end;     {procedure WriteHeader}


procedure WriteLineOfOutput(ID, Water, Bacteria: integer;
                            Mon1, Mon2, Day1, Day2,
                            Yr1, Yr2: char;
                            Ratio: real;
                            Warning: boolean);
{produces a line of output in the table corresponding to one
reading - echoes input data and writes warning message if
warranted}
  begin     {procedure WriteLineOfOutput}
    write(ID:5, Mon1:6, Mon2, '/', Day1, Day2, '/', Yr1, Yr2);
    write(Water:8, ' ml', Bacteria:9, Ratio:11:2);

    if Warning then
      write('    ** HIGH  **');
    writeln;
  end;        {procedure WriteLineOfOutput}

begin     {main program}

  n := 0;
  repeat
    n := n + 1;

    GetInput(SiteData[n,ID], SiteData[n,Water],
             SiteData[n,Bacteria], Month[n,1], Month[n,2],
             Day[n,1], Day[n,2], Year[n,1], Year[n,2]);

    Level[n] := Ratio(SiteData[n,Bacteria], SiteData[n,Water]);

    writeln;
    writeln;
    if (n < MaxNoOfReadings) then
      begin {room for more data}
        writeln('Do you have more sites to process?');
        writeln('(Answer Y or N): ');
        readln(Continue);
      end {room for more data}
    else
```

```
        begin {array full}
          writeln('Maximum number of readings entered. ');
          write('Adjust program constant MaxNoOfReadings ');
          writeln('if this is a problem.');
        end;    {array full}

    until (Continue = 'N') or (Continue =  'n')
                        or (n = MaxNoOfReadings);

    {all the input has been gathered and stored in the arrays,
     now print out table of results}

    WriteHeader;
    for i := 1 to n do
      begin {produce line i of the output table}
        CheckThreshold(Level[i], Warning);
        WriteLineOfOutput(SiteData[i,ID],  SiteData[i,Water],
                          SiteData[i,Bacteria], Month[i,1],
                          Month[i,2],  Day[i,1], Day[i,2],
                          Year[i,1], Year[i,2],
                          Level[i], Warning);
      end; {line i has been written}
  end.      {main program}
```

RUNNING THE PROGRAM...

```
        Enter the site ID number: 3240
        Check the site ID number and enter again: 320

        Enter the date of this sample.
        Use month/date/year format: 22/13/87
        Please enter the date again: 12/13/87

        Enter the amount of water in sample (in ml): 700

        Enter the bacteria count found in this sample: 1100


        Do you have more sites to process?
        (Answer Y or N):
        y

        Enter the site ID number: 556

        Enter the date of this sample.
        Use month/date/year format: 07/36/89
        Please enter the date again: 07/26/89

        Enter the amount of water in sample (in ml): 520
```

Enter the bacteria count found in this sample: 1340

Do you have more sites to process?
(Answer Y or N):
y

Enter the site ID number: 128

Enter the date of this sample.
Use month/date/year format: 11/22/87

Enter the amount of water in sample (in ml): 920

Enter the bacteria count found in this sample: 1870

Do you have more sites to process?
(Answer Y or N):
y

Enter the site ID number: 239

Enter the date of this sample.
Use month/date/year format: 04/15/90

Enter the amount of water in sample (in ml): 640

Enter the bacteria count found in this sample: 2170

Do you have more sites to process?
(Answer Y or N):
y

Enter the site ID number: 450

Enter the date of this sample.
Use month/date/year format: 07/18/88

Enter the amount of water in sample (in ml): 550

Enter the bacteria count found in this sample: 940

Do you have more sites to process?
(Answer Y or N):
n

Site ID	Date	Water		Bacteria	Level	Warning	
320	12/13/87	700	ml	1100	1.57		
556	07/26/89	520	ml	1340	2.58	** HIGH	**
128	11/22/87	920	ml	1870	2.03	** HIGH	**
239	04/15/90	640	ml	2170	3.39	** HIGH	**
450	07/18/88	550	ml	940	1.71		

CASE STUDY TWO

View #9

Modify the hypertension clinic program to collect the data from all patients first and then display a table of all of the results. Do not change the program's user interface.

EXERCISES

For Exercises 1-7, use the following:

```
type
    TableType  =  array [0..6,'P'..'R'] of integer;
var
    Table : TableType;
```

#1. How many memory locations will *Table* require?

#2. Write an assignment statement to give the first element in the first row of *Table* the value 1.

3. What is wrong with the following statement to write the values of column 'P' of *Table*?

```
for i := Table[0,'P'] to Table[6,'P'] do
  writeln(i);
```

#4. Write a statement that will print out the third row of *Table*.

5. Write a statement that will print out the second column of *Table*.

6. Write a section of code to initialize all the values of *Table* to 0.

7. What will be the output from the following section of code?

```
Table[6,'R'] := 0;
for i := 6 downto 1 do
  begin    {for loop with index i}
    for j := 'Q' downto 'P' do
      begin {for loop with index j}
        Table[i, j] := 1 + Table[i,succ(j)];
      end; {for loop with index j}
    Table[i - 1,'R'] := Table[i,'P'];
  end;     {for loop with index i}
writeln(Table[1,'Q']);
```

#8. What could go wrong with the following section of code to search an array *A* of integers indexed from 1 to 10 for an integer value *X*?

```
i := 1;
while (i <= 10) and (A[i] <> X) do
  i := i+1;
if (A[i] = X) then
  writeln('X found at index ',i)
else
  writeln('X not in array');
```

SKILL BUILDERS

1. A multiple-choice test has 10 questions, each with a choice of answers from "a" to "d." The correct answers are:

b c a b d c b a a d

Write a program to read a student's answers and output them with an X beside each wrong answer; also give the total correct score.

#2. Write a program to read in a matrix (two-dimensional array) of integers of maximum size 10 x 20 and output both the matrix and its transpose.

3. Write a program to read in two square matrices *A* and *B* of integers of maximum size 8 x 8 and compute and write out the product matrices *A*∗*B* and *B*∗*A*.

4. Write a program to read in an unsorted list of integers (maximum 20 numbers) and a particular input value *X*. The program should search the list for the value *X* and return the first position in the list at which *X* occurs or a message saying that *X* does not occur at all. (Note Exercise 8 above.)

5. A *magic square* is a square array of integers with the property that the elements of each row, each column, and each of the two main diagonals sum to the same value. Write a program to test 3 x 3 arrays to see if they are magic squares. Test your program at least on the arrays

```
2 1 5    5 7 3
5 3 0    3 5 7
1 4 3    7 3 5
```

SOFTWARE DEVELOPMENT PROJECTS

1. Develop software that asks the user to supply two lists of integers. The program should sort each of the two lists in increasing order, then *merge* (combine) the elements in the two lists, and write out the result in sorted order, eliminating any duplicates. (In the merge process, do *not* sort a third array.)

2. Develop software that asks the user for a paragraph of text and outputs the paragraph with each line except the last right justified by inserting the necessary number of spaces between words. The added spaces should be distributed more or less evenly across the line.

3. Rework program *Bacteria* on page 159. This time the output should be a graph with the values of time along the horizontal axis and the number of bacteria along the vertical axis. The vertical scale should go from 0 to 9000 in such a way that differences of 100 can be detected in the graph.

4. Develop software that acts as a family budget/financial record for one month. The user can select up to fifteen budget categories (rent, food, insurance, etc.). The user can set budgeted totals for each category and can make at most one entry for each category/date combination. The user can also select from any of the following report options:

1. The total amount spent on any date of the month.
2. The total amount spent for the month in any one category.
3. The grand total spent for the month.
4. The amount over or under the budgeted amount in any one category or in all categories.
5. A bar graph of the amount spent compared to the amount budgeted by category for all categories.

5. (This problem was used in the 1982 Association for Computing Machinery Scholastic Programming Contest.) Develop software that reads English text, maximum 60 characters per line, until a terminating symbol of * is read as the first character in a line. The program then reads coded text under the same conditions. The program determines the frequency of each letter of the alphabet in the English text and in the coded text. The relative frequencies provide the decoding key; for example, if "E" is the most frequent letter in the English text, and "M" is the most frequent letter in the coded text, then all Ms in the coded text should be decoded as Es. Finally, the program writes out the decoded paragraph. Test this program with the following data:

THIS DATA SET HAS BEEN CREATED FOR THE PROBLEM ENTITLED "BREAKING
A CIPHER" FOR THE 1982 ACM NATIONAL SCHOLASTIC PROGRAMMING
CONTEST. IN ORDER TO TEST THE CONTESTANTS' PROGRAMS, SOME OF THE
DATA IN THIS SET IS CONTRIVED. FOR EXAMPLE, NEXT IS A COMPLETELY
BLANK LINE.

IN ORDER TO GUARANTEE THAT THE ALPHABET IS COMPLETELY
REPRESENTED, THE STRAIGHT ALPHABET OCCURS HERE:
ABCDEFGHIJKLM NOPQRSTUVWXYZ. IN A REALISTIC SITUATION, THE
MESSAGES NEEDED IN BREAKING A CIPHER WOULD HAVE TO BE QUITE LONG.
HOWEVER, IN THIS CONTEST SITUATION, SINCE IT IS POSSIBLE TO
INCLUDE STRANGE WORDS AS NEEDED, THE MESSAGES WILL BE RELATIVELY
SHORT. THE FOLLOWING WORDS ARE PRESENT ONLY TO MAKE THE
ANSWERS CORRECT:
THE QUEEN OF ALBUQUERQUE GROWS JOJOBA BEANS.
JUDY, JERRY, JACKIE, JEFFREY, AND JOHNNY KICKED A VERY BIG BALL.
JEFF WILL PUT A PIE IN HIS FACE.

THE BUM IN A MUUMUU BOBBLED THE BUBBLE.
PETER PIPER PIPES PAPER PIPES.
DID DAD BID BAD BUD?
SASSY SNOWS OF NOON YET?
THIS IS THE LAST LINE.
*

N U Y G M   V S F L O   C W P H J   X R I D Z   T A Q K E B

ZFM WLHM NUJAM LD LHZMHGMG ZJ PNCM ZFM OTGSLHS ND MNDE ND
XJDDLUWM, DLHYM ZFM MHZLIM PMDDNSM LD YJIIMYZ LV NHG JHWE LV ZFM
VLIDZ WLHM LD ZFM NWXFNUMZ. ZFM XIJUWMP DZNZMD, LH XNIZ: N
PMDDNSM FND UMMH MHYLXFMIMG TDLHS N DLPXWM DTUDZLZTZLJH YLXFMI.
ZFLD PMNGD ZFNZ N XMIPTZNZLJH JV ZFM NWXFNUMZ FND UMMH YFJDMH,
NHG MNYF WMZZMI JV ZFM JILSLHNW PMDDNSM FND UMMH IMXWNYMG UE ZFM
YJIIMDXJHGLHS WMZZMI JV ZFM XMIPTZMG NWXFNUMZ.

   ZJ PNCM ZFM NHDQMID YJIIMYZ, ZFM VJWWJQLHS QJIGD FNAM UMMH
NGGMG: NWUTRTMIRTM NKJWJZW OTHCVJJG AMWJYLZE OJOJUN QNZMIVNWW
ZILMG VIJSSE QNIZ, XIJG EJTI XTGGWM DLWZ, ONYC QLWWE YNULH
PTPUWM.
*

**TESTING
AND
MAINTENANCE
DEPARTMENT**

1. Test the behavior of program *Player* on an empty input list, i.e., when the terminating symbol * is the first input entered.

2. Test the behavior of program *Player* when the user attempts to enter more players than allowed (reduce the constant *MaxArraySize* to make this test).

3. Modify program *MirrorWriting* of this chapter to write the reversed message on two separate lines of roughly equal length.

4. Modify program *Dive* on page 203 to use arrays and loop structures.

5. Modify procedure *SelectionSort* to create a procedure that sorts in decreasing, rather than increasing, order. Write a driver and test the new procedure.

6. Modify program *MirrorWriting* of this chapter to create a program that asks the user for a word or phrase of length 1 to 60 characters and reports whether the input is a palindrome (reads the same forward and backward).

7. Modify program *BankStatement* on page 247 to include as part of the output summary statement a list of all the checks written (the check number, date, and amount of each check) in increasing order of check number.

**DEBUGGING
CLINIC**

1. Change the body of procedure *SortName* in program *Player* of this chapter to the following:

```
for i : = Length downto 2 do
  begin {for loop}
    ExchangeName(Name[i], Name[MaxIndexName(Name,i)]);
    ExchangeGPA(GPA[i], GPA[MaxIndexName(Name,i)]);
  end;   {for loop}
```

Test the new version; what happens, and why?

CHAPTER TEN
RECORDS AND SETS

10.1 The Record Data Type

Program *Player* of Chapter 9 used parallel arrays to store players' names (strings of characters) and grade point averages (real numbers). As one of these arrays was sorted, the program had to perform identical rearrangements on the other array. If the coach at Touchdown Tech had been doing this task manually, he might have written the information on index cards, one player's name and GPA per card. As the cards are sorted by order according to the player's name, i.e., as the cards are physically rearranged, the GPA automatically gets moved right along with the player's name. The "index card" is a common mental model of related variables (a data structure), and it can be implemented by the Pascal **record** data type.

10.1.1 *The Record Type Declaration*

A record is a collection of related items of data; unlike an array, however, these related items can have different data types. Each item is called a ***field*** of the record. To declare a record data type, we must name the type, indicate that it is a record type, and also name each field and declare its data type.

Suppose that an apartment rental agency keeps an index card for each available apartment that lists the area in which it is located, the address, the number of bedrooms, and the monthly rent. A typical index card could look like Figure 10.1, which describes a two-bedroom apartment on the east side that rents for $425 per month.

East   1340 Dogwood Court #5   2   425

FIGURE 10.1 Typical apartment rental data.

313

The type declaration for a record data type that reflects this structure could look like this:

```
type
    String = packed array [1..25] of char;
    LocaleType = (East, West, North, South);
    Apartment = record
      Locale : LocaleType;
      Address : String;
      Bedrooms, Rent : integer;
      end;    {Apartment}
```

In a record type declaration, each field must have a name and data type; don't forget the "end."

This declaration specifies that legitimate values of type *Apartment* will be records with four fields, a *Locale* field that contains enumerated type data, an *Address* field that contains string data, a *Bedrooms* field that contains an integer value, and a *Rent* field that contains an integer value (see Fig. 10.2). A field can be of any data type. The list of fields and their data types must be terminated with **end,** otherwise the field declarations can't be separated from other type declarations that may follow. Two fields of the same type can be listed together, as *Bedrooms* and *Rent* above. Two different fields in a single record type cannot, of course, have the same name, but fields in two different record types can have the same name, or a field name can be the same as some other program variable name.

A shortcut is allowed in record declarations. The indicator for the data type of a field may itself be a type declaration. The following declaration describes records with exactly the same characteristics as those of type *Apartment*, but in this declaration the string and enumerated data type are not previously declared.

```
type
    Another = record
      Locale : (East, West, North, South);
      Address : packed array [1..25] of char;
      Bedrooms, Rent : integer;
      end;    {Another}
```

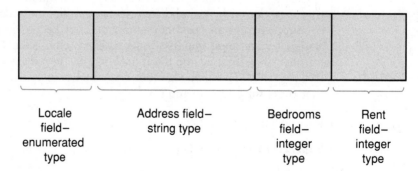

FIGURE   10.2 The *Apartment* record type.

One disadvantage to this shortcut is that no variable or formal parameter can be declared to be of the same enumerated type as the *Locale* field because no name has been given to this data type. For this reason, we'll stick with the longer form.

The order in which record fields are declared is irrelevant, so the following declaration is still another way to describe records with the characteristics we desire.

```
type
    String = packed array [1..25] of char;
    LocaleType = (East, West, North, South);
    AThird = record
      Bedrooms, Rent : integer;
      Address : String;
      Locale : LocaleType;
    end;    {AThird}
```

CHECKUP 10.1   Give a type declaration for a record to store data about recipes; the record should contain the name of the recipe, the number of servings, and the total cost of the ingredients.

10.1.2 *Referencing Fields of Records*

After the above type declaration for *Apartment*, variables of type *Apartment* can be declared as usual:

```
var
    Apt1, Apt2 : Apartment;
```

Record fields are referenced by "recordname. fieldname" notation.

Like arrays, records are structured data types. Therefore a variable of record type can be thought of as a single entity (*Apt1*) or as a collection of component variables (the four fields of *Apt1*). In order to reference an individual component of a record, we give the record name, followed by a period, followed by the name of the field. For example, if the information shown in Figure 9.1 has been stored in *Apt1*, then the output from the statement

```
writeln(Apt1.Bedrooms);
```

would be 2. These individual record components can be used just like any other simple variable—in read and write statements, as part of an expression, in comparisons, etc.

Given the declarations

```
type
    Info = record
        Weight : integer;
        Kind : char;
        end; {Info}
var
    Front, Back : Info;
```

what is the output from the following section of code?

```
Front.Kind := 'A';
Front.Weight := 12;
Back.Weight := 2*Front.Weight;
Back.Kind := succ(Front.Kind);
writeln(Back.Kind, Back.Weight);
```

10.1.3 Records as Single Variables

Records are treated as single entities in the same two situations we treated arrays as single entities—in assignment statements and as parameters. The statement

```
Apt2 := Apt1;
```

makes each field of *Apt2* agree with the corresponding field of *Apt1*. Such an assignment statement is only allowed between two variables of the same record type. As with arrays, this means that the type identifier of the two variables must be the same. An assignment of a record of type *Another* to a record of type *Apartment,* for example, is illegal, even though both records reflect the same mental model.

A record name can be treated as a single variable in an assignment statement or in a parameter list.

A record can be passed as a single actual parameter to a program module (procedure or function). Within the module, the individual fields (i.e., *Apt1.Bedrooms*) can be referenced just as if they had been passed as individual parameters. This not only shortens the parameter list, it is consistent with the top-down design philosophy that modules represent—the details of what is done with individual record fields are confined to the module.

All other situations require processing the individual record fields. Writing out the contents of a record, for example, must be done on a field-by-field basis. The following procedure writes out the data from a record of type *Apartment.* Note that the formal parameter indicates that a single record will be passed to the procedure, yet within the procedure individual fields of the record are referenced. A **case** statement serves as a translation table to effectively write out the enumerated-type variable that is the *Locale* field. The *Address* field can be written out directly because it is a packed array.

procedure WriteApartmentRecord(Apt: Apartment);
{writes out all fields of one record of Apartment type}

```
   begin    {procedure WriteApartmentRecord}
     write('Locale:            ');
     case Apt.Locale of
       North  :  writeln('North');
       South  :  writeln('South');
       East   :  writeln('East');
       West   :  writeln('West');
     end;    {case statement}
     writeln('Address:         ', Apt.Address);
     writeln;
     writeln('Number of Bedrooms: ', Apt.Bedrooms:1);
     writeln('Monthly Rent: $ ', Apt.Rent:3);
   end;       {procedure WriteApartmentRecord}
```

10.2 Records and Arrays

10.2.1 *Records of Arrays*

Because packed arrays can be written out as single entities, procedure *WriteApartmentRecord* somewhat obscures the fact that the *Address* field of records of type *Apartment* is itself an array. When reading records of type *Apartment,* this array has to be loaded one element at a time. As with any array, the index of the array is used to identify the array element. For example, *Apt1.Address[3]* refers to the third element in the array that is the *Address* field of record *Apt1;* this will contain the third character in the address. If *Apt1.Address* has the value

   '1340 Dogwood Court #5   '

then *Apt1.Address[3]* has the value '4'. Procedure *ReadApartmentRecord* below reads one record. It uses a local *char* variable to represent the enumerated-type variable *Apt.Locale.*

procedure ReadApartmentRecord(**var** Apt: Apartment);
{reads all fields of one record of Apartment type}

var
```
     Location : char;      {abbreviation for Locale}
     i : integer;          {index in address array}

   begin    {procedure ReadApartmentRecord}
     writeln('Apartment location');
     write('(enter N, S, E, or W for ');
```

```
    write('North, South, East, West): ');
    readln(Location);
    case Location of
      'N','n' : Locale := North;
      'S','s' : Locale := South;
      'E','e' : Locale := East;
      'W','w': Locale := West;
    end;    {case statement}

    for i := 1 to 25 do
      Apt.Address[i] := ' ';
    writeln('Enter apartment street address :');
    i := 0;
    while (not eoln) and (i < 25) do
      begin
        i := i + 1;
        read(Apt.Address[i]);
      end;
    readln;

    write('Number of bedrooms: ');
    readln(Apt.Bedrooms);

    write('Monthly Rent: $ ');
    readln(Apt.Rent);
  end;      {procedure ReadApartmentRecord}
```

10.2.2 *Arrays of Records*

Arrays of records implement the mental model of a box of index cards.

Our mental model of index cards almost always has a number of these cards arranged in a collection. This data structure is implemented by an array whose elements are records. Arrays of records are a very useful construct in Pascal programs. The apartment rental agency, for example, keeps a collection of records, one for each available apartment. Program *Rental* below arranges this data as an array *Listings,* where each array element is a record of type *Apartment.* Program *Rental* collects the data on available apartments. (Typically, this data would be stored in a permanent file, so that it does not have to be re-entered each time the program is run.) Then, at the user's request, the program displays data by locale, highlighting the listing in that locale with the lowest monthly rent. It uses the procedures that we wrote earlier to read and write records (except that the character translation part of the read procedure has been pulled out as a separate procedure). An individual record is now an element of array *Listings.* To refer to a record, we must know its index within the *Listings* array. As an example,

    Listings[5]

is the fifth record in the array.

    Listings[5].Rent

Fields of a record can be of any data type, including arrays or other records; references are read left to right from major items to subitems.

is the *Rent* field of this record. And

Listings[5].Address[3]

is the third character in the *Address* field of the fifth record in the array *Listing!* (See Fig. 10.3.) If this seems confusing, just note that the description reads hierarchically from left to right, major items to subitems. **Listings[5].Address[3]** first gives the array name (*Listings*), then the element in this array (index 5), then, because this array element is a record, the field in this record (*Address*), and finally, because this field is an array, the element in this array (index 3).

```
program Rental(input, output);
{collects data on available apartments - their locale, address,
 number of bedrooms, and monthly rent; user can select display
 of listings for any locale, minimum rent in that locale is
 highlighted}

const
    MaxArraySize = 50;    {maximum number of apartments}
    Highlight = '*****************************************';
```

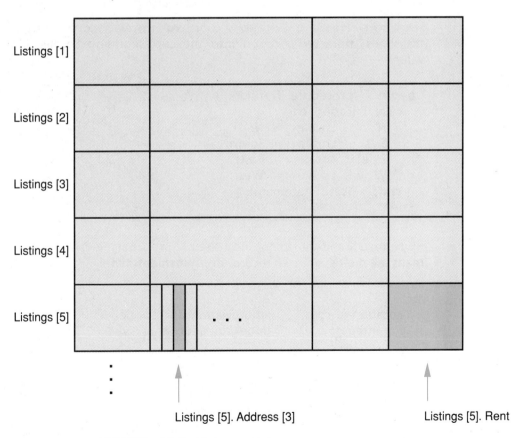

FIGURE 10.3 The array *Listings.*

```
type
    String = packed array [1..25] of char;
    LocaleType = (East, West, North, South);
    Apartment = record
      Locale :    LocaleType;
      Address : String;
      Bedrooms, Rent : integer;
      end;    {Apartment}
    Index = 1..MaxArraySize;
    TypeListings = array [Index] of Apartment;
    Range = 0..MaxArraySize;


var
    Listings : TypeListings;     {array of apt. records}
    Count : Index;               {number of records in array}
    i : Index;                   {array index}
    Min: Range;                  {index of minimum rent for desired
                                   locale}
    Location : char;             {abbreviation for locale}
    Key : LocaleType;            {translated form of Location}


procedure Translate (Location: char; var Locale:  LocaleType);
{translates character Location into the corresponding Locale
 value}

  begin    {procedure Translate}
  case Location of
    'N','n' : Locale := North;
    'S','s' : Locale := South;
    'E','e' : Locale := East;
    'W','w': Locale := West;
  end;    {case statement}
  end;    {procedure Translate}


procedure ReadApartmentRecord(var Apt: Apartment);
{reads all fields of one record of Apartment type}

var
    Location : char;    {abbreviation for Locale}
    i : integer;        {index in address array}

  begin    {procedure ReadApartmentRecord}
  writeln('Apartment location');
  write('(enter N, S, E, or W for ');
  write('North, South, East, West): ');
  readln(Location);
  Translate(Location, Apt.Locale);
```

```
      for i := 1 to 25 do
        Apt.Address[i] := ' ';
      writeln('Enter apartment street address :');
      i := 0;
      while (not eoln) and (i < 25) do
        begin
          i := i + 1;
          read(Apt.Address[i]);
        end;
      readln;

      write('Number of bedrooms: ');
      readln(Apt.Bedrooms);

      write('Monthly Rent: $ ');
      readln(Apt.Rent);
    end;        {procedure ReadApartmentRecord}

  procedure WriteApartmentRecord(Apt: Apartment);
  {writes out all fields of one record of Apartment type}

      begin     {procedure WriteApartmentRecord}
        write('Locale:              ');
        case Apt.Locale of
          North : writeln('North');
          South : writeln('South');
          East  : writeln('East');
          West  : writeln('West');
        end;    {case statement}
        writeln('Address:            ', Apt.Address);
        writeln;
        writeln('Number of Bedrooms: ', Apt.Bedrooms:1);
        writeln('Monthly Rent: $ ', Apt.Rent:3);
      end;        {procedure WriteApartmentRecord}

  procedure Minimum(Listings: TypeListings; n: Index;
                    Key: LocaleType; var Which: Range);
  {returns index Which in array Listings, with n entries, at which
   minimum rent for locale Key occurs; Which is 0 if no entries for
   this locale}

  var
      CurrentMin: integer;        {current minimum rent}
      i : Index;                  {array index}

    begin     {procedure Minimum}
      Which := 0;
      CurrentMin := 10000;
      for i := 1 to n do
```

```
        begin {for loop to traverse array}
          if (Listings[i].Locale = Key) and
             (Listings[i].Rent < CurrentMin) then
              begin
                CurrentMin := Listings[i].Rent;
                Which := i;
              end;
        end;    {for loop to traverse array}
     end;    {procedure Minimum}

begin    {main program}
  write('How many listings are there? (maximum 50) ');
  readln(Count);
  writeln;
  writeln('Enter the information on each available apartment;');
  for i := 1 to Count do
    begin
      writeln;
      ReadApartmentRecord(Listings[i]);
    end;
  writeln;
  writeln ('All data entered.');
  writeln;

  write('Select locale desired (N, S, E, or W): ');
  readln(Location);
  writeln;
  Translate(Location, Key);
  writeln('Information for this locale follows:');

  {now write out records for Locale Key, highlighting minimum
   rent}

  Minimum(Listings, Count, Key, Min);
  if Min = 0 then
    begin
      writeln;
      writeln('No entries for this locale');
    end
  else
    for i := 1 to Count do
      if Listings[i].Locale = Key then
        begin    {entry for this locale}
          if i <> Min then
            begin
              Writeln;
              WriteApartmentRecord(Listings[i]);
            end
```

```
            else {minimum rent for this locale}
              begin
                writeln;
                writeln;
                writeln(Highlight);
                WriteApartmentRecord(Listings[i]);
                writeln(Highlight);
                writeln;
              end;   {minimum rent}
          end;   {entry for this locale}
      {end of for statement and array traversal}
  end.   {main program}
```

RUNNING THE PROGRAM...

How many listings are there? (maximum 50) 4

Enter the information on each available apartment;

Apartment location
(enter N, S, E, or W for North, South, East, West): n
Enter apartment street address :
430 Forest Drive
Number of bedrooms: 3
Monthly Rent: $ 425

Apartment location
(enter N, S, E, or W for North, South, East, West): e
Enter apartment street address :
1534 E. 71st St. #7
Number of bedrooms: 2
Monthly Rent: $ 350

Apartment location
(enter N, S, E, or W for North, South, East, West): n
Enter apartment street address :
7412 Winding Way #320
Number of bedrooms: 2
Monthly Rent: $ 350

Apartment location
(enter N, S, E, or W for North, South, East, West): n
Enter apartment street address :
1300 N. Vernon #44
Number of bedrooms: 2
Monthly Rent: $ 395

All data entered.

Select locale desired (N, S, E, or W): n

Information for this locale follows:

Locale: North
Address: 430 Forest Drive

Number of Bedrooms: 3
Monthly Rent: $ 425

****
Locale: North
Address: 7412 Winding Way #320

Number of Bedrooms: 2
Monthly Rent: $ 350
****

Locale: North
Address: 1300 N. Vernon #44

Number of Bedrooms: 2
Monthly Rent: $ 395

It is clear that some very complicated structures are possible—arrays of records of records of arrays of records, etc.! One could reference the bottom element in a hierarchy of this form by something like

array[i].fieldj.fieldk[p].fieldq

(see Fig. 10.4). However, the data structure of which this is the implementation seems overly complicated. A simpler structure may be possible. Even if not, expressions like the one above should not have to occur. Use of procedures to deal with each level of the hierarchy means that we can pass structured variables as entire entities and have successive procedures break them down.

CHECKUP 10.3   Given the declarations

```
type
    ArrayType = array ['A'..'P',1..4] of integer;
    Entry = record
      Key : char;
      Display : ArrayType;
```

Continued

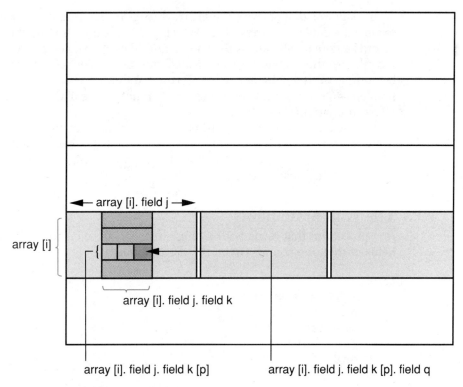

FIGURE 10.4 A complicated data structure.

CHECKUP 10.3   Continued

```
                Value : real;
        end;    {Entry}
        ListType  =  array [1..10] of Entry;

    var
        List : ListType;
        Key : char;
```

a. Write a reference for the *Value* field of the fourth record in *List*.
b. Write a reference for the number stored in row C, column 3 of the array *Display* in the first record of *List*.
c. Write a statement to assign to the variable *Key* the value of the *Key* field of the second record of *List*.

10.2.3 *Alternative Data Structures*

The choice of data structure to represent a problem will occupy more of our time as we have more alternatives. In program *Player* of Chapter 9, our view of the data was that of two parallel arrays (Fig. 10.5a). Another possibility is to view the data as an array of records (Fig. 10.5b); then sorting the array of records automatically keeps the "horizontal" data items, i.e., the data in one record, together. That idea motivated our discussion of records at the beginning of this chapter. (See Testing and Maintenance Department problem #6 on how this new view can eliminate some of the duplication of effort in program *Player*.)

On the other hand, a spreadsheet (a table of data for financial analysis) could be viewed as an array of records, but is probably better implemented as a two-dimensional array, making it easy to reference any entry in a nonhierarchical manner.

10.3 **The** With **Statement**

Any procedure that deals with a single record will often reference several fields of that one record. Given the declarations

type
    Pattern = **record**
        Number : integer;
        UnitCost : real;
        Total : real;
    end;

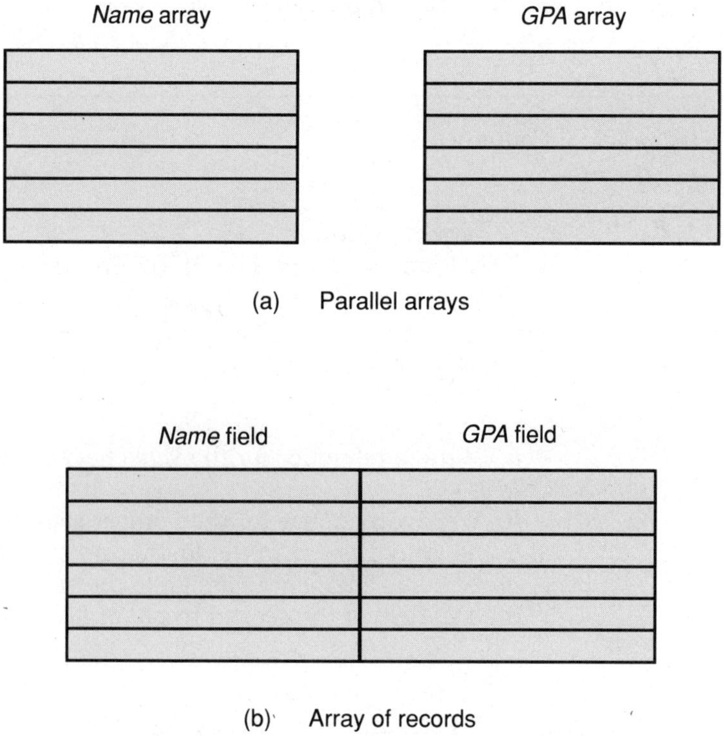

(a)   Parallel arrays

(b)   Array of records

FIGURE   10.5 Alternative data structures for program *Player*.

```
var
    Entry : Pattern;
    AnotherEntry : Pattern;
```

a procedure to process the single record *Entry* might contain a statement such as

```
Entry.Total := Entry.Number * Entry.UnitCost;
```

The Pascal **with** statement allows us to specify the record name *Entry* and, within the scope of that specification, use the field names without the record identifier. The form of the **with** statement here would be

```
with Entry do
    Total := Number * UnitCost;
```

The general form of the **with** statement is

```
with record identifier do
    (compound) statement;
```

If many manipulations are done with the fields of one record, the with statement saves having to write the record name each time.

Within the body of the **with** statement, all references to fields of the record named in the statement heading can be made by just giving the field name. The body of procedure *ReadApartmentRecord* discussed earlier could be made the body of a **with** statement that names *Apt* as the referenced record; then the prefix "Apt." could be dropped from all the field references.

Although the **with** statement saves a little typing tedium, it also takes away from clarity. It is no longer obvious at a glance, particularly if the body of the **with** statement is long, that references are being made to fields of a record, as opposed to totally unrelated simple variables. **With** statements can also be nested; the rules of scope for the record names involved act as one might expect, that is, the most local record named takes precedence. The following section of code

```
with Entry do
    with AnotherEntry do
        Number := 5;
```

has the effect of assigning 5 to *AnotherEntry.Number* (not to *Entry.Number*). Worse, the nesting can be replaced by an ordered list of record identifiers, so that the following code is equivalent to that above

```
with Entry, AnotherEntry do
    Number := 5;
```

but

```
with AnotherEntry, Entry do
    Number := 5;
```

changes the *Number* field in *Entry* rather than in *AnotherEntry*. Needless to say, this convention asks too much of the human reader of the program. Such a construction should be avoided.

The identification of the record in a **with** statement may involve a variable. If there is an array *List* of records of type *Pattern*, then

```
with List[i] do
  Number := 5;
```

is legitimate. However, the record name is evaluated at the beginning of the **with** statement, and any changes in the body of the **with** statement will not affect this evaluation. Suppose we want to set the *Number* field in each record of array *List*. The code below will *not* work; it will repeatedly set the *Number* field of the first record.

```
i := 1;
with List[i] do
  begin
    while i <= n do
      begin
        Number := 5;
        i := i + 1;
      end;    {while}
  end;    {with}
```

The following code will do the job.

```
i := 1;
while i <= n do
  begin
    with List[i] do
      begin
        Number := 5;
      end;    {with}
    i := i + 1;
  end;    {while}
```

CHECKUP 10.4   Using the declarations of CHECKUP 10.3, write a **with** statement that assigns the value 'Q' to the *Key* field and the value 6.4 to the *Value* field of the third record in *List*.

10.4 Variant Records (Optional)

Much as we've talked about type declarations serving as fixed descriptions for variables of that type, Pascal does allow some flexibility in describing records. **Variant records** allow a description of a record type to be broken into two parts, a fixed part and a variant part. The fixed part describes fields that will appear in all records of this data type. The fixed part ends with a **tag field.** The value of the tag field in any given record determines the form of the remaining fields of the record, the variant part. The declaration

```
type
    String = packed array [1..10] of char;
    AgeType = (New, Used);
    Condition = (Good, Fair, Poor);
    CarType = record
      Make : String;
      case Age : AgeType of
        New : (Price : real);
        Used : (Miles : integer; Rating : Condition);
      end;    {CarType}
```

In a variant-record type declaration, a single end terminates both the case-like variant part and the entire record declaration.

specifies that all records of type *CarType* have a *Make* field. Then comes the field *Age*, which is a tag field. The rest of the format for a record of *CarType* is not known until a value is assigned to the tag field. If that value is New, then there is one more field, *Price*. If that value is Used, then there are two more fields, *Miles* and *Rating*. Note that there is only one **end** statement that serves to end both the variant part and the entire record type declaration.

In variant-record type declarations the order in which the fields are specified does matter: the nontag fixed fields are declared first, then the tag field, then the variant fields. The field names must all be unique; for example, because *Price* is a field name under the New variant above, it would be illegal to have a *Price* field under the Used variant. The fixed part of the record can be empty except for the tag field; then the type declaration begins with the tag field. One of the variant cases may have no variant fields. This is indicated by putting an empty list of field names in parentheses behind this case of the tag field, as in

```
    AgeType = (New, Used, Totaled);
    Condition = (Good, Fair, Poor);
    CarType = record
      Make : String;
      case Age : AgeType of
        New : (Price : real);
        Used : (Miles : integer; Rating : Condition);
        Totaled : ( );
      end;    {CarType}
```

Processing variant records is neatly done by using a case statement.

Processing variant records, for example, reading values into them, is handled nicely by a **case** statement. In pseudocode form, reading a record of type *CarType* can be done by

read *Make* field
read *Age* field

case *Age* **of**
   New : read *Price* field
   Used : read *Miles* **and** *Rating* fields
end;   {Age}

Variable declarations have to do with storage allocation assigned when the program is compiled. The amount of storage to allocate cannot depend on a value to be computed during program execution. In the case of variant records, storage is allocated for the longest possible record. Each record of type *CarType* has storage allocated for the fixed part and the tag field, and enough storage to accommodate two extra fields in case the tag field gets the value Used. Only part of this storage will be needed if the tag field gets the value New (see Fig. 10.6). This saves storage over the alternative of using three fields for each record (*Price, Miles,* and *Rating*) and referencing only those that are appropriate for the value of the tag field. Unless there will be a lot of data, however, saving storage will not be a concern. Instead, variant records are useful because they indicate more clearly which attributes are important for which subclass of records. Another way to do this would be to declare different record types for each variant, such as two different record types for new cars and used cars, respectively. In this case, however, reading a record would require storing information in temporary storage until the tag field had been read, then assigning the information to the fields of a record of the appropriate type. Furthermore, there would have to be separate procedures to perform operations on these records, one for each type, as opposed to a single procedure with a **case** statement.

It is up to the programmer to manage use of variant records correctly. On most systems, reference to a variant field that does not exist for the current value of the tag field will not produce an error message but may have unexpected results.

10.5 The Set Data Type

We've used sets together with the **in** relational operator to validate input data. For example, code of the form

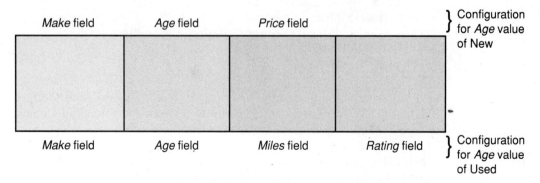

FIGURE 10.6 Variant record type *CarType*.

```
repeat
  prompt;
  readln(Value);
until Value in [1..5];
```

or

```
prompt;
readln(Value);
while not (Value in [1..5]) do
  begin
    prompt;
    readln(Value);
  end;
```

guarantees that *Value* will have an integer value from 1 through 5 before processing proceeds. (In the second form above, note the construction

```
while not (Value in  [1..5])
```

—this cannot be written as

```
while Value not in [1..5]
```

as a direct translation from English might suggest.) We've also used the **in** operator in **case** statements to guarantee that only values from the case label lists are passed to the **case** statement, as in the following code:

```
if Initial in ['H'..'M'] then
  case Initial of
    'H','I','J'  : writeln('Group Alpha');
    'K','L','M' : writeln('Group Beta');
  end    {case statement}
else
  writeln('Initial not valid');
```

Expressions such as [1..5] or ['H'..'M'] are set constants, i.e., fixed sets. Pascal also provides a **set** data type so that variables can be declared to be sets and the content of such variables can change during program execution. To declare a set data type, we name the type, indicate that it is a set type, and give the underlying ordinal data type from which the set elements will come. (Recall from Chapter 7 that all the elements of a set must belong to the same ordinal type.) Some typical set-type declarations are

```
type
  Digit  =  0..9;
  NumeralType  =  set of Digit;
  CharValues  =  set of char;
  Story  =  (Western, Gothic, Mystery, Romance, SciFi);
  Shelf  =  set of Story;
```

A system-dependent limit will be imposed on the size of the underlying ordinal type. This limit is usually fairly small (256 is a common limit). It is illegal, for example, to use *integer* as the ordinal type for set elements because it would allow the creation of arbitrarily large sets. Most systems allow for sets that can contain all of the character set, as we have assumed in declaring *CharValues* above. Two set data types are compatible if the underlying ordinal data types are compatible.

Given the above type declarations, variable declarations such as the following are legal:

```
var
    Numerals : NumeralType;
    Letters1, Letters2 : CharValues;
    Books : Shelf;
```

Square brackets are used with set constants, but not with set-type variables.

A legitimate value for *Numerals* is any set whose elements have the data type *Digit*. The assignment

```
Numerals := [0..3,5];
```

which is equivalent to

```
Numerals := [0,1,2,3,5];
```

A set variable can have as a value any set of elements from the underlying ordinal type; there are no duplicates and order does not matter.

can be made. Because elements in a set are not repeated, and there is no order associated with set elements,

```
Numerals := [3,0,1,5,2,0];
```

has exactly the same effect as the previous assignment. Furthermore, set elements can be named by expressions of the proper data type. If *Number* is a variable of type *Digit* that currently has the value 5, then

```
Numerals := [0..3,Number];
```

is still another way to assign the same set value to *Numerals*. As usual, assignments can be made between variables of the same (or compatible) type, as in

```
Letters1 := ['a'..'m','N'..'Z'];
Letters2 := Letters1;
```

Set elements, unlike array elements or record elements, cannot be referenced directly.

Sets are structured data types, like arrays and records. Each set is an entity in itself yet is made up of component parts, the set elements. Unlike arrays, set components are not arranged in any order. Unlike both arrays and records, set components cannot be referenced individually. Also unlike arrays and records, however, "arithmetic" operations exist that can be carried out on sets as entities.

10.5.1 *Set Operations*

The three set operations are **set union, set difference,** and **set intersection,** represented by the symbols "+," "−," and "*," respectively. These operations must be done on type-compatible set variables. The results are defined by

$A + B$ = the set of all elements in set A or set B or both
$A - B$ = the set of all elements in set A but not in set B
$A*B$ = the set of all elements in both sets A and B

Operations of union, difference, and intersection can be performed on type-compatible set variables.

The **Venn diagrams** of Figure 10.7 clarify these operations.

Sets that have no common elements are called **disjoint.** If sets A and B are disjoint, then $A*B$ results in the **empty set.** This set, denoted by [ ], is a set with no elements. The empty set is useful to initialize a set to which we will later add values by performing the union operation. Suppose, for example, that *NextDigit* is a variable of type *Digit,* and that we initialize *Numerals* by

```
Numerals := [ ];
```

Every time we read a new value for *NextDigit,* we execute the statement

```
Numerals := Numerals + [NextDigit];
```

This will have the effect of collecting in the set *Numerals* all of the distinct digit values read in; duplicates are ignored because a set has no duplicate values. (Notice that the set *Numerals* is not helpful if, for instance, you want to keep a count of how many times each digit is read.) This process is the only way to read elements into a set variable. Writing out the elements of a set variable is also somewhat awkward, as one must traverse the underlying ordinal values checking for those that are in the set:

```
for NextDigit := 0 to 9 do
  if NextDigit in Numerals then
    write(NextDigit);
```

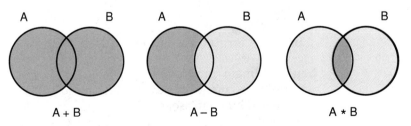

FIGURE 10.7 Set operations of union, difference, and intersection.

The following program might be used by a dietician in meal planning. Basic nutritional requirements (vitamins and minerals) are grouped into twelve categories, numbered 1-12. Each dish in the planned meal is evaluated for which of the requirements it satisfies, and the program's output shows any nutritional categories that are still missing. The set *Included* is initialized to the empty set and then constructed by a series of set unions as elements are read in. *Missing* is the set difference between the set of all nutritional requirements and *Included*.

```
program Nutrition(input, output);
{collects integer categories for nutrients in each dish of a
 menu; outputs list of missing categories}

type
    Category = 1..12;
    Nutrients = set of Category;

var
    Included, Missing : Nutrients;      {the sets of nutrients
                                         included in, and missing
                                         from, the menu}

    NumberOfDishes, i : integer;
    Counter : Category;

procedure ProcessDish(DishNumber: integer;
                      var Included: Nutrients);
{collects and adds to set Included the nutritional categories for
 dish DishNumber}

var
    CurrentNutrient : Category;

  begin    {procedure ProcessDish}
    write('Enter the integer categories for the nutrients ');
    writeln('dish number ', DishNumber:1);
    write('provides - all on one line please, no commas: ');
    while not eoln do
      begin
        read(CurrentNutrient);
        Included := Included + [CurrentNutrient];
      end;
    readln;
    writeln;
  end;      {procedure ProcessDish}

begin    {main program}
  write('How many dishes in this menu? ');
  readln(NumberOfDishes);
  writeln;
  Included := [ ];
```

```
      for i := 1 to NumberOfDishes do
        ProcessDish(i, Included);
      Missing := [1..12] — Included;
      write('This menu does not include nutrient categories ');
      for Counter := 1 to 12 do
        if Counter in Missing then
          write(Counter:2,', ');
      writeln;
    end.   {main program}
```

RUNNING THE PROGRAM...

How many dishes in this menu? 2

Enter the integer categories for the nutrients dish number 1 provides - all on one line please, no commas: 5 2 6 10 8

Enter the integer categories for the nutrients dish number 2 provides - all on one line please, no commas: 2 3 6 12

This menu does not include nutrient categories 1, 4, 7, 9, 11,

---

CHECKUP 10.5   Let *A*, *B*, and *C* be variables of type *NumeralType*, with $A = [2,3,7]$, $B = [0,2,4,6,8]$, and $C = [2,3,6,7,8]$. What is the content of each set below?

  a. $A + B$
  b. $A - B$
  c. $B*C$
  d. $A - (B+C)$

10.5.2 *Relations on Sets*

Relational operators can be applied to type-compatible set variables. The relations = and <> test whether two sets are or are not the same (contain the same elements). The relations <= and >= test whether one set is included in another. The relation $A <= B$ is true if every element in set *A* is also an element of set *B*. The relation $A >= B$ is true if every element in set *B* is also an element of set *A*.

Note that [ ] <= *B* will be true for any set *B* because there are no elements in the empty set that are not also elements of set *B* (since there are no elements in the empty set at all).

CHECKUP 10.6   Let *A*, *B*, and *C* be as in CHECKUP 10.5. Which of the following
boolean expressions are true?

a. A = [7,3,1*4 − 2]
b. C <= A
c. A <= C
d. A <= (A + B)
e. [ ] **in** B

10.6 Sample Software Development Project—Payroll

Problem Statement

Before-tax weekly pay amounts are computed differently for salaried and
hourly employees. Write a program to collect the information for each
employee, then print out a list of the salaried employees and a list of the
hourly employees, each sorted by increasing pre-tax weekly pay.

Problem Specification

The information to be collected for each employee is the employee's name,
address, Social Security number, and a salaried/hourly indicator. In addition, salaried employees have a weekly pay rate; this amount constitutes
their pre-tax weekly pay, regardless of the number of hours worked. Hourly
employees have an hourly pay rate and an overtime rate. The hourly rate is
paid on time worked up to and including 40 hours per week, and hours in
excess of 40 are paid at the overtime rate. It is assumed that there are no
fractional hours of work, therefore hours worked can be an integer. A
maximum of 30 employees is assumed, as is a limit of 20 characters each on
the employee's name, street address, etc. In the interests of meeting the
development deadline, a decision is made to include only minimal input
validation. [Editorial comment: Buyer Beware Software is proud of always
meeting its development deadlines.] Input termination is to be user-
controlled through answering a query for more data. The two sorted lists
should include the name, address, Social Security number, and pre-tax
weekly pay for each employee.

Input: each employee's name, address, and Social Security number; an
         indication of whether the employee is a salaried or an hourly
         worker; if salaried, the weekly pay rate; if hourly, the hourly pay
         rate, overtime pay rate, and number of hours worked for the week

Output: a list of the salaried workers, including name, address, Social
         Security number, and pre-tax weekly pay for each one, sorted in
         order of increasing pay

         a list of the hourly workers, including name, address, Social
         Security number, and pre-tax weekly pay for each one, sorted in
         order of increasing pay

Algorithm and Data Structure Development

We'll begin by thinking of an appropriate data structure for the information. Because the data on the employees is to be sorted, it must be stored rather than repeatedly read into the same variables. This suggests an array of records, one record per employee. If the output is to be two sorted lists, perhaps there should be two arrays, one for salaried employees and one for hourly employees. This would make reading records awkward: until the salary/hourly indicator is read, we would not know which array to load the current record into. Furthermore, two arrays are not necessary because if we sort a single array, each subclass of records within it will also be in sorted order. We'll settle on one array of records. The array will be a onedimensional array of size 30, but we'll make this limit a program constant for easy modification.

Each record must contain all of the information on each employee. We'll use the following fields—name, address, Social Security number, salaried/hourly indicator, weekly pay rate, hourly pay rate, overtime rate, hours worked, and weekly pay. The hourly pay rate, overtime rate, and hours worked fields are not of interest if the employee is salaried, and the weekly pay rate field is not of interest if the employee is an hourly worker. (See Testing and Maintenance Department problem #7 on using variant records here.)

The address field will have three parts—street address, city, state/Zipcode. Each of these will be a string, a packed array of characters. These strings could be the elements of an array, or they could be fields in a record. Because nothing gets done with these strings other than reading them in and writing them out, the choice is rather arbitrary. We'll use a record structure. This means that the address field of the main record is itself a record with fields of street address, city, state/Zipcode that are packed arrays of characters.

We should address a further detail of reading and writing strings. The program below allocates space for 20-character string arrays, but we will not read 20 characters each time. There are two choices of how to deal with this problem. We can initialize the string array with blanks, read the string, and then write out all 20 characters (this is what we did with the *Address* field in program *Rental* earlier). This can leave many blank spaces in the output, particularly noticeable if several strings are written on one line. A better choice is to keep track of the number of characters read in and then only write out that number of characters. This requires an extra integer for each string array to indicate the number of characters. A neat way to store these two related items of data is in a record with two fields, one for the string and one for the length of the string.

The following type declarations reflect these decisions.

```
const
    MaxWorkers = 30;        {maximum no. of employees}
    MaxLine = 20;           {max. length each line of data}

type
    WorkerRange = 1..MaxWorkers;
    LineRange = 1..MaxLine;
    String = packed array [LineRange] of char;
    StringHolder = record
```

```
        Message : String;
        Length : integer;
        end; {record StringHolder}

   AddressType = record
        Street, City, StateZip: StringHolder;
        end; {record Address}

   ConditionOfEmployment = (Salaried, Hourly);

   WorkerType = record
        Name, SocialSecurity : StringHolder;
        Address : AddressType;
        Status : ConditionOfEmployment
        WeeklyPayRate : real;
        HourlyPayRate  : real;
        OvertimeRate   : real;
        HoursWorked    : integer;
        Pay : real;
        end;    {WorkerType}

   ArrayType = array [WorkerRange] of WorkerType;
   ArrayRange = 0..MaxWorkers;
```

Note that we have spent a lot of time talking about an appropriate data structure and how to implement it. Only now are we getting around to developing an algorithm as a hierarchy of tasks and subtasks. That's why this section in the Sample Software Development Projects has been changed to *Algorithm and Data Structure Development*. These processes will go hand and hand from now on. Sometimes (as in this case) the data structure takes a bit of thought but the algorithm is fairly obvious; in other cases (most of the programs we've done up to now) the ratio is reversed, but there are aspects of each in every programming problem.

The major tasks the algorithm must perform are shown in the structure chart of Figure 10.8. The tasks of reading and writing records and computing weekly pay will be done within loops that traverse the array. The sort algorithm will be the selection sort from Chapter 9; comparisons will be done on the pay field of the employee records, but entire records will be exchanged.

The *Status* field is an enumerated-type variable, so some conversion has to be done from a character that is the salaried/hourly indicator to the value of the internal enumerated-type variable. Because so much string data has to be read, we'll put that task in a little module as well. Figure 10.9 shows the refined structure chart.

Read Record
This procedure reads an employee record and passes it back to the main program through a variable formal parameter of type *WorkerType*. The corresponding actual parameter when the

Continued

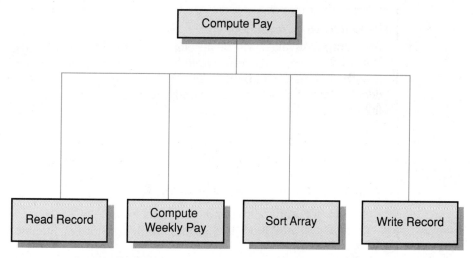

FIGURE 10.8 Structure chart for program *ComputePay*.

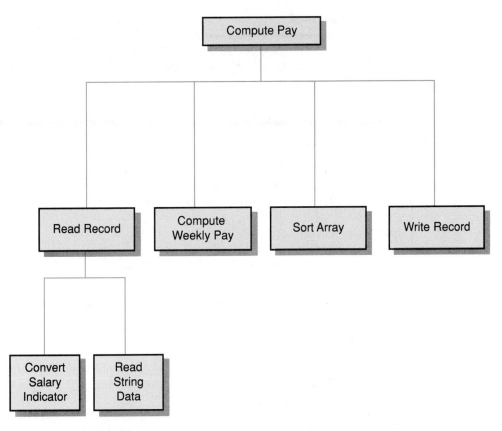

FIGURE 10.9 Refined structure chart for program *ComputePay*.

Read Record—Continued

procedure is invoked will be an element of the array of records. Within the procedure, multiple fields of a single record are read, so a **with** statement will be helpful. Also, a **case** statement is used to decide which fields to read, depending on the value of the *Status* field.

procedure ReadRecord(**var** Worker: WorkerType);
{reads and returns a record of type WorkerType}

begin   {procedure ReadRecord}

    prompt for and read the string for *Name*
    prompt for and read the string for *Address.Street, Address.City, Address.StateZip*
    prompt for and read the string for *SocialSecurity*
    prompt for and read the *Status* character; convert it to type *ConditionOfEmployment*
    case Status **of**
      Salaried : prompt for and read weekly pay rate
      Hourly   : prompt for and read hourly pay rate, overtime rate, and hours worked

end;   {procedure ReadRecord}

Convert Salary Indicator

A **case** statement is used to change a character into an internal variable of type *ConditionOfEmployment*.

procedure Convert(Symbol: char;
                      var Internal: ConditionOfEmployment);
{changes Symbol to corresponding Internal (enumerated-type) value}

Read String Data

This procedure enters data into a variable of type *StringHolder;* the corresponding actual parameter will be a record field.

procedure ReadString(**var** CharArray: Stringholder);
{reads one character at a time - maximum MaxLine - into the Message field of CharArray; the Length field holds the number of characters read}

Continued

Read String Data—Continued
begin   {procedure ReadString};

   initialize counter to 0
while not end-of-line **and not** *MaxLine* characters,
increment counter and read character
   set *Length* field equal to counter

end;   {procedure ReadString}

Compute Weekly Pay
This procedure computes the *Pay* field of an employee record based
on the value of the *Status* field. It uses a **with** statement and a
case statement.

procedure ComputeWeeklyPay(**var** Worker: WorkerType);
{computes Worker.Pay based on Worker.Status}

begin   {procedure ComputeWeeklyPay}

  case Status **of**
    Salaried : *Pay* is weekly pay rate
    Hourly   : *Pay* is hours worked times hourly rate
if <= 40 hours, otherwise add excess hours over
40 times overtime rate

end;   {procedure ComputeWeeklyPay}

Write Record
Because the fields to be written from each record are the same,
there is no need to distinguish between salaried and hourly workers.

procedure WriteRecord(Worker: WorkerType);
{writes appropriate fields of an employee record}

begin   {procedure WriteRecord}

  write fields *Name, Address.Street, Address.City,*
Address.StateZip, SocialSecurity, Pay

end;   {procedure WriteRecord}

Main program

repeat *ReadRecord* **until** the user chooses
to stop **or** array length exceeded
    maintain *Count* as number of records in array
    process array from 1 **to** *Count* by invoking
ComputeWeeklyPay
    sort array
    from 1 **to** *Count* invoke *WriteRecord* for
those records with *Status* field Salaried
    from 1 **to** *Count* invoke *WriteRecord* for
those records with *Status* field Hourly

The data flow diagram appears in Figure 10.10. The complete program
follows.

program ComputePay(input, output);
{collects data on salaried and hourly employees, computes weekly
pay for each employee, outputs lists of salaried and hourly
workers sorted in order of increasing pay}

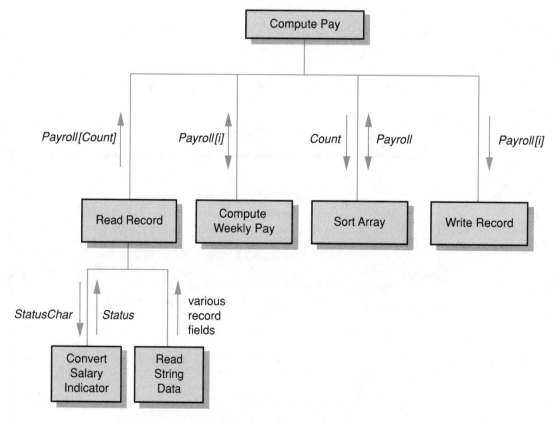

FIGURE   10.10   Data flow diagram for program *ComputePay.*

```
const
    MaxWorkers = 30;        {maximum no. of employees}
    MaxLine = 20;           {max. length each line of data}

type
    WorkerRange = 1..MaxWorkers;
    LineRange = 1..MaxLine;
    String = packed array [LineRange] of char;
    StringHolder = record
      Message : String;
      Length : integer;
    end; {record StringHolder}

    AddressType = record
      Street, City, StateZip: StringHolder;
    end; {record Address}

    ConditionOfEmployment = (Salaried, Hourly);
    WorkerType = record
      Name, SocialSecurity : StringHolder;
      Address : AddressType;
      Status : ConditionOfEmployment;
      WeeklyPayRate : real;
      HourlyPayRate : real;
      OvertimeRate : real;
      HoursWorked : integer;
      Pay : real;
    end;    {WorkerType}

    ArrayType = array [WorkerRange] of WorkerType;
    ArrayRange = 0..MaxWorkers;

var
    Payroll : ArrayType;        {array of employee records}
    Count : ArrayRange;         {number of employee records
                                 entered}
    StopSignal : char;          {terminates record entry}
    i : WorkerRange;            {index in array of records}

procedure Convert(Symbol: char;
                  var Internal: ConditionOfEmployment);
{changes Symbol to corresponding Internal (enumerated-type)
value}

  begin     {procedure Convert}
    while not (Symbol in ['S','s','H','h']) do
      begin
        writeln('Enter S or H');
        readln(Symbol);
      end;    {valid Symbol obtained}
```

```
      case Symbol of
        'S','s' : Internal := Salaried;
        'H','h' : Internal := Hourly;
      end {case statement}
    end;    {procedure Convert}
```

```
procedure ReadString(var CharArray: Stringholder);
{reads one character at a time - maximum MaxLine - into the
Message field of CharArray; the Length field holds the number
of characters read}

type
    LengthRange = 0..MaxLine;

var
    i : LengthRange;           {counter for length of string read}

  begin    {procedure ReadString}
    i := 0;
    while (not eoln) and (i < MaxLine) do
      begin
        i := i + 1;
        read(CharArray.Message[i]);
      end;
    CharArray.Length := i;
    end;     {procedure ReadString}
```

```
procedure ReadRecord(var Worker: WorkerType);
{reads and returns a record of type WorkerType}

var
    StatusChar : char;      {input symbol for Status}

  begin     {procedure ReadRecord}
    with Worker do
      begin     {with Worker}
        writeln;
        write('Employee' 's name: ');
        ReadString(Name);
        readln;
        writeln;

        writeln('Address (3 lines) :');
        ReadString(Address.Street);
        readln;
        ReadString(Address.City);
        readln;
        ReadString(Address.StateZip);
        readln;
        writeln;
```

```
            writeln('Social Security number: ');
            ReadString(SocialSecurity);
            readln;
            writeln;

            write('Enter S for salaried employee, ');
            write('H for hourly employee: ');
            readln(StatusChar);
            Convert(StatusChar,Status);

            case Status of
              Salaried : begin
                            write('Enter weekly pay rate: ');
                            readln(WeeklyPayRate);
                         end;
              Hourly :   begin
                            write('Enter hourly pay rate: ');
                            readln(HourlyPayRate)
                            write('Enter overtime rate: ');
                            readln(OvertimeRate);
                            write('Enter hours worked this week: ');
                            readln(HoursWorked);
                         end;
            end;     {case}

        end;     {with Worker}
  end;      {procedure ReadRecord}

procedure ComputeWeeklyPay(var Worker: WorkerType);
{computes Worker.Pay based on Worker.Status}

function HourPay(Base, Over: real; Hours: integer): real;
{computes Pay for the hourly worker}

  begin     {function HourPay}
    if Hours > 40 then
      HourPay := (Hours - 40)*Over + 40*Base
    else
      HourPay := Hours*Base;
  end;      {function HourPay}

  begin     {procedure ComputeWeeklyPay}
    with Worker do
      begin    {with Worker}
        case Status of
          Salaried : Pay := WeeklyPayRate;
          Hourly :   Pay := HourPay(HourlyPayRate,
                                    OvertimeRate,
                                    HoursWorked);
        end; {case}
```

```
        end;    {with Worker}
    end;    {procedure ComputeWeeklyPay}


procedure Sort(var A: ArrayType; n: ArrayRange);
{uses a selection sort to sort the first n records in array A in
 increasing order according to the real field Pay}

var
    i : integer;      {index in array A}

function MaxIndex(A: ArrayType; i: integer): integer;
{finds the index of the maximum value from 1 to i in array A}

var
    CurrentMaxIndex : integer;    {index of current max. value}
    j : integer;                  {array index}

  begin    {function MaxIndex}
    CurrentMaxIndex := 1;
    for j := 2 to i do
      begin
        if A[j].Pay > A[CurrentMaxIndex].Pay  then
          CurrentMaxIndex := j;
      end;
    MaxIndex := CurrentMaxIndex;
  end;    {function MaxIndex}


procedure Exchange(var X, Y: WorkerType);
{exchanges records X and Y}

var
    Temporary : WorkerType;

  begin    {procedure Exchange}
    Temporary := X;
    X := Y;
    Y := Temporary;
  end;    {procedure Exchange}

  begin    {procedure Sort}
    for i := Count downto 2 do
      begin
        Exchange(A[i], A[MaxIndex(A,i)]);
      end;    {for loop}
  end;    {procedure Sort}


procedure WriteRecord(Worker: WorkerType);
{writes appropriate fields of an employee record}
```

```
begin    {procedure WriteRecord}
  with Worker do
    begin    {with Worker}
      writeln;
      writeln(Name.Message:Name.Length);

      write(Address.Street.Message:Address.Street.Length);
      write(', ', Address.City.Message:Address.City.Length);
      writeln(', ', Address.StateZip.Message:
                    Address.StateZip.Length);

      write('Social Security Number: ',
            SocialSecurity.Message:SocialSecurity.Length);

      writeln(' Pre-Tax Weekly Pay: ', Pay:7:2);
    end;    {with Worker}
end;    {procedure WriteRecord}


begin    {main program}
  {read records into Payroll array}
  Count := 0;
  repeat
    Count := Count + 1;
    ReadRecord(Payroll[Count]);
    write('Type S to stop, C to continue: ');
    readln(StopSignal);
  until (StopSignal = 'S') or (StopSignal = 's')
                          or (Count = MaxWorkers);
  if Count = MaxWorkers then
    writeln('Maximum number of workers entered');

  {compute weekly pay for each employee}
  for i := 1 to Count do
    begin    {for loop}
      ComputeWeeklyPay(Payroll[i]);
    end;    {for loop}

  {sort the payroll array in order of increasing pay}
  Sort(Payroll, Count);

  {write the output}
  writeln;
  writeln('        Salaried Employees and Pre-Tax Weekly  Pay');
  for i := 1 to Count do
    begin    {for loop}
      if Payroll[i].Status = Salaried then
        WriteRecord(Payroll[i]);
    end;    {for loop}
```

```
    writeln;
    writeln('            Hourly Employees and Pre-Tax Weekly  Pay');
    for i : = 1 to Count do
      begin    {for loop}
        if Payroll[i].Status  =  Hourly then
          WriteRecord(Payroll[i]);
      end;    {for loop}

  end.    {main program}
```

RUNNING THE PROGRAM...

Employee's name: Ivan Abrams

Address (3 lines) :
45 Heather Lane
Curtisville
Iowa 47865

Social Security number:
999-23-4567

Enter S for salaried employee, H for hourly employee: s
Enter weekly pay rate: 390.00
Type S to stop, C to continue; c

Employee's name: Betty Bradley

Address (3 lines) :
750 Wimple Street
Cornrover
Iowa 46983

Social Security number:
456-22-6543

Enter S for salaried employee, H for hourly employee: h
Enter hourly pay rate: 4.80
Enter overtime rate: 6.00
Enter hours worked this week: 50
Type S to stop, C to continue; c

Employee's name: Sam Sterling

Address (3 lines) :
1372 E. Fifth Street, Apt. 8
Curtisville
Iowa 47655

Social Security number:
999-00-8766

Enter S for salaried employee, H for hourly employee: h
Enter hourly pay rate: 4.50
Enter overtime rate: 5.80
Enter hours worked this week: 30
Type S to stop, C to continue; c

Employee's name: Houston James

Address (3 lines) :
87 Hilltop
Burger
Iowa 46598

Social Security number:
674-88-7250

Enter S for salaried employee, H for hourly employee: s
Enter weekly pay rate: 350.00
Type S to stop, C to continue; s

                    Salaried Employees and Pre-Tax Weekly Pay

Houston James
87 Hilltop, Burger, Iowa 46598
Social Security Number: 674-88-7250 Pre-Tax Weekly Pay: 350.00

Ivan Abrams
45 Heather Lane, Curtisville, Iowa 47865
Social Security Number: 999-23-4567 Pre-Tax Weekly Pay: 390.00

                    Hourly Employees and Pre-Tax Weekly Pay

Sam Sterling
1372 E. Fifth Street, Curtisville, Iowa 47655
Social Security Number: 999-00-8766 Pre-Tax Weekly Pay: 135.00

Betty Bradley
750 Wimple Street, Cornrover, Iowa 46983
Social Security Number: 456-22-6543 Pre-Tax Weekly Pay: 252.00

**CASE
STUDY
ONE**   **View #10**

An additional feature required of the semiannual reports from the Lodestone County Water Pollution Department is a statement of the percentage

of readings in the report that indicate bacteria level violations. In addition to enhancing the existing program's capabilities by adding this feature, you decide to change the data structure view used in the program from a collection of parallel arrays of various data types to a single array of records, one record per reading. This will be more convenient should the individual site reports ever have to be sorted in some way; the change can be done with minimal effort and with no impact on the existing user interface.

Notice in the program below that the tasks of the program remain the same as before (except for the new feature), but the data items that used to be elements of the individual parallel arrays are now fields in a single record. The warning signal is also made a field of the record, rather than a single variable that gets recomputed for each reading. The record structure greatly simplifies parameter passing to the input and output procedures, yet within these procedures, by use of the **with** statement, individual statements look almost identical to those in the previous version. Other modules can be lifted unchanged from the previous version.

```pascal
program WaterPollution(input, output);
{tests water sample from a site against a pollution threshold,
 issues a warning if the bacteria level is too high; processes
 multiple sites and readings in this way and prints results in
 tabular form, along with a statement of the percent of
 violations. An array of records, one record per reading, is used
 to store the data.}

const
    Threshold = 2.0;              {200 bacteria per 100 ml water}
    MaxNoOfReadings = 30;         {maximum number of readings
                                   program can handle}

type
    TwoCharArray = array[1..2] of char;

    Reading = record
       ID, Water, Bacteria : integer;
       Mon, Day, Yr: TwoCharArray;
       Level : real;             {pollution level}
       Warning : boolean;        {flag for warning message}
       end;    {Reading}
    Index = 1..MaxNoOfReadings;
    ArrayType = array [Index] of Reading;

var
    Report : ArrayType;          {holds all the report data}
    Continue : char;             {signal to terminate execution}
    n : integer;                 {number of readings to process}
    i : integer;                 {array index}
```

```pascal
procedure GetInput(var OneSite: Reading);
{procedure to collect input for water pollution data; amount
 Water of water and count Bacteria of bacteria were
 obtained from  site ID on date Mon1Mon2/Day1Day2/Yr1Yr2}

var
    Slash : char;      {separating / in date format}

function Value(FirstChar, SecondChar: char): integer;
{function to convert two characters to a two-digit integer}

var
    FirstDigit    : integer;     {the integer equivalents}
    SecondDigit : integer;     {of numerical characters}

  begin   {function Value}
    FirstDigit := ord(FirstChar) − ord('0');
    SecondDigit := ord(SecondChar) − ord('0');
    Value := 10*FirstDigit + SecondDigit;
  end;    {function Value}

function ValidDate(Mon1, Mon2, Day1, Day2: char): boolean;
{function to do some validation on date entered}

var
    MonthValue : integer;     {numerical value for month}
    DayValue : integer;       {numerical value for day}
    ValidMonth : boolean;     {MonthValue in range 1–12}
    ValidDay : boolean;       {DayValue in range 1–31}

  begin   {function ValidDate}
    MonthValue := Value(Mon1, Mon2);
    DayValue := Value(Day1, Day2);

    ValidMonth := (0 < MonthValue) and (MonthValue < 13);
    ValidDay := (0 < DayValue) and (DayValue <  32);

    ValidDate := ValidMonth and ValidDay;
  end;    {function ValidDate}

  begin    {procedure GetInput}
    with OneSite do
      begin   {with OneSite}
        writeln;
        write('Enter the site ID number: ');
        readln(ID);
        while not((1 <= ID) and (ID <=  1000)) do
```

```
      begin {ID out of range}
        write('Check the site ID number ');
        write('and enter again: ');
        readln(ID);
      end;  {ID out of range}
    writeln;

    writeln('Enter the date of this sample.');
    write('Use month/date/year format: ');
    readln(Mon[1], Mon[2], Slash, Day[1], Day[2],
          Slash, Yr[1], Yr[2]);
    while not ValidDate(Mon[1], Mon[2],
                          Day[1], Day[2]) do
      begin {error in date input}
        write('Please enter the date again: ');
        readln(Mon[1], Mon[2], Slash,
              Day[1], Day[2], Slash, Yr[1], Yr[2]);
      end;  {error in date input}
    writeln;

    write('Enter the amount of water in sample (in ml): ');
    readln(Water);
    while not (Water > 0) do
      begin    {error in amount of water}
        write('Check the amount of water & ');
        write('enter again: ');
        readln(Water);
      end;     {error in amount of water}
    writeln;

    write('Enter the bacteria count found in this sample:  ');
    readln(Bacteria);
    while not (Bacteria >= 0) do
      begin    {error in bacteria count}
        write('Check the bacteria count & ');
        write('enter again: ');
        readln(Bacteria);
      end;     {error in bacteria count}

    end;    {with OneSite}

  end;    {procedure GetInput}

function Ratio(Bacteria, Water: integer): real;
{computes the Ratio of Bacteria to Water}

  begin      {function Ratio}
    Ratio := Bacteria/Water;
  end;       {function Ratio}
```

```
procedure CheckThreshold(Ratio: real;
                              var Over: Boolean);
{compares Ratio to the global constant Threshold and sets Over
 to  true if that limit is exceeded}

   begin     {procedure CheckThreshold}
     Over := false;   {initialize Over}
     if Ratio > Threshold then
       Over := true;
   end;     {procedure CheckThreshold}

procedure WriteHeader;
{writes output table heading}

   begin    {procedure WriteHeader}
     writeln;
     writeln;
     write('Site ID', 'Date':8, 'Water':12, 'Bacteria':13);
     writeln('Level':9, 'Warning':10);
     write('_____');
     writeln('_____');
     writeln;
   end;     {procedure WriteHeader}

procedure WriteLineOfOutput(OneSite: Reading);
{produces a line of output in the table corresponding to one
 reading - echoes input data and writes warning message if
 warranted}

   begin     {procedure WriteLineOfOutput}
     with OneSite do
       begin    {with OneSite}
         write(ID:5, Mon[1]:6, Mon[2], '/', Day[1],  Day[2],
                '/', Yr[1], Yr[2]);
         write(Water:8, ' ml', Bacteria:9, Level:11:2);

         if Warning then
           write('     ** HIGH **');
         writeln;
       end;     {with OneSite}
   end;     {procedure WriteLineOfOutput}

procedure Percent(Report: ArrayType; n: integer);
{computes and writes out the percentage of readings with high
 bacteria}

var
     Total : integer;      {number of high readings}
```

```
      i : integer;          {array index}
      Percentage : real;    {percent of high readings}


  begin    {function Percent}
    Total := 0;
    for i:= 1 to n do
      begin    {count violators}
        if Report[i].Warning then
          Total := Total + 1;
      end;      {count violators}

    Percentage := (Total/n) * 100;
    writeln;
    write('The percentage of readings in violation is: ');
    writeln(Percentage:6:2);
  end;      {function Percent}


begin      {main program}
  n := 0;
  repeat
    n := n + 1;

    GetInput(Report[n]);

    with Report[n] do
      Level := Ratio(Bacteria, Water);

    writeln;
    writeln;
    if (n < MaxNoOfReadings) then
      begin {room for more data}
        writeln('Do you have more sites to process?');
        writeln('(Answer Y or N): ');
        readln(Continue);
      end    {room for more data}
    else
      begin {array full}
        writeln('Maximum number of readings entered. ');
        write('Adjust program constant MaxNoOfReadings ');
        writeln('if this is a problem.');
      end;   {array full}

  until (Continue = 'N') or (Continue  = 'n')
                      or (n = MaxNoOfReadings);

  {all the input has been gathered and stored in the array,
   now print out table of results}

  WriteHeader;
```

```
    for i := 1 to n do
      begin {produce line i of the output table}
        CheckThreshold(Report[i].Level, Report[i].Warning);
        WriteLineOfOutput(Report[i]);
      end; {line i has been written}

    Percent(Report, n);
  end.      {main program}
```

RUNNING THE PROGRAM...

Enter the site ID number: 82

Enter the date of this sample.
Use month/date/year format: 04/16/89

Enter the amount of water in sample (in ml): 1350

Enter the bacteria count found in this sample: 1800

Do you have more sites to process?
(Answer Y or N):
y

Enter the site ID number: 209

Enter the date of this sample.
Use month/date/year format: 04/17/89

Enter the amount of water in sample (in ml): 800

Enter the bacteria count found in this sample: 2100

Do you have more sites to process?
(Answer Y or N):
n

Site ID	Date	Water	Bacteria	Level	Warning
82	04/16/89	1350 ml	1800	1.33	
209	04/17/89	800 ml	2100	2.63	** HIGH **

The percentage of readings in violation is: 50.00

**CASE
STUDY
TWO**

View #10

Modify the hypertension clinic program to maintain patient data in an array
of records, and to print a summary statement giving the percentage of

readings in each of the categories of normal, mild, moderate, or severe hypertensive.

(Items marked with * make use of optional material on Variant Records.)

EXERCISES

#1. Draw a diagram in the style of Figure 10.4 for the structure determined by the following type declaration:

```
type
    SmallRecord = record
      NumberOne : integer;
      NumberTwo : integer;
      end;    {SmallRecord}
    BiggerRecord = record
      OneField : SmallRecord;
      TwoField : real;
      ThreeField : char;
      end;    {BiggerRecord}
    Bunch = array [1..5] of BiggerRecord;
    BiggestRecord = record
      OneField : char;
      TwoField : integer;
      ThreeField : Bunch;
      end;    {BiggestRecord}
```

2. What is wrong with the following program?

```
program Quiz(input, output);

type
    Event = record
      Date1 : integer;
      Date2 : integer;
      Sum : integer;
      Kind : char;
      end;    {Event}

begin    {main program}
  with Event do
    begin    {with Event}
      Date1 := 92;
      Date2 := 20;
      Sum := Date1 + Date2;
      Kind := 'K';
      writeln(Sum, Kind);
    end;    {with Event}
end.    {main program}
```

#3. In program *Rental* of this chapter, why is the variable *Min* declared to be of type *Range* instead of type *Index*?

#4. Consider the following declarations:

type
    Display = **array** [1..3] **of** integer;
    Duet = **record**
      View : char;
      Cluster : Display;
      end;   {Duet}
    TwoSome = **record**
      Field1 : integer;
      Field2 : Duet;
      end;   {TwoSome}
    Bunch = **array** [1..3] **of** TwoSome;

var
    ABunch : Bunch;

Figure 10.11 shows the partial contents of *ABunch*. At this point, what would be the output from the following statements?

a. writeln(ABunch[1].Field1);
b. writeln(ABunch[1].Field2.View);
c. writeln(ABunch[1].Field2.Cluster[1]);

5. Given the declarations of Exercise 4 above,

a. Write a statement that will write out the number 7 as shown in Figure 10.11.
b. Write a statement that will write out the character item in the second record in *ABunch*.

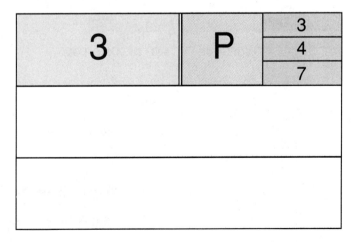

FIGURE 10.11 Partial contents of *ABunch*.

6. What is the output from the following program?

```
program McDonald(input, output);

type
    StockType = record
        Horses : integer;
        Cattle : integer;
        end;    {StockType}

var
    Farm1, Farm2 : StockType;

begin
  with Farm1 do
    begin    {with Farm1}
      Horses := 15;
      Cattle := 30;
    end;    {with Farm1}
  Farm2 := Farm1;
  writeln(Farm2.Horses);
  with Farm1 do
    begin    {with Farm1}
      Cattle := 40;
      with Farm2 do
        begin {with Farm2}
          Horses := Cattle;
        end;    {with Farm2}
    end;    {with Farm1}
  writeln(Farm1.Horses, Farm2.Horses);
end.
```

#7. Consider the following declarations:

```
type
    ColorList = (Red, Blue, Green, Violet, Yellow);
    ColorsType = set of ColorList;

var
    Colors : ColorsType;
```

What will be the content of *Colors* after executing the following section of code?

```
Colors := [ ];
Colors := Colors + ([Red..Green]*[Blue..Yellow]);
```

*8. What is the error in the following program?

```
program OhOh(input, output);

type
    Weather = record
      Temp : integer;
      case Season : char of
        'S' : (Rain : real; High, Humidity : integer);
        'W' : (Snow, Low : integer);
      end; {Weather}

var
    Day : Weather;

begin
    Day.Temp := 72;
    Day.Season := 'S';
    Day.High := 75;
    Day.Low := 58;
    with Day do
      writeln(Temp, Season, High, Low);
end.
```

SKILL BUILDERS

#1. Write a program to prompt for, read, and write a single record that stores the following information: name, age, sex, height, weight.

2. Given the type declarations below, write a procedure that initializes all of the *Group* values in each entry of array *Books* to 0.

```
type
    GroupType = array [1..20] of integer;
    Statement = record
      Bottom : integer;
      Kind : char;
      Group : GroupType;
      end;   {Statement}
    BookType = array [1..50] of Statement;

var
    Books : BookType;
```

3. Given the type declarations below, write a procedure that checks for a given credit card number (*Number*) against those in array *Cards* and writes out the agreeing record or a message that the number does not appear. You may assume that all string variables have been initialized with blanks.

```
type
   String = packed array [1..15] of char;
   Entry = record
     Name, Address, Phone, CreditCard : String;
     end;    {Entry}
   CardsType = array [1..100] of Entry;

var
   Cards : CardsType;
   Number : String;              {credit card number to check}
```

4. Write a program that reads a line of text and writes out all the capital letters contained in that line; use set variables.

*5. A patient's medical record for a particular condition contains the patient's name and a flag for an allergic reaction to a specific drug. If the patient is not allergic, the record contains the dosage of that drug; if the patient is allergic, the record contains the dosage for each of two alternate drugs. Write a program to prompt for, read, and write a single variant record that stores this information.

SOFTWARE DEVELOPMENT PROJECTS

1. An attorney's electronic appointment calendar maintains information for four five-day weeks at a time. In each day, thirty-minute appointments can be scheduled on the hour or half hour from 9:00 A.M. to 4:30 P.M. The user should be allowed to enter as many appointments as desired by specifying the week (1 to 4), the day (Monday to Friday), the time of the appointment, the name of whom the appointment is with, and the case number the appointment pertains to. Then the user should be able to continue to choose one of three types of queries (or to stop). The types of queries are

  i. name and case number for appointment at a given date (week/day) and time, or information that there is no appointment then,

  ii. list of all times, names, and case numbers for appointments on a given date (week/day),

  iii. list of all times and dates (week/day) of any appointments with a person of a given name or about a given case.

Be sure to display appropriate prompts and menu choices. Also check for duplicate appointment entries, issue an appropriate message, and allow for re-entry.

2. Develop a missile-interceptor launch program that reads a series of two-dimensional fixed-point coordinates and, for each fixed point, a series of coordinates for radar readings. When the user specifies the radius of a circle, the program determines if any of the radar reading locations associated with any fixed point fall within a circle of this radius around that fixed point. If so, the program generates a launch signal and terminates. As long as no launch signal is generated, the user should be able to process the data repeatedly with various values for the circle radius or terminate the program.

3. Develop software that maintains a clothing store inventory. For each item there is an item number and a price, and also a list of sizes for that item. For each size, the number in stock of each of several colors is kept. The user should be able to choose from along the following activities:

    i. Set up the original inventory information (specify item number, price, and number in stock of each color for each size).

    ii. Query about the number in stock of a given color and size for a given item.

    iii. Enter information for the sale of an item and adjust the inventory accordingly.

    iv. Enter information for the receipt of a shipment of items and adjust the inventory accordingly.

    v. Stop.

4. New cars can be ordered with options that are bundled into various packages. Develop software that reads in the option packages available, followed by a list of options the customer desires. The output of the program should be the package that most closely matches the customer's desired options, i.e., it should include all the desired options along with the fewest extra options. If no such package exists, the program should find the combination of option packages that gives the closest match. (If there is more than one "closest match," the program should give all the possibilities.)

5. Develop software to play a hand of four-handed poker. Each of four players gets five cards. The user "deals" the hands in rotation by entering each card in English, i.e., "three of diamonds." Poker hands are ranked as follows (worst to best), with some tie-breaking rules, although tied hands are still possible.

Ranking	Description
no pair	none of the other rankings; between two such hands, high card wins; if the high card is a tie, the next high card wins, etc.
1 pair	2 cards with same denomination (3, king, etc.); between two such hands, the pair with highest cards wins; if this is a tie, decision is based on high card among the remaining three cards, if this is a tie, next high card, etc.
2 pairs	2 pairs of 2 cards with same denomination; between two such hands, highest-ranking pair wins; if this is a tie, highest-ranking second pair wins, then highest fifth card
3 of a kind	3 cards with same denomination; between two such hands, the highest-ranking three-of-a-kind wins
straight	5 cards in consecutive denomination (3,4,5,6,7); between two such hands, straight with highest- ranking card wins
flush	5 cards of same suit; between two such hands, highest-ranking card wins; if this is a tie, the next high card wins, etc.
full house	3 of a kind plus 1 pair; between two such hands, the highest-ranking three-of-a-kind wins

Ranking	Description
4 of a kind	4 cards with same denomination; between two such hands, the highest-ranking four-of-a-kind wins
straight flush	5 cards of same suit in consecutive denomination; between two such hands, straight with highest-ranking card wins

The program should check for illegal data entry (for example, "for" instead of "four" or "dimonds" instead of "diamonds") and should not allow duplicate cards to be dealt. The output should be the four player hands, together with the number of the player with the winning hand (or player numbers in case of tie). (Hint: An internal representation of the denominations in integer form would allow sorting to more easily count cards of the same denomination and runs of consecutive denominations; the same idea can be used for the suit.)

TESTING AND MAINTENANCE DEPARTMENT

1. Develop test data sets for program *ComputePay*. Be sure to consider such situations as filling the arrays, no hourly employees, illegal status indicator, etc. Run the program on these test sets.

2. Modify program *ComputePay* to produce two sorted lists based on after-tax pay rather than pre-tax pay. Figure Social Security deductions at 7.3%. Figure federal income tax deduction at 15% for before-tax weekly pay of $350 or less, 28% for before-tax weekly pay above $350. Figure state income tax deduction at 3%. The output for each employee should show the pre-tax pay and the various deductions, as well as the after-tax pay.

3. Modify program *Rental* of this chapter to include input validation and warning messages when arrays are filled.

4. Modify program *Rental* of this chapter to output the listings for the chosen locale in order of increasing rent; do not highlight the minimum rent.

5. Modify program *Rental* of this chapter to allow the user to request information on multiple locales, one at a time.

6. Rewrite program *Player* on page 295 to use an array of records rather than parallel arrays. Replace functions *MaxIndexName* and *MaxIndexGPA* with a single function *MaxIndex* that finds the index in an array of records of the maximum value in one of two fields; the choice of which field to use is passed as a parameter. Replace procedures *SortName* and *SortGPA* with a single procedure *Sort* that sorts an array of records on one of two fields; the choice of which field to sort on is passed as a parameter. Replace procedures *ExchangeName* and *ExchangeGPA* with a single procedure *Exchange* that exchanges two records.

*7. Redo program *ComputePay* to use variant records, where *ConditionOfEmployment* is the tag field.

DEBUGGING CLINIC

1. In procedure *ReadApartmentRecord* of program *Rental,* replace

```
i := 0;
while (not eoln) and (i < 25) do
  begin
    i := i + 1;
    read(Apt.Address[i]);
  end;
```

with

```
for i := 1 to 25 do
  begin
    read(Apt.Address[i]);
  end;
```

Test the new version. What happens, and why?

2. Replace the same section of code as above with

```
i := 1;
while (not eoln) and (i < 25) do
  begin
    read(Apt.Address[i]);
    i := i + 1;
  end;
```

Test the new version. What happens, and why?

CHAPTER ELEVEN

FILES

We are familiar with files for permanent storage in auxiliary memory; after all, our Pascal programs are stored in files. Permanent files for input and output data would also be convenient. We do not want to enter the same large quantity of data over and over every time we run a program (as we had to do for program *Rental* in the previous chapter), and we would like a more permanent repository for output results than the terminal screen.

11.1 Using Files

Pascal provides the standard files *input,* for keyboard input, and *output,* for screen output. It is easy enough to have our programs communicate with other files, but to do so, we must perform several tasks that Pascal automatically does for us in the case of *input* and *output.* These are

1. Files must be declared in a variable declaration.
2. File names must be referenced in statements that read data from or write data to such files, and in the *eoln* and *eof* functions.
3. Files must be "opened" before they can be used in a program.

In addition, permanent files must be referenced in the program heading, just as we have to do now for *input* and *output.*

We'll look at each of these three tasks in turn.

Pascal provides one standard file data type called *text.* A text file may be thought of as lines of characters, each line terminating with the end-of-line character, and the entire file terminating with the end-of-file marker. Because *text* is a predefined data type, no type declaration is needed, and

var
    MailingList : text;

365

*Files other than
input and output
must be declared
as program
variables.*

is sufficient to declare a variable *MailingList* to be a file of type *text*. Unlike other variable declarations, which allocate memory space to hold the contents of the variable, this declaration does not reserve space in main memory for the file; files reside in secondary storage. *Input* and *output* are special text files that don't reside in secondary storage and don't require declarations in the program.

The fact that a file is a text file does not mean that data from that file can only be treated as type *char*. It means that the data contained in that file has been transformed from the computer's internal binary representation to an external representation convenient for humans to read, i.e., character form. Data of type *integer*, for example, can be read from any text file, just as it can be read from file *input*. If the number 12 appears in a text file and is read into a type *integer* variable *Number*, then the character string 12 is converted into the binary internal representation of the number 12. The process is reversed when the content of *Number* is written to a text file. As a consequence, asking the computer system to type the content of a text file produces a readable result.

*Files created
with a system
editor are text
files.*

Whenever you use the system editor to create a file, you create a text file. Hitting the RETURN key inserts an end-of-line character into the file. The system requirements for naming files may be different from the Pascal requirements for identifiers. Some Pascal implementations allow the system file name to be left alone, provided a statement is included within the program to associate that file with a Pascal file identifier used in the program. We'll assume in our examples that the system file name is the same as the Pascal program file identifier.

Although other file types can exist, we'll consider for now only files of type *text*. The statements *read, readln, write,* and *writeln* behave exactly as before, except now the name of the file must be given as the first identifier in the variable list of the statement. When no file name is given, the *read* and *readln* statements read from file *input,* and the *write* and *writeln* statements write to file *output.*

*When read,
readln, eoln, or
eof are to apply
to files other
than input, the
file name must
be the first
parameter given;
similarly with
write or writeln
applied to files
other than
output.*

Suppose that *Item* has been declared as an integer variable. Then

readln(MailingList, Item);

reads an integer value from file *MailingList* and assigns that value to *Item,* after which the read "pointer" in file *MailingList* proceeds to the beginning of the next line of the file. Note that from the syntax of the above statement alone, the program might be reading two values from file *input,* one for a variable called *MailingList* and the other for *Item.* It is the declaration of *MailingList* as a file variable that prevents this interpretation. The file name must also be given with the *eoln* or *eof* function if a file other than *input* is being referenced.

Opening a file is done with a statement of the form

reset(filename);

or

rewrite(filename);

depending on whether we wish to read from the file or write to the file, respectively. This hints at some peculiarities—opening a file seems to dedicate it to a certain type of use. Indeed, a file that has been named in a *reset* statement cannot be written to unless a later *rewrite* statement has named that file. Similarly, a file named in a *rewrite* statement cannot be read from unless a later *reset* statement has again prepared the file for reading. A *reset* statement moves the read "pointer" to the beginning of the file. A *rewrite* statement moves the write "pointer" to the beginning of the file *after erasing any previous contents of the file;* the "erasure" is actually accomplished by moving the end-of-file marker to the beginning of the file. Because of the way files are opened, reading from and writing to the same file must be done with care. We'll see some examples later. The files *input* and *output* are automatically opened for reading and writing, respectively.

11.1.1 Text File Examples

First, let's look at some simple situations. The program below writes nonzero integer values entered at the keyboard into a text file. Note the declaration of the text file, and its inclusion in the program heading. The *rewrite* statement creates an empty file *NumberList* if this file did not exist before. If the file did exist before, it is now empty. In either case, the pointer is positioned at the beginning of the file and the file is open to be written to. In an empty file, the beginning of the file is also the end of the file, and *eof(NumberList)* is true. Each *writeln* to the file inserts a value followed by an end-of-line character at the current end of the file, pushing the end-of-file marker—and the write pointer—farther away from the beginning of the file; *eof(NumberList)* continues to be true. Figure 11.1 illustrates what happens during the sample program execution below.

```
program WriteAFile(input, output, NumberList);
{writes nonzero integer values, one per line, to text file
 NumberList}

var
     NumberList : text;      {file to receive integer values}
     Number : integer;

begin
  rewrite(NumberList);
  writeln('Enter a list of nonzero integers (no commas, please);');
  writeln('terminate with 0.');
  read(Number);
  while (Number <> 0) do
     begin
        writeln(NumberList, Number);
        read(Number);
     end;
  write('These numbers are stored one per line ');
  writeln('in file NumberList.');
end.
```

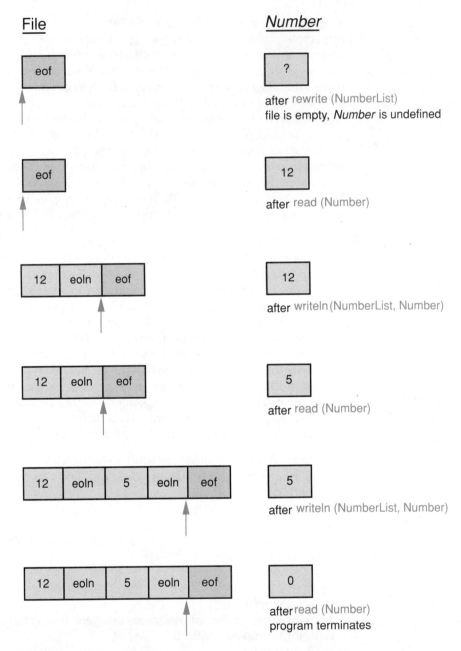

FIGURE 11.1 Viewing sample execution of program *WriteAFile*.

RUNNING THE PROGRAM...

Enter a list of nonzero integers (no commas, please);
terminate with 0.
12 5 0
These numbers are stored one per line in file NumberList. ·

As program *WriteAFile* shows, a text file can be created by a Pascal program, as well as by use of the system editor.

The next program reads integer values from a text file and displays them on the screen. The file is assumed to have one integer value per line. This file could have been created by the previous program. Because of the *eof* test at the beginning of the loop, the program will still cope if the file is empty. (Recall from Chapter 8 that it is an error to attempt to read the end-of-file marker.) "Running the Program..." and Figure 11.2 illustrate execution of this program on the file created in the previous sample program execution.

```
program ReadAFile(NumberList, output);
{reads integers from file NumberList, writes them to the screen}

var
    NumberList : text;          {file containing one integer per line}
    Number : integer;

begin
  reset(NumberList);            {opens NumberList for reading}
  writeln('The values in file NumberList are');
  while not eof(NumberList) do
    begin
      readln(NumberList, Number);
      writeln(Number);
    end;
end.
```

RUNNING THE PROGRAM...

```
The values in file NumberList are
12
5
```

The next program copies text from file *Source* into file *Target*. The main program writes reassuring messages to the user on the progress of the program; otherwise the user would see nothing at all on the screen. It also opens the files and invokes the *FileCopy* procedure, which is simply a reworking of program *ReadWriteText* from Chapter 8. *FileCopy* illustrates that a file can be passed as a parameter, but it *must always be a variable parameter*, not a value parameter. Because a file can be arbitrarily large, a main memory copy of a file (which use of a value parameter would create) is not possible.

File parameters must be variable parameters.

```
program CopyCat(Source, Target, output);
{program to copy the text file Source into Target}

var
    Source, Target : text;
```

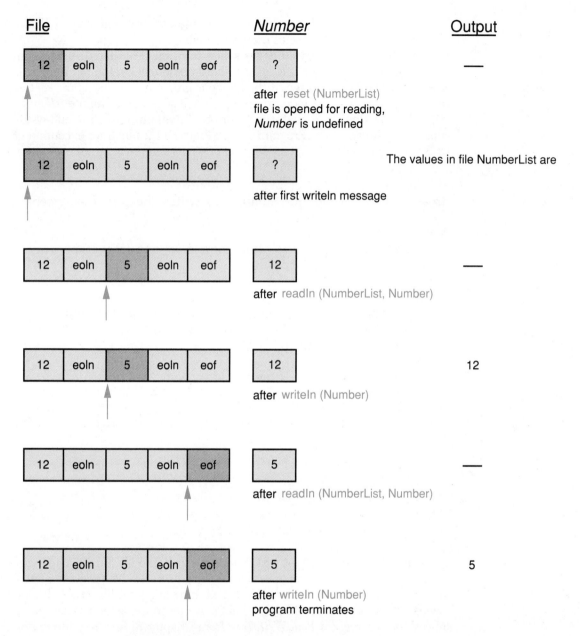

FIGURE 11.2 Viewing execution of program *ReadAFile* on file *NumberList*.

procedure FileCopy(**var** Old, New: text);
{copies contents of opened file Old into opened file New}

var
    NextCharacter : char;   {next character in file}

  begin   {procedure FileCopy}
    while not eof(Old) **do**

```
begin      {while not eof}
  while not eoln(Old) do
    begin {while not eoln}
      read(Old, NextCharacter);
      write(New, NextCharacter);
    end;   {while not eoln}

    {now deal with end-of-line character}
    readln(Old);   {read eoln & go to next line}
    writeln(New); {advance to next line in output}
  end;       {while not eof}
end;    {procedure FileCopy}

begin
  reset(Source);
  rewrite(Target);
  writeln('Program running');
  FileCopy(Source, Target);
  writeln('Program complete');
end.
```

Note that *FileCopy* uses a variable *NextCharacter* in main memory to pass a value from the old file to the new file. Such **buffer variables** (temporary holding locations) are required because direct transfer of items between files is not possible.

11.1.2 *File Modification*

Suppose we want to do something slightly harder—read some data from a file, perform some manipulations on it, and return it *to the same file*. A false start for this task is proposed in the following CHECKUP.

CHECKUP 11.1   What will be the content of *NumberList* after execution of the following program, assuming that *NumberList* originally contains the values

5

30

(Recall the peculiar properties of the *reset* and *rewrite* statements.)

```
program WatchOut(NumberList);
{is supposed to read two integers from NumberList, double
 them, and write the results back in NumberList}

var
  NumberList : text;
  Number, i : integer;
```

Continued

```
begin
  reset(NumberList);
  for i := 1 to 2 do
    begin
      readln(NumberList, Number);
      Number := 2*Number;
      rewrite(NumberList);
      writeln(NumberList, Number);
      reset(NumberList);
    end;
end.
```

The best way to handle file modification is to introduce a temporary file that exists only while the program is executing. Such files, called **internal files** or **scratch files,** are treated like other files except that they are not listed in the program heading. The following program reads military times from a text file *Times* and converts them to standard times as it stores them in a temporary file. Then the temporary file is copied back into the original file, using the *FileCopy* procedure from the previous program. After the program terminates, only file *Times* exists.

```
program TimeConverter(Times, output);
{converts entries in file Times from military to standard time;
 assumes entries in Times are stored one per line in the form
 15:30}

var
    Times : text;
    Temp : text;    {temporary file}

procedure ProcessNextTime(var Times, Temp: text);

var
    Hours : integer;
    Colon, Min1, Min2 : char;

  begin {procedure ProcessNextTime}
    readln(Times, Hours, Colon, Min1, Min2);
    if Hours < 12 then
      begin   {A.M. time}
        write(Temp, Hours:2, ':', Min1, Min2);
        writeln(Temp, ' A.M.');
      end     {A.M. time}
```

```
        else
          begin   {P.M. time}
            write(Temp, (Hours − 12):2, ':', Min1, Min2);
            writeln(Temp, ' P.M.');
          end;     {P.M. time}
    end;    {procedure ProcessNextTime}

procedure FileCopy(var Old, New: text);
{copies contents of opened file Old into opened file New}

var
    NextCharacter : char;       {next character in file}

  begin      {procedure FileCopy}
    while not eof(Old) do
      begin   {while not eof}
        while not eoln(Old) do
          begin   {while not eoln}
            read(Old, NextCharacter);
            write(New, NextCharacter);
          end;      {while not eoln}

        {now deal with end-of-line character}
        readln(Old);   {read eoln & go to next line}
        writeln(New); {advance to next line in output}
      end;      {while not eof}
  end;        {procedure FileCopy}

begin
  writeln('Starting');
  reset(Times);
  rewrite(Temp);
  while not eof(Times) do
    ProcessNextTime(Times, Temp);
  reset(Temp);
  rewrite(Times);
  FileCopy(Temp, Times);
  writeln('Done');
end.
```

If *Times* originally contains
09:30
14:00
22:00
11:59

then after execution of program *TimeConverter*, *Times* contains

```
 9:30 A.M.
 2:00 P.M.
10:00 P.M.
11:59 A.M.
```

11.1.3 *Issues in Using Text Files*

We'll add three final thoughts about text files. First, text files can be created (or modified) by a system editor or by a Pascal program. Allowing the user to create or modify the data file for a program with an editor opens the door for a file that is not in the correct format. Having a program control the process of building or modifying the file enforces the file format (although it still does not prevent all typing errors). An applications program may therefore consist of two parts, building (or modifying) the data file and running the application on the resulting file.

Second, reading numeric data from text files can be tricky. If the file is formatted with one numeric value per line, then

```
while not eof(filename) do
  begin
    readln(filename, Number);
    - - -
  end;
```

will work, just as in program *ReadAFile* earlier. (If your program controls creation of the text file, you may wish to enforce the one-value-per-line format.) Suppose, however, that the file is formatted with more than one numeric value per line. Then we can't use *readln* because we will miss successive values on a line. Consider

```
while not eof(filename) do
  begin
    read(filename, Number);
    - - -
  end;
```

After reading the last numeric value in the file, the read "pointer" is positioned just after that value. An end-of-line character is still ahead, so the end-of-file marker is not seen, and the loop will be executed again. The *read* statement will read and ignore the end-of-line character and attempt to read the end-of-file marker on its search for more numeric data. An error results. Perhaps the code in Checkup 11.2 will solve the problem.

CHECKUP 11.2   Will the following code correctly read numeric values from a text file?

```
while not eof(filename) do
  begin
    while not eoln(filename) do
```

Continued

CHECKUP 11.2   Continued

```
        begin
          read(filename, Number);
          - - -
        end;

      {now deal with end-of-line character}
      readln(filename);
    end;
```

(Hint: What if there are blanks in the last line of the file after the last numeric value?)

Although some Pascal implementations provide a measure of protection in these situations, the safest technique is to shift after

```
read(filename, Number);
```

to a character-by-character mode, examining and discarding blank characters until the next numeric value (or the end-of-file marker) is found. Later in this chapter we'll see how use of a "file window" can be helpful here.

Watch out for blanks and empty lines in text files; watch out for empty files of any type.

Third, as we've just seen in CHECKUP 11.2, blanks in text files must be accounted for. Blanks at the beginning or at the end of a line of text are just as much a part of the file as nonblank characters and must be properly read and disposed of. Because the end-of-line character can be read and written out just as if it were a blank, special care is needed to deal with the line-oriented structure of the file. Programs should be able to successfully handle empty lines and empty files. The *eoln* and *eof* functions are valuable safeguards.

11.2 Binary Files

File components must all have the same data type.

Text files contain characters (formatted into lines). However, files can have components of any single data type that does not itself involve type **file** (files of files are illegal, as are files of records with file fields, etc.). Nontext files require a type declaration. The statements

```
type
    IntFile = file of integer;
var
    Values : IntFile;
```

Binary files require a type declaration.

declare a file *Values* whose components are integers. Because this is not a text file, the values stored in *Values* are the internal binary representations of integers. Such a file is called a **binary file;** it is machine-readable but not "human-readable." It can only be created from within a program, not, in general, by using the system editor. Binary files still have an end-of-file marker that can be tested with the *eof* function, but there is no end-of-line character. The values are simply stored in one long stream. As a consequence, *readln*, *writeln*, and *eoln* cannot reference binary files, but *read*, *write*, and *eof* can still be used. As with text files, the first identifier in the variable list for a *read* or *write* statement must be the file name. Subsequent variables in a *read* statement, and variables or expressions in a *write* statement, must have the data type of the file component. Incidentally, enumerated-type variables can't be written to or read from text files because they have no character representation, but they can be written to or read from binary files with enumerated-type components.

Slight changes in our previous programs *WriteAFile* and *ReadAFile* will allow them to work for binary files. Therefore it is easy to display any binary file in a form that we can read, provided we know the format of the file components. This should alleviate our disquiet at having data stored in files that are only machine-readable.

CHECKUP 11.3   **a.** Rewrite program *WriteAFile* to create a binary file of integers with values entered at the keyboard.
b. Rewrite program *ReadAFile* to read a binary file of integers and display the integers (in human-readable form, of course) on the screen.

11.2.1 *Why Use Binary Files?*

Binary files can have real components, array components, etc. Files of records are especially useful, just as arrays of records are often useful data structures for internal storage. The *read* and *write* statements move entire file components, even if these components are structured data types. Suppose that the following declarations have been made:

```
type
    String = packed array [1..25] of char;
    IDTag = record
      Name, Make : String;
      Model : integer;
      end;   {IDTag}
    IDTagFile = file of IDTag;

var
    Products : IDTagFile;
    OneIDTag : IDTag;
```

and that records have been written into the *Products* file. The *read* statement

```
read(Products, OneIDTag);
```

retrieves a component of the file, which is a record. The fields of this record can then be accessed in the usual way. The statement

```
writeln(OneIDTag.Model);
```

writes to the screen the integer that is the model number in the particular record read.

A file of a structured data type thus preserves the structure of its components. We could store the information contained in a record of type *IDTag* in one line of a text file, but the three fields would be simply three data items in a line of characters. We would have to read and discard the two string fields, character by character, before we could read the model number. Some advantage seems to accrue, then, by using a binary file to store structured data types.

What about files of type *integer* or *real*? Why bother with binary files in those cases? For one thing, **file access time**—the time it takes to read values from or write values to the file—will be faster with a binary file because no conversion of the data between binary and character form is required. Binary representation also saves space over character representation and, in addition, no end-of-line characters need to be stored. Finally, real numbers stored as character data in a text file may lose some of their accuracy in the translation, and this problem is compounded if the same value is moved in and out of the file a number of times.

11.3 Sequential Access

Files, as we've noted, have the advantage of providing permanent storage. They also have the advantage of being essentially unbounded in size, subject only to the limits on secondary storage. These advantages come at a price, however. Pascal files are **sequential access** files, meaning that to access a single item in a file (even if we know it is, for example, the seventeenth item), all preceding items must be read (and ignored). To modify a single item in a file requires the following steps:

1. Copy all preceding items into a temporary file.
2. Read the item in question, change it, and write the changed item in the temporary file.
3. Copy the rest of the original file into the temporary file.
4. Copy the entire temporary file back into the original file.

For text files, a version of *FileCopy* can be used for step 1, but some test must be incorporated to stop copying at the specified item. *FileCopy* can be used directly for steps 3 and 4. Copying binary files is a bit simpler than *FileCopy* because there is no line structure to preserve.

Nevertheless, this process is much more work than, say, directly referencing the seventeenth item in an array and changing it (recall that arrays are random-access structures).[†]

[†]Some versions of Pascal do provide random access to files, but this is not standard. As usual, the convenience of such a feature must be weighed against the constraints it places on a program's portability.

CHECKUP 11.4   The following is an outline for processing the fifth item in a text file *oldfile* with items stored one per line. Insert the necessary *reset* and *rewrite* statements.

```
for i := 1 to 4 do
  begin
    readln(oldfile, item);
    writeln(tempfile, item);
  end;
readln(oldfile, item);
process item;
writeln(tempfile, item);
FileCopy(oldfile, tempfile);
FileCopy(tempfile, oldfile);
```

CHECKUP 11.5   Assume that *Old* and *New* have been declared to be files of real values. Write a procedure to copy binary file *Old* into binary file *New*.

11.4 File Windows

We have used regular variables declared within our programs as buffer variables to hold a file component after it is read from a file or before it is written to a file. Pascal provides built-in file buffers, called **file windows.** File windows are variables that automatically become available when files are declared and opened, and they must not be declared as separate program variables. The file window has the same data type as the file components.

The file window (filename) holds the next file component after the file "pointer."

A file window is denoted by giving the file identifier followed by an up-arrow (↑) or a caret (^), depending on the system. The file window contains the next component in the file after the "pointer." Files being written to and files being read from operate differently in this regard. If *Values* is a binary file of integers that has just been opened with

rewrite(Values);

then *Values* is an empty file, *Values*^ is undefined, and *eof(Values)* is true (see Fig. 11.3a). The statement

write(Values, 12);

serves to add a component to the end of the file and move the end-of-file marker and the file pointer farther along; *Values*^ is still undefined, and

File   File Window

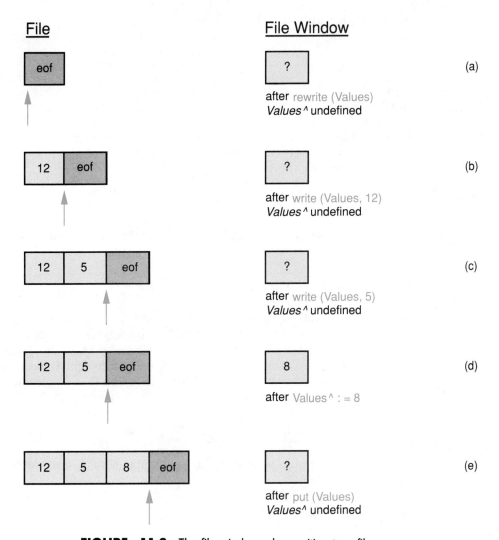

FIGURE 11.3 The file window when writing to a file.

eof(Values) is still true (Fig. 11.3b). *Values^* remains undefined through subsequent *write* statements (Fig. 11.3c).

The effect of the *write* statement is twofold—to append a component to the end of the file and then move the pointer. This can also be achieved by assigning the value of the component to the file window (the file window is, after all, a variable) and then using the Pascal procedure *put*. The *put* procedure has the syntax

put(filename);

Put appends the current content of the file window to the file and advances the file pointer. Therefore write(Values, 8);

and

Values^: = 8;
put(Values);

have identical effects (see Figs. 11.3d and 11.3e). Note that *Values^*, after the *put* statement, is again undefined.

If we now open the file *Values* for reading by the statement

reset(Values);

the file window contains the first component of the file (see Fig. 11.4a). The statement

read(Values, OneNumber);

has a twofold effect—the current content of the file window is assigned to *OneNumber*, and the pointer is advanced to the second component of the file, thereby changing the value of the file window (Fig. 11.4b). This can also be achieved by using an assignment statement to copy the content of the file window into *OneNumber*, and then using the Pascal procedure *get*. The *get* procedure has the syntax

An assignment to the file window followed by a put statement has the same effect as a write statement; an assignment from the file window followed by a get statement has the same effect as a read statement.

get(filename)

This advances the file pointer to the next component. Consequently, the effect of the statement

read(Values, OneNumber);

is duplicated by

OneNumber : = Values^;
get(Values);

(See Figs. 11.4c and 11.4d).

If a text file is being read, it is possible for the file window to contain the end-of-line character. This is what makes the *eoln* function true. The *eof* function is true, in either a text file or a binary file, whenever the file window has been moved beyond the last file component, i.e., when the file pointer occurs just before the end-of-file marker. The file window is undefined when *eof* is true, and the *get* procedure (like the *read* procedure) is not appropriate because it tries to move the pointer past the end-of-file marker.

Read and *write* statements seem easier to use than the two-step equivalents involving *get* and *put*. Indeed, the use of file windows and *get*

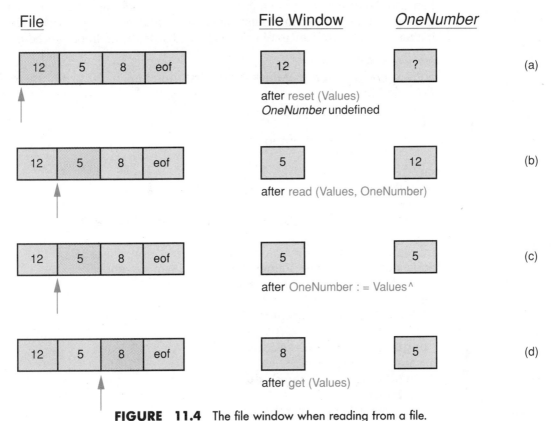

FIGURE 11.4 The file window when reading from a file.

and *put* is optional; there is never a case where their use is required.[†] However, use of the file window is convenient in one type of situation. Suppose we are reading from a file and want to pursue different courses of action, e.g., execute different procedures, based on the value of the next file component. (For example, we discussed earlier that when looking for successive numeric values in a text file, we want to proceed differently depending on whether the next character in the file is a blank or the start of the next numeric value.) The file window allows us to see the value of the next file component without advancing the file pointer past that component, as the *read* statement would. Based on the file window value, we can branch to the appropriate procedure and *then* read the file component. If we actually read the file component (with a *read* statement) in order to make the decision, we must then pass the value read to the appropriate procedure for its use, and the procedures are less logically self-contained. This defeats the modularity that procedures are intended to enforce.

As another example, suppose we want to scan the file of integers *Values* and add the numbers together beginning with the first value that is greater

---

†Some implementations of Pascal do not support *read* and *write* for nontext files and so *get* and *put* must be used. On the other hand, some versions of Pascal do not support *get* and *put*!

than 100. We want to invoke a procedure to do the adding. Using the *read* statement alone, we get the following version; note how we must pass the first term in the sum (since we've already read it) to the addition procedure.

```pascal
program Add1(Values, output);
{adds numbers in file Values from first number > 100; no use of
 file window}

type
    IntFile = file of integer;

var
    Values : IntFile;
    Number : integer;
    Flag : boolean;    {set to true if any numbers > 100}

procedure AddUp(var Values: IntFile; FirstTerm: integer);
{adds numbers in file Values from FirstTerm to end}

var
    Sum, Number : integer;

  begin      {procedure AddUp}
    Sum := FirstTerm;
    while not eof(Values) do
      begin
        read(Values, Number);
        Sum := Sum + Number;
      end;
    writeln('The sum of the numbers in file Values');
    writeln('from the first value greater than 100 to');
    writeln('the end of the file is ', Sum);
  end;      {procedure AddUp}

begin
  Flag := false;
  reset(Values);
  while not eof(Values) do
    begin
      read(Values, Number);
      if Number > 100 then
        begin
          AddUp(Values, Number);
          Flag := true;
        end;
    end;
  if not Flag then
    writeln('No values >  100 in file');
end.
```

Using the file window, we get the following version, where procedure *AddUp* does the entire reading-and-adding task.

```pascal
program Add2(Values, output);
{adds numbers in file Values from first number > 100; uses file
 window}

type
    IntFile = file of integer;

var
    Values : IntFile;
    Flag : boolean;    {set to true if any numbers > 100}


procedure AddUp(var Values: IntFile);
{adds numbers in file Values from current file pointer to  end}

var
    Sum, Number : integer;

  begin      {procedure AddUp}
    Sum := 0;
    while not eof(Values) do
      begin
        read(Values, Number);
        Sum := Sum + Number;
      end;
    writeln('The sum of the numbers in file Values');
    writeln('from the first value greater than 100 to');
    writeln('the end of the file is ', Sum);
  end;       {procedure AddUp}

begin
  Flag := false;
  reset(Values);
  while not eof(Values) do
    begin
      if Values^ > 100 then
        begin
          AddUp(Values);
          Flag := true;
        end
      else
        get(Values);
    end;
  if not Flag then
    writeln('No values >  100 in file');
end.
```

11.5 Sample Software Development Project— Student Data Base

Problem Statement

Write a program to maintain a simple student data base for the academic counselors at State University. Information on each student should include the student's name, student ID number, major, and courses in which the student is registered for the current semester. A counselor should be able to add or delete student records, view information for a particular student, and make changes in the information for a particular student.

Problem Specification

In the manual system of recordkeeping used up to now, counselors at State have marked student file folders with student names in the form last name, comma, first name, as in

Lopez, Janet

Student names should be stored in this format. When the counselor wants to access information for a particular student, either to view or modify the information, or to delete the student's record, only the name should be required. If there are no duplicate names, information on the only student with that name will be displayed; if there are duplicates, the program should then ask for the student ID number. This number is a Social Security number in the format

xxx-xx-xxxx

Of course, the counselor must supply all of the information when a student record is added to the data base. The program should issue a warning if the name and student ID duplicates a record already in the data base.

The student's major is given by a four-letter code for each academic department—PHYS for physics, ECON for economics, etc. Because the counselors at State are relatively forgetful, we'll add a feature that allows the counselor to type in a code and get the department name, or to type in the department name and get the corresponding code.

Classes are identified by the department code and a three-digit course number, as in PHYS 252. We'll assume a maximum of six courses per semester for a given student.

The program should display a menu of choices (Add, Delete, View, Modify) from which the counselor can select. The counselor should be able to call up the department/code correspondence help feature from the menu, and also at appropriate times when performing the subtasks. A "Stop" choice, used to stop the program, should also be part of the menu. Whenever the user wants to modify or delete a student record, the record should first be displayed before it is changed or erased. Then some sort of double-check with the user should be done before the changes to the record are made permanent, or before the record is deleted.

Algorithm and Data Structure Development

The term student "record" crept into our description of the problem. One record for each student is certainly a reasonable choice. What should be the fields of each record? For the student name, we'll use one field, a packed array of type *char*. We'll impose a length limit of 25 characters. The student ID number will be a packed array of *char* of length 11, and the major field will be a packed array of *char* of length 4.

Rather than use a separate field for each course the student is taking, let's use a little array (maximum 6 elements) of records, where the form of each record is the four-character department code followed by the three-digit integer. Figure 11.5 illustrates the form of a single student record.

Because we want to save the student data base in permanent storage, we will use a file of such records. Using a file has the added advantage that we do not have to impose an artificial limit on the number of student records. (We're talking here about a file of record-type components, so it is a binary file, not a text file.) In order to save space, we'll leave the declarations that reflect these data structure decisions for the actual program.

As far as the algorithm development is concerned, there are some obvious major subtasks that are part of the original problem statement,

Name	ID	Major	Classes	
			Department	Number
Lopez, Janet	287-24-1109	PSYC	ENGL	100
			PSYC	102
packed array of char of length 25	packed array of char of length 11	packed array of char of length 4	HIST	150
			MATH	180
			SOCI	121
			—	—

packed array of char of length 4   integer

array of 6 records with 2 fields

FIGURE   11.5 A single student record in program *Students.*

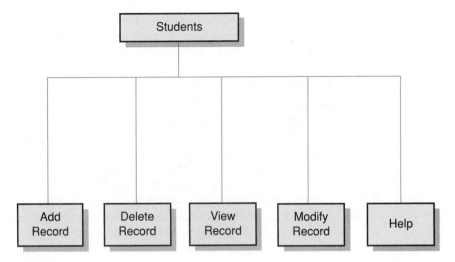

FIGURE 11.6 Structure chart for program *Students*.

namely, adding, deleting, viewing, or modifying student records. In addition, we have decided to add a "Help" feature for departments and their codes. Figure 11.6 shows the first breakdown of the problem. One might think that creating the initial external file should be a separate task, but this can be done by repeatedly adding records, beginning with an empty file; actually, there is a slight problem with this approach, as we will see presently.

Because we are adding, deleting, or modifying elements in a file, a file copy procedure similar to that written for CHECKUP 11.5 will be necessary. Then there are the tasks of managing the menu and collecting the user's choices. We envision this as a screen-oriented program, where the program occasionally clears the screen and presents new output in a nice display, uncluttered by old material. Therefore, we need a procedure to clear the screen. Figure 11.7 adds the new subtasks.

Just to be different, let's start with a discussion of the main program.

Main program
The main program must repeatedly display a menu, collect the user's choice, and invoke the appropriate procedure until the user selects the STOP option. The structure of the main program is very simple, as it should be:

        clear screen & display menu
        collect valid user's response & clear screen
     while response **not** STOP
        begin
           invoke *Add, Delete, View, Modify,* **or** *Help*
           clear screen & display menu
           collect valid user's response & clear screen
        end

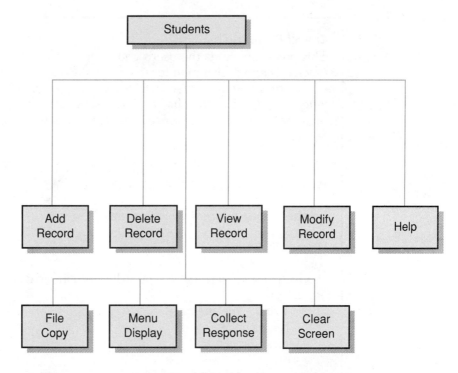

FIGURE   11.7   Refined structure chart for program *Students*.

Now let's look at the subtasks.

Clear Screen

This procedure clears the screen by writing twenty-four blank lines. *ClearScreen* will be invoked by other procedures as appropriate. It is a parameterless procedure because it neither needs information from nor will it return information to the procedure that invokes it.

Menu Display

This procedure invokes *ClearScreen* and then writes the menu of user choices. These choices are Add, Delete, View, Modify, Help, Stop. The display for the menu should give some brief explanation of each of the choices. *MenuDisplay* is also a parameterless procedure. Writing this procedure is a matter of designing a nice screen display, and it may take a little trial and error to produce an attractive arrangement. The details of a truly sophisticated screen-management program that allows us to clear the screen, write the menu, and reposition the cursor somewhere in the middle of the menu are highly system-dependent, and we won't go that far here. As a result, the cursor must always remain at the end of the most recent screen output, typically at the bottom of the screen.

Collect Response

This procedure reads the user's choice of action and then invokes *ClearScreen* in preparation for that action. Because the user choices start with different letters, we can use a single character—the first letter—to represent the choice. This character is returned to the main program. A check is made that the user's response is legitimate.

```
procedure CollectResponse (var Choice: char);
{collects the user's choice of action}

begin    {procedure CollectResponse}

   read choice
   clear screen
   while choice not in set of valid responses do
     begin
        write error message
        read choice
        clear screen
     end

end;    {procedure CollectResponse}
```

Help

The user must be able to request help in translating between department names and four-letter department codes. A table for this translation should be available to the program, something like
Psychology PSYC
Mathematics MATH
Computer Science CSCI
   etc.
The information in this table is not apt to change frequently, and we do not want to recreate it every time we run the data base program. We'll assume that it is available as a permanent file *Table* of two-field records, the first field containing the department name (a string of *MaxDeptName* characters) and the second field containing the code. (The file was created by another program.)

   The *Help* procedure must process the user's request for help in using the table. The request can be issued while the user is at the menu or from within the *Add* or *Modify* procedures.

   When the user invokes the help option, the choice of action is either to encode a department name or to decode a department

Continued

Help—Continued

abbreviation. The desired help is written to the user, not passed back to the invoking program, so the only parameter is the file *Table,* passed as a variable parameter.

procedure Help(**var** Table: CodeFile);
{reads department 4-character code, outputs department name; reads department name, outputs corresponding 4-character code; this information stored as two-field records in already existing binary file Table}

begin   {procedure Help}

  prompt for and read valid user request

  if the user wants to find the code corresponding to a name, collect the name, search the file for the name (field 1) and output the corresponding code (field 2); give error message if no such name; handle all this in an *Encode* procedure

  if the user wants to find the name corresponding to a code, collect the code, search the file for the code (field 2), and output the corresponding name (field 1); give error message if no such code; handle all this in a *Decode* procedure

end;   {procedure Help}

Add Record

The *Add* procedure allows the user to add a student record to the file. The file will be passed as a variable parameter to the procedure. The general outline of the file handling is to open the existing, permanent file for reading, open a temporary file for writing, and copy the old file into the temporary file. At the end of the copy, the write "pointer" in the temporary file is at the end of the file, and the new record can be added. Then after appropriate statements to reopen the files, the temporary file, containing the new record, is copied back into the permanent file.

  We noted above that there is a slight problem with creating the initial student record file using the *Add* procedure. It is the following. Suppose this is the first time the program is being run, and we want to enter the first record. The student record file (*DataBase*) is declared in the program but does not really exist until a call of *rewrite* creates an empty file ready to be written to.

Continued

Add Record—Continued

Therefore, when the first record to go into the *DataBase* file is being created, the program must first *rewrite* the file. Now suppose that *DataBase* exists, and a record is being added to the file. Here we must avoid the *rewrite* statement because that will destroy the existing file! We will solve this problem by asking the user whether this is the first record to be added to the file; as a safeguard, we'll double-check, warning the user of the consequences of a wrong answer.

The user should be prompted for the data to build the new student record, *NewRecord,* which consists of the name, student ID, major code, and list of classes for the semester. Because the name, ID, major, and classes will have to be collected from the user for other applications as well, we will make procedures for these tasks global. These procedures will be invoked from procedure *Add* with the variable parameter *NewRecord*; each procedure will contribute one of the fields to *NewRecord.*

Once the name field and ID field have been entered, a check should be made for duplicate records; this will require reading the entries in the file. Because we don't want to have to read the file twice, the name and ID data should be collected before the file manipulations are done. Then the permanent file can be read into the temporary file and checked for duplicates at the same time. If a duplicate is found, the *Add* process is terminated (with no change having been made in the permanent file). If there is no duplication, then the remaining fields of *NewRecord* can be collected and the file processing completed.

```
procedure Add (var DataBase: FileType;
                var Table:  CodeTable);
{allows user to add a student record to file DataBase; Table
 needed only if the Help procedure is invoked}

begin    {procedure Add}

   if first record, rewrite the file
   collect student's name
   collect student's ID
   check for duplicate record
   if duplicate then
      quit
   else
      collect student's major
      collect student's classes
      complete file manipulation

end;     {procedure Add}
```

Get Name

The student name is stored as a packed array but must be read in one character at a time. The name field should be initialized to blanks before reading the name, and the user should be warned if the name length is exceeded.

Get ID

The student ID field is also a packed array of characters. Error checking should occur on the student ID field to see that the data entered conforms to a Social Security number format, i.e., that it has digits and dashes in the right places. The user should be able to re-enter the ID until it is in the proper form.

Check Duplicate

This procedure begins the file copying, checking for duplicate name and ID fields. It will be local to procedure *Add*. As parameters, it needs the *DataBase* file and the temporary file, local to procedure *Add*, that is used for the file copying. It also needs *NewRecord*, which at this point contains pertinent information only in the name and ID fields. The procedure returns a boolean flag to signal duplication. If duplication occurs, the file copying is terminated and the procedure is exited. If there is no duplication, the file copying is completed, so that when the procedure is exited the write "pointer" for the temporary file is at the end of the file, ready to receive the new record.

```
procedure CheckDuplicate(var DataBase, TempFile:  FileType;
                         NewRecord: Student;
                         var Duplicate:  boolean)
{begins copy of DataBase into TempFile, setting flag Duplicate
 and terminating copy if Name/ID of NewRecord already in
 DataBase}

var
    OldRecord : Student;     {record already in file}

begin     {procedure CheckDuplicate}

  reset(DataBase);
  rewrite(TempFile);
  Duplicate: =  false;
```

Continued

Check Duplicate—Continued

while (not Duplicate) **and   (not** eof(DataBase)) **do**

  read *OldRecord* from *DataBase*
  compare *Name* **and** *ID* fields of *OldRecord* and *NewRecord*
  set *Duplicate,* if duplication
  write *OldRecord* to *TempFile*

end;   {procedure CheckDuplicate}

Get Major
This procedure collects the four-letter code for the student's major
and enters it in the proper field of *NewRecord*. The counselor may
want to use the Help option in order to determine the correct code
for the major department, so the table of department names and
corresponding codes must be passed as a parameter.

procedure GetMajor (**var** NewRecord: Student;
                var Table: CodeTable);
{fills Major field in NewRecord; Help option should be
 available here, hence Table parameter}

Get Classes
This procedure fills the array of classes for the current semester.
The Help option should be available here as well.

procedure GetClasses(**var** NewRecord: Student;
                var Table: CodeTable);
{fills classes array in NewRecord; Help option should be
 available here, hence Table parameter}

begin   {procedure GetClasses}

  initialize *Classes* array in *NewRecord* with blanks
  prompt and collect response for number of classes—validate
that response is in range
  read the correct number of department codes (allow Help
option) and class numbers

end;   {procedure GetClasses}

A structure chart for the major subtask *Add* would look like Figure 11.8. Similar structure charts can also be drawn for the other major subtasks of *View, Delete,* and *Modify.*

View Record

Procedure *View* allows the user to select a record to be displayed. The user enters the student's name. If there is a unique record in the file with that name, it is displayed. If more than one record in the file has that name, the user is asked for the student ID in order to identify the correct record. If there is no such record in the file, a message to that effect is displayed.

View will be used as a subtask by *Delete* and *Modify.* These applications will require that *View* return a boolean flag indicating whether the requested record exists in the file, and a copy of that record if it exists. This affects *View*'s parameter list; without *Delete* and *Modify,* the parameters *RecordExists* and *ViewRecord* would not be required. Because the *View* procedure has some interesting nested control structures, we'll write the pseudocode version in some detail.

```
procedure View (var DataBase: FileType;
                var ViewRecord: Student;
                var RecordExists: boolean);
{collects student name; if duplicate records exist with this
 name, collects ID to identify record; displays record
 (ViewRecord) or gives message that record does not exist;
 returns  displayed record and boolean flag}
```

Continued

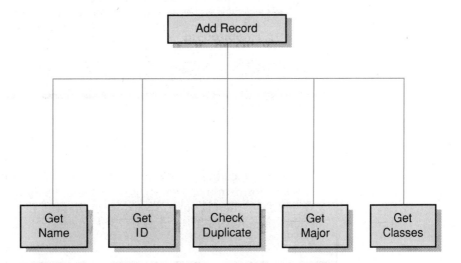

FIGURE   11.8   Structure chart for the *Add* subtask of program *Students.*

View Record—Continued

var
    FindRecord : Student;   {holds name and ID of record
                                    to be displayed}
    OldRecord : Student;   {record read from file, compared
                                    against FindRecord}
    Match : boolean;   {flag to indicate match with
                                    FindRecord}

begin   {procedure View}

  RecordExists : = false;
  GetName(FindRecord);
  reset(DataBase);
  Match : = false;

  while no match **and not** eof **do**
      read *OldRecord* from *DataBase*
      compare name fields of *OldRecord* and *FindRecord*

  if match **then**
      copy matching record into *ViewRecord*
      reset match flag
      while no match **and not** eof **do**
        read *OldRecord* from file
        compare name fields of *OldRecord* and *FindRecord*
      if match **then**
        write message
        GetID(FindRecord);
        compare against *ViewRecord,* current record,
and succeeding records **until** a match occurs **or** eof
        if match **then**
           copy into *ViewRecord* and display
         else (eof) write message - no such record
       else (eof - no duplicates) display *ViewRecord*
     else (eof) write message - no such record

  end;   {procedure View}

Delete Record
The *Delete* procedure begins by invoking the *View* procedure. This
collects information to identify a record and displays that record if it
exists. *Delete* then checks to make sure that the user indeed wants
to delete the record. If so, a *KillRecord* procedure is invoked.

Continued

Delete Record—Continued

KillRecord copies the *DataBase* file into a temporary file until the target record is read. This record is not copied, but the remaining records in *DataBase* are copied. Finally, the temporary file (without the target record) is read back into *DataBase*.

Modify Record

The *Modify* procedure also invokes the *View* procedure as its initial action. Once the record is identified and displayed, the user is led through a series of questions about modifications, one for each field of the record. If the user chooses to modify a field, the appropriate subtask (*GetName, GetID,* etc.) can be used to collect the new information for that field. If either the name or the ID is changed, the modified record might duplicate an existing record in the data base; this is checked and the *Modify* procedure terminated if such is the case.

Once the modified record has been created (making sure it does not duplicate an existing record), it is displayed and the user is asked if this is indeed to replace the original record. If so, the necessary file modifications are carried out.

```
program Students (input, output, DataBase, Table);
{maintains a student data base with each student's name, ID,
major, and classes for current semester; records can be viewed,
added, deleted, or modified}

const
    MaxName = 25;          {maximum length of student name}
    MaxCourses = 6;        {maximum number of current
                            courses}
    MaxDeptName = 30;      {maximum dept. name length}

type

{declare the data structure for the file of student records}
    NameString = packed array [1..MaxName] of char;
    SSNumber = packed array [1..11] of char;
    CodeString = packed array [1..4] of char;

    Course = record
      Department : CodeString;
      Number : integer;
      end;      {Course}
```

```
        Semester = array [1..MaxCourses] of Course;
        Student = record
          Name : NameString;      {student name, last name first}
          ID : SSNumber;          {student ID - Social Security
                                     number}
          Major : CodeString;     {student's major department}
          Classes : Semester;     {current classes - dept. code and
                                     course number}
          end;      {Student}

        FileType = file of Student;

{now declare the data structure for the translation table file}
        String = packed array [1..MaxDeptName] of char;
        Translation = record
          Name : String;
          Code : CodeString;
          end;    {Translation}
        CodeTable = file of Translation;

var
        DataBase : FileType;      {binary file of student records}
        Action : Char;            {activity to be carried out for user}
        Table : CodeTable;        {existing binary file of dept.
                                     name/code correspondence}
        ViewRecord : Student;     {record selected by user}
        Exists : boolean;         {identifies whether ViewRecord exists
                                     in DataBase}

procedure ClearScreen;
{clears the screen by writing 24 blank lines}

var
    i : integer;

    begin    {procedure ClearScreen}
    for i := 1 to 24 do
      writeln;
    end;      {procedure ClearScreen}

procedure MenuDisplay;
{displays the menu of actions from which the user can choose}

    begin    {procedure MenuDisplay}
    ClearScreen;

    {now "paint" the screen with the menu of choices}
    writeln;
    writeln('                         State University');
```

```
    writeln('                              Student Data Base');
    writeln;
    write('                  You may choose one of these four');
    writeln(' tasks:');
    writeln;    writeln;
    writeln('          Add (A)        Add a new student record');
    writeln;
    writeln('          Delete (D)     Delete a student record');
    writeln;
    writeln('          View (V)       View a student record');
    writeln;
    writeln('          Modify (M)     Modify (change) a student record';)
    writeln;
    write    ('          Help   (H)     Dept. name/Dept. code ');
    writeln('translation');
    writeln;
    writeln('          Stop (S)       Stop the program');
    writeln;
    write('          Enter your choice (A, D, V, M, H, or S):  ');
  end;    {procedure MenuDisplay}

procedure CollectResponse (var Choice: char);
{collects the user's choice of action}

type
    ResponseType = set of char;

var
    Valid : ResponseType;

  begin    {procedure CollectResponse}
    Valid := ['A','D','V','M','H','S','a','d','v','m','h','s'];
    readln(Choice);
    ClearScreen;
    while not (Choice in Valid) do
      begin
        writeln('Your choices are:');
        writeln;
        writeln('     A:   Add a record');
        writeln;
        writeln('     D:   Delete a record');
        writeln;
        writeln('     V:   View a record');
        writeln;
        writeln('     M:   Modify a record');
        writeln;
        writeln('     H:   Dept. name/Dept. code');
        writeln;
        writeln('     S:   Stop the program');
```

```
            writeln;
            write('Enter your choice (A, D, V, M, H, or S): ');
            readln(Choice);
            ClearScreen;
          end;
      end;    {procedure CollectResponse}

procedure Help(var Table: CodeTable);
{reads department 4-character code, outputs department name;
 reads department name, outputs corresponding 4-character code;
 this information stored as two-field records in already existing
 binary file Table}

var

    Task : char;        {user's choice of action to encode or
                          decode}

procedure Encode(var Table: CodeTable);
{collects department name, outputs corresponding code}

var
    Key : String;              {department name user gives}
    i : integer;               {array index}
    OneLine : Translation;     {one record in file Table}
    Found : boolean;           {flag to indicate whether name
                                found}

  begin    {procedure Encode}
    {blank out the name array before reading in}
    for i := 1 to MaxDeptName do
      Key[i] := ' ';

    {read in user department name}
    writeln;
    writeln('Give the name of the department');
    writeln;
    i := 0;
    while (i < MaxDeptName) and (not eoln) do
      begin
        i := i + 1;
        read(Key[i]);
      end;
    if (i = MaxDeptName) and (not eoln) then
      begin    {name too long}
        writeln;
        write('Name too long, only first ', MaxDeptName:2);
        writeln(' characters used');
      end;    {name too long}
    readln;
```

```
{now search file Table for match with Key}
reset(Table);
Found := false;
while (not eof(Table)) and (not Found) do
  begin    {search file for name}
    read(Table, OneLine);
    if OneLine.Name = Key then
      begin    {name found}
        writeln;
        write('The code for department ');
        writeln(Key, ' is');
        writeln;
        writeln('                  ', OneLine.Code);
        Found := true;
      end;    {name found}
  end;    {search file for name}

if not Found then
  begin    {error message}
    writeln;
    writeln('This department name not in file. ');
    writeln;
    write('To learn how to add to the file, see');
   •writeln(' your user' 's manual, page 13.');
    write('If you just made a typographical error, ');
    writeln('select the help option again.');
  end;    {error message}

writeln;
writeln('Hit RETURN to continue');
readln;
end;    {procedure Encode}


procedure Decode(var Table: CodeTable);
{collects department code, outputs corresponding name}

var
  Key : CodeString;        {department code user gives}
  OneLine : Translation;   {one record in file Table}
  Found : boolean;         {flag to indicate whether code
                            found}


procedure GetCode(var Key: CodeString);
{collects Key, a 4-character dept. code}

var
  CodeOK : boolean;    {flag to indicate 4-char. code  read}
  i : integer;         {array index}
```

```
begin    {procedure GetCode}
  CodeOK := false;
  while not CodeOK do
    begin     {while not CodeOK}
      i := 0;
      while (i < 4) and (not eoln) do
        begin
          i := i + 1;
          read(key[i]);
          CodeOK := true;
        end;
      if (i = 4) and (not eoln) then
        begin    {code too long}
          write('Code too long, only first 4');
          writeln(' characters used');
        end;    {code too long}
      if i < 4 then
        begin
          writeln('Codes must be 4 characters,');
          writeln('enter code again');
          CodeOK := false;    {make loop execute again}
        end;
      readln;
    end;    {end while, code is OK}
end;    {procedure GetCode}


begin    {procedure Decode}

  {read in user department code}
  writeln;
  writeln('Give the code for the department');
  writeln;
  GetCode(Key);

  {now search file Table for match with Key}
  reset(Table);
  found := false;
  while (not eof(Table)) and (not found) do
    begin    {search file for code}
      read(Table, OneLine);
      if OneLine.Code = Key then
        begin    {code found}
          writeln;
          write('The name for the department with');
          writeln(' code ', Key, ' is');
          writeln;
          writeln('              ', OneLine.Name);
          found := true;
```

```
        end;      {code found}
      end;     {search file for code}

  if not found then
    begin     {error message}
      writeln;
      writeln('This code not in file. ');
      writeln;
      write('To learn how to add to the file, see');
      writeln(' your user' 's manual, page 13.');
      write('If you just made a typographical error, ');
      writeln('select the help option again.');
    end;     {error message}

  writeln;
  writeln('Hit RETURN to continue');
  readln;
end;    {procedure Decode}


begin    {procedure Help}
  writeln('Which do you want to do?');
  writeln;
  writeln('Encode - find the code for a department');
  writeln('Decode - find the department for a code');
  writeln;
  write('Enter E (Encode) or D (Decode): ');
  readln(Task);
  while not (Task in ['E','e','D','d']) do
    begin
      write('Enter E (Encode) or D (Decode): ');
      readln(Task);
    end;
  {valid user response obtained, now process request}

  case Task of
    'E','e' : Encode(Table);
    'D','d': Decode(Table);
  end;    {case statement}
end;    {procedure Help}


procedure FileCopy(var Old, New: FileType);
{copies contents of opened file Old into opened file New}

var
    Item : Student;      {file component}

  begin    {FileCopy}
```

```
      while not eof(Old) do
        begin
          read(Old, Item);
          write(New, Item);
        end;
    end;     {FileCopy}

procedure GetName(var KeyRecord: Student);
{collects student name from user to build KeyRecord}

var
    i : integer;                {array index}
    NextChar : char;            {next character to be read}

  begin     {procedure GetName}

    {initialize name field to blanks}
    for i := 1 to MaxName do
      begin
        KeyRecord.Name[i] := ' ';
      end;

    {collect student's name in form Last, First}
    writeln;
    writeln('Give student' 's name in form ''Last, First''  :');
    i := 0;
    repeat
      i := i + 1;
      read(KeyRecord.Name[i]);
    until (i = MaxName) or eoln;
    if (i = MaxName) and (not eoln) then
      begin     {name exceeds MaxName}
        write('Name length exceeded, only first ');
        writeln(Maxname:2, ' characters used');
      end;     {end if}
    readln;
  end;     {procedure GetName}

procedure GetID(var KeyRecord: Student);
{collects student ID from user to build KeyRecord; verifies form
 of ID using function Valid}

var
    i : integer;                {array index}

function Valid (SS: SSNumber): boolean;
{checks string SS for valid form of Social Security number}

type
    DigitType = set of char;
```

```
var
    i : integer;                    {array index}
    digit : DigitType;             {legitimate digit characters}


  begin    {function Valid}
    digit := ['0'..'9'];    {fix legitimate digit characters}
    Valid := true;
    for i := 1 to 3 do
      begin
    .   if not (SS[i] in digit) then Valid := false;
      end;
    for i := 5 to 6 do
      begin
        if not (SS[i] in digit)  then Valid := false;
      end;
    for i := 8 to 11 do
      begin
        if not (SS[i] in digit) then Valid := false;
      end;
    if (SS[4] <> '-') or (SS[7]  <> '-') then
      Valid := false;
  end;      {function Valid}



  begin    {procedure GetID}
    writeln;
    write('Enter student ID number: ');
    for i := 1 to 11 do
      begin
        read(KeyRecord.ID[i]);
      end;
    readln;

    while not Valid(KeyRecord.ID) do
      begin    {re-enter until valid ID}
        writeln;
        writeln('Student ID not in proper form.');
        write('Please check and enter again: ');
        for i := 1 to 11 do
          begin
            read(KeyRecord.ID[i]);
          end;
        readln;
      end;       {valid ID obtained, exit procedure}
  end;      {procedure GetID}



procedure Quit;
{record to be added or modified duplicates Name/ID already in
 DataBase, terminate Add or Modify process}
```

```
begin    {procedure Quit}
  writeln;
  write('Record for this name/ID already in ');
  writeln('database.    Add or Modify process terminated.');
  writeln('Hit RETURN to continue');
  readln;
end;    {procedure Quit}

procedure GetMajor(var NewRecord: Student;
                   var Table:  CodeTable);
{fills major field in NewRecord; Help option should be available
 here, hence Table parameter}

var
  i : integer;              {array index}
  NextChar : char;          {next character to read}

begin    {procedure GetMajor}
  writeln;
  write('Enter 4-letter code for student' 's ');
  writeln('major or "H" for code help: ');
  read(NextChar);
  if ((NextChar = 'H') or (NextChar = 'h')) and eoln then
    begin    {invoke Help}
      readln;
      ClearScreen;
      Help(Table);
      ClearScreen;
      write('Enter 4-letter code for student' 's major: ');
      read(NextChar);
    end;    {Help done}

  {NextChar now first one in major code}
  NewRecord.Major[1] := NextChar;
  for i := 2 to 4 do
    begin
      read(NewRecord.Major[i]);
    end;
  readln;
end;    {procedure GetMajor}

procedure GetClasses(var NewRecord: Student;
                     var Table:  CodeTable);
{fills classes array in NewRecord; Help option should be
 available here, hence Table parameter}

var
  i, j : integer;           {array indices}
  NextChar : char;          {next character to read}
  n: integer;               {number of classes this semester}
```

```
begin    {procedure GetClasses}
  {initialize classes array}
  for i := 1 to MaxCourses do
    begin
      with NewRecord.Classes[i] do Department := '    ';
    end;

  {find the number of classes}
  writeln;
  write('Enter number of classes for this semester ');
  write('(maximum ', MaxCourses:1,'):');
  readln(n);
  while not ((1 <= n) and (n <=  MaxCourses)) do
    begin    {error in number of classes}
      write('Number of classes must be between 1 and ');
      writeln(MaxCourses:1, ' please enter again: ');
      readln(n);
    end;     {n is now in right range}

  {read data for classes array}
  writeln;
  write('Enter student' 's classes for this ');
  writeln('semester; use form "DEPT XXX" ');
  writeln('Type H for dept. code help');
  for i := 1 to n do
    begin    {collect classes}
      write('Class ', i:2, ':');
      read(NextChar);
      if ((NextChar = 'H') or (NextChar =  'h'))
          and eoln then
        begin    {invoke Help}
          readln;
          ClearScreen;
          Help(Table);
          ClearScreen;
          write('Enter class ', i:2, ';');
          write(' use form "DEPT XXX" : ');
          read(NextChar);
        end;     {Help done}

      {NextChar now first char in class i}
      NewRecord.Classes[i].Department[1] :=  NextChar;
      for j := 2 to 4 do
        read(NewRecord.Classes[i].Department[j]);
      read(NextChar);    {separating blank}
      readln(NewRecord.Classes[i].Number)
    end;       {collect classes}
end;     {procedure GetClasses}
```

```
procedure Add (var DataBase: FileType; var Table:  CodeTable);
{allows user to add a student record to file DataBase; Table
 needed only if the Help procedure is invoked}

var
    TempFile : FileType;        {temporary file to allow file
                                 modification}
    NewRecord : Student;        {new record to be added to file}
    Duplicate   : boolean;      {flag for duplicate name/ID
                                 between new record to be added
                                 and some existing record}
    FirstTime : char;           {user response to query if this is
                                 very first record in DataBase}

procedure CheckDuplicate(var DataBase, TempFile:  FileType;
                             NewRecord: Student;
                         var Duplicate: boolean);
{begins copy of DataBase into TempFile, setting flag Duplicate
 and terminating copy if Name/ID of NewRecord already in
 DataBase}

var
    OldRecord : Student;        {record already in file}

  begin     {procedure CheckDuplicate}
    reset(DataBase);
    rewrite(TempFile);
    Duplicate := false;
    while (not Duplicate) and (not eof(DataBase)) do
      begin
        read (DataBase, OldRecord);
        if (OldRecord.Name = NewRecord.Name) and
           (OldRecord.ID = NewRecord.ID) then
          begin
            Duplicate := true;
          end;
        write(TempFile, OldRecord);
      end;
  end;     {procedure CheckDuplicate}


  begin     {procedure Add}

    {handle details of creating DataBase to receive first  record}

    writeln('Are you adding the very first record to ');
    write('build file DataBase? (Y or N): ');
    readln(FirstTime);
    if (FirstTime = 'Y') or (FirstTime =  'y') then
```

```
begin
  writeln;
  write('Are you sure? A Y here will destroy ');
  writeln('the DataBase file if it already exists.');
  write('If you only want to add a record to the ');
  writeln('existing file DataBase, type N');
  writeln('Are you adding the very first record to ');
  write('build file DataBase? (Y or N): ');
  readln(FirstTime);
  if (FirstTime = 'Y') or (FirstTime = 'y') then
    rewrite(DataBase);    {DataBase now empty file}
end;

{build NewRecord to add}
GetName(NewRecord);
GetID(NewRecord);
rewrite(TempFile);
CheckDuplicate(DataBase, TempFile, NewRecord, Duplicate);
if Duplicate then
  Quit
else   {collect rest of NewRecord and complete  file
        processing}
  begin    {good record}
    GetMajor(NewRecord, Table);
    GetClasses(NewRecord, Table);

    {NewRecord complete, add it to TempFile, then copy
     TempFile back into DataBase}

    write(TempFile, NewRecord);
    reset(TempFile);
    rewrite(DataBase);
    FileCopy(TempFile, DataBase);
  end;     {good record}
end;     {procedure Add}


procedure Display(var KeyRecord: Student);
{displays a student record on the screen}

var
  i : integer;     {array index}

begin     {procedure Display}
  with KeyRecord do
    begin
      writeln;
      writeln(Name);
      writeln(ID);
```

```
writeln;
writeln('Major: ', Major);
writeln;
writeln('Classes this semester:');
i := 1;
while Classes[i].Department <> '     ' do
  begin
    write(Classes[i].Department, ' ');
    writeln(Classes[i].Number:3);
    i := i + 1;
  end;
writeln;
writeln('Hit RETURN to continue');
readln;
    end;
end;     {procedure Display}


procedure View (var DataBase: FileType;
                var ViewRecord: Student;
                var RecordExists: boolean);
```

{collects student name; if duplicate records exist with this
name, collects ID to identify record; displays record
(ViewRecord) or gives message that record does not exist; returns
displayed record and boolean flag}

```
var
    FindRecord : Student;        {holds name and ID of record to
                                   be displayed}
    OldRecord  : Student;        {record read from file,
                                   compared against FindRecord}
    Match : boolean;             {flag to indicate match with
                                   FindRecord}


begin     {procedure View}

    {get name field of record to view}
    RecordExists := false;
    writeln('Describe record.');
    writeln;
    GetName(FindRecord);
    reset(DataBase);
    Match := false;
    while (not Match) and (not eof(DataBase)) do
      begin
        read(DataBase, OldRecord);
        if OldRecord.Name = FindRecord.Name then
          begin
            Match := true;
          end;
      end;
```

```
if Match then
  begin    {initial match}
    {store the match in ViewRecord and look for other
     records with duplicate name}

    ViewRecord := OldRecord;
    Match := false;
    while (not Match) and (not eof(DataBase)) do
      begin
        read(DataBase, OldRecord);
        if OldRecord.Name = FindRecord.Name then
          begin
            Match := true;
          end;
      end;

  if Match then
    begin    {duplicate name found, collect ID}
      writeln;
      write('More than one record with ');
      writeln('this name exists.');
      GetID(FindRecord);

      Match := false;
      {now look for record with this name and ID; current
       ViewRecord and OldRecord have the right name}

      if ViewRecord.ID = FindRecord.ID then
        begin
          Match := true;
        end;
      if OldRecord.ID = FindRecord.ID then
        begin
          Match := true;
          ViewRecord := OldRecord;
        end;
      while (not Match) and (not eof(DataBase)) do
        begin
          read(DataBase, OldRecord);
          if (OldRecord.name = FindRecord.Name) and
             (OldRecord.ID = FindRecord.ID) then
            begin
              match := true;
              ViewRecord := OldRecord;
            end;
        end;    {while}

      if Match then
        begin    {ViewRecord holds the right stuff}
```

```
                        Display(ViewRecord);
                        RecordExists := true;
                      end
                  else {eof - no such record}
                    begin
                      writeln;
                      writeln('No such record in DataBase');
                      writeln('Hit RETURN to continue');
                      readln;
                    end;
                end    {duplicate name found}

            else {eof - no duplicates}
              begin
                Display(ViewRecord);
                RecordExists := true;
              end;
          end    {initial match}

      else {eof - no initial match}
        begin
          writeln;
          writeln('No such record in DataBase');
          writeln('Hit RETURN to continue');
          readln;
        end;

end;    {Procedure View}

procedure Delete(var DataBase: FileType);
{collects information on a record to be deleted; displays the
record and double-checks for deletion; if user still wants to
delete, returns DataBase with this record deleted}

var
    KeyRecord : Student;      {record to delete}
    Response : char;          {checks user's intention to delete
                               this record}
    Exists : boolean;         {flag to see if record exists}

procedure KillRecord(var DataBase: FileType; Target: Student);
{deletes record Target from DataBase - we know DataBase
 contains Target}

var
    TempFile : FileType;      {temporary file to allow file
                               modification}
    Buffer : Student;         {holds record read from file}
```

begin {procedure KillRecord}

{find Target record}
reset(DataBase);
rewrite(TempFile);
read(DataBase, Buffer);
while (Buffer.Name <> Target.Name) **or**
        (Buffer.ID <> Target.ID) **do**
  begin {haven't found Target record yet}
    write(TempFile, Buffer);
    read(DataBase, Buffer);
  end;

{Buffer = Target, do not read Buffer into TempFile, but
 continue FileCopy from this point on, then copy TempFile
 back into DataBase}
FileCopy(DataBase, TempFile);
reset(TempFile);
rewrite(Database);
FileCopy(TempFile, DataBase);
end; {procedure KillRecord}

begin {procedure Delete}

{find the record}
Exists : = false;
View(DataBase, KeyRecord, Exists);
if Exists **then**
  begin {record exists}
    writeln;
    writeln('Do you want to delete this record (Y or N): ');
    readln(Response);
    if (Response = 'Y') **or** (Response = 'y') **then**
      begin {double check}
        writeln('Are you sure?');
        readln(Response);
        if (Response = 'Y') **or** (Response = 'y') **then**
          begin
            KillRecord(DataBase, KeyRecord);
            writeln('Record deleted from DataBase.');
            writeln;
            writeln('Hit RETURN to continue');
            readln;
          end;
      end; {double check}
  end; {record exists}
end; {procedure Delete}

```
procedure Modify(var DataBase: FileType;
                 var Table:  CodeTable);
{collects information from user on record to modify and changes
to be made; displays copy of changed record and asks for
confirmation, then actually makes the change in DataBase. Table
needed only if the Help procedure is invoked}

var
    KeyRecord : Student;        {record to modify}
    Response : char;           {Y to modify}
    Exists : boolean;          {flag to see if record exists}
    NewRecord : Student;       {modified version of KeyRecord}
    TempFile : FileType;       {temporary file to allow file
                                 modification}
    i : integer;               {array index}
    Length : integer;          {number of classes in KeyRecord}
    Duplicate : boolean;       {flag for duplicate name/ID between
                                 modified version of record and
                                 some existing record}

procedure Scan(var DataBase: FileType; NewRecord: Student;
               var Duplicate: boolean);
{scans DataBase for record with same name and ID as
NewRecord; sets boolean flag Duplicate if match found - file
DataBase is not changed upon exit}

var
    OldRecord : Student;        {record from file DataBase}

  begin    {procedure Scan}
    reset(DataBase);
    Duplicate := false;
    while (not Duplicate) and (not eof(DataBase)) do
      begin
        read(DataBase, OldRecord);
        if (OldRecord.Name = NewRecord.Name) and
           (OldRecord.ID = NewRecord.ID) then
          begin
            Duplicate := true;
          end;
      end;
  end;    {procedure Scan}

procedure FileMod(var DataBase: FileType;
                  KeyRecord, NewRecord: Student);
{replaces KeyRecord with NewRecord in file DataBase; we know
 DataBase contains KeyRecord}

var
    TempFile : FileType;    {temporary file for file modification}
    OldRecord : Student;    {record already in file}
```

```
begin     {procedure FileMod}

  {find KeyRecord}
  reset(DataBase);
  rewrite(TempFile);
  read(DataBase, OldRecord);
  while (OldRecord.Name <> KeyRecord.Name) or
        (OldRecord.ID <> KeyRecord.ID) do
    begin {haven't found KeyRecord yet}
      write(TempFile, OldRecord);
      read(DataBase, OldRecord);
    end;

  {OldRecord is now KeyRecord, write NewRecord to file
   instead}
  write(TempFile, NewRecord);

  {now finish file copy to TempFile, then copy TempFile
   back into DataBase}
  FileCopy(DataBase, TempFile);
  reset(TempFile);
  rewrite(Database);
  FileCopy(TempFile, DataBase);

end;     {procedure FileMod}


begin   {procedure Modify}

  {find the record}
  Exists := false;
  View(DataBase, KeyRecord, Exists);
  if Exists then
    begin     {record exists}
      writeln;
      writeln('Do you want to modify this record (Y or N): ');
      readln(Response);
      if (Response = 'Y') or (Response = 'y') then
        begin     {modify}

          {deal with name}
          writeln;
          writeln('Name: ', KeyRecord.Name);
          write('Change? (Y or N): ');
          readln(Response);
          if (Response = 'Y') or (Response = 'y') then
            begin
              GetName(NewRecord);
            end
```

```
    else     {use existing name}
      begin
        NewRecord.Name := KeyRecord.Name;
      end;

    {deal with ID}
    writeln;
    writeln('ID: ', KeyRecord.ID);
    write('Change? (Y or N): ');
    readln(Response);
    if (Response = 'Y') or (Response = 'y') then
      begin
        GetID(NewRecord);
      end
    else     {use existing ID}
      begin
        NewRecord.ID := KeyRecord.ID;
      end;

    {if the name or ID is changed, it may duplicate an
     existing record, check this}

    Duplicate := false;
    if (NewRecord.Name <> KeyRecord.Name) or
       (NewRecord.ID <> KeyRecord.ID) then
      begin
        Scan(DataBase, NewRecord, Duplicate);
      end;
    if Duplicate then
      Quit
    else
      begin     {continue with modification}

        {deal with major}
        writeln;
        writeln('Major: ', KeyRecord.Major);
        write('Change? (Y or N): ');
        readln(Response);
        if (Response = 'Y') or (Response = 'y') then
          begin
            GetMajor(NewRecord, Table);
          end
        else     {use existing major}
          begin
            NewRecord.Major := KeyRecord.Major;
          end;

        {deal with classes}
        writeln;
```

```
with KeyRecord do
  begin
    i := 1;
    while Classes[i].Department <> '    ' do
      begin
        write(Classes[i].Department, ' ');
        writeln(Classes[i].Number:3);
        i := i + 1;
      end;
    Length := i - 1;    {number of classes}
  end;
write('Change? (Y or N): ');
readln(Response);
if (Response = 'Y') or (Response =  'y') then
  begin
    GetClasses(NewRecord, Table);
  end
else    {use existing classes but initialize array first}
  begin    {else}
    for i := 1 to MaxCourses do
      begin
        with NewRecord.Classes[i] do
          Department := '    ';
      end;
    for i := 1 to Length do
      begin
        NewRecord.Classes[i].Department :=
          KeyRecord.Classes[i].Department;
        NewRecord.Classes[i].Number :=
          KeyRecord.Classes[i].Number;
      end;
  end;    {else}
{record modification complete, do final check with
user before modifying the file to replace KeyRecord
with NewRecord}

writeln('The modified record now reads');
Display(NewRecord);
writeln;
writeln('Do you want to replace the original record');
write('with this one? (Y or N):');
readln(Response);
if (Response = 'Y') or (Response =  'y') then
  begin
    FileMod(DataBase, KeyRecord, NewRecord);
    writeln;
    writeln('Record modified in DataBase.');
    writeln;
```

```
                            writeln('Hit RETURN to continue');
                            readln;
                        end;
                    end;    {continue with modification}
                end;    {modify}
            end;    {record exists}
        end;      {procedure Modify}


    begin    {main program}

        MenuDisplay;
        CollectResponse(Action);
        while not ((Action = 'S') or (Action = 's')) do
            begin
                case Action of
                    'A','a':  Add(DataBase, Table);
                    'D','d':  Delete(DataBase);
                    'V','v':  View(DataBase, ViewRecord, Exists);
                    'M','m':  Modify(DataBase, Table);
                    'H','h':  Help(Table);
                end; {case}
                MenuDisplay;
                CollectResponse(Action);
            end; {while}

        {Action is STOP, terminate program}
    end.      {main program}
```

RUNNING THE PROGRAM...

This program allows many different activities to take place, and we won't attempt to trace an entire actual working session here. Instead, we'll just present a snapshot of part of the screen when a record modification has been done and the user is asked whether the modified record is to replace the original one.

```
The modified record now reads

Walker, Louise
327-46-9328

Major: CHEM

Classes this semester:
CHEM 240
MATH 345
ENGL 390
```

Hit RETURN to continue

Do you want to replace the original record
with this one? (Y or N):

**CASE
STUDY
ONE**

View #11

The Lodestone County Water Pollution Department wants to keep permanent records of all site readings. The department has asked Sterling Software Systems to make the necessary changes in the water pollution program to support file storage for the data. The department specifies that the data input process remain unchanged; the new readings collected are to be added to the file. The output display table for readings collected during a given session of program execution should be retained, but the percentage of violators per session is not very meaningful information and should be dropped. Instead, the user should be able to display all readings in the file that are in violation, together with the total number of readings in the file and the percentage of total readings that are in violation. Sterling hands this project back to your department.

These changes are relatively easy to make. The first thing the program below does is give the user a menu of choices for the two tasks—either collect and display data and append it to the file, or search the file for violations. The previous version of the program constitutes most of the first task. Because readings for a session of program execution are to be displayed as before, the internal array of records used to store the data entered during that session is kept. However, these records are also appended to a file of records. In the program below, we assume that file *DataH2O* already exists (see program *Students* in this chapter to see how to handle the problem of creating the file for the first time vs. adding records to an existing file).

The second task involves displaying data for readings in the file that are in violation. This will involve searching the file for records with the warning flag turned on. (For report-generating purposes, these records would be written to a separate file, but we'll simply display them.) In addition, the program is to compute the percentage of the readings in the file that are in violation.

```
program WaterPollution(input, output, DataH2O);
{maintains a file DataH2O of records of water samples from
 various sites; each record contains site ID, date of sample,
 amount of water, and bacteria count, also the bacteria/water
 ratio and a warning if the bacteria level is too high. User may
 choose to enter new records (these are displayed in tabular
 form and appended to the file), or to display all records from
 file that are in violation together with the total number of
 readings in the file and the percentage of total readings
 that are in violation.}
```

```pascal
const
    Threshold = 2.0;                {200 bacteria per 100 ml  water}
    MaxNoOfReadings = 30;           {maximum number of readings
                                      per session program can handle}

type
    TwoCharArray = array [1..2] of char;

    Reading = record
      ID, Water, Bacteria : integer;
      Mon, Day, Yr : TwoCharArray;
      Level : real;                 {pollution level}
      Warning : boolean;            {flag for warning message}
      end;    {Reading}
    Index = 1..MaxNoOfReadings;
    ArrayType = array [Index] of Reading;
    FileType = file of Reading;

var
    DataH2O : FileType;         {file of site readings}
    Task : char;                {user task selection from menu}

procedure ClearScreen;
{clears the screen by writing 24 blank lines}

var
    i : integer;

  begin    {procedure ClearScreen}
  for i := 1 to 24 do
    writeln;
  end;     {procedure ClearScreen}

procedure MenuDisplay;
{displays menu of tasks from which user can choose}

  begin    {procedure MenuDisplay}
  ClearScreen;
  writeln;
  writeln('                    Water Pollution Record Keeper');
  writeln;
  writeln('                              written by');
  writeln('                    Sterling Software Systems');
  writeln;
  writeln('                       Choose task to be done:');
  writeln; writeln;
  writeln('          Enter (E)        Enter new data for  file');
  writeln;
  write('          Violators (V)     Display pollution  violation');
```

```
        writeln(' records from file');
        writeln;
        writeln('            Quit (Q)              Quit program');
        writeln;
        write('               Enter your choice (E, V, or Q): ');
    end;      {procedure MenuDisplay}

procedure CollectResponse(var Choice: char);
{collects the user's choice of action}

type
    Response = set of char;

var
    Valid : Response;

    begin      {procedure CollectResponse}
    valid := ['E','V','Q','e','v','q'];
    readln(Choice);
    ClearScreen;
    while not (Choice in Valid) do
      begin
        writeln('Your choices are E, V, Q, try again: ');
        readln(Choice);
        ClearScreen;
      end;
    end;         {procedure CollectResponse}

procedure GetInput(var OneSite: Reading);
{procedure to collect input for water pollution data; amount
Water of water and count Bacteria of bacteria were obtained
from  site ID on date Mon1Mon2/Day1Day2/Yr1Yr2}

var
    Slash : char;      {separating / in date format}

function Value(FirstChar, SecondChar: char): integer;
{function to convert two characters to a two-digit integer}

var
    FirstDigit    : integer;    {the integer equivalents}
    SecondDigit : integer;      {of numerical characters}

    begin   {function Value}
    FirstDigit := ord(FirstChar) − ord('0');
    SecondDigit := ord(SecondChar) − ord('0');
    Value := 10*FirstDigit + SecondDigit;
    end;     {function Value}

function ValidDate(Mon1, Mon2, Day1, Day2: char): boolean;
{function to do some validation on date entered}
```

```
var
    MonthValue : integer;        {numerical value for month}
    DayValue : integer;          {numerical value for day}
    ValidMonth : boolean;        {MonthValue in range 1-12}
    ValidDay : boolean;          {DayValue in range 1-31}

begin    {function ValidDate}
    MonthValue := Value(Mon1, Mon2);
    DayValue := Value(Day1, Day2);

    ValidMonth := (0 < MonthValue) and (MonthValue < 13);
    ValidDay := (0 < DayValue) and (DayValue < 32);

    ValidDate := ValidMonth and ValidDay;
end;     {function ValidDate}


begin      {procedure GetInput}
  with OneSite do
    begin    {with OneSite}
      writeln;
      write('Enter the site ID number: ');
      readln(ID);
      while not((1 <= ID) and (ID <= 1000)) do
        begin {ID out of range}
          write('Check the site ID number ');
          write('and enter again: ');
          readln(ID);
        end;   {ID out of range}
      writeln;

      writeln('Enter the date of this sample.');
      write('Use month/date/year format: ');
      readln(Mon[1], Mon[2], Slash, Day[1],
             Day[2], Slash, Yr[1], Yr[2]);

      while not ValidDate(Mon[1], Mon[2],
                          Day[1], Day[2]) do
        begin {error in date input}
          write('Please enter the date again: ');
          readln(Mon[1], Mon[2], Slash,
                 Day[1], Day[2], Slash, Yr[1], Yr[2]);
        end;   {error in date input}
      writeln;

      write('Enter the amount of water in sample (in ml): ');
      readln(Water);
      while not (Water > 0) do
```

```
            begin {error in amount of water}
              write('Check the amount of water & ');
              write('enter again: ');
              readln(Water);
            end; {error in amount of water}
          writeln;

          write('Enter the bacteria count found in this sample: ');
          readln(Bacteria);
          while not (Bacteria >= 0) do
            begin    {error in bacteria count}
              write('Check the bacteria count & ');
              write('enter again: ');
              readln(Bacteria);
            end;      {error in bacteria count}
        end;    {with OneSite}

   end;      {procedure GetInput}


function Ratio(Bacteria, Water: integer): real;
{computes the Ratio of Bacteria to Water}

   begin      {function Ratio}
     Ratio := Bacteria/Water;
   end;         {function Ratio}


procedure CheckThreshold(Ratio: real;
                           var Over:  Boolean);
{compares Ratio to the global constant Threshold and sets Over
to true if that limit is exceeded}

   begin      {procedure CheckThreshold}
     Over := false;    {initialize Over}
     if Ratio > Threshold then
       Over := true;
   end;        {procedure CheckThreshold}

procedure WriteHeader;
{writes output table heading}

   begin     {procedure WriteHeader}
     writeln;
     writeln;
     write('Site ID', 'Date':8, 'Water':12, 'Bacteria':13);
     writeln('Level':9, 'Warning':10);
     write('_____');
     writeln('_____');
     writeln;
   end;       {procedure WriteHeader}
```

```
procedure WriteLineOfOutput(OneSite: Reading);
{produces a line of output in the table corresponding to one
reading - echoes input data and writes warning message if
warranted}

  begin      {procedure WriteLineOfOutput}
    with OneSite do
      begin    {with OneSite}
        write(ID:5, Mon[1]:6, Mon[2], '/', Day[1],
              Day[2], '/', Yr[1], Yr[2]);
        write(Water:8, ' ml', Bacteria:9, Level:11:2);

        if Warning then
          write('    ** HIGH **');
        writeln;
      end;      {with OneSite}
  end;        {procedure WriteLineOfOutput}

procedure NewData(var DataH2O: FileType);
{handles collection and display of new records and appends them
to already existing file DataH2O}

var
    Session : ArrayType;      {holds records entered in
                               current program session}
    Continue : char;          {signal to terminate data entry}
    n : integer;              {number of readings to process}
    i : integer;              {array index}
    Temp : FileType;          {temporary file for file copy}
    Entry : Reading;          {record in file}

  begin      {procedure NewData}

    n := 0;
    repeat
      n := n + 1;

      GetInput(Session[n]);

      with Session[n] do
        Level := Ratio(Bacteria, Water);

      writeln;
      writeln;
      if (n < MaxNoOfReadings) then
        begin {room for more data}
          writeln('Do you have more sites to process?');
          writeln('(Answer Y or N): ');
          readln(Continue);
        end    {room for more data}
```

```
        else
          begin {array full}
            writeln('Maximum number of readings entered. ');
            write('Adjust program constant MaxNoOfReadings ');
            writeln('if this is a problem.');
          end;   {array full}

      until (Continue = 'N') or (Continue  = 'n') or
            (n = MaxNoOfReadings);

{all the input has been gathered and stored in the array,
 now print out table}

      write('The following new records will be appended');
      writeln(' to file DataH2O.');

      WriteHeader;
      for i := 1 to n do
        begin {produce line i of the output table}
          CheckThreshold(Session[i].Level,  Session[i].Warning);
          WriteLineOfOutput(Session[i]);
        end;   {line i has been written}
      writeln;
      writeln('Hit RETURN to continue');
      readln;

{now append these records to file DataH2O}
      reset(DataH2O);
      rewrite(Temp);
      while not eof(DataH2O) do
        begin
          read(DataH2O, Entry);
          write(Temp, Entry);
        end;

{old file copied, now append new records}
      for i := 1 to n do
        begin
          write(Temp, Session[i]);
        end;   {new records appended}

{now copy back to DataH2O}
      reset(Temp);
      rewrite(DataH2O);
      while not eof(Temp) do
        begin
          read(Temp, Entry);
          write(DataH2O, Entry);
        end;    {DataH2O now complete}
   end;       {procedure NewData}
```

```
procedure Violators(var DataH2O: FileType);
{displays all records in file DataH2O with pollution levels above
 threshold}

var
    Entry : Reading;           {record in file}
    Count : integer;           {number of records in file}
    Bad : integer;             {number of violation records in
                                file}
    Percentage : real;         {percent violation records}

 begin    {procedure Violators}
   reset(DataH2O);
   writeln('Readings from file that are in violation:');
   writeln;
   Count := 0;
   Bad := 0;
   WriteHeader;
   while not eof(DataH2O) do
     begin
       read(DataH2O, Entry);
       if Entry.Warning then
         begin
           WriteLineOfOutput(Entry);
           Bad := Bad + 1;
         end;
       Count := Count + 1;
     end;   {while not eof}
   writeln;
   if Count = 0 then
     begin
       writeln('File DataH2O is empty');
       writeln('Hit RETURN to continue');
       readln;
     end
   else
     begin
       write('Total number of readings in file: ');
       writeln(Count:3);
       writeln('Percentage of readings in file ');
       write('that are in violation: ');
       Percentage := (Bad/Count)*100;
       writeln(Percentage:6:2);
       writeln('Hit RETURN to continue');
       readln;
     end;
 end;    {procedure Violators}
```

```
begin     {main program}

  MenuDisplay;
  CollectResponse(Task);
  while not ((Task = 'Q') or (Task =  'q')) do
    begin
      case Task of
        'E','e':  NewData(DataH2O);
        'V','v':  Violators(DataH2O);
      end; {case}
      MenuDisplay;
      CollectResponse(Task);
    end;    {while}

  {Task is QUIT, terminate program}
end.     {main program}
```

RUNNING THE PROGRAM...

Again, we'll just present some screen snapshots. The menu screen looks like this when the user chooses to view records that are in violation:

Water Pollution Record Keeper

written by
Sterling Software Systems

Choose task to be done:

Enter (E)   Enter new data for file

Violators (V)   Display pollution violation records from file

Quit (Q)   Quit program

Enter your choice (E, V, or Q): v

The next screen has the form

Readings from file that are in violation:

Site ID	Date	Water	Bacteria	Level	Warning
382	12/01/88	840 ml	1900	2.26	** HIGH **
520	09/17/88	1100 ml	2300	2.09	** HIGH **
255	05/16/89	750 ml	1800	2.40	** HIGH **

Total number of readings in file: 7
Percentage of readings in file
that are in violation: 42.86
Hit RETURN to continue

| CASE STUDY TWO | View #11 |

Modify the hypertension clinic program to maintain a file. The user should be able to append new data to the file, or to print the records for patients in any of the three categories of mild, moderate, or severe hypertensive and obtain a percentage of the total file records for the category.

EXERCISES

#1. What is the difference between a text file and a binary file with components of type *char*?

2. What will be the contents of text file *Guess* after the following section of code has been executed?

```
writeln(Guess, 1);
rewrite(Guess);
writeln(2);
writeln('Guess', 3);
write(Guess, 4);
writeln(Guess, 5);
```

#3. Suppose that text file *DuckSoup* begins with

chicken 12(eoln)pea5(eoln)minestrone6(eoln)

What is the output from the following program?

```
program YumYum(DuckSoup, output);

var
    DuckSoup : text;
    Char1, Char2, Char3 : char;
    Number : integer;

begin
  reset(DuckSoup);
  readln(DuckSoup, Char1, Char2);
  writeln(Char1, Char2);
  readln(DuckSoup, Char1, Char2, Char3, Number);
  writeln(Number:2);
  read(DuckSoup, Char1);
  while not eoln(DuckSoup) do
```

```
      begin
        read(DuckSoup, Char1);
        write(Char1);
      end;
    readln(DuckSoup);
  end.
```

4. Modify procedure *FileCopy* for text files so that every odd line of the original file is written to file *Odd* and every even line is written to file *Even*. Assume that the original file has an even number of lines.

5. Redo Exercise #4 above without assuming that the original file has an even number of lines.

#6. Write a type declaration for a file of inventory records. Each record will contain the name of an item (at most ten characters), the number of items on hand, and the price per item.

7. Given the following declarations and assuming that *Mail* has been opened for reading, find statements that will write out the contents of the *State* field and the third entry in array *Zips* for the record currently in the file window.

```
type
    String  =  packed array  [1..25] of char;
    StateCode  =  packed array  [1..2] of char;
    ZipCode  =  packed array  [1..5] of char;
    ZipArray  =  array  [1..10] of ZipCode;
    Locale  =  record
       City  :  String;
       State  :  StateCode;
       Zips  :  ZipArray;
       end;     {Locale}
    MailFile  =  file of Locale;

var
    Mail  :  MailFile;
```

8. *NumberList* is a binary file of integers with at least K entries. Find statements that will cause double the Kth entry to be written to the screen.

#9. Modify your answer to CHECKUP 11.5 so that your procedure copies a binary file of real values, *Old*, both into binary file *New* and onto the screen.

#10. What is wrong with the following program?

```
program Triplets(input, output, List);
{creates a binary file List of positive integers, three to a line}

type
    ListType  =  file of integer;

var
    List  :  ListType;
```

```
        Num1, Num2, Num3 : integer;

begin
  rewrite(List);
  writeln('Enter triplets of positive integers;');
  writeln('terminate with 0');
  read(Num1);
  while(Num1 <> 0) do
    begin
      readln(Num2, Num3);
      writeln(List, Num1, Num2, Num3);
      writeln('Next triplet: ');
      read(Num1);
    end;
end.
```

11. A binary file *List* of integers contains the values

5 14 6 9 52 31 7 eof

What is the content of *List*^ and of *Number* after the following statements have been executed?

```
  reset(List);
  read(List, Number);
  List^ := 7;
  read(List, Number);
  get(List);
```

SKILL BUILDERS

1. Use the system editor to create a three-line text file, where the first two lines are strings of characters and the third line is an integer. Write a program to read this file and display the three lines on the screen.

2. Write a program that allows the user to create a three-line text file as described in Skill Builder #1 above, then reads this file and displays the three lines on the screen.

3. Write a program that uses *NumberList,* a binary file of integers. After program execution, *NumberList* will contain the same values as before, but each pair of values will be reversed. Thus

    12 5 63 47 18 eof

will become

    5 12 47 63 18 eof

(Your answers to CHECKUP 11.3 will help you test your program.)

#4. Write a program to create a file *Table* of department names and codes for use with program *Students.*

5. Redo program *SearchList* on page 222 assuming that the ticket numbers have been stored, one per line, in a text file.

6. Suppose that files *List1* and *List2* are text files storing one integer per line, and that these integers are stored in sorted order. Write a program that merges these two files, producing a third file *List3* in sorted order with no duplicate entries. (This problem is similar to Software Development Project #1 in Chapter 9. How the files *List1* and *List2* got sorted to begin with is another story—see Software Development Project #6 below.)

SOFTWARE DEVELOPMENT PROJECTS

1. The Sleazy Sales Corporation needs software for a junk mail generator. Junk mail consists of a form letter, individualized at certain points with a name or a name and address obtained from a file of names and addresses. Develop the junk mail generator.

2. Develop a data base system for an employment agency. The agency wants to maintain a file of job descriptions, and a file of job applicants. The data base must allow for new records to be created and old records to be deleted or modified in each of these files. In addition, the system should allow the user to select a job applicant and search the job description file for a suitable match, or to select a job description and search the applicant file for a suitable match. (For simplicity, the job description itself can be one word, such as "accountant," but a job description record must also contain items such as employer and salary.)

3. Develop part of a word-processing system. The program is to search a text file for all instances of a key word that the user enters. When each instance is found, the user can leave the word alone or replace it with another word the user then enters.

4. As another part of the word-processing system begun in #3 above, develop software that reformats a text file that has been generated as a single-spaced document with lines up to eighty columns long. The user should be able to enter the new line width (between forty and eighty columns), and the result should be a double-spaced text file with text right-justified within this line width.

5. A message is to be sent in encoded form for security reasons. (For simplicity, assume that the message contains only uppercase letters, no blanks, and no punctuation marks.) Encoding the message requires first translating each alphabetic character into a unique number between 0 and 25. The simplest such translation function is

$f(A) = 0$
$f(B) = 1$
$f(C) = 2$

.
.

$f(Z) = 25$

Then f is a one-to-one function, and the inverse function f^{-1} exists and reverses this translation ($f^{-1}(0) = $ A, etc.) Another part of the encoding process involves a 2×2 matrix M of integers such that if arithmetic is done modulo 26, then M has an inverse matrix M^{-1} with integer elements. (***Arithmetic modulo 26*** means that values 26 or bigger are first reduced by 26 or multiples of 26. For example, 29 becomes $29 - 26 = 3$ in arithmetic modulo 26.) Such a matrix is

$$M = \begin{bmatrix} 3 & 2 \\ 7 & 5 \end{bmatrix}$$

with

$$M^{-1} = \begin{bmatrix} 5 & 24 \\ 19 & 3 \end{bmatrix}$$

because (in arithmetic modulo 26)

$$\begin{bmatrix} 3 & 2 \\ 7 & 5 \end{bmatrix} \cdot \begin{bmatrix} 5 & 24 \\ 19 & 3 \end{bmatrix} = \begin{bmatrix} 1 & 0 \\ 0 & 1 \end{bmatrix}$$

To encode a word, break it into blocks of length 2, and for each block X, compute $f^{-1}(f(X) \times M)$, that is, apply f, multiply by M, and apply f^{-1}, doing all arithmetic modulo 26. For example, the block TO becomes

$$f^{-1}(f(\text{T O}) \times M) = f^{-1}((19\ 14) \times \begin{bmatrix} 3 & 2 \\ 7 & 5 \end{bmatrix})$$

$$= f^{-1}(25\ 4)$$

$$= \text{ZE}$$

To decode a word, break it into blocks of length 2, and for each block X, compute $f^{-1}(f(X) \times M^{-1})$. Thus ZE becomes

$$f^{-1}(f(\text{Z E}) \times M^{-1})) = f^{-1}((25\ 4) \times \begin{bmatrix} 5 & 24 \\ 19 & 3 \end{bmatrix})$$

$$= f^{-1}(19\ 14)$$
$$= \text{TO}$$

Develop software to code and decode text files. Use the matrix M given above, but allow the user to enter the translation function f.

6. Given an external file that contains, say, integers, how can this file be sorted? One solution is to read the file into an internal array and sort the array, a problem we have done before. However, this assumes that the maximum length of the file is known, and that it is small enough to fit into main memory. Another solution is to emulate the selection sort on the file. Thus we could search the file for the smallest entry, remove that entry from the file, and make it the first entry in a new file, and then repeat the process. This is incredibly inefficient because it requires searching the entire file many times.

A better solution is to break the file in half and store each half in files *One* and *Two*. After this is done, files *One* and *Two* are within one entry of equal length. We then consider each file as a succession of groups of entries with one entry per group and do a succession of merges between groups in each file, writing the results alternately to files *Three* and *Four*. After this is done, *Three* and *Four* may be thought of as successions of groups of entries with two entries per group; furthermore, each group is sorted. For example, if the original file contains

    24 6 7 8 9 21 25 4 6 12 19

then *One* and *Two* look like

    24 | 7 | 9 | 25 | 6 | 19
    6 | 8 | 21 | 4 | 12

After merging the singleton groups from the two files and storing the results in *Three* and *Four, Three* and *Four* will look like

    6 24 | 9 21 | 6 12
    7 8 | 4 25 | 19

Now repeat this process. Merge each sorted two-length group into sorted four-length groups; these can be stored in *One* and *Two*, since we do not need the previous contents of those files. After this, *One* and *Two* look like

    6 7 8 24 | 6 12 19
    4 9 21 25

After merging the four-length groups, *Three* and *Four* contain

    4 6 7 8 9 21 24 25
    6 12 19

and a final merge produces file *One* containing

    4 6 7 8 9 12 19 21 24 25

which is the original file in sorted order.

Develop software to carry out external file sorting.

TESTING AND MAINTENANCE DEPARTMENT

1. Devise scenarios to thoroughly test program *Students*.

2. Write both a user's manual and a technical reference manual for program *Students*.

3. Rewrite Software Development Project #2 from Chapter 10, this time reading the coordinates for fixed points and radar readings from a file.

4. Rewrite Software Development Project #3 from Chapter 10, this time keeping the store inventory in a file.

5. Modify program *Students* to allow the user to query the database for
   a. A list of all students who are taking a particular course (i.e., all students taking CSCI 482).
   b. A list of all students who are taking all of some list of courses (i.e., all students taking CSCI 482 and MATH 351).
   c. A list of all students who are taking any from some list of courses (i.e., all students taking CSCI 482 or MATH 351).

6. Devise a scenario that will cause program *Nutrition* from Chapter 10 to fail and test the program under this scenario. Then, rewrite the program so as to correct the problem.

DEBUGGING CLINIC

1. What is wrong with the following program?

```
program DebugA(input, output, Names);
{creates and reads back file Names of names}

type
    String = packed array [1..10] of char;
    Name = String;
    FileType = file of Name;

var
    Names : FileType;
    CurrentName : Name;
    i : integer;

begin
    rewrite(Names);
    writeln('Enter names to go into file, one name per line.');
    writeln('End list with DONE');

    CurrentName := '          ';
    i := 1;
    while (not eoln) and (i <=  10) do
      begin
        read(CurrentName[i]);
         i := i + 1;
      end;
```

```
      readln;
      while CurrentName <> 'DONE          '  do
        begin
          write(Names, CurrentName);
          CurrentName := '              ';
          i := 1;
          while (not eoln) and (i <=  10) do
            begin
              read(CurrentName[i]);
              i := i + 1;
            end;
          readln;
        end;
      {file Names created, now to read it back}

      reset(Names);
      writeln('The names in the file are:');
      while not eof do
        begin
          read(Names, CurrentName);
          writeln(CurrentName);
        end;
end.
```

2. Devise test data that can cause the following program to fail. Then correct the problem.

```
program DebugB(input, output, NumberList);
{reads already-existing binary file NumberList of integers}

type
    IntFile = file of integer;

var
    NumberList : IntFile;
    CurrentNumber : integer;

begin
  reset(NumberList);
  writeln('Contents of file NumberList');
  repeat
    read(NumberList, CurrentNumber);
    writeln(CurrentNumber);
  until eof(NumberList);
end.
```

CHAPTER TWELVE

RECURSION

Unlike previous chapters, this chapter does not introduce any new Pascal as such. What it does is discuss a new method of thinking, a method that the Pascal language supports. We'll begin with a little story.

12.1 A Fable

Once upon a time, there lived a princess with long, beautiful hair. She longed to have a golden comb for her hair. Such a comb was hanging by a chain in the castle dungeon, but no one knew how to release it. One night a wily fox came to her in a dream and told her that the big wooden box in the dungeon had a most peculiar lock. If she could only get the key to this lock and lock the box, that would release the comb.

"But how will I get the key to the lock?" asked the princess. "Aha," said the fox. "To *lock* the box, you must *lock* the smaller box inside it; locking that box will release the key to lock the bigger box."

When the princess awoke the next morning, she could hardly wait to hurry to the dungeon and open the big box. Sure enough, there was a smaller box inside, but there was no key to that box's lock. The princess sighed; her task of locking the big box had reappeared in a smaller version—she now had to lock a smaller box. Then a brilliant idea struck her. What if this really were the exact same problem, and the key to the smaller box depended on locking a still smaller box inside? Opening the box, she did indeed find another box inside.

The princess continued opening the nested boxes, each time leaving the task of locking a box unfinished to turn her attention to the task of locking the smaller box inside. "Goodness," she complained after opening twenty-seven boxes, "I wonder where this will all end?"

At last the princess came to a very small box to be locked. Opening this box, she discovered a tiny golden key that just fit the lock to the tiny box,

435

which she was then able to lock. "Hooray," she thought, "I have finally finished a box-locking task." As soon as the tiny box was locked, another golden key fell from its padlock. This key exactly fit the next bigger box in which the tiny box nested, so its locking task could also be completed. Sure enough, that released the key to the next larger box.

Soon the princess was able to complete, in reverse order, each of the box-locking tasks she had left unfinished. At last she locked the outside box, whereupon the golden comb was released from its chain, and the princess lived happily ever after.

12.2 The Idea of Recursion

Think about a recursive solution if the problem can be solved once a smaller version of the same problem has been solved, and if there is a trivial smallest case that can easily be solved.

What is the moral of the fable? Sometimes a problem can be solved by solving a "smaller" version of the same problem. For this to work, there must be a "smallest" version of the problem that is immediately solvable. This process of repeatedly solving smaller versions of the same type of problem is called ***recursion,*** and the smallest version, to which there is an immediate solution, is the ***base step*** of the recursion.

To put this in the context of programming, a procedure or function is written to solve the problem. This module is invoked with certain parameter values. The module often does some preliminary work but then suspends its work until the smaller version of the problem has been solved. To solve the smaller version, the module invokes itself, with different ("smaller") parameter values than used in the initial invocation. The module may be invoked many times with successively smaller parameter values. Each time the module is invoked, it must first check to see whether the parameters are such that this invocation is the base step. If it is, the computation is completed without another invocation of the module. Completion of the base step releases values to be used in completion of the previous invocation, and so forth, until finally the initial invocation can be completed.

An outline of a recursive module appears below:

```
module (parameters):
declarations
  begin
    if parameters are such that this is the base step then
      solve base step;
    else
      begin
        do some preliminary work
        invoke module ("smaller" parameters)
        complete work based on values returned by the above
          invocation
      end;
  end;
```

Each invocation of the module causes an activation record for that invocation to be placed on top of a stack. (Recall from Chapter 3 that an activation record is added to a stack whenever a module is invoked, whether recursion is involved or not.) This activation record provides memory for local variables and also for any value formal parameters. If the module does some preliminary work, values in the activation record are updated accordingly. When another invocation of the module takes place, a new activation record is placed on top of the stack. The base step corresponds to the final invocation of the module, and the topmost activation record on the stack. As each invocation is completed, the corresponding activation record is removed from the stack and the "local environment" information for the previous invocation becomes available at the top of the stack.

Each invocation of a procedure or function causes an activation record of local data values to be added to a stack, so recursion can rapidly consume memory.

The programmer need not worry about the stacking mechanism, as this is all handled automatically. The only point in mentioning the stack is to observe that recursion can consume a lot of memory. For example, suppose that the base step is reached on the twenty-fifth invocation of a recursive module, and that the module needs values for 5 local variables to do its computation. Each invocation of the module causes a new activation record with storage for 5 variables to be put on top of the stack. Altogether, 125 values will have to be stored for this module when it initially appears that only 5 are needed! A "stack overflow" error message may result if the stack requires more memory space than the system allocation for stack memory. (This will surely happen if the base step of the recursion is omitted or somehow never executed. The recursion will go on indefinitely, with each new invocation adding values to the stack. This **infinite descent recursion** is an error to be avoided.)

It is clear that recursion can be expensive in terms of consumed resources. Some programming languages do not even support recursion, that is, they do not allow a module to invoke itself. Any problem that can be done recursively can also be done in a nonrecursive manner, usually by a looping process, hence the nonrecursive version is often called an **iterative** version. What, then, is the advantage to recursion?

Any problem solved by recursion can also be solved without recursion, but the nonrecursive solution may be much more complex.

The advantage is that a problem solution may be short, simple, and elegant when viewed recursively, but long and complex when viewed nonrecursively. This simplicity is worth the price in resources. (Remember we always take the view that human resources—the effort needed to understand the algorithm, for example—are more precious than machine resources.)

Nonetheless, it does take some practice to learn to think recursively, and to spot problems for which recursion provides an elegant solution. We'll begin with some examples of recursive functions and then look at a recursive procedure.

12.3 Recursive Functions

12.3.1 *The Power Function*

The first function we'll look at is very simple. It is the function $f(x) = x^n$, where n is a nonnegative integer. The function needs two parameters, the values of x and n. (Before invoking the function, the invoking program segment should check that it is not the case that both x and n are zero, as zero to the zero power is undefined.) A nonrecursive solution is easy to write:

```
function Power1(x: real; n: integer): real;
{computes x to the power n, nonrecursively; n ≥ 0}

var
    i : integer;              {counter variable}
    CurrentValue : real;      {current function value}

  begin
    CurrentValue := 1.0;
    if   n > 0 then
      for i := 1 to n do
        CurrentValue := CurrentValue * x;
    Power1 := CurrentValue;
  end;
```

A recursive solution makes use of the observation that for $n > 0$,

$$x^n = x * x^{n-1}$$

We can compute the power function with parameter values x and n as soon as we know the value of the power function with parameter values x and $n-1$. The "smaller" version of the problem is to invoke the power function with parameters x and $n-1$. What is the base step, the point at which we can directly compute the answer without further recursion? This occurs when the second of the two parameters, which has successive values n, $n-1$, ..., reaches the value 0. At this point the value 1.0 is assigned to the function identifier. The recursive version is

```
function Power2(x: real; n: integer): real;
{computes x to the power n, recursively; n ≥ 0}

  begin
    if n = 0 then
      Power2 := 1.0
    else
      Power2 := x * Power2(x, n-1);
  end;
```

Let us trace the execution of *Power2*(x, n) to compute $(3.0)^2$. There are no local variables in *Power2*, but there are two value parameters, x and n.

Initial invocation: Power2(3.0, 2)

Value of x: 3.0
Value of n: 2

An activation record is created on the stack to hold the current values for x and n (Fig. 12.1a). Because n is not 0, *Power2* is invoked again with parameters x and $n-1$. When this invocation occurs, work on the initial invocation is suspended.

Second invocation: Power2(3.0, 1)

> Value of x: 3.0
> Value of n: 1

A second activation record holds the values for x and n associated with the second invocation (Fig. 12.1b). Because n is not 0, *Power2* is invoked again with parameters x and $n-1$. Work on the second invocation is suspended.

Third invocation: Power2(3.0, 0)

> Value of x: 3.0
> Value of n: 0

A third activation record is added to the stack. Because n is now 0, the third invocation can complete its work and assign the value 1.0 to the function name *Power2* (Fig. 12.1c). Then the third activation record is removed from the stack.

Second invocation resumed: Control reverts back to the second invocation. The second invocation was suspended when attempting to carry out

> Power2 := x * Power2(x, $n-1$);

Now that the value of *Power2(x, $n-1$)* is available, the second invocation can complete its work. The activation record associated with the second invocation is now the top of the stack (Fig. 12.1d) and its values are once again available to the second invocation. (In this example, the current value of n is not directly used in completing the computation, only the value of x.) A value is assigned to the function name by

> Power2 := 3.0 * 1.0 = 3.0

Then the second activation record is removed from the stack.

Initial invocation resumed: Control is returned to the initial invocation. The initial activation record is now the top of the stack (Fig. 12.1e). Its values are available to the initial invocation, which assigns a value to the function name by

> Power2 := 3.0 * 3.0 = 9.0

The initial invocation of the function is now complete, and the final value of the function has been computed. Finally, the stack is emptied.

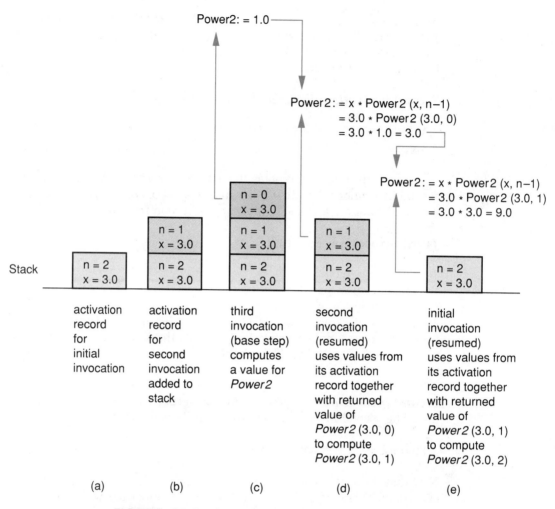

FIGURE   12.1   The stack to support recursion in the *Power2* function.

Note that although there can be multiple values for the same variable on the stack at any one time, there is no confusion because only the top set of values is available for use.

The recursive version of the power function is not appreciably shorter, simpler, or more elegant than the nonrecursive version, although it eliminates the counting loop that steps through the various multiplications. (From tracing the execution of *Power2*, we know that these multiplications are still performed, but it is the stack—rather than the local variable i of *Power1*—that does the counting.) The next function lends itself more naturally to recursion.

12.3.2 *The Fibonacci Function*

A sequence of integers that appears surprisingly often in nature is described as follows: The first and second values are both 1. Successive values after that are found by adding together the two previous values in the sequence.

Therefore the sequence consists of

1, 1, 2, 3, 5, 8, 13, 21,...

and the following facts are true, where Fibonacci(n) denotes the nth number in the sequence:

Fibonacci(1) = 1
Fibonacci(2) = 1
Fibonacci(n) = Fibonacci($n-1$) + Fibonacci($n-2$) for $n > 2$

A recursive function to compute Fibonacci(n) is:

```
function Fibonacci(n: integer): integer;
{computes the nth value in the Fibonacci sequence}

  begin
    if (n = 1) or (n = 2) then
      Fibonacci := 1
    else
      Fibonacci := Fibonacci(n-1) + Fibonacci(n-2);
  end;
```

This recursive approach to computing the nth value in the sequence is simple and natural in that it follows directly from the definition of the sequence. It is also elegant when compared with a nonrecursive version (see Exercise 3). It is expensive, however, because previous values must be recomputed many times (see CHECKUP 12.1 below).

CHECKUP 12.1 Trace the execution of *Fibonacci(5)*. How many times is *Fibonacci* invoked (counting the initial invocation)? How many times does *Fibonacci(2)* get computed? How many times does *Fibonacci(3)* get computed?

12.3.3 *Palindrome Checker*

A **palindrome** is a string of characters that reads the same forwards and backwards, for example, IUPUI is a palindrome. We want to write a program to check for palindromes. The program should read in and write out a string of characters along with a message indicating whether the string is a palindrome. (Testing and Maintenance Department problem #6 in Chapter 9 asked for a nonrecursive solution to this problem.) We decide to store the characters in a one-dimensional array and pass the array as a parameter to a palindrome-testing function. Because the array may not be full, the function also needs the index in the array where the last valid character is stored.

The recursive view of the problem is as follows. Examine the first and last characters in the string. If these do not match, the string is not a palindrome. If they do match, then the question of whether the string is a palindrome hinges on whether the string remaining after knocking off the first and last symbol is a palindrome (see Fig. 12.2). Here is the "smaller" version of the problem. If we give the function three parameters—the array, the index of the first character in the string to be considered, and the index of the last character in the string to be considered—we can then see how to call the function recursively. The initial invocation will pass ARRAY, 1, N (where there are N valid characters in the array). The next invocation will pass ARRAY, 2, N − 1, so that the string to be tested is the original string minus its first and last symbols. The length of the string being tested shrinks with each succeeding invocation.

What is the base step? The base step occurs when the string length has shrunk to 0 or 1 characters. Because the string is shortened by two at each invocation, whether it ends up with 0 or 1 characters depends on whether the original length was even or odd. In either case the string is at that point a (trivial) palindrome. Again, recursive thinking leads to a conceptually elegant solution.

The complete program follows. Note that the test for string length is easily done by comparing the first and last index values. Also note that the array is passed to the function as a variable parameter, even though its value will not be changed by the function and its size is relatively small. The reason is that the function is recursive and may be invoked a number of times. If the array parameter is passed as a value parameter, then each function invocation creates yet another copy of the array, needlessly consuming memory.

```
program Palindrome(input, output);
{tests strings up to length MaxLength for palindromes}

const
    MaxLength = 30;                    {maximum length string to
                                       test}

type
    ArrayType = array [1..MaxLength] of char;
```

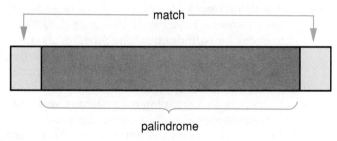

FIGURE 12.2 Recursive view of a palindrome.

```
var
    Word : ArrayType;          {array to hold string}
    n : integer;               {length of string}
    i : integer;               {array index}

procedure GetInput(var Word: ArrayType; var n: integer);
{reads in string to be tested, stores it in array Word, notes its
 length as n}

var
    NextChar : char;                {current char read}

    begin    {procedure GetInput}
    writeln('Enter string of characters to test for');
    writeln('palindrome (max. 30 characters).');
    writeln;
    n := 0;
    while(not eoln) and (n < 30) do
      begin
        read(NextChar);
        n := n + 1;
        Word[n] := NextChar;
      end;
    readln;
    end;     {procedure GetInput}

function Test(var Word: ArrayType;
                Front, Back: integer): boolean;
{tests string stored in Word[Front] to Word[Back] for palindrome}

    begin    {function Test}
    if (Back - Front <= 0) then
      Test := True
    else
      if Word[Front] <> Word[Back] then
        Test := False
      else
        Test := Test(Word, Front+1, Back-1);
    end;     {function Test}

begin    {main program}
  GetInput(Word, n);
  writeln;
  write('The string ');
  for i := 1 to n do
    write(Word[i]);
  if Test(Word, 1, n) then
    writeln(' is a palindrome')
```

else
writeln(' is not a palindrome');
end   {main program}.

RUNNING THE PROGRAM. . .

Enter string of characters to test for palindrome (max. 30 characters).

atoyota

The string atoyota is a palindrome

12.4 Recursive Procedures

12.4.1 *Generating Permutations*

Consider a string of four characters, ABCD. There are twenty-four different arrangements or **permutations** of these four characters. Some of the permutations are:

ABCD   ABDC   ACBD   ACDB   ADBC   ADCB
BACD   etc.

CHECKUP 12.2

a. Write all of the permutations of ABCD.
b. Prove that the number of permutations of n characters is $n!$ (n factorial), where $n! = n*(n-1)*. . .*3*2*1$. (Hint: How many choices are there for the first character?)

Six of the twenty-four permutations begin with the letter A. These six can be generated by fixing the leading A and then generating all possible permutations of the remaining three characters. The same thing works for a leading character of B, C, and D, respectively. Here is where the recursive thinking comes in—finding all the permutations of four characters, with no leading characters fixed, involves four instances of finding all the permutations of four characters with one leading character fixed. The base step occurs when the problem is reduced to finding all permutations of four characters with three leading characters fixed. In this trivial case, the character string itself is the only permutation, and it can be written out.

In the program below, a packed array *String* stores the character string. The *GeneratePermutations* procedure receives as parameters the array to be processed, *String,* and the index i in the array that tells where to begin permuting characters, i.e., the $i - 1$ leading characters are fixed. (For the initial invocation of *GeneratePermutations, i* has the value 1.) The **for** loop within *GeneratePermutations* puts each of the other $4-(i-1)$ characters in turn in position i (using the *Exchange* procedure) and for each such arrangement invokes *GeneratePermutations* to permute the remaining characters in the array.

```pascal
program Permutations(input, output);
{writes all permutations of the four-character string ABCD}

type
    StringType = packed array [1..4] of char;

var
    String : StringType;      {string to be permuted}

procedure Exchange(var String: StringType; i, j: integer);
{exchanges character in position i of String with character in
 position j}

var
    Temp : char;          {temporary holder for array element}

  begin   {procedure Exchange}
    Temp := String[i];
    String[i] := String[j];
    String[j] := Temp;
  end;      {procedure Exchange}

procedure GeneratePermutations (String: StringType; i: integer);
{writes out all permutations of String with first i - 1
 characters fixed}

var
    j : integer;      {array index}

  begin   {GeneratePermutations}
    if i = 4 then
      writeln(String)
    else
      for j := i to 4 do
        begin
          Exchange(String, i, j);
          GeneratePermutations (String, i + 1);
        end;
  end;      {GeneratePermutations}

begin   {main program}
  String[1] := 'A';
  String[2] := 'B';
  String[3] := 'C';
  String[4] := 'D';

  GeneratePermutations(String, 1);

end.      {main program}
```

> **CHECKUP 12.3**   Explain why *String* is a variable formal parameter in procedure *Exchange* above, while *String* is a value formal parameter in procedure *GeneratePermutations*.

12.4.2 *Forward Declarations (Optional)*

Recursion allows a module to be invoked from within itself. In the examples we have seen, this has occurred directly by module *X* containing a statement that invokes module *X*. Recursion can occur more indirectly, however. Suppose that module *X* invokes module *Y*, which in turn invokes module *X*. Then *X* is still invoked within itself (as is *Y*). Modules *X* and *Y* are said to be ***mutually recursive.***

Program modules can be mutually recursive, in which case a forward declaration is required.

There is nothing fundamentally different about this kind of recursion, but it does present one tiny technical problem. Where are modules *X* and *Y* to be declared? Because *X* invokes *Y*, *Y* would normally be declared before *X*, but because *Y* invokes *X*, *X* would normally be declared before *Y*! It seems to be a standoff. The solution is the following. The declaration for *X* can precede the declaration for *Y* as long as a **forward** declaration for *Y* is inserted before *X*'s declaration. This consists of the complete heading for *Y*, including its formal parameter list, followed by the reserved word **forward.** The **forward** declaration notifies the compiler that *Y* will indeed be declared later on; otherwise the compiler would signal an error at the point in *X* where *Y* is invoked, thinking that *Y* is undefined. After *X*'s declaration comes *Y*'s declaration, but without the parameter list this time. (If *Y* is a function, the function type is also omitted in this second heading.) The sequence of declarations looks like

```
procedure Y (formal parameter list for Y); forward;
procedure X (formal parameter list for X);
              .
              .
              .
    Y(actual parameter list);   {Y is invoked}
              .
              .
              .
end;   {procedure X}
procedure Y; {a comment giving the formal parameter list for Y would
              be informative here}
              .
              .
              .
    X(actual parameter list);   {X is invoked}
              .
              .
              .
end;   {procedure Y}
```

Mutual recursion requires an "out of order" function or procedure declaration, but "out of order" declarations can be used as part of program documentation. For example, grouping certain declarations together may improve program readability. The **forward** declaration again comes to the rescue.

12.5 Recursive vs. Iterative Solutions

As we remarked earlier, recursion is not a necessity. If thinking about the problem recursively seems natural and simple, then the capability to write a recursive function or procedure is valuable. Using recursion masks the counting, manipulation of indices and local variables, etc., that the corresponding iterative solution would require. This sort of work is done instead by stacking activation records. Therefore as far as machine resources—memory requirements and execution time—a recursive solution is almost always less efficient than an iterative solution. How much less efficient depends on how "deep" the recursion has to go, which in turn will usually depend not only on the problem but also on the input parameters to the problem. Computing *Power2*(3.0, 0) requires no recursive calls at all, while computing *Power2*(3.0, 17) will put eighteen activation records on the stack.

The payoff for the inefficient use of system resources comes in the simpler conceptual view of the problem solution. How much recursion buys us again depends on the particular problem. *Power2* is not a big improvement over *Power1* in this regard, but the recursive version of *Fibonacci(n)* is crystal clear compared to an iterative version. Some problems are so well suited to a recursive solution that it is hard to imagine how to construct an iterative solution (see Software Development Project #5 for an archetypical example). On the other hand, there are problems where imposing recursion seems to cloud, rather than clarify, the solution (see Skill Builder #2).

In conclusion, the question of the relative merits of recursive vs. iterative solutions doesn't have an easy answer. Recursion is simply another programming tool, a point of view, a thought process with which you should be familiar and that you should apply when it seems appropriate.

12.6 Sample Software Development Project— Natural Language Processing

Problem Statement

Natural language processing, that is, the ability for a computer to "understand" instructions or text expressed in an ordinary human language, as opposed to a restricted programming language, has long been an ideal of computer scientists. It is a difficult goal to achieve because of the complexities, ambiguities, and shades of meaning in English and other "natural" languages. Nonetheless, it is possible to recognize at least a small subset of correctly constructed English sentences. This is done by setting up rules for how the component parts of a sentence can legally be combined, and then ***parsing*** sentences—breaking them into their component parts—to determine whether they fit the rules. Develop a parser for a simple subset of the English language.

Problem Specification

We will first establish the rules for valid sentence forms. Our first rule is that a sentence must be composed of a noun phrase followed by a verb phrase followed by a delimiter. Symbolically, we write

<sentence> --> <noun phrase> <verb phrase> delimiter

The brackets < > denote an item that can be further broken down into components. Items without brackets will denote "atomic components"— those that cannot be further broken down, such as "delimiter" above.

A noun phrase can have any of several forms (read the vertical line below as "or"):

<noun phrase> -->article noun|
               article adjective noun|
               preposition <noun phrase>

As indicated, "article" and "noun" are atomic components, and one valid form for a noun phrase is an article followed by a noun (example: "a book"). Another valid form is an article followed by an adjective followed by a noun (example: "a good book"). The third valid form is recursive, as it includes <noun phrase> as part of the definition of a valid <noun phrase> (example: "from a good book").

The forms for a verb phrase are:

<verb phrase> --> verb|
              verb <noun phrase>|

The atomic components are thus:

article
adjective
noun
preposition
verb
delimiter

We must identify acceptable instances of atomic components, in effect setting up a dictionary. Suppose we define the following dictionary:

Instance	Atomic Component
a	article
the	article
good	adjective
black	adjective
book	noun
cat	noun
in	preposition
of	preposition
eats	verb
(period)	delimiter

Then

the good cat eats of the book.

is a valid sentence, but

a cat eats from a good book.

is not valid ("from" is not in the dictionary). Our language is restricted not only by the size of the dictionary, but also by the limited rules we have adopted. For example, a noun phrase does not allow for more than one adjective, so

the good black cat eats of the book.

is also not valid. Some nonsensical phrases are ruled out:

a book of cat eats.

is not a legitimate sentence. According to our rules, however.

a cat eats of of of a book.

is legal!

We will let the user create the dictionary, but we will limit the number of instances of each atomic component type. We will also limit the length of each word in a sentence. The program will then consider sentences input by the user and determine, in each case, whether the sentence is valid. If it is not valid, the program will try to diagnose where it fails to satisfy the rules.

Algorithm and Data Structure Development

A convenient data structure for the dictionary is an array of records, with each record having an "instance" field holding a defined word and a "kind" field (the kind field gives the particular atomic component of which this is an instance). Words can be packed arrays of char. The "kind" values can constitute an enumerated data type, except it will be handy to have an additional value of "nomatch" to indicate when a dictionary search for a word has failed. We will also need a small array to hold the current word read from the sentence, but we don't need a data structure for the entire sentence because we never need to see the sentence all at once. This also means that we don't need to limit the size of the sentence.

Major subtasks involved in this problem are: building the dictionary, getting words from the input sentence, and parsing the sentence. The parsing task has several subtasks, namely, it must test in turn for noun phrase, verb phrase, and delimiter. Each of these can be boolean-valued functions, returning a true value if the conditions for that component are satisfied. The noun phrase function will be recursive, in accordance with the definition of a noun phrase. In addition, we'll make searching the dictionary for a given word a separate subtask because the noun phrase and verb phrase tasks must do this for each word. The diagnosis will be handled by setting message flags in a boolean array for various types of rule violations. Figure 12.3 shows our view of the problem at this point.

Preliminary data structure declarations are

type
    KindType = (article, adjective, noun, preposition, verb,
                 delimiter, nomatch);
    WordType = **packed array** [1..12] **of** char;
    Entry = **record**
      Instance : WordType;   {instance of atomic component}
      Kind : KindType;   {kind of atomic component}
      end;   {Entry}
    DicType = **array** [1..26] **of** Entry;   {3 articles, 3 delimiters,
                                   5 of each other kind
                                   except   nomatch}

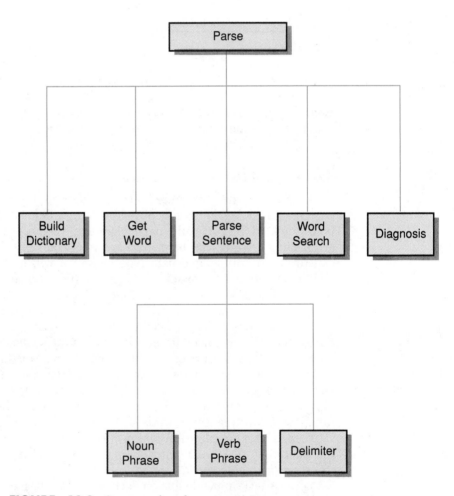

FIGURE 12.3 Structure chart for program *Parse*.

BitArray = **array** [1..6] **of** boolean; {6 kinds of messages}

var
    Dictionary : DicType;   {user-built dictionary of legal
                              instances of atomic components}

    Message : BitArray;   {message array for diagnostic
                            messages}

Build Dictionary
The user is asked to build the dictionary, supplying a limited
number of words that are instances of each kind of atomic
component. Because there are only three articles ("a," "an," and
"the"), we'll build these into the dictionary up front (and so inform
the user). We'll also include three delimiters (period, question mark,
exclamation point).

We'll give brief instructions to the user, then supply a series of
prompts, one for each kind of atomic component. After each prompt,
we'll read in the instances of that kind that the user wishes to
include in the dictionary. Words that are shorter than twelve
characters are automatically padded with blanks. The dictionary
will, of course, be passed as a variable parameter because the rest of
the program needs access to it.

procedure BuildDictionary(**var** Dictionary: DicType);
{prompts the user for instances of each kind of atomic
component, stores these in Dictionary}

var
    Word: WordType   {holds current word entered}

begin   {procedure BuildDictionary}

    give the user general info. about the dictionary
    initialize dictionary with articles and delimiters, load
blanks in the remaining word fields and the appropriate kind
value in the kind fields
    for each of the other kinds **do**
        for each of 5 entries **do**
            while user has more entries **and**
limit not exceeded **do**
                prompt user for instance (RETURN for no entry)
                read word (max. 12 characters)
                load into instance field

end;   {procedure BuildDictionary}

Get Word

The *GetWord* procedure will be used to isolate the next word from the sentence being tested. Note that although this word is the same type as the dictionary entries—a packed array of 12 characters—this is not the procedure used to read the dictionary words. The dictionary entries are given as isolated words, whereas *GetWord* must read the input string from the current position until the next blank (or a delimiter) is found. The final *NextChar*—the blank or delimiter—is returned to a global variable *LastChar* and will be used as a check on whether a delimiter has been seen. A boolean flag *TooLong* will signal when the word exceeds the twelve-character limit; if this is ever set to true, it should cause the sentence to be invalid. It should also set a bit in the *Message* array so that the appropriate message will eventually be printed out.

```
procedure GetWord(var Word: WordType;
                  var NextChar: char;
                  var TooLong: boolean;
                  var Message: BitArray);
{reads the next word Word in the sentence input string;
returns final NextChar value, which is of interest only if it
is a delimiter; TooLong is set to true for word exceeding
12 chars}

begin    {procedure GetWord}

    read NextChar until first nonblank found
    read nonblank characters into Word until blank or
delimiter found or length exceeded
    if length exceeded, set TooLong and the correct Message
bit

end;    {procedure GetWord}
```

Delimiter

The *Delim* function only needs to check the value of *LastChar* because that is the last character read by the most recent application of *GetWord*. *LastChar* will be padded with blanks and then compared with the dictionary records of kind "delimiter." The function value is set to true if a match occurs.

Word Search

This procedure compares a word against the dictionary, returning the kind of the word if it is found, and setting a message flag otherwise.

procedure WordSearch(**var** Dictionary: DicType;
Word: WordType;
var Kind: KindType;
var Message: BitArray);
{compares Word with Dictionary instances; if a match is found, Kind returns the kind of atomic component for Word, otherwise Kind has value nomatch}

Noun Phrase

The function *NounPhrase* does a succession of *GetWord* calls and matches the words against the legal forms for a noun phrase. *NounPhrase* needs access to the dictionary array; it will not modify the dictionary, but because *NounPhrase* is a recursive function, we'll make *Dictionary* a variable parameter so as not to consume so much memory. For the same reason, *Dictionary* is a variable parameter in *WordSearch*, which is invoked by *NounPhrase*. *NounPhrase* passes the flag *TooLong* back and forth between *GetWord* and the main program. It also updates the *Message* array in case violations occur. We'll initialize a boolean value *OK* to false and then change this value if a noun phrase is seen; *OK* will eventually be the function value.

function NounPhrase(**var** Dictionary: DicType;
var TooLong: boolean;
var Message: BitArray): boolean;
{tests part of input string for valid noun phrase form,
 returns true if valid form found, false otherwise}

var
    Word : WordType;   {current word being tested}
    OK : boolean;   {will be function value}
    Kind : KindType;   {Word kind}

begin   {function NounPhrase}
   initialize OK false
   do *GetWord* and *WordSearch*

Continued

Noun Phrase—Continued

```
if Word kind is an article or a preposition, then
    case Kind of
        article: begin    {article}
                do GetWord and WordSearch
                if Word kind is a noun then OK
                else
                    if Word kind is an adjective then
                        do GetWord and WordSearch
                        if Word kind is a noun then  OK
                        else set a Message flag-3rd word
                                not noun
                    else set a Message flag - 2nd word
                            not noun or adjective
            end;    {article}
        preposition: OK := NounPhrase(Dictionary, TooLong,
                                                Message);
        end;    {case statement}
    else
        set a Message flag
    NounPhrase := OK
end;    {function NounPhrase}
```

Verb Phrase

The *VerbPhrase* procedure works exactly like the *NounPhrase* procedure, again testing a succession of words against the legal verb phrase forms. The only trick here is that while looking for a noun phrase after a verb, we may instead read the delimiter. The flag *EndFound* will carry this information back to the main program so that it does not attempt to read the delimiter again.

```
function VerbPhrase(Dictionary: DicType;
                    var TooLong: boolean;
                    var EndFound: boolean;
                    var Message: BitArray):  boolean;
{tests part of input string for valid verb phrase form, returns
 true if valid form found, false otherwise}
```

Main program

The main program builds the dictionary and then, for as many sentences as the user wishes to enter, checks in turn for true values to *NounPhrase*, *VerbPhrase*, and *Delim*. If any of these values are not

Continued

Main Program—Continued

true, it consults the *Message* array to see what diagnostic messages to print.

```
begin      {main program}
  BuildDictionary(Dictionary);
  while user wants to do more sentences
    prompt for sentence
    initialize flags
    check NounPhrase, VerbPhrase, Delimiter
    write message about whether sentence is valid
    if invalid sentence, write diagnostic messages

end.      {main program}
```

The data flow diagram is shown in Figure 12.4. *Dictionary* is shown as an "input/output" parameter for *NounPhrase* because it is passed as a variable parameter, even though modification of *Dictionary* by *NounPhrase* would be an undesirable side effect.

```
program parse(input, output);
{recognizes restricted subset of English sentences}

type
    KindType  = (article, adjective, noun, preposition, verb,
                    delimiter, nomatch);
    WordType  = packed array [1..12] of char;
    Entry = record
      Instance : WordType;       {instance of atomic component}
      Kind : KindType;           {kind of atomic component}
      end;     {Entry}
    DicType = array [1..26] of Entry; {3 articles, 3 delimiters,
                                       5 of each other kind
                                       except nomatch}
    BitArray = array [1..6] of boolean;    {6 kinds of messages}

var
    Dictionary : DicType;    {user-built dictionary of legal
                                instances of atomic components}
    LastChar : char;         {last character read from sentence -
                                may be delimiter or separating blank}
    TooLong : boolean;       {set to true whenever a too-
                                long word is encountered}
    EndFound : boolean;      {set to true if delimiter already read}
```

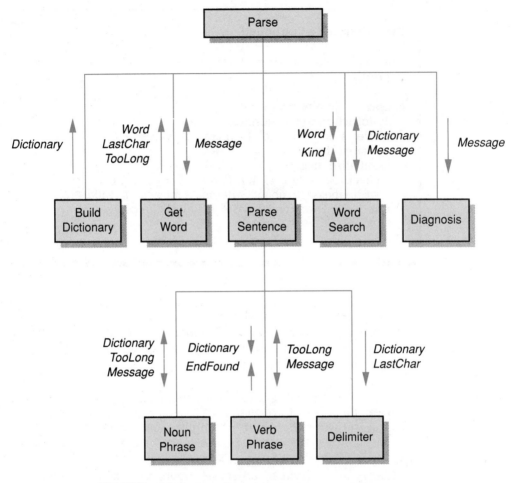

FIGURE 12.4 Data flow diagram for program *Parse*.

Good : boolean;	{set to false if sentence form <noun phrase><verb phrase>delimiter not found}
Response : char;	{response to process more sentences}
Message : BitArray;	{message array for diagnostic messages}
i: integer;	{array index}

procedure BuildDictionary(**var** Dictionary: DicType);
{prompts the user for instances of each kind of atomic component, stores these in Dictionary}

var

Word : WordType;	{holds current word entered}
i, j, n : integer;	{array indices and counters}
symbol : char;	{next character read}

```
Index : integer;          {index in Dictionary for this  word}
Blank : WordType;         {used to initialize array}

begin    {procedure BuildDictionary}
  writeln('In order to use this program to recognize sentences,');
  writeln('you must build a dictionary of valid words. These');
  writeln('words will be of the following types:  article,');
  writeln('adjective, noun, preposition, verb, and');
  writeln('delimiter.   For example, a noun could be ''cat'' or');
  writeln('''windmill'', a preposition could be ''of''
          or ''to'', and');
  writeln('a delimiter could be   .   (a period). The dictionary');
  writeln('automatically includes three articles - a, an,  the,');
  writeln('and 3 delimiters - period, question mark, and ');
  writeln('exclamation point. You must supply the  other entries,');
  writeln('up to 5 of each type.');
  writeln;

  {initialize the dictionary}
  Blank := '            ';     {12 blanks to initialize
                                Instance fields in Dictionary}
  Dictionary[1].Instance := 'a          ';
  Dictionary[2].Instance := 'an         ';
  Dictionary[3].Instance := 'the        ';
  for i := 1 to 3 do
    Dictionary[i].Kind := article;

  for i := 4 to 23 do
    Dictionary[i].Instance := Blank;
  for i := 4 to 8 do
    Dictionary[i].Kind := adjective;
  for i := 9 to 13 do
    Dictionary[i].Kind := noun;
  for i := 14 to 18 do
    Dictionary[i].Kind := preposition;
  for i := 19 to 23 do
    Dictionary[i].Kind := verb;

  Dictionary[24].Instance := '.          ';
  Dictionary[25].Instance := '?          ';
  Dictionary[26].instance := '!          ';
  for i := 24 to 26 do
    Dictionary[i].Kind := delimiter;

  {now load the dictionary}
  for i := 1 to 4 do
    begin    {i = 1 to 4}
      writeln;
      writeln('Enter up to 5 words of this type, one per line,');
      writeln('max. 12 characters each. ');
```

```
            writeln('Hit RETURN for no entry.');
            writeln;
            case i of
              1: writeln('Adjective');
              2: writeln('Noun');
              3: writeln('Preposition');
              4: writeln('Verb');
              end;     {case statement}


            for n := 1 to 5 do
              begin     {collect nth word of kind i}
                writeln;
                writeln('Word', n:2, ' of this type: ');
                j := 0;
                while (not eoln) and (j < 12) do
                  begin     {while}
                    j := j + 1;
                    Index := 3 + 5*(i - 1) + n;
                    read(Dictionary[Index].Instance[j]);
                  end;      {while}
                if (j = 12) and (not eoln) then
                  writeln('Only first 12 characters used');
                readln;
              end;      {collect nth word of kind i}
          end;      {i = 1 to 4}


  end;     {procedure BuildDictionary}


procedure GetWord(var Word: WordType;
                  var NextChar:  char;
                  var TooLong: boolean;
                  var Message: BitArray);
{reads the next word Word in the sentence input string; returns
final NextChar value, which is of interest only if it is a
delimiter; TooLong is set to true for word exceeding 12 chars}

  begin {procedure GetWord}
    {initialize Word to blanks}
    Word := '               ';
    {skip any initial blanks}
    read(NextChar);
    while (NextChar = ' ') do
      read(NextChar);

    {beginning of next word}
    i := 1;
    while (NextChar <> ' ') and (NextChar <> '.') and
          (NextChar <> '?') and (NextChar <> '!') and
          (i <= 12) do
```

```
    begin      {while}
      Word[i] := NextChar;
      i := i + 1;
      read(NextChar);
    end;       {while}
```

{NextChar should be a blank or delimiter, otherwise
 word too long}
```
    if (NextChar <> ' ') and (NextChar <> '.') and
       (NextChar <> '?') and (NextChar <> '!') then
      begin    {word too long}
        TooLong := true;
        Message[1] := true;
      end;       {word too long}
  end;   {procedure GetWord}
```

```
function Delim(Dictionary: DicType; LastChar: char): boolean;
```
{tests LastChar to see if it is a delimiter as stored in
 records 24-26 of Dictionary}

```
var
    Word : WordType;    {padded form of LastChar}
    i, j : integer;          {array indices}

  begin    {function Delimiter}
    Word[1] := LastChar;
    for i := 2 to 12 do
      Word[i] := ' ';
    if (Word = Dictionary[24].Instance) or
       (Word = Dictionary[25].Instance) or
       (Word = Dictionary[26].Instance) then
          Delim := true
    else
          Delim := false;
  end;      {function Delimiter}
```

```
procedure WordSearch(var Dictionary: DicType;
                         Word: WordType;
                         var Kind: KindType;
                         var Message: BitArray);
```
{compares Word with Dictionary instances; if a match is
 found, Kind returns the kind of atomic component for
 Word, otherwise Kind has value nomatch}

```
var
    i : integer;      {array index}

  begin    {procedure WordSearch}
    Kind := nomatch;
    i := 0;
```

```
    while (Kind = nomatch) and (i < 26) do
      begin   {while}
        i := i + 1;
        if Word = Dictionary[i].Instance then
          begin
            Kind := Dictionary[i].Kind;
          end;
      end;   {while}
    if Kind = nomatch then
      Message[2] := true;
end;   {procedure WordSearch}

function NounPhrase(var Dictionary: DicType;
                    var TooLong: boolean;
                    var Message: BitArray): boolean;
{tests part of input string for valid noun phrase form,
returns true if valid form found, false otherwise}

var
    Word : WordType;      {current word being tested}
    OK : boolean;         {will be function value}
    Kind : KindType;      {Word kind}

  begin   {function NounPhrase}
    OK := false;
    GetWord(Word, LastChar, TooLong, Message);
    WordSearch(Dictionary, Word, Kind, Message);
    if (Kind = article) or (Kind = preposition) then
      case Kind of

        article : begin   {1st word article}
          GetWord(Word, LastChar, TooLong, Message);
          WordSearch(Dictionary, Word, Kind, Message);
          if (Kind = noun) then
            OK := true   {article-noun form}
          else
            if (Kind = adjective) then
              begin   {2nd word adjective}
                GetWord(Word, LastChar, TooLong, Message);
                WordSearch(Dictionary, Word, Kind, Message);
                if (Kind = noun) then
                  OK := true   {article-adjective-noun form}
                else {3rd word not noun - OK still false}
                  Message[5] := true;
              end   {2nd word adjective}
            else   {2nd word not noun or adjective - OK still false}
              Message[4] := true;
        end;   {1st word article}
```

```
                   preposition : OK := NounPhrase(Dictionary, TooLong, Message);
          end    {case}
       else
          begin {1st word wrong kind or no match - OK still  false}
             if Kind <> nomatch then
                Message[3] := true
          end;   {1st word wrong kind or no match}
       NounPhrase := OK;   {give NounPhrase the appropriate  value}
    end;    {function NounPhrase}


function VerbPhrase(Dictionary: DicType;
                    var TooLong:  boolean;
                    var EndFound: boolean;
                    var Message: BitArray):
{tests part of input string for valid verb phrase form, returns
 true if valid form found, false otherwise}


var
    Word : WordType;      {current word being tested}
    OK : boolean;         {will be function value}
    Kind : KindType;      {kind of Word}


  begin    {function VerbPhrase}
    OK := false;
    GetWord(Word, LastChar, TooLong, Message);
    WordSearch(Dictionary, Word, Kind, Message);
    if (Kind = verb) then
       begin   {1st word verb}
          if not Delim(Dictionary, LastChar) then
             begin {more follows the verb}
                OK := NounPhrase(Dictionary, TooLong, Message);
             end    {more follows the verb}
          else
             begin {2nd word delimiter}
                OK := true;   {verb form}
                EndFound := true;   {delimiter already read}
             end;   {2nd word delimiter}
       end    {1st word verb}

    else
       begin {1st word not verb, OK still false}
          if Kind <> nomatch then
             Message[6] := true;
       end;   {1st word not verb, OK still false}
    VerbPhrase := OK;     {give VerbPhrase the appropriate  value}
  end;    {function VerbPhrase}

procedure Diagnosis(Message: BitArray);
{gives error message as to why sentence is not valid}
```

```
begin    {procedure Diagnosis}
  if Message[1] then
    writeln('some word exceeds 12 characters');
  if Message[2] then
    writeln('some word not in dictionary');
  if Message[3] then
    writeln('first word in noun phrase not article or  prep.');
  if Message[4] then
    writeln('word after article not noun or adjective');
  if Message[5] then
    writeln('word after adjective not a noun');
  if Message[6] then
    writeln('first word in verb phrase not a verb');
end;      {procedure Diagnosis}


begin    {main program}
  BuildDictionary(Dictionary);
  write('Do you have a sentence to test? (Y or N): ');
  readln(Response);
  while (Response = 'Y') or (Response = 'y') do
    begin    {more sentences to test}
    writeln('Enter sentence');
    writeln;
      TooLong := false;
      EndFound := false;
      for i := 1 to 6 do
        Message[i] := false;
      Good := true;
      if not NounPhrase(Dictionary, TooLong, Message) then
        Good := false;
      if not VerbPhrase(Dictionary, TooLong, EndFound, Message) then
        Good := false;
      if not EndFound then    {delimiter not yet read}
        if not Delim(Dictionary, LastChar) then
          Good := false;

    readln;
    writeln;
    if Good and (not TooLong) then
      writeln('This is a sentence')
    else
      begin
        writeln('This is not a sentence');
        writeln;
        Diagnosis(Message);
        writeln;
      end;
```

```
        writeln;
        writeln('Do you have another sentence');
        write('to test? (Y or N): ');
        readln(Response);
      end;    {more sentences to test}

  end.    {main program}
```

RUNNING THE PROGRAM. . .

Suppose that the dictionary has already been built and contains the following words:

Adjectives: hungry, swift, lazy, tall, green
Nouns: lion, zebra, monkey, tree, grass
Prepositions: from, to, in, over
Verbs: eats, attacks, swings, runs, jumps

Then the following interaction can occur:

Do you have a sentence to test? (Y or N): y
Enter sentence

the hungry lion attacks the swift zebra.

This is a sentence

Do you have another sentence
to test? (Y or N): y
Enter sentence

a monkey swings in a tall tree!

This is a sentence

Do you have another sentence
to test? (Y or N): y

Enter sentence

the tall giraffe eats the green grass.

This is not a sentence

some word not in dictionary
word after adjective not a noun

Do you have another sentence
to test? (Y or N): n

View #12

The State Board of Environmental Affairs has changed its reporting requirements. In the future the Lodestone County Water Pollution Department must be prepared to supply data on all readings from a given start date to a given ending date, together with the percentage of violations that occurred during this period.

The major change needed to support this capability is to keep the file *DataH2O* in date-sorted order. To facilitate sorting by date, the record data structure will be changed to store the date in a single packed array of 6 characters, YYMMDD. Then the string 870915 precedes 880423, as desired. We will assume that the file *DataH2O* contains records with this new data structure already sorted by date. We will date-sort the array of entries for the current session and then merge these records into the already sorted file. (This sort-merge operation is the classic solution to the file-update problem that occurs in many business applications—updating a customer mailing list, for example.)

If this process is done from the creation of the data file, then the first merge will put the sorted array in the previously empty file, and from then on the file will be sorted, as assumed. If a large body of unsorted data already exists in the file, then the file itself will have to be sorted before the file-update program can be used (see Software Development Project #6 in the previous chapter for a discussion of how to sort an already existing external file). Furthermore, if this large file contains data in the old date format, then either these records must be modified, or we must approach the problem constrained by the existing data structure. These are difficulties frequently encountered when additional features are required of software far down the road from the design of the original data structure.

As the project manager at Sterling, you choose to date-sort the array of entries for the current session using a recursive version of the selection sort. The recursion works on the principle that if the largest entry is placed in the nth (last) array position, then the problem reduces to that of sorting the first $n - 1$ elements, a smaller array. As a base step, a one-element array is already sorted. Note in the *Sort* procedure below that function *MaxIndex* and procedure *Exchange* are virtually unchanged from the nonrecursive sort done in program *ComputePay* of Chapter 10.

In the *Merge* procedure below, the next record from the data file is compared to the next record from the array; the record with the lower date is the next one merged into *Temp*, the new data file being built. If the array is exhausted while there are more records in the data file, these remaining records are simply appended to the end of *Temp*. Whenever the end-of-file marker is reached, however, a record with an artificially high date field is created so that any remaining records will be added from the array.

Another option will be added to the menu, that of seeing all records within a range of dates. Upon choosing this option, the user must specify the range. (Although these records are written to the screen in the program below, they could also be written to a file for purposes of report generation.)

The previous option of viewing all violators in the file will work just as it did before, except that now the records will be in date-sorted order.

```pascal
program WaterPollution(input, output, DataH2O);
{maintains a file DataH2O of records of water samples from
 various sites; each record contains site ID, date of sample,
 amount of water, and bacteria count, also the bacteria/water
 ratio and a warning if the bacteria level is too high. The file
 is maintained in sorted order by date of sample. The user may
 choose to enter new records (these are displayed in tabular form,
 sorted, and merged into the file), to display all records from
 file that are in violation together with the total number
 of readings in the file and the percentage of total readings
 that are in violation, or to display all readings within a given
 range of dates together with the percentage of violations
 during this period.}

const
     Threshold = 2.0;              {200 bacteria per 100 ml water}
     MaxNoOfReadings = 30;  {maximum number of readings per
                                    session program can handle}

type
     DateArray = packed array [1..6] of char;
     Reading = record
       ID, Water, Bacteria : integer;
       Date : DateArray;
       Level : real;              {pollution level}
       Warning : boolean;         {flag for warning message}
       end;    {Reading}
     Index = 1..MaxNoOfReadings;
     ArrayType = array [Index] of Reading;
     FileType = file of Reading;

var
     DataH2O : FileType;          {file of site readings}
     Task : char;                 {user task selection from menu}

procedure ClearScreen;
{clears the screen by writing 24 blank lines}

var
     i : integer;

  begin    {procedure ClearScreen}
    for i := 1 to 24 do
      writeln;
  end;    {procedure ClearScreen}
```

```
procedure MenuDisplay;
{displays menu of tasks from which user can choose}

  begin    {procedure MenuDisplay}
    ClearScreen;
    writeln;
    writeln('                    Water Pollution Record Keeper');
    writeln;
    writeln('                              written by');
    writeln('                  Sterling Software Systems.');
    writeln;
    writeln('                       Choose task to be done:');
    writeln; writeln;
    writeln('         Enter (E)        Enter new data for file');
    writeln;
    write('         Violators (V)    Display pollution violation');
    writeln(' records from file');
    writeln;
    write('         Display (D)      Display all records within');
    writeln(' given date range');
    writeln;
    writeln('         Quit (Q)         Quit program');
    writeln;
    write('         Enter your choice (E, V, D, or Q): ');
  end;     {procedure MenuDisplay}

procedure CollectResponse(var Choice: char);
{collects the user's choice of action}

type
    Response = set of char;

var
    Valid : Response;

  begin      {procedure CollectResponse}
    valid := ['E','V','D','Q','e','v','d','q'];
    readln(Choice);
    ClearScreen;
    while not (Choice in Valid) do
      begin
        writeln('Your choices are E, V, D, Q, try again: ');
        readln(Choice);
        ClearScreen;
      end;
  end;       {procedure CollectResponse}

procedure DateInput(var Date: DateArray);
{collects date in month/date/year format, returns as YYMMDD in
 array Date}
```

```
type
    TwoCharArray = array[1..2] of char;

var
    Mon, Day, Yr: TwoCharArray;
    Slash : char;      {separating / in date format}

function Value(FirstChar, SecondChar: char): integer;
{function to convert two characters to a two-digit integer}

var
    FirstDigit    : integer;    {the integer equivalents}
    SecondDigit : integer;    {of numerical characters}

  begin   {function Value}
    FirstDigit := ord(FirstChar) − ord('0');
    SecondDigit := ord(SecondChar) − ord('0');
    Value := 10*FirstDigit + SecondDigit;
  end;    {function Value}

function ValidDate(Mon1, Mon2, Day1, Day2: char): boolean;
{function to do some validation on date entered}

var
    MonthValue : integer;    {numerical value for month}
    DayValue : integer;      {numerical value for day}
    ValidMonth : boolean;    {MonthValue in range 1-12}
    ValidDay : boolean;      {DayValue in range 1-31}

  begin    {function ValidDate}
    MonthValue := Value(Mon1, Mon2);
    DayValue := Value(Day1, Day2);

    ValidMonth := (0 < MonthValue) and (MonthValue < 13);
    ValidDay := (0 < DayValue) and (DayValue < 32);

    ValidDate := ValidMonth and ValidDay;
  end;    {function ValidDate}

begin    {procedure DateInput}

    write('Use month/date/year format: ');
    readln(Mon[1], Mon[2], Slash, Day[1], Day[2],
          Slash, Yr[1], Yr[2]);

    while not ValidDate(Mon[1], Mon[2], Day[1], Day[2]) do
      begin {error in date input}
        write('Please enter the date again: ');
        readln(Mon[1], Mon[2], Slash,
              Day[1], Day[2], Slash, Yr[1], Yr[2]);
      end; {error in date input}
```

```
      {date OK, now put it in Date array in YYMMDD form}
      Date[1] := Yr[1];
      Date[2] := Yr[2];
      Date[3] := Mon[1];
      Date[4] := Mon[2];
      Date[5] := Day[1];
      Date[6] := Day[2];
  end;     {procedure DateInput}

procedure GetInput(var OneSite: Reading);
{procedure to collect input for water pollution data; amount
Water of water and count Bacteria of bacteria were obtained
from site ID on date Date (YYMMDD)}

  begin     {procedure GetInput}
    with OneSite do
      begin    {with OneSite}
        writeln;
        write('Enter the site ID number: ');
        readln(ID);
        while not((1 <= ID) and (ID <= 1000)) do
          begin {ID out of range}
            write('Check the site ID number ');
            write('and enter again: ');
            readln(ID);
          end;  {ID out of range}
        writeln;

        writeln('Enter the date of this sample.');
        DateInput(Date);

        writeln;
        write('Enter the amount of water in sample (in ml): ');
        readln(Water);
        while not (Water > 0) do
          begin   {error in amount of water}
            write('Check the amount of water & ');
            write('enter again: ');
            readln(Water);
          end;     {error in amount of water}
        writeln;

        write('Enter the bacteria count found in this sample: ');
        readln(Bacteria);
        while not (Bacteria >= 0) do
          begin   {error in bacteria count}
            write('Check the bacteria count & ');
```

```
            write('enter again: ');
            readln(Bacteria);
        end;   {error in bacteria count}
    end;   {with OneSite}

  end;      {procedure GetInput}


function Ratio(Bacteria, Water: integer): real;


  begin      {function Ratio}
    Ratio := Bacteria/Water;
  end;       {function Ratio}

procedure CheckThreshold(Ratio: real; var Over: Boolean);
{compares Ratio to the global constant Threshold and sets
Over to true if that limit is exceeded}

  begin      {procedure CheckThreshold}
    Over := false;    {initialize Over}
    if Ratio > Threshold then
      Over := true;
  end;       {procedure CheckThreshold}


procedure WriteHeader;
{writes output table heading}

  begin     {procedure WriteHeader}
    writeln;
    writeln;
    write('Site ID', 'Date':8, 'Water':12, 'Bacteria':13);
    writeln('Level':9, 'Warning':10);
    write('_____');
    writeln('_____');
    writeln;
  end; {procedure WriteHeader}


procedure WriteLineOfOutput(OneSite: Reading);
{produces a line of output in the table corresponding to one
reading - echoes input data and writes warning message if
warranted}

  begin      {procedure WriteLineOfOutput}
    with OneSite do
      begin    {with OneSite}
        write(ID:5, Date[3]:6, Date[4], '/', Date[5],
            Date[6], '/', Date[1], Date[2]);
        write(Water:8, ' ml', Bacteria:9, Level:11:2);
```

```
        if Warning then
          write('     ** HIGH **');
        writeln;
      end;    {with OneSite}
  end;      {procedure WriteLineOfOutput}
```

```
procedure Sort(var A: ArrayType; n: integer);
{recursive selection sort on array A, sorting records from 1 to n
 on Date field}
```

```
var
    i : integer;                    {index in array A}
```

```
function MaxIndex(A: ArrayType; i: integer): integer;
{finds the index of the maximum value from 1 to i in array A}
```

```
var
    CurrentMaxIndex : integer;      {index of current max value}
    j : integer;                    {array index}

  begin    {function MaxIndex}
    CurrentMaxIndex := 1;
    for j := 2 to i do
      begin
        if A[j].Date > A[CurrentMaxIndex].Date then
            CurrentMaxIndex := j;
      end;
    MaxIndex := CurrentMaxIndex;
  end;     {function MaxIndex}
```

```
procedure Exchange(var X, Y: Reading);
{exchanges records X and Y}
```

```
var
    Temporary : Reading;

  begin    {procedure Exchange}
    Temporary := X;
    X := Y;
    Y := Temporary;
  end;     {procedure Exchange}
```

```
  begin    {procedure Sort}
    if n > 1 then
      begin    {array length > 1}
        Exchange(A[n], A[MaxIndex(A, n)]);
        Sort(A, n−1);
      end;    {array length > 1}
```

```
  end;    {procedure Sort}

procedure Merge(var DataH2O, Temp: FileType;
                var Session: ArrayType; n: integer);
{merges records from sorted file DataH2O and sorted array Session
(with n entries) into file Temp}

var
    i : integer;          {array index}
    Entry : Reading;      {record in file}

  begin    {procedure Merge}

    reset(DataH2O);
    rewrite(Temp);
    i := 1;
    if not eof(DataH2O) then
      read(DataH2O, Entry)
    else Entry.Date := '999999';

    while (i <= n) do
      begin    {more items left in array}

        if Entry.Date <= Session[i].Date then
          begin    {write record from file into Temp}
            write(Temp, Entry);
            if not eof(DataH2O) then
              read(DataH2O, Entry)
            else Entry.Date := '999999';
          end     {write record from file into Temp}
        else
          begin    {write record from array into Temp}
            write(Temp, Session[i]);
            i := i + 1;
          end;    {write record from array into Temp}
      end;    {more items left in array}

{the array is exhausted, put any remaining legitimate
 records from the file into Temp}

    while Entry.Date <> '999999' do
      begin
        write(Temp, Entry);
        if not eof(DataH2O) then
          read(DataH2O, Entry)
        else Entry.Date := '999999';
      end;
  end;       {procedure Merge}
```

```
procedure NewData(var DataH2O: FileType);
{handles collection and display of new records, sorts them by
date, and merges them with already existing sorted file
DataH2O}

var
    Session : ArrayType;      {holds records entered in current
                               program session}
    Continue : char;          {signal to terminate data entry}
    n : integer;              {number of readings to process}
    i : integer;              {array index}
    Temp : FileType;          {temporary file for file copy}
    Entry : Reading;          {record in file}

begin    {procedure NewData}

    n := 0;
    repeat
      n := n + 1;

      GetInput(Session[n]);

      with Session[n] do
        Level := Ratio(Bacteria, Water);

      writeln;
      writeln;
      if (n < MaxNoOfReadings) then
        begin {room for more data}
          writeln('Do you have more sites to process?');
          writeln('(Answer Y or N): ');
          readln(Continue);
        end    {room for more data}
      else
        begin {array full}
          writeln('Maximum number of readings entered. ');
          write('Adjust program constant MaxNoOfReadings ');
          writeln('if this is a problem.');
        end;    {array full}

    until (Continue = 'N') or (Continue = 'n') or
          (n = MaxNoOfReadings);

  {all the input has been gathered and stored in the array, now
  print out table}

    write('The following new records will be merged');
    writeln(' into file DataH2O.');
```

```
      WriteHeader;
      for i := 1 to n do
        begin {produce line i of the output table}
           CheckThreshold(Session[i].Level, Session[i] Warning);
           WriteLineOfOutput(Session[i]);
        end;   {line i has been written}
      writeln;
      writeln('Hit RETURN to continue');
      readln;

   {now sort this array by date}
      Sort (Session, n);

   {now merge these records into sorted file DataH2O}
      Merge(DataH2O, Temp, Session, n);

   {merge complete, now copy back to DataH2O}
      reset(Temp);
      rewrite(DataH2O);
      while not eof(Temp) do
        begin
           read(Temp, Entry);
           write(DataH2O, Entry);
        end;     {DataH2O now complete}

   end;      {procedure NewData}

procedure Violators(var DataH2O: FileType);
{displays all records in file DataH2O with pollution levels above
 threshold}

var
      Entry : Reading;            {record in file}
      Count : integer;            {number of records in file}
      Bad : integer;              {number of violation records in
                                    file}
      Percentage : real;          {percent violation records}

   begin    {procedure Violators}
      reset(DataH2O);
      writeln('Readings from file that are in violation:');
      writeln;
      Count := 0;
      Bad := 0;
      WriteHeader;
      while not eof(DataH2O) do
        begin
           read(DataH2O, Entry);
```

```
    if Entry.Warning then
      begin
        WriteLineOfOutput(Entry);
        Bad := Bad + 1;
      end;
    Count := Count + 1;
  end;    {while not eof}
writeln;
if Count = 0 then
  begin
    writeln('File DataH2O is empty');
    writeln('Hit RETURN to continue');
    readln;
  end
else
  begin
    write('Total number of readings in file: ');
    writeln(Count:3);
    writeln('Percentage of readings in file ');
    write('that are in violation: ');
    Percentage := (Bad/Count)*100;
    writeln(Percentage:6:2);
    writeln('Hit RETURN to continue');
    readln;
  end;
end;    {procedure Violators}


procedure Display(var DataH2O: FileType);
{displays all records in file DataH2O within a given range of
dates; gives percent of these records with pollution levels above
threshold}

var
    StartDate, EndDate : DateArray;      {range of dates for
                                          display}
    RangeBegin, RangeEnd : boolean;      {flags for marking
                                          beginning and end of
                                          range as file is read}
    Entry : Reading;                     {record in file}
    Count : integer;                     {number of records in range}
    Bad : integer;                       {number of violation records
                                          in range}
    Percentage : real;                   {percent violation records in
                                          range}

begin    {procedure Display}
    writeln('Enter starting date for display of records;');
    DateInput(StartDate);
    writeln;
```

```
writeln('Enter ending date for display of records;');
DateInput(EndDate);
writeln;
while StartDate > EndDate do
  begin    {bad range dates}
    writeln('Starting date must precede ending date.');
    writeln('Please try again.');
    writeln('Enter starting date for display of records;');
    DateInput(StartDate);
    writeln;
    writeln('Enter ending date for display of records;');
    DateInput(EndDate);
    writeln;
  end;    {bad range dates}
reset(DataH2O);
RangeBegin := false;
RangeEnd := false;
writeln('Readings from file within this range of dates:');
writeln;
Count := 0;
Bad := 0;
WriteHeader;

if eof(DataH2O) then
  begin
    writeln('File DataH2O is empty');
    writeln('Hit RETURN to continue');
    readln;
  end
else
  begin    {file not empty}

    while (not eof(DataH2O)) and (not RangeBegin) do
      begin    {looking for first record in range}
        read(DataH2O, Entry);
        if (Entry.Date >= StartDate) and
           (Entry.Date <= EndDate) then
          begin    {first record in range found}
            RangeBegin := true;
            WriteLineOfOutput(Entry);
            if Entry.Warning then
              Bad := Bad + 1;
            Count := Count + 1;
          end;    {first record in range found}
      end;    {looking for first record in range}

    while (not eof(DataH2O)) and (not RangeEnd) do
      begin    {processing records in range}
        read(DataH2O, Entry);
```

```
           if Entry.Date <= EndDate then
             begin    {this record in range}
               WriteLineOfOutput(Entry);
               if Entry.Warning then
                 Bad := Bad + 1;
               Count := Count + 1;
             end      {this record in range}
           else    {turn off processing}
             RangeEnd := true;
         end;    {processing records in range}

     writeln;
     if Count = 0 then
       begin
         writeln('No records within this range');
         writeln('Hit RETURN to continue');
         readln;
       end
     else
       begin
         writeln('Percentage of readings in range ');
         write('that are in violation: ');
         Percentage := (Bad/Count)*100;
         writeln(Percentage:6:2);
         writeln('Hit RETURN to continue');
         readln;
       end;
   end;    {file not empty}
 end;    {procedure Display}




begin    {main program}

  MenuDisplay;
  CollectResponse(Task);
  while not ((Task = 'Q') or (Task = 'q')) do
    begin
      case Task of
        'E','e': NewData(DataH2O);
        'V','v': Violators(DataH2O);
        'D','d': Display(DataH2O);
      end; {case}
      MenuDisplay;
      CollectResponse(Task);
    end;    {while}

  {Task is QUIT, terminate program}
end.    {main program}
```

RUNNING THE PROGRAM. . .

If the user chooses to view records within a range of dates, the following
interaction could occur.

Water Pollution Record Keeper

written by
Sterling Software Systems

Choose task to be done:

Enter (E)   Enter new data for file

Violators (V)   Display pollution violation records from file

Display (D)   Display all records within given date range

Quit (Q)   Quit program

Enter your choice (E, V, D, or Q): d

Enter starting date for display of records;
Use month/date/year format: 01/01/75

Enter ending date for display of records;
Use month/date/year format: 12/31/78

Readings from file within this range of dates:

Site ID	Date	Water	Bacteria	Level	Warning
412	06/15/75	790 ml	1920	2.43	** HIGH **
210	04/30/77	1200 ml	720	0.60	
340	08/12/77	900 ml	2200	2.44	** HIGH **

Percentage of readings in range
that are in violation: 66.67
Hit RETURN to continue

**CASE
STUDY
TWO**   **View #12**

Modify the hypertension clinic program to maintain the file of patient
records sorted by date of visit. The user should be able to specify a range of
dates and see all records within this range, together with the percentage of

records within this range in each of the three hypertensive categories. In addition, all records in the file for each of these categories should be available, as before.

EXERCISES

#1. What function is computed by the following:

```
function f(n: integer): integer;
  begin
    if n = 1 then
      f := 1
    else
      f := f(n − 1) + 1;
  end;
```

2. The following function is initially invoked with an i value of 1. *List* is a one-dimensional array of ten integers. What does the function do?

```
function g(List: Arraytype; i, x: integer): boolean;
  begin
    if i > 10 then
      g := false
    else
      if List[i] = x then
        g := true
      else
        g := g(List, i + 1, x);
  end;
```

#3. Write a nonrecursive version of function Fibonacci from this chapter.

4. Write still another version of function Fibonacci using the fact that the nth Fibonacci number is given by the formula

$$F(n) = \frac{\sqrt{5}}{5}\left(\frac{1 + \sqrt{5}}{2}\right)^n - \frac{\sqrt{5}}{5}\left(\frac{1 - \sqrt{5}}{2}\right)^n$$

5. For the recursive function

$$f(0,y) = y$$
$$f(x,0) = x$$
$$f(x,y) = f(x − 1,y) + f(x,y − 1)$$

compute the value of $f(2,3)$. How many times is function f invoked (counting the initial invocation)?

6. Ackermann's function is a recursive function defined by

$$A(0,y) = 1$$
$$A(1,0) = 2$$

$$A(x,0) = x + 2 \quad \text{for } x \geq 2$$
$$A(x+1,y+1) = A(A(x,y+1),y)$$

It is an example of a function that grows extremely rapidly.

#a. Find a general expression $f(x)$ for $A(x,1)$, $x \geq 1$.

b. Find a general expression $g(x)$ for $A(x,2)$, $x \geq 1$.

c. Compute the value of $A(4,3)$.

SKILL BUILDERS

1. Write a recursive function to compute $f(n) = n!$, where $0! = 1$ and for $n \geq 1$, $n! = n*(n-1)*\ldots*3*2*1$.

#2. a. Write a recursive procedure to double all the elements in a one-dimensional array of integers of size 5.

b. Write an iterative version of this procedure.

c. Comment on the relative merits of the two approaches.

3. Write recursive functions to compute

a. $g(n,m) = n + m$

b. $h(n,m) = n*m$

#4. a. The number of **combinations** of (groups consisting of) r objects out of a set of n objects, $C(n,r)$, is given by the formula

$$C(n,r) = \frac{n}{r!(n-r)!}$$

Prove that this can be expressed recursively as

$$C(n,0) = 1$$
$$C(n,n) = 1$$
$$C(n,r) = C(n-1,r) + C(n-1,r-1) \quad \text{for } n > r > 0$$

b. Write a recursive function to compute $C(n,r)$.

5. Write a recursive function to evaluate a specific polynomial

$$p(x) = a_n x^n + a_{n-1} x^{n-1} + \cdots + a_1 x + a_0$$

for a given value of x.

SOFTWARE DEVELOPMENT PROJECTS

1. Develop a program (using recursion) that requests a positive integer and computes the sum of its digits.

2. The **greatest common divisor** of two integers n and m, $\gcd(n,m)$, is the largest integer that divides both n and m. Suppose m is smaller than n. If m divides n, then $\gcd(n,m) = m$. Otherwise, $\gcd(n,m)$ is equal to the greatest common divisor of m and the remainder when n is divided by m. (This is

Euclid's algorithm, not a self-evident fact.) Suppose m is not smaller than n; in this case, note that $\gcd(n,m) = \gcd(m,n)$. Develop software that collects two positive integers from the user and invokes a recursive function to compute their greatest common divisor.

3. The determinant of an n x n matrix A is defined in terms of minors and cofactors. The ***minor*** of element $A[i,j]$ is the determinant of the $(n-1) \times (n-1)$ matrix obtained from A by crossing out the elements in row i and column j; we'll denote the minor by M_{ij}. The ***cofactor*** of element $A[i, j]$, C_{ij}, is defined by

$$C_{ij} = (-1)^{i+j} M_{ij}$$

The ***determinant*** of A is computed by multiplying all the elements in some fixed row of A by their respective cofactors and summing the results. For example, if the first row is used, then the determinant of A is given by

$$\sum_{j=1}^{n} (A[k,j])(C_{kj})$$

Develop software to read in the size n of a square matrix and collect the matrix elements, then recursively compute the value of the determinant.

4. Develop software that allows the user to enter a set and writes out all of the subsets of that set. (If there are n elements in the set, there will be 2^n subsets.)

5. A classic example of a problem with an elegant recursive solution is the Towers of Hanoi game. This game consists of three pegs, A, B, and C, with a series of rings stacked on peg A; the rings are of different sizes and are stacked from bottom to top in order of decreasing size (Fig. 12.5a). A legitimate move in the game consists of removing the top ring from a peg and putting it on another peg. However, a ring can only be placed on top of a larger ring. The object of the game is to end up with all the rings in order on peg B (Fig. 12.5b). Peg C can be used for temporary storage. Develop software to solve the Towers of Hanoi for n rings, where the user chooses n. The solution should illustrate the sequence of moves that takes place.

TESTING AND MAINTENANCE DEPARTMENT

1. Test your solution to the recursive determinant evaluator (Software Development Project #3 above) for various values of n. Is there a limit on the size of the matrix (and hence the number of recursive invocations) that your machine can handle before a stack overflow occurs? (Unlike program *Palindrome* of this chapter, it is not sufficient to maintain one "global" copy of the original matrix and pass it as a variable parameter. Each invocation of the determinant evaluation function needs its own matrix, hence each activation record must store the entries of the local matrix. This can quickly eat up a lot of memory.)

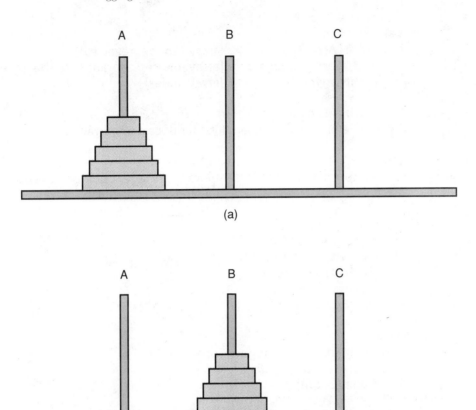

FIGURE 12.5 Towers of Hanoi.

2. Modify function *Power2* of this chapter to handle negative exponents.

3. In the *Merge* procedure of program *WaterPollution* (Case Study One) of this chapter, the end of file is handled by creating a phony record with an artificially high date field. Modify this procedure to use a file window, eliminating the need for the phony record.

4. Devise data sets to thoroughly test program *Parse*.

DEBUGGING CLINIC

1. Find the difficulty with the following program and correct it.

```
program   Reverse(input, output);
{collects 10-element list of integers and reverses it}

type
    ArrayType  =  array  [1..10] of integer;
```

```
var
    List : ArrayType;        {array to be reversed}
    First, Last : integer;   {array indices − range to be reversed}
    i : integer;             {array index}

procedure Exchange(var List: ArrayType; First, Last: integer);
{reverse elements between First and Last in array List}

var
    Temp : integer;     {temporary storage used while switching
                         two values}

  begin {Exchange}
    Temp := List[First];
    List[Last] := List[First];
    List[First] := Temp;
    Exchange(List, First + 1, Last − 1);
  end; {Exchange}

begin
  writeln('Enter 10 integers, one per line.');
  for i := 1 to 10 do
    readln(List[i]);
  First := 1;
  Last := 10;
  Exchange(List, First, Last);
  writeln('Reversed list is:');
  for i := 1 to 10 do
    writeln(List[i]);
end.
```

CHAPTER THIRTEEN

DYNAMIC VARIABLES; ABSTRACT DATA TYPES; SORTING AND SEARCHING

13.1 Dynamic Variables

The variables used so far in our Pascal programs have been **static variables.** Static variables are declared in the program, and the declarations serve to allocate memory locations to hold their values. Using only static variables means that the program's memory allocation requirements (except for the stack to implement recursion) are known when the program is compiled. Pascal does provide mechanisms to request additional memory locations during program execution and to release the locations when they are no longer needed. The variables that use these memory locations created "on the fly" are called **dynamic variables.**

Dynamic variables are not declared (otherwise they would be static variables) and, as a consequence, have no identifier. How is it possible, then, to manipulate these variables—assign them values, write out their values, and so forth? Dynamic variables are manipulated indirectly, by the use of **pointer variables.** A pointer variable is declared, has a name, and is used to "point to" a dynamic variable. It does this by having as its value the address in memory where the dynamic variable is stored. Figure 13.1a illustrates this idea. Here *P* is a pointer variable; the value of this variable is an address in memory. Stored at that address is the value of a dynamic variable of type *integer*. The programmer is never concerned with what the address really is; in fact, pointer variable values cannot be written out, so there is no way to even see this address. We can think of the pointer variable having a rope that connects it to the location to which it points. We never know the true name of the location, but we can get there just the same by following the rope. Figure 13.1b illustrates this conceptual view.

Dynamic variables can have any data type (except a type involving files). However, a given pointer variable can only point to dynamic variables of a particular type, specified in the type declaration for that pointer variable.

The value of a pointer variable can't be written out.

483

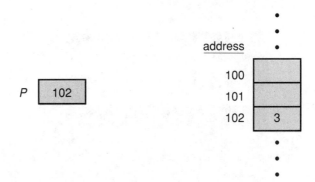

FIGURE 13.1A How a pointer variable works.

FIGURE 13.1B How we can imagine a pointer variable works.

The declarations

The type declaration for a pointer variable identifies the data type of the dynamic variables to which it can point.

type
    NumberPointer = ^integer;
    LetterPointer = ^char;

var
    P, Q : NumberPointer;
    R, S : LetterPointer;

declare two types of pointer variables, those that can point to dynamic variables with integer values, and those that can point to dynamic variables with character values. (An up arrow ↑ can also be used instead of ^ in the type declaration.) Two pointer variables of each type are declared. As with any other variable, a pointer variable's value is initially undefined, so the situation at this point is pictured in Figure 13.2a.

The standard procedure *new* is used to create a memory location for a pointer variable to point to. The statements

    new(P);
    new(R);
    new(S);

have the effect of allocating three memory locations of the proper type (*integer, char,* and *char,* respectively), and assigning the memory addresses of those locations to *P, R,* and *S,* respectively. *P, R,* and *S* now have values;

conceptually, they now point to memory locations (see Fig. 13.2b). The contents of those memory locations, that is, the values of the dynamic variables just created, are still undefined.

These (unnamed) dynamic variables are referenced through the pointer variables that point to them. A pointer variable identifier followed by ^ (or ↑) refers to the dynamic variable pointed to. Using this notation, all the usual things can be done with dynamic variables. For example, the statements

If P is a pointer variable, then P^ is the dynamic variable P points to.

```
P^ := 3;
R^ := 'A';
S^ := 'B';
```

assign values of the appropriate type to the referenced dynamic variables (see Fig. 13.2c).

CHECKUP 13.1   Write a statement that will cause the value of the dynamic variable to which *P* is currently pointing to be written out.

An important distinction in notation should be emphasized. *P* refers to the pointer variable itself, while *P^* refers to what *P* is pointing to. The statement

```
S^ := R^;
```

assigns to the dynamic variable to which *S* points the value of the dynamic variable to which *R* points, resulting in Figure 13.2d. The statement

```
Q := P;
```

assigns to the pointer variable *Q* the value that *P* has, resulting in Figure 13.2e.

CHECKUP 13.2   Given the situation shown in Figure 13.2e, what's the effect of each statement in the following sequence?
 a. P^ := 7;
 b. writeln(Q^);
 c. **writeln(R);**
 d. S := 'B';
 e. S := R;
 f. R^ := 'C';
 g. writeln(S^);
 h. S := Q;

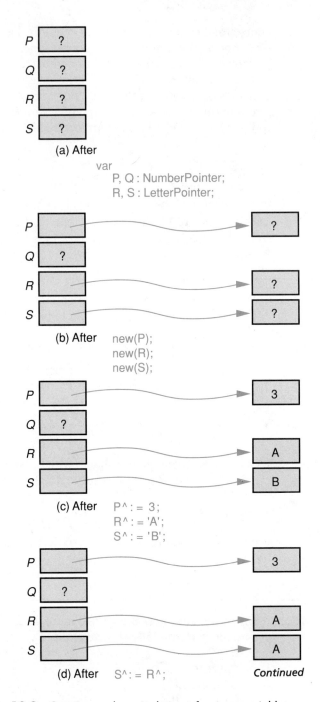

FIGURE 13.2 Creation and manipulation of pointer variables.

A value can be assigned to a pointer variable in one of three ways:

1. By using the *new* procedure. The statement

new(P);

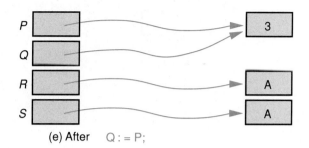

(e) After   Q : = P;

FIGURE 13.2 Creation and manipulation of pointer variables—Continued.

makes *P* point to a new memory location, whose value is undefined.

2. By using the assignment statement between pointer variables of the same type. The statement

    P := Q;

makes *P* point to wherever *Q* is currently pointing.

3. By assigning the value **nil.** The statement

    P := **nil;**

P^ is undefined if P's current value is the nil pointer.

conceptually coils up the pointer rope and stores it in *P*. *P* is not undefined, but it's not currently pointing anywhere either. Therefore when *P* = **nil,** *P^* is undefined. *P* can be tested for the **nil** value, as in

    if (P <> nil) then
        writeln('P points to the value ', P^)
    else
        writeln('P doesn't point anywhere');

It is easy to "lose" things when working with pointer variables. Suppose, for example, that *P* and *Q* are declared as before, and they point to two distinct memory locations, as in Figure 13.3a. If we want to exchange *P* and *Q* so they point to each other's values, the following will *not* work:

When changing pointer values, be careful of the order in which values are changed; use auxiliary pointers if needed so as not to leave some location unreferenced.

    Q := P;
    P := Q;

It helps to think of pointers as ropes. The first statement above unties *Q*'s rope from the location it was pointing to and, following *P*'s rope, ties it where *P* is pointing, resulting in Figure 13.3b. The second statement unties *P*'s rope and, following *Q*'s rope, ties it where *Q* is pointing—the same place as before. The second statement has no effect. To accomplish the switch, we have to use an auxiliary pointer to the location *Q* points to, tying its rope in place before we untie the rope from *Q*.

(a) *P* and *Q* Point to Separate Memory Locations

(b) After   Q : = P;   *Q* and *P* point to the same location.
Now P : = Q has no effect and the
location to which *Q* previously
pointed is "lost"

FIGURE   13.3   Redirecting pointer variables.

CHECKUP 13.3   Assume that *Temp* has been declared as a variable of type
NumberPointer, and write three statements that will switch pointers
P and *Q*. Draw diagrams to illustrate the effect of each statement.

After the statement **Q := P** above, the location to which Q previously
pointed is "lost." It cannot be accessed. Perhaps this is fine, and the program
no longer needs to use the value stored there. However, this value is still
taking up allocated space, and this space can't be reclaimed for further use
by, for example, a subsequent *new* statement. If this sort of thing happens
a great deal during program execution, memory will be littered with
inaccessible and unreclaimable storage locations, known as **garbage.** (Yes,
this is the technical term!) The program may even run out of memory
unless some sort of **garbage collection** is done to reclaim these locations.
The programmer can assist in garbage collection by using the *dispose*
procedure. If R is a pointer variable, the statement

   dispose(R);

releases the location pointed to by R, so that it may be reallocated later.
Given the situation in Figure 13.3a, the sequence

   dispose(Q);
   Q := P;

releases the location to which Q originally points—leaving Q temporarily
undefined—and then redirects Q to point to the same location as P. The

dispose procedure must be done first, before the location to which Q originally points becomes inaccessible.

Suppose that a location is pointed to by more than one pointer variable, say, Q and R. Then

dispose(Q);

renders R as well as Q undefined.†

A pointer variable is usually used to point to a dynamic variable that is a record type, with one field of the record itself being a pointer variable to the record type. Then one can link the dynamic variables together in a chain, as illustrated in Figure 13.4. Records linked together like this are often referred to as **nodes.** We'll look at this idea in more detail shortly, but for now, let's just get the notation straight.

The following declarations define a type *Node* for records that contain three fields; one of these fields is a pointer to records of type *Node*. The type declaration for such pointer variables is given first, even though it references *Node*, which has not yet been declared. Reversing the record and pointer type declarations would make the record declaration reference the pointer type before it had been declared, so this is a circular problem. Pascal allows the form given below, but not the reverse.

Declare the pointer type to a record with a pointer field before declaring the record type.

type
 String = **packed array** [1..5] **of** char;
 NodePointer = ^Node;
 Node = **record**
  Color : String;
  Quantity : integer;
  Link : NodePointer;
  end; {Node}

var
 Head : NodePointer;

Now the statement

new(Head);

allocates storage for a record of type *Node* to which *Head* points. *Head^.Color* references the *Color* field of this record, and *Head^.Quantity* references the

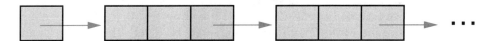

FIGURE 13.4 Records (nodes) linked by pointer variables.

---

† Some versions of Pascal do not implement the *dispose* procedure, and some older versions do so in a peculiar way, such as releasing not only the intended location but also all locations subsequently allocated by *new!*

Quantity field. *Head^.Link* references the pointer field. The value of each of these fields is currently undefined; the *Head^.Link* field can be given a value by

    new(Head^.Link);

Now the pointer in the first record points to a second record, whose fields can be referenced by *Head^.Link^.Color,* etc. (This is nothing new—it's just an exercise in following the ropes!)

13.2 Abstract Data Types

By now we're quite familiar with data structures—mental models of related variables. For instance, a table of values is a mental model that can be implemented by the Pascal **array** data type. In some cases, various operations seem natural to perform on a given data structure. An ***abstract data type*** consists of a data structure together with such operations. It is abstract because it has nothing to do with a programming language (just as the mental model of a table of values exists apart from the Pascal **array** data type). We then have to find ways to implement the abstract data type with the tools available in the programming language at hand. The abstract data types we will discuss here can be implemented in various ways, but the dynamic variables and pointers available in Pascal are particularly useful.

13.2.1 *Lists*

Lists of items are common entities. Such items are related in that there is a first one, followed by a second one, etc. At this point, we may seem to be simply talking about a data structure that can be implemented as a one-dimensional array, which certainly has a first element, a second element, etc. To elevate this idea to an abstract data type, we add the natural operations we might want to perform on a list. We should be able to

Natural operations to perform on a linked list are traversal, search, insert, and delete.

- ■ ***Traverse*** the list—visit each element in turn and write out its value
- ■ ***Search*** the list—inspect each element in turn until a particular element is found
- ■ ***Insert*** an element anywhere in the list
- ■ ***Delete*** an element from anywhere in the list

Even with these operations, an array implementation of a list is possible. Traversing an array or searching an array for a particular entry are tasks we talked about back in Chapter 9. Inserting and deleting array elements is awkward, however. Suppose we wish to delete the third element in a ten-element array *A* indexed from 1 to 10. This has a ripple effect: the element in *A[4]* must be moved to *A[3]*, the element in *A[5]* must be moved to *A[4]*, and so forth. It is awkward to have to readjust all these array indices, even though this work can be carried out within a loop. The amount of work the loop must perform depends on the size of the array and where the deletion takes place. Readjustments are also required if a new element is to be inserted as *A[3]* (assuming the array was not full to begin with). Elements from *A[3]* on must be shifted to make room for the new entry; this has to be done in reverse order, because moving *A[3]* to *A[4]*, for example, overwrites the value of *A[4]*. Again, the amount of work can grow with the size of the array. Finally, as we've noted before, the array occupies a fixed number of memory locations. If the list is shorter than the array capacity, space is wasted; if the list fills the array, no more insertions can be made.

Dynamic variables and pointers provide an alternative list implementation that avoids the fixed memory space allocation of an array. Figure 13.5 illustrates a typical list implemented as a ***linked list,*** so called because of the pointers from one node to the next. A pointer variable called *Head* points to the first node in the list; the end of the list is denoted by the **nil** pointer. An auxiliary pointer to mark our current place in the list is often convenient. Inserting and deleting nodes becomes a simple matter of untying and retying a couple of ropes, i.e., manipulating one or two pointer variables, no matter how large the list currently is or where the insertion or deletion takes place. Auxiliary pointers are also needed in order to keep from "losing" an element while pointer values are being changed. Memory space is allocated (using *new*) when needed for a new node and released (using *dispose*) when no longer needed. As a consequence, a linked list can grow arbitrarily large (subject to main memory limitations, of course), and its use avoids the allocated-but-unused wasted space possible in an array implementation. However, it is also true that each node must have a pointer field, each of which uses a memory location that is not holding useful data.

Inserting and deleting nodes in a linked list does not require the juggling that array insertions and deletions do, and the size of the list is not fixed.

13.2.2 Implementing List Operations

Let's look at procedures to carry out list operations in a linked-list implementation. These procedures will be presented in pseudocode form, as generic operations suitable for any linked list. The details will depend on the nature of the node records. *NodePointer* is used as the identifier of an appropriate pointer type, *Node* is a record type, and *Link* is the pointer field in each node. In general, *Head* will be a pointer to the first node in the list. Passing a list as a parameter to a procedure is accomplished by passing *Head*, because from *Head* the entire rest of the list can be accessed. The last node in the list will contain the **nil** pointer. The list is empty if *Head* itself is the **nil** pointer. This condition for an empty list should be tested. It is possible to empty a list

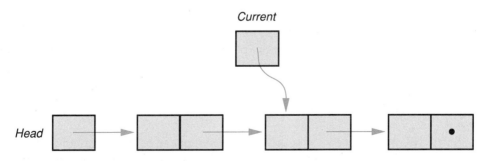

FIGURE 13.5 A linked list.

Test programs that process linked lists for their behavior on empty lists.

using the *Delete* procedure, and a new list, created by the statement

Head := **nil;**

is initially empty. A program should be robust enough to work for empty lists, just as it should work for empty files or empty lines in a text file.

Traversal: To traverse the entire list simply involves following the pointers. In order to avoid notations like

Head^.Link^.Link^.Link^.Field

an auxiliary pointer *Current* will move along in the list. *Current* points to the next node in the list, if there is a next node, or has the value **nil** if the end of the list has been reached.

procedure Traverse(Head: NodePointer);
{traverses entire linked list to which Head points and writes out each element}

var
Current : NodePointer;

begin   {procedure Traverse}
initialize *Current* to *Head*
if empty list **then** write message
else
repeat
write the contents of *Current*^
advance *Current*
until end of list
end;   {procedure Traverse}

In the above pseudocode, "if empty list" is tested by

if Head = **nil**

(or **if** Current = **nil).** "End of list" is recognized by the condition

Current = **nil**

As long as this condition is not true, then *Current*^ exists and its contents can be written out. "Advance Current" moves the *Current* pointer through the list by making it point where the next *Link* field points:

Current := Current^.Link;

In procedure *Traverse,* the *Current* pointer can be avoided by advancing *Head* through the list. Because *Head* is a value parameter, it will still have its original value when the procedure is exited. Use of the auxiliary pointer seems clearer, however, as there is no chance of confusion about somehow losing the pointer to the start of the list. Figure 13.6 illustrates procedure *Traverse* for a short linked list.

Search: The search operation can be implemented as a function. The function needs access to the list (through *Head*) and it needs the target element. The function returns the value **nil** if the list is empty or if the target element is not in the list; it returns a pointer value to the target element if that element is in the list.

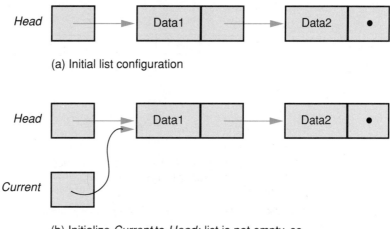

(a) Initial list configuration

(b) Initialize *Current* to *Head*; list is not empty, so enter **repeat** loop

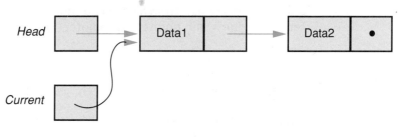

(c) Write out *Data1*

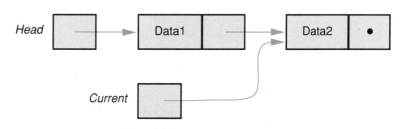

(d) Advance C*urrent*; not end of list, so execute **repeat** loop again

Continued

FIGURE 13.6 Traversing a linked list.

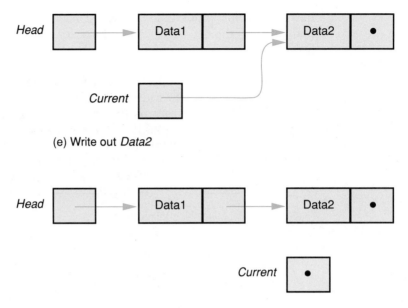

(e) Write out *Data2*

(f) Advance *Current*; end of list reached,
exit **repeat** loop and procedure

FIGURE   13.6   Traversing a linked list—Continued.

```
function Search(Head: NodePointer; Target: Node):  NodePointer;
{searches linked list to which Head points for target element
 Target; returns nil pointer or pointer to Target}

var
    Current : NodePointer;
    Temp : NodePointer;     {Search gets value Temp at exit}

  begin   {function Search}
    initialize Current to Head
    initialize Temp to nil
    while Temp is nil and not end  of list do
      begin
        if Current^ equals Target data, set Temp to Current
        advance Current
      end
    set Search to Temp
  end;     {function Search}
```

Insert: The insert procedure will need as its parameters the element to be inserted in the list and a marker *AfterThis* for the location in the list where the insertion is to take place. *AfterThis* will be a pointer to the node that will ultimately precede the new node. Figure 13.7 illustrates the insertion process. The *new* procedure is invoked to create memory space to

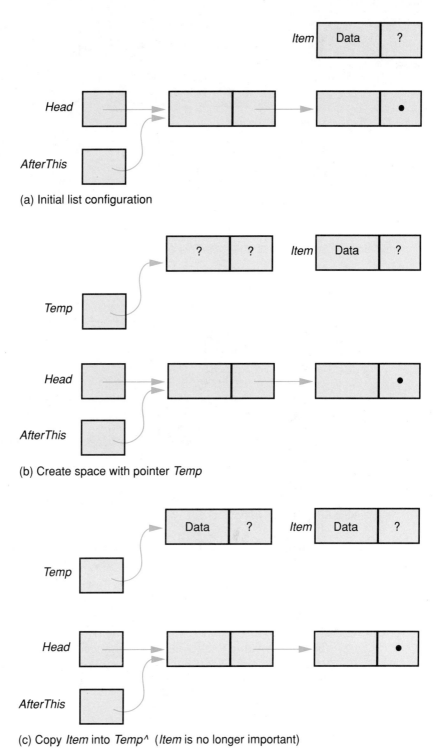

(a) Initial list configuration

(b) Create space with pointer *Temp*

(c) Copy *Item* into *Temp^* (*Item* is no longer important)

Continued

FIGURE 13.7 Inserting a node in a linked list.

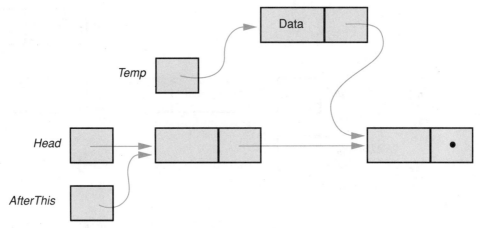

(d) Connect *Temp^* to node after *AfterThis^*

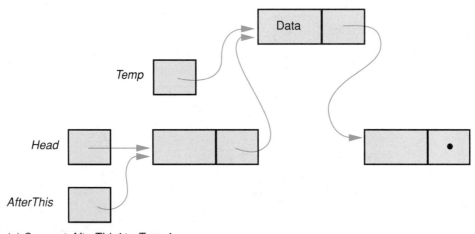

(e) Connect *AfterThis^* to *Temp^*

FIGURE 13.7 Inserting a node in a linked list—Continued.

which *Temp* points. Data from *Item* is copied into *Temp^*, and then the pointers are adjusted to tie *Temp^* into the list.

The following procedure incorporates these steps. This procedure will change the link field in *AfterThis^*, the node to which *AfterThis* points, but the pointer value itself will not be changed. Therefore, *AfterThis* can be a value parameter. Note that using a value parameter for a pointer variable does not safeguard against side effects caused by changes in the node to which that pointer variable points.

```
procedure Insert(AfterThis: NodePointer; Item:  Node);
{a node containing the data from Item gets inserted in a linked
 list after the node pointed to by AfterThis}
```

var
      Temp : NodePointer;

   begin   {procedure Insert}
     allocate space, pointed to by *Temp*
     copy *Item* into *Temp^*
     connect *Temp^* to node after *AfterThis^*
     connect *AfterThis^* to *Temp^*
   end;   {procedure Insert}

CHECKUP 13.4   Write program statements to implement
        connect *Temp^* to node after *AfterThis^*
    and
        connect *AfterThis^* to *Temp^*

CHECKUP 13.5   Trace through procedure *Insert* in the case where *AfterThis^* is the last node in the linked list. Modify the procedure, if necessary, to handle this case as well.

Although procedure *Insert* works for "most" cases, it is not completely general. It does not allow for insertion of a new node as the first node in a list. Even if *AfterThis* has the value *Head* when the procedure is invoked, *Insert* will still insert the new node after the node pointed to by *AfterThis*, i.e., after the node pointed to by *Head*. This would make the new node the second one in the list, not the first. In fact, this is exactly the situation pictured in Figure 13.7. We can modify procedure *Insert* so that invoking it with a value of **nil** for *AfterThis* will cause the new node to be added as the first node.

CHECKUP 13.6   Modify procedure *Insert* so that when it is invoked with a value of **nil** for *AfterThis*, the new node is added as the first node. Make sure the modified procedure works if the list is initially empty.

Delete: For the delete procedure, parameters of *Head* and *AfterThis* are passed. *AfterThis* points to the node *before* the node to be deleted, rather than to the node to be deleted. This is necessary so that the pointer field from the previous node is available to reconnect to the node after the one to be deleted. A particular version of the delete procedure is requested in Skill

Builder #1, but the general idea is shown in Figure 13.8. The *Temp* pointer is used so that the *dispose* procedure can be invoked for the deleted node.

Now let's put some of these pieces together in an example. The following program builds a linked list of three-letter names entered by the user. Each new name is inserted in the proper place so that the names are in alphabetical order. When the list is complete, it is written out. The only part that does not follow directly from the list operations we have discussed is the function *Place* that locates where the insertion should occur. *Place* computes the value for *AfterThis* that will be passed to procedure *Insert*. Within function *Place*, as the *Temp* pointer moves along looking for where to put the new node, the loop condition we really want is

```
while (Temp^.Link <> nil) and
      (Temp^.Link^.Name <= NextName.Name) do
      {advance Temp}
```

However, this can get us into trouble if the end of the list is ever reached. At that point, *Temp^.Link* is **nil** and *Temp^.Link^* is undefined (remember that usually both conditions in an **and** statement are evaluated, even when one of them is false).

```
program NameList(input, output);
{requests names from the user, builds a linked list with these
 names in alphabetical order, writes out the list}

const
     Delimiter = 'End';      {string marking end of data}

type
     String = packed array [1..3] of char;
     NodePointer = ^Node;
     Node = record
       Name : String;
       Link : NodePointer;
       end;      {Node}

var
     Head : NodePointer;        {pointer to linked list}
     NextName : Node;           {record to hold name read in}
     AfterThis : NodePointer;   {pointer to mark insertion spot}

procedure GetName(var NextName: Node);
{collects next name, stores it in Name field of NextName}

var
     i : integer;      {array index}


  begin    {procedure GetName}
    for i := 1 to 3 do
```

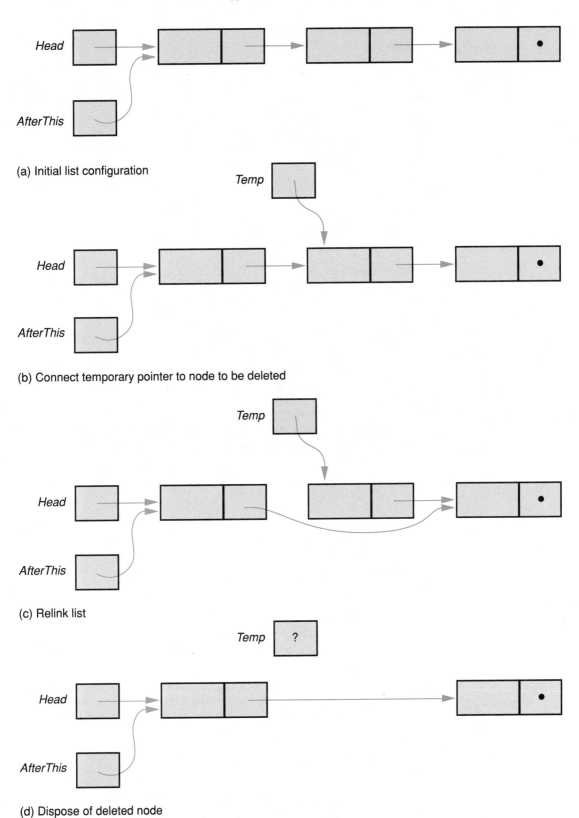

(a) Initial list configuration

(b) Connect temporary pointer to node to be deleted

(c) Relink list

(d) Dispose of deleted node

FIGURE 13.8 Deleting a node in a linked list.

```
        read(NextName.Name[i]);
     readln;
   end;      {procedure GetName}

function Place(Head: NodePointer;
             NextName: Node): NodePointer;
{NextName should be inserted alphabetically after node to which
Place points; if NextName should be inserted as first node-
, Place  is set to nil}

var
     Temp : NodePointer;       {pointer through list; Place will get
                                value Temp at exit}
     Stop: boolean;            {flag for loop exit}

   begin    {function Place}
     if Head = nil then
       Temp := nil    {new element goes first in empty list}
     else    {nonempty list}
       if (Head^.Name >= NextName.Name) then
         Temp := nil    {new element goes first}
       else
         begin    {else}
           Temp := Head;
           Stop := false;
           while (Temp^.Link <> nil) and (not Stop) do
             if (Temp^.Link^.Name <= NextName.Name) then

               {advance Temp}
               Temp := Temp^.Link
             else

               {exit loop, Temp points to correct node}
               Stop := true;
         end;    {else}
     Place := Temp;
   end;    {function Place}

procedure Insert(var Head: NodePointer;
               AfterThis: NodePointer;
               Item: Node);
{in linked list to which Head points, a node containing the data
from Item gets inserted after the node pointed to by After-
This;  if AfterThis is nil, the new node becomes the first node}

var
     Temp : NodePointer;
```

```
  begin     {procedure Insert}
    new(Temp);
    Temp^ := Item;
    if AfterThis = nil then
      begin
        Temp^.Link := Head;
        Head := Temp;
      end
    else
      begin
        Temp^.Link := AfterThis^.Link;
        AfterThis^.Link := Temp;
      end
  end;      {procedure Insert}

procedure Traverse(Head: NodePointer);
{traverses entire linked list to which Head points and writes out
 each element}

var
    Current : NodePointer;

  begin     {procedure Traverse}
    Current := Head;
    if Head = nil then
      writeln('List is empty')
    else
      repeat
        writeln(Current^.Name);
        Current := Current^.Link;
      until Current = nil;
  end;      {procedure Traverse}


begin    {main program}
  writeln('Enter a list of 3-letter names, one per  line.');
  writeln('Terminate the list with "End". ');
  writeln;

  {create empty list}
  Head := nil;

  {build list}
  GetName(NextName);
  while NextName.Name <> Delimiter do
    begin   {valid name to enter in list}
      AfterThis := Place(Head, NextName);
      Insert(Head, AfterThis, NextName);
      GetName(NextName);
    end;     {valid name to enter in list}
```

```
{List complete, now write it out}
writeln;
writeln('The names, in alphabetical order, are:');
Traverse(Head);
end.     {main program}
```

RUNNING THE PROGRAM...

Enter a list of 3-letter names, one per line.
Terminate the list with "End".

Jan
Lee
Bob
Tim
Tom
Ann
End

The names, in alphabetical order, are:
Ann
Bob
Jan
Lee
Tim
Tom

Our procedures for linked-list operations were general ones, able to handle the special cases of empty lists, insertion of the first element in a list, etc. Simpler procedures can be used if artificial first and last elements are created for the specific application. For example, in the *NameList* program, artificial records containing the names AAA and ZZZ could be put in place as permanent first and last list elements when the list is first created. Then the list-processing procedures will never encounter an empty list, a legitimate record will never have to be inserted as the first element in the list, etc. This simply moves part of the work out of the list-processing procedures into some other section of the program and makes the procedures themselves less portable. Moreover, it seems a rather contrived approach.

13.2.3 *Stacks and Queues*

A **stack** is an arrangement of items characterized by the properties that a new item can only be added to the top of the stack, and only the top item can be removed from the stack. The last item added to the stack (the current top-of-stack) is therefore the first item to be removed from the stack, so a stack is sometimes called a LIFO (Last-In, First-Out) structure. Although a common illustration of a stack is a pile of plates in a cafeteria, stacks have many practical applications. We know, for example, that a stack is used to store activation records corresponding to procedure invocations.

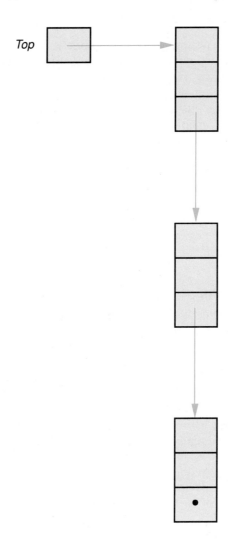

FIGURE 13.9 A stack implemented as a linked list.

A stack can be implemented as a variation of a linked list: think of the list "vertically," so that what we have called the head becomes the top, and insertions and deletions take place only at the top. Figure 13.9 illustrates a linked-list implementation of a stack. Because insertions and deletions take place at the top, *Top* is the only pointer needed to locate where activity is to take place. Stack insertions and deletions have their own names. An element is ***pushed*** onto the top of the stack (inserted), or the top element is ***popped*** off the stack (deleted).

The natural operations to perform on a stack are therefore

- ***Push*** an element onto the stack
- ***Pop*** the stack
- ***View*** the current top element on the stack

A stack is a last-in, first-out list; natural operations to perform on a stack are push, pop, and view (the top element).

When a stack is implemented as a linked list, the push and pop procedures are simplifications of the *Insert* and *Delete* procedures we've already outlined.

CHECKUP 13.7   Assume that push(x) pushes element x onto a stack, pop deletes the top element of the stack, and write(top) writes out the current stack top. What is the output from the following sequence of operations?

push(3)
push(7)
pop
write(top)
push(2)
push(5)
write(top)
pop
pop
write(top)

Program *MirrorWriting* on page 270 reads in a string of characters and writes it out in reverse order. This is clearly a last-in, first-out situation. *MirrorWriting* uses an array to store the characters, but we'll rewrite the program using a stack. Each new character read is pushed onto the stack. When the input is complete, the characters are popped off the stack. *MirrorWritingTwo* below sets up the appropriate data structure and the overall program logic. It will function properly once the push and pop procedures are implemented. Because the linked list can grow indefinitely, the *MirrorWriting* requirement of establishing a maximum number of characters in the string is removed.

```
program MirrorWritingTwo(input, output);
{reads in a line of characters, stores the characters in a stack,
 and writes them out in reverse order}

const
    Terminator  =  '#';

type
    NodePointer  =  ^Node;
    Node  =  record
      Character : char;
      Link : NodePointer;
      end;      {Node}

var
    Top : NodePointer;        {pointer to top of stack}
    Symbol : char;            {current character}

procedure Push(var Top: NodePointer; Symbol: char);
{inserts new node with Symbol data at top of stack pointed to
 by Top, adjusts Top accordingly}
```

```
    begin    {procedure Push}

      {not implemented}

    end;      {procedure Push}

procedure Pop(var Top: NodePointer; var Symbol:  char);
{removes node at top of stack pointed to by Top, returns its
 data as Symbol; adjusts Top accordingly}

    begin     {procedure Pop}

      {not implemented}

    end;      {procedure Pop}

begin     {main program}
  {create empty stack}
  Top := nil;

  {build stack}
  writeln('Write the line of characters that you want');
  writeln('MirrorWritingTwo to reverse.');
  writeln('Use # to denote the end of the message.');
  writeln;

  read(Symbol);
  while (Symbol <> Terminator) do
    begin
      Push(Top, Symbol);
      read(Symbol);
    end;
  {input complete}

  {empty the stack and write out the characters in reverse
   order}
  writeln('The reverse of your message is:');
  while (Top <> nil) do
    begin    {stack not empty}
      Pop(Top, Symbol);
      write(Symbol);
    end;      {stack not empty}
  writeln;
end.      {main program}
```

A *queue* is a list where all insertions are done at the back and all deletions are done from the front. A queue can represent, for example, a line of customers at a service window. New customers are added at the back of the line, and customers are "deleted" from the front of the line after they are

A queue is a first-in, first-out list; natural operations to perform on a queue are enqueue and dequeue.

served. A queue is sometimes called a FIFO (First-In, First-Out) structure. The natural queue operations are

- **Enqueue** an element (add it to the back of the queue)
- **Dequeue** an element (remove it from the front of the queue)

Once again, a linked-list implementation is convenient, with enqueue and dequeue special forms of *Insert* and *Delete*. In addition to a *Front* pointer, it is convenient to maintain an auxiliary *Back* pointer to facilitate the enqueue operation. Figure 13.10 illustrates a linked-list queue implementation.

13.2.4 Trees

A **tree** is a collection of items where one distinguished node serves as the **root** of the tree, and each node may have a number of **children** nodes. A node is the **parent** of its children nodes. Nodes with no children are called **leaves** of the tree. Figure 13.11 illustrates a tree. Node 1 is the root, and nodes 3, 5, 6, and 7 are leaves. (Notice that computer scientists grow trees with the root at the top!) Node 2 is the parent of nodes 5 and 6. Nodes 5 and 6, having the same parent, are **siblings.** The root is the **ancestor** of all other nodes, each of which is a **descendant** of the root. There are three levels, or **generations,** in this tree.

The tree data structure becomes an abstract data type when we include the natural tree operations. We should be able to perform the same operations we do for lists:

- **Traverse** the tree—visit each node and write out its value
- **Search** the tree—determine whether a particular element is a node in the tree
- **Insert** a new node into the tree
- **Delete** a node from the tree

Unlike the list structure, where the items have an inherent ordering, the order in which we should traverse the tree or where we should insert a new node is not clear. In fact, there are several possibilities depending on what the tree is being used to represent. A tree could represent, for example, the

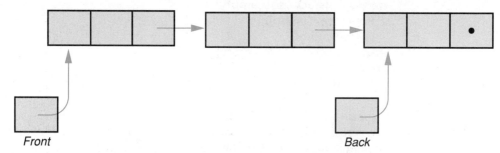

FIGURE 13.10 A queue implemented as a linked list.

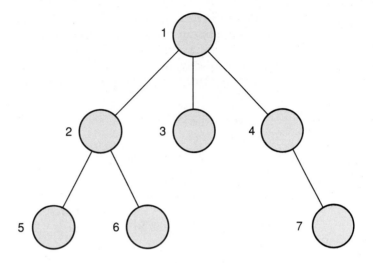

(a) A Three-Generation Tree

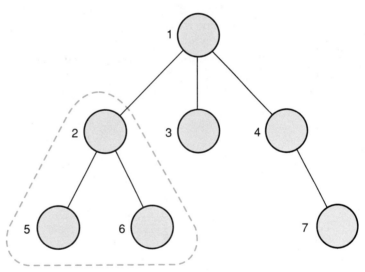

(b) The Same Tree Showing the Subtree with Root 2

FIGURE 13.11 A tree data structure.

reporting structure in the management of a business, a sorted collection of items (more on this later), or the result of a compiler's analysis of the syntax of a programming language instruction (a **parse tree**).

Whatever it is representing, a tree can be viewed as a recursive structure in that each node in a tree is the root of a tree composed of itself and its descendants. The leftmost subtree below node 1 in Figure 13.11a has root 2 and is shown in Figure 13.11b. This means that a tree operation can often be performed by a procedure that processes a root as the base step and recursively invokes itself on that root's subtrees. We will limit our discussion of trees to **binary trees,** where each node can have at most two children, a **left child** and a **right child,** that serve as roots of a left subtree and a right subtree, respectively.

One tree traversal algorithm proceeds recursively in three steps:

1. Traverse the left subtree.
2. Visit the root.
3. Traverse the right subtree.

This traversal algorithm is called an **inorder traversal.** Writing out the contents of each node visited in an inorder traversal of the binary tree shown in Figure 13.12 results in the output

        c a i d d g c e j a c f

Pointer variables and record nodes again provide a convenient tree implementation. Each record needs two pointer fields, one for the left subtree and one for the right subtree. A pointer *Root* to the root node serves to access the whole tree, much as the *Head* pointer for a linked list allows access to the entire list. The following declarations could be used for the tree in Figure 13.12.

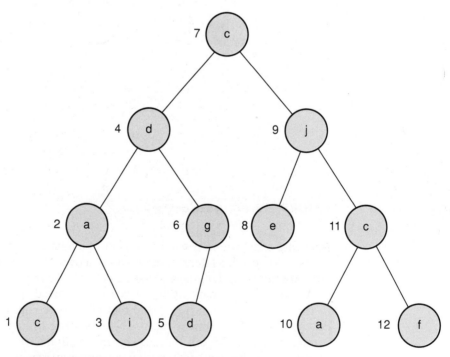

FIGURE 13.12 A binary tree showing inorder traversal.

```
type
   NodePointer = ^Node;
   Node = record
     Left, Right : NodePointer;
     Value : char;
     end;      {Node}

var
   Root : NodePointer;
```

The *Left* and *Right* pointers are set to **nil** if there is no corresponding subtree.

CHECKUP 13.8   Draw the tree of Figure 13.12 using the data structure of the above declarations and showing all of the pointers.

The inorder traversal of a binary tree with these declarations can then be carried out by the following recursive procedure, which first checks to see that the tree exists, i.e., that the pointer to its root is not the **nil** pointer.

procedure Inorder (Root: NodePointer);
{does an inorder traversal of binary tree with root pointed to by Root; writes out the value of each node visited}

```
   begin    {procedure Inorder}
     if Root <> nil then
       begin    {tree exists}
         Inorder(Root^.Left);
         write(Root^.Value);
         Inorder(Root^.Right);
       end;      {tree exists}
   end;       {procedure Inorder}
```

Without recursion, the inorder traversal algorithm would be messy, requiring a loop to travel along pointers until the **nil** pointer is reached, and enough auxiliary pointers to "backtrack" easily up the tree.

13.2.5 *Binary Search Trees*

An inorder traversal of a binary search tree writes out the nodes in sorted order.

A binary tree is useful for maintaining a sorted collection of items. A tree used for such a purpose is called a ***binary search tree.*** In a binary search tree, new items that precede a node are stored as nodes in the left subtree of that node. New items that succeed the node are stored in the right subtree. Because an inorder traversal processes the left subtree, then the node, then the right subtree, it has the effect of writing out the elements in sorted order. Creating a binary search tree requires that each new node be inserted into the tree in the proper place, determined by comparing its value with the values of existing nodes. Program *NameTree* is a version of *NameList* that stores the names in a binary search tree and uses an inorder traversal to write them out in sorted order.

```pascal
program NameTree(input, output);
{requests names from the user and builds them into a binary
search tree, does an inorder traversal to write the names in
alphabetical order}

const
    Delimiter = 'End';     {string marking end of data}

type
    String = packed array [1..3] of char;
    NodePointer = ^Node;
    Node = record
      Name : String;
      Left, Right : NodePointer;
      end;     {Node}

var
    Root : NodePointer;      {pointer to root of binary tree}
    NextName : Node;         {record to hold name read in}

procedure GetName(var NextName: Node);
{collects next name, stores it in Name field of NextName}

var
    i : integer;      {array index}

  begin    {procedure GetName}
  for i := 1 to 3 do
    read(NextName.Name[i]);
  readln;
  end;      {procedure GetName}

procedure Insert(var Root: NodePointer; Item: Node);
{inserts node containing the data from Item in binary search tree
to which Root points}

  begin    {procedure Insert}
  if Root = nil then
    begin    {empty tree, attach node Item}
    new(Root);
    Root^.Name := Item.Name;
    Root^.Left := nil;
    Root^.Right := nil;
    end    {empty tree, attach node Item}
```

```
    else
      if (Item.Name < Root^.Name) then
        {insert node Item in left subtree}
        Insert(Root^.Left, Item)
      else
        {insert node Item in right subtree}
        Insert(Root^.Right, Item);
  end;      {procedure Insert}


procedure Inorder(Root: NodePointer);
{performs inorder traversal of binary tree to which Root points,
 writes out each element}


    begin    {procedure Inorder}
      if Root <> nil then
        begin
          Inorder(Root^.Left);
          writeln(Root^.Name);
          Inorder(Root^.Right);
        end;
  end;      {procedure Inorder}


begin    {main program}
  writeln('Enter a list of 3-letter names, one per line.');
  writeln('Terminate the list with "End". ');
  writeln;

  {create empty tree}
  Root := nil;

  {build tree}
  GetName(NextName);
  while NextName.Name <> Delimiter do
    begin    {valid name to enter in list}
      Insert(Root, NextName);
      GetName(NextName);
    end;      {valid name to enter in list}

  {Tree complete, now do inorder traversal}
  writeln;
  writeln('The names, in alphabetical order, are:');
  if Root = nil then
    writeln('No names')
  else
    Inorder(Root);
end.      {main program}
```

CHECKUP 13.9   A binary search tree containing a certain set of elements as its node values is not unique. The structure of the tree will depend on the order in which the nodes are inserted. Construct the binary search trees that result when the integers from 1 through 6 are inserted in the following orders (left to right):

a. 3, 5, 2, 4, 6, 1

b. 2, 6, 3, 1, 5, 4

Searching a binary search tree for a particular item involves comparisons of the target item against the node values. Such a comparison can have three outcomes:

1. The target value equals the node value, in which case the search is over.
2. The target value is less than the node value, in which case the search can be restricted to the left subtree.
3. The target value is greater than the node value, in which case the search can be restricted to the right subtree.

This suggests that a recursive search function would be appropriate. As before, such a function should return **nil** if the tree is empty or the target element is not in the tree, and should return a pointer to the appropriate node if the target element is found. The search can begin by examining the root; if the root is **nil,** the tree is empty and the function exits. When a search has progressed unsuccessfully from the original root down through a leaf, the next "subtree," i.e., the left or right pointer from the leaf, is **nil,** which terminates the recursion. An outline of the search function follows.

```
function TreeSearch(Root: NodePointer;
                    Target: Node): NodePointer;
{searches binary search tree to which Root points for target
 element Target; returns nil pointer or pointer to Target}

    begin    {function TreeSearch}

      if Root = nil then number is not in tree
      else if Target value = Root value then success
      else if Target value < Root value then search left subtree
      else search right subtree

    end;     {function TreeSearch}
```

CHECKUP 13.10   Write a binary search function for program *NameTree.*

During a binary tree search, an unsuccessful comparison against a single node directs the search process to a subtree. This eliminates other nodes (all those in the other subtree) from consideration. Examine the two binary search trees formed in Checkup 13.9. Tree (a) is **balanced**—the left and right subtrees of each node contain approximately the same number of elements. Tree (b) is not balanced. In searching a balanced tree, a comparison of the target element against any node eliminates roughly half of the remaining nodes. In contrast, the linked-list search described earlier is a **sequential search** in which each node in the list must be examined in turn until the target value is found or the whole list has been examined. The binary tree search algorithm may therefore require less work than the sequential search algorithm to perform the same task, namely, to search a pool of n items for a target element. The amount of work an algorithm requires is a matter of considerable interest for such common tasks as sorting and searching. We'll discuss this idea further in the next section.

13.3 Sorting and Searching

Suppose that we have a collection of n data items stored internally in an array, and we wish to sort these items. The items may be records that we want to sort on a particular field that contains data that can be ordered—integer, real, character, enumerated-type, or string data, for example. The data type will dictate how the relative ordering of two items is determined. If the data is type *integer* or *real*, the usual numerical ordering will be used. If it is string or character data, the ordering depends on the collating sequence. If it is enumerated-type, the type declaration defines the ordering. None of these details affects the overall approach of algorithms for sorting, so we will simply assume that we have an array of n integers, created under the following declarations. The objective is to sort the array in increasing order.

```
type
    ArrayType = array [1..n] of integer;

var
    A : ArrayType;
```

13.3.1 Selection Sort

In Chapter 9, we discussed the selection sort algorithm. The general idea of this approach is to make multiple passes through the array. On each pass through those elements not yet properly positioned in the array, the largest element is selected and positioned in its rightful place. Eventually all elements are properly positioned and the array is sorted. The code for a procedure to implement selection sort follows (this is the answer to CHECKUP 9.8).

```
procedure SelectionSort(var A: ArrayType; n: integer);
{sorts first n elements in array A}
```

```
var
    i : integer;                            {index in array A}
```

```
function MaxIndex(A: ArrayType; i: integer):  integer;
{finds the index of the maximum value from 1 to i in array A}
```

```
var
    CurrentMaxIndex : integer;        {index of current max. value}
    j : integer;                               {array index}

  begin    {function MaxIndex}
    CurrentMaxIndex := 1;
    for j := 2 to i do
      begin
        if A[j] > A[CurrentMaxIndex] then
          CurrentMaxIndex := j;
      end;
    MaxIndex := CurrentMaxIndex;
  end;      {function MaxIndex}
```

```
procedure Exchange(var X, Y: integer);
{exchanges elements X and Y}
```

```
var
    Temporary : integer;

  begin    {procedure Exchange}
    Temporary := X;
    X := Y;
    Y := Temporary;
  end;       {procedure Exchange}
```

```
  begin    {procedure SelectionSort}
    for i := n downto 2 do
      begin    {for loop}
        Exchange(A[i], A[MaxIndex(A,i)]);
      end;       {for loop}
  end;       {procedure SelectionSort}
```

13.3.2 *Insertion Sort*

In the selection sort, a section of the array that contains properly positioned elements grows from back to front. Once properly positioned, an element is not moved again. In the ***insertion sort*** algorithm, a section of the array grows—again from back to front—so that the entries in that section are in relative sorted order but are not necessarily in their final positions. When the section expands to include a new element, all of the elements in the section are subject to readjustment as the new element is inserted into its proper relative position. Finally the section includes the entire array, and the array is then sorted.

Figure 13.13 illustrates the insertion sort. In Figure 13.13a, the initial array configuration, the section consisting of just the last element *A[4]* is obviously in sorted order. When the section expands to include *A[3]* and *A[4]*, the entries 1 and 7 are still in relative sorted order, so no changes occur (Fig. 13.13b). When the section expands to include *A[2]*, *A[3]*, and *A[4]*, the new element, 9, is out of order. It is exchanged in turn with element 1 and element 7, and the section is then sorted (Fig. 13.13c-e). Finally, the section expands to include the entire array, and the new element, 3, is exchanged with element 1 (Fig. 13.13g). At this point, the entire array is sorted.

The procedure below references the *Exchange* procedure that can be taken directly from the selection sort code. However, it is only fair to announce that this procedure as written can lead to a run-time error under the right conditions.

```
procedure InsertionSort(var A: ArrayType; n: integer);
{sorts first n elements in array A}

var
    i, j : integer;                    {index in array A}

    begin    {procedure InsertionSort}
      for i := n − 1 downto 1 do
        begin
          j := i;                      {A[j] is new element to insert}

        while (j < n) and (A[j] > A[j + 1]) do
```

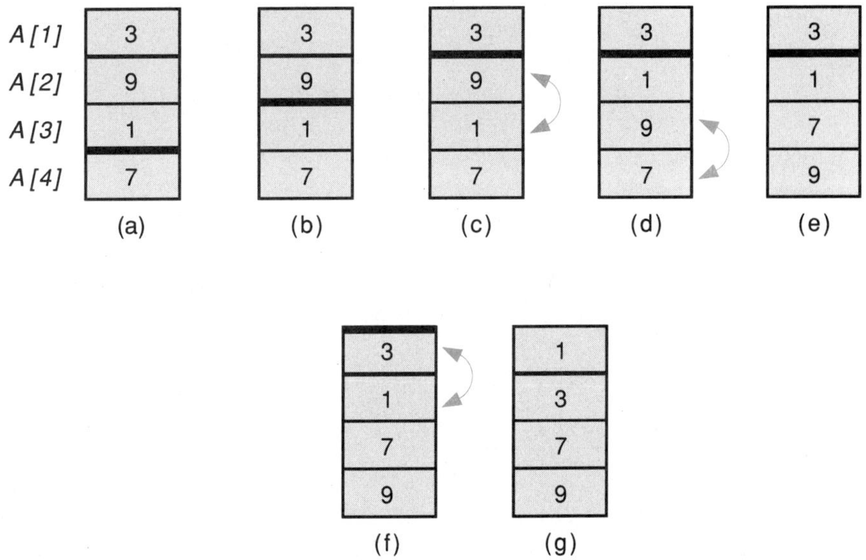

FIGURE   13.13 Insertion sort.

```
begin    {inserting A[j]}
   Exchange(A[j], A[j + 1]);
   j := j + 1;
end;      {inserting A[j]}


end;    {for loop}
end;      {procedure InsertionSort}
```

CHECKUP 13.11   What is the difficulty with procedure *InsertionSort* above? What conditions can lead to a run-time error?

13.3.3 *Bubble Sort*

In the **bubble sort** algorithm, we make one pass through the entire array, examining pairs of adjacent elements and exchanging any two that are not in relative sorted order. At the end of the first pass, the largest element will have "bubbled" its way to the back of the array. On the next pass the process is repeated, except that the last element (already in its correct position) is not examined. Each successive pass through the array can stop one element sooner, until finally the entire array is sorted.

The bubble sort algorithm is illustrated in Figure 13.14. Figure 13.14a shows the exchanges that are done on the first pass. No exchange is needed between elements *A[1]* and *A[2]*, but elements *A[2]* and *A[3]*, and then *A[3]* and *A[4]*, get exchanged. At the end of this pass, the fourth element (the value 9) is correctly positioned. In Figure 13.14b, on the second pass, elements *A[1]* and *A[2]* are exchanged, *A[2]* and *A[3]* are not. On the third pass, Figure 13.14c, only elements *A[1]* and *A[2]* are considered, and they do not need to be exchanged.

```
procedure BubbleSort(var A: ArrayType; n: integer);
{sorts first n elements in array A}

var
    i, j : integer;        {array indices}

begin    {procedure BubbleSort}
   for i := n downto 2 do
     for j := 1 to i − 1 do
       if A[j] > A[j + 1] then
         Exchange(A[j], A[j + 1]);
end;      {procedure BubbleSort}
```

13.3.4 *Quicksort*

The *Quicksort* algorithm is recursive; it cleverly breaks the sorting problem down into two "smaller" sorting problems. An element is chosen as the **pivot element,** and the array elements are rearranged such that all array

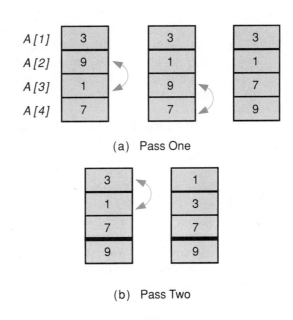

(a) Pass One

(b) Pass Two

(c) Pass Three

FIGURE 13.14 Bubble sort.

elements smaller than the pivot element precede the pivot in the array, and all array elements larger than the pivot element follow the pivot in the array. At this point the pivot element occupies its correct position, and the elements on either side occupy the correct "half" of the array, but are not necessarily in sorted order. The process is then repeated on each "half" of the array, i.e., on the elements preceding the pivot element and on the elements after the pivot element. (Unless the pivot element happens to end up as the middle element of the array, the two subarrays will not actually be halves of the original array.) Termination occurs when the section to be sorted is only one element long.

Rearranging the array into smaller elements, followed by the pivot element, followed by larger elements, constitutes a major part of the effort in this algorithm. We'll assume that the first array element is always the one used as the pivot. Then, two index markers i and j move along the array. Marker i moves through the array from front to back until it finds an element larger than the pivot element. Marker j moves through the array from back to front until it finds an element smaller than the pivot element. At this point, the two elements found are exchanged in the array, and i and *j* resume their progress. Eventually *i* and *j* will cross. When this happens, all elements smaller than the pivot have been positioned in the array so that their indices are now $\leq j$, and all elements larger than the pivot now have indices $\geq i$. Exchanging *A[First]* (the pivot element) and *A[j]* will put the pivot element in its correct position. An example should clarify how this works.

In Figure 13.15a, the array *A* is indexed from *First* to *Last*, and *A[First]* is the pivot element. The marker *i* moves right from *First* looking for a value that exceeds the pivot. When *i* finds such a value, it stops while *j* moves left from *Last* looking for a value less than or equal to the pivot. Two such values have been found in Figure 13.15b. These two values are exchanged, resulting in Figure 13.15c. Markers *i* and *j* proceed as before, finding another pair of values in Figure 13.15d. These are exchanged (Fig. 13.15e), and *i* and *j* proceed as before. The next time *i* and *j* stop, *i* exceeds *j* (Fig. 3.15f). An exchange of *A[First]* and *A[j]* puts the 7 in the correct place, and the entire process can be repeated on the subarrays to the left of 7 and to the right of 7 (Fig. 13.15g).

The parameters to the *Quicksort* procedure include not only the array, but also the *First* and *Last* index in the array that specify the range of values to sort. When *Quicksort* is initially invoked, these indices will be 1 and *n*, respectively, but invoking *Quicksort* on the subarrays will require different indices as parameters. The first thing *Quicksort* does is to check these parameters to detect a one-element array, in which case the procedure terminates.

In the procedure below, repeat loops are used to move the markers *i* and *j*. These markers are initialized to *First* and *Last* + 1, respectively, so that when the repeat loops are entered, elements *A[First + 1]* and *A[Last]* are examined.

```
procedure Quicksort(var A: ArrayType; First, Last: integer);
{sorts array A between A[First] and A[Last]; locates
 pivot element, A[First], in its proper position with all
 smaller elements before it, all larger elements after it, then
 calls Quicksort on the two subarrays before and after pivot}

var
     i, j : integer;     {array indices}
     Pivot : integer;    {pivot element of array}

  begin    {procedure Quicksort}
    if First < Last then
      begin    {array to sort has more than one element}

        {select the pivot value}
        Pivot := A[First];

        {set markers i and j}
        i := First;
        j := Last + 1;
```

Pivot = 7

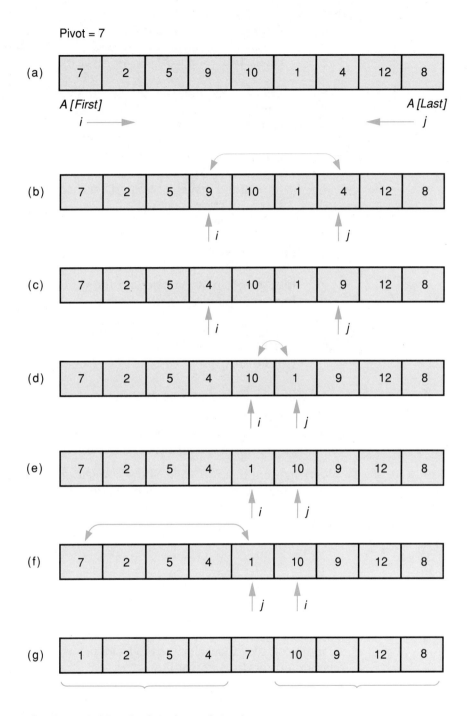

FIGURE 13.15 The first phase of *Quicksort*.

repeat
    {move i to element larger than Pivot, but don't let i
    move off the end of the array}

```
          repeat
            i := i + 1
          until (A[i] > Pivot) or (i = Last);

          {move j to element smaller than Pivot, but don't let j
           move off the end of the array}
          repeat
            j := j - 1
          until (A[j] < Pivot) or (j = First);

          {if i and j haven't crossed, exchange}
          if i < j then
            Exchange(A[i], A[j]);

        until i >= j;

        {put pivot in its correct position}
        Exchange(A[First], A[j]);

        {array partitioned, now sort subarrays}
        Quicksort(A, First, j-1);
        Quicksort(A, j+1, Last);

      end;     {array to sort has more than one  element}
  end;   {procedure Quicksort}
```

CHECKUP 13.12   Working from Figure 13.15g, show how *Quicksort* would finish the sort by illustrating the array after each exchange of elements. (Some "exchanges" swap an element with itself, producing no visible effect; you need not show these!)

13.3.5 *Analysis of Sorting Algorithms*

We have now discussed four algorithms for sorting an array of elements: selection sort, insertion sort, bubble sort, and quicksort. Earlier in this chapter, we saw how to build two different data structures—linked lists and binary trees—that allow elements to be sorted as they are read in from the keyboard or from an external file.

What are the relative merits of these algorithms? One quality of a "good" algorithm is that it is easy to understand how the algorithm works. The selection sort and the insertion sort probably score highest in this category. Other factors on which to judge an algorithm have to do with the resources consumed by executing the algorithm. These resources could be memory space or execution time. For example, one variation on the selection sort would be to build a second copy of the array, putting a copy of the current largest element in the original array into place in the new array at each pass, rather than exchanging it with some other element in the original array. This might have a slight advantage over our version of the selection sort in terms of being easy to understand, but it would certainly consume resources. Space would be required for twice the size of the original array, rather than just the original array plus one temporary location to aid in the exchange of elements.

The exact execution time of an algorithm depends on the type of computer used, so that is not a particularly helpful measure. However, it can be assumed that in comparing two algorithms to do the same task, one that performs fewer steps than the other would require less execution time on any given machine. The number of steps or operations an algorithm performs is a measure of the algorithm's **efficiency.** A study of algorithm efficiency is called **analysis of algorithms.** We will do a brief analysis of our various sorting algorithms.

Obviously, the number of steps required to carry out an array sort depends on the number n of elements in the array. Therefore, we expect our efficiency measure to be a function of n, $f(n)$. Even knowing the size of the array does not give us all the answers. The amount of work an algorithm does can also depend on what the original array looks like. For example, the insertion sort does not have to perform any exchanges if the array is already in sorted order, but if the array is in reverse sorted order, it has to perform the maximum number of exchanges. We might ask, then, what is the worst-case efficiency of an algorithm, i.e., given that the n elements are initially arranged in a way that requires that algorithm to work hardest, what is $f(n)$? We might also try to ascertain some measure of the amount of work required "on the average," although this is more difficult because it is hard to determine what constitutes "average" input data.

Finally, even for the worst-case function, we will only give an order-of-magnitude description. This means that we will describe $f(n)$ as, for example, $O(n)$ (order n), which means that f is a linear function, proportional to n, or as $O(n^2)$, proportional to n^2. The functions

$$g(n) = n \quad \text{and} \quad h(n) = 300n + 15$$

are $O(n)$. The functions

$$q(n) = n^2 \quad \text{and} \quad r(n) = 0.5n^2 + 42n - 20$$

are $O(n^2)$. Why not be more precise? For one thing, it is difficult to determine what the exact coefficients might be. More importantly, we are only concerned about algorithm efficiency if n is large. In this case, the coefficients do not have nearly the impact that the order of magnitude does. To understand this, let's imagine that each operation the algorithm performs takes only 0.0001 seconds. The following table computes the time required to carry out algorithms of various efficiency on various size inputs n. We see that for large n $(n = 10,000)$, the $O(n^2)$ function $q(n)$ far outdistances the $O(n)$ function $h(n)$, even though the leading coefficient in $h(n)$ is large.

Algorithm efficiency is measured by giving an order-of-magnitude function of the amount n of input.

	n = 10	n = 100	n = 10,000
g(n) = n	0.001s	0.01s	1.0 s
h(n) = 300n + 15	0.3 s	3.0 s	5 min
q(n) = n²	0.01 s	1.0 s	2.78 hr

element requires comparing the current maximum, initially set to $A[1]$, against the remaining $n - 1$ values in the array. On the next pass, the current maximum is compared against $n - 2$ values. On each pass, the number of comparisons required is reduced by 1, so the total number of comparisons is

$$(n - 1) + (n - 2) + \ldots + 1$$

Mathematical induction can be used to prove that

$$(n - 1) + (n - 2) + \ldots + 1 = n(n - 1)/2$$

which is $O(n^2)$. In addition, $n - 1$ exchanges are required, one on each pass, which still leaves $O(n^2)$ total work to do. The selection sort behaves the same way whether the original array is in sorted order, reverse sorted order, or is completely random.

As we mentioned earlier, the worst case for the insertion sort occurs when the array starts out in reverse sorted order. Then the maximum number of comparisons and exchanges must be done, namely, one comparison (and one exchange) on the first pass, two comparisons and exchanges on the second pass, etc. The amount of work is

$$2(1 + 2 + \ldots + (n - 2) + (n - 1))$$

which is again $O(n^2)$. On an already sorted array, however, the insertion sort requires only one comparison for each of the first $n - 1$ elements in the array and no exchanges, so its best-case performance is $O(n)$. The "average" performance over all possible arrangements of input is still $O(n^2)$.

In the bubble sort, the first pass requires $n - 1$ comparisons, the second pass $n - 2$ comparisons, etc. The total number of comparisons is

$$(n - 1) + (n - 2) + \ldots + 1$$

which is $O(n^2)$. The number of exchanges depends on how the original array elements are ordered. If the original array is already in sorted order, no exchanges are required; the maximum number of exchanges is required if the original array is in reverse sorted order. Even in the worst case, there is at most one exchange for every comparison, which does not change the $O(n^2)$ work estimate. Therefore, the total work done by the bubble sort algorithm, for both best case and worst case, is $O(n^2)$.

The worst cases for the quicksort approach occur when the subarrays to be sorted are very unbalanced in size. If the pivot element ends up as the first (or last) element in an array of size k, then there is a $k - 1$ length subarray to sort. This will happen on each invocation if the array is originally in sorted order or in reverse sorted order. For each subarray to be sorted, the i and j marker together travel the entire subarray, involving roughly k comparisons. The total number of comparisons is therefore

$$n + (n - 1) + \ldots + 2$$

which again is $O(n^2)$. The number of exchanges will not exceed the number of comparisons, resulting in the conclusion that *Quicksort* is, in the worst case, $O(n^2)$. What, then, is so quick about *Quicksort*? *Quicksort* is so named because if the data is relatively random to begin with, then the subarrays will be more balanced in size. Suppose that $n = 2^p$. The first pass will require about n comparisons. Then, the two subarrays of approximate size $n/2$ will each require about $n/2$ comparisons. Next there will be four subarrays of size $n/4$ requiring about $n/4$ comparisons. The total number of comparisons is therefore

$$n + 2(n/2) + 4(n/4) + \ldots + 2^{p-1}(n/2^{p-1})$$
$$= n + n + n + \ldots + n \quad (p \text{ terms})$$
$$= np$$

Another way of saying that $n = 2^p$ is that $p = \log_2 n$. The number of comparisons is then

$$n \log_2 n$$

Quicksort is $O(n^2)$ in the worst case, when the array is already sorted or in reverse sorted order, but is $O(n \log_2 n)$ on the average.

The number of exchanges does not affect the order of magnitude of the work involved. Even if n is not a power of 2, and even if the subarrays do not form balanced halves each time, the quicksort algorithm is still $O(n \log_2 n)$ for data that is not close to already sorted or reverse sorted. The "average" performance over all possible arrangements of input is $O(n \log_2 n)$. The value of $n \log_2 n$ is worse than n but better than n^2. The improvement of $n \log_2 n$ over n^2 increases for large n, as seen in the following table.

n	n log$_2$ n	n^2
8	24	64
64	384	4096
256	2048	65,536
1024	10,240	1,048,576

Linked lists and binary trees for sorting exact a space penalty because of the storage required for pointers. In terms of execution time, the major portion of the work consists of finding the correct place to insert the new list element or the new tree node. Once the correct location is found, inserting the element involves minimal work of setting one or two pointers.

Sorting by reading elements into a linked list in sorted order is an $O(n^2)$ process in the worst case.

In the linked list, the worst case occurs if the elements read in are already in sorted order. Then each new element gets inserted at the end of the list, involving a comparison with each element already in the list. The first element requires no comparisons, the second element requires one comparison against the element already in place, and so forth. The number of comparisons to process n elements is thus given by

$$1 + 2 + \ldots (n - 1) = O(n^2)$$

Sorting by building a binary search tree is $O(n^2)$ in the worst case, but is $O(n \log_2 n)$ on the average.

In the binary search tree, already sorted elements cause the binary tree to grow in a lopsided fashion, with new nodes added only as right children. Here also, a comparison with all nodes already in the tree must be done for each new node, an $O(n^2)$ job. Relatively random data mean that the binary tree remains balanced as it is created, and if $n = 2^p$ elements have been inserted in the tree, each branch contains approximately $\log_2 n$ nodes. New nodes to be inserted require comparisons only with the nodes along a single branch. The total amount of work to insert n nodes in the tree turns out to be $O(n \log_2 n)$. As with *Quicksort*, this improved efficiency holds for all but the worst cases.

13.3.6 *Searching*

Searching an array for a particular target value, say X, is, like sorting, a common task. If the array elements are unordered, then a sequential search must be performed, where X is compared against each array element in turn until a match occurs or the array is exhausted. The worst case occurs if X is not in the array or is the last array element. In either of these cases, if the array contains n elements, then all n array elements must be examined, requiring a total of n comparisons. A sequential search is therefore an $O(n)$ algorithm in the worst case.

A sequential search is an $O(n)$ algorithm in the worst case.

A binary search is $O(\log_2 n)$ in the worst case.

If the array is already in sorted order, then we can use a **binary search** algorithm to reduce the amount of work required. In a binary search, the middle element of the list is compared to X. If its value is the same as X, then X has been found. If the middle value is larger than the value of X, then X (if it appears at all) is in the first half of the list; if the middle value is smaller than the value of X, then X (if it appears at all) is in the last half of the list. At each unsuccessful comparison, half of the remaining elements are discarded as potential matches. In the worst case, where X is not in the list, $O(\log_2 n)$ comparisons are required. The following table illustrates the improvement of $\log_2 n$ over n for various values of n.

n	$\log_2 n$
64	6
256	8
1024	10
1,048,576	20

Although a binary search is efficient on a sorted array, the cost of maintaining the array in sorted order if the array entries are subject to change must be considered.

The following function implements a binary search on an array A of integers, returning the index in the array of element X if X is found, or returning 0 if X is not in the array. The segment of the array being searched is bounded by indices *First* and *Last;* these will be set to 1 and n, respectively, when the function is initially invoked. The function is recursive and terminates when *First* and *Last* have overlapped, i.e., when the current segment has shrunk below length one.

```
function Search(var A: ArrayType;
                X, First, Last: integer): integer;
{performs a binary search on sorted array A between A[First]
and A[Last] for element X; returns index of X in array, or 0
if not found}

var
    Midpoint : integer;        {middle index in the array segment
                                being searched}

    begin    {function Search}
     if First > Last then
       Search := 0      {X not in array}
     else
       begin    {search this section}
         Midpoint := (First + Last) div 2;
         if X = A[Midpoint] then
           Search := Midpoint    {X found}
         else
          if X < A[Midpoint] then
            {search first half}
            Search := Search(A, X, First, Midpoint − 1)
          else
            {search second half}
            Search := Search(A, X, Midpoint + 1, Last);
       end;      {search this section}
    end;      {function Search}
```

If the elements to be searched are already stored in a relatively balanced binary search tree, then the search process resembles the binary search on a sorted array. This requires $O(\log_2 n)$ comparisons. If the tree is highly unbalanced (if, for example, the entries are in sorted order when the tree is constructed), then the binary tree search degenerates into a sequential search, requiring $O(n)$ comparisons.

13.4 Sample Software Development Project— Message Forwarding

Problem Statement

One node in a computer network must forward messages it receives to an adjacent node in the network. If node A is forwarding messages to node B,

A stores a copy of each message sent in a **buffer** (allocated memory space) until it receives an acknowledgment from B that the message has been received. Once an acknowledgment for a given message is received, the copy of that message is no longer needed and its buffer space can be reused. It takes time for the message to travel to B and for the acknowledgment to travel back to A. Instead of sitting idle until the acknowledgment is received, A continues to send new messages until it runs out of space to store the copies. Simulate the contents of A's buffer space as messages are sent and acknowledgments received.

Problem Specification

The buffer space that A uses to store message copies is limited in size. Realistically, the amount of space for a given message would depend on the length of the message, but we will assume that all messages take the same amount of storage. The number of messages the buffer can hold will be a program constant. Messages will be distinguished from one another by a sequence number. Assuming that acknowledgments will be received in the order in which the messages were sent, the first message sent will be the first one released from the buffer. New message copies will be added to the back of the buffer, to work their way to the front as older copies are released. This suggests a first-in, first-out structure—a queue. The simulation will run on a timed basis, with the contents of the buffer displayed at each "clock tick."

The computer network is not 100 percent reliable, and messages and acknowledgments can be lost en route. Therefore A has a time-out interval (a program constant) and associates an elapsed time since transmission with each message. The time-out interval should be long enough to allow a message to get to B and the acknowledgment to get back to A. If the elapsed time for a message in the buffer exceeds the time-out interval, it is assumed that either the message or the acknowledgment was lost. The message is then retransmitted (it remains on the queue and its elapsed time is reset). (In a real network, node B would have to do some work to keep track of what messages it has received. If a message is received and passed on by B but its acknowledgment is lost, then A will eventually time-out on this message and retransmit it. B should not pass on a duplicate copy.) We will assume that node A always has a new message to transmit at each clock tick, provided that there is room in the buffer to store the copy and that A is not occupied by a retransmission due to a time-out during this clock tick.

The user controls the clock by supplying input. The input can either signal the arrival of an acknowledgment, which will also advance the clock, or simply advance the clock without an acknowledgment arriving. Each of these two actions will trigger a series of events.

a. Signal arrival of an acknowledgment: If the acknowledgment is for a message in the buffer, that message is removed from the buffer. All elapsed-time counters for remaining messages are incremented by one, and any message that has timed out is retransmitted. If possible, a new message is transmitted.

b. Advance the clock: All elapsed-time counters are incremented by one, any message that has timed out is retransmitted, and, if possible, a new message is transmitted.

The screen display should show the buffer contents at each clock tick, namely, the sequence numbers and elapsed times for messages currently in the buffer. A comment about any event that has caused the buffer contents to change, such as "acknowledgment received for message #3" or "message #5 timed out, retransmitted," should also appear.

Because messages or acknowledgments can be lost, acknowledgments may not arrive in the same order in which messages were sent. Therefore the queue model for the buffer is only partially accurate—new messages will always be appended to the back of the queue, but deletions may not always occur at the front.

Algorithm and Data Structure Development

We will maintain the buffer as a queue in the sense that we will use a linked list with both front and back pointers. However, as we noted above, deletions will not always take place from the front, although additions will always occur at the back. Another feature of the buffer, as opposed to an arbitrary queue, is that it is limited in size. Therefore we will include as part of the buffer structure a count of the number of records currently in the buffer.

Each record in the buffer represents a message that has been sent but not acknowledged. There must be a field for the sequence number of the message, a field for the elapsed-time counter for that message, and a link field. We will omit a "data" field to hold the actual message contents, as in our simulation we don't really care what the messages are. The following declarations will serve as a starting point.

```
const
    BufferSize  =  10;
    TimeLimit  =  5;                        {time-out limit}

type
    CountType  :  1..BufferSize;
    TimeType  :  0..TimeLimit;
    posinteger  :  1..maxint;

    NodePointer  =  ^Node;
    Node  =  record
        Number : posinteger;                {message sequence number}
        TimeCount : TimeType;               {message elapsed-time
                                              count}

        Link : NodePointer;
    end;        {Node}

    BufferType  =  record
        Count : CountType;                  {current buffer size}
        Front, Back : NodePointer;          {pointers into buffer}
    end;        {BufferType}
```

var
Buffer : BufferType;	{buffer to store messages}
Ack : posinteger;	{message number acknowledged}
Symbol : char;	{user input at clock tick}

The major tasks are summarized in the structure chart of Figure 13.16. Process Timeout has been made a subtask to Advance Clock because at any clock tick, the elapsed times are advanced before messages are checked for time-out. The main program will process inputs in a loop until the user exercises a "Quit" option. We'll look at an outline of the main program first.

Main program

The main program simulates sending the first message by putting message #1 in the buffer and displaying the initial output. It then repeatedly gets the user's input, invokes appropriate procedures, and displays the buffer and accompanying comments until the user selects the QUIT option.

    initialize and display buffer for message #1
    get input
    while response **not** Quit
      begin
        if acknowledgment arrives, invoke
            Acknowledge, AdvanceClock **and** *Transmit*
        otherwise, invoke *AdvanceClock* **and** *Transmit*
        display buffer and comments
        get input
      end

Process Acknowledgment

If the user indicates that an acknowledgment has arrived, the sequence number of the acknowledgment is checked against the numbers currently in the buffer. If that sequence number is found, the appropriate record is deleted from the buffer, otherwise an error message is written. The procedure needs the buffer passed as a variable parameter, as well as the sequence number of the message acknowledged. The procedure works like a combination of the search and delete procedures for a linked list. (Recall that the node to be removed may not be at the front of the buffer.)

Continued

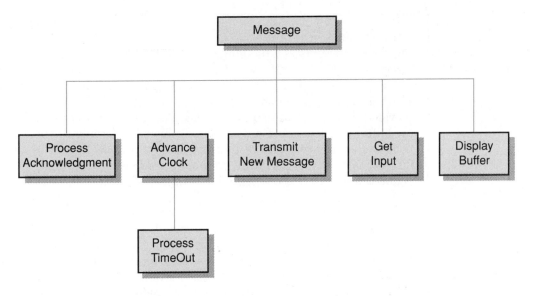

FIGURE 13.16 Structure chart for program *Message*.

Process Acknowledgment—Continued

procedure Acknowledge(**var** Buffer: BufferType;
                               Ack: posinteger);
{removes from buffer the message node with acknowledgment
 number Ack}

var
    Temp : NodePointer;   {pointer through buffer}

begin   {procedure Acknowledge};

  set *Temp* equal to front pointer
  if first node is message # *Ack*, delete this node
  otherwise
      while matching sequence number **not** found **and**
          not end of list, advance *Temp*
      if sequence number found, delete node
      otherwise (end of list), write error message

end;   {procedure Acknowledge}

Advance Clock

This requires traversing the buffer list and increasing the *TimeCount* field in each node. The *AdvanceClock* procedure needs access to *Buffer,* and it will process a time-out event as a subtask. The buffer list can be maintained in decreasing order of *TimeCount,* provided that retransmitted messages are deleted from the front of the buffer and reinserted at the back. If this is done, only the first node in the buffer is subject to timing out when *TimeCount* is incremented. The elapsed time in the first node is checked first, before the times are incremented. If a time-out is about to occur, the first node's elapsed time is set to 0. Then, when all of the time counts are incremented, the node to be retransmitted will have an elapsed time of 1, as desired. In the event that a message times out and is retransmitted, no new message can be transmitted during that clock tick. We'll use a boolean variable *SlotUsed* to indicate this. *TimeOut,* if invoked, will set *SlotUsed* to true; *AdvanceClock* will pass this value back to the main program, and *Transmit* will check *SlotUsed* before sending a new message.

```
procedure AdvanceClock(var Buffer: BufferType;
                       var SlotUsed: boolean);
{advances TimeCount field in each node of Buffer; invokes
 TimeOut if the first node's TimeCount field exceeds
 TimeLimit; if first node is retransmitted, SlotUsed is true}

begin    {procedure AdvanceClock}

  if TimeCount in first node equals TimeLimit
     set TimeCount to 0
     increment all the TimeCount fields
     invoke TimeOut
  otherwise
     increment all the TimeCount fields

end;     {procedure AdvanceClock}
```

Process TimeOut

This procedure will be invoked by *AdvanceClock* to dequeue the first node from the buffer and enqueue it at the back of the buffer, setting the *SlotUsed* flag to true.

Continued

Process TimeOut—Continued

```
procedure TimeOut(var Buffer: BufferType;
                  var SlotUsed: boolean);
```
{remove first node from nonempty Buffer, add it to end, set SlotUsed to prevent another transmission in this time slot}

Transmit

Transmit first checks whether the buffer is currently full or whether *SlotUsed* is true. If not, it enqueues a new message at the end of the buffer and gives it the next sequence number and a *TimeCount* value of 1. This suggests that a program variable holding the current highest sequence number should be available. This variable and the buffer count must each be incremented by one.

```
procedure Transmit(var Buffer: BufferType;
                   var HighNumber: posinteger;
                       SlotUsed: boolean);
```
{if room and SlotUsed false, adds new node to end of Buffer with Number field HighNumber + 1}

begin   {procedure Transmit}

   if buffer **not** full **and** *SlotUsed* **not** true, **then**
      add new message node to end of queue
      increment *Buffer.Count* by 1
      increment *HighNumber* by 1

end;   {procedure Transmit}

Display Buffer

Displaying the buffer is just a list traversal operation.

The following completed program also uses a *Comment* procedure to take care of writing the output comments that describe events that changed the buffer (acknowledgment arrived, time-out and retransmission occurred, new message was sent). *Comment* is invoked by the procedures that process these events.

```
program Message(input, output);

const
    BufferSize = 10;
    TimeLimit  = 5;                    {time-out limit}
```

```
type
    CountType  =  1..BufferSize;
    TimeType  =  0..TimeLimit;
    posinteger  =  1..maxint;

    NodePointer  =  ^Node;
    Node  =  record
        Number : posinteger;            {message sequence number}
        TimeCount : TimeType;           {message elapsed-time count}
        Link : NodePointer;
    end;      {Node}

    BufferType  =  record
        Count : CountType;              {current buffer size}
        Front, Back : NodePointer;      {pointers into buffer}
    end;      {BufferType}

    EventType  =  (AckReceived, TimedOut, NewMessage);

var
    Buffer : BufferType;                {buffer to store messages}
    Ack : posinteger;                   {message number
                                         acknowledged}

    Symbol : char;                      {user input at clock tick}
    HighNumber : posinteger;            {current high sequence
                                         number}

    Event : EventType;                  {event that changed buffer}
    SlotUsed : boolean;                 {flag to signal retransmission
                                         in a time slot so no new
                                         message can be sent then}
```

```
procedure DisplayBuffer(Buffer: BufferType);
{traverses and writes out the buffer list}

var
    Current : NodePointer;

    begin    {procedure DisplayBuffer}
    writeln;
    writeln('      Current contents of message buffer:');
    write('        ');
    Current := Buffer.Front;
    if Buffer.Front = nil then
        writeln('Buffer is empty')
    else
        repeat
            write(Current^.Number:1, '(');
            write(Current^.TimeCount:1, ')     ');
            Current := Current^.Link;
```

```
        until Current = nil;
      writeln;
      writeln;
    end;      {procedure DisplayBuffer}


procedure Comment(Event: EventType; Number: integer);
{writes output messages for events that change buffer}

  begin    {procedure Comment}
    case Event of
      AckReceived :   begin    {AckReceived}
                        writeln;
                        write('Acknowledgment received for ');
                        writeln('message # ', Number:1);
                      end;     {AckReceived}
      TimedOut :      begin    {TimedOut}
                        writeln;
                        write('Message # ', Number:1, ' timed ');
                        writeln('out, retransmitted');
                      end;     {TimedOut}
      NewMessage :    begin    {NewMessage}
                        writeln;
                        writeln('Message # ', Number:1, ' sent');
                      end;     {NewMessage}
    end;      {case}
  end;       {procedure Comment}

procedure GetInput(var Symbol: char);
{displays menu of choices and collects user response Symbol}

  begin    {procedure GetInput}
    writeln;
    writeln('Enter:    A (acknowledgment arrives)');
    writeln('          T (advance timer)');
    writeln('          Q (Quit simulation)');
    writeln;
    write('          ');
    readln(Symbol);
  end;       {procedure GetInput}

procedure Acknowledge(var Buffer: BufferType;
                          Ack: posinteger);
{removes from buffer the message node with acknowledgment
 number Ack}

var
    Temp : NodePointer;    {pointer through buffer}
    found : boolean;       {flag for loop exit}
```

```
begin    {procedure Acknowledge};
  if Buffer.Front <> nil then
    begin    {list not empty}
      Temp := Buffer.Front;
      if Temp^.Number = Ack then
        begin    {delete first node}
          Buffer.Front := Buffer.Front^.Link;
          Buffer.Count := Buffer.Count - 1;
          Comment(AckReceived, Ack)
        end    {delete first node}
      else
        begin    {Ack not for first node}
          found := false;
          while (Temp^.Link <> nil) and (not found) do
            if (Temp^.Link^.Number <> Ack) then

              {advance Temp}
              Temp := Temp^.Link
            else

              {exit loop, Temp^.Link
               points to Ack node}
              found := true;

          if found then
            begin    {delete Temp^.Link node}
              Temp^.Link := Temp^.Link^.Link;
              if Temp^.Link = nil then
                {deleted last node}
                Buffer.Back := Temp;
              Buffer.Count := Buffer.Count - 1;
              Comment(AckReceived, Ack);
            end    {delete Temp^.Link node}
          else
            begin    {Ack message not in buffer}
              write('Message #', Ack:1);
              writeln(' not in buffer');
            end;    {Ack message not in buffer}

        end;    {Ack not for first node}
    end;    {list not empty}
end;    {procedure Acknowledge}

procedure AdvanceClock(var Buffer: BufferType;
                       var SlotUsed: boolean);
{advances TimeCount field in each node of Buffer; invokes
TimeOut if the first node's TimeCount field exceeds TimeLimit;
if first node is retransmitted, SlotUsed is true}
```

```
procedure IncrementTimers(var Buffer: BufferType);
{increments TimeCount fields in all nodes of nonempty buffer}

var
    Temp : NodePointer;

  begin    {procedure IncrementTimers}
    Temp := Buffer.Front;
    repeat
      Temp^.TimeCount := Temp^.TimeCount + 1;
      Temp := Temp^.Link;
    until Temp = nil;
  end;      {procedure IncrementTimers}

procedure TimeOut(var Buffer: BufferType;
                  var SlotUsed: boolean);
{remove first node from nonempty Buffer, add it to end, set
SlotUsed to prevent another transmission in this time slot}

  begin    {procedure TimeOut}
    if Buffer.Front <> Buffer.Back then
      begin    {list has more than one element}
        Buffer.Back^.Link := Buffer.Front;
        Buffer.Front := Buffer.Front^.Link;
        Buffer.Back := Buffer.Back^.Link;
        Buffer.Back^.Link := nil;
      end;        {list has more than one element}

    SlotUsed := true;
  end;      {procedure TimeOut}

  begin    {procedure AdvanceClock}

    if Buffer.Front <> nil then
      begin    {list not empty}

        if Buffer.Front^.TimeCount = TimeLimit then
          begin    {first node times out}
            Buffer.Front^.TimeCount := 0;
            IncrementTimers(Buffer);
            TimeOut(Buffer, SlotUsed);
            Comment(TimedOut, Buffer.Back^.Number);
          end      {first node times out}

        else    {no node times out}
          IncrementTimers(Buffer);

      end;      {list not empty}
  end;        {procedure AdvanceClock}
```

```
procedure Transmit(var Buffer:  BufferType;
                   var HighNumber: posinteger;
                   SlotUsed: boolean);
{if room and SlotUsed false, adds new node to end of Buffer
with Number field HighNumber + 1}


var
    Temp : NodePointer;

  begin    {procedure Transmit}

    if (Buffer.Count < BufferSize) and (not SlotUsed) then
      begin    {buffer not full and free time slot - can
                send new message}

      {prepare new node}
      new(Temp);
      Temp^.Number := HighNumber + 1;
      Temp^.TimeCount := 1;
      Temp^.Link := nil;

      {enqueue new node}
      if Buffer.Front <> nil then
        begin    {list not empty, add node to back}
          Buffer.Back^.Link := Temp;
          Buffer.Back := Temp;
        end    {list not empty, add node to back}
      else
        begin    {add node to empty list}
          Buffer.Front := Temp;
          Buffer.Back := Temp;
        end;    {add node to empty list}

      {update buffer node count}
      Buffer.Count := Buffer.Count + 1;

      {update current high sequence number}
      HighNumber := HighNumber + 1;

      Comment(NewMessage, HighNumber);
      end;    {can send new message}

    end;    {procedure Transmit}


begin    {main program}

  {opening remark}
```

```
writeln('This program simulates message passing in a computer ');
writeln('network.   The output shows the buffer where the');
writeln('sending node stores messages by sequence number');
writeln('until each message is acknowledged.');
writeln;
writeln;

{send first message, initialize buffer queue}
new(Buffer.Front);
Buffer.Front^.Number := 1;
Buffer.Front^.TimeCount := 1;
Buffer.Front^.Link := nil;
Buffer.Back := Buffer.Front;
Buffer.Count := 1;
HighNumber := 1;

{display output}
Comment(NewMessage, 1);
DisplayBuffer(Buffer);

{start simulation}
GetInput(Symbol);
SlotUsed := false;
while (Symbol <> 'Q') and (Symbol <> 'q') do
  begin    {while not Quit}
    if (Symbol = 'A') or (Symbol = 'a') then
      begin    {process acknowledgment}

        writeln;
        write('Sequence number for acknowledgment: ');
        readln(Ack);
        Acknowledge(Buffer, Ack);
        AdvanceClock(Buffer, SlotUsed);
        Transmit(Buffer, HighNumber, SlotUsed);

      end        {process acknowledgment}
    else
      begin    {advance timer}

        AdvanceClock(Buffer, SlotUsed);
        Transmit(Buffer, HighNumber, SlotUsed);

      end;      {advance timer}

    DisplayBuffer(Buffer);
    GetInput(Symbol);
    SlotUsed := false;
  end;      {while not Quit}
```

```
            {option is QUIT, terminate program}
            writeln ('End of message passing simulation');
end.      {main program}
```

RUNNING THE PROGRAM...

This program simulates message passing in a computer
network. The output shows the buffer where the
sending node stores messages by sequence number
until each message is acknowledged.

Message # 1 sent

        Current contents of message buffer:
        1(1)

    Enter: A (acknowledgment arrives)
              T (advance timer)
              Q (Quit simulation)

              t

Message # 2 sent

        Current contents of message buffer:
        1(2)   2(1)

    Enter: A (acknowledgment arrives)
              T (advance timer)
              Q (Quit simulation)

              t

Message # 3 sent

        Current contents of message buffer:
        1(3)   2(2)   3(1)

    Enter: A (acknowledgment arrives)
              T (advance timer)
              Q (Quit simulation)

              a

Sequence number for acknowledgment: 2

Acknowledgment received for message # 2

Message # 4 sent

    Current contents of message buffer:
    1(4)   3(2)   4(1)

Enter: A (acknowledgment arrives)
           T (advance timer)
           Q (Quit simulation)

        t

Message # 5 sent

    Current contents of message buffer:
    1(5)   3(3)   4(2)   5(1)

Enter: A (acknowledgment arrives)
           T (advance timer)
           Q (Quit simulation)

        t

Message # 1 timed out, retransmitted

    Current contents of message buffer:
    3(4)   4(3)   5(2)   1(1)

Enter: A (acknowledgment arrives)
           T (advance timer)
           Q (Quit simulation)

        a

Sequence number for acknowledgment: 3

Acknowledgment received for message # 3

Message # 6 sent

    Current contents of message buffer:
    4(4)   5(3)   1(2)   6(1)

Enter: A (acknowledgment arrives)
           T (advance timer)
           Q (Quit simulation)

        q
End of message passing simulation

**CASE
STUDY
ONE**   **View #13**

The Lodestone County Water Pollution Department has made one final request for program modification. In order to aid in identifying causes of high pollution levels, the department would like the option of printing out the pollution levels and associated reading dates for any given site in order of increasing levels.

Sterling Software Systems agrees to modify the program, and you are given this task on the eve of your retirement from Sterling. The existing data file contains records from all sites, sorted by date. The number of records pertaining to a given site is unknown, and these records will have to be reordered by pollution level. You decide to scan the file for records for the site and build them into a binary search tree based on pollution level. Then, an inorder traversal of the binary search tree can be used to generate the output. The nodes of the tree need not contain all of the record data; only the pollution level and reading date are necessary.

Much of the code in procedure *Site* below is very similar to that of program *Nametree* earlier in this chapter. The only additional changes required to carry out this modification occurred in the *MenuDisplay* and *CollectResponse* procedures, as well as the main program.

```
program WaterPollution(input, output, DataH2O);
{maintains a file DataH2O of records of water samples from
various sites; each record contains site ID, date of sample,
amount of water, and bacteria count, also the bacteria/water
ratio and a warning if the bacteria level is too high. The file
is maintained in sorted order by date of sample. The user may
choose to enter new records (these are displayed in tabular form,
sorted, and merged into the file), to display all records from
file that are in violation together with the total number of
readings in the file and the percentage of total readings that
are in violation, to display all readings within a given range of
dates together with the percentage of violations during this
period, or to display all entries from a particular site, in
order of pollution level.}

const
    Threshold = 2.0;              {200 bacteria per 100 ml water}
    MaxNoOfReadings = 30;  {maximum number of readings
                            per session
                            program can handle}

type
    DateArray = packed array [1..6] of char;
    Reading = record
      ID, Water, Bacteria : integer;
      Date : DateArray;
      Level : real;                  {pollution level}
```

```
            Warning : boolean;          {flag for warning message}
          end;      {Reading}
        Index  =  1..MaxNoOfReadings;
        ArrayType  =  array [Index] of Reading;
        FileType  =  file of Reading;

var
        DataH2O : FileType;          {file of site readings}
        Task : char;                 {user task selection from menu}

procedure ClearScreen;
{clears the screen by writing 24 blank lines}

var
        i : integer;

    begin    {procedure ClearScreen}
      for i := 1 to 24 do
        writeln;
    end;      {procedure ClearScreen}


procedure MenuDisplay;
{displays menu of tasks from which user can choose}

    begin    {procedure MenuDisplay}
      ClearScreen;
      writeln;
      writeln('                  Water Pollution Record Keeper');
      writeln;
      writeln('                              written by');
      writeln('                       Sterling Software Systems.');
      writeln;
      writeln('                       Choose task to be done:');
      writeln; writeln;
      writeln('          Enter (E)        Enter new data for file');
      writeln;
      write('          Violators (V)     Display pollution violation');
      writeln(' records from file');
      writeln;
      write('          Display (D)       Display all records within');
      writeln(' given date range');
      writeln;
      write('          Site (S)          Display pollution levels/dates');
      writeln(' for a given site');
      writeln;
      writeln('          Quit (Q)            Quit program');
      writeln;
      write('          Enter your choice (E, V, D, S, or Q):  ');
    end;      {procedure MenuDisplay}
```

```
procedure CollectResponse(var Choice: char);
{collects the user's choice of action}

type
    Response = set of char;

var
    Valid : Response;

  begin      {procedure CollectResponse}
    valid := ['E','V','D','S','Q','e','v','d','s','q'];
    readln(Choice);
    ClearScreen;
    while not (Choice in Valid) do
      begin
        writeln('Your choices are E, V, D, S, Q, try again: ');
        readln(Choice);
        ClearScreen;
      end;
    end;      {procedure CollectResponse}

procedure DateInput(var Date: DateArray);
{collects date in month/date/year format, returns as YYMMDD in
 array Date}

type
    TwoCharArray = array[1..2] of char;

var
    Mon, Day, Yr: TwoCharArray;
    Slash : char;      {separating / in date format}

function Value(FirstChar, SecondChar: char): integer;
{function to convert two characters to a two-digit integer}

var
    FirstDigit    : integer;      {the integer equivalents}
    SecondDigit : integer;      {of numerical characters}

  begin    {function Value}
    FirstDigit := ord(FirstChar) − ord('0');
    SecondDigit := ord(SecondChar) − ord('0');
    Value := 10*FirstDigit + SecondDigit;
    end;      {function Value}

function ValidDate(Mon1, Mon2, Day1, Day2: char): boolean;
{function to do some validation on date entered}

var
    MonthValue : integer;      {numerical value for month}
```

```
      DayValue : integer;        {numerical value for day}
      ValidMonth : boolean;      {MonthValue in range 1-12}
      ValidDay : boolean;        {DayValue in range 1-31}

   begin   {function ValidDate}
     MonthValue := Value(Mon1, Mon2);
     DayValue := Value(Day1, Day2);

     ValidMonth := (0 < MonthValue) and (MonthValue < 13);
     ValidDay := (0 < DayValue) and (DayValue < 32);

     ValidDate := ValidMonth and ValidDay;
   end;      {function ValidDate}


   begin    {procedure DateInput}
     write('Use month/date/year format: ');
     readln(Mon[1], Mon[2], Slash, Day[1], Day[2],
            Slash, Yr[1], Yr[2]);

     while not ValidDate(Mon[1], Mon[2], Day[1], Day[2]) do
       begin {error in date input}
         write('Please enter the date again: ');
         readln(Mon[1], Mon[2], Slash,
                Day[1], Day[2],
                Slash, Yr[1], Yr[2]);
       end;  {error in date input}

     {date OK, now put it in Date array in YYMMDD form}
     Date[1] := Yr[1];
     Date[2] := Yr[2];
     Date[3] := Mon[1];
     Date[4] := Mon[2];
     Date[5] := Day[1];
     Date[6] := Day[2];
   end;      {procedure DateInput}

procedure GetInput(var OneSite: Reading);
{procedure to collect input for water pollution data; amount
 Water of water and count Bacteria of bacteria were obtained
 from site ID on date Date (YYMMDD)}

   begin      {procedure GetInput}
     with OneSite do
       begin    {with OneSite}
         writeln;
         write('Enter the site ID number: ');
         readln(ID);
         while not((1 <= ID) and (ID <= 1000)) do
```

```
        begin {ID out of range}
          write('Check the site ID number ');
          write('and enter again: ');
          readln(ID);
        end;     {ID out of range}
      writeln;

      writeln('Enter the date of this sample.');
      DateInput(Date);

      writeln;
      write('Enter the amount of water in sample (in ml): ');
      readln(Water);
      while not (Water > 0) do
        begin    {error in amount of water}
          write('Check the amount of water & ');
          write('enter again: ');
          readln(Water);
        end;       {error in amount of water}
      writeln;

      write('Enter the bacteria count found in this sample: ');
      readln(Bacteria);
      while not (Bacteria >= 0) do
        begin    {error in bacteria count}
          write('Check the bacteria count & ');
          write('enter again: ');
          readln(Bacteria);
        end;       {error in bacteria count}
    end;      {with OneSite}

  end;        {procedure GetInput}

function Ratio(Bacteria, Water: integer): real;
{computes the Ratio of Bacteria to Water}

  begin      {function Ratio}
    Ratio := Bacteria/Water;
  end;        {function Ratio}

procedure CheckThreshold(Ratio: real;
                            var Over: Boolean);
{compares Ratio to the global constant Threshold and sets Over
 to true if that limit is exceeded}

  begin      {procedure CheckThreshold}
    Over := false;   {initialize Over}
    if Ratio > Threshold then
      Over := true;
  end;        {procedure CheckThreshold}
```

```
procedure WriteHeader;
{writes output table heading}

   begin      {procedure WriteHeader}
     writeln;
     writeln;
     write('Site ID', 'Date':8, 'Water':12, 'Bacteria':13);
     writeln('Level':9, 'Warning':10);
     write('_____');
     writeln('_____');
     writeln;
   end;    {procedure WriteHeader}

procedure WriteLineOfOutput(OneSite: Reading);
{produces a line of output in the table corresponding to one
reading - echoes input data and writes warning message if
warranted}

   begin      {procedure WriteLineOfOutput}
     with OneSite do
       begin    {with OneSite}
         write(ID:5, Date[3]:6, Date[4], '/', Date[5], Date[6],
               '/', Date[1], Date[2]);
         write(Water:8, ' ml', Bacteria:9, Level:11:2);

         if Warning then
           write('      ** HIGH **');
         writeln;
       end;     {with OneSite}
   end;         {procedure WriteLineOfOutput}

procedure Sort(var A: ArrayType; n: integer);
{recursive selection sort on array A, sorting records from 1 to n
on Date field}

var
     i : integer;                  {index in array A}

function MaxIndex(A: ArrayType; i: integer): integer;
{finds the index of the maximum value from 1 to i in array A}

var
     CurrentMaxIndex : integer;     {index of current max value}
     j : integer;                   {array index}

   begin    {function MaxIndex}
     CurrentMaxIndex := 1;
     for j := 2 to i do
```

```
      begin
        if A[j].Date > A[CurrentMaxIndex].Date then
          CurrentMaxIndex := j;
      end;
   MaxIndex := CurrentMaxIndex;
 end;      {function MaxIndex}

procedure Exchange(var X, Y: Reading);
{exchanges records X and Y}

var
    Temporary : Reading;

  begin    {procedure Exchange}
   Temporary := X;
   X := Y;
   Y := Temporary;
 end;      {procedure Exchange}

 begin    {procedure Sort}
   if n > 1 then
     begin    {array length > 1}
       Exchange(A[n], A[MaxIndex(A, n)]);
       Sort(A, n − 1);
     end;      {array length > 1}

 end;      {procedure Sort}

procedure Merge(var DataH2O, Temp: FileType;
                    var Session: ArrayType; n: integer);
{merges records from sorted file DataH2O and sorted array
 Session (with n entries) into file Temp}

var
    i : integer;          {array index}
    Entry : Reading;      {record in file}

  begin    {procedure Merge}

   reset(DataH2O);
   rewrite(Temp);
   i := 1;
   if not eof(DataH2O) then
     read(DataH2O, Entry)
   else Entry.Date := '999999';

   while (i <= n) do
     begin    {more items left in array}
```

```
     if Entry.Date <= Session[i].Date then
       begin    {write record from file into Temp}
         write(Temp, Entry);
         if not eof(DataH2O) then
           read(DataH2O, Entry)
         else Entry.Date := '999999';
       end     {write record from file into Temp}
     else
       begin    {write record from array into Temp}
         write(Temp, Session[i]);
         i := i + 1;
       end;      {write record from array into Temp}
   end;      {more items left in array}
```

{the array is exhausted, put any remaining legitimate records from the file into Temp}

```
  while Entry.Date <> '999999' do
    begin
      write(Temp, Entry);
      if not eof(DataH2O) then
        read(DataH2O, Entry)
      else Entry.Date := '999999';
    end;

end;        {procedure Merge}

procedure NewData(var DataH2O: FileType);
```
{handles collection and display of new records, sorts them by date, and merges them with already existing sorted file DataH2O}

```
var
    Session : ArrayType;      {holds records entered in current
                                program session}
    Continue : char;          {signal to terminate data entry}
    n : integer;              {number of readings to process}
    i : integer;              {array index}
    Temp : FileType;          {temporary file for file copy}
    Entry : Reading;          {record in file}

  begin     {procedure NewData}

  n := 0;
  repeat
    n := n + 1;

    GetInput(Session[n]);
```

```
        with Session[n] do
          Level := Ratio(Bacteria, Water);

        writeln;
        writeln;
        if (n < MaxNoOfReadings) then
          begin {room for more data}
            writeln('Do you have more sites to process?');
            writeln('(Answer Y or N): ');
            readln(Continue);
          end    {room for more data}
        else
          begin {array full}
            writeln('Maximum number of readings entered. ');
            write('Adjust program constant MaxNoOfReadings ');
            writeln('if this is a problem.');
          end;   {array full}

      until (Continue = 'N') or (Continue  = 'n') or
            (n = MaxNoOfReadings);

{all the input has been gathered and stored in the array,
 now print out table}

      write('The following new records will be merged');
      writeln(' into file DataH2O.');

      WriteHeader;
      for i := 1 to n do
        begin {produce line i of the output table}
          CheckThreshold(Session[i].Level, Session[i].Warning);
          WriteLineOfOutput(Session[i]);
        end;   {line i has been written}
      writeln;
      writeln('Hit RETURN to continue');
      readln;

{now sort this array by date}
      Sort(Session, n);

{now merge these records into sorted file DataH2O}
      Merge(DataH2O, Temp, Session, n);

{merge complete, now copy back to DataH2O}
      reset(Temp);
      rewrite(DataH2O);
      while not eof(Temp) do
        begin
          read(Temp, Entry);
```

```
            write(DataH2O, Entry);
         end;      {DataH2O now complete}

   end;           {procedure NewData}

procedure Violators(var DataH2O: FileType);
{displays all records in file DataH2O with pollution levels above
 threshold}

var
      Entry : Reading;          {record in file}
      Count : integer;          {number of records in file}
      Bad : integer;            {number of violation records in
                                 file}
      Percentage : real;        {percent violation records}

   begin     {procedure Violators}
   reset(DataH2O);
   writeln('Readings from file that are in violation:');
   writeln;
   Count := 0;
   Bad := 0;
   WriteHeader;
   while not eof(DataH2O) do
      begin
         read(DataH2O, Entry);
         if Entry.Warning then
            begin
              WriteLineOfOutput(Entry);
              Bad := Bad + 1;
            end;
         Count := Count + 1;
      end;      {while not eof}
   writeln;
   if Count = 0 then
      begin
        writeln('File DataH2O is empty');
        writeln('Hit RETURN to continue');
        readln;
      end
   else
      begin
        write('Total number of readings in file: ');
        writeln(Count:3);
        writeln('Percentage of readings in file ');
        write('that are in violation: ');
        Percentage := (Bad/Count)*100;
        writeln(Percentage:6:2);
        writeln('Hit RETURN to continue');
```

```
        readln;
      end;
  end;      {procedure Violators}

procedure Display(var DataH2O: FileType);
{displays all records in file DataH2O within a given range of
dates; gives percent of those records with pollution levels above
threshold}

var
      StartDate, EndDate : DateArray;      {range of dates for
                                            display}
      RangeBegin, RangeEnd : boolean;      {flags for marking
                                            beginning and end of
                                            range as file is read}
      Entry : Reading;                     {record in file}
      Count : integer;                     {number of records in range}
      Bad : integer;                       {number of violation records
                                            in range}

      Percentage : real;                   {percent violation records
                                            in range}

  begin     {procedure Display}
    writeln('Enter starting date for display of records;');
    DateInput(StartDate);
    writeln;
    writeln('Enter ending date for display of records;');
    DateInput(EndDate);
    writeln;
    while StartDate > EndDate do
      begin     {bad range dates}
        writeln('Starting date must precede ending date.');
        writeln('Please try again.');
        writeln('Enter starting date for display of records;');
        DateInput(StartDate);
        writeln;
        writeln('Enter ending date for display of records;');
        DateInput(EndDate);
        writeln;
      end;     {bad range dates}
    reset(DataH2O);
    RangeBegin := false;
    RangeEnd := false;
    writeln('Readings from file within this range of dates:');
    writeln;
    Count := 0;
    Bad := 0;
    WriteHeader;
```

```
if eof(DataH2O) then
  begin
    writeln('File DataH2O is empty');
    writeln('Hit RETURN to continue');
    readln;
  end
else
  begin     {file not empty}

    while (not eof(DataH2O)) and (not RangeBegin) do
      begin    {looking for first record in range}
        read(DataH2O, Entry);
        if (Entry.Date >= StartDate) and
           (Entry.Date <= EndDate) then
          begin    {first record in range found}
            RangeBegin := true;
            WriteLineOfOutput(Entry);
            if Entry.Warning then
              Bad := Bad + 1;
            Count := Count + 1;
          end;     {first record in range found}
      end;     {looking for first record in range}

    while (not eof(DataH2O)) and (not RangeEnd) do
      begin    {processing records in range}
        read(DataH2O, Entry);
        if Entry.Date <= EndDate then
          begin    {this record in range}
            WriteLineOfOutput(Entry);
            if Entry.Warning then
              Bad := Bad + 1;
            Count := Count + 1;
          end        {this record in range}
        else    {turn off processing}
          RangeEnd := true;
      end;      {processing records in range}

    writeln;
    if Count = 0 then
      begin
        writeln('No records within this range');
        writeln('Hit RETURN to continue');
        readln;
      end
    else
      begin
        writeln('Percentage of readings in range ');
        write('that are in violation: ');
        Percentage := (Bad/Count)*100;
```

```
            writeln(Percentage:6:2);
            writeln('Hit RETURN to continue');
            readln;
          end;
        end;     {file not empty}
    end;      {procedure Display}


procedure Site(var DataH2O: FileType);
{builds binary search tree with pollution level/date information
for a given site, ordered by level; does inorder traversal to
display data sorted by level and gives percent of entries with
level above threshold}

type
    NodePointer = ^Node;
    Node = record
      Level : real;
      Date : DateArray;
      Left, Right : NodePointer;
      end;      {Node}

var
    ID : integer;          {ID for site to examine}
    Count : integer;       {number of readings for this site}
    Bad : integer;         {number of violation readings for this
                              site}
    Percentage : real;     {percent violation nodes}
    Root : NodePointer;    {pointer to root of binary tree}

procedure Insert(var Root: NodePointer; Entry:  Reading);
{inserts level and date data from Entry into binary search tree
ordered by level}

  begin    {procedure Insert}
    if Root = nil then
      begin    {empty tree, attach node}
        new(Root);
        Root^.Level := Entry.Level;
        Root^.Date := Entry.Date;
        Root^.Left := nil;
        Root^.Right := nil;
      end      {empty tree, attach node}
    else
      if Entry.Level < Root^.Level then
        {insert node in left subtree}
        Insert(Root^.Left, Entry)
      else
        {insert node in right subtree}
        Insert(Root^.Right, Entry);
    end;      {procedure Insert}
```

```
procedure BuildTree(var DataH2O: FileType;
                    var Root:  NodePointer; ID: integer;
                    var Count, Bad: integer);
{creates the binary search tree for site data from records in
file DataH2O; also returns total number of nodes, Count, and
number of nodes in violation, Bad}

var
    Entry : Reading;       {record in file}

  begin    {procedure BuildTree}
    reset(DataH2O);
    while not eof(DataH2O) do
      begin    {while not eof}
        read(DataH2O, Entry);
        if Entry.ID = ID then
          begin    {record for this site}
            Insert(Root, Entry);
            Count := Count + 1;
            if Entry.Warning then
              Bad := Bad + 1;
          end;    {record for this site}
      end;    {while not eof}
  end;    {procedure BuildTree}

procedure Inorder(Root: NodePointer);
{does inorder traversal of binary search tree to which Root
points, writes out node values - these will be sorted by
pollution level}

  begin    {procedure Inorder}
    if Root <> nil then
      begin    {Root not nil}
        Inorder(Root^.Left);
        with Root^ do
          begin    {write level and date}
            write(Level:5:2);
            writeln(Date[3]:6, Date[4], '/', Date[5],
                    Date[6], '/', Date[1], Date[2]);
          end;    {write level and date}
        Inorder(Root^.Right);
      end;    {Root not nil}
  end;    {procedure Inorder}


  begin    {procedure Site}
    {determine site}
    write('Enter the site ID number: ');
    readln(ID);
```

```
      while not((1 <= ID) and (ID <= 1000)) do
        begin {ID out of range}
          write('Check the site ID number ');
          write('and enter again: ');
          readln(ID);
        end;  {ID out of range}
      writeln;

      {initialize}
      Root := nil;
      Count := 0;
      Bad := 0;

      {build binary search tree for this site}
      BuildTree(DataH2O, Root, ID, Count, Bad);

      {display results}
      writeln('Pollution levels and dates for site ',ID:5);
      Inorder(Root);
      writeln;
      if Count = 0 then
        begin
          writeln('No records in file for this site');
          writeln('Hit RETURN to continue');
          readln;
        end
      else
        begin
          writeln('Percentage of readings for this site ');
          write('that are in violation: ');
          Percentage := (Bad/Count)*100;
          writeln(Percentage:6:2);
          writeln('Hit RETURN to continue');
          readln;
        end;

    end;    {procedure Site}

begin    {main program}

  MenuDisplay;
  CollectResponse(Task);
  while not ((Task = 'Q') or (Task = 'q')) do
    begin
      case Task of
        'E','e': NewData(DataH2O);
        'V','v': Violators(DataH2O);
        'D','d': Display(DataH2O);
        'S','s':  Site(DataH2O);
      end;    {case}
```

```
        MenuDisplay;
        CollectResponse(Task);
    end;    {while}

    {Task is QUIT, terminate program}
    end.    {main program}
```

RUNNING THE PROGRAM...

If the user chooses to view data for a given site, the following interaction could occur.

```
            Water  Pollution  Record  Keeper

                        written  by
                Sterling  Software  Systems

                Choose  task  to  be  done:

        Enter (E)        Enter  new  data  for  file

        Violators (V)    Display  pollution  violation  records  from  file

        Display (D)      Display  all  records  within  given  date  range

        Site (S)         Display  pollution  levels/data  for  a  given  site

        Quit (Q)         Quit  program

            Enter  your  choice  (E,  V,  D,  S,  or  Q):  s

    Enter  the  site  ID  number:  121


    Pollution  levels  and  data  for  site     121
        0.80        09/22/82
        2.03        08/20/82
        3.52        11/01/85

    Percentage  of  readings  for  this  site
    that  are  in  violation:     66.67
    Hit  RETURN  to  continue
```

(Note: The Lodestone County Water Pollution Department has worked closely with Sterling Software Systems over the life of this project. The department manager is so pleased with the work Sterling has done that when a friend in the Lodestone County Air Quality Control Department mentions that they are looking for someone to do software development, the manager recommends Sterling.)

CASE STUDY TWO

View #13

Modify the program for the Lodestone County Hospital Hypertension Clinic to allow the user to display, for a given patient, average pressure and date of visit, ordered by increasing diastolic pressure. In addition, the percentage of readings for this patient in each of the three hypertensive categories should be part of the output for this option.

EXERCISES

For Exercises 1-5, assume the following declarations:

```
type
    NodePointer = ^Node;
    Node = record
      Value : integer;
      Category : char;
      Link : NodePointer;
      end;      {Node}
var
    Head, Temp : NodePointer;
```

#1. What is the output from the following section of code?

```
new(Temp);
Temp^.Value := 3;
Head := Temp;
writeln(Head^.Value);
```

2. What is the output from the following section of code?

```
new(Head);
new(Temp);
Head^.Category := 'A';
Temp^.Category := 'B';
Head^.Link := Temp;
writeln(Head^.Link^.Category);
```

3. Write a statement to make *Head* and *Temp* both point to the record pointed to by *Head.*

#4. Write a statement to make the *Value* field of the record that *Head* points to the same as the *Value* field of the record that *Temp* points to.

#5. Draw a diagram that represents the situation after execution of the following section of code.

```
new(Temp);
Temp^.Value := 7;
Temp^.Category := 'S';
Head := Temp;
new(Temp);
Temp^.Value := 12;
Temp^.Category := 'T';
Head^.Link := Temp;
Temp^.Link := Head;
Head := nil;
```

6. Given two linked lists with pointers *Head1* and *Head2* to the heads of the lists, write a procedure to concatenate list #2 behind list #1.

#7. Write a variation of the *Traverse* procedure for program *NameList* that writes out only every other name.

8. Complete the *Push* and *Pop* procedures for *MirrorWritingTwo*.

9. Write the values output by an inorder traversal of the tree shown in Figure 13.17.

10. Other tree-traversal algorithms are **preorder** and **postorder.** In a preorder traversal of a binary tree, the node is visited first, then the left subtree is traversed, followed by the right subtree. In a postorder traversal, the left and right subtrees are traversed, and then the node is visited. Using the following declarations for a binary tree

```
type
    NodePointer = ^Node;
    Node = record
      Left, Right : NodePointer;
      Value : char;
      end;      {Node}
var
    Root : NodePointer;
```

a. Write a procedure for a preorder traversal.
b. Write a procedure for a postorder traversal.

11. Preorder and postorder traversals of a binary tree are defined in Exercise #10. Referring to the tree shown in Figure 13.17,

a. Write the values output by a preorder traversal.
b. Write the values output by a postorder traversal.

#12. Binary trees are useful representations of arithmetic expressions. The leaves of the tree hold constant or single variable values. Nodes with two children denote a binary operator that acts on the two subtrees as operands.

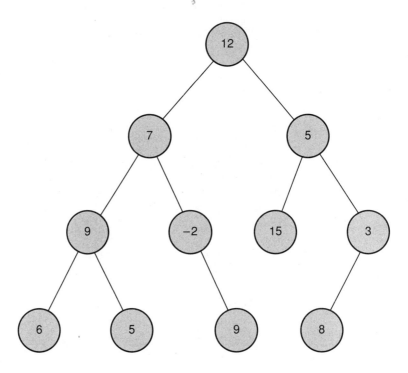

FIGURE 13.17

For example, the arithmetic expression

$$A * (B + C) - 4 \tag{1}$$

can be represented by the **_expression tree_** of Figure 13.18. An inorder traversal of this tree yields the string

$$A * B + C - 4$$

Although the order of operations imposed by the parentheses in expression (1) is contained in the tree structure, this information is lost in the inorder traversal because parentheses are not present. Expression (1) is written in **_infix_** notation, where the binary operator symbol is located between the two operands. In **_prefix_** notation, a binary operator symbol precedes its two operands, while in **_postfix_** notation, the operator symbol follows the two operands. The advantage to the prefix and postfix forms is that parentheses are not required in order to clarify the order of operations. The preorder and postorder traversals (see Exercise #10) of an expression tree yield prefix and postfix forms for the expression, respectively.

    _a._ Write the prefix form for expression (1) by doing a preorder traversal of the expression tree in Figure 13.18.

    _b._ Write the postfix form for expression (1) by doing a postorder traversal of the expression tree in Figure 13.18.

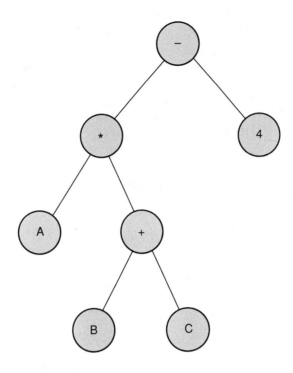

FIGURE 13.18 An expression tree.

#13. Draw figures similar to Figures 9.5, 13.13, and 13.14 to illustrate the selection sort, insertion sort, and bubble sort, respectively, on the elements

    9 0 14 5 7 3 −2 5

14. Illustrate the quicksort algorithm on the elements

    4 6 3 0 3 9 5   .

by showing the array after each exchange of elements that modifies the array.

15. The following comments refer to sorting an array. Each comment describes one or more of selection sort, insertion sort, bubble sort, quicksort. Provide the correct answer or answers for each comment.

    a. Does the same operations regardless of what original array looks like.

  #b. Best case occurs when original array is already sorted.

    c. Worst case occurs when original array is already sorted.

    d. Worst case does $O(n^2)$ work.

    e. Best case does $O(n^2)$ work.

    f. Best case does $O(n)$ work.

    g. All but worst cases require $O(n \log_2 n)$ work.

SKILL BUILDERS

#1. Write a *Delete* procedure for program *NameList*. Be sure your procedure is general enough to cover special cases, such as the list is empty when the procedure is invoked, the element to be deleted is the first one in the list, or *AfterThis* points to the last node in the list when the procedure is invoked.

2. A nonrecursive version of a function to search a linked list and return **nil** or a pointer to a target element was described on page 494. Write a recursive *Search* function for program *NameList*.

3. Write a procedure that reverses the links in a linked list. The procedure receives a pointer *Head* to the head of the list as a parameter; upon exit, *Head* should point to the new head of the list. Assume that the list items are integers.

4. Given two sorted linked lists of integers with pointers *Head1* and *Head2* to the heads of the lists, write a procedure to merge the two lists into one sorted linked list.

5. A *doubly linked list* maintains pointers from the tail to the head of the list, as well as from the head to the tail. This makes it easy to traverse the list in either direction. Write the declarations for a doubly linked list of integers. Write procedures to insert and delete elements from a doubly linked list.

6. Write a procedure to delete a node from a binary search tree in such a way that the result is still a binary search tree. (Hint: Consider three cases, one where the node to be deleted is a leaf, one where it has a single descendant, and one where it has two descendants.)

#7. Write a corrected version of procedure *InsertionSort* (see CHECKUP 13.11).

8. In the bubble sort algorithm, once a complete pass of the array is made in which no exchanges occur, the array is in sorted order. Examining the array for further exchanges is not necessary. Modify procedure *BubbleSort* to monitor this condition and terminate if it occurs.

SOFTWARE DEVELOPMENT PROJECTS

1. Develop software to determine whether an arithmetic expression is *well formed* with respect to grouping symbols. There are two types of grouping symbols, parentheses and brackets. The expression

$$[A * (B + C)] - D$$

is well formed, while the expression

$$(A * [B + C) - D]$$

is not. (Hint: Use a stack.)

2. The Dumpsterbreath Used Car Agency maintains a computerized file of information on cars on the lot that are available for sale. Data on each car include an identification number, the sale price, and the class (subcompact,

compact, midsize, or luxury). The file is maintained in sorted order on sale price within a class. At the start of a business day, Dumpsterbreath wants this information available in main memory for faster processing; insertions will be made for autos taken in trade on that day, and deletions done for autos sold. Queries on the availability of an auto in a particular class or particular price range should be possible. Various reporting capabilities such as number of autos purchased or sold that day or number of available autos in a particular class should also be included. At the end of the business day, the updated information should be rewritten to the file. Develop software to maintain the Dumpsterbreath data base.

3. A list can be implemented using an array structure as a simulation of a linked list. Unlike the ordinary array implementation where list elements are stored sequentially, a simulated linked list uses an array of records with one field of the record acting as the link field in a linked list. The contents of this field will be an array index where the next node is stored. If the array is indexed from 1 to n, a zero can be used to denote the **nil** pointer. An integer variable giving the array index of the first element in a list acts like the *Head* pointer in the linked-list implementation. To simulate the *new* and *dispose* procedures, an ***available list*** of unused array entries must be maintained.

This implementation shares one shortcoming with the ordinary array implementation because a fixed amount of storage is dedicated to the list. However, it shares one advantage with the linked-list implementation: the amount of work required for list insertions and deletions is independent of the size of the list.

Rewrite program *NameList* using this implementation. Also include a *Search* function and a *Delete* procedure.

4. A ***sparse matrix*** is a matrix where many of the entries are zero. If the matrix is large, it may save storage space to represent it as a series of linked lists where only the nonzero elements are nodes, as opposed to using an $n \times m$ array where most of the entries are 0. A *Row* array can store n pointers to n linked lists, one for each row. The list pointed to by *Row[i]* contains nodes for the nonzero elements in row i. Each node contains a data value and a column number for that value, as well as a link field. A *Column* array can store m pointers to m linked lists, one for each column. The nodes here contain a data value and a row number. Develop software to:

    a. Collect the entries for a sparse matrix and store them as described above.

    b. Display as an $n \times m$ array a matrix stored as described above.

    c. Add two sparse matrices.

    d. Multiply two sparse matrices.

5. An array-sorting method that improves upon the insertion sort is the ***shell sort,*** named after its discoverer, D. L. Shell. The shell sort is also called the ***diminishing increment sort.*** In this sorting method, a series of decreasing positive integers is chosen, with the initial value less than the size of the array and the final value equal to 1. Any value in this sequence, say k, represents an increment, or step size, in the array. The k subarrays made up of elements from the original array that are k values apart are sorted using an insertion sort. For example, if the value of k is 5, then the five subarrays consisting of elements

$A[1]$, $A[6]$, $A[11]$, $A[16]$, ...
$A[2]$, $A[7]$, $A[12]$, $A[17]$, ...
$A[3]$, $A[8]$, $A[13]$, $A[18]$, ...
$A[4]$, $A[9]$, $A[14]$, $A[19]$, ...
$A[5]$, $A[10]$, $A[15]$, $A[20]$, ...

are each sorted. (Depending on the size of the original array, these subarrays may not all be exactly the same length.)

This process is repeated for each decreasing value of k. For each value of k, there will be fewer, but longer, subarrays to sort. However, the successive subarrays are more nearly in sorted order as k decreases. For the final pass, when $k = 1$, the entire array is sorted using the insertion sort, but its elements are "close to" sorted order, which is the condition under which insertion sort is highly efficient.

Develop software to implement the shell sort using values of k that are approximately $n/2$, $n/4$, $n/8$,..., 1. For testing purposes, a driver program will be needed to read in the array values and display the results of the sort.

TESTING AND MAINTENANCE DEPARTMENT

1. Run program *Message* for various values of *TimeLimit*. You should be able to observe that if *TimeLimit* is too small, the node spends most of its time retransmitting messages; if *TimeLimit* is too large and messages or acknowledgments are frequently lost, then the node is blocked from activity because the buffer stays full.

2. Modify the binary search function to return the set of all indices in the array where element X occurs, or the empty set if X is not in the array.

3. In program *Message,* a new message is automatically transmitted at each clock tick provided that there is room in the buffer and that no retransmission has taken place during that clock tick. As a consequence, the buffer queue can never empty, and indeed only shrinks in size if one message times-out and an acknowledgment for a different message arrives in the same time slot. Modify program *Message* so that transmitting a new message is a user option. Test the new version; note that the buffer queue can now become empty during the simulation.

4. Rewrite program *Player* on page 295 to store a player's name and GPA in a record with two additional pointer fields. One pointer field is used to maintain a linked list of players in sorted order by name, the other pointer field is used to maintain a linked list of players in sorted order by GPA. As each record is read in, it is inserted in its proper position in both linked lists. The output is then obtained by traversing each of the two linked lists.

DEBUGGING CLINIC

Run and debug the following program, which is supposed to build a linked list of integers and then "cut" the list, an operation similar to "cutting" a deck of cards. The back part of the list, after the "cut," gets moved to the front of the list. For example, if the list entries are (left to right)

5 4 8 2 7

and the list is "cut" after the third node, then the new list is (left to right)

2 7 5 4 8

```pascal
program Debug13(input, output);
{builds linked list, contains procedure to "cut" list}

type
    NodePointer = ^Node;
    Node = record
      Value : integer;
      Link : NodePointer;
      end;       {Node}

var
    Head : NodePointer;      {pointer to linked list}
    Last : NodePointer;      {pointer to last node in list}
    Cut : NodePointer;       {pointer to last node before cut}
    Where : integer;         {user's choice to locate Cut}
    i : integer;             {loop index}

procedure BuildList(var Head: NodePointer;
                    var Last:  NodePointer);
{creates linked list from user input; on exit Head points to
 first node, Last points to last node}

var
    Temp : NodePointer;
    Number : integer;

  begin    {procedure BuildList}
    writeln('Enter list of positive integers, terminate with 0');
    read(Number);
    while (Number <> 0) do
      begin    {valid node to insert}
        new(Temp);
        Temp^.Value := Number;
        Temp^.Link := nil;
        if Head = nil then
          begin    {this is the first node to insert}
            Head := Temp;
            Last := Temp;
          end;       {this is the first node to insert}
        Last^.Link := Temp;
        Last := Temp;
        read(Number);
      end;       {valid node to insert}
```

```
      readln;
  end;      {procedure BuildList}
```

```
procedure WriteList(Head: NodePointer);
{traverses and writes out linked list}

var
    Current : NodePointer;

  begin    {procedure WriteList}
    Current := Head;
    if Head = nil then
      writeln ('List is empty')
    else
      repeat
        writeln(Current^.Value);
        Current := Current^.Link;
      until Current = nil;
  end;      {procedure WriteList}
```

```
procedure CutList(var Head, Last: NodePointer;
```

{on entry, Head points to head of list, Last points to last node
in list, Cut points to a node in the list; procedure "cuts"
list so that nodes after Cut^ move to the front of the list,
nodes from Head^ to Cut^ move to the back of the list; on exit,
Head points to head of new list, Last points to last node of new
list}

```
  begin    {procedure CutList}
    Last^.Link := Head;
    Cut^.Link := nil;
    Head := Cut^.Link;
    Last := Cut;
  end;      {procedure CutList}
```

```
begin    {main program}
  {create empty list}
  Head := nil;
  Last := Head;

  BuildList(Head, Last);

  writeln('The original list is:');
  writeln;
  WriteList(Head);

  write('Enter number of node in list where cut should ');
```

```
writeln('take  place:  ');
readln(Where);

Cut  :=  Head;
for  i  :=  2  to  Where  do
  Cut  :=  Cut^.Link;

CutList(Head,  Last,  Cut);

writeln;
writeln('The  new  list  is:');
WriteList(Head);
end.     {main  program}
```

GLOSSARY

Abstract data type   a data structure and its associated operations (Chap. 9 and 13)

Activation record   the memory storage used for local variables and constants and for value parameters when a procedure or function is invoked (Chap. 3)

Actual parameter   a quantity in a procedure or function invocation that passes a value to, or receives a value from, the procedure or function (Chap. 3)

Ada   a programming language developed for standardization purposes by the Department of Defense (Prologue)

Algorithm   a procedure to do a certain task, presented as a series of actions that can be mechanistically executed (Chap. 1)

Alpha test site   in-house users of a new program, other than the program developers, who test the program to detect errors (Chap.7)

Analysis of algorithms   the study of algorithm efficiency (Chap. 13)

Ancestor   node A in a tree is an ancestor of node B if B is in a subtree rooted at A (Chap. 13)

Argument   an input value to a function (Chap. 6)

Arithmetic expression   a syntactically legal combination of numeric constants, numeric variables, and arithmetic operators (Chap. 5)

Arithmetic-logic unit (ALU)   the part of the CPU that performs basic arithmetic and comparisons between two values (Prologue)

Array element   the value stored at a particular array index (Chap. 9)

Array index   the location of a particular element in an array (Chap. 9)

Assembler   system software that translates an assembly language program into machine language (Prologue)

Assembly language   a machine-dependent language that uses English abbreviations for its instructions, but requires the programmer to keep track of memory locations (Prologue)

Assertion   a statement about relations between program variables that should hold at a certain point in the program; used in program verification (Chap. 8)

Assignment statement   a Pascal statement that gives a value to a variable (Chap. 2)

Auxiliary memory (secondary storage)   storage outside of the computer's main memory, such as on disk or tape (Prologue)

Available list   a list of unused memory locations maintained by the programmer in an array implementation of a linked list (Chap. 13)

Balanced tree   a binary tree where the left and right subtrees of each node contain approximately the same number of elements (Chap. 13)

Base step   the part of a recursive procedure or function where there is an immediate solution without having to invoke the procedure or function again (Chap. 12)

BASIC   an easy-to-learn general programming language widely available on microcomputers (Prologue)

Batch processing   the computing mode wherein the user has no interaction with the computer during program execution (Prologue)

Beta test site   selected external users of a new program who test the program to detect errors (Chap. 7)

Binary file   a non-text file, where the elements, all of one data type, are stored in machine-readable (binary) form (Chap. 11)

Binary operation   an arithmetic operation that acts upon two operands to produce a third value (Chap. 5)

Binary search   an algorithm for searching a sorted list; the target element is compared with the middle element in the list; if the middle element is not the target, then the binary search is continued on the first or last half of the list (Chap. 13)

Binary search tree   a binary tree that maintains a sorted collection of items; new items preceding a node are stored in the left subtree of the node, new items succeeding the node are stored in the right subtree of the node (Chap. 13)

Binary form   the representation of information within a computer as a sequence of 0s and 1s (Prologue)

Binary tree a tree where each node has at most two children (Chap. 13)

Bit a binary digit, i.e., a 0 or 1 (Chap. 2)

Black-box testing testing a program by assuming no internal knowledge of the program, but examining output for various classes of input (Chap. 7)

Body of a loop the section of code that may be executed many times in a **while** or **repeat** loop (Chap. 8)

Boolean expression an expression with an associated truth value, made up of boolean constants or variables perhaps combined with relational operators and boolean operators (Chap. 7)

Boolean operators the logical connectives **and, or,** and **not** that can be used to combine boolean expressions (Chap. 7)

Bottom-up testing individual program modules are tested as they are developed and then integrated together (Chap. 7)

Brute force a straightforward, non-elegant solution method that cranks through a computation to produce the result (Chap. 3)

Bubble sort a sorting algorithm where on each pass pairs of successive elements are placed in order (Chap. 13)

Buffer variable a temporary storage location, for example, to hold a variable being moved from one file to another (Chap. 11 and 13)

Bug an error in a computer program (Chap. 1)

Building firewalls the process of carefully controlling the flow of data across module interfaces, intended to limit the spread of erroneous data (Chap. 3)

C originally a systems programming language, now used in a variety of applications (Prologue)

Cascading errors a succession of "errors" that are the result of one error earlier in the program, and that will go away once that error is corrected (Chap. 1)

Case label list the list of values that will initiate a certain action in a case statement when the expression being evaluated takes on one of those values (Chap. 7)

Central processing unit (CPU) that part of the computer that actually carries out program instructions, composed of the control unit and the arithmetic-logic unit (Prologue)

Children nodes the immediate descendants of a node in a tree (Chap. 13)

COBOL a programming language used primarily for business data processing (Prologue)

Collating sequence   the enumeration of character data used in a particular machine (Chap. 6)

Comment   a program item that serves to convey information about the program but is ignored by the compiler; must be enclosed within braces { and }, or within (* and *) (Chap. 2)

Compatible data types   two data types that draw their values from the same underlying set, as in two subrange data types that both have integer values (Chap. 7)

Compiler   system software that translates a program from a higher level language into machine language (Prologue)

Computer code   statements in a programming language (Chap. 1)

Conditional flow of control   allows one section of code to be executed while other sections are omitted based upon a condition evaluated during program execution (Chap. 7)

Constant   a quantity in a program whose value is fixed and known before program execution (Chap. 2)

Control structures   program statements that redirect the flow of control out of sequential mode (Chap. 3 and 7)

Control unit   the part of the CPU that sequences events for carrying out a program instruction, such as fetching the next instruction and needed data from memory, passing these to the arithmetic-logic unit, and storing the results in memory (Prologue)

Counting loop (definite loop)   a loop to be executed a fixed number of times that can be determined before the loop begins (Chap. 8)

Dangling else   a possible ambiguity involving nested **if** statements that is resolved by associating an **else** with the nearest preceding **then** statement not already associated with an **else** (Chap. 7)

Data flow diagram   a graphical illustration of the information passed into or out of a module interface (Chap. 2)

Data structure   a mental model of a collection of organized and related data items (Chap. 3 and 9)

Data validation   the process of using program statements to check on the validity of input data and detect errors (Chap. 7)

Debugging   the process of locating and correcting errors in a computer program (Chap. 1)

Defensive programming   the attitude on the part of the programmer that input errors are a fact of life and that the program should be written to protect against them (Chap. 7)

Definite loop (counting loop)   a loop to be executed a fixed number of times that can be determined before the loop begins (Chap. 8)

Dequeue   the operation of removing an element from the front of a queue (Chap. 13)

Descendant   node B in a tree is a descendant of node A if B is in a subtree rooted at A (Chap. 13)

Desk check   a debugging tool that consists of "executing" the program by hand on some data (Chap. 6)

Diagnostic statements   *writeln* statements within the program whose purpose is to help in debugging by providing information on the value of program variables at various points during execution (Chap. 6)

Disjoint sets   sets with no elements in common (Chap. 10)

Disk   an auxiliary memory medium for storage outside the main memory of the computer (Prologue)

Disk drive   an input/output device that stores information in the computer's main memory on a disk or reads information from the disk back into the computer's main memory (Prologue)

Divide-and-conquer   the strategy of dividing a problem into a sequence of smaller, easily-solved subtasks (Chap. 3)

Documentation   all information that contributes to understanding a program (Chap. 1)

Doubly linked list   a linked list where pointers are maintained from the tail to the head of the list, as well as from the head to the tail (Chap. 13)

Driver   a section of code that provides the minimal framework needed to execute and test a completed program module (Chap. 4)

Dynamic variable   a variable that uses memory locations created and released during program execution (Chap. 13)

Editor   a piece of system software that allows the computer user to create and edit files (Prologue)

Efficiency   a property of an algorithm measured by the number of operations the algorithm performs (Chap. 13)

Empty set   a set with no elements (Chap. 10)

Enqueue   the operation of adding an element to the back of a queue (Chap. 13)

Enumerated data type (user-defined data type)   a data type whose legitimate values are those listed in a finite, ordered list (Chap. 7)

Exponentiation   raising a quantity to a power (Chap. 5)

Expression tree   a binary tree that represents an arithmetic expression, where the leaves are constants or single variables and the remaining nodes denote binary operators (Chap. 13)

External documentation   documentation outside the program itself, such as a user's manual or a technical reference manual (Chap. 1 and 8)

Fault-tolerant software   software that is able to continue functioning even when deeply hidden bugs appear (Chap. 7)

Field   a component of a record (Chap. 10)

Field width   the number of horizontal spaces in which a value is printed (Chap. 2)

File   a collection of related items of information in auxiliary memory (Prologue)

File access time   the time it takes to read values from or write values to a file (Chap. 11)

File window   a buffer variable automatically associated with a file that contains the next component in the file after the file "pointer" (Chap. 11)

Floating-point number   another name for a real number, so called because of the way the decimal point can move when writing the number in E format (Chap. 2)

Floating-point overflow   an attempt to store a real number that is too large in absolute value, i.e., has a positive exponent in E format that is too large to store in one memory location (Chap. 2)

Floating-point underflow   an attempt to store a real number that is too close to zero, i.e., has a negative exponent in E format that is too large to store in one memory location (Chap. 2)

Flow of control   the path traced through the program by following the current statement being executed (Chap. 7)

Formal parameter   a variable name in a procedure or function heading that receives a value from, or passes a value to, the rest of the program (Chap. 3)

FORTRAN   a programming language especially suited to scientific and engineering applications (Prologue)

Free-format language   a language, like Pascal, where program statements need not appear in any fixed position on a line and blanks between words are ignored (Chap. 2)

Function   a unit or module of Pascal code, usually designed to compute a specific value (Chap. 3)

Function designator   the function name and actual parameter list that invokes the function and then is replaced by the computed function value (Chap. 6)

Functional requirements a description of what a program is to do, including what the input and output will be, or a description of what a program module is to do, including a description of the module interface (Chap. 2)

Garbage memory locations that cannot be accessed or used (Chap. 13)

Garbage collection the process of reclaiming inaccessible memory locations and making them available for use again (Chap. 13)

Generations the levels in a tree structure (Chap. 13)

Global variable a variable declared in the main program and available to the entire program, including all program modules (Chap. 4)

Graphics tablet an input device that accepts information traced on its surface (Prologue)

Hard copy printed output from a computer (Prologue)

Hardware the physical components of a computing system (Prologue)

Higher level language (programming language) a machine-independent language, such as Pascal, that allows the programmer to write instructions in a more natural form than assembly language (Prologue)

Histogram a graph with the independent variable along the vertical axis and the dependent variable graphed horizontally (Chap. 6)

Identifier the name of an object within a program, used to designate one or more memory locations; an identifier can be any string of letters and digits starting with a letter, provided it is not a reserved word (Chap. 2)

Infinite descent recursion a never-ending recursion occurring because the conditions for the base step are never attained (Chap. 12)

Infinite loop a loop from which the program never exits, generally because the value of the boolean expression controlling the loop is not modified within the loop (Chap. 8)

Infix notation the form for writing an arithmetic expression where a binary operator symbol appears between the two operands (Chap. 13)

Information hiding the concept of keeping the details of implementing a particular subtask within a program module, limiting that module's communication with the rest of the program to the module interface (Chap. 3)

Initialization of variables the process of assigning variables a value before they are used in a program (Chap. 5)

Inorder traversal a tree traversal algorithm that traverses a binary tree by traversing the left subtree, then the root, then the right subtree (Chap. 13)

Input the data on which a program will act (Chap. 1)

Input device   a computing system peripheral device that translates information from the form in which it is entered into the binary form that is the computer's internal representation (Prologue)

Input echo   the process of writing out input values as soon as they are read in to confirm that they have been read correctly (Chap. 6)

Insertion sort   a sorting algorithm where successively larger sections of the array are put in relative sorted order (Chap. 13)

Integer overflow   an attempt to store an integer that is too large to fit in one memory location (Chap. 2)

Integration testing   the process of testing code that combines modules that were already individually tested (Chap. 7)

Interactive computing   the computing mode wherein the user can supply input while a program is executing (Prologue)

Internal documentation   documentation incorporated within the program, such as comments, use of white space, choice of informative identifiers, etc. (Chap. 1 and 5)

Internal file (scratch file)   a file that is declared within the program but is not listed in the program heading and exists only while the program is executing (Chap. 11)

Interpreted language   a programming language where each program instruction is translated into machine language and executed every time the program is run, as opposed to compiling the program once and keeping the object code (Prologue)

Iterative version   a nonrecursive algorithm that is the equivalent of a recursive solution (Chap. 12)

Leaf   a tree node with no children (Chap. 13)

Left child   the left direct descendant of a node in a binary tree (Chap. 13)

Linked list   a collection of records linked by pointer variables, with a special "head" pointer to the first record in the list (Chap. 13)

LISP   a programming language widely used for artificial intelligence (Prologue)

Local constant or variable   a constant or variable declared within a procedure or function and not existing outside the scope of that module (Chap. 3)

Logic error   an error in the algorithm design, so that the resulting algorithm does not solve the problem at hand (Chap. 1)

Loop invariant   an assertion about relations between program variables that holds before the loop is entered and remains true after each loop iteration; used in program verification (Chap. 8)

Looping   repeated execution of a section of code (Chap. 7)

Machine language   the earliest computing language where all instructions are in binary form; still the internal language of the computer (Prologue)

Main memory   the storage area within the computer itself (Prologue)

Mainframe   a large computer, usually requiring special air-conditioning and power facilities, that serves many users at once (Prologue)

Maxint   the largest integer that can be stored in a single memory location on a given machine, (Chap. 2)

Microcomputer   a desk-top or lap-size machine serving one user at a time (Prologue)

Minicomputer   a computer the size of a small cabinet that may satisfy the computing needs of a small or medium-sized business, often serving more than one user at a time (Prologue)

Modula-2   a programming language designed to expand Pascal's capabilities (Prologue)

Module   a section of program code to accomplish a specific subtask, i.e., a Pascal procedure or function (Chap. 3)

Mutual recursion   the situation where module X invokes module Y which in turn invokes module X (Chap. 12)

n factorial   the product of the positive integers from 1 to n (Chap. 12)

Nested if statements   the situation that results when an **if** statement appears in the **then** or **else** clause of another **if** statement (Chap. 7)

Nested loops   the situation that results when a loop statement appears in the body of another loop statement (Chap. 8)

Nested procedures   the situation that results when a procedure is declared within another procedure (Chap. 4)

Node   an individual record in a linked structure of records (Chap. 13)

Null statement   a statement inserted by Pascal solely to allow a compound statement with a semicolon after **begin** or before **end** to conform to the syntax for a compound statement Chap. 2)

Object code   the machine language version of a program, after compilation (Prologue)

Off-by-one   an error that occurs when using a loop by initializing the loop variable incorrectly or by using the wrong condition for loop exit (Chap. 8)

Operand   a quantity upon which an arithmetic operator acts (Chap. 5)

Operating system   a piece of system software that manages the computer's resources and responds to user commands (Prologue)

Ordinal data type   a data type that carries a standard enumeration; examples are *integer* and *char*, although *char* enumeration depends on the collating sequence of the machine (Chap. 6)

Ordinal number   the integer that is the position of a value within the enumeration of an ordinal data type (Chap. 6)

Output   the results after executing a program (Chap. 1)

Output device   a computing system peripheral device that translates information from the binary form that is the computer's internal representation into a form that humans can read (Prologue)

Palindrome   a string of characters that reads the same forwards and backwards (Chap. 12)

Parallel arrays   two or more arrays where related items are stored at the same index in each array (Chap. 9)

Parent node   the immediate ancestor of a node in a tree (Chap. 13)

Parse   to break a sentence into its component parts according to the rules of grammar (Chap. 12)

Parse tree   a tree that represents the decomposition of a program instruction according to the syntax of the programming language (Chap. 13)

Pascal   a programming language developed in the early 1970s as an easy but powerful language that would encourage good programming techniques (Prologue)

Peripheral device   a component of a computing system, such as an input or output device, that is not part of the computer itself (Prologue)

Permutation   an ordered arrangement of objects (Chap. 12)

Pivot element   a list element selected as the breaking point between two sublists in the quicksort algorithm (Chap. 13)

Pointer variable   a variable that contains the address in memory of a dynamic variable (Chap. 13)

Pop   the operation of removing an element from the top of a stack (Chap. 13)

Postfix notation   the form for writing an arithmetic expression where a binary operator symbol follows the two operands (Chap. 13)

Postorder traversal   a tree traversal algorithm that traverses a binary tree by traversing the left subtree, then the right subtree, then the root (Chap. 13)

Precedence   conventions about which operators are applied first in the absence of parentheses (Chap. 5 and 7)

Prefix notation   the form for writing an arithmetic expression where a binary operator symbol precedes the two operands (Chap. 13)

Preorder traversal   a tree traversal algorithm that traverses a binary tree by visiting the root, then traversing the left subtree, then the right subtree (Chap. 13)

Pretty printer   software that reformats an existing program with a consistent indentation style (Chap. 5)

Procedure   a unit or module of Pascal code, usually designed to carry out a specific subtask (Chap. 3)

Program verification (proof of correctness)   a formal mathematical proof that a section of code conforms to its specification requirements (Chap. 8)

Programming language (higher level language)   a machine-independent language, such as Pascal, that allows the programmer to write instructions in a more natural form than assembly language (Prologue)

Programming style   the sum of the overall program details that reflect individual choices made by the programmer (Chap. 4)

PROLOG   a programming language that simulates deductive reasoning (Prologue)

Prologue comment   the opening comment of a program or program module that gives a general description of the task to be done, any restrictions or assumptions, important modifications, and any other useful information (Chap. 5)

Prompt   a message to the user in an interactive program to indicate that data values are expected (Chap. 2)

Proof of correctness (program verification)   a formal mathematical proof that a section of code conforms to its specification requirements (Chap. 8)

Prototype software   a preliminary version of a piece of software that can be developed quickly in order to illustrate the user interface and the form of the output (Chap. 2)

Pseudocode   an intermediate "language" for describing a problem solution, a mixture of English and a programming language (Chap. 1)

Push   the operation of adding an element to the top of a stack (Chap. 13)

Queue   a list where all insertions are done at the back and all deletions are done from the front (Chap. 13)

Quicksort   a recursive sorting algorithm where elements smaller than a pivot element are placed before the pivot element in the list and elements larger than the pivot are placed after the pivot element in the list, then the left and right sublists are sorted (Chap. 13)

Random-access   the property of a data structure such as an array that allows an individual element to be accessed directly (Chap. 9)

Real-time system   a computing system (hardware and software) that must produce output almost instantaneously after receiving input (Chap. 2)

Recursion   the process whereby a procedure or function invokes itself with successively "smaller" parameters (Chap. 4 and 12)

Relational operators   relations that compare two quantities of the same data type to determine whether they are equal or one precedes the other (Chap. 7)

Reserved word   a word that can only be used for a special purpose in a Pascal program; examples are **program, begin, var, while** (Chap. 2)

Response time   on a multi-user system, the time it takes the computer to carry out some work for a particular user (Prologue)

Right child   the right direct descendant of a node in a binary tree (Chap. 13)

Robustness   the degree to which a program can accept any erroneous input without "crashing" (Chap. 2 and 7)

Round-off errors   accumulated errors due to the limit on the number of significant digits of a real number that the computer can store (Chap. 5)

Run-time error   an error that results from an attempt to do an illegal operation with data, such as dividing by zero (Chap. 1)

Scope   the range of a program in which an identifier has meaning (Chap. 4)

Scratch file (internal file)   a file that is declared within the program but is not listed in the program heading and exists only while the program is executing (Chap. 11)

Searching   the process of looking for a given item in a list of items (Chap. 3)

Secondary storage (auxiliary storage)   storage outside of the computer's main memory, such as on disk or tape (Prologue)

Selection sort   a sorting algorithm where each pass selects the maximum value in the unsorted portion of the array and moves it into place (Chap. 9 and 13)

Self-documenting code   code whose internal elements, such as meaningful identifiers, help provide program documentation (Chap. 5)

Sentinel value (trailer value)   a special value to signal the end of legitimate data (Chap. 8)

Sequential access   the property of a data structure such as a file that allows an individual element to be accessed only after all preceding elements have been read and discarded (Chap. 11)

Sequential flow of control   the default flow of control in which program statements are executed in the order in which they occur in the code (Chap. 7)

Sequential search   a list search algorithm that proceeds by examining each element in turn until the target value is found or the whole list has been examined (Chap. 13)

Set difference   an operation on two set variables that results in a set containing only the elements in the first set that are not in the second set (Chap. 10)

Set intersection   an operation on two set variables that results in a set containing only the elements in both of the two sets (Chap. 10)

Set union   an operation on two set variables that results in a set containing all the elements in either of the two sets (Chap. 10)

Sibling nodes   two or more nodes in a tree that have the same parent node (Chap. 13)

Side effect   an inadvertent change to a value outside a program module caused by some action within the module (Chap. 4)

Simple data type   a data type, such as *integer,* where a variable of that type is one indivisible item of data (Chap. 9)

Single-stepping   halting to display the contents of the program's variables after every executable statement; used for debugging (Chap. 6)

Software   computer programs (Prologue)

Sorting   the process of putting a list of items into numerical or alphabetical order (Chap. 3)

Source code   program code in a higher level language, before compilation (Prologue)

Stack   an arrangement of data items that always grows or shrinks from the top (Chap. 3 and 13)

Stand-alone   the mode of operation of a single-user computer, such as a microcomputer (Prologue)

Standard data type   one of the Pascal data types *integer, real, char,* or *boolean,* for which no type declaration is required (Chap. 2)

Standard function   a function supplied by the Pascal library for which no function declaration is required (Chap. 6)

Standard identifier   an identifier that has a default meaning in the absence of identical user-defined identifiers; examples are *read, write,* and *odd* (Chap. 2)

Static scoping   the scope of variables is determined when the program is compiled by where procedures, functions, and variables are declared (Chap. 4)

Static variable   a variable declared in the program, for which space is allocated when the program is compiled (Chap. 13)

Stepwise refinement (top-down design)   the process of attacking a problem by breaking it down into a succession of smaller subtasks (Chap. 1)

Strongly typed language   a programming language like Pascal where every variable has a fixed data type determined when the program is compiled (Chap. 2)

Structure chart   a graphical representation of the subtasks identified in a top-down design (Chap. 1)

Structured data type   a data type, such as **array,** where a variable of that type can be thought of as a single variable or as a collection of component variables (Chap. 9)

Stub   a preliminary section of code for a module that tests the module interface but does not actually do any of the work of the module (Chap. 4)

Subrange data type   a data type whose legitimate values are a section of values from an ordinal type (Chap. 7)

Supercomputer   a machine with the maximum computing power, often found in government or research installations where massive amounts of computation are done (Prologue)

Syntax chart (syntax diagram)   a graphical representation of a syntax rule (Chap. 2)

Syntax error   an error resulting from a combination of symbols illegal in the programming language; the compiler will detect syntax errors (Chap. 1)

Syntax rules   rules for legal combinations of symbols in the programming language (Chap. 2)

System software   computer programs, such as an operating system or an editor, written for a particular computing system that allow that system to function (Prologue)

Tag field   the field in a variant record whose value determines which variant fields are present in the rest of the record (Chap. 10)

Tape   an auxiliary memory medium for storage outside the main memory of the computer (Prologue)

Tape drive   an input/output device that stores information in the computer's main memory on a tape or reads information from the tape back into the computer's main memory (Prologue)

Technical reference manual   external program documentation that details the problem specification, the program structure, the algorithms used, the history of program testing and modification, and other useful information of a technical nature (Chap. 8)

Terminal a device connected to a mainframe computer that allows input to be entered at a keyboard and output to be received on a screen or printer (Prologue)

Test-set generation the task of constructing sets of data for black-box or white-box program testing (Chap. 7)

Text processing treating the data file entirely as lines of characters (Chap. 8)

Timesharing the mode of operation wherein a mainframe computer services many users by doing a small amount of work for each user in turn (Prologue)

Top-down design (stepwise refinement) the process of attacking a problem by breaking it down into a succession of smaller subtasks (Chap. 1)

Top-down testing Tests the entire program in successive levels of detail, first using stubs for modules and then inserting module code as it is completed (Chap. 7)

Trace program part of the system debugging software that tells at any point during execution what module is being executed, what module invoked the current module, etc. (Chap. 6)

Trailer value (sentinel value) a special value to signal the end of legitimate data (Chap. 8)

Transparent change a change in a program (or program module) that is not apparent to the program user (or to the rest of the program) (Chap. 3 and 9)

Traversal the operation of visiting each element in a list in turn and writing out its value (Chap. 13)

Tree a collection of data items with one distinguished node that is the root and where each node may have children nodes (Chap. 13)

Truth table a summary of the effects of a boolean operator based on the truth values of the boolean operands (Chap. 7)

Truth value the value *true* or *false* associated with a boolean expression (Chap. 7)

Type checking the compiler's action to check that the data type of a value to be given to a variable matches the data type of that variable (Chap. 2)

Type clash occurs when attempting to give a value to a variable that does not agree with the data type of the variable (Chap. 2)

Unary operation an arithmetic operation that acts upon one operand to produce a second value (Chap. 5)

Used-car syndrome the tendency to hang on to bad code at all costs (Chap. 6)

User interface that part of a program that interacts with the user to collect input or display output (Chap. 2 and 9)

User's manual   external program documentation that describes how to run the program, the form for input and output, restrictions on input data, and other useful information for the program user (Chap. 8)

User-defined data type (enumerated data type)   a data type whose legitimate values are those listed in a finite, ordered list (Chap. 7)

User-defined function   a function defined by a function declaration within the program (Chap. 6)

Value formal parameter   a module parameter that receives a value from the invoking program segment in a new, temporary memory location; upon exiting the module, the content of this memory location is no longer available (Chap. 3 and 4)

Variable   a quantity in a program whose value is not known until the program executes on some data (Chap. 2)

Variable formal parameter   a module parameter that temporarily adds another label to an existing memory space for the duration of module execution; upon exiting the module, a change made to the value of this memory location will persist (Chap. 3 and 4)

Variant assertion   an assertion that some quantity changes will loop iterations so that the loop exit condition will eventually be satisfied; used in program verification (Chap. 8)

Variant record   a record data type where the field descriptions can vary according to the value of a tag field (Chap. 10)

Venn diagram   a pictorial representation of a set operation (Chap. 10)

White-box testing   testing a program by making use of its internal structure to select test data that will exercise different paths through the program (Chap. 7)

White space   the margins, blank lines, and indentations that can contribute to internal program documentation (Chap. 5)

APPENDICES

RESERVED WORDS

and	array	begin	case
const	div	do	downto
else	end	file	for
forward	function	goto	if
in	label	mod	nil
not	of	or	packed
procedure	program	record	repeat
set	then	to	type
until	var	while	with

APPENDIX B

STANDARD IDENTIFIERS

Constants:
false, true, maxint

Types:
integer, real, char, boolean, text

File variables:
input, output

Procedures:
read, readln, write, writeln,
reset, rewrite, get, put,
new, dispose, pack, unpack, page

Functions:
abs, arctan, chr, cos, eof, eoln,
exp, ln, odd, ord, pred, round, sin,
sqr, sqrt, succ, trunc

APPENDIX C

STANDARD FUNCTIONS

Function Name	Purpose	Argument Type	Value Type
Mathematical functions			
sin(x)	computes the sine of x (x in radians)	real or integer	real
cos(x)	computes the cosine of x (x in radians)	real or integer	real
arctan(x)	computes the arctangent of x, result in radians	real or integer	real
exp(x)	computes e^x	real or integer	real
ln(x)	computes the natural logarithm of x (x > 0)	real or integer	real
abs(x)	computes the absolute value of x	real or integer	same as x
sqr(x)	computes x^2	real or integer	same as x
sqrt(x)	computes $\sqrt{x}$ (x ≥ 0)	real or integer	real
round(x)	rounds x to nearest integer	real	integer
trunc(x)	truncates (drops the decimal part of) x	real	integer
Boolean functions			
odd(x)	true if x is odd	integer	boolean
eoln(x)	true if no more data on current line of file x	file	boolean
eof(x)	true if no more data in file x	file	boolean
Ordinal functions			
succ(x)	gives value after x in standard enumeration of x's data type	ordinal type	same as x
pred(x)	gives value before x in standard enumeration of x's data type	ordinal type	same as x
ord(x)	gives position of x in standard enumeration of x's data type	ordinal type	integer
chr(x)	gives char data item with ordinal number x	integer	char

APPENDIX D

ADDITIONAL PASCAL

This Appendix describes three additional capabilities supported within ISO Standard Pascal that are not often called upon.

The Goto Statement

The **if** statement and the **case** statement implement conditional flow of control within a program. The point to which control is transferred, i.e., the section of code to be executed next, is based upon the evaluation of an expression—a boolean expression in the **if** statement, and an ordinal expression in the **case** statement. Pascal provides a mechanism for *unconditional transfer of control,* the **goto** statement. In order to use a **goto** statement, certain program statements are marked with a numerical label. Any integers between 0 and 9999 can be used as statement labels, but they must be declared as labels in the declarations section of the program or module where they appear, immediately after the heading. This declaration takes the form

    label 100, 200;

A program statement could then be marked with one of these labels and a colon, as in

    100: writeln ('the jig is up');

Then the statement

    goto 100;

causes an immediate transfer of control to the statement labeled 100. Execution then continues on from this statement; there is no automatic return to the vicinity of the original **goto** statement. In all other respects, the label on a statement is ignored, so that the statement labeled 100 will also be executed if sequential flow of control arrives there.

The only requirement on use of the **goto** statement is that control cannot be transferred from outside to inside a structure, say, from outside a loop to inside the loop. Control can be transferred from inside a structure to outside that structure, or from one statement to another statement in the same level of nesting.

Unrestrained use of the **goto** statement can cause control to transfer hither and thither in a program. This could destroy the entire structure of the program, which would no longer proceed smoothly in a logical sequence of subtasks from beginning to end, and could in fact make the logic of the program so convoluted that it would be extremely difficult to understand. The **goto** statement was one of the only mechanisms available to direct flow of control in early programming languages, such as BASIC or FORTRAN. In Pascal, however, more elegant mechanisms, such as the **if** statement, the

case statement, and the various looping statements, are available. These mechanisms are more elegant exactly because they help ensure that the flow of control proceeds smoothly and logically in well-defined blocks; the presence of these mechanisms allows Pascal to be classified as a ***structured language.*** Because of these more elegant control structures, Pascal does not need the **goto** statement. Its potential for harm causes many people to feel that a **goto** statement should *never* be allowed in a Pascal program. This is probably good advice, especially for beginning programmers.

However, a **goto** statement, used judiciously, can be beneficial. It can provide a quick exit from a loop or a procedure when some unusual terminating condition, such as an error condition, arises and it is pointless to execute the rest of the loop or procedure. We can use boolean flags to accomplish this task in a loop:

set boolean flag to false
while condition **and not** flag **do**
  begin
    processing . . .
    if error condition set boolean flag to true
    processing . . .
  end;
if error condition **then . . .**

Setting the boolean flag to true will cause an exit from the loop when control gets back up to the top to test for loop continuation. In order to avoid the bottom block of processing, which we might have to "undo" after exit, we would like to be able to exit the loop as soon as the error condition becomes true. The programming language Ada, for example, provides an **exit when** statement that allows a construct such as

while condition **do**
  begin
    processing . . .
    exit when error condition
    processing . . .
  end;
if error condition **then** . . .

The Pascal **goto** statement can be used in the same way, provided that control is transferred to the very next statement after the loop. This would look like

while condition **do**
  begin
    processing . . .
    if error condition **then**
      goto 100; {exit loop}
    processing . . .
  end;
100: **if** error condition **then** . . .

Note that we have been very careful to limit use of the **goto** statement to a very restricted type of situation.

The Pack and Unpack Procedures

A packed array can save storage over the same array in an unpacked configuration, although manipulating individual elements in a packed array will take longer than for an unpacked array. In a large program where memory space may be a concern, perhaps there is a particular phase of program execution when, for example, many dynamic variables are being created that involve an array and consume a lot of memory. During such a phase, it would save space to utilize packed storage for the array. During other phases of the program execution, when memory is not a constraint but a lot of array element processing is occurring, having the array in an unpacked configuration would speed up the processing. The standard Pascal procedures *pack* and *unpack* allow the programmer to switch back and forth between a packed and an unpacked configuration.

Suppose that *PackedArray* is declared as a packed array and *Unpacked-Array* is declared as an ordinary (unpacked) array that is at least as large as *PackedArray* and has the same component type. The procedure invocation

unpack(PackedArray, UnpackedArray, I);

will cause the elements in *PackedArray* to be stored in sequence, in unpacked form, in *UnpackedArray* beginning at index I. The procedure invocation

pack(UnpackedArray, I, PackedArray);

does just the opposite - it stores elements from *UnpackedArray,* beginning with *UnpackedArray[I],* in order and in packed from in *PackedArray* until *PackedArray* is filled.

Conformant Array Parameters

In program *Player* of Chapter 9, we noted how inconvenient it was to have to use two nearly identical sort procedures because the arrays to be sorted had two different component types. This occurred because arrays with different component types are not the same array type, and the data type of the array must be given as part of the procedure's formal parameter list. It is even more annoying to realize that the same problem exists if the two arrays have the same component type but merely differ in size. The following two declarations do indeed specify different data types:

type
    FirstType = **array** [1..10] **of** char;
    SecondType = **array** [1..5] **of** char;

In order to read in the values of these two arrays, two different procedures have to be written, even though the body of each procedure has the form

```
    prompt;
  for i : = start to stop do
    read array[i];
```

Level 1 ISO Pascal, an extension to Level 0 ISO Pascal, provides for a formal parameter that exactly describes the components of an array but uses variables for the range of index values, i.e., the dimensions, of the array. Such a parameter is called a ***conformant array parameter,*** and it may be used in either a procedure or a function heading. The corresponding actual parameter can be any array that "conforms" to the description. The effect is to allow procedures or functions to accept arrays of variable size.

Using a conformant array parameter, we can write a single procedure that reads an array of either *FirstType* or *SecondType*, allowing the following construction:

```
program Example(input, output);
{illustrates use of conformant array types}

type
    FirstType = array[1..10] of char;
    SecondType = array [1..5] of char;

var
    ArrayOne : FirstType;
    ArrayTwo : SecondType;

procedure ReadArray (var List: array [start..stop: integer] of char);
{loads values into a one-dimensional character array with integer
 indices}

var
    i : integer;        {array index}

  begin      {procedure ReadArray}
    writeln ('Enter the ', stop - start + 1, ' array elements.');
    for i : = start to stop do
      read List[i];
    readln;
  end;         {procedure ReadArray}
    .
    .
    .


begin {main program}
    .
    .
    .
  ReadArray (ArrayOne);
  ReadArray (ArrayTwo);
    .
    .
    .
end. {main program}
```

The conformant array parameter in the above example is

var List: **array** [start..stop: integer] **of** char

Not all Pascal systems support this extension to Level 0 Pascal, but if conformant array types are an option, they can be used for either packed or unpacked arrays of any component type and with dimensions of any ordinal type. Conformant array types can also be used with multidimensional arrays.

APPENDIX E

SYNTAX DIAGRAMS

array type

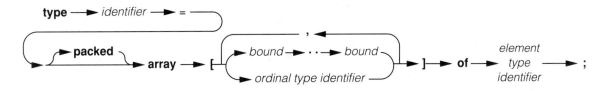

case statement

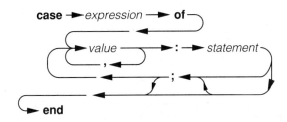

compound statement

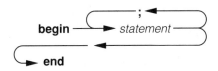

constant declaration

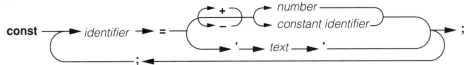

enumerated type declaration

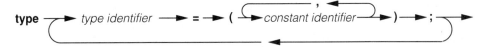

field list

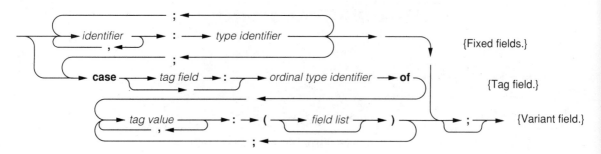

{Fixed fields.}

{Tag field.}

{Variant field.}

file *type*

for *statement*

function *heading*

identifier

if *statement*

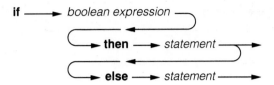

label *declaration*

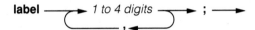

ordinal subrange

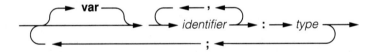

parameter list

pointer type

type ⟶ *identifier* ⟶ **=** ⟶ ↑ ⟶ *identifier* ⟶ **;**

procedure *heading*

procedure ⟶ *identifier* ⟶ **(** ⟶ *parameter list* ⟶ **)** ⟶ **;**

program

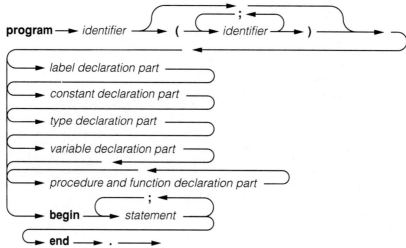

read and readln

real

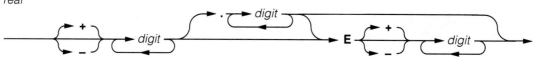

record _type (simple)_

type ⟶ _identifier_ ⟶ = ⟶ **record**

↳ _field list_

⟶ **end** ⟶ ;

record *type*

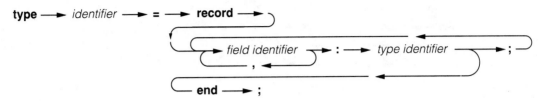

repeat *statement*

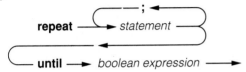

set *type*

type ⟶ *identifier* ⟶ = ⟶ **set of** ⟶ *base type identifier* ⟶ ;

type *declaration*

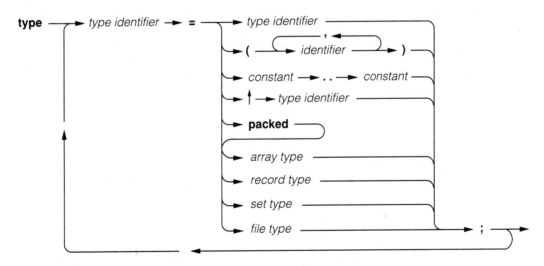

variable declaration

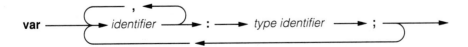

while *statement*

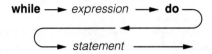

with *statement*

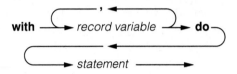

write and writeln

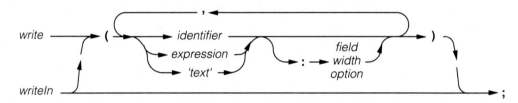

APPENDIX F

SUMMARY OF SYNTAX AND SEMANTICS

This Appendix provides a reference for the syntax (form) and semantics (meaning) of various Pascal constructs.

Array Type Declaration

Syntax:

type
    identifier = **array** [list of dimension indicators] **of** type-identifier;

or

type
    identifier = **packed array** [list of dimension indicators] **of**
        type-identifier;

where
    "dimension indicator" is an ordinal type identifier
    or a subrange of values from an ordinal type

Semantics

Defines a new data type whose legitimate values are arrays of the fixed size and shape given by the dimension indicators, and all of whose elements are of type *type-identifier*. Variables of this type can now be declared.

A variable that is a packed array of component type *char* can be written out with a single write statement, can be filled by using a single assignment statement employing an appropriate string constant, and can be used as an operand with relational operators.

Restriction:

The ordinal type identifier *integer* cannot be used as a dimension indicator because it would imply an array unbounded in size.

Examples:

type
    Battleship = **array** [char, 1..100] **of** boolean;
    Unemployment = **array** [CityRange, PercentRange] **of** real;
    Name = **packed array** [1..25] **of** char;

Assignment Statement

Syntax:

variable identifier : = expression;

Semantics:

The variable named on the left side of the assignment statement receives the current value of the expression.

Restriction:

The data type of the expression must be the same as or compatible with the data type of the variable. Exception: integer values can be assigned to type *real* variables.

Examples:

```
OldValue : = NewValue;
Triple : = 3*Item;
```

Boolean Data Type

Syntax:

boolean

Semantics:

Boolean is one of the standard data types provided in Pascal, so no type declaration is required. Variables of type *boolean* can take on only the values *true* or *false*.

Restrictions:

Boolean values may not be read in as data.

Example:

```
var
    Terminate : boolean;
```

Case Statement

Syntax:

case ordinal-valued expression **of**
    case label list 1 : statement1;

```
   case label list 2 : statement2;
        etc.
end;
```

Semantics:

The case label lists are searched for a match with the value of the expression. If the expression value appears in case label list *i*, then statement*i* is executed. Then control passes to the statement following the **case** statement.

Restrictions:

A real-valued expression is not an ordinal-valued expression, so it cannot be used in a **case** statement.

Values in the case label lists must be constants of the same data type as the expression.

A given constant cannot appear in more than one case label list.

In standard Pascal, an error occurs if the expression value does not appear in any of the case label lists.

Example:

```
case Choice of
  'a','A' : AddToInventory(Item, StockNumber);
  'd','D': DecreaseInventory(Item, StockNumber);
end; {case}
```

Character Data Type

Syntax:

char

Semantics:

Char is one of the standard data types provided in Pascal, so no type declaration is required. Variables of type *char* can take on values of any single character on the keyboard.

Restrictions:

A variable of type *char* holds only one character, not a character string. Examples of legitimate *char* values are:

'J' '8' '?'

Example:

var
    NextMenuChoice : char;

Comment

Syntax:

{any informational message}

or

(*any informational message*)

Semantics:

Used to provide internal documentation, i.e., describe the use of program identifiers, and what is accomplished by various sections of code. The compiler treats anything appearing between braces as a comment, and ignores it.

Restrictions:

A comment cannot be nested within another comment.

Examples:

{This procedure computes the total sales for the month}

var
    Quantity : integer; {Quantity is the number ordered}

Compound Statement

Syntax:

begin
    s_1;
    s_2;
    s_3;
    .
    .
    .
    s_k
end

Semantics:

A compound statement allows a sequence of statements to be executed in order, and can be used anywhere a single (non compound) statement can be used. A semicolon can appear between s_k and **end.** Any statement in a compound statement can itself be a compound statement.

Example:

```
begin
   readln(x);
   x := 2*x;
   writeln(x);
end;
```

Constant Declaration

Syntax:

```
const
      identifier = constant value;
```

Semantics:

Provides names for values that are known before program execution and will remain fixed throughout program execution. Naming constants may improve program readability, and declaring a constant can minimize the amount of work required in a subsequent program modification should the constant value change.

Examples:

```
const
   Pi = 3.1416;
   PageHeader = 'Ergonomics Study, Part III';
```

Dispose **Statement**

Syntax:

```
dispose(identifier);
```

Semantics:

Releases the memory location to which *identifier* points, leaving the value of *identifier* undefined.

Restriction:

The variable *identifier* must be a variable of pointer type.

Example:

dispose(TemporaryPointer);

Enumerated Data Type Declaration

Syntax:

type
         identifier = (list of identifiers);

Semantics:

Defines a new data whose legitimate values are given by the identifiers in the list. The list provides an ordering for these identifiers. Variables of this type can now be declared.

Restrictions:

No identifier can appear in more than one enumerated-type declaration list.

Variables of enumerated type cannot be read from or written to text files.

Example:

type
         Class = (Freshman, Sophomore, Junior, Senior);

Eof Function

Syntax:

    eof(filename)

or

    eof

Semantics:

The boolean function designator *eof*(filename) is true whenever the read "pointer" in file *filename* is positioned just before the end-of-file marker, i.e., there is no more data in the file. If *filename* is omitted, the file is *input*.

Restriction:

In a file being read from, the value of the file window is undefined when *eof*(filename) is true, and a *read, readln,* or *get* procedure will cause a "tried to read past end-of-file" error.

Example:

```
while not eof(datafile) do
  begin
    readln(datafile, NextNumber);
    Sum : = Sum + NextNumber;
  end;
```

Eoln Function

Syntax:

eoln(filename)

or

eoln

Semantics:

The boolean function designator *eoln*(filename) is true whatever the read "pointer" in text file *filename* is positioned so that the next character is the end-of-line character (i.e., the file window contains the end-of-line character). If *filename* is omitted, the file is *input*.

Restriction:

eoln cannot have a binary (non text-type) file as an argument.

Example:

```
while (not eoln (datafile) and (i < 30)) do
  begin
    read(datafile, Name[i]);
    i : = i + 1;
  end;
```

File Type Declaration

Syntax:

```
type
    identifier = file of component type;
```

Semantics:

Defines a new data type whose legitimate values are files with components of the indicated type. These are binary (non text-type) files. Variables of this type can now be declared.

Restrictions:

The component type of a file cannot itself be of type **file** or include components of type **file.**

Binary files are only machine-readable.

Writeln, readln, and *eoln* cannot be used with binary files.

Examples:

type
    NumberList = **file of** integer;
    RollCall = **file of** StudentRecordType;

File Window

Syntax:

filename^

Semantics:

The file window for a file is a buffer variable of type file-component that automatically exists when the file is declared and opened. In a file being written to, assigning a value to the file window and then applying the *put* procedure has the same effect as writing the value to the file. In a file being read from, the file window contains the next file component after the read "pointer".

Restriction:

In a file being read from, the value of the file window is undefined when *eof* is true.

Examples:

    Datafile^ := NextNumber;
    put(Datafile);

    if Datafile^ <> 0 **then**
     Sum := Sum + Datafile^ ;

For Statement

Syntax:

for loop-control-variable : = initial-exp. **to** final-exp. **do**
   statement S;

or

for loop-control-variable : = initial-exp. **downto** final-exp. **do**
   statement S;

Semantics:

First form: The loop control variable is set equal to the value of the initial expression and then incremented to the value of the final expression. For each value of the loop control variable, statement S is executed. If the initial expression value exceeds the final expression value, statement S is not executed at all, and control passes immediately to the statement following the **for** statement.

Second form: The loop control variable is set equal to the value of the initial expression and then decremented to the value of the final expression. For each value of the loop control variable, statement S is executed. If the initial expression value is less than the final expression value, statement S is not executed at all, and control passes immediately to the statement following the **for** statement.

Restrictions:

The initial expression, final expression, and loop control variable must all be of the same ordinal type. The loop control variable is incremented or decremented according to the enumeration scheme of this ordinal type.

Within the body of the loop (statement S - which can be a compound statement), no statement can change the value of the loop control variable.

If the **for** statement appears within a procedure or function, the loop control variable must be a local variable.

The value of the loop control variable is undefined once the **for** statement is exited.

Example:

```
for i : = 1 to 100 do
   write(A[i]:3);
```

```
for Place : = Last downto First do
  begin
    ComputeOdds(Place);
    writeln(Winner[Place]);
  end;
```

Forward Declaration

Syntax:

procedure heading for Y; **forward;**
declaration for procedure X that invokes procedure Y
procedure Y;
   rest of declaration for procedure Y

Semantics:

Allows procedure X to be declared before procedure Y even though X invokes Y.

Example:

```
procedure DoSecond(n: integer); forward;
procedure DoFirst (n: integer);
  begin {procedure DoFirst}
    n : = n - 1;
    if n > 0 then
      DoSecond(n);
  end;  {procedure DoFirst}
procedure DoSecond;
  begin {procedure DoSecond}
    writeln(n);
    DoFirst(n);
  end;  {procedure DoSecond}
```

Function Designator

Syntax:

identifier (actual parameter list)

Semantics:

The function designator occurs within another program statement wherever the function value is desired. It invokes the function named by the identifier and passes to that function the values of the quantities given in the actual parameter list. The computed function value then replaces the function designator in the program statement.

Restrictions:

The actual parameter list must match the formal parameter list in number, order, and type. Exception: an actual parameter corresponding to a value formal parameter need only be type-compatible with the formal parameter.

Actual parameters that correspond to value formal parameters can be expressions, but those that correspond to variable formal parameters must be variable identifiers.

The function designator must be used only in statements where the data type of the function value is appropriate.

Example:

writeln('The result is ', ObtainAnswer(Value1, Value2));

Function Format

Syntax:

function heading
declarations
   begin
      statements
   end;

Semantics:

A user-defined function must follow this format. The declarations section includes, in order, any of the following:

   label declarations
   constant declarations
   type declarations
   variable declarations
   procedure and other function declarations

Restrictions:

Within the body of the function, a value must be assigned to the function identifier.

Example:

function SalesTax(Price: real): real;
{computes sales tax on an item of price Price}

```
const
    TaxRate = 0.05; {sales tax rate}

begin
    SalesTax : = TaxRate * Price;
end;
```

Function Heading

Syntax:

function identifier(formal parameter list): data type;

Semantics:

Provides a name for the function and indicates the internal names (formal parameters) the function will use to reference quantities passed to it from the invoking program segment. The formal parameter list also provides information on the data types of these quantities. The data type of the function value is the last piece of information specified in the function heading.

Example:

```
function Maximum(List: ArrayType): integer;
```

Get Statement

Syntax:

get(filename);

Semantics:

In a file being read from, advances the file pointer one file component.

Restriction:

The *get* procedure cannot be applied to a file when *eof* is true.

Example:

```
while not eof(Datafile) do
    if Datafile^ = 0 then
        get(Datafile);
```

Goto Statement

Syntax:

   goto integer;

Semantics:

Execution of this statement causes unconditional transfer of control to the program statement labeled *integer.*

Restriction:

A **goto** statement cannot be used to transfer control from outside to inside a structure, for example, from outside to inside a loop.

Example:

   goto 50;

Identifier

Syntax:

   a string of letters and digits starting with a letter

Semantics:

Used to name programs and objects used by programs, such as procedures, functions, variables, constants, and types.

Restriction:

   An identifier cannot be a reserved word.

Examples:

   Time
   Value2
   NumberToOrder

If Statement

Syntax:

   if boolean expression **then**
     statement1

else
    statement2;

or

if boolean expression **then**
    statement1;

Semantics:

First form: If the value of the boolean expression is *true*, then statement1 is executed and statement2 is not; if the value of the expression is *false*, then statement1 is not executed but statement2 is. In either case, control then passes to the statement following the **if** statement.

Second form (empty **else**): If the value of the boolean expression is *true*, then statement1 is executed, after which control passes to the statement following the **if** statement; if the value of the expression is *false*, then control passes directly to the statement following the **if** statement.

Restrictions:

In the **if-then-else** form, a semicolon cannot precede the **else.**

An **else** is always associated with the nearest preceding **then** statement not already associated with an **else** (the "dangling **else** convention").

Examples:

```
if (Count > 100) then
   writeln('Too many')
else
   begin {Count < = 100}
      BoxSize : = 10;
      writeln('Count < 100, use small box size.');
   end;  {Count < = 100}

if ((Time < 5.5) and (Class = 'A')) then
   writeln('Accept');
```

Integer Data Type

Syntax:

integer

Semantics:

Integer is one of the standard data types provided in Pascal, so no type declaration is required. Variables of type *integer* can take on zero, or positive or negative counting-number values. Integer values must fall within the system-dependent range − *maxint* to *maxint*, otherwise an "integer overflow" error may result. An integer value has an exact internal representation.

Restrictions:

Integer values cannot include a comma, nor is a plus sign used for positive values. Examples of legitimate integer values are:

12   −445   0   1892

Example:

var
        Age, Class : integer;

Label Declaration

Syntax:

label list of integers;

Semantics:

Declares numerical labels that can be used to mark statements as destinations in a **goto** statement.

Restriction:

The integers in the label list must be between 0 and 9999.

Example:

label 50, 100;

New Statement

Syntax:

    new(identifier);

Semantics:

Creates a memory location to which *identifier* now points.

Restriction:

The variable *identifier* must be a variable of pointer type.

The value of the dynamic variable *identifier*ˆ is undefined directly after a *new* statement is executed.

Example:

```
new(Link);
```

Nil

Syntax:

identifier : = **nil;**

Semantics:

Puts a "nil" value in pointer variable *identifier*, so that *identifier*ˆ is undefined.

Restriction:

The variable *identifier* must be a variable of pointer type.

Example:

```
Link : = nil;
```

Pack Statement

Syntax:
pack(identifier1, identifier2, identifier3);

Semantics:

Stores elements from unpacked array *identifier1*, beginning at the element indexed by *identifier2*, in packed form in *identifier3*.

Restriction:

The variables *identifier1* and *identifier3* must be type **array** and **packed array,** respectively, with the same array component type; *identifier2* must have the value of an index for *identifier1*.

The indicated segment of *Identifier1* must be at least as large as *identifier3*.

Example:

pack(BigArray, 1, SmallArray);

Pointer Type Declaration

Syntax:

type
     identifier = ^type-identifier;

or

type
     identifier = ↑ type-identifier;

Syntax:

Defines a new data type whose legitimate values are variables containing the address of (pointing to) dynamic variables of type *type-identifier*. Variables of this type can now be declared.

Restrictions:

The type-identifier of the dynamic variables cannot involve type **file**.

Pointer variables cannot be written out.

Example:

type
     NodePointer = ^ListRecord;

Procedure Format

Syntax:

procedure heading
declarations
   begin
     statements
   end;

Semantics:

Any Pascal procedure must follow this format. The declarations section includes, in order, any of the following:

label declarations

constant declarations
type declarations
variable declarations
other procedure and function declarations

Example:

```
procedure Little(var time: integer);
{a quick procedure}

  begin
    writeln('How long does it take to blink an eye?');
    readln(time);
  end;
```

Procedure Heading

Syntax:

procedure identifier(formal parameter list);

Semantics:

Provides a name for the procedure and indicates the internal names (formal parameters) the procedure will use to reference quantities passed across the interface between it and the invoking program segment. The formal parameter list also provides information on the data types of these quantities.

Restrictions:

Only formal parameter identifiers preceded in the formal parameter list by **var** can carry the effects of a procedure's actions back to the invoking program segment.

Example:

procedure Example(**var** TakeBack: integer; KeepLocal: char);

Procedure Invocation

Syntax:

identifier (actual parameter list);

Semantics:

Invokes the procedure named by the identifier and passes to that procedure the values of the quantities given in the actual parameter list.

Restrictions:

The actual parameter list must match the formal parameter list in number, order, and type. Exception: an actual parameter corresponding to a value formal parameter need only be type-compatible with the formal parameter.

Actual parameters that correspond to value formal parameters can be expressions, but those that correspond to variable formal parameters must be variable identifiers.

Example:

UpdateSales(ItemNumber, 100*Quantity, Charge);

Program Format

Syntax:

program heading
declarations
begin
   statements
end.

Semantics:

Any Pascal program must follow this format. The declarations section includes, in order, any of the following:

   label declarations
   constant declarations
   type declarations
   variable declarations
   procedure and function declarations

Restrictions:

The final **end** must be followed by a period.

Example:

program Simple(input, output);
{a really simple Pascal program}

```
var
      Initial1, Initial2 : char;

begin
   writeln('Enter your first and last initial: ');
   readln(Initial1, Initial2);
   write('Glad to meet you, ');
   writeln(Initial1, Initial2);
end.
```

Program Heading

Syntax:

program identifier (list of file identifiers);

Semantics:

Provides a name for the program and indicates the files the program will access during its execution. The file identifier list includes *input* and *output* if data is to be collected from the keyboard and results written to the screen, but may include other external files as well.

Examples:

```
program Snoopy(input, output);

program Calculate(output, DataFile);
```

Put Statement

Syntax:

put(filename);

Semantics:

In a file being written to, appends the current value of the file window to the end of the file and advances the file pointer.

Example:

```
Datafile^ : = NextNumber;
put(Datafile);
```

Read Statement

Syntax:

   read (filename, variable₁, variable₂,..., variable_k);

or

   read (variable₁, variable₂,..., variable_k);

Semantics:

Reads values from the file *filename* and assigns them in order to the variables in the list. If *filename* is omitted, values are read from the *input* file. In a text file, after reading the value for the last variable, the read "pointer" does not advance in the file and additional values on that line can be read with a subsequent *read* or *readln* statement. If there are not enough values in the file to assign to all the variables in the variable list, an interactive program will "hang," and a batch program will generate a "tried to read past end-of-file" error.

Restrictions:

The value read for a variable must be the same data type as the variable. Exception: integer values can be read for type *real* variables.

Read cannot be done on a file when *eof* is true.

Examples:

```
read(DataFile, Number);
read(FirstValue, SecondValue);
```

Readln Statement

Syntax:

   readln(filename, variable₁, variable₂,...,variable_k);

or
   readln(variable₁, variable₂,..., variable_k);

Semantics:

Reads values from the file *filename* and assigns them in order to the variables in the list. If *filename* is omitted, values are read from the *input* file. After reading the value for the last variable, the read "pointer" advances to the beginning of the next line of the file and additional values on the previous line cannot be read. If there are not enough values in the file to assign to all the variables in the variable list, an interactive program will "hang," and a batch program will generate a "tried to read past end-of-file" error.

Restrictions:

The value read for a variable must be the same data type as the variable. Exception: integer values can be read for type *real* variables.

Readln is not allowed with binary (non text-type) files.

Readln cannot be done on a file when *eof* is true.

Examples:

```
readln(DataFile, Number);
readln(FirstValue, SecondValue);
```

Real Data Type

Syntax:

   real

Semantics:

Real is one of the standard data types provided in Pascal, so no type declaration is required. Variables of type *real* can take on decimal number values. Real values that are too large in absolute value may cause a "floating-point overflow" error, those that are too small in absolute value may cause a "floating-point underflow" error. Real values may be expressed either in decimal or exponential (E) format. Real values frequently do not have an exact internal representation.

Restrictions:

Real values expressed in decimal form must have at least one digit before and after the decimal point. Examples of legitimate real values are:

-18.9 4.0 $82.3E02$ $-75E$-03

Example:

var
     PricePerBarrel : real;

Record Type Declaration

Syntax:

type
    identifier = **record**
        list of field identifiers : data type;
        list of field identifiers : data type;
        etc.

        end;

Semantics:

Defines a new data type whose legitimate values are records with the field names and field data types given. Variables of this type can now be declared.

Restriction:

Two different fields in a given record type cannot have the same identifier.

Example:

type
    IndexCard = **record**
        Name : NameArray;
        Score : integer;
        Grade : char;
        end; {IndexCard}

Repeat Statement

Syntax:

repeat
    body of loop
until boolean expression;

Semantics:

The loop body is executed and then the boolean expression is evaluated; if the expression is false, the loop body is executed again, and the expression is evaluated again. This process continues until the boolean expression evaluates to true, at which time control passes to the statement following the **repeat** statement.

Restrictions:

Within the body of the loop some change must take place that affects the boolean expression; otherwise an infinite loop can occur.

The loop body is always executed at least once.

Example:

```
repeat
   Count : = Count + 1;
   writeln('Nuts to you');
until Count > 50;
```

Reset Statement

Syntax:

reset(filename);

Semantics:

Opens file *filename* for reading, placing the read "pointer" at the beginning of the file.

Restriction:

A file named in a *reset* statement cannot be written to unless a later *rewrite* statement names that file.

Example:

```
reset(DataFile);
```

Rewrite Statement

Syntax:

rewrite(filename);

Semantics:

Opens file *filename* for writing, placing the write "pointer" (and the end-of-file marker) at the beginning of the file.

Restrictions:

A file named in a *rewrite* statement cannot be read from unless a later *reset* statement names that file.

A *rewrite* statement applied to an existing file erases the previous contents of the file. A *rewrite* statement applied to a declared but nonexistent file creates an empty file.

Example:

```
rewrite(DataFile);
```

Set Type Declaration

Syntax:

type
        identifier : **set of** ordinal type identifier;

Semantics:

Defines a new data type whose legitimate values are sets with components from the ordinal type. Variables of this type can now be declared.

Restriction:

The ordinal type must have a relatively small number of values in order to limit the size of sets of this type.

Example:

```
type
    Smallset = set of 1..10;
    Monogram = set of char;
```

Subrange Type Declaration

Syntax:

type
        identifier = ordinal value1..ordinal value2;

Semantics:

Defines a new data type whose legitimate values are all the members of the ordinal type between *value1* and *value2*, inclusive. Variables of this type can now be declared.

Restrictions:

Value1 and *value2* must belong to the same ordinal type, and *value1* must precede or equal *value2*.

Examples:

type
    PositiveInt = 1..maxint;
    EndOfAlphabet = 'W'..'Z';

Text Data Type

Syntax:

  text

Semantics:

The file data type *text* is one of the standard data types provided in Pascal, so no type declaration is required. Files of type *text* can be thought of as consisting of lines of characters, each line terminating with the end-of-line character.

Example:

var
    Paragraph : text;

Unpack Statement

Syntax:

  unpack(identifier1, identifier2, identifier3);

Semantics:

Stores elements from packed array *identifier1* in unpacked form in *identifier2* beginning at index *identifier3*.

Restrictions:

The variables *identifier1* and *identifier2* must be type **packed array** and **array,** respectively, with the same array component type; *identifier3* must have the value of an index for *identifier2*.

The segment of *identifier2* in which *identifier1* will be stored must be large enough to accommodate all of *identifier1*.

Example:

```
unpack(SmallArray, BigArray, 5);
```

Variable Declaration

Syntax:

var
      list of identifiers : data type;
      list of identifiers : data type;
         etc.

Semantics:

Gives names to (and sets aside memory space for) quantities whose values are unknown before program execution or whose values will change during program execution. All the variables in a given list of identifiers will receive the data type for that list.

Examples:

var
      Average : real;
      TimeIn, TimeOut : integer;

Variant-Record Type Declaration

Syntax:

type
    identifier = **record**
        list of field identifiers : data type;
        list of field identifiers : data type;
        etc.
        case tag field identifier : data type **of**
            list of tag field values : (list of field descriptors);
            list of tag field values : (list of field descriptors);
            etc.

        end;

Semantics:

Defines a new data type whose legitimate values are records. All records of this type have certain fixed fields, as described before the **case** statement, and a tag field, as described in the heading of the **case** statement. When the tag field is evaluated, its value will be located in one of the lists of tag field values, and the corresponding list of field descriptors determines the remaining fields of the record. An empty list of field descriptors means that no additional fields exist for this value(s) of the tag field. Variables of this type can now be declared.

Restrictions:

Fixed field declarations must precede the **case** part of the record type declaration.

Two different fields in a given record type cannot have the same identifier.

Example:

```
type
    StockType = record
        Name : String;
        Value : real;
        case Market : Range of
            Low : (NumberOfShares : integer);
            High : (SharePrice : real; Volume : integer);
            Volatile :( );
        end; {StockType}
```

While Statement

Syntax:

while boolean expression **do**
    statement S;

Semantics:

The boolean expression is evaluated; if it is true, statement S is executed, then the boolean expression is evaluated again. This process continues as long as the boolean expression remains true. If the expression ever evaluates to false, statement S is not executed and control passes to the statement following the **while** statement.

Restrictions:

Within the body of the loop (statement S–which can be a compound statement), some change must take place that affects the boolean expression; otherwise an infinite loop can occur.

If the boolean expression is initially false, statement S is never executed.

Examples:

while A < 10 **do**

```
begin
  read(A):
  Total : = Total + A;
end;
```

```
while (Gate = Open) and (Signal = Low) do
  IncrementSignal(Signal);
```

With Statement

Syntax:

with record identifier **do**
    statement S;

Semantics:

Within the body of the **with** statement, i.e., within (compound) statement S, a field identifier for the record named in the **with** statement can be given by itself, without having to use the
    record identifier.field identifier
format.

Restriction:

In nested **with** statements where different records have identical field identifiers, the most local record named takes precedence.

Example:

```
with WeatherRecord do
  begin
    writeln(Temperature);
    writeln(Pressure);
  end;
```

Write Statement

Syntax:

write(filename,
    list of constants, variables,
    and expressions
    with optional field width specifications);

or

write(list of constants, variables,

and expressions
with optional field width specifications);

Semantics:

Writes to the file *filename* values obtained in order from the list. If *filename* is omitted, values are written to the *output* file. In a text file, after writing the last value in the list, the write "pointer" does not advance in the file and a subsequent *write* or *writeln* statement will put additional values on the same line. Also in a text file, field width specifications control the amount of horizontal space in which a value will be written.

Restrictions:

A string constant to be written cannot be split over two lines.

Two single quote marks must be used within a string constant in order to print an apostrophe.

When writing to a binary (non text-type) file, the data type of the values from the list must match the data type of the file components.

Field width specifications cannot be used with binary files.

Examples:

```
write(ResultsFile, 'Bonus points: ', (New-Old):3);

write('Enter the next number: ');
```

Writeln Statement

Syntax:

writeln(filename,
   list of constants, variables,
   and expressions,
   with optional field width specifications);
or

writeln(list of constants, variables,
   and expressions,
   with optional field width specifications);

Semantics:

Writes to the file *filename* values obtained in order from the list. If *filename* is omitted, values are written to the *output* file. After writing the last value in the list, the write "pointer" advances to the beginning of the next line of the file and a subsequent *write* or *writeln* statement will put values on this new line. Field width specifications control the amount of horizontal space in which a value will be written.

Restrictions:

A string constant to be written cannot be split over two lines.

Two single quote marks must be used within a string constant in order to print an apostrophe.

Writeln is not allowed with binary (non text-type) files.

Examples:

writeln(ResultsFile, 'Average is ', Average:6:2);

writeln('You earned ', (New-Old):3, ' bonus points.');

APPENDIX G

CHARACTER SETS

The following tables give the collating sequences for the most commonly-used character sets: ASCII (American Standard Code for Information Interchange), EBCDIC (Extended Binary Coded Decimal Interchange Code), and CDC Scientific. Only printable characters are shown. The blank character is denoted by "□". The ordinal number for each character is shown in decimal form. For example, in the ASCII character set, ord('j') = 106.

Left Digit(s) \ Right Digit	0	1	2	3	4	5	6	7	8	9
3			□	!	"	#	$	%	&	'
4	(	)	*	+	,	-	.	/	0	1
5	2	3	4	5	6	7	8	9	:	;
6	<	=	>	?	@	A	B	C	D	E
7	F	G	H	I	J	K	L	M	N	O
8	P	Q	R	S	T	U	V	W	X	Y
9	Z	[	\	]	^	—	`	a	b	c
10	d	e	f	g	h	i	j	k	l	m
11	n	o	p	q	r	s	t	u	v	w
12	x	y	z	{	|	}	~			

(Header spanning columns 0–9: ASCII)

Codes 00–31 and 127 are nonprintable control characters.

Left Digit(s)	0	1	2	3	4	5	6	7	8	9
						EBCDIC				
6					□					
7					¢	.	<	(	+	|
8	&									
9	!	$	*	)	;	¬	-	/		
10							^	,	%	−
11	>	?								
12			:	#	@	'	=	"		a
13	b	c	d	e	f	g	h	i		
14						j	k	l	m	n
15	o	p	q	r						
16			s	t	u	v	w	x	y	z
17								\	{	}
18	[	]								
19				A	B	C	D	E	F	G
20	H	I								J
21	K	L	M	N	O	P	Q	R		
22							S	T	U	V
23	W	X	Y	Z						
24	0	1	2	3	4	5	6	7	8	9

Codes 00–63 and 250–255 are nonprintable control characters.

Left Digit(s)	0	1	2	3	4	5	6	7	8	9
						CDC				
0	:	A	B	C	D	E	F	G	H	I
1	J	K	L	M	N	O	P	Q	R	S
2	T	U	V	W	X	Y	Z	0	1	2
3	3	4	5	6	7	8	9	+	−	*
4	/	(	)	$	=	□	,	.	≡	[
5	]	%	≠	↦	∨	∧	↑	↓	<	>
6	≤	≥	¬	;						

APPENDIX H

RULES OF OPERATOR PRECEDENCE

First do
    parenthesized expressions   (inner to outer)

then do
    not

then do
    *   /   **div**   **mod**   **and**   (left to right)

then do
    +   −   **or**   (left to right)

then do
    =   < >   <   <=   >   >=

APPENDIX I

TURBO PASCAL

TURBO Pascal[†] is a version of Pascal for microcomputers, such as IBM/PC compatibles, that use the DOS operating system. TURBO Pascal supports most of the standard Pascal features described in the text, as well as many extensions. TURBO also provides a complete "programming environment," that is, in addition to the compiler, it also provides facilities for editing and managing files.

The TURBO system

The TURBO environment is invoked by typing "turbo" at the operating system prompt. The system inquires

Include error messages (Y/N)?

Answer "y" (lower case is perfectly acceptable and no RETURN is necessary) in order to see complete error messages during program development.

The next screen contains a menu of choices:

Work file:
Main file:

Edit   Compile Run Save
Dir   Quit   compiler Options

Each command is invoked by typing the associated first letter (no RETURN). Thus, "s" saves the current version of the work file, "c" compiles the current version of the work file, "q" exits the TURBO environment, etc.

The initial task at this menu is to choose a work file by typing "w" and then specifying a file name, which consists of up to eight characters, a dot, and a three-character extension. A Pascal program should use PAS as the extension. For example, PROG1.PAS is a legitimate file name. If a file with this name already exists, it will be loaded into main memory from the disk; if no such file exists, a new file with this name will be created. If an existing file is edited and then saved, the previous version of that file is saved as a back-up copy with the extension BAK, as in PROG1.BAK.

Editing a file (including putting something in a new file) is accomplished by using the "e" command. The system editor is a full-screen editor that uses commands based on the WordStar[††] word processing system. Moving the cursor around within the file is accomplished by the use of the Control or Ctrl key on the keyboard in conjunction with other keys. Thus Ctrl-E means to hold down the Ctrl key and press the "e" (but not the Shift key) at the same time.

[†]TURBO Pascal is a trademark of Borland International, Inc.

[††]WordStar is a trademark of MicroPro International Corporation.

Basic cursor movement commands are:

Ctrl-E: move cursor up one line
Ctrl-X: move cursor down one line
Ctrl-D: move cursor right one character
Ctrl-S: move cursor left one character

Note that the four characters used in cursor movement are located on the keyboard in positions that are suggestive of their respective directions:

```
            E (up)
   S (left)      D (right)
            X (down)
```

Correcting a typing error can be done by moving the cursor to the incorrect character and hitting the Delete key or Ctrl-G, which erases the character under the cursor. Inserting a new character just involves typing it in at the correct location. As an alternative to erasing characters and inserting new ones, hitting Ctrl-V invokes the "overwrite" mode, where a new character replaces the existing character under the cursor. Hitting Ctrl-V again reverts to the "insert" mode.

When typing in a Pascal program, the RETURN key is used to move to the next line. TURBO imposes a pseudo-indentation system by beginning the next line at the same level of indentation at which the previous line was entered. If this is not satisfactory, then the cursor can be moved before the line is typed.

The command Ctrl-K followed by D (Ctrl-K D) exits the editor. (It does not, however, save the file to disk, which must be done by the Save command.) After exiting the editor, the program can be run using the Run command.

This description of the Turbo editor is enough to get you started, but there are many other useful editing commands available, such as commands that move or copy blocks of text within the file, that search within the file for a specified string, etc. You should consult a Turbo Pascal manual for further information.

Modifying existing programs to TURBO

Some of the programs contained in this book will not run on TURBO Pascal without modifications. Problem areas include:

■ "string" is a reserved word in TURBO, and is therefore not available to use in a type statement such as

type
      String = **packed array** [1..10] **of** char;

A modification such as changing "String" to "SString" throughout the program will get around this difficulty. ("String" is a predefined data type in

TURBO that handles string manipulations better than a packed array of characters does—see the following section on TURBO extensions.)

■ Any program that uses the *read* statement is almost sure to behave in a peculiar fashion. To correct this problem, insert

    {$B −}

as the first line of the program file, before the program heading. This **compiler directive** instructs the compiler to treat the *read* statement as described in the text. The *readln* statement presents no problems whether the compiler directive is inserted or not.

■ A program that uses a file other than *input* or *output* requires two additional statements. The statement

    assign(Data, 'Data.Old');

associates the external system file named *Data.Old* with the program file identifier *Data*. This is the only statement in which the system file name appears. All other references within the program use the identifier *Data* with the same syntax for file handling as described in the text. The *assign* statement is required even if the system file name is the same as the file identifier, as in

    assign(Data, 'Data');

The *assign* statement must precede any executable statements involving the file. After all executable statements involving the file, the file should be closed with the statement

    close (Data);

■ TURBO requires that a numeric value that is to be read with a *read* statement (because additional data appears on that same line) must be followed by a blank. For example, in program *TimeConverter* of Chapter 11, data items representing military time are stored in file *Times* in the form 15:30. The statement to read such a data item is

    readln(Times, Hours, Colon, Min1, Min2);

where *Hours* is an integer and *Colon*, *Min1*, and *Min2* are *char* data. TURBO will generate an I/O error when trying to read the integer value for *Hours* because that value is not followed by a blank.

■ TURBO disregards a field width specification in a *write* statement for a **packed array of** *char*, and writes out the entire array. If the string entered is less than the array length and the array is not padded with blanks, then the rest of the array contains leftover garbage that nonetheless gets printed. Therefore program *ComputePay* of Chapter 10 can produce a lot of garbage mixed in with the real output. (TURBO does support a field width specification for data of type *string*.)

■ TURBO Pascal does not allow functions or procedures to be passed as parameters. Therefore, program *FunctionCompute* of Chapter 6 will not run under TURBO.

■ File windows and the *get* and *put* procedures are not supported.

TURBO extensions

TURBO Pascal supports capabilities that are extensions to standard Pascal. For the most part, these are such good ideas that one wishes they were supported in all versions of Pascal. They include:

Strings

We've already noted that TURBO supports a *String* data type. The statement

var
    Name : string [10];

declares *Name* to be a *string* variable whose maximum length is 10 characters. The maximum string length in a declaration can be any integer from 1 through 255.

Like variables that are type **packed array of** *char*, variables that are type *string* can be written out with a single *write* or *writeln* statement, can receive values in a single assignment statement, and can be compared against each other using relational operators. In addition, however, variables of type *string* can be read in with a single *read* or *readln* statement. There are also convenient built-in string manipulation procedures and functions available. These are invoked as follows:

String Procedures

        Delete(SourceString, Position, Number)

removes a substring of *Number* characters from the string *SourceString* beginning at position *Position*. *Position* and *Number* have integer values.

        Insert(SourceString, TargetString, Position)

inserts the string *SourceString* into the string *TargetString* at position *Position*. *Position* has an integer value.

        Str(Value, TargetString)

converts the numeric value *Value* into a string and assigns that string to *TargetString*. *Value* may include field width specifications. For example, the invocation

Str(48:3, TargetString)

results in *TargetString* having the value ' 48'.

Val(SourceString, Value, Error)

is essentially the inverse of the *Str* procedure. It converts a numeric string *SourceString* into its *real* or *integer* value *Value*. *Error* indicates the position in the string where a character that is not part of a numeric string is encountered, and has the value 0 if the string is indeed a numeric string. No blanks are allowed in the string. For example, the invocation

Val('82', Value, Error)

results in *Value* receiving the integer value 82 and Error receiving the value 0.

String Functions

Copy(SourceString, Position, Number)

returns the substring of string *SourceString* that begins at position *Position* and contains *Number* characters. *Position* and *Number* have integer values.

Concat(String1, String2,...,Stringk)

returns the concatenation of the *string* values in the order given.

Length(SourceString)

returns the number of characters in string *SourceString*.

Pos(Pattern, TargetString)

returns the integer value that is the first position in *TargetString* at which the substring *Pattern* begins. If *Pattern* does not occur in *TargetString*, the value 0 is returned.

Else clause in case statement

TURBO supports the use of an **else** clause in a **case** statement. The syntax is

```
case expression of
  case label list 1 : statement1;
  case label list 2 : statement2;
                 •
                 •
                 •
  case label list k : statementk;
  else : statement;
end;
```

The statement following **else** is executed if the expression evaluates to a value not in any of the case label lists.

Random-access binary files

Random access for binary files is possible with the use of the built-in TURBO procedure *seek*. The statement

```
seek(Filename, n);
```

positions the file pointer at component number n of the binary file *Filename*. File components are numbered from 0, so

```
seek(Filename, 5);
```

actually locates the pointer at the sixth component.

TURBO allows a binary file opened for reading with the *reset* procedure to be written to without a subsequent *rewrite* procedure. To modify the sixth component in file *Filename* can therefore be done by the following steps:

```
reset(Filename);
seek(Filename, 5);
read(Filename, Component);
modify Component;
seek(Filename, 5);
write(Filename, Component);
```

where *Component* is a variable of file-component type. The second invocation of the *seek* procedure is necessary because the *read* statement advances the file pointer to the next component. Note that this method for modifying a single file component entirely avoids temporary files and file copy operations.

The *seek* procedure will accept a value of n that is one more than the last file component number, thereby placing the file pointer at the end of the file. The function designator

```
filesize(Filename)
```

returns an integer that is the number of components in the file. This integer is one more than the last component number. Together with the *seek* procedure, this makes it easy to move to the end of a file in preparation for further additions to the file. The statement

    seek(Filename, filesize(Filename));

does the job.

Identifiers

Turbo allows underscores as part of an identifier. Therefore,

Miles_to_kilometers_conversion

is a legal identifier in TURBO Pascal.

Besides the reserved words of standard Pascal, TURBO has additional reserved words that may not be used as user-declared identifiers. These additional reserved words are:

absolute	**shl**
external	**shr**
inline	**string**
overlay	**xor**

Because of the additional procedures and functions provided in TURBO Pascal, there are also additional standard identifiers above those of standard Pascal. For example, we have already discussed the following:

assign	**insert**
close	**length**
concat	**pos**
copy	**seek**
delete	**str**
filesize	**val**

As usual, the user may choose a standard identifier for a program identifier, but the built-in capability provided by the standard identifier will be lost.

Miscellaneous Notes on TURBO

■ File names (*input, output,* or other filenames) are not required in program headings.
■ To terminate input from the keyboard and enter an end-of-file marker, use Ctrl-Z.
■ The default condition is that range checking (for out-of-range array indices or out-of-range assignments to subrange or enumerated data types) is not done. To activate range-checking, insert the compiler directive {$R + } before the program code. Range-checking should be activated during program development, but may be deactivated for faster program execution once the program reaches a mature state.

■ Section 11.1.3 discusses a situation in which a *read* statement with a numeric-type argument will, at the end of a text file, read the last end-of-line character and attempt to read the end-of-file marker, causing an error. In TURBO Pascal, if *eoln* or *eof* is true when such a *read* statement is encountered, the end-of-line character or end-of-file marker is consumed and no error results; the numeric variable retains its previous value.

■ Sets (set constants or variables of **set** data type) cannot contain integer values outside of the range 0 through 255.

TURBO Pascal has many features we have not touched on in this brief introduction. In particular, it provides numerous graphics capabilities. Newer versions of TURBO also provide additional numeric data types, "windows" to aid on-screen editing, use of function keys to provide a one-key shortcut for entering commands, the ability to compile program units (modules) separately and then use them with various programs as needed without recompiling, and "short-circuit" boolean expression evaluation. This latter means that in the boolean expression

X **and** Y

evaluation will terminate as soon as X is found to have the value *false;* Y will not be evaluated. This will avoid the sort of work-around we had to use in case Y becomes undefined, out-of-range, etc., exactly when X becomes false.

APPENDIX J

ANSWERS TO CHECKUPS

Chapter 2

2.1 A_Robin, 2Robin, Robin.x (A_Robin is valid in many implementations)

2.2 a. 2.34
b. 38900.0
c. −0.00024

2.3 .60 (need a digit on each side of the decimal point)
42. (need a digit on each side of the decimal point)
2.59 E+01 (no space allowed)
4.67E+1.0 (exponent not an integer)

2.4 a. X: 2, Y: 7, Z: 1.4
b. X: 2, Y: 7, Z: 3.5
c. X: 2, Y: type clash!

2.5 _____ 46   (3 blanks, then 46)
_____231__2.43 (4 blanks, then 231, then 2 blanks before 2.43)

2.6

writeln(' Size = ', Size:5:2,' Cost = $', Cost:6:2);

2.7 4

Chapter 3

3.1
Here's a message from all your friends:

Happy Birthday to You!
Happy Birthday to You!
Happy Birthday, Happy Birthday
Happy Birthday to You!

3.2 See Figure J-1.
3.3 C, F, G
3.4 7, 19; 12, −3
3.5 8
3.6

program Quizzes(input, output);
{collects grades for each of 10 quizzes and writes out
 the number of such grades that are below 70}

var
    Number : integer   {counting variable for the 10 quizzes}
    Grade : integer;   {grade for a quiz}
    Count : integer;   {number of quiz grades that are
                          below 70}

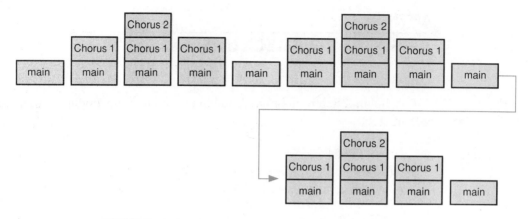

FIGURE J–1

```
procedure GetData(Number:  integer;  var Grade: integer);
{collects grade Grade for quiz Number}

   begin    {procedure GetData}
     write('Enter the grade for quiz number ');
     writeln(Number:1);
     readln(Grade);
   end;     {procedure GetData}

begin    {main program}
  Count := 0;
  for Number := 1 to 10 do
    begin
      GetData(Number, Grade);
      if Grade < 70 then
        Count := Count + 1;
    end;
  writeln;
  write('The number of quizzes with grades below 70 is ');
  writeln(Count:2);
end.    {main program}
```

Chapter 4

4.1 4   7
4.2 5   15
        7   10
        5   10

Chapter 5

5.1 a. 8.5
        b. 1.4

c. -1.6

d. 42

e. run-time error — attempt to divide by zero.

In the original expression, quantities in parentheses are evaluated first, giving

$$2*Z \textbf{ div } 0/(-1.0)*X$$

These operations have equal precedence, so using the left to right rule, we get

$$6 \textbf{ div } 0/(-1.0)*X$$

and the next operation to be attempted is 6 **div** 0.

5.2 b, c, and e are not legal

Chapter 6

6.1 No. A function designator must be used within a program statement.

Average(Value1, Value2, Value3);

stands for the computed function value *Average*. Thus the above statement is similar in form to the statement

Average;

which is not a legal statement. The second statement,

writeln(Average:25:3);

is also illegal because it attempts to use the function name like an ordinary variable name.

6.2   a. 5

b. 49

c. 49.0

d. 4

e. n

f. -6

6.3

exp(x*ln(2)) + sqr(b) + 4*sin(x)

Chapter 7

7.1   a. true

b. true

c. false

d. illegal—*Class* is type *char*, *Time* + *Key* is type *real*

      e. illegal, unless X has been declared as a *char* variable or
a *char* constant and currently has the value 'X'

      f. true

7.2   a. true

      b. false

      c. true

7.3   a. false

      b. false

      c. true

7.4   big A

      Next time make A smaller

      small A

      Next time make A smaller

      big A

      Next time make A smaller

Note that "Next time make A smaller" will always appear as part of the output; despite the indenting, there is only one statement in the **else** clause; the statement

    writeln('Next time make A smaller');

follows the entire **if** statement and will always be executed

7.5   ODD

7.6   illegal—the integer constants in the case label lists are not the same data type as the case expression

7.7

```
if (transaction = 'D') or (transaction = 'd') then
    DepositProcess
else
  if (transaction = 'W') or (transaction = 'w') then
      WithdrawalProcess
    else
      if (transaction = 'B') or (transaction = 'b') then
          BalanceProcess
        else
          writeln('Request not valid, try again.');
```

7.8   a, c, and d are legal; b is not legal because it tries to assign a constant value to a type, rather than to a variable; e is not legal because it tries to write out an enumerated constant value; f is not legal because it tries to compare a constant value with a type, rather than with a variable of that type

Chapter 8

8.1 As explained in the text, the value of *Amount* is unknown at the beginning of the **while** loop.

8.2 It adds the (negative) sentinel value to *Sum*.

8.3
12 11 10 9 8 7

8.4
  1 3 5 **

(Note that the statement **write(' ** ');** is not part of the body of the **for** loop.)

8.5
  2 4 6 8 10

```
for number := 1 to 5 do
  write(2*number:3);
```

8.6 a. correct

b. the value of *I* gets changed before it's added to *Sum*, so 1 fails to get added in, but when *I* = 5 on the last loop execution, *I* = 6 gets added to *Sum*

c. correct

d. when *I* = 5, the loop does a final execution during which *I* = 6 gets added to *Sum*

e. this time the loop does one too few passes and *I* = 5 does not get added to *Sum*

f. As in e, the loop is exited one pass too soon and *I* = 5 does not get added to *Sum*

8.7
```
Sum := 0;
for I := 1 to 5 do
  Sum := Sum + I;
```

8.8

```
program ReceiptTotal4(input, output);
{is supposed to add up the day's receipts}

var
    Sum, Amount: real;

begin
  writeln('Enter the day' 's receipts - do not separate ');
  writeln('values with commas; use a negative number ');
  writeln('as the last value.');
  writeln;
  Sum := 0.0;
  repeat
    read(Amount);
```

```
      writeln(Amount);    {diagnostic}
      Sum := Sum + Amount;
      writeln(Sum);         {diagnostic}
   until Amount <= 0.0;
   readln;
   writeln;
   writeln('The total receipts for the day add to $', Sum:8:2);
end.
```

Chapter 9

9.1   a. 6
     b. 15
     c. 416

9.2

a.
```
type
   Array1 = array [1..2,1..3] of char;
```
b.
```
type
   Array2 = array [1..3,1..2] of integer;
```

9.3   a. writes the value 'r'
     b. writes the value 0
     c. error—array index out of range
     d. assigns the value 18 to the element in row 1, column 3 of *Box*
     e. writes the value 9

9.4
  −5
d

9.5

```
writeln(Box[2,4]);
```

9.6   The program works correctly; *n* retains the value 0 and the **for** loop in procedure *WriteReverse* is not executed; nothing is written out for the reverse of the message.

9.7   a. No—string constant too short to assign to *name*
     b. OK
     c. No—must read one character at a time
     d. OK

9.8   l
     i
     j
     CurrentMaxIndex
     MaxIndex

```
        X    Y
        n downto 2
        A[i]    A    i
```

Chapter 10

10.1

```
type      String = packed array [1..20] of char;
          RecipeType = record
              Name : String
              Servings : integer;
              Cost : real;
              end; {RecipeType}
```

10.2 B   24

10.3   a. List[4].Value
       b. List[1].Display['C',3]
       c. Key := List[2].Key;

10.4

```
with List[3] do
  begin
    Key := 'Q'
    Value := 6.4;
  end;
```

10.5   a. $A + B = [0,2,3,4,6,7,8]$
       b. $A - B = [3,7]$
       c. $B*C = [2,6,8]$
       d. $A - (B + C) = [\ ]$

10.6   a. true
       b. false
       c. true
       d. true
       e. this results in a type mismatch as the elements of B are not a set type

Chapter 11

11.1   20 (On the first pass through the loop, the value 5 is read from the file and doubled to 10. The *rewrite* procedure empties the file, and then 10 is written to the file. The file is then reset so that on the second pass through the loop, the first (and only) value in the file, 10, is read and doubled to 20. The next rewrite empties the file and then 20 is written to the file. The file is then opened for reading, but nothing more is done in the program.)

11.2   If there are blanks in the last line of the file after the last numeric value then, after reading the last numeric value, *eoln* is not true and the read statement will consume the blanks and the end-of-line character while looking for a number, and attempt to read the end-of-file marker, resulting in an error.

11.3 a.

```pascal
program WriteBinary(input, output, NumberList);
{writes nonzero integer values to integer file NumberList}

type
    IntFile = file of integer;

var
    NumberList : IntFile    {file}
    Number : integer;

begin
  rewrite(NumberList);
  write('Enter a list of nonzero integers, ');
  writeln('terminate with 0.');
  read(Number);
  while(Number <> 0) do
    begin
      write(NumberList, Number);
      read(Number);
    end;
  write('These numbers are stored in binary');
  writeln(' file NumberList');
end.
```

b.

```pascal
program ReadBinary(NumberList, output);
{reads integers from binary file NumberList, writes them to the
 screen}

type
    Intfile = file of integer;

var
    NumberList : IntFile;
    Number : integer;

begin
  reset(NumberList);
  writeln('The values in binary file NumberList are');
  while not eof (NumberList) do
    begin
      read(NumberList, Number);
      writeln(Number);
    end;
end.
```

11.4
```
reset (oldfile);
rewrite(tempfile);
for i := 1 to 4 do
  begin
    readln(oldfile, item);
    writeln(tempfile, item);
  end;
readln(oldfile, item);
process item;
writeln(tempfile, item);
FileCopy(oldfile, tempfile);
reset(tempfile);
rewrite (oldfile);
FileCopy(tempfile, oldfile);
```

(Note that *reset* and *rewrite* do not belong before the first *FileCopy* invocation. Resetting *oldfile* would put the pointer back at the beginning of *oldfile*, and rewriting *tempfile* would erase the 5 entries it contains.)

11.5
```
procedure CopyBin(var Old, New: RealFile);
{copies contents of opened binary file Old into opened binary file
 New}

var
    item : real;

  begin     {procedure CopyBin}
    while not eof(Old) do
      begin
        read(Old, item);
        write(New, item);
      end;
  end;     {procedure CopyBin}
```

11.6   yes—if *Item* is declared to be an integer variable, then

```
read(Values, Item);
```

could replace the *get* statement; *Item* would be ignored.

Chapter 12

12.1

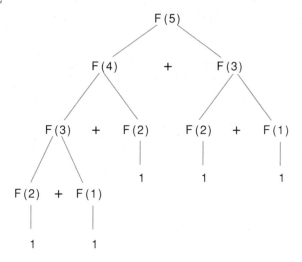

Fibonacci gets invoked 9 times, Fibonacci(2) is computed 3 times, and Fibonacci(3) is computed 2 times.

12.2   a. ABCD   ABDC   ACBD   ACDB   ADBC   ADCB

BACD   BADC   BCAD   BCDA   BDAC   BDCA

CABD   CADB   CBAD   CBDA   CDAB   CDBA

DABC   DACB   DBAC   DBCA   DCAB   DCBA

b.   Any of the n characters may come first, so there are n choices. Then there are $n-1$ choices for the second character, $n-2$ choices for the third character, etc. The total number of arrangements is the product of these choices,

$$n*(n-1)*(n-2)*..*3*2*1$$

This can be seen most easily by drawing a tree. For example, with three characters, A, B, and C, there are $3*2*1 = 6$ permutations, represented by the "leaves" of the tree

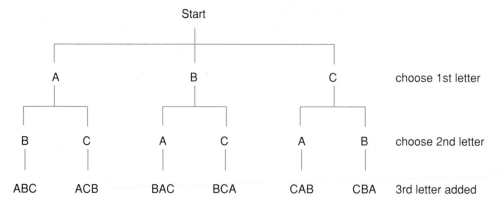

12.3 *Exchange* sets the fixed leading characters; the results of its work must be available to procedure *GeneratePermutations*. Within the **for** loop, once *Exchange* has set the leading characters, the array must still look the same after the new invocation of *GeneratePermutations* is completed. *GeneratePermutations* can make local changes in the array in order to write out the permutations, but must return the same array in order for the **for** loop to know what it's working with.

Chapter 13

13.1   writeln(P^);

13.2   a. changes the value to which *P* points to 7
           b. writes out the value 7 (*Q* points to the same place as *P*)
           c. illegal; can't write out the value of a pointer variable
           d. illegal; can assign the value 'B' to *S^*, but not to *S*
           e. makes *S* point where *R* is pointing
           f. changes the value to which *R* points to 'C'
           g. writes out the value 'C'
           h. illegal; *S* and *Q* are not the same data type

13.3

```
Temp := Q;
Q := P;
P := Temp;
```

See Figure J-2

13.4

Temp^.Link := AfterThis^.Link;

AfterThis^.Link := Temp;

13.5   The procedure will still work. If *AfterThis^* is the last node, then *AfterThis^.Link* is **nil**. The statement

Temp^.Link := AfterThis^.Link;

sets the *Link* field in the new node to **nil,** which is correct, as the new node will be the last one in the list.

13.6

```
procedure Insert(var Head: NodePointer; AfterThis: NodePointer;
                    Item: Node);
{in linked list to which Head points, a node containing the
 data from Item gets inserted after the node pointed to
 by AfterThis; if AfterThis is nil, the new node becomes
 the first node}
```

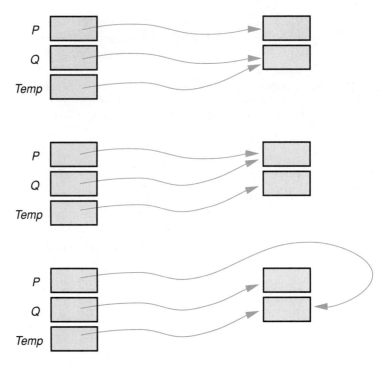

FIGURE J–2

```
var
    Temp : NodePointer;

begin    {procedure Insert}
    allocate space, pointed to by Temp
    copy Item into Temp^
    if AfterThis = nil then
      begin
        connect Temp^ to node pointed to by Head
        point Head to Temp^
      end
    else
      begin
        connect Temp^ to node after AfterThis^
        connect AfterThis^ to Temp^
      end
end;    {procedure Insert}
```

Note that this version of *Insert* needs to know the value of *Head* and can change that value, so *Head* must be a variable parameter. The procedure still works if *Head* is **nil,** i.e., the list is empty, when the procedure is invoked.

13.7   3
         5
         3

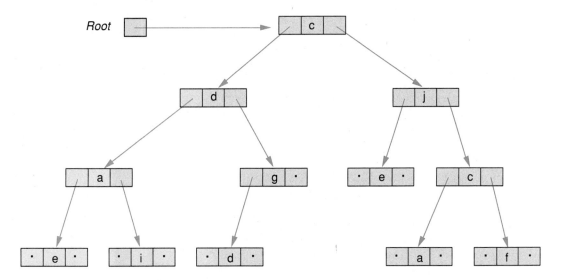

FIGURE J–3

13.8   See Figure J-3.

13.9   a. See Figure J-4
           b. See Figure J-5

13.10
function   TreeSearch(Root: NodePointer; Target: Node):
            NodePointer;
{searches binary search tree to which Root points for target
 element Target; returns nil pointer or pointer to Target}

```
begin    {function TreeSearch}
  if Root = nil then   {Target not found}
    TreeSearch := nil
  else
    if Target.Name = Root^.Name then   {Target at Root^}
      TreeSearch := Root
```

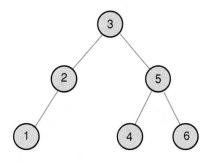

FIGURE   J–4

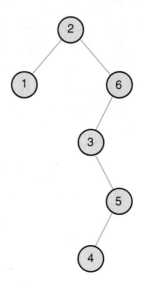

FIGURE   J–5

else
  if Target.Name < Root^.Name **then**   {try left subtree}
    TreeSearch := TreeSearch(Root^.Left, Target)
  else   {try right subtree}
    TreeSearch := TreeSearch(Root^.Right, Target);

 end; {function TreeSearch}

13.11   The problem occurs with the compound boolean expression

(j < n) and (A[j] > A[j+1])

that governs the **while** loop. Consider the case where $j = n-1$ and element $A[n-1]$ is greater than element $A[n]$. Within the **while** loop these two elements are exchanged and j is incremented to n. Then the boolean expression is tested again. Although $j < n$ is now false, the condition $A[j] > A[j+1]$ is also tested, and $A[j+1]$ results in an array index out of range.

13.12

| 1 | 2 | 5 | 4 | 7 | 10 | 9 | 12 | 8 | (Fig. 13.15g)
|---|---|---|---|---|----|---|----|---|

1	2	4	5	7	10	9	12	8

1	2	4	5	7	10	9	8	12

1	2	4	5	7	8	9	10	12

APPENDIX K

ANSWERS TO SELECTED EXERCISES AND SKILL BUILDERS

Chapter 1

1.1. a. A more complete problem specification could include the following comments:

Names will be given in the form

first name   middle initial   last name

as in

Suzanne P. Twaddle

Ages will be rounded to the nearest year

Alphabetical ordering of names will be by last name; if the two people have the same last name, then by first name; if the two people have the same last name and the same first name, then by middle initial

If two people have exactly the same name, the age of the person whose name was given first will be used to compute the output

If a nonpositive age occurs, the program should write out an error message to that effect and then stop

The output should also include the name of the person whose age has been doubled

If a name is given without a middle initial, it is assumed to precede alphabetically the same first and last name with an initial

Chapter 2

2.1 *M:* 74   *N:* − 14   *P:* 26   *Q:* 62

2.4 _− 35
  _46.79_2

2.5 3   4

2.7
program Month(input, output);

```
var
    name1 : char;
    name2 : char;
    name3 : char;

begin
  writeln('What month is this?');
  read(name1);
  read(name2);
  readln(name3);
  write('The month is now ');
  writeln(name1, name2, name3)
end.
```

2.9 line 1:   program name missing

line 3:   a colon should be used, not =; data type is "integer", not "integers"

line 6:   "print" is not a legitimate statement for writing output, and the field width specification :7:2 is illegal for an integer value

line 7:   "capital" is misspelled and does not match the variable declaration, so is an undeclared variable

2.13 How are students identified, how many grades per student will there be, are all grades weighted equally, what is the range of average for each letter grade, etc.

Skill Builder 2.4

```
program MyNumbers(output) ;
{prints out the values assigned to two integer variables}

var
    X, Y : integer;     {the two values}

begin

  {assign the values}
  X := 3;
  Y := 2150;

  {write the output}
  writeln('    X = ', X:1);
  writeln;
  writeln('    Y = ', Y:4);
end.
```

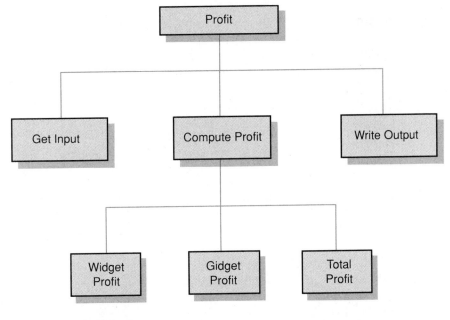

FIGURE K–1

Chapter 3
3.1 See Figure K-1

3.3 *A:* 12   *B:* 39   *C:* 8.9

3.5 *Volume* must be a variable parameter because the procedure must pass this value back to the rest of the program; *Length, Width, Height* can be value parameters.

***3.8** 21;   10

Skill Builder 3.3

```
program Double(input, output);
{reads an integer, doubles it, writes the result}

var
    Number : integer;          {original number}
    TwiceNumber : integer;     {number after doubling}

procedure TwiceIt(Number: integer; var TwiceNumber: integer);
{doubles the value of Number, returns result as TwiceNumber}

  begin    {procedure TwiceIt}
    TwiceNumber := 2*Number;
  end;     {procedure TwiceIt}
```

```
begin    {main program}

  {read input}
  write('Enter an integer value: ');
  readln(Number);

  {double it}
  TwiceIt(Number, TwiceNumber);

  {write output}
  writeln;
  writeln('Twice this value is: ', TwiceNumber:6);
end.     {main program}
```

Chapter 4

4.1 *Sum* is an input/output parameter; for each invocation of procedure *ComputeTotal*, *Sum* receives the current value of *Total* and returns a modified value.

4.2 *A: B*   *B: 79*   *C: 7*

4.4 12
   0

4.6 19
  2
  7   7
  7
  5

Skill Builder 4.4

```
procedure FindArea(Radius: real; var Area: real);
{computes  surface area Area of a sphere of radius Radius)

const
    pi = 3.1416;
  begin    {procedure FindArea}
    Area := 4*pi*Radius*Radius;
  end;     {procedure FindArea}
```

Chapter 5

5.2 Yes
5.4 real
5.5 28.0
5.8 See Figure K-2

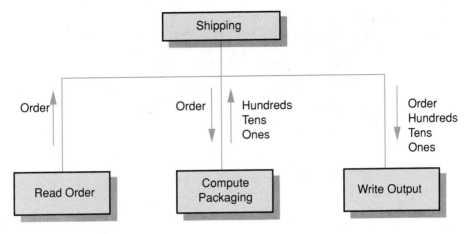

FIGURE K-2

Skill Builder 5.3

program Evaluator(input, output);
{reads a real value and computes an algebraic expression using
 that value}

var
   x : real;   {value to use in expression}
   Expression : real;   {result of computation}

procedure GetInput(**var** x: real);
{gets value of real number x and returns it to main program}

  begin   {procedure GetInput}
    write('Enter real number: ');
    readln(x);
  end;   {procedure GetInput}

procedure Compute(x: real; **var** Expression: real);
{computes the value of Expression using x}

var
   Numerator, Denominator: real;   {components of
                                the expression}
  begin   {procedure Compute}
    Numerator := 2*x − 1;
    Denominator := 4*x − 2;
    Expression := Numerator/Denominator;
  end;   {procedure Compute}

procedure WriteOutput(Expression: real);
{writes the value of Expression}

```
begin    {procedure WriteOutput}
  writeln('The result of using this value in the expression');
  writeln;
  writeln('                         2x  −  1');
  writeln('                         _____');
  writeln('                         4x  −  2');
  writeln;
  writeln('is (to two decimal places)');
  writeln;
  writeln('                              ', Expression:8:2);
end;     {procedure WriteOutput}


begin    {main program}
  GetInput(x);
  Compute(x, Expression);
  WriteOutput(Expression);
end.     {main program}
```

Note that the expression that this program computes is undefined when x = 0.5; a run-time error will occur for attempting to divide by zero. Also, the expression reduces to $1/2 = 0.5$ whenever $x \neq 0$. Therefore, using the **if** statement, another version of this program would be the following, where the statement following the **if** statement in procedure *WriteOutput* is a compound statement.

```
program Evaluator(input, output);
{reads a real value and computes an algebraic expression using
 that value}

var
    x : real;            {value to use in expression}
    Expression : real;   {result of computation}

procedure GetInput(var x: real);
{gets value of real number x and returns it to main program)

  begin    {procedure GetInput}
    write('Enter real number: ');
    readln(x);
  end;     {procedure GetInput}

procedure Compute(x: real; var Expression: real);
{computes the value of Expression using  x}

  begin    {procedure Compute}
    if x = 0.5 then
      Expression := 0.0
    else
      Expression := 0.5;
  end;     {procedure Compute}
```

```
procedure WriteOutput (Expression: real);
{writes the value of Expression}

  begin {procedure WriteOutput}
    if Expression = 0.5 then
      begin   {Expression = 0.5}
        write('The result of using this value ');
        writeln('in the expression');
        writeln;
        writeln('                        2x  −  1');
        writeln('                        _____');
        writeln('                        4x  −  2');
        writeln;
        writeln('is');
        writeln;
        writeln('            0.5');
      end     {Expression = 0.5}
    else
      writeln('Expression undefined for this value.')
  end;    {procedure WriteOutput}

begin   {main program}
  GetInput(x);
  Compute(x, Expression);
  WriteOutput(Expression);
end.    {main program}
```

Chapter 6

6.2 illegal — *pred* cannot have a real value as an argument

6.3 2.0

6.5 24

*6.7 exp(8*1n(x))

Skill Builder 6.2

```
program NextCharacter(input, output);
{reads in a character between a and s, outputs next character}

var
    Symbol : char;   {character read in}

begin
  write('Enter a single character between a and s: ');
  readln(Symbol);
  writeln('The next alphabetical character is ', succ(Symbol));
end.
```

Chapter 7

7.1 false; true

7.2 **if** Temp > 98 **then**
     writeln('too hot');

7.3 **if** Temp > 98 **then**
     writeln('too hot')
   else
     writeln('just right');

7.7
type
         DayType = (Monday, Tuesday, Wednesday, Thursday,
                     Friday, Saturday, Sunday);
         WeekDayType = Monday..Friday;
var
         PayDay : WeekDayType;

Skill Builder 7.1

```
program Compare(input, output);
{collects and compares two character values}

var
    ValueOne, ValueTwo : char;    {the two characters}

procedure GetInput(var x, y: char);
{collects two character values from user}

  begin   {procedure GetInput}
    writeln('Enter two character values.');
    write('First character: ');
    readln(x);
    write('Second character:  ');
    readln(y);
  end;    {procedure GetInput}

procedure Decide(x, y: char);
{compares x and y and writes appropriate message}

  begin   {procedure Decide}
    write('The characters ', x, ' and ', y, ' are ');
    if x = y then
      writeln('the same.')
    else
      writeln('different.');
  end;    {procedure Decide}
```

```
begin    {main program}
  GetInput(ValueOne, ValueTwo);
  Decide(ValueOne, ValueTwo);
end.    {main program}
```

Chapter 8

8.1 It will lead to an infinite loop because the value of *score* is never changed within the loop body.

8.3
```
Total := 0;
while Total <= 100 do
  begin
    read(Number);
    Total := Total + Number;
  end;
writeln('The total is ', Total);
```

8.6
```
    if A <= B then...
```

or

```
    if C > D then ...
```

i.e., a statement to distinguish which of the two possible conditions led to exiting the loop

8.9 $X + 2 > Y$

Skill Builder 8.4

```
program Multiples(output);
{writes out multiples of 10 from 0 to 100}

var
    i : integer;    {loop index}

begin
  writeln('The multiples of 10 from 0 to 100 are');
  writeln;
  for i := 0 to 10 do
    write('        ', 10*i:2);
  writeln;
end.
```

Chapter 9
9.1 21
9.2 Table[0,'P'] := 1;

9.4 for j := 'P' to 'R' **do**
    writeln(Table[2,j]);

9.8 If X is not in array A, then the loop is executed when i has the value 10. Within the loop, i gets incremented to 11. When the loop test is made again, $i <= 10$ is false, but if both boolean operands are evaluated before the loop is exited, then A[i] <> X will produce an index-out-of-range error.

Skill Builder 9.2

```
program matrix(input, output);
{reads in maximum 10 × 20 integer matrix, outputs matrix
 and transpose}

type
    MaxRowSize = 1..10;
    MaxColSize = 1..20;
    MatrixType = array [MaxRowSize, MaxColSize] of integer;
var
    Matrix : MatrixType;    {original matrix}
    Transpose : MatrixType;    {transpose of original matrix}
    RowSize, ColSize : integer;    {rows and columns
                                     in original matrix}

procedure GetInput (var Matrix: MatrixType;
                     var RowSize, ColSize: integer);
{reads in maximum 10 × 20 array Matrix of integers}

var
    i, j: integer;    {loop indices}

  begin   {procedure GetInput}
    writeln('You will enter the integer entries of an array.');

    write('Specify the number of rows (maximum 10): ');
    readln(RowSize);
    while not (RowSize in [1..10]) do
      begin    {while loop for row size}
        write('Maximum 10 rows; enter number of ');
        write('rows again: ');
        readln(RowSize);
      end;    {while loop for row size}

    write('Specify the number of columns (maximum 20): ');
    readln(ColSize);
    while not (ColSize in [1..20]) do
      begin   {while loop for column size}
        write('Maximum 20 columns; enter number of ');
```

```
            write('columns again: ');
            readln(ColSize);
        end;    {while loop for column size}

    for i := 1 to RowSize do
      begin    {outer loop − by row}
        writeln;
        writeln('Enter the ', ColSize:1, ' values for row ', i:1)
        for j := 1 to ColSize do
          begin    {inner loop − by column}
            read(Matrix[i,j]);
          end;    {inner loop − by column}
        readln;
      end;    {outer loop − by row}
  end;    {procedure GetInput)}

procedure FindTranspose(Matrix: MatrixType;
                        var Transpose: MatrixType;
                        RowSize, ColSize: integer);
{finds the transpose of Matrix, stores it in Transpose}

var
    i, j : integer;    {loop indices}

  begin    {procedure FindTranspose}
    for i := 1 to RowSize do
      for j := 1 to ColSize do
        Transpose[j,i] := Maxtrix[i,j];
  end;    {procedure FindTranspose}

procedure WriteOutput(Matrix, Transpose: MatrixType;
                      RowSize, ColSize: integer);
{writes out the original matrix Matrix and its transpose Transpose}

var
    i, j: integer;    {loop indices}
    Temp: integer;    {placeholder}

  begin    {procedure WriteOutput}

    {write original matrix}
    writeln;
    writeln('The original matrix is:');
    for i := 1 to RowSize do
      begin    {outer loop - by row}
        writeln;
        for j := 1 to ColSize do
          begin    {inner loop - by column}
            write(Matrix[i,j]:5);
```

```
        end;    {inner loop - by column}
     end;   {outer loop - by row}
       writeln;

       {adjust dimensions for the transpose matrix}
       Temp := RowSize;
       RowSize := ColSize;
       ColSize := Temp;

       {write transpose matrix}
       writeln;
       writeln('The transpose matrix is:');
       for i := 1 to RowSize do
          begin   {outer loop - by row}
            writeln;
            for j := 1 to ColSize do
               begin   {inner loop - by column}
                 write(Transpose[i,j]:5);
               end;    {inner loop - by column}
            end;    {outer loop - by row}
          writeln;
       end;   {procedure WriteOutput}


    begin   {main program}
      GetInput(Matrix, RowSize, ColSize);
      FindTranspose(Matrix, Transpose, RowSize, ColSize);
      WriteOutput(Matrix, Transpose, RowSize, ColSize);
    end.   {main program}
```

Chapter 10

10.1 See Figure K-3

10.3 *Min* must be allowed to have the value 0 to signify no listings for the chosen locale.

10.4 a) 3
b) P
c) 3

10.7 Colors = [Blue, Green]

Skill Builder 10.1

```
program FileCard(input, output);
{reads and writes a single record with individual data}

type
    String = packed array [1..30] of char;
    HeightType = array [1..2] of integer;
    InfoType = record
      Name : String;
      Age : integer;
```

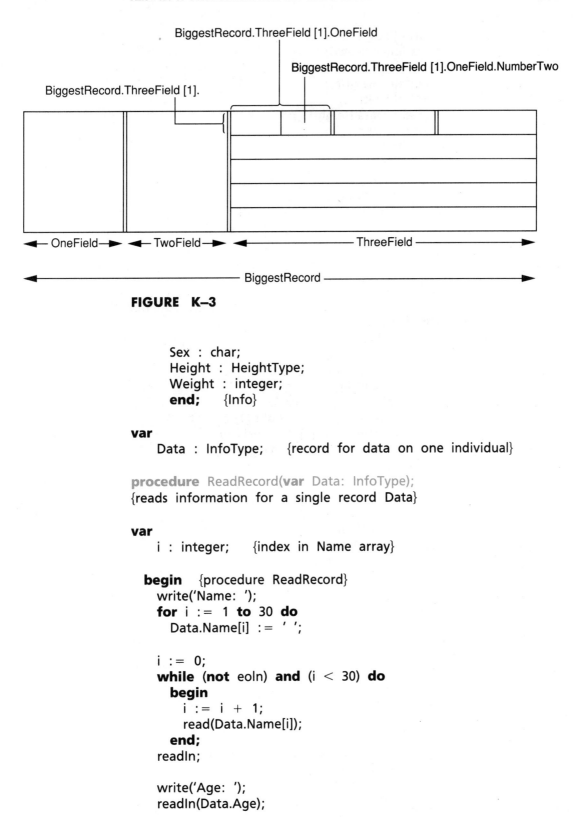

FIGURE K–3

```
        Sex : char;
        Height : HeightType;
        Weight : integer;
        end;    {Info}


var
        Data : InfoType;    {record for data on one individual}

procedure ReadRecord(var Data: InfoType);
{reads information for a single record Data}

var
        i : integer;    {index in Name array}

  begin    {procedure ReadRecord}
    write('Name: ');
    for i := 1 to 30 do
      Data.Name[i] := ' ';

    i := 0;
    while (not eoln) and (i < 30) do
      begin
        i := i + 1;
        read(Data.Name[i]);
      end;
    readln;

    write('Age: ');
    readln(Data.Age);
```

```
        write('Sex  (M  or  F):  ');
        readln(Data.Sex);

        writeln('Height');
        write('Feet:  ');
        readln(Data.Height[1]);
        write('Inches:  ');
        readln(Data.Height[2]);

        write('Weight:  ');
        readln(Data.Weight);
      end;     {procedure  ReadRecord}

procedure WriteRecord(Data:  Infotype);


      writeln;
      writeln('The  following  data  has  been  obtained.');
      writeln;
      with Data do
        begin     {with}
          writeln('Name:  ',  Name);
          writeln('Age:  ',  Age:2);
          writeln('Sex:  ',  Sex:1);
          write('Height:  ',  Height [1]:1,  '  ft.,  ');
          writeln(Height[2]:2,  '  inches');
          writeln('Weight:  ',  Weight:3);
        end;     {with}
      end;     {procedure  WriteRecord}

begin     {main  program}
  ReadRecord(Data);
  WriteRecord(Data);
end.     {main  program}
```

Chapter 11

11.1 A text file is organized into lines of characters separated by end-of-line characters, while a binary file of *char* components is one long string of characters.

11.3 ch

     5

11.6

```
type
    String  =  packed array [1..10] of char;
    Item  =  record
      Name  :  String;
      Quantity  :  integer;
```

```
        Price : real;
      end;    {Item}
   FileType = file of Item;
```

11.9

```
procedure CopyBin(var Old, New: RealFile);
{copies contents of opened binary file Old into opened binary file
 New and also writes it onto the screen}

var
   item : real;

  begin    {procedure CopyBin}
    while not eof(Old) do
      begin
        read(Old, item);
        write(New, item);
        writeln(item);
      end;
  end;    {procedure CopyBin}
```

11.10 A *writeln* statement can only be used with a text file, not a binary file.

Skill Builder 11.4

```
program Maketable(input, output, table);
{creates a binary file Table of dept. name/code records}

const
   MaxDeptName = 30;

type
   String = packed array [1..MaxDeptName] of char;
   Codestring = packed array [1..4] of char;
   Translation = record    {Translation}
     Name : String;
     Code : Codestring;
     end;    {of Translation}
   Codetable = file of translation;

var
   Table : Codetable;
   Name : String;
   Code : Codestring;
   Oneline : Translation;
   i, j : integer;
```

```
begin
  rewrite(Table);
  write('Enter department name, maximum ', MaxDeptName);
  writeln(' characters, then a semicolon, then the');
  writeln('department code, 4 capital letters');
  writeln('Continue list; terminate list with *');
  writeln;
  i := 1;
  read(Name[i]);
  while (Name[i] <> '*') do
    begin   {valid name, enter in Table}
      repeat
        i := i + 1;
        read(Name[i]);
      until Name[i] = ';';
      for j := i to MaxDeptName do
        begin   {blank out semicolon & rest of
                  name field}
          Name[j] := ' ';
        end;
      for i := 1 to 4 do
        begin
          read(Code[i]);
        end;
      readln;
      Oneline.Name := Name;
      Oneline.Code := Code;
      write(Table, Oneline);

      {start on next entry}
      i := 1;
      read(Name [i]);
    end;   {while loop}
end.
```

Chapter 12

12.1 $f(n) = n$ for $n \geq 1$

12.3
```
function Fibonacci(n: integer): integer;
{computes the nth value in the Fibonacci sequence - nonrecursive}

var
    Sum : integer;        {current value in Fibonacci sequence}
    Index : integer;      {marks term in Fibonacci sequence
                            being computed}
    OneBack, TwoBack : integer;   {two previous terms in
                                    sequence}
```

```
begin   {function Fibonacci}
  if (n = 1) or (n = 2) then
    Sum := 1
  else
    begin
      OneBack := 1;
      TwoBack := 1;
      Index := 3;
      while Index <= n do
        begin
          Sum := OneBack + TwoBack;
          Index := Index + 1;
          TwoBack := OneBack;
          OneBack := Sum;
        end;
    end;
  Fibonacci := Sum;
end;    {function Fibonacci}
```

12.6 a) 2*x

Skill Builder 12.2

a.
```
procedure RecursiveListDoubler(var List: ArrayType;
                                   i: integer);
{recursive procedure to double the entries in List from i to 5}

  begin   {procedure RecursiveListDoubler}
    if i <= 5 then
      begin   {List length > 0}
        List[i] := 2*List[i];
        RecursiveListDoubler(List, i + 1);
      end;    {List length > 0}
  end;    {procedure RecursiveListDoubler}
```

b.
```
procedure IterativeListDoubler(var List: ArrayType);
{iterative procedure to double the entries in List from 1 to 5}

  begin   {procedure IterativeListDoubler}
    for i := 1 to 5 do
      List[i] := 2*List[i];
  end;    {procedure IterativeListDoubler}
```

c. In this case, the iterative approach is clear and straightforward, while the recursive approach seems unnatural and complex.

Chapter 13
13.1 3

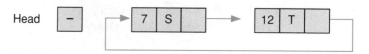

FIGURE K–4

13.4 Head^.Value := Temp^.Value;
13.5 See Figure K-4
13.7
procedure NewTraverse(Head: NodePointer);
{traverses entire linked list to which Head points and writes out every other element}

var
    Current : NodePointer;

```
  begin   {procedure NewTraverse}
    Current := Head;
    if Head = nil then
      writeln('List is empty')
    else
      repeat
        writeln(Current^.Name);
        Current := Current^.Link;
        if Current <> nil then   {advance again}
          Current := Current^.Link;
      until Current = nil;
  end;   {procedure NewTraverse}
```

13.12
    a. −   *   A   +   B   C   4

    b. A   B   C   +   *   4   −
13.13 See Figure K-5
13.15 b. insertion sort, bubble sort

Skill Builder 13.1

```
procedure Delete(var Head: NodePointer; AfterThis: NodePointer);
{In list pointed to by Head, deletes node after AfterThis^; if
 AfterList is  nil, deletes first element}

var
    Temp : NodePointer;   {used to dispose of deleted
                                      element}
  begin   {procedure Delete}
    if Head = nil then
```

a) Selection Sort

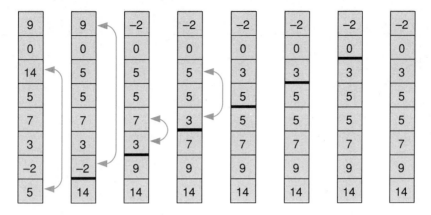

b) Insertion Sort

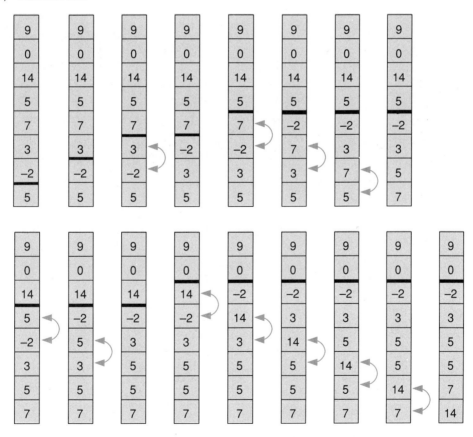

FIGURE   K–5

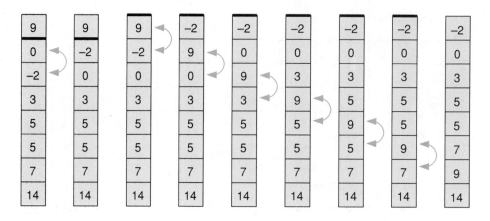

c) Bubble Sort

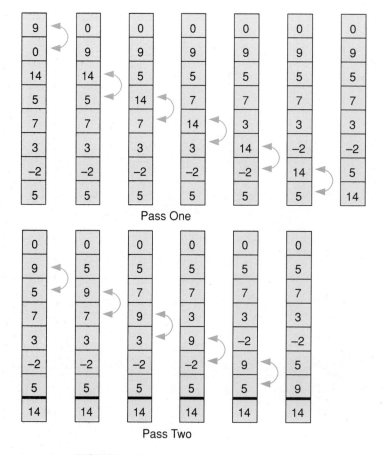

Pass One

Pass Two

FIGURE   K–5   Continued

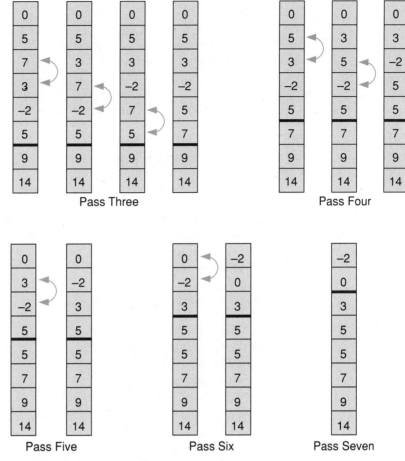

Pass Three

Pass Four

Pass Five

Pass Six

Pass Seven

FIGURE K–5 Continued

```
            writeln('Empty list, no deletions possible')
          else
            if AfterThis = nil then
              begin   {delete first element}
                Temp := Head;
                Head := Temp^.Link;
                dispose(Temp);
              end   {delete first element}
            else
              if AfterThis^.Link = nil then
                {no node after AfterThis^}
                writeln('Can' 't do this deletion')
              else
                begin   {delete node after AfterThis^}
                  Temp := AfterThis^.Link;
                  AfterThis^.Link := Temp^.Link;
                  dispose(Temp);
                end;   {delete node after AfterThis^}
        end;   {procedure Delete}
```

Skill Builder 13.7

```
procedure InsertionSort(var A: ArrayType; n: integer);
{sorts first n elements in array A}

var
          i, j : integer;    {index in array A}

begin   {procedure InsertionSort}
  for i := n - 1 downto 1 do
    begin
      j := i;    {A[j] is new element to insert}

      while (j < n − 1) and (A[j] > A[j + 1]) do
        begin   {insert A[j] by considering elements
                 through A[n − 1]}
          Exchange (A[j], A[j + 1]);
          j := j + 1;
        end;    {insert A[j] through A[n − 1]}

      {take care of A[n] case}
      if (A[n − 1] > A[n]) then
        Exchange(A[n − 1], A[n]);
    end;    {for loop}
end;    {procedure InsertionSort}
```

INDEX